YO-AFW-596

Children's Writer Guide to 1998

INSTITUTE *of*
CHILDREN'S
LITERATURE

Editor: Susan Tierney

Senior Editor: Kristi Vaughan

Coordinating Editor: Jean Lewis

Reporters:
Elaine Marie Alphin
Victoria Hambleton
Mark Haverstock
Catherine Frey Murphy
Patricia Curtis Pfitsch

Contributing Writers:
Cheryl Bowlan
Ginger Roberts Brackett
Joan Broerman
Sandy Fox
Donna Freedman
Donald R. Gordon
Jane Kurtz
Norma Jean Lutz
Ellen Macauley
Bobi Martin
Dorothy Mock
Pegi Deitz Shea
Carolyn Yoder

Copy Editor: Cheryl de la Guéronnière
Research Assistant: Cynthia Marron

Cover Art: Dolph LeMoult
Illustrations: Jennifer Hayden
Profile drawings: Joanna Schorling

Publisher: Prescott V. Kelly

Copyright © Institute of Children's Literature® 1998.
All rights reserved.

The material contained herein is protected by copyright. Quotations up to 40 words are permitted when *Children's Writer Guide to 1998* is clearly identified as the source. Otherwise, no part of *Children's Writer Guide to 1998* may be republished, copied, reproduced, or adapted without the express written permission of the Institute of Children's Literature, 93 Long Ridge Road, West Redding, CT 06896-0811.

Printed and bound in Canada.

1998
Table of Contents

Introduction, v

Part 1: Timeline
News of the Year, 3

Part 2: Key News for 1998
Queries for Fiction?, 21
How to Walk the Multicultural Tightrope, 27
A Surge in the Teen Market, 37

Part 3: Market Overviews
Book Publishing: A Forward Momentum, 47
Magazine Publishing: A Boom Market: Crowded but Open, 61
Tales that Teach: Writing Opportunities in Education, 75
New Panoramas in Parenting and Family, 85
Packagers: Making Books Happen, 95

Part 4: The Business Side
Contracts: When Words Mean Business, 105
Promotion: How Authors Sell, 119
Payment: Show Writers the Money, 135
The Profit in Market Research, 145
Children's Book Agents, 155

Part 5: Style & Technique
Editors on Plot: What Makes for Story?, 171
Submissions: Proposing in Style, 179
Sidebars: Snagging Sales on the Side, 185
The Descriptive Zone: Beyond Adjectives & Adverbs, 189
Editing and Revision: Anyone for Rigor?, 195

Part 6: Reference & Research
Photo Research: Detectives Nonpareil, 203
Interviews: An Expert Voice to Bring Nonfiction to Life, 217
Steps on the Research Road, 227

Electronic Research: The Tools You Need to Find What You Want, **235**
Annotated Research Primer, **245**

Part 7: Profiles

Joanna Cole: A Simple, Natural Progression, **261**
Barbara Cooney: The Chain of Story, **265**
Christina Ferrari: In the Big Arena, **269**
E. L. Konigsburg: Starting with Water, **273**
Ursula K. Le Guin: Cultivating a Fantastic Garden, **277**
Arthur A. Levine: The Books that Matter, **281**
Lois Lowry: Playing with Words, **285**
Eloise Jarvis McGraw: Inventing Other Times, Other Worlds, **289**
Joan Lowery Nixon: Kids Love a Mystery, **293**
J.D. Owen: Moving Through the Ranks, **297**
Katherine Paterson: Building Characters and Miracles, **301**
E. Russell Primm III: A Constant Devotion, **305**
Anita Silvey: A Circle of Books, **309**
Judy Wilson: From the Ground Up, **313**

Part 8: Contests & Conferences

Children's Writing Contests and Awards, **319**
Writers' Conferences, **371**
    Conferences Devoted to Writing for Children, General, **371**
    Conferences Devoted to Writing for Children, SCBWI, **376**
    Conferences with Sessions on Writing for Children, University or Regional, **383**
    Conferences with Sessions on Writing for Children, Religious Writing, **393**

Part 9: Idea Generation

Let Inspiration Lead, **399**
Idea Development: From Seed to Full Bloom, **407**
Milestones, **423**

Index, **457**

Introduction

An introductory college class on linguistics: We covered phonemes, Grimm's law, and the concept of studying language diachronically and synchronically. As fascinating as much of the course was, only parts had staying power for this student. Yet years later, the possibility of looking at a subject—children's publishing—both synchronically and diachronically can still illuminate.

Children's Writer Guide to 1998 takes a single point in time and looks at it, synchronically, to ask: What is the most up-to-date state of children's publishing as we close this comprehensive review? Diachronically, the *Guide* surveys the entire year and anticipates the year, and more, to come. The marketplace of children's publishing appears to be at a pivotal point; light falls on a corner being turned. Today, the industry is solidifying, stabilizing in a way that is leading to growth that is already visible.

We approached this third annual *Guide* with a determination to give it even more clarity, accessibility, and immediate practicality, and to add even more analysis and perspective on the near future in children's publishing. We began with a reorganization. The *Guide* now opens with a timeline, the News of the Year, which is a baseline for the information and analysis in the remaining 400-plus pages.

Key News for 1998, a new section, pulls out issues undergoing particularly notable change. While in the past, editors expected queries for nonfiction, they always required manuscripts, or at least sample chapters, for fiction. As "Queries for Fiction?" shows, those submissions requirements can no longer be assumed. "How to Walk the Multicultural Tightrope" takes an honest and timely look at a niche that is redefining itself after a burst of growth.

An emphasis on teens in this year's *Guide* begins in "The Surge in Teen Magazines." At this single point, the subject of young adults in the marketplace is especially timely, since their sheer number is expanding. Historically, these children of the baby boomers are entering early maturity. That young maturity is also reflected in the Market Overviews on trade books, magazines, educational publishing, family magazines, and packagers. Throughout, editors express a sense of renewed focus in their needs and the direction of their companies.

As for the most practical side of being a writer, The Business Side, this *Guide* section offers detailed looks at book contracts and magazine rights, in "Contracts: When Words Mean Business," and at authors' roles in promoting themselves and their books, in "How Authors Sell." Real numbers and author tips mark "Show Writers the Money," while "The Profit in Market Research" is a convincing argument for the reward in taking magazine market research as far as possible. The listing of children's book agents at the end of part four has been updated and expanded.

For that linguistics student of years ago, an English major like many reading this *Guide,* the Style and Technique articles should prove *utile et dulce*—useful and sweet. Editors wax almost poetic and philosophical about plot in "What Makes for Story?" "The Descriptive Zone: Beyond Adjectives and Adverbs" and "Editing and Revision: Anyone for Rigor?" should strike a chord with anyone who loves language; the articles offer advice for treasuring words and form. The section is filled out with choice suggestions for integrating love of writing and sales in "Proposing in Style" and "Sidebars: Snagging Sales on the Side."

One of the most striking qualities about the current marketplace, for books and magazines, is the much augmented accent on research, and particularly on photographs and primary sources. "Photo Research: Detectives Nonpareil" is full of specific advice from experienced photo researchers and editors. Finding and optimizing expert sources is the subject of "Interviews: An Expert Voice to Bring Nonfiction to Life." This extensive section also includes two vital resources: "Electronic Research: The Tools You Need to Find What You Want," and the updated "Annotated Research Primer." A writer must grapple with all this information—photos, experts, primary sources, print, technology—and then deal with an editor besides. "Steps on the Research Road" provides a strategy.

Armed with strategies and sources, writers still need inspiration to strike in some form today. The *Guide* offers profiles of fourteen writers and editors, all with motivating, challenging stories. Or, writers can enter a contest or attend a conference for inspiration and practical information. Comprehensive listings of both make up part eight. More pointedly, the purpose of the Idea Generation section is to spur creativity, keeping in mind topics likely to be of interest to editors in coming years.

The wave in time that children's publishing is now riding—diachronically—is leaving behind uncertainty and erratic growth and moving toward quality and identity. It can be a very good time to be a writer for children.

TIMELINE

Part
1

1997 Publishing News

Winter 1997

Anniversaries

■ 1997 is the twenty-fifth anniversary of the **Margaret K. McElderry** imprint and **Aladdin** paperbacks at **Simon & Schuster.**

■ *Misty of Chincoteague,* by *Marguerite Henry,* celebrates its fiftieth anniversary. Henry will die later in the year.

■ **Random House** declares 1997 The Year of *The Cat in the Hat* as that celebrated title turns forty. Company-sponsored birthday parties, stickers, and more are accompanied by a new line of books, The Wubbulous World of Dr. Seuss.

■ **Doubleday** celebrates 100 years of publishing.

Books

■ **Planet Dexter**, an imprint of the educational publisher **Addison Wesley Longman,** names *Michael Cirone* Director of Product Development.

■ The **American Library Association** (ALA) is the lead plaintiff in a suit to obtain an injunction against a New York statute that makes it a crime to disseminate materials that are harmful to minors through any computer communications network.

■ *Elise Howard* is named Executive Editor of **Avon Books.**

■ **Cahners Publishing** purchases **BookWire**, the largest book information site on the Web for about $1 million from Individual Inc. The site will include publishing and book news and job opportunities as well as new features.

■ *Elizabeth Bicknell* is named Editor-in-Chief at **Candlewick Press.** Formerly with Harcourt Brace's Red Wagon imprint, Bicknell replaces *Amy Ehrlich.*

■ **Charlesbridge Publishing**, a fast-growing small publisher, announces it will launch an imprint in the fall to concentrate on fiction picture books for children three to eight. It also expands its nonfiction picture book line for this age.

■ Religious publishing company **David C. Cook** buys **Victor Books**.

■ **Dorling Kindersley** emphatically rejects allegations of conspiracy with three former editors from **Orchard Books**, a **Grolier** company, to "divert and expropriate" the children's imprints' entire list and destroy Orchard's business.
    The new **Dorling Kindersley** publishing imprint is given a name: **DK Ink.**

■ **Element Books** launches a new children's line headed up by *Barry Cunningham* and *Elinor Bagenal*, from Rockport, Maine.

■ *Patty Sullivan* is promoted to Executive Vice President and Publisher of Children's Publishing Group at **Golden Books.** She had been Executive Vice President of Sales, Marketing, and Licensing. *Thea Feldman*, Vice President and Editorial Director of Mass-Market Formats, assumes responsibility for the mass-market story book group and coloring and activity group.
    Golden sells its party goods unit, Penn Corporation, to Peacock Papers. It doesn't fit in with owner *Richard Snyder*'s goal of forming a multiple media family entertainment company.

■ **Grolier** forms a new subsidiary, **inKNOWvations**, headed by *Stephen Zrike*, to do direct sales—the Tupperware way. **World Book** is doing the same; General Manager of Group Sales for World Book's direct selling unit, **The Learning Journey**, is *Peter Fisher*. To date, only **Educational Development Corporation** and **Dorling Kindersley Family Learning** had sold book sales this way.
    Sales expectations for Grolier are more than $1 million in the first year, through 250 distributors. Grolier offers 231 titles from **Orchard, Children's Press**, and **Franklin Watts.** World Book has 150 products, and already has 200 representa-

tives. Dorling Kindersley sells about 400 titles through 9,000 distributors. Sales hit $16 million in 1995. Educational Development has 8,400 sales reps and hopes for sales of $16 million.

■ *Judy Wilson* is named to head **Grolier's Orchard Books.**

■ **Harcourt Brace** launches a new imprint, **Silver Whistle Books.** *Paula Wiseman* is the Editor.
    David Nelson is appointed Vice President and Director of Sales for the **Harcourt Brace** trade division, which encompasses all the children's imprints.

■ **HarperCollins** announces a new imprint, later named **HarperActive,** under Editorial Director *Hope Innelli.* The mass-market line will offer original works and licensed books originally published by companion imprints **HarperTrophy,** which concentrates on trade books, and **HarperFestival,** a line of merchandise and novelty books not considered mass-market.

■ *Margery Cuyler* leaves her position as Associate Publisher of **Henry Holt Books for Young Readers.** *Laura Godwin* is named to the position.

■ With $250,000, **Hyperion Books** outbids seven competitors for reprint rights to *The Cuckoo's Child,* a first novel by *Suzanne Freeman,* originally published by **Greenwillow Books.** Freeman was a book reviewer before she became an author.

■ **K-III Holdings** acquires **Gareth Stevens,** a Milwaukee publisher in the supplemental and school library market.

■ **Marshall Cavendish,** primarily a curriculum-based publisher, launches a line of children's trade books. The first list will have fourteen titles, fiction and nonfiction, but the concentration will be on picture books.

■ *Marc Gave* is named Editorial Director at **McClanahan and Company.** Plans are announced to increase the size of the list in 1998.

■ **The Millbrook Press** goes public with an offering of 1.5 million shares of common stock at $5 a share. $2.6 million goes to product development, including expanding trade lines through novelty, early reader, and popular children's reference and chapter books. Plans call for new hires in marketing and beefing up direct mail, telemarketing, and the in-house sales force.

■ **William Morrow** announces a new, nonreturnable, 50 percent discount for qualified retail accounts.

■ **Northland Publishing** announces the launch of a new children's imprint, **Rising Moon.** It will publish picture books, middle-grade novels, and young adult books. All future Northland children's titles will be published under the Rising Moon imprint.

■ **Putnam Berkely** sells to **Pearson** for $336 million, making the new company, **Penguin Putnam,** the second largest children's book publisher, after Scholastic. Sales are more than $150 million. The official name of the resulting company after the Putnam & Penguin merger is **Penguin Putnam, Inc.** The parent company takes a $163 million charge against earnings in connection with accounting irregularities at Penguin USA.

    Phyllis Grann, Putnam's Chairman, becomes President of combined Penguin/Putnam operations, reporting to *Michael Lynton,* Chairman and Chief Executive Officer (CEO) worldwide. *Lara Bergen* is promoted to Executive Editor at **Grosset & Dunlap.**

■ *Nancy Pines* is named Vice President and Publisher of **Archway Paperbacks** and **Minstrel Books,** imprints of **Pocket Books.** She had been Associate Publisher, and previously had been at Bantam and Scholastic.

■ **Random House** announces a new paperback imprint, **Knopf Paperbacks.** *Joan Slattery* is the Editor.

    Random House agrees to sell back its 50 percent stake in **Living Books** to offer the joint venture with Broderbund Software a better chance to grow.

    Ruth Koeppel is named Senior Editor of **Random House's Stepping Stones** beginning reader series.

■ **Reader's Digest Young Families** enters into a licensing agreement with **Fisher Price** to publish and market **Little People PlayBooks,** beginning with seventeen interactive titles.

■ **Saint Mary's Press** announces a line of young adult novels, the company's first move into children's books.

■ **Scholastic's Cartwheel Books** announces the signing of *Robert Munsch,* author of *Paper Bag Princess* and *Love You Forever,* to a multibook, hardcover and paperback deal.

    Cartwheel's series of beginning-to-read books written by *Bill Cosby* are published. The books for ages seven to ten are multi-ethnic and deal with subjects important to kids.

    Scholastic announces its partnership with the American Lung Association to publish *The Berenstain BearScouts* and *The Sinister Smoke Ring.* Former Surgeon General C. Everett Koop is present at the debut.

■ *David Wan* is named President of **Simon & Schuster**'s kindergarten to grade twelve publishing group. The group combines *Silver Burdett Ginn, Prentice Hall School,* and *Globe Fearon* into one entity.

■ The **Anne Schwartz** list debuts at **Simon & Schuster**.

■ **Torstar Corporation** buys **Delta Education** of Nashua, New Hampshire. Torstar has been building its line of supplemental materials, which this acquisition furthers, particularly in math and science. Delta's products are activity-based and support basal and supplemental science and math curriculum. *Donna Hayes* is Vice President and General Manager of Torstar's Children's Supplementary Educational Products Division.

■ **TSR Books** launches its first serial novel, *The Double Diamond Triangle,* part of the **Forgotten Realm** series. The first of the nine monthly books is to sell for 99 cents, and subsequent books for $1.99. *Peter Archer* is the Senior Editor.

Magazines

■ The **National Association of At-Home Mothers** announces plans to launch *At Home Mothering*, for mothers at home, or those who want to be at home and need help making choices and arrangements.

■ *Boys' Life* divides into two editions, more closely age-targeted to younger and older readers.

■ *Connections,* a weekly newspaper, launches. *Mary Yoo,* inspired by a book, *Why Our Schools Are Failing and What We Can Learn from Japanese and Chinese Education,* focuses on high expectations for all children. Initial circulation is quite small.

■ *Crystal Ball,* a science and technology quarterly for ten-to-fourteen-year-old readers, premieres.

■ *My Friend* takes a new upbeat turn and adds departments under new Managing Editor *Sister Kathryn James.*

■ *Parenting* magazine moves to New York. *Janet Chan* is named Editor.

■ *People* magazine announces plans to develop *Teen People*. *Christina Ferrari,* formerly of *YM,* is Editor.

■ **Petersen Publishing,** publishers of *'Teen* and the now defunct *Sassy,* among others, is acquired by **Willis Stein & Partners.**

■ *Sports Illustrated For Kids* begins to publish an insert directed specifically at girls. The inserts appear in subscription issues identified as going to female subscribers.

■ *Your Big Backyard* changes format and raises the top of the readership range to appeal not only to toddlers, but to beginning readers.

Awards

■ John **Newbery** Medal goes to *E.L. Konigsburg* for *The View from Saturday,* published by Jean Karl Books, an imprint of Atheneum. Randolph **Caldecott** Medal goes to *David Wisniewski* for *Golem.*

Newbery Honor authors: *Nancy Farmer,* for *A Girl Named Disaster,* (Orchard/Jackson); *Eloise McGraw,* for *The Moorchild* (McElderry Books); *Megan Whalen Turner,* for *The Thief* (Greenwillow Books), and *Ruth White,* for *Belle Prater's Boy* (Frances Foster Books).

Caldecott Honor artists: *Holly Meade,* for *Hush! a Thai Lullaby,* by Minfong Ho (Orchard/ Kroupa); *David Pelletier,* for *The Graphic Alphabet* (Orchard); *Dav Pilkey,* for *The Paperboy* (Orchard/Jackson); and *Peter Sis,* for *Starry Messenger* (Frances Foster Books).

■ **Coretta Scott King Award** goes to author *Walter Dean Meyers,* for *Slam!* (Scholastic); illustrator, *Jerry Pinkney* for *Monty: A Story of Young Harriet Tubman* (Dial).

■ **New England Book Award** for Editorial Excellence for children's books goes to *Natalie Kinsey-Warnock,* for *The Fiddler of the Northern Lights* (Dutton).

Deaths

■ *Margaret Rey* co-creator, with her husband H.A. Rey, of the *Curious George* books, dies at 90 years old.

■ *Edith Hurd,* who worked with husband Clement Hurd and co-authored a few books with Margaret Wise Brown under the pen name Juniper Sage, dies.

Spring 1997

TIMELINE

Books

■ **Avisson Press** announces plans to expand into young adult market. It looks for biographies for teens.

■ Avon launches the **Avon Hardcover** line of general children's fiction.
  Gwen Montgomery resigns as Editorial Director of **Avon Books**. *Ruth Katcher* becomes Senior Editor; she had been with Knopf and with Aladdin.

■ Publisher *Craig Virden* adds the title of President of **Bantam Doubleday Dell Books for Young Readers.** *William Whalen,* former President, is now Vice President for New Business Development.

■ **Berlitz Kids** imprint launches with *The Missing Cat,* the premiere title in the *Adventures with Nicholas* book and cassette series.

■ The **Books of Wonder** trade list, announced a year earlier, has launched and numbers about thirty titles. Another new series, is announced: **Classic Frights**, will introduce kids to works of classic horror writers. Company co-owner *Peter Glassman* expects the publishing segment of the book-selling company to become more significant in the next few years.
  Co-founder *James Whaley* dies.

■ **Grolier** and **DK** set a court date for July 8 in their battle over editors accused of expropriating books from the list of **Orchard Books**, a Grolier company.

■ *Margery Cuyler* takes a consulting position with **Golden Family Entertainment** to develop a hardcover line of children's books.
  Golden begins an adult imprint, its first title Steven Covey's *The Seven Habits of Highly Effective Families.*
  The company continues to report a loss: $197 million for an eleven-month period.

■ *Stephanie Spinner* leaves **HarperCollins**. *Mary Alice Moore* is named Editor of **HarperTrophy** in addition to **HarperFestival.**
  HarperCollins posts a $7 million loss for the quarter.

■ *Alessandra Balzer* is named Associate Editor of **Hyperion Books** and **Disney Press.**

■ **Kids Can Press**, a Canadian publisher, announces plans to begin distributing in the U.S. market. Although it does not yet accept manuscripts from U.S. authors, the company says that is a future possibility.

■ **The Millbrook Press** announces a major expansion program. It looks for acquisitions, and strategic alliances and joint ventures.

Judy Korman joins the company as Publisher of trade books.

■ **Richard C. Owen Publishers** adds a second line of easy-to-read books, for older kids.

■ **Penguin Putnam** announces it will close the Los Angeles office of **Price Stern Sloan** and move operations to New York City. *Lara Bergen* is named Editorial Director of Price Stern Sloan, *Daniel Weismann,* Editor.

Douglas Whiteman is named Executive Vice President of Penguin Putnam, responsible for the operations of the combined children's divisions.

■ After announcing a sizeable loss for the first quarter, led by a decline in *Goosebumps* sales, **Scholastic** revamps its book group.

Jean Feiwel adds the title of Publisher.

The company says it will boost marketing of its trade book business by developing such promising series as *Animorphs* and *Dear America* and through titles such as *I Spy Challenger, Miss Spider's New Car,* and the new Bill Cosby series.

■ *Stephanie Owens Lurie* is promoted to Associate Publisher and Editorial Director of **Simon & Schuster Books for Young Readers.**

The company announces a new imprint, **Simon Spotlight.**

Viacom says Simon & Schuster increased its sales 7.4 percent.

■ **Troll** shakes up its executive ranks: Gone are *David Green* and *Patty Jensen.* Rumors circulate that the company is about to be sold. Potential buyers at this time are said to be **Pearson** and **Golden.**

Magazines

■ *Chirp* begins publishing. It is the newest publication from **Owl Communications**, and is targeted to a three-to-six-year-old audience.

■ A new magazine from the **Cricket Magazine Group**, *Click,* is announced to debut in the fall. The bimonthly for two-to-six-year-olds will focus on nonfiction.

■ *Clubhouse* announces that, for financial reasons, it is no longer accepting manuscripts and is, instead, recycling previous works.

■ *Glossy* launches online. It is directed at girls twelve to twenty, and covers the usual topics: beauty, boys, being a teen. It plans to launch a print version in 1998.

■ *Carolyn Yoder* is named Senior Editor, History, at **Highlights for Children**.

■ The key to **Scholastic**'s plan for regaining profitability is eliminating 400 jobs in non-core areas and the closing of three magazines, including *Agenda, Superscience Red,* and *Math Power.*

■ *'Teen* begins publishing a sixteen-page insert representing editorial content of the former *Sassy* magazine

■ *Time For Kids* announces plans for younger and older editions, *Time For Kids Primary Edition* and *InTime.*

■ *Lesley Seymour* joins *YM* as an Editor-in-Chief.

Awards

■ Nominees for the **American Booksellers Book of the Year** (ABBY) Award are announced: *Falling Up,* by *Shel Silverstein* (HarperCollins); *The Golden Compass,* by *Philip Pullman* (Knopf); *Lilly's Purple Plastic Purse,* by *Kevin Henkes* (Greenwillow); *My Many Colored Days,* by *Dr. Seuss* (Knopf); and *My Very First Mother Goose,* edited by *Iona Opie* (Candlewick). The award goes to *Lilly's Purple Plastic Purse.*

■ The Child Study Children's Book Committee at **Bank Street College** gave its **Children's Book Award** for titles that "deal realistically and in a positive way with problems in their world" to *The Cuckoo's Child,* by *Suzanne Freeman* (Greenwillow).

■ *Maisy's House* wins the **Children's Book Award** at the **Bologna Book Fair.**

■ Annual **Literary Market Place Awards:** Individual Achievement Awards in children's publishing went to *Joanna Cotler,* Joanna Cotler Books/HarperCollins Children's Books and *Frances Foster,* Frances Foster Books/Farrar, Straus & Giroux. The corporate award for children went to **Scholastic Press.**

■ **Scott O'Dell Award** for historical fiction is presented to *Katherine Paterson* for *Jip: His Story* (Lodestar).

Deaths

■ *Ethel L. Heins,* former Editor of the *Horn Book* and children's literature champion, dies.

■ *Lyll Becerra de Jenkins,* author of *The Honorable Prison,* dies.

Anniversaries

■ The seventy-fifth anniversary of the **Newbery Medal** is celebrated at the 116th Annual Conference of the **American Library Association.**

Books

■ *Harold Underdown* becomes Senior Editor at **Charlesbridge Publishing.**

■ **CINAR Films**, a Quebec-based company buys the Greensboro, North Carolina, **Carson-Dellosa**, which produces specialty school supplies and classroom materials for the preschool-to-grade-six market.

■ The **Children's Book Council** unveils its first *Not Just for Children Anymore* catalogue of "110 Children's Books that Adults Will Enjoy and Buy for Themselves."

■ Signs of trouble appear at **Dove Entertainment.** A comprehensive review of the printed book publishing segment is made. Fifteen children's books are slated for the year but a spokesperson says that if little support arises for certain books, they will be dropped. The net loss for the first quarter is $3.4 million.

In mid-June, **Media Equities International** (MEI) takes control of the company through a purchase of stock from founders *Michael* and *Deborah Raffin Viner.* The Viners will be consultants. Dove CEO *Rod Lightstone* announces that the company is deciding on a new, but unspecified, direction.

■ **Golden Family Entertainment** has a new book line, *Smart Pages,* which has a patented in-the-page sound technology that allows children to interact with characters. The first books are *Disney's Hercules: Zero to Hero* and *Hercules: The Heart of a Hero.*

Golden announces that it is embarking on a new sales strategy that will include expanded distribution channels, fact-based selling, intelligent category management, and an integrated sales and marketing approach to account management.

Richard Collins is named Executive Vice President of Sales and Retail Marketing, North America, for the children's publishing group. He comes from Unilever/Lipton.

■ **Grolier** and **Dorling Kindersley** settle the lawsuit. DK pays an undisclosed amount and enters into future arrangements with Grolier "concerning electronic publishing."

■ **GT Publishing**, which entered the children's mass-market business a year earlier, launches a new imprint, **Inchworm Press**. It features storybooks, novelty books, and books plus.

■ **HarperCollins** cancels contracts for a number of books when authors have not met deadlines or otherwise met their obligations and as part of the company's continuing effort to refocus on what it does best, including children's books. The **Authors' Guild** sends 7,500 postcards to its members warning them to seek professional advice before signing any legal waivers in connection with contracts canceled by HarperCollins.

Rupert Murdoch denies rumors that HarperCollins is up for sale. Nonetheless, the **BDD** parent company, **Bertelsmann**, is said to be a suitor. HarperCollins takes a $270 million charge against earnings, one of the largest taken in the publishing industry. The charge was largely for inventories of returned books and author advances for unprofitable books. *Jo Keiner,* the Chief Operating Officer, says the company is likely to publish fewer than 1,000 books in 1998, down more than 600 books from 1996.

Marilyn Kriney leaves. She had been Senior Vice President and Publisher-at-large of HarperCollins Children's Books.

■ *Ken Geist* is promoted to Vice President and Associate Publisher of **Hyperion Books for Children** and **Disney Press**. His new job includes overseeing marketing, acquiring authors, and developing new series.

■ **Klutz Press** is now marketing all books as "100-percent Klutz Certified," to differentiate them from imitations.

■ At **National Geographic Books**, Senior Vice President for Publications, *Nina Hoffman,* plans to add more children's titles to the list of twenty-four now published.

■ **Pages Inc.** announces it will launch four new targeted school book fairs: Bargain Fairs, Corporate Fairs, the Good Book Program, and Pages Plus. They are designed to hit specific interests. The Good Book Fair, for instance, emphasizes positive childhood experiences that reinforce solid family values.

■ **Scholastic** consolidates its instructional units into one group, the Scholastic School Group, which includes instructional publishing, classroom magazines, and the professional publishing and early childhood divisions. Key personnel includes: *Margery Mayer,* Executive Vice President of Instructional Publishing, who oversees Literacy Place, and the development of new core reading and literacy products; *Linda Kroons,* Vice President and Publisher of Supplemental Publishing, including early childhood, professional publishing, and supplemental products;

Claudia Cohl, Vice President of Editorial Planning and Development; and *Hugh Roome,* Executive Vice President of Promotion and Sales. All report to Chairman *Richard Robinson.*

Scholastic steps up the publishing schedule for *Animorphs* and announces that it has a tie-in live-action television series in preproduction, scheduled for release on Nickelodeon in fall 1998.

Scholastic also steps up marketing for the *Goosebumps* series with special promotions.

Scholastic stock begins a comeback.

■ Cutbacks are made at **Sierra Club Books** where *Helen Sweetland* moves from Director of Children's Books to Publisher of Sierra Club Books. The adult list is cut in half, to sixteen titles in 1998; the children's list is cut from twelve to ten.

■ **Troll** is sold to **Torstar.**

■ **TSR, Inc.** is purchased by **Wizards of the Coast,** in Renton, Washington.

Magazines

■ *Sarah Jane Brian* is named Editor of *American Girl.*

■ After the parent company of Canada's **Owl Communications** collapses and the publications and staff are put on hiatus, **Bayard Presse Canada** and **Coscient Group** purchase Owl and publication resumes. Bayard announces plans for expansion.

Editor *Susie Berg* resigns. *Chickadee* is redesigned.

■ *Dinosaurus* launches in July. The bimonthly for six-to-twelve-year-olds intends to use the universal juvenile interest in dinosaurs to entertain and teach in a variety of disciplines.

■ *Jane,* the latest incarnation from *Jane Pratt,* hits the newsstands. The target range is eighteen to thirty-one, but particularly women in their twenties.

■ *Jump,* for teen girls "who dare," debuts. The basic slant is on health and fitness, but the magazine, the first for this young audience by **Weider Publishing**, the company that produces *Living Fit* and *Shape,* covers all the topics of interest to teens. *Lori Berger* is named Editor.

■ *KidStyle,* a kids' fashion magazine for moms and grandmothers, launches.

■ *SNAP!,* a magazine for teen girls that covers real life, dating, fashion, celebrities, and entertainment is launched by **Bauer Publishing,** which publishes *First for*

Women and *Soap Opera Digest. Jonathan Small* is Executive Editor; *Lisa Lombardi* is Editor-in-Chief. The magazine is soon renamed **Twist.**

■ The new owners of **Petersen Publishing** — publishers of *'Teen*— announce that they will file an initial public offering (IPO) for as much as $172 million in stock in the next few months. Rumors are that some of the money will be used to repay debt, and some to buy other periodicals.

■ The **U.S. Tennis Association** announces plans to launch a magazine for juniors. called **Topspin.**

■ *Time Machine* suspends publication pending the finding of alternate financing.

Fall 1997

Anniversaries
■ **HarperCollins** marks forty years of *I Can Read Books.* The first title in the series, launched by the almost legendary editor *Ursula Nordstrom,* was *Else Holmelund Minarik's Little Bear,* illustrated by *Maurice Sendak.* More than 200 beginning readers in the I Can Read Books series have been published, including *Frog and Toad, Danny and the Dinosaur,* and *Amelia Bedelia.* Editorial Director *Sally Doherty* now oversees the line.

■ **Houghton Mifflin** celebrates the twenty-fifth anniversary of the publication of the picture book *George and Martha,* by author and illustrator *James Marshall.* Marshall produced a series of George and Martha books, as well as series on the Stupids, the Cut-ups, the Fox easy readers, and others.

■ *Junior Scholastic* magazine reaches its sixtieth year.

Books
■ The **American Booksellers Association, Scholastic,** and participating pediatricians join in a national Read to Your Bunny program to promote literacy. *Rosemary Wells's* new book, *Read to Your Bunny,* is at the program's center.

In a comparable literacy drive, **Random House Children's Publishing** signs up booksellers for its reading encouragement program, Babies Bloom and Big Kids Blossom with Books.

Scholastic, Disney Publishing, and **HarperCollins** are providing books to Boys & Girls Clubs of America in the All Books for Children program.

The **National Children's Book and Literacy Alliance** is formed, and begins promoting its campaign, Literacy Through Literature. A primary purpose of the group is to support and promote existing children's literacy groups nationally.

These campaigns have been undertaken in response to a challenge by President and Mrs. Clinton at a White House Summit on early childhood learning.

■ **Blackbirch Press** announces the launch of a new line of illustrated fiction, **blackbirch picturebooks.** The picture book line for ages two to five debuts with four titles in fall 1998, with eight more following in spring 1999, and a projected twelve each season by 2000. The line will be marketed to Blackbirch's primary audience, schools and libraries, but also to the trade outlets.

■ **Dove Entertainment** loses the lawsuit brought against it by Simon & Schuster. Dove is forbidden from selling any products with the title "The Book of Virtues." The company had published *The Children's Book of Virtues* and *The Children's Audiobook of Virtues,* which were found to have infringed on the trademark rights of *The Book of Virtues* series, by *William Bennett,* and published by **Simon & Schuster.**

■ *E. Russell Primm* leaves **Grolier** to begin his own company, book producer **Editorial Directions.**

■ *Margery Cuyler* joins **Golden Family Entertainment** full-time as Vice President of Children's Publishing and Director of Trade Publishing. She will help launch a hardcover picture book line and develop nonfiction, collectibles, and gift lines. Six hardcover titles are planned for release in winter 1999, including new formats of titles from Golden's backlist as well as books from new authors and illustrators.

Golden also renews an extensive licensing agreement with **Walt Disney Corporation,** to run through 2001, with the possibility of extension through 2002.

■ **HarperCollins** has scheduled the February debut of **Growing Tree**, an imprint directed at the very youngest children, the nonreaders from infants to toddlers. Produced after several years of research, the line begins by offering twelve books in six development age groups from birth to three. The books are literature-based, not concept books: They are to consist of stories, songs, and poems that will cultivate language development. Growing Tree's Senior Editor is *Simone Kaplan,* and *Ellen Stein* is the Associate Editor.

■ **The Millbrook Press** acquires **Twenty-First Century Books**, a line of high school nonfiction for the library market, from **Henry Holt.**

■ *Rosemary Brosnan-Workman* joins **Morrow Junior Books** as Executive Editor. She was previously at Lodestar Books.

■ **Pleasant Company** publishes a six-book series on a new character, Josefina Montoya, a Mexican-American girl of 1824. Five new **American Girl** activity books and a CD-ROM are also produced.

■ **Penguin Putnam** closes two imprints, **Cobblehill Books** and **Lodestar Books** after performing a study that reveals other imprints sell better across various markets. The two, now defunct, lines sold primarily to institutional markets. As a result, *Virginia Buckley* and *Joe Ann Daly* left the company.

Penguin's **Dutton Children's Books** is reorganized, with the following personnel: *Lucia Monfried*, Associate Publisher and Editor-in-Chief; *Donna Brooks*, Editorial Director, Children's Trade; *Joan Powers*, Director, Children's Merchandise, including Winnie the Pooh products; *Susan Van Metre*, Senior Editor, trade titles and Playskool Books.

■ *Kristina Peterson* is named Executive Vice President of **Random House's** children's division, responsible for selling and marketing, subrights, client distribution, and business development. Most recently she was CEO at DK Publishing, for less than a year.

■ **Scholastic** announces the reorganization of its book group is complete. *Michael Jacobs* becomes Vice President, Trade, under Executive Vice President *Barbara Marcus*.

■ **Simon & Schuster** plans to launch books based on two popular **Nickelodeon** series, *Rugrats* and *Real Monsters*. Books based on licenses of *Rocky and His Friends* will be published by **Simon Spotlight**, as will **Weather Channel** books.

■ **Winslow Press**, a new publishing arm of the nonprofit **Foundation for Concepts in Education**, announces it will launch its first line of books in the fall. It will publish children's fiction and nonfiction for all ages. The first list will have seven titles. The Publisher is *Diane Kessenich*. *Josephine Nobisso* is Managing Editor.

■ **Reader's Digest** Chairman *George Grune* says he expects big growth possibilities for the company in children's books.

■ A new publisher of licensed products, **Ziccardi Publishing Group**, offers board books based on **Royal Doulton's** well-known children's china, *Bunnykins*.

Awards

■ *Small Steps: The Year I Got Polio*, by *Peg Kehret*, (Albert Whitman & Co) wins the **PEN Center USA West Award** for children's literature.

■ *Kevin Henkes*, author-illustrator of *Lilly's Purple Plastic Purse*, receives the first **Humpty Dumpty Award** given by **Mid-South Independent Booksellers for Children Association.**

■ The winners of the **National Book Awards** are announced: *Han Nolan* wins in the category of Young People's Literature, for *Dancing on the Edge* (Harcourt). The other nominees are *Brock Cole, The Facts Speak for Themselves* (Front Street); *Adele Griffin, Sons of Liberty* (Hyperion); *Mary Ann McGuigan, Where You Belong* (Atheneum); and *Tor Seidler, Mean Margaret* (HarperCollins).

■ **Scholastic Classroom Magazines and Professional Publications** win a total of twenty-eight **EdPress Awards**, including the EdPress Golden Lamp Award for *Scholastic Literary Cavalcade*. This is the second time Scholastic has won the award.

Magazines

■ **Cobblestone Publishing**, a **Simon & Schuster** company, announces plans to launch three magazines in 1998: ***AppleSeeds, California Cobblestone,*** and, under a working title, ***African-American Heritage and Achievement.*** The first two will echo the theme-based magazines for which Cobblestone is known, *AppleSeeds,* for grades three and four and *California Cobblestone* with a specific focus on state history. *African-American Heritage and Achievement* will target middle school and provide resource material on its title subject.

■ *Freeze* magazine, a ski magazine for fourteen-to-twenty-five-year-olds begins publication by **Times Mirror Magazines.**

■ *Dance Spirit*, for dance teams on campus and in dance studios, launches. It will appear quarterly.

■ *Lacrosse* magazine plans to launch quarterly children's version.

Deaths

■ *Matt Christopher,* author of more than 120 children's books spanning a wide variety of sports, died due to complications following surgery for a brain tumor.

■ *Marguerite Henry,* author of *Misty of Chincoteague,* dies.

KEY NEWS FOR 1998

Part 2

Submissions

Queries for Fiction?

By Bobi Martin

What sets a professional author apart from an amateur? Ask a nonfiction writer and the response is likely to be, "a query letter." Professional nonfiction authors query first and then write only after an editor expresses interest in the piece. Amateurs write a piece and then try to find a magazine whose needs fit what they wrote about.

While an editor's yes to a query isn't a guarantee of a sale, using the query approach, most published authors sell about 75 percent of what they write.

But what about fiction? Are query letters useful there, too? While traditionally queries and fiction didn't go together, many editors and authors are saying they now do. With the growing number of publishers who are closing their doors temporarily (however long that may be) to unsolicited manu-scripts, a well-written query letter can open a window of opportunity.

"I think fiction queries to 'closed' houses are a good idea," agrees Rosemary Brosnan-Workman, Executive Editor at Morrow Junior Books and formerly with Lodestar Books, an imprint closed after the massive merger of Putnam and Penguin. They allow editors to "see quickly if we're interested in a topic or not." Publishers that don't take unsolicited manuscripts, Brosnan-Workman suggests, may be glad to get short fiction queries, which represent something of "a door still open."

Bantam Doubleday Dell doesn't accept unsolicited manuscripts, but Editor Karen Wojtyla finds fiction queries helpful for long projects like middle-grade and young adult novels. "Keep the query brief," she cautions. "Tell me in a couple of lines the general idea of

Put Your Best Query Forward

If you decide a query letter or package is in your best interest, these tips will help en-sure a favorable response.

- **Keep the letter brief.** Be able to describe the plot or theme of your book, and tell something about the main character, in three or fewer lines. "My book is about a thirteen-year-old girl who is kidnapped by her father two years after her parents' bitter divorce" is enough. You don't have to go into what the main character learns or describe several scenes: That's the job of a synopsis.
- **For novels, let the editor know how many pages the manuscript is.** "My novel, geared for older middle-grade readers, is about 120 pages." Know the average length of manuscripts in the genre you've chosen. A twenty-five page manuscript is too long to be a picture book, and not long enough to be a middle-grade novel. (See sidebar, Know Your Lengths, page 25.)
- **List publishing credits, if you have them.** If your only sale so far is a short story and this submission is a young adult novel, you might say something like, "My most recent sale is a short story to *Top Kid* magazine." If you have no credits, say nothing. Don't say, "I haven't published anything yet," or worse, "If you buy this, it will be my first sale!"
- **Do mention college or university writing courses you have taken or membership in writing organizations.** This shows you take writing seriously. If you've heard the editor speak at a conference, mention this. "I enjoyed hearing you speak last October at the Society of Children's Book Writers and Illustrators conference in northern California." (Noting that you've taken adult education or other, non-college, courses get mixed responses from editors—better leave them out.)
- **Be professional.** Don't get chatty and try to make friends with the editor by sharing your life story: "I'm the divorced mom of two children in elementary school and writing gives me a creative outlet." Don't give the editor the impres-sion that this is a passing hobby, rather than a serious endeavor: "I was at a barbecue last week when I got this idea, and the story just poured out when I got home."
- **Avoid the most used—and most hated—lines editors have seen, in all their variations.** Examples are "I've read this story to my third-grade class," or "My kids never tire of hearing this story."
- **Create a positive first impression.** Use a decent quality paper and a standard font in a standard size. Proofread for complete sentences, proper punctuation, and spelling. Make sure you've spelled the editor's name correctly. Always include a self-addressed, stamped envelope or postcard.

the book: 'I've written a young adult novel about a fifteen-year-old boy who is affected by his father getting AIDS' tells me the main idea of the book in one sentence."

Wojtyla likes an estimate of length, by pages. "If the author says they've written a 500-page middle-grade novel, I know right off that this book isn't for us, and that the author hasn't checked out common lengths," she says.

Brosnan-Workman recommends keeping fiction queries to one page, with a partial synopsis of the theme, something about the main character, and a little about the author, including any publication credits, magazine sales, or contest awards. An author without sales could mention workshops or writing courses they've taken.

Simon & Schuster Books for Young Readers is also 'closed' to unsolicited manuscripts, but 'open' to queries. "A well-written query letter lets us see if your idea fits for us and allows us to respond quickly," says Vice President and Editorial Director Stephanie Owens Lurie. For middle-grade and young adult books, Lurie likes the query, a synopsis, and one chapter. The letter, she says, should "describe your book. Tell me briefly what prompted you to write it, and let me know which of our books is similar to yours."

A Faster Read

A big plus of queries, from the authors' standpoint, is that their brevity makes it likely they will be read sooner than manuscripts.

Laura Atkins, Assistant Production Editor at Children's Book Press, says, "We like getting queries because we can respond to these more quickly than we can to full manuscripts. If a story is completely off, I'll let the author know, and if a story really interests me, I might add a note encouraging the author." She also sends along a copy of their guidelines.

While Greenwillow's Robin Roy prefers to see complete manuscripts, she concedes that queries generally do get faster responses. "Query letters get shifted to a different pile," she says. "We respond to queries in about a month, whereas manuscripts take much longer."

Roy also understands that a query package saves authors hefty postage expenses on middle-grade and young adult manuscripts. The ideal query package for her contains a query letter with a synopsis and three chapters. "A good query will quickly tell me something about the plot and main character and then let me know if the author has been published before," she says."Whether the author lists publication credits or not, the manuscript will still get read," she adds.

Beth Troop, Manuscript Coordinator at Boyds Mills Press, agrees that queries for middle-grade and young adult novels get a faster response. Troop also prefers a query package rather than just a letter. "We want to see the author's fiction writing style, and that doesn't come through in a query letter," she explains.

If queries can be read more quickly and save authors time, postage, and paper, why don't all editors like them? The problem, as Troop and others say, is that editors can't judge the quality of an author's fiction writing without seeing at least part of the actual manuscript. "After all," Roy points out, "it's the actual writing that counts.

"You can't tell if the writing is good or if the theme is well developed from a query letter," says Albert Whitman and Company's Senior Editor, Abby Levine. "We prefer a synopsis and three chapters. This gives us a better idea of plot development and writing style."

Time Wasting

Although queries are often a foot in the door at publishers that are not taking unsolicited manuscripts, the door is wide open at those that do, and queries there may not be as useful.

Sarah Hines Stephens, Submission Coordinator at Houghton Mifflin, says queries to Houghton waste the author's time. "A house that accepts unsolicited manuscripts already has a blanket *send* statement," she says. "For us, a query is more work. Nine times out of ten, we'll tell the author to send the whole manuscript."

A major complaint from editors, whether a submission comes in the form of a full manuscript or a query, is that the author hasn't bothered to learn what the company publishes. According to Atkins, "Nearly 90 percent of the submissions received by Children's Book Press are unrelated to what we buy."

Atkins likes getting queries and prefers a one-page letter in which the author briefly describes the book and shows in two or three sentences why it is right for Children's Book Press. "Show that you know what we publish," Atkins says. By way of example, she offers: "My story is about a Chinese-American girl growing up in an area where there are no other Chinese families. As you are looking for contemporary stories about Asian children, I believe your company would be a good home for this manuscript."

Regina Griffen, Editor-in-Chief at Holiday House, says, "When I get a letter proposing a fiction series, the author has wasted my time and theirs. Holiday House doesn't publish series fiction, and authors submitting to us should know that."

A query that can show the editor that the author is familiar with what that particular house publishes has a definite edge. "When a query letter comes in from someone who has clearly looked at our company's list, and they comment on a particular book of ours that is similar to theirs and say that's why they chose us—I can see that person has done their homework," says Griffen.

Not So Short

Almost everyone agrees that queries are seldom useful for picture books and short stories. Since these can often be sent in the same size envelope and for the same amount of postage as a query, authors aren't saving there, plus these short manuscripts can be read about as quickly as a letter.

"We don't give priority to queries. Picture book manuscripts are just as easy and fast to read," says Liz Szabla, Editor-in-Chief at Lee & Low, which publishes picture books.

Mary Lou Carney, Editor of the magazine *Guideposts for Kids*, thinks queries to them for stories are a waste of time and postage. "The only way for me to know if I want the story is to read the whole thing," she says.

Carney knows authors who query think they're getting a faster response to their work. "And I can often know quickly if an idea isn't right for us," she says, "but they might sell themselves short. If I received a query pitching a horse story, and we'd just bought one of those, I'd probably decline the query. But if I'm looking at a manuscript and the first three lines of the story grab me—if the story is particularly well written—I might see other layers that move the submission beyond another horse story, and buy it."

Judy Burke, an Assistant Editor at *Highlights for Children,* says, "Unless we can tell right off that the idea isn't right for us, we'll ask to see the story. A query can't tell us if this particular story will touch a child in a special way; that's in the style of the author's writing."

Then there is *Focus on the Family Clubhouse,* which neither accepts nor declines queries, according to Assistant Editor Annette Bourland. "We respond with a form letter asking to see the whole story," she says.

As the diverse perspectives of the editors show, there are few 'rules' about query letters. Some editors welcome them, some tolerate them, some discourage them. Carefully reading publishers' listings in market directories will help authors determine which editors are most receptive to a query letter or package—and which houses are really open.

Know Your Lengths

Part of doing your homework is knowing the average manuscript length for the age and genre. The following are manuscript pages, not the number of printed pages in the finished book. Note that the average double-spaced manuscript page is considered to be 250 words.

	Ms. Pages
Board book	1
Picture book	2-4
Picture storybook	6-9
Easy reader	10-20
Early chapter book	40-60
Nonfiction, early readers	10-20
Middle-grade novels	100-150
Middle-grade nonfiction	60-100
Young adult novels	175-200
Young adult nonfiction	100-150

KEY NEWS

Niches and Genres

How to Walk the Multicultural Tightrope

By Jane Kurtz

KEY NEWS

Not too long ago, *multicultural* was a magic word in children's books. It all started in the late 1980s and early 1990s when, according to Stephanie Owens Lurie, Vice President and Editorial Director of Simon & Schuster Books for Young Readers, different ethnic groups were "quickly becoming a larger segment of the U.S. population." At the same time, more and more people "were concerned that there weren't enough books that reflected the lives and interests of people of color."

As teachers, librarians, parents, and grandparents led the hue and cry for more multicultural books, publishers were eager to respond. In 1992, when James Cross Giblin, long-time Editor of Clarion Books and author of children's nonfiction books, was asked at a writers' conference if he knew of any "hot" topics for which editors were currently looking, his immediate response was, "Well, multicultural, of course."

In the rush to expand the borders of the children's book world, editors began to look hard for books that would illuminate the lives and environments of children of diverse backgrounds. New publishing houses were even started with the express aim of broadening the perspective of children's literature.

When Cheryl and Wade Hudson were unable to find a picture book with illustrations of black children for their daughter, Katura, they decided to start their own company. By 1990, Just Us Books was selling $270,000 worth of books aimed at the African-American audience.

Lee & Low Books, where the telephones are answered "award-winning

Don't Forget Nonfiction

One clear avenue for multicultural books today is in nonfiction. Since schools and libraries are still seeking books with multicultural subjects, publishing houses that target institutional markets find that a multicultural touch often still helps in setting a book apart. Multicultural nonfiction trade books are also doing well. In fact, Phillip Lee of Lee & Low Books says, "We consistently find that they are among our most popular books."

Lee notes that the company's picture book biographies have been strong sellers, in stores as well as to libraries. A recent nonfiction release, *Passage to Freedom: The Sugihara Story,* by Ken Mochizuki, sold out its first printing before the book was even launched. It tells the true and powerful story of Chiune Sugihara, a Japanese diplomat who had the courage to save the lives of thousands of Polish Jews. The trade magazine *American Bookseller* called *Passage to Freedom* "a powerful story that needs to be told" and said it was "a touching account of how one person's courage can make a difference." Such reviews illustrate the attention that an important and well-done multicultural book can still attract in the marketplace.

publisher of multicultural books," is another publishing house with a mission of diversity. The company was started to publish books for ages four to ten, "with themes that address children of color and promote a greater understanding of one another."

While publishers were looking for good multicultural books, authors were also looking hard—for that special something that would make their manuscripts stand out. Sometimes a multicultural touch was the answer. I was one author who rode the tail end of the multicultural wave into publication. After ten agonizing years of submitting to editors without reaching my goal of a book contract with a major publishing company, in the early 1990s my picture book retellings of two Ethiopian folktales, *Fire on the Mountain* and *Pulling the Lion's Tail,* suddenly

sparked that long coveted call: a two-book contract with Simon & Schuster.

Not Just Multicultural Anymore

Sometimes I ask myself if my two break-through books would find their way into print if I had written them today. Alas, I've concluded the answer may well be "no."

Aaron Shepard, whose most recently published folktale is *The Sea King's Daughter: A Russian Legend* (Atheneum), agrees that folktales are hardly an open path to publication anymore. "My advice to beginners is, 'Don't do it!'—unless you're really compelled," he says. "You couldn't think of a harder way to break into the business right now."

One of the issues, as Lurie says, is that in response to the call for multicultural books, "publishers flooded the market, sometimes, unfortunately, with books that weren't of high quality." Melanie Kroupa, Editor at DK Ink, put it this way: "Everybody climbed on the multicultural bandwagon. It's not enough, anymore, for a story just to be multicultural. Multicultural is not a substitute for a good story or an unusual perspective or great writing."

Bookstores have also changed. The late 1980s and early 1990s, boom times for children's books in general, saw bookstores springing up everywhere to connect eager book buyers with the approximately 5,000 new books published every year. By 1992, about 350 children's bookstores were open nationwide. The owners and staff of these stores, who tended to be knowledgeable and passionate about children's books, enjoyed hand selling books they found particularly appealing or important, including a number of multicultural books.

The middle of this decade, however, has seen a gobbling of bookstore customers by huge superstores, often staffed by people with little training in children's literature. Kroupa pointed out that while staff in the best independent bookstores always filed a book in several different places, many superstores simply have a multicultural "shelf." A customer not specifically looking for a multicultural book might never find a book pigeonholed that way.

Today's booksellers, Lurie says, "seem wary of books about other cultures. We are hearing that customers aren't interested in multicultural folktales with lengthy texts, or in books that are historically accurate but show people of color being oppressed. These books still sell to schools and libraries, but it is difficult to get wide retail distribution for them."

Does that mean that multicultural writing is "dead"? No, said Lurie. "One bookseller recently challenged us with the question 'What are you publishing for the burgeoning Latino population?' Luckily, we had a series of novels already under way!"

Continuing Commitment

Certainly, the commitment of many, many librarians and teachers to multicultural books remains firm. For proof of that, look at such books as *Golem,* by David Wisniewski (Clarion); *The View from Saturday,* by E.L. Konigsburg (Jean Karl/Atheneum), winners of the prestigious Caldecott and Newbery awards given by the American Library Association. Look, too, at the year's Newbery and Caldecott Honor Books: *Hush! A Thai Lullaby,* by Minfong Ho (Melanie Kroupa/Orchard); and *A Girl Named Disaster,* by Nancy Farmer (Richard Jackson/Orchard).

Hush! A Thai Lullaby, Kroupa says, illustrates much of what works well in a multicultural book. "It's a simple, rhythmic, engaging picture book text that touches young children where they're at. Most children won't have had the experiences of the child in the book, but every child has experienced resistance between a mother and baby, where the mother thinks she's in charge and the baby is off in the background, being himself." Holly Meade's art, Kroupa adds, "extends the text in a wonderful way. It's fresh in that it takes its impetus from Thai culture, but

Meade has brought something of her own to it, too." Kroupa also points out that the decision not to put the subtitle, "A Thai Lullaby," on the jacket was deliberate—a way to try to avoid the book's being pigeonholed on the multicultural shelf.

Clearly, a great multicultural story still has a good chance of becoming a book. Lurie said that if Simon & Schuster editors come across a story that is "entertaining, beautifully written, and also happens to expose readers to another world, then we will publish it, even though there is some resistance out there."

Philip Lee notes that Lee & Low is actively looking for stories that are compelling, with believable characters and universal appeal: "elements that are no different from any other story."

Sounds easy, deceptively easy. With a folktale, the plot is already in place. But a writer who sets out to write a contemporary multicultural story, Lee says, "has to work harder." In fact, when the Lee & Low editors were starting up their list, they had to read nearly 300 manuscripts before they found what they considered to be five good stories.

What Doesn't Work

Lee said the problem in the manuscripts he sees is often that an author has written an "ethnic interest book," but has not looked hard enough for the larger story behind the book. "Mung or Vietnamese are not stories in themselves," he says. "Our most successful books have ethnic American characters, but they are *about* fathers or *about* baseball. They're not pumped out because there is a need for a story about a certain ethnic group." Or sometimes, he says, an author sends him a story and says, "This story could be set in any ethnic group." His response? "If it's that generic, it's probably about nothing at all."

Lee is also quick to point out that "too many publishers have published too much folklore." His company doesn't do folktales at all anymore.

Shepard agrees, "It's definitely tough to sell folktales today, unless you're one of the top two or three in the field." He notes that Atheneum, the only publisher buying folktales from him, decided a few years ago that "if they were going to publish folktales profitably, the tales should be (1) unusual; (2) educational; and (3) illustrated by artists with big names or otherwise outstanding."

So why even think about writing a multicultural story? "Being on the cusp of a culture," says Kroupa, "is an interesting place. Voices that echo that ethnic experience are often interesting voices."

As one of three editors charged with starting a new fiction line at Dorling Kindersley, Kroupa adds that she is "keen to find fresh, new voices" and "eager to work with a voice that has promise." In searching for the "gems" in a mass of mediocre stories, she has kept her eyes open for "books that explore the edges, the gray areas that make life real and interesting. Multicultural provides many gray areas. Books that aren't black and white are always the most illuminating and resonant."

An Insider's Story

When Haemi Balgassi was eight or nine

Multicultural Markets: Book Publishers

A&B Books
African American Images
Annick Press
Arroyo Projects Studio
Avisson Press
Baker's Plays
Benchmark Books
Bess Press
Beyond Words
Blackbirch Press
Blue Bird Pub.
Borealis Press
Bureau for At-Risk Youth
Carson-Dellosa
Charlesbridge Pub.
Chelsea House
Cherubic Press
Children's Book Press
China Books
Chronicle Books
Clear Light Pub.
Council for Indian Educ.
Crabtree Pub.
Creative Teaching Press
Crocodile Books
DawnSign Press
Delmar Pub.
Didax Educ. Resources
Displays for Schools
Eakin Press
Educators Pub. Service
Facts on File
Fairview Press
Flatland Tales Pub.
Forest House
Fulcrum Kids
Gage Educ. Pub.
Golden Meteorite Press
Gryphon House

Gumbs & Thomas
Hampton-Brown Books
Holloway House
Impact Pub.
Incentive Pub.
Jonathan David Pub.
Jewish Pub. Society
Key Porter Books
Alfred A. Knopf Books
Lee & Low Books
Lindsey Pub.
Linnet Books
Lion Books
Lollipop Power Books
James Lorimer
Lothrop, Lee & Shepard
Lucent Books
Mage Pub.
McClanahan and Co.
Midwest Traditions
Milkweed Editions
The Millbrook Press
Mitchell Lane Pub.
Morehouse Pub.
Morgan Reynolds
New Hope
New Seed Press
Northland Pub.
Open Hand Pub.
Orchard Books
Our Child Press
Richard C. Owen Pub.
Pacific Educ. Press
Pacific View Press
Paws IV Pub.
Peachtree Pub.
Peartree
Pelican Pub.
Pemmican Pub.

Piñata Books
The Place in the Woods
Polychrome Pub.
QED
Ragweed Press
Raspberry Pub.
Rayve Productions
Rosen Pub.
Salina Bookshelf
Sasquatch Books
Scarecrow Press
Seedling Pub.
Sierra Oaks Pub.
Silver Moon Press
Social Science Educ.
SpanPress
Storytellers Ink
Sundance Pub.
Teacher Created Materials
Theytus Books
Third World Press
Thomasson-Grant
Tilbury House
Tradewind Books
Treasure Chest
Tundra Books
Twenty-First Century
Volcano Press
Ward Hill Press
Weigl Educ. Pub.
Williamson Pub.
Winston-Derek Pub.
Wolfhound Press
Zino Press

years old, her mother told her about a piece of her family history, "a rooftop ride on a freight train in the middle of a harsh winter and war." That story inspired Balgassi's first book, *Peacebound Trains* (Clarion).

"The details of the story left a vivid impression on me," Balgassi says, "and I knew from a young age that I would try to write down the story some day." In fact, her first attempt to do so was published when Balgassi was still in high school, in the form of an essay called "War Child" for the school literary magazine. Although the heart of the story was family history, Balgassi also did research on the Korean War to write *Peacebound Trains*.

The research for her second book, *Tae's Sonata* (Clarion), "was much more personal—digging up memories mostly." When she submitted a picture book version of the story, her editor at Clarion, Dorothy Briley, asked if Balgassi would be interested in turning the story into a longer piece. The novel, published in 1997, focuses on the life of a Korean-American girl five years after her arrival in the United States, the period of Balgassi's own childhood "when I felt the most conflicted and unsettled."

"Tae, in many ways, is based on myself," she adds. "In writing the story, there were times when I felt like I was visiting the girl I used to be." At the same time, Balgassi noticed that it was more comfortable to revisit that child now that she was wearing "adult shoes." She says, "I understand myself better now, and feel a sense of peace about my heritage that I struggled for in childhood."

Writing about her own cultural experience, she says, was "a bit like staring into a mirror. You look long enough, and the flaws jump out at you." She finds herself wanting to write and show "all the good things," but knows that to have an honest and good story, she has "to show the wrinkles, too."

An Outsider's Story

During the boom time for multicultural books, one of the debates that raged was whether it was legitimate for European-American authors to write about a culture other than their own. While critics have sometimes drawn clear lines in the sand on this highly charged issue, a senior editor at one small publisher points out that very few editors really take a rigid stance.

"I may prefer to find authors writing from within their own cultures," he says, "but I make no rule about it, even though I am tempted to sometimes, as when I got a story set in contemporary India by someone who had never been there," as the lack of direct knowledge showed.

Can it be done? Author Laurie Anderson is an example of an author who has been successful in writing about a place she had never been. Her first picture book, *Ndito Runs* (Henry Holt), set in Kenya, was named an American Booksellers Association Pick of the Lists and has recently been translated into Zulu, Xhosa, Lesotho, and Afrikaans. She got the idea for the story when she was lying in bed one morning, listening to National Public Radio (NPR), and a story came on about female runners in Kenya.

Multicultural Markets: Magazines

Adoptive Families
AIM
The ALAN Review
Alaska Parenting
American Baby
American Girl
Atlanta Parent
Bay Area Parent
Birth to Three
Black Child
The Black Collegian
Book Links
The Book Report
Bridges
Brilliant Star
Careers & Majors
Challenge
Christteen
Cleveland/Akron Family
Cobblestone
College PreView
Colorado Kids
Creative Classroom
DirectAIM
The Drinking Gourd
Early Childhood Today
Educational Oasis
Education Today
Essence
Faces
First Opportunity
First Word Bulletin
Florida Leader
Girls' Life
Harambee
High Adventure

The High School Magazine
High School Writer
Hip Mama
Holidays & Seasonal
    Celebrations
i propaganda
Journal for a Just and
    Caring Education
Juniorway
Kid Connection
KIDS
Launch Pad
Library Talk
Mahoning Valley Parent
The McGuffey Writer
Middle School Journal
Montessori LIFE
National Geographic
    World
New Moon
Nineteenth Avenue
Parenting for Peace &
    Justice
Parents and Children
    Together Online
Parents' Press
Pockets
PTV Families
Read, America!
Scholastic Math Power
Scholastic Update
The School Librarian's
    Workshop
Sharing Space
Shofar
Shoofly

Single-Parent Family
Skipping Stones
Sports Illustrated For Kids
Stepfamilies
Story Friends
Storytelling
Student Travels
Successful Black Parenting
Teaching Elementary
    Physical Education
TEACHING Exceptional
    Children
Teaching Secondary
    Physical Education
Teaching Tolerance
Teen Life
Teen Voices
Tomorrow's Morning
Totally Fox Kids
Valley Parent
The Whole Idea
With
Writing Teacher
Young Adult Today
Young Children
Young Salvationist
Youth

The reporter who did the research for the NPR story interviewed Kenyan children who ran back and forth to school every day. One morning, he thought he would join the young runners. "These nine- and ten-year-old girls just cruised comfortably, while he struggled and puffed to keep up," Anderson says. "And the girls laughed and giggled."

Listening to the sound of their laughter, Anderson wondered what the girls were thinking and dreaming about as they ran through the countryside. "When I was a girl," she says, "trudging through the snow to get to school in Syracuse, New York, I pretended to be different kinds of animals to relieve the boredom. I think that imagining oneself as an animal is a core childhood experience that transcends culture."

To get the details right, Anderson spent "months researching Kenya, reading everything in the academic libraries of Philadelphia, viewing films, interviewing people who lived there, calling a principal of a school in the highlands." After she had her manuscript written, she sent it to the Kenyan Embassy "to make sure the facts and sense of place were correct and respectfully done." Interesting research tidbits she was unable to use in the book ended up on her web page (www.voicent.com/laurie).

Inside/Outside Connection

Anyone who would draw clear lines, in the interest of cultural authenticity, underestimates just how complicated it can be, anyway, to decide who is writing from their own culture.

I am an example. My parents took me to Ethiopia when I was only two, and I spent most of my childhood there as what is sometimes called a third-culture kid—someone being raised outside the country of her parents' culture, but not totally belonging to the culture of the country where she is being raised. As an adult, I lived in the U.S. But as I began to barrel toward the big forty, I developed a longing to reconnect with Ethiopia. Luckily, at the time, a number of editors were also longing to have books that showed young readers what life was like in a faraway place like Ethiopia.

Even someone who has spent a great deal of time in another country or with another ethnic group, however, has to be sensitive to the complexities of crossing cultural lines. In the process of writing *Pulling the Lion's Tail* (Simon & Schuster), I called an Ethiopian friend to ask what it would really be like for a stepchild in Ethiopia who was learning to get along with a new mother. It was when I heard what she had to say that my story found its real conflict.

I've researched countless details about Ethiopian life in the process of writing my books. The hardest task of all is to enter into the mind and heart (or the stomach, as an Ethiopian would say) of someone from another culture. Such a challenge can have rich rewards, but it should never be undertaken lightly.

Peace Corps, church work, romance, study abroad, emigration: A multitude of situations pull people into intense contact with cultures not their own. Third-culture kids and global nomads are everywhere these days, eager to tell their stories.

While it may no longer be possible to publish a fully illustrated retelling of that folktale from another country, a well-written picture book story of contemporary life could well find a home—such as happened with *Only a Pigeon* (Simon & Schuster), which my brother and I wrote from the perspective of a street kid in Addis Ababa, raising pigeons. "At last," said one review, "a book set in an African city." Novels like *The Ear, the Eye, and the Arm,* by Nancy Farmer (Orchard) and *Shabanu: Daughter of the Wind,* by Suzanne Fisher Staples (Alfred A. Knopf)—both Newbery Honor books—attest to the power that having been immersed in another culture can give an author's writing.

Yes, although multicultural books may face a somewhat rockier road than they did when multicultural was a magic word, they continue to have strong advocates. Dr. Francenia L. Emery, a former school principal in the Philadelphia school system, has made it her mission, through the Multicultural Resource Center, to introduce good children's books, not only to teachers and parents but to hospitals, ministerial groups, adoption agencies, social workers. "I have such passion about this!" she says. "All children need to see themselves reflected in the literature they read. They also need to learn about people who may be different in some ways. Literature is one of the best ways to reduce prejudice in children. After all, everybody loves a good story."

If there is any bit of advice for writers on what still works in multicultural writing it's echoed in Emery's words: Write a good story. "The best books that could fit into the classification of multicultural," Kroupa says, "really work as wonderful books. They speak to the more universal—often just what it is to be a human being, brought alive through a specific character in a specific setting."

Magazines

A Surge in the Teen Market

By Victoria Hambleton

KEY NEWS

Some writers look for the new and different, a chance to be on the cutting edge. Others prefer to grow a career with solid writing on tried-and-true subjects of proven interest to readers. For both approaches, the mushrooming teen magazine market offers the possibility of a high yield.

In one year, an unbelievable five new teen consumer magazines hit the stands—*Jump, Twist, Teen People, Guideposts for Teens,* and *Glossy*—as did a handful of special interest publications aimed at young adults—*Crystal Ball,* on science and technology, for ages ten to fourteen; *Freeze,* on skiing, ages fourteen to twenty-five; *Dance Spirit,* by the publishers of *American Cheerleader,* for school dance teams; and, *Topspin,* sponsored by the U.S. Tennis Association, for ages eight to sixteen. Making its debut at the American Library Association

1998 summer meeting is *Cicada,* a teen literary magazine by the Cricket Group.

This new crop owes much to current demographics on teens, as any of the new publications' editors will explain. U.S. Census figures indicate that the teen population, ages twelve to nineteen, is now estimated at 29 million and that it will grow to 34 million by 2010. Add to that the fact that thirteen–to-nineteen-year-olds spent an estimated $68.8 billion on personal items in 1995, the last year for which figures are available, and it's not hard to imagine advertisers lining up to hawk their wares.

Yet another demographic truth of the teen magazine market concerns gender: It is the girls who buy magazines, who read regularly. Teen boys may pick up the adult *Sports Illustrated* like their fathers and coaches, and dedicated scouts have *Scouting,* but say

"teen magazine" and for the most part you're saying "girl."

What better place to attract the attention of teenage girls than in that entity sacrosanct to maturing girls—the beauty and fashion magazine. For decades, it has been a monthly ritual to pore over *Seventeen* behind closed doors, alone or with friends. Yes, once upon a time the primary fodder of such publications was Yardley City Slickers and Twiggy in a tartan plaid skirt. The most pressing question in their pages was not much more serious than whether or not to put pennies in your loafers. But loafers are oddly back in style and the enduring popularity of *Seventeen*, *YM*, and *'Teen* prove that the old formula of fashion, make-up, and boys still works.

A Real Service?

What's different in the new species of teen magazines, all the editors say, is the *real-girl* slant. Whether that translates to using regular people for models or using first-person narratives by girls to touch on the more serious issues of growing up, all the new publications tap into this perspective, each, it hopes, in a unique way.

Lori Berger, Editor-in-Chief of Weider Publication's *Jump*, is a veteran of the teen magazine industry who has held top positions at both *YM* and the now defunct *Sassy*. "There's a formula to teen magazines," she says, "and it's boys, beauty, fashion, and boys. To be a player these days in the teen field, you have to distinguish yourself beyond the basic formula. We take a pretty intense real-girl approach with *Jump*. We use real girls in beauty and fashion and I would say 50 percent of our features are first-person stories."

Sassy pioneered this use of the first-person voice in the early 1990s. Ahead of its time, the magazine featured such stories on abortion, gay couples, and birth control, and as a result had many consumers and advertisers up in arms.

The new teen magazines are taking the approach and topics farther still. Cover lines for a given month's new publications include: "My Boyfriend Gave Me an STD," "He Raped Me But I Fought Back," and "What Happens When Relationships Turn Deadly." Other stories involve self-mutilation, alcoholism, liposuction, teen HIV, and abuse.

To anyone who hasn't picked up a teen magazine in a while, the subject matter is disturbing. Yet the editors definitively argue that such subjects should be standard fare, even in magazines that aim to be entertaining, too.

Christina Ferrari is Editor of the new *Teen People*. The magazine borrows much of its approach from its parent publication, *People:* a healthy mix of celebrity features, photos, and gossip. But it also looks at the more serious side of teen life because, Ferrari notes, topics like date rape and eating disorders are a reality. "It's sad to say, but these issues are prevalent in this age," she says. "I think many magazines feel that they have a responsibility to talk about the scary, depressing issues because many teenagers don't have anywhere else to turn for information. I think if you present them in a responsible way, as a service, then they are important issues to tackle."

Teen People's Investigation column deals with just these kind of problems. But Ferrari is quick to point out that the magazine also stresses positive stories about what real teens are doing with their lives. The Local Hero department showcases a teen who has done something extraordinary in the community or as a volunteer. Success Story looks at teens who have made a name for themselves by entrepreneurship.

Jump took on the issue of self-mutilation through a first-person story in a regular column, My So-Called Life. The second issue featured an article about a girl beaten to death by her boyfriend. Berger justifies these stories by saying she is responding to what the audience wants. "We have to demonstrate that we are real and in touch with what's out there. If we were to pretend that these issues didn't exist, we wouldn't be relevant to our readers' lives."

More Power to You

But *Jump* is a magazine of the Weider group, publishers of numerous fitness

magazines, most notably *Shape.* The new teen magazine naturally shares that slant. While not neglecting the demonstrated appeal of stories on beauty and fashion, *Jump* tries to incorporate these into a mix that also promotes self-esteem and empowerment.

"I think *Jump* is setting trends," says Berger. "The established recipe for teen magazines—including celebrities, lots of boys, and beauty tips—clearly sells magazines. But what we've tried to do, and I think successfully, is take these ingredients and give them an empowering edge. Our stories are all generated with the intention of making girls feel better about themselves. Our message is get involved, play sports, be a part of your community. We don't ever come out and talk about self-esteem but we subliminally suggest it. Whatever the subject—health, fitness, sex, boys—the message is the same: Feel good about yourself." So far, the plan seems to be

Teen Magazines

Title	Frequency	Circ.	Free-lance*	Topics
American Careers	3x/yr	N.A.	15	Careers, computers, nature, health, math, science.
American Cheerleader	bimonthly	200,000	3	Cheerleading competition, school, health, pop culture.
Blue Jean	bimonthly	20,000	25%	Teen girls. Careers, social issues. Written mostly by readers.
Breakaway	monthly	90,000	30	Christian boys. Self-esteem. Profiles, sports, how-to, religion.
Brio	monthly	110,000	40	Christian, girls. Self-esteem. Profiles, family, how-to, religion.
Campus Life	9x/yr	100,000	15	Leading a Christian life. Fiction, nonfiction.
Careers & Colleges	4x/yr	125,000	20	Newly revamped. High school juniors and seniors.
Career World	7x/yr	200,000	56	How-to, self-help, education, college, career, ethics.
Dramatics	9x/yr	37,000	60	Theater personalities, drama, acting, production, directing.
Exploring	quarterly	350,000	15	Boy Scouts. Profiles, high-adventure sports, leadership.
Freeze	4x/yr	N.A.	30%	Skiing, for ages 14-25. Lifestyle, humor.
Hit Parader	monthly	150,000	5	Music, especially heavy metal and hard rock.
Inside Sports	monthly	859,000	15	Sports, health, pop culture, technology, in relation to sports
InSights	monthly	58,000	40	Junior members of the National Rifle Association.
Keynoter	7x/yr	182,000	20	Promote activities of Key Club. Self-help, service.

(continued on next page)

* Number of freelance submissions purchased yearly, or if that number is not available, the percentage of the magazine written by nonstaff writers.   N.A.: not available.

Teen Magazines *continued*

Title	Frequency	Circ.	Free-lance*	Topics
Listen	monthly	40,000	45	Healthy alternatives to drugs, alcohol, cigarettes.
react	weekly	4 million	90%	Interactive newsmagazine; voice of teens.
Scholastic Choices	8x/yr	100,000	5	School-based. Health, home, lifestyle.
Scholastic MATH	14x/yr	200,000	3	Math in the real world, problem-solving skills.
Scholastic Scope	20x/yr	850,000	5	Classic and contemporary literature.
Scholastic Update	14x/yr	185,000	20	News, social issues.
Science World	biweekly	400,000	30	Pub. in school year. Life, earth, physical, sciences.
Seventeen	monthly	2 million	50%	Health, pop. culture, friendship, family, self-help, boys.
Slap	monthly	60,000	5	Boys. Music, hip-hop, skateboarding.
'Teen	monthly	1.1 million	39	Fashion, beauty, social issues, lifestyle, sports, health.
Teen Beat	monthly	350,000	2	Entertainment, celebrities.
Tiger Beat	bimonthly	200,000	2	Film, TV, music, for girls.
Thrasher	monthly	150,000	20	Boys. Skateboarding, snowboarding, sports, music.
Topspin	quarterly	N.A.	N.A.	U.S. Tennis Assn. Tennis for junior players.
YM	14x/yr	2.3 million	12	Friends, dating, health, social issues, entertainment, beauty.

KEY NEWS

Religious Teen Magazines

Breakaway, Focus on the Family, boys
Brigade Leader, Christian Service Brigade
Brio, Focus on the Family, girls
Campus Life, Christianity Today
Challenge, Brotherhood Commission, Southern Baptist Convention, boys
Christteen, interdenominational, African-American teens
Club Connection, Assemblies of God, girls, ages 5-17
The Conqueror, United Pentecostal Church International
Crusader, Calvinist Cadet Corps, boys
Guide, Review and Herald Publishing, Seventh-day Adventist Church
High Adventure, Assemblies of God, Royal Ranger boys, ages 5-17
I.D., David C. Cook Publishing, Pentecostal and nondenominational versions
Insight, Christ-centered
The New Era, Church of Jesus Christ of Latter-day Saints
On Course, Assemblies of God
On the Line, Mennonite Publishing House
Partners, Mennonite Publishing House
Sharing the Victory, Fellowship of Christian Athletes
SPIRIT, Sisters of St. Joseph of Carondelet
Straight, Standard Publishing Company
Take Five, Assemblies of God
TC,(Teenage Christian), Christian Publishing
Teen Life, Assemblies of God
Teens on Target, Word Aflame Publications
Today's Christian Teen, Bible-based
Touch, GEMS girls (formerly known as Calvinettes)
With, Mennonite
YOU!, Catholic moral framework
Young Adult Today, Bible-based, African-American
Young & Alive, blind or visually impaired young Christians
Young Salvationist, The Salvation Army
Youth Challenge, Pentecostal Publishing House
Youth 98, House of White Birches
Youth Update, St. Anthony Messenger Press

working. *Jump* premiered as a bimonthly in August and quickly turned monthly.

The Mainstay

Empowerment is a word that Mary Lou Carney, Editor of the highly successful Christian magazine for younger children, *Guideposts for Kids,* used as her mainstay when she came up with the idea of *Guideposts for Teens.* "*Guidepost's* social agenda," she explains, "has always been to offer a practical guide for successful living. It's the pragmatic side of faith. Surely no group needs empowerment more than teens. We created *Guideposts for Teens* to give them that by sharing stories of faith at work."

Faith at work translates, again, to first-person narratives. They are the backbone of the first issue of *Guideposts for Teens,* which debuted with a December/January issue. In it there are eight such fortifying stories: Carney describes them as "911 with a purpose."

"We all like a good story," she adds. "That's really what I think the magazine capitalizes on. We take those stories and wrap them in a package where the faith angle is part of the story. I think that a teen magazine should address issues teens face in their daily lives. As a nonpolitical publication, there are stories we would not do (for example, abortion or sexuality) but there are plenty of other tough topics to tackle."

Catering to readers aged thirteen to seventeen, *Guideposts for Teens* hopes to cross the gender gap and appeal to teenage boys as well as girls. To that end, it will not feature any fashion or beauty.

Sensory Overload

Twist and *Glossy* are banking on the suc-

cessful formulas of "old-timers," *Seventeen* and *YM.* At the same time, they are also investing in the belief that today's teens are readers with a difference.

Twist is published by Bauer Publishing, which has successfully produced teen magazines in Europe. Of all the new entries, it sports the most visual translation of the theory that teens read differently than their parents. Its layout is highly charged with color and bits of information cramming every page, cartoon style. Even the articles, which are rarely longer than 1,500 words, are highly visual, with bold pull-quotes accompanied by color photos and color text.

Editor-in-Chief Lisa Lombardi describes the magazine's look as "an intentional attempt at sensory overload." "I think teens read a magazine the way they visit a website: Click here, click there, read this, move on, skip to this, now go back, then forward. They access information in a nonlinear way."

Twist, a monthly as of April, addresses serious issues in its Real Life column, but by and large, it is a more traditional teen magazine. Since teen girls tend to buy more than one magazine, *Twist* is expecting another beauty book to appeal to a majority of them. "Our magazine covers many of the areas that the others do because fashion, beauty, celebrities, these are what teen girls love," says Lombardi. "We're trying to let our readers dictate to a large extent what we are doing. At a certain point, I think publishers will get a little wary of entering a crowded market, but I think if the magazines are done well, they can all survive."

Glossy, which existed first as a website and later launched its print version, makes no bones about the fact that it is "fluff and entertainment." The aim, says Editor-in-Chief Sarah Goldsmith, is to be "the first fashion magazine" for teenagers with an editorial content that is 60 percent fashion. "We want to produce a magazine that has the sophistication of *Vogue* or *W.*" *Glossy* has its cap set on the "trendsetting" fourteen- and-fifteen-year-olds that research indicates "read up" to magazines like *Vogue, Harper's Bazaar,* and *Allure.*

Who's Talking?

The frenzy of activity in the teen market is, on the one hand, a purely business response to demographics and buying patterns. Whether anything truly new and exciting will emerge is still anybody's guess. For the moment at least, the new magazines are answering trends rather than setting them.

But what is new and different is the voice with which the magazines are responding. Where once the tone was like a mother's, saying, "Do wear that, don't wear the other," today's magazines speak in the voice of a teen's peers. Caring adults can only hope those voices are filtered through the responsible guidance of editors. Nineties society as a whole seems to hunger for the true story, the baring of the soul, as a means of communication. While there are good reasons to present stories on the tough issues facing teens today, most editors stress that their magazines are first and foremost entertainment and not self-help manuals.

"When magazines start dissecting teens' lives, they sometimes forget that being a teenager is supposed to be fun," says Lombardi. "It's all about your friends and secrets and acting silly and having a good time."

Editors acknowledge that it is a fine line to walk between presenting information and passing judgment. "When you ask if teen magazines should have a social responsibility," says Ferrari, "I think you get onto dangerous ground. You attach a moral purpose to something that is really a consumer product. I try never to forget that we are here to sell magazines and entertain people, not tell them what is right and what is wrong."

If you want to know what teenage life is all about, look no further than the pile of magazines you can find under most teen girls' beds. If you are looking for answers to the issues that teens confront in the real world, read on, and keep looking.

MARKET OVERVIEWS

Part
3

OVERVIEWS

Book Publishing

A Forward Momentum

By Kristi Vaughan

OVERVIEWS

Psst! Don't tell the naysayers, but children's book publishing isn't in the tough shape that some might have you believe. In fact, if you look beyond the bad news headlines, you will find underlying optimism and considerable forward momentum.

New imprints have launched at HarperCollins, Simon & Schuster, and Marshall Cavendish, among others. Small publishers, including Northland and Charlesbridge, continue their growth trends. New writers are still welcomed at such houses as Houghton Mifflin's Children's Books, The Millbrook Press, and HarperCollins Children's Books.

"I think all of the markets are starting to come back," says Margaret Raymo, Senior Editor at Houghton Mifflin. "There is just a more positive feeling out there now."

John Keller, Vice President and Publisher of Children's Books at Little, Brown and Company, which just a year ago was slashing its list by 40 percent, concurs: "We're feeling very happy and optimistic."

While the sales numbers of some publishers certainly run against this tide, overall the figures show growth. In its most recent study on consumer research, The Book Industry Study Group found that annual sales of children's books rose 5 percent. According to the most current Veronis, Suhler & Associates Communications Industry Forecast, annual unit sales of juvenile trade books grew by nearly 9 percent and paperback sales by 12.1 percent.

The American Association of Publishers recorded a 2.2 percent rise in juvenile hardcover sales year-to-date, according to the latest figures available at presstime, and returns were down more than 4 percent. The downside was in juvenile paperback sales: They were off 22 percent for the year and returns were up by 25 percent. Much of the paperback decline was attributed to a relative slump in sales of Scholastic's enormous success, Goosebumps.

As optimism returns to the children's book market, several key factors could affect the market's direction and growth. These include:

■ The ability of publishers to iden-tify and maintain the focus of their publishing programs.

■ The growing importance of licensed characters and entertainment tie-ins.

■ The increased attention on marketing and new sales outlets.

Healthy Pruning

The strategy for the latter part of the 1990s at many publishing houses is to determine who they are and want to be. Wilting under high returns and lower

New Imprints, Lines, and Series

Name	Parent Company	Description
Adventures with Nicholas	Berlitz Kids	Books and cassettes. The first title: *The Missing Cat.*
	Avisson Press	The company expands into the YA market for the first time. Biographies.
Avon Hardcover	Avon Books	General fiction; no picture books.
Classic Frights	Books of Wonder	Introduces children to classic horror writers.
DK Ink	Dorling Kindersley	Primarily picture books and middle-grade and older fiction. 20 books a season. Some adult titles and nonfiction.
Forgotten Realm	TSR Books	Series of nine monthly books. Publisher of science fiction, fantasy, horror.
HarperActive	HarperCollins	Hardcover, paperback, novelty, mass-market imprint.
Knopf Paperbacks	Random House	Largely a reprint line.
Inchworm Press	GT Publishing	Storybooks, novelty books, books plus.

(continued on next page)

than expected profits earlier in the decade, segments of the industry have acquired a "return to roots" mentality.

Gardeners know that clipping a rose bush or a fruit tree in the wrong place is useless or even harmful, but pruning in the right places and ways creates a healthier, better-producing, longer-lasting plant. Publishers today believe the pruning of lists means the same. Editors are therefore taking an even closer look at what will sell and what won't, what to prune, and what to fos-ter. "We previously trimmed the list to a more manageable number. Now we are trying to give each book the right focus and attention," comments Andrea Cascardi, Associate Publishing Director, Knopf and Crown Books for Young Readers.

"I think that everybody has been publishing too much and that has been extremely detrimental," says Jean Feiwel, Publisher and Senior Vice President of the Scholastic Book Group. The result, at least as it affects writers, is de-

New Imprints, Lines, and Series *continued*

Name	Parent Company	Description
	Marshall Cavendish	Curriculum publisher launches first line of trade books. 14 titles, fiction and nonfiction, but stress on picture books.
	Richard C. Owen	Second line of easy-to-read books, for older children.
Rising Moon	Northland Pub.	Picture books, middle-grade novels, YA books.
	Saint Mary's Press	YA novels. First juvenile books by this publisher.
Simon Spotlight	Simon & Schuster	Media tie-ins, licensed characters, and other books in a variety of formats.
Smart Pages	Golden Books	Books have in-the-page sound technology allowing children to interact with characters.
Talewinds	Charlesbridge Publishing	Fiction picture books, ages 3-8
	Winslow Press	A new line of books from the nonprofit Foundation for Concepts in Education.

Projected Juvenile Book Units

The number of trade books estimated to be shipped yearly:

Hardcover Books			Paperbacks		
	Trade Books	*Change*		*Trade Books*	*Change*
1997	180 million	-3.7%	1997	188 million	-6.0%
1998	178 million	-1.1%	1998	185 million	-1.6%
1999	181 million	1.7%	1999	187 million	1.1%
2000	185 million	2.2%	2000	190 million	1.6%
2001	191 million	3.2%	2001	196 million	3.2%

Source: Based on data from the Veronis, Suhler & Associates Communications Industry Forecast. Veronis, Suhler & Associates, Wilkofsky Fruen Associates, Book Industry Study Group.

creases in list sizes and the closing of some imprints. "We are, for the first time, pruning our list in a way we haven't before," Feiwel continues. "I think that is a sensible and not entirely hurtful thing to do. It allows us to focus more and spread our marketing dollars more effectively."

"Certainly one of the biggest influences on the future of the children's market is one that we have been seeing for the last few years, and that is an overall reduction in the number of titles being accepted in the marketplace," says Douglas Whiteman, Executive Vice President of Penguin Putnam and President and Publisher of The Putnam and Grosset Group. In the aftermath of the merger of the two large houses, an analysis by Putnam Penguin of its imprints resulted in the closing of Lodestar Books and Cobblehill Books, which sold to schools and libraries.

As Penguin Putnam cuts back its list over the next three years from about 900 titles to between 700 and 750, the company will be looking for books that have a broad appeal, says Whiteman. "We're not reducing our interest in the institutional market, but we're really focusing our energies on books and lines that sell in all marketplaces." The remaining imprints include Dial, Dutton, Grosset & Dunlap, PaperStar, Philomel, Price Stern Sloan, Puffin, Putnam, and Viking.

The pruning of lists probably does mean that so-called midlist writers will struggle, but Feiwel is quick to say that list cutbacks don't mean an end to innovation. "We still have to go after

tribute was strong sales and marketing," says Rick Richter, who joined the company as President and Publisher of the Children's Division after establishing the successful Candlewick Press. "I felt we were undermarketed and undersold. From an editorial standpoint, it seemed to me that we really needed to raise up and hold high the identity of each of the imprints, to show how Atheneum is different from Simon & Schuster Books for Young Readers, which is different from Margaret McElderry Books."

In Simon & Schuster's paperback field, Richter is taking what once was a catchall and drawing clear lines. Licensed books, for example, previously were mixed in with paperback reprints. Richter established Simon Spotlight as an umbrella for novelty books and books associated with licensed characters. Aladdin paperbacks are becoming more differentiated: They have enlarged logos and are classified into middle-grade and young adult books in distinct categories. Banners running across the bottom of the books state whether they are humor, action, adventure, or any one of six other categories.

books that are risky because that has tremendous upside potential. If we are merely doing what we did last year except in a bigger size or at a higher price point, that is not entirely interesting or ultimately profitable." For many, a willingness to take risks comes only after the structure is in place to support a healthy bottom line.

"We're really looking for exceptional works to publish because we don't publish as many titles as we once did," says Cascardi. "This is good for writers because it encourages them to think about whether they are doing everything they can to make their books the best they can be."

Clear Identity

After the less vibrant growth has been removed, publishers turn to the biggest bloom: They focus energy on creating or refining an identity, and supporting it through strong marketing.

"When I came to Simon & Schuster, the most important thing I could con-

A Populist View

That new, strong, clear look for Aladdin's books has particular advantages in a changing marketplace, and other publishers are working on the same enhancement of graphics and presentation.

At Putnam Penguin, Whiteman says, "something like 24 percent of all books purchased last year were purchased outside of the traditional mar-

Following Trends—or Not

As attuned as publishers try to be to kids' interests, they have to be careful not to jump on fads. "What is hot today could fizzle out tomorrow," says Michelle Poploff, Editorial Director of Bantam Doubleday Dell Books for Young Readers. Company representatives out in "the field will mail us something about what kids are doing—for example Beanie Babies or Nano Babies. Unless we publish practically overnight, the fad may be over and kids will be on to a different trend."

The fine line of trends must be carefully trod. "We have a lot of ears to a lot of different ground, " says Jean Feiwel, Publisher and Senior Vice President of the Scholastic Book Group. "We listen to people in-house, in sales, marketing, publicity, and editorial."

Clearly, marketing staff input on acquisition decisions at some houses has increased. "We are very integrated in what we do," says Jeanne Finestone, Vice President for Marketing and General Manager, McClanahan & Company, a mass-market publisher of workbooks, activity books, board and novelty books, all of which are educationally driven. "We have a weekly or biweekly meeting at which marketing, sales production, design, and editorial get together," Finestone says. "Editorial takes the lead in developing material but it is incumbent on everybody to come in with an idea. We bring in that outside perspective to hone and fine tune a product from being merely good to being absolutely the best it can be."

Andrea Cascardi, Associate Publishing Director of Alfred A. Knopf, says that marketing involvement comes earlier now at Alfred A. Knopf as well. "Editorially, we require ourselves to think very strongly right from the beginning about all of the possibilities for a book, and not just expect somebody else to think about what to do with it once it is done." Marketing programs can include adding reading guides for fiction, or creating supporting sales materials and organizing author tours. But even the best of marketing plans won't compensate for a less than great book. "You have to have a brilliant book to start with," says Joan Abramowitz, Vice President of Marketing at Random House Children's Publishing. "Ultimately, it is difficult to make a book that doesn't have editorial merit a success."

---

kets. We think it will be 30 percent next year, so that, obviously, is an area we have to concentrate on. Most of the sales through those areas require real visibility; they are not books that sell just because the title sounds nice." Those nontraditional markets include "big box" stores like Price Costco and WalMart, catalogues, direct mail, and specialty outlets. Chain stores of course remain a significant part of the market, as well.

"I believe it is our responsibility to bring books to kids and parents wherever they are," says Richter. "That is fundamentally a populist view, but one that I really believe in. So, for instance, in the future, I would expect to find us pioneering nontraditional markets while at the same time building programs for each of the discrete markets we already serve."

Brand identity and visuals will continue to weigh in heavily. Covers are more colorful and graphic, so books will stand out on a crowded shelf. Even well-known titles are going through visual changes to make them more appealing and noticeable. The sports books of Matt Christopher, who died in late 1997, have long been a Little, Brown staple. Now the books will carry a tag line: "Number one sports writer for kids." Hyperion Books, too, has given titles a flashier, more graphic spine design that makes them instantly recognizable.

The practical, knowing, but committed voice of Scholastic's Feiwel explains, "We have to be mindful of the fact that books can be sold almost as tonnage in certain accounts and the retail environment of ten years ago is not there anymore." But, she adds, "to tailor our publishing program to the environment is to go down a dead end eventually. I think you have to publish what you believe in. There has to be something in there that is a spark all its own."

The Paperback Bloom

In publishing, 1997 is likely to be remembered as the year the bloom came off the paperbacks. The double-digit growth of early in the decade transformed to double-digit declines early that year. Most dramatically, returns of Scholastic's Goosebumps proved to be considerably higher than the company anticipated. "Goosebumps was just an

enormous phenomenon that ultimately was hard to sustain," says Robert Broadwater, Managing Director of the communications industry investment company, Veronis Suhler. That doesn't mean publishers are pulling up all their roots in paperbacks. Far from it.

"Goosebumps is not all there is in paperback," says Harold Underdown, Senior Editor of Charlesbridge Publishing, "When I came into publishing in 1989, paperback publishing was confined to a few companies doing reprints. Many of the trade houses didn't do paperbacks. Since then, just about every trade publisher has started publishing paperback reprints of picture books and novels and, very often, hard/soft publications."

Indeed, David Reuther, Editor-in-Chief of Morrow Junior Books, says that as more rights revert back to Morrow he expects the company's Beechtree imprint to increase its paperback publishing program. Alfred A. Knopf Books for Young Readers started Knopf Paperbacks largely as a reprint line. And Keller sees Little, Brown doing more paperback publishing by the year 2000, although he doubts much of it will be original.

"Paperbacks are friendlier to the retail market," says Underdown. "Maybe a parent can afford one hardcover but you can buy three paperbacks. Since publishers can no longer rely on the library market, they are going more to paperback."

He continues, "Charlesbridge anticipated this trend. We've always published in paperback and, while we're moving more in the direction of hardcover, that is from a place where 80 to 85 percent of our sales are in paper."

More Known Quantities

The drive to focus a company's identity, and of course increase profits, is sending many children's publishers back to their backlists, where they find tried-and-true books that they can "reinvent" as board books, books plus, or even television series—which, if all goes well, will then spawn a new interest in the books. Just look at what Marc Brown's *Arthur* has done for Little, Brown.

While the *Arthur* books have been around a while, and were certainly well liked, *Arthur* premiered as a PBS show about a year ago. Now the books are selling like hot cakes. "*Arthur* is a huge hit," agrees Little, Brown's Keller, who doesn't want to use that success to mask other problems. "There is no question that things are tough out there in the trade, so we are still sticking with the 'fewer but better' idea and books with more commercial appeal."

Little, Brown is not alone in capitalizing on past success. A look at *Publishers Weekly*'s list of children's bestsellers consistently finds board book versions of *Guess How Much I Love You* and *Brown Bear, Brown Bear, What Do You See?* "There has been a big boom in publishing picture books in board book format," says Steve Geck, Director of Children's Books at Barnes and Noble and former Executive Editor of the Children's Book of the Month Club. "It has been such a success that publishers are taking other picture books with longer text, editing them, and turning them into board books."

Even publishers who pride them-selves on literary quality rather than quantity are stepping into this arena. Houghton Mifflin had obtained the rights to the *Curious George* books before Margaret Rey's death in December 1996, and is now creating *Curious George* board books. "Margaret Rey always had approval of what we did," says Raymo. "Now, we have more freedom, but we are still being scrupulous about what we publish." Even so, says Geck, "This is already one of those areas where so many people are doing it that we have to wonder if it isn't becoming saturated. We are watching sales closely."

Another current recycling of success involves branding and licensed characters. Licensing is the reality of business today, particularly as the mass-market business grows. "The bookstore market is flat," says. "The big numbers are in the mass market." While that doesn't please writers, or many parents and teachers who look for good writing, says Joan Abramowitz, Vice President of Marketing at Random House Children's Publishing, "The fact is, parents are buying the licensed products in the mass-market and in the supermarkets. While licensed books do show up in the trade, they are the bread and butter of mass-market and supermarket." She also says that while many assume the writing in licensed books isn't particularly good, some of it is.

Mass-market potential has attracted such trade publishers as HarperCollins and Simon & Schuster, which launched the HarperActive and Simon Spotlight imprints, respectively, in response to growth in this area. When Whiteman says that Penguin Putnam is likely to

Mass-Market Publishers at a Glance

Mass-market books are sold in retail outlets such as discount stores (K-Mart, Walmart, Caldor's, Ames) and supermarkets. Most books with licensed characters (Barney, Sesame Street, Disney, Star Wars) are mass-market, as are many board and novelty books. Trade books usually have higher production values, more literary quality, and are sold in bookstores. Some publishers, such as Golden Books, publish mass-market books almost exclusively. Others, like HarperCollins and Penguin Putnam, publish a mix of trade and mass-market titles, sometimes under dedicated imprints and sometimes not.

Company	List Size	Description
Archway/Minstrel	200	Imprints of Pocket Books. Archway: ages 12-16. Minstrel: Ages 7-11. Suspense/thrillers, romantic sagas, comedy, scary humor, biographies of celebrities and sports figures. Licensed characters.
Bantam Doubleday Dell	350 (all imprints)	Publishes a broad range of books, from high-quality trade to mass-market. Last year it published 70 reprint or licensed books.
Golden Books	175	To age 12. Fiction, nonfiction, picture books, activity books. See sidebar, page 56, on developments at Golden. Licensed characters.
HarperActive	—	Imprint of HarperCollins, which has both trade and mass-market lines. It started the HarperActive line specifically to focus on its mass-market licensed products. HarperFestival publishes merchandise and novelty books not considered mass-market.
McClanahan & Company	60	To age 11. Board, novelty, activity and workbooks, interactive nonfiction. Educational. Owned by Scott Foresman-Addison Wesley.
Modern Publishing	250	Specializes in series. Publishes storybooks, board books, coloring and activity books, novelty books, for children 2-8.

Penguin Putnam:
   Grosset & Dunlap
   Price Stern Sloan
	
	90
	85
		To age 12. Fiction and nonfiction; activity, board, concept, picture, novelty, lift-the-flap books; chapter books. Fantasy, humor, adventure, fairy tales, science, sports, crafts. 50 of PSS's titles were reprints or licensed. Penguin Putnam is likely to add an imprint soon.

Simon & Schuster
   Simon Spotlight
   Little Simon
	
	33
	150
		6 months to 8 years. Simon Spotlight: new imprint dedicated to media tie-ins and licensed characters. Little Simon: novelty books with no tie-ins.

A Golden Future?

A new force in the children's market is Golden Books/Family Entertainment. So far, the company hasn't altered the face of children's publishing but many are carefully watching. Richard Snyder's efforts are directed at leveraging the well-known Golden Book brand name into a diverse publishing and entertainment company that offers children and adults more than mass-marketed storybooks.

"Clearly they are changing the shape of their company and getting into some things they weren't doing before, but until it rolls out in a significant way, I am unconvinced they will have a huge directional influence," says Douglas Whiteman, Executive Vice President of Penguin Putnam and President and Publisher of The Putnam and Grosset Group.

Significant moves of the past year have included the launch of an adult line, starting with Steven Covey's *The Seven Habits of Highly Effective Families;* a revival of the Lassie series for television and books; the introduction of its Smart Pages line of books; and a focus on merchandising based on such well-known books as *Pat the Bunny* and *The Poky Little Puppy.* Upcoming is a hardcover list being developed by Margery Cuyler, Vice President and Editorial Director of Trade Publishing. Cuyler is experienced at building new lists, having done it at Holiday House, where she was Editor-in-Chief before moving to Henry Holt, and then to Golden.

Of particular note to industry observers has been the amount of money Golden has paid for products and alliances. Golden, for example, acquired Shari Lewis Enterprises, complete with rights to Lamb Chop and Hush Puppy. The amount wasn't revealed, but the publishing industry took note of another deal, too: one with R.L. Stine. *Publishers Weekly* reported that Stine signed a deal for 65 new titles in the Fear Street, Ghosts of Fear Street, and Fear Street Sagas, worth $13 million. In addition to getting a big name author on its list, this extends Golden's reach into the eight-to-fourteen-year-old market for the first time.

Golden's big spending "hasn't yet had an influence elsewhere," says Whiteman. "I think people are still unsure of where they are going. I have seen cases where either an author or a licensee didn't go to Golden even though the money may have been higher because of uncertainty. If they are able to pull it off and continue to spend the money they have been offering, then two or three years from now we may see the effect."

add an imprint in the near future, he is talking about negotiations that are underway for a licensing partnership with a major movie studio.

Burned by past excesses, however, publishers express caution. "Right now we are turning down licensing proposals that don't have evergreen potential or real hit potential," says Simon & Schuster's Richter. Many times, rather than spend big money for a new license, publishers are leveraging what they already have. "Character development is another primary driving influence on the children's market," says Whiteman. "We have a lot of characters, some of whom have been exploited more than others, and I see a much greater focus on doing character-driven projects."

This is a trend that may hurt writers by taking away publishers' resources, but it may also give publishers enough income to produce a financial freedom to take risks on new projects.

A Necessary Balance

HarperCollins is representative of the leading publishers facing the two-pronged challenge: publishing in appropriate quantities for general consumption, and publishing with appropriate quality and innovation to promote the company's identity. "We're known in the industry as having the best backlist because we have such powerful authors as Shel Silverstein, Margaret Wise Brown, and Maurice Sendak," says Susan Katz, President and Publisher of HarperCollins Children's Books. "So the challenge for us is to keep the backlist alive but branch out and find new talent."

While keeping immediate profits in mind, publishers are sensibly continuing to look to the long term by making room for new authors and ideas. "There is definitely a quantity of titles that are designated for new people," says Whiteman, of Penguin Putnam. "We are always looking for new blood. This is not a situation where it is impossible for someone to walk in the door." Much the same is heard at Simon & Schuster. "Down the road you will see no shortage of investment in the future," Richter says. "A third of our list will always be investing in new talent, a third will build on people with a track record, and a third will be aiming for best sellers. This is a necessary balance to run a profitable publishing house, which ultimately is in the best interest of everyone."

"We always welcome new voices," says Michelle Poploff, Editorial Director of Bantam Doubleday Dell Books for Young Readers. But because the industry can't afford to go out on a limb for an unknown, the printruns for titles by new authors are usually smaller. "Hopefully, they will get good reviews and will go back for further printings."

The search for new voices, however, doesn't mean doors are completely open, however. Even as it looks for new authors, using its annual Marguerite de Angeli and Delacorte contests as vehicles for reaching new writers, BDD is not accepting unsolicited manuscripts. Neither is Simon & Schuster. At Hyperion and Disney Press, Vice President and Associate Publisher Ken Geist says, "Writers need to have a great manuscript or unusual idea and do their homework."

The reality is that, despite the chances taken on new authors, they will have to prove themselves. With some larger, publically owned companies often looking for a fast return on investments, books are expected to find success quickly or they are off the shelves. "It is sort of the way movies have changed," says Geck. "I think publishers look at the money they have spent on a book and they need to see a quick turnaround. If they don't see it right away they write it off and move on."

Whiteman agrees that the parameters for success are getting tougher. "Whereas maybe in the past we would have taken five to seven books to give an author or series a chance to work, now we are talking maybe three to four books," he says. Those most hurt by such demands will continue to be new writers and writers whose work doesn't have an editor's passionate backing. "For writers it is a struggle," says Abramowitz. "The real struggle is building a body of work and getting known."

The Other Side

The children's book market is far from a dying industry. It has been through some recent ups and downs and it will continue to have them going forward. The key is that forward momentum.

"We are going in fourteen different directions but all of them are straight ahead," says Scholastic's Feiwel. "I think we have come through a difficult time. I stress to the editorial board that we can learn a lesson from our setbacks but that doesn't mean we should shrink up and die."

Much the same can be said for writers. Marketing and genre trends will come and go, but writers who stop writing just because the market isn't storming ahead will never find true success. The same goes for writers who try to jump on every trend.

"Just because the market has changed, a writer shouldn't try to write a particular kind of book," says Underdown. "When he does, all he ends up with is something that doesn't come naturally. Writers should be writing the best they can. They should be reading as much as they can to soak up other people's writing. They should be networking, going to conferences, and talking to other writers. Those are the basic things they have to do and those haven't changed."

Book Manuscript Purchases

The number of manuscripts purchased by selected book publishers in 1997:

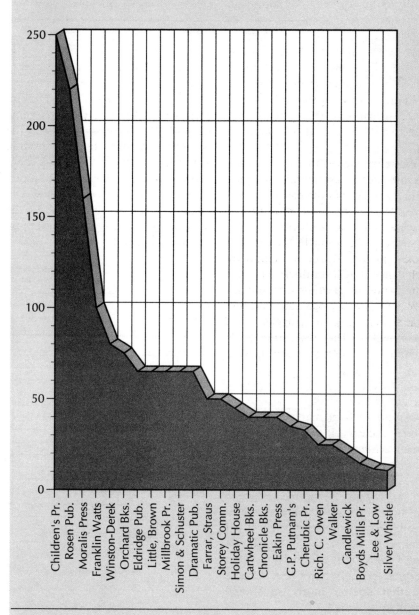

Book Publisher List Sizes

The number of books published by selected children's book publishers in 1997:

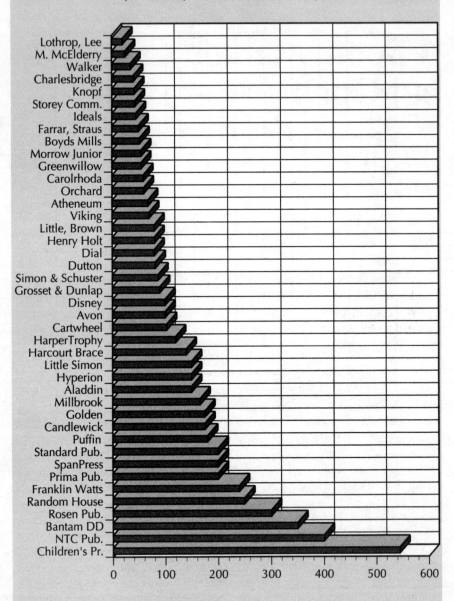

Magazine Publishing

A Boom Market: Crowded but Open

By Kristi Vaughan

I t is a time of dynamic growth for children's magazines. After a number of years of looking for the long-term good news, predicting it would come, but sounding cautious, publishing observers can say that the time has arrived. New publications are popping up with regularity. Even if, in this vibrant environment, some small magazines come and go quickly, it is because opportunities for markets are being newly defined and the free enterprise system is working at its what-the-market-can-bear best.

Jump, Chirp, Click, Real Kids, Topspin, Twist, and a primary edition of *Time For Kids* launched (and *Real Kids* closed, at least temporarily). A major expansion is occurring at Cobblestone Publishing in 1998. Cricket Magazine Group is expanding upward in its age-targeting with a new publication. *Teen People,* from Time, Inc., will debut in the next year.

"It has become a much more crowded marketplace over the last year or so," says David Goddy, Vice President and Editor-in-Chief of Scholastic magazines. He points out that many of the newcomers have what they think is an original idea for a magazine but, after they embark on their enterprise, they learn that there are others competing for the same audience. This makes success much harder. Existing publications *are* all over the field. Some are specialty or niche magazines created with a narrow, distinct market in mind. They include *Topspin*, which is aimed at young tennis players, and *Freeze,* for teenage skiers. *Real Kids* was started by Joe Leahy because he felt there was a need for a magazine to fill the gap between secular and religious magazines. Yet others seek a broader

Magazine Circulations

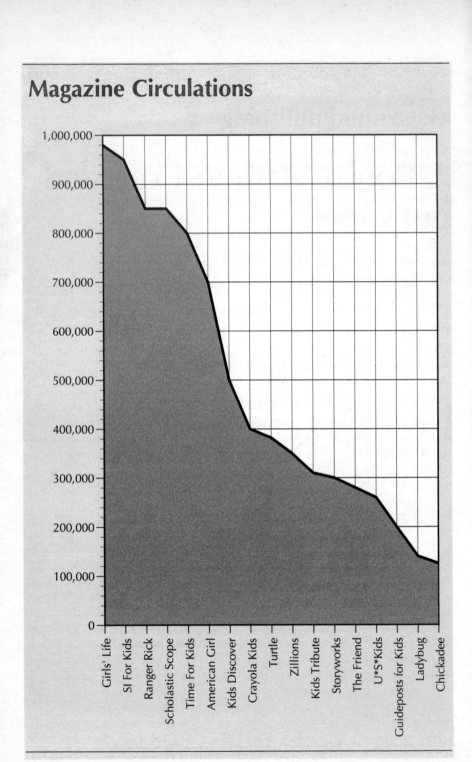

audience and, like *Twist* (formerly known as *SNAP!*) or *Time For Kids Primary Edition,* have a general consumer or educational slant.

Most of these magazines, for now at least, are actively seeking freelance submissions. According to figures compiled by *Children's Writer,* over the past year more than 20,000 freelance manuscripts were accepted by magazines answering the survey. Of these, about 7,000 submissions came from authors new to the magazine and more than 4,500 were by previously unpublished writers. The latest statistics compiled by the Magazine Publishers of America show that the categories of baby, children, family, and youth magazines included 785 magazines, up 34 from the year before and more than double the number in 1990. The numbers for 1997 and 1998 are likely to be even higher.

On the Horizon
With the rapid expansion, however, come predictions of consolidation. Charlene Gaynor, Executive Director of EdPress, says she believes that magazine publishing, like all businesses, runs in cycles. "I think the publishing industry, in general, is moving toward a consolidation period. I think there will be some consolidation, where the big guys will buy up the small guys and

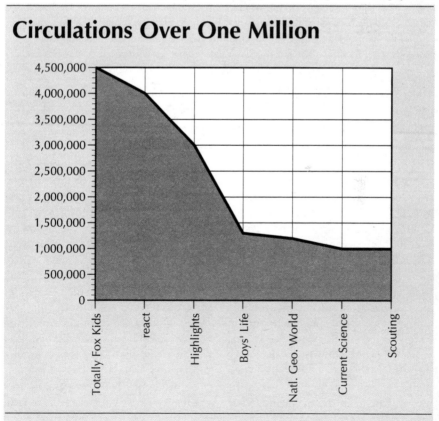

Circulations Over One Million

Up and Coming

While the big news for this and coming years is in the teen and adolescent market, magazines for the younger set continue to develop.

Your Big Backyard has changed its format and raised its target audience by a year. The nature monthly is now directed to ages three to six, and it is using more text.

Even the Owl Communcications, where financial difficulties and a summer of uncertainty ended with a corporate purchase, continued with its new publication for two-to-six-year-olds, *Chirp*. After a couple of months of catch-up at Owl, Publisher Diane Davy says all is returning to "business as usual." The *Chickadee* redesign process is being completed, showing a stronger voice and identity as a magazine for six-to-nine-year-olds. Like its older siblings, *Chirp* encourages children's interest and understanding of the world around them. Each issue contains puzzles, games, rhymes, crafts, and stories on animals, nature, letters, numbers, and more.

Also aimed at the younger market of ages three to seven is *Click,* yet another new Cricket publication. The bimonthly nonfiction magazine is described as a junior *Muse*. "*Muse* is very much liked," says Carus. "The kids love it because it is fun. It is also very serious as far as the science and technology is concerned. The underlying principle is that ideas and concepts are more important than just facts that they have to learn by rote. *Click* has the same philosophy for younger kids. It is not just facts but the process of how you arrive at a conclusion, how you study things so you get an idea of how they work."

a few strong umbrella companies will emerge. And there will be some shake-outs."

"I think the field is just too crowded," says Marianne Carus, Editor-in-Chief of the Cricket Magazine Group. "When we started *Cricket* twenty-five years ago, there were about a hundred magazines. There are many more good magazines around now than when we started *Cricket,* but there are some that shouldn't be around." Unlike book publishers, who might have a project in the works for several years, magazine publishers can change direction, or go out of existence, in a matter of months. "I think that's the biggest danger in the magazine field,"

Carus says. "Many magazines are started all the time."

Just ask Leahy, whose *Real Kids,* ceased publication in October. Then there were the difficulties of last summer, at the Owl Communications. Citing financial difficulties, the company went looking for a buyer. Two were found in Bayard Presse Canada, which took over the print publications, and Coscient Group Inc., which is acquiring Owl's television division. *Time Machine,* a joint venture of American Historical Publications and the Smithsonian's National Museum of American History, folded for lack of money. "The difference between passion and the reality of carrying a magazine year after year is dramatic," says Gaynor. "There are some good trends that portend well for children's magazines, but I think the business realities are tough."

Don Stoll, Gaynor's predecessor as Executive Director of EdPress and now a Professor of Education at Rowan University in New Jersey, says today's realities include the fact that expenses drive more and more magazine publishers to accept advertising. "There are not enough dollars in subscriptions to match the costs," he says.

While venerable magazines such as *Highlights for Children* continue to flourish without advertising, many of the newer magazines are accepting advertisements. These include *Muse,* the Cricket Magazine Group's joint venture with *Smithsonian,* and "brand" publications such as the Disney magazines and *Nickelodeon,* as well as most of the sports magazines and the teen magazines.

Gaynor believes the biggest upheavals will come in three to five years, as some of the new publications reach the point of turning a profit—or not. "In general, there has been a proliferation of magazines for kids and teens that carry advertising," she says. "But unless they can find a niche that is very specific, it is unlikely that they can survive on advertising alone. The question is, 'Can a magazine survive on circulation alone or does it need advertising?'" Gaynor is placing her survival bets on hobby and sports magazines, which have dedicated audiences.

Goddy, who oversees Scholastic's forty magazines, expects the shakeout in children's magazines to arrive even earlier than Gaynor's predicted three-to-five year horizon. "There is much less willingness these days to wait for a magazine to take hold editorially and financially," Goddy says. "If you want to get into this market, you must be into it for the long term. It also is almost mandatory to work with an organization with deep pockets that is willing to lose money for the first several years."

A Key Group

One of the most vigorous growth areas in publishing is teen magazines. Adult sports magazines such as *Skiing* are going after younger audiences with dedicated publications like *Freeze* and the U.S. Tennis Association's *Topspin,* for young, predominantly teenaged, tennis players.

Drawn by the potential of advertising revenue, adult magazine publishers such as Weider Publications have launched teen magazines. "The sheer numbers show that this group is growing," says Kathy Nenneker, Associate Publisher and Creative Director for the Women's Publishing Group at Weider, which in mid-1997 launched *Jump,* aimed at teenage girls. Weider also publishes *Shape, Living Fit,* and *Fit Pregnancy* for women, as well as several men's health and fitness magazines. Other new entries in, or contiguous with this market are *Twist,* a fashion, celebrity, and beauty magazine from Bauer Publishing, and, in the slightly older age range of eighteen to thirty-one, *Jane,* from Fairchild Publications.

Then there is the latest expansion of the Cricket Magazine Group, which publishes its handful of high-quality magazines for children from birth to adolescence. It is creating a new magazine to keep progressing with its audience, which has now grown older.

"Fifteen-to-twenty-four-year-olds are one of the fastest growing groups," Nenneker says. "They are growing at twice the rate of the overall population." Most important, this group has money to spend. "They are a key consumer group for the next decade." When Weider surveyed teens, it found many open niches in publications serving the age group, especially when compared to the scores of publications aimed at women eighteen and older. "We felt the teen market was underserved," says Nenneker.

In an attempt to stay away from that corner of the market already controlled by *YM* and *Seventeen,* Weider is going for a more "real girl" approach. Editor-in-Chief Lori Berger, says *Jump* is "a sort of health and fitness magazine for young women, but in the loosest sense." Editors of the new publications for young adults are pitching their titles as more reality-based. *Jump,* for example, intends to include real girls in fashion articles, and beauty articles will have a health-oriented approach. "If we can give beauty a health slant, we will," says Berger.

Teen People, scheduled for a February launch will focus on celebrities, like its adult namesake, but it will also concentrate on lifestyle issues that concern teenagers. "There is a lot of competition out there, with existing magazines and a few newcomers that are arriving, but we think that *Teen People* will have a real advantage in that it is the only one that is really different," says Editor Christina Ferrari. (See the profile of Ferrari, page 269.) She says celebrity articles will be intermingled with coverage of "ordinary teenagers who have done incredible things in volunteerism, starting their own business, their own web companies, or just making their mark in the world. This is where teens can read about themselves." (See "A Surge in the Teen Market," page 37.)

Catch-up

At least one editor thinks these magazines are just the big companies catching up, however. "In many other magazines that have started we are seeing verbiage and concepts that sound very much like *New Moon,*" says Managing Editor Joe Kelly. "To me, this is a sign of us affecting others."

Kelly doesn't think this real-girl approach is a trend: "I would call it a fad. I think it is good that the message is getting out there, but I don't think they are using it in a real way." Started five years ago, *New Moon*'s philosophy has been to give girls eight to fourteen a forum for expressing themselves about all aspects of their lives, not just beauty, fashion, and boys. *New Moon* is edited and largely written by girls and is as likely to contain an article about architecture as it is boys and friendships.

"One of our regular editors says a girl's life is like a circle and it has 360 degrees on it. Most magazines focus on four to five degrees of that life," says Kelly. *New Moon* is not about saying those are unimportant, but that there are hundreds of other things that are ignored, for the most part, in other media aimed at adolescent girls. We are

Launches at a Glance

Periodical	Age	Description
African-American Heritage & Achievement	Middle-grade	Cobblestone Pub. Resource for classrooms. Black experience in America.
AppleSeeds	Gr. 3-4	Cobblestone Pub. Theme-based. Similar to *Cobblestone,* for younger audience.
At-Home Mothering	Adults	Quarterly for mothers at home, or those who wish to be at home. Advice, inspiration.
California Cobblestone	Middle-grade	Cobblestone Pub. State history.
Chirp	3-8	Owl Pub. Animals, nature, letters, numbers, stories, puzzles, crafts, rhymes.
Click	3-6	Carus Pub. Nonfiction bimonthly. Arts, sciences, culture, history, environment.
Connections	7-12	Weekly newspaper that promotes high expectations for children
Crystal Ball	10-14	Quarterly on science and technology.
Dance Spirit	YA	Quarterly by the publishers of American Cheerleader for school and dance studio dance teams.
DINOSAURUS	6-12	Focus on dinosaurs, but articles have several layers—e.g, geography or technology, etc.
Freeze	14-25	Skiing.
Glossy	12-20	Originally on Web. For girls. Fashion, beauty, boys, teen interests.
Jane	YA, Adults	For young women, but especially those in their twenties.
Jump	YA	For girls. Fashion, beauty, boys, teen interests.
KidStyle	Adults	Kids' fashion, for parents and grandparents.
Teen People	YA	Time, Inc. Entertainment, celebrities, profiles teens who have done something exceptional.
Time For Kids Primary Edition, InTime	Gr. 3, 6-9	Expansion of *Time For Kids* to lower grade. Launch of *InTime,* for grades 6-9, is tentative.
Topspin	8-16	Tennis. Sponsored by the U.S. Tennis Association.
Twist	14-19	Real life, fashion, entertainment, dating.

Magazine Submissions and Purchases

The number of submissions received and purchases made by selected publications in 1997, as reported to the publishers of Children's Writer Guide:

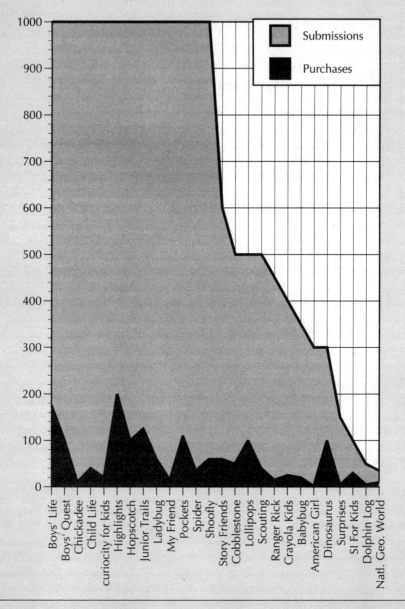

Legend:
- Submissions
- Purchases

Y-axis: 0, 100, 200, 300, 400, 500, 600, 700, 800, 900, 1000

X-axis categories: Boys' Life, Boys' Quest, Chickadee, Child Life, curiosity for kids, Highlights, Hopscotch, Junior Trails, Ladybug, My Friend, Pockets, Spider, Shoofly, Story Friends, Cobblestone, Lollipops, Scouting, Ranger Rick, Crayola Kids, Babybug, American Girl, Dinosaurus, Surprises, SI For Kids, Dolphin Log, Natl. Geo. World about trying to put it all in perspective."

Hitting a similar market is *Blue Jean Magazine,* established in 1996. "We're looking forward to an amazing year," says Victoria Nam, Executive Editor. She believes the magazine's success—circulation has reached 30,000—is due in large part to its philosophy. "We have a mission statement that we strongly adhere to. We want to provide the reader with quality writing that is not found elsewhere." The bimonthly provides articles on activities, careers, adventures, social issues, and social events.

So far, *New Moon* has stuck with its original market, but Kelly says requests have come for an older publication as well as one for boys. "We are thinking about projects where we might reach older and younger girls," says Kelly. "Our longer-term goal is to do something for boys, but we would only do that if it is an alternative to what is already out there for boys."

Loyalty Extended

Another obvious reality of the children's magazine market is that children grow older and lose interest in the magazines they once loved. Now brand loyalty is a marketing concept that magazine publishers are looking to embrace. The idea is to get kids interested while they are young and then keep them as "consumers" as long as possible.

The Cricket Magazine Group began with *Cricket,* now directed at readers nine to fourteen, then added *Ladybug* (ages two to six) and *Spider* (ages six to nine), and just a few years ago, started *Babybug* (six months to two years). Potentially, parents and toddling readers-to-be are captured by *Babybug* and progress through the other magazines. Now the company is hoping to hold onto those readers who are growing out of *Cricket.* These older children are willing to stay, apparently. "These kids were absolutely insulted when we started *Babybug,*" says Carus. "They wanted to know why *they* weren't getting a magazine."

"Because of passionate reader requests," Carus admits, "the Cricket Group is taking one of our biggest gambles with a magazine for teens. We really want to satisfy the wishes of our former *Cricket* readers who say there is nothing for them. They want to have a solid literature magazine." The magazine, named *Cicada,* launches at the American Library Association's June meeting. The editors are still determining the mix of stories that the magazine will contain, but Carus says *Cicada* will include classics and teen problem stories, "if they are sensitively written. We won't include one just for shock value."

Also extending its market is *Time For Kids.* The magazine quickly reached one million in circulation and Time Inc. followed up with a younger version, *Time For Kids Primary Edition,* in September 1997. An older version for high school readers was also considered but is apparently on hold. The primary grade edition has a circulation of about 400,000 and climbing.

"I think we brought a number of things to this market that nobody else could," says Managing Editor Claudia Wallis. "Timely news is something our competitors can't match. We happen to be part of a big news organization, *Time* magazine, and that gives us access to reporters and economies of scale."

Scholastic does not plan to expand its list of magazines this year, but Goddy is quick to say that, for the future, they are looking at several different magazine proposals. This year the investment priorities are *Scholastic News* and *Junior Scholastic,* the publisher's major news and current events magazines. Scholastic has added editorial pages, redesigned the magazines, and shortened the publishing time.

Stoll thinks there is more age expansion downward possible as well, and the issue is one of quality. "The big trend is in the thirteen-to-fifteen-year-old range, but a subsection is tied to that—the eight-to-twelve-year-old market. More and more people are finding out that eight-to-twelve-year-olds have money," says Stoll. "Look at what has happened with Pleasant Rowland and American Girl, how she has gone from being a book company to being a fashion catalogue because she is creating credibility with readers and parents."

Knowledge Growth

Also going strong are children's magazines aimed, in large part, at the school and library market. Cobblestone Publishing is introducing three new magazines in 1998. A niche publication on dinosaurs began publishing in July. The Cricket Magazine Group is growing not just in age but in topical coverage: It has announced plans to launch two new magazines, for younger and older readers.

"We're very excited," says Cobblestone Publishing Managing Editor Denise Babcock. "And this is just the beginning. We have plans on the drawing board for more publications." All three new magazines are based on feedback from the educational readership. "What I keep hearing from teachers is that they want to get away from the traditional textbooks, so theme-based publications are exactly what they are looking for," says Babcock. The company is therefore offering *AppleSeeds,* a magazine that will cover social studies, reading, language, and math for grades three and four; a magazine on the American black experience, which has the working title of *African-American Heritage and Achievement;* and *California Cobblestone*, a state-specific magazine written by and for Californians. If successful, Cobblestone is looking forward to more launches of magazines aimed at individual states. "We have known for a while that various states needed some help in terms of having material available for state histories," says Babcock. "It's just a question of getting that information to them at a price they can afford and that we can afford to produce."

The growth in nonfiction magazines that has been occurring over the past several years continues to extend into science. As schools struggle to improve science education, says Stoll, he predicts a greater emphasis on science writing and the development of publications with specific science concentrations. "I see a lot of emphasis on science and creativity," he says. "For example, organizations like Odyssey of the Mind are just blossoming. That says to me that there is pressure on programs that are helping children develop workplace skills. I see this developing more science publications, not a million of them, but there will be some exploration."

One recently launched science-oriented magazine is *Dinosaurus,* a bimonthly for six-to-twelve-year-olds. Early response has been good, reports Editor Vanessa Etherington, and it has been bolstered by children's dinosaur exhibits in New York and California.

Stoll observes that it is very hard to find a good children's science writer. Cobblestone's Babcock agrees: "Much of what we do deals with scientists who are not writers, " she says. "People who can write about what these scientists are doing or thinking, even just to the point of making an editor understand it, are very valuable."

Amidst the comings and goings, the centrality of that skill remains: Good writing, well thought out, well researched and well presented, opens doors. The markets are there. It is up to each writer to offer only the best of what he or she can do.

Magazine Market Overview

Preschool & Up	Frequency	Circulation	Free-lance*	Topics
Babybug	9x/yr	45,000	18	Simple readaloud stories.
Chirp	9x/yr	new	new	Animals, nature, the world around. Readers, 3-8.
Click	bimonthly	new	new	Nonfiction.
Highlights for Children	monthly	3 million	200	Readers are 2-12. All age-appropriate fiction, nonfiction.
Humpty Dumpty	8x/yr	236,000	50	Health. Fiction and nonfiction.
Ladybug	monthly	140,000	60	Readers are 2-6. All age-appropriate fiction, nonfiction.
Our Little Friend	weekly	46,000	40	Spiritually based stories.
Shoofly	quarterly	500	60	Audiomagazine. Stories, songs, poems.
Together Time	weekly	7,500	100-200	Fiction and poetry with religious themes.
Turtle	8x/yr	382,000	75	Health. Fiction and nonfiction.
Your Big Backyard	monthly	350,000	20	Activities, crafts, readaloud. Readers, 2-9.
Early Readers				
Chickadee	9x/yr	125,000	9	Nature, science. Readers, 6-9.
Children's Playmate	8x/yr	115,000	50	Easy-to-read fiction, poems, nonfiction, focus on health.
Dinosaurus	bimonthly	75,000	100	Ages 6-12. Everything about dinosaurs; geography, science.
Spider	monthly	92,000	35	Literary fiction, nonfiction for beginning readers.
U*S*Kids	8x/yr	260,000	24	Fiction, nonfiction, focus on health.

(continued on next page)
* Number of freelance submissions purchased yearly, or if not available, the percentage of published pieces from freelancers. N.A.: not available.

Magazine Market Overview *continued*

Middle-Grade	Frequency	Circulation	Free-lance*	Topics
American Girl	bimonthly	700,000	2	Contemporary and historical fiction; nonfiction; profiles.
Boys' Life	monthly	1.3 million	175	Nature, history, humor, sports, science.
Boys' Quest	bimonthly	5,000	100	Adventure, humor, multicultural, nature, sports.
Cobblestone, Faces, Calliope, Odyssey	5-10x/yr	10,000-36,000	20-50 each	Cobblestone Pub. mags on history, people, science.
Children's Digest Jack And Jill	8x/yr	115,000 370,000	100 each	Fiction and nonfiction, focus on health. Ages10-13, 7-10.
Cricket Muse	bimonthly	80,000 N.A.	150 N.A.	*Cricket:* literary fiction, nonfiction. *Muse:* nonfiction.
Dolphin Log	bimonthly	80,000	6-18	Science, natural history, marine biology, ecology.
Girls' Life	bimonthly	980,000	15	Pop culture, friendships, sports, news, entertainment.
Hopscotch	bimonthly	10,000	100	Nature, pets, hobbies, sports, careers.
Kids Discover	10x/yr	500,000	10	Science, technology, history, geography, nature, entertainment.
National Geographic World	monthly	1 million	75%	Science, technology, adventure, sports, nature, multicultural.
OWL	10x/yr	104,000	5	Nature, science, technology, travel, geography.
Ranger Rick	monthly	850,000	15	Fiction, nonfiction. Environment, outdoor adventure, science.
Soccer JR.	bimonthly	100,000	6	Skills, strategies, profiles.
Sports Illustrated For Kids	monthly	950,000	30	Athletes, sports tips, hobbies, health, science, news, history.
Storyworks	6x/yr	300,000	75%	Fiction and nonfiction.
3-2-1-Contact	10x/yr	N.A.	20%	Science and technology.
Totally Fox Kids	quarterly	4.5 million	10-12	Fox television characters.
Zillions	bimonthly	350,000	6	Saving, spending, earning money; hobbies; environment; advertising.

OVERVIEWS

School Markets

Tales that Teach: Writing Opportunities in Education

By Catherine Frey Murphy

Boring textbooks, endless drills, and dull worksheets: You might associate the phrase *educational publishing* with childhood memories of classroom tedium. But in educational publishing today, *boring* definitively is no longer the operative word. Educators need lively material to reach kids who grow up with *Sesame Street*, Nintendo, and the Internet.

Across the country, teachers need resources to help them explore and understand a wide variety of educational practices and philosophies. To meet the market's demands, publishers look for help from writers who understand children and education, and who can translate that understanding into the kind of writing that engages, excites, and educates today's kids.

The market for traditional classroom textbooks is strong. Educators who combine professional experience with subject-matter expertise and writing ability will find publishers for textbooks, reading series, study guides, teachers' manuals, tests, and other materials. But across the curriculum, and especially in language arts, new opportunities have also sprung up for children's writers whose primary expertise is in the telling of tales, particularly if they combine their gifts for words with backgrounds in education.

"This evolved out of the whole-language movement," says Pat Moore, Vice President of Educational Materials for Publicom, Inc., a development company that creates educational materials for many publishers. Schools that subscribe to the whole-language philosophy teach reading with picture books and novels, not just basal reading primers, on the theory that good, exciting reading makes good, excited readers. With the growth of the whole-language movement in the 1980s, Moore says, "Schools went into trade books wanting to give kids authentic reading experiences." But as the movement developed, teachers found that they needed reading materials that served specialized needs.

That gave rise to a thriving market for supplementary materials, often called *emergent readers, big books,* or *little books*. These are storybooks created for classroom use that may use limited vocabularies, or may include words intended to teach a particular element of phonics, such as the long-a vowel sound, or the *th* combination. They look so much like ordinary trade children's books that it can be hard to distinguish them, but hidden in the lively language are lessons in phonics, vocabulary, or subject content.

Niches to Explore

Although many districts are still committed to the whole-language approach, Moore says, more traditional phonics-based methods have also come back into favor. "There's a clamoring for back-to-basics from some states. The whole spectrum is going to be out there. The bottom line is always instructional, but there are forums available today for children's writers with engaging style and flair."

"It's very much a mixed market," agrees Ed Bloor, Senior Editor in Reading and Language Arts at Harcourt Brace School Publishers. "The practices vary almost district by district. There are so many niches that we haven't even thought of them all yet, especially in technology. That's why so many little publishing companies are springing up and succeeding."

In response, some children's writers have built specialties in writing for the educational market. The field has grown more competitive, especially in recent years, as "down-sized" editors have launched writing careers. But educational writers who have proven their skills and reliability find ample freelance employment, and they say that the work is challenging, flexible, and rewarding.

Until a few years ago, Fay Robinson was an editor at Scott Foresman, one of the country's leading educational publishers. "I wanted time and energy to write my own picture books," she says, "and working in-house wasn't leaving me enough energy for my own writing. As an editor, I worked with freelancers, and their lifestyle looked appealing." In addition to her editorial experience, Robinson had previously worked as a teacher. Besides, she says, "I love to write stories."

Robinson launched her freelance career by mass-mailing her credentials in writing, editing, and teaching to educational publishers and development companies. "My preference is to write stories for kindergarten through second grade, mostly reading and language arts materials," she says. "But, in dry spells, I'll work on teachers' guides, too." As she had hoped, her new career has also allowed her to write and publish several of her own trade children's books, including *Where Did All the Dragons Go?* (Bridgewater Books), and *Great Snakes* and *Mighty Spiders* (both from Scholastic). Robinson often writes *little books.* "There used to be more of a free rein on vocabulary," she says, "but it's changing. There's some backlash against whole language, and the publishers are more phonics-driven now. But even as schools revise their philosophies, they're still including little books."

As an editor in educational publishing, Robinson learned "how important it is to know what teachers want." To keep herself aware of up-to-the-minute classroom needs and practices, she volunteers in schools and occasionally attends teachers' conferences.

Specification Variables

Like Robinson, Deb Eaton specializes in educational writing. "I was writing training packages for a computer-based company, until, with a friend, we decided to form a writing company," she says. Eaton and her partner spent several months on interviews and phone calls before they landed their first job. Now, Eaton freelances full-time, writing and editing little books, workbooks, and other materials to accompany reading programs. Creativity counts in her work, she says, along with the ability to work within someone else's structure. "If you're somebody who can work within tight limits and still be creative, you can get a lot of work."

In a typical project, Eaton might be asked to adapt an African folktale, using a phonics-based text. She might be required to use a specific phonics sound, such as *air*, a number of times in the text, and to include review sounds previously taught in other stories.

"They'll tell me the page count, the line count per page, and exactly how many characters per line. In educational publishing, you do your own art specifications, so they'll also tell you how many art spots to plan for. They'll give you a general reading level, like the first half of grade two. Then they'll check it with a readability formula."

Eaton advises, "You do need either educational background, or someone to coach you. For one thing, there's a lot of jargon, and you show that you're a beginner if you can't use that language. It's amazing how many times writers who are at too much of a remove from the classroom will set up a teacher doing two things at once, because they can't put themselves in that position. I've heard that it's very unusual to do this writing without a teaching background. I wasn't a teacher, but I've always been able to put myself in the place of kids, and I've spent time in classrooms observing teachers."

In texts for public schools, where book purchases are influenced by community moral standards and constitutional concerns, Eaton adds, "There are many rules. You can't mention churches, cookies, or witches. Well, cookies are okay in Texas, but they're not in California. For a while, gerbils were okay, but hamsters weren't—I never knew why. A friend of mine in production at a large educational publisher told me about book covers in which they had to airbrush out the cow udders."

In addition to following the rules, Eaton warns, writers in this market may have to give up the sense of creative ownership they're used to in trade publishing. "You can't feel like you own anything. The publishers will change your work any way they need to." But she's invigorated by the challenge of this kind of writing. "I've had editors call at 3:00 P.M. to say, 'I need a little book by 4:00!' You have to be quick on your feet, ready to summon up creativity at any moment. You can get anything thrown at you. It builds up your self-confidence."

Positive Strictures

Many children's writers who don't specialize in education do occasional projects for educational publishers. Patricia Curtis Pfitsch has written extensively for children's magazines, and her first children's novel, *Keeper of the Light,* was published by Simon & Schuster in the fall of 1997. Recently she created twenty-six audio scripts for a Scott Foresman-Addison Wesley, spelling workbook.

"My job was to look at each lesson's spelling list, and pick six of the words to use in the script. Though they didn't give me specific readability lists, they asked me to write for a fifth-grade audience." Pfitsch found the project enjoyable and challenging. "Writing a script is very different from writing a story. It had to be all dialogue, and there had to be a certain kind of sound effects. I love doing research, and I got to read up on a number of topics I was interested in: finding a 1,000-year-old body in a bog in England, the Loch Ness Monster, the Pyramids. It also made me focus on fifth-graders and get in touch with what interests them. It's good for writers to think about the audience—it keeps us humble!"

Linda Wirkner, author of several children's books, wrote an adaptation of the classic novel, *Moby Dick*, on a fifth-grade reading level. "Writing with a controlled vocabulary was a real challenge," she says. "I learned to write much leaner and tighter than I ever had before. And, because many jobs for educational publishers include deadlines, you learn to write and research more quickly and efficiently."

Sheri Cooper Sinykin, author of many middle-grade novels and several books in the Magic Attic Club series, wrote fourteen short fiction pieces for an educational publisher in a month. She says, "It was a great experience, proving to myself that I could write on deadline, and come up with story ideas on an as-needed basis. The entire experience really built up my self-confidence about my ability to produce on demand, which may be why I had the courage to try the Magic Attic books."

Picture book author and illustrator Anne Sibley O'Brien has written many emergent readers. "I really enjoy this work," she says. "It's great for learning how to create a story. You have to learn, what is a story? What's a beginning, a middle, an end?"

This writing can be like solving a puzzle, says O'Brien, as the writer deals with limitations on ideas, phonics, vocabulary, grade level, word count, line count, character count, and more. "The more of these elements there are in demand, the trickier the puzzle," she says.

"The deadlines are always ridiculous, too, but that's actually part of the fun. It's always a crisis!" But to O'Brien, the stories are more than puzzles. "My goal is to try to make the whole struc-

Educational Publishers

The number of books published in 1997, by publisher:

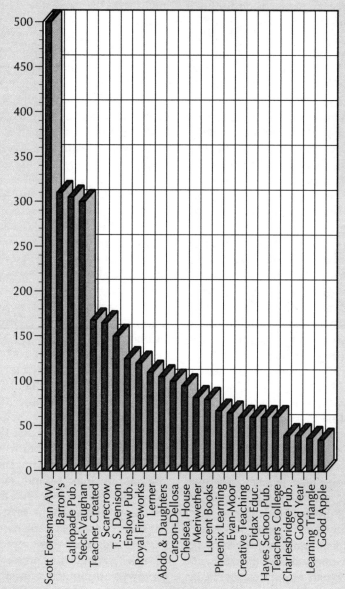

ture disappear, so the limitations don't show," she says. "I want to write a story that a child will enjoy."

Project Development

The main texts used in most schools come from the best-known publishers: Scholastic, Harcourt Brace, Henry Holt, and other industry leaders. But freelance writers aren't likely to receive many assignments directly from the largest publishers. That's because of the growing importance in the educational publishing world of development companies, also known as packagers. These companies develop books for publishers in all sorts of genres, from series paperbacks to educational materials. Packagers may develop books from the original idea through final production, or they may simply execute them for publishers who have already conceptualized the text and format in precise detail. (See "Packagers, Making Books Happen," page 95, on packagers and trade and mass-market publishing.)

"The premise of our company is that no publisher can keep on staff the number of freelance people needed when it's time to develop a new series," explains Moore at Publicom. "They'd go out of business if they did." When federal education funding dropped in the 1980s, publishers began reducing their payrolls. Now, most large publishers don't have enough employees to handle the heavy, but irregular demand for professional expertise that's imposed by a new reading program. A development house steps in to fill the gap, providing writers, illustrators, and any other staff or services a publisher may need to turn pedagogical concepts into published books.

Nancy Pernick, Managing Editor for Kirchoff/Wohlberg, Inc., says her development company has created educational projects for "all the major publishers. We think there is an increase in the use of development companies such as ours."

"We problem-solve for our clients," explains Gale Clifford at Brown Publishing Network, Inc., which lists Scholastic, Houghton Mifflin, Harcourt Brace, and Macmillan/McGraw-Hill among the many publishers it has recently worked with. "The governor of California may say, 'We are going to mandate that phonics will be used in our classrooms starting in 1998.' All the educational publishers scramble in response. They hire people like us, who can be an extension of their own staff, to get that project done fast, so they can go to California and say, here's the tool you need."

That trend is evident at Harcourt Brace, Bloor says. "When I started here, I would contact a writer and we'd develop a textbook together. I might have had a writer who always handled all of grade five, for instance. But now, it's almost all funnelled through development companies." Bloor stresses that this trend doesn't mean that Harcourt Brace, or any other publisher, allows other companies to control the pedagogical principles behind its school materials. Before the development company is called in, he says, editors work with educators to plan out their projects in detail. "We conceptualize to the nth degree, creating prototype after prototype, using focus groups, and working with our authors and teachers. By the time it goes to the development house, we know everything, down to the character and line count."

But the use of development companies does mean that they can be excellent markets for freelance writers looking for opportunities in educational writing. At Kirchoff/Wohlberg, for instance, Pernick says, "We use many, many freelance writers of various skills, depending on the project. We welcome résumés, though we don't particularly welcome phone calls!"

"We keep a file of writers who've written for the school and library market before," says Lelia Mander of Media Projects, Inc., which has produced books for Scholastic, The Millbrook Press, Silver Burdett, and other publishers. "Include as much information as possible on your résumé about your teaching or library experience, and your familiarity with the market. We'd also like to know what you've published, and your areas of expertise."

"What drives our success is the talent of our freelance writers," says Clifford. "You want the writer to have wonderful creative ideas, something that will just light up the page. Also, they need a sound background in the pedagogy: How do kids learn to decode? How do they know whether the letter with a circle and a little stick on one side makes the sound *buh* or *duh*? The general rule of thumb is that the writers have to have been in this business, usually as teachers."

Qualifications

As with educational publishers, most freelance writers come to the attention of development companies by sending a well-written cover letter and a résumé. Make sure your résumé highlights your educational credentials, along with any subject-matter expertise you may have, and your writing credits. "We are looking for experience, clear writing, the ability to write to specifications, and deadline reliability," says Pernick. The last criterion is especially important, she says, since "we're most often called in on a very tight schedule." Prior publication is usually necessary, too, she says, "unless someone has a particular talent—perhaps a very creative math teacher, who can show us the ability to put ideas into writing."

Moore says, "We want writers who know the educational market, who know kids and schools, and who know how to write for different grade levels. We love to see samples, if writers have worked with other development houses." Networking helps, too, she adds. "Freelancers are a community. They tell us about each other."

Unlike publishers, the names and addresses of development companies often don't appear in the books they produce. A directory of book packagers, including a capsule description of each company's business and a list of some of its recent publications, can be obtained free of charge by writing to the American Book Producers Association, 160 5th Ave., New York, NY 10010. Writers can also find a list of packagers specializing in educational publishing in *Literary Market Place,* a reference book available in libraries. In addition, the Society of Children's Book Writers and Illustrators (SCBWI) makes a list of development companies available to its members for the cost of postage.

Not all major publishers work exclusively with development companies. Scott Foresman-Addison Wesley, publishes educational materials of every description for kindergarten to grade twelve, and Tom Lenz, Director of Editorial Administration, says, "We have used a number of freelance writers in the past few years. They are involved to some extent in every new program. We've developed a network of writers, editors, and teachers throughout the country, and we're always looking for prospective writers who are or have been teachers."

In the summer of 1997, Lenz says, Scott Foresman-Addison Wesley's parent company, Addison Wesley Longman, acquired McClanahan & Company, a development company located in New York. McClanahan has been one of the most active development companies in educational publishing, working with many leading publishers. Now its editorial staff will put McClanahan's large network of freelancers to work on Scott Foresman-Addison Wesley products.

At Barron's Educational Series, Managing Editor Grace Freedson says, "We publish for the whole educational market, including the preschool and early school market." Submissions may come in as complete manuscripts or queries, or Freedson may assign projects to development companies or directly to writers. Get Ready, Get Set, Read! is Barron's phonics-based reading program. "The author submitted the first title," says Freedson. "After its success, we expanded on it."

Freedson says the skills she looks for depend on the demands of the project.

"Currently, I'm looking for beginning chapter books for a phonics program that goes beyond Get Ready," she says. For that project, writers need to demonstrate phonics-based writing experience.

The School Division of Charlesbridge Publishing, which publishes books for elementary schools in the areas of reading, writing, and mathematics, works directly with freelancers, says Don Robb, Vice President for School Markets. Manuscripts often come in as queries or completed submissions, but just as often, a publisher develops a concept and assigns freelance writers to carry it out. For example, he says, "In the schools right now, there's a lot of interest in taking literature across the curriculum, such as material that makes a connection between literature and mathematics. We might recruit writers to work on a project like that."

"We find that teaching experience is virtually essential," says Robb. "You have to understand the climate: What's appropriate in third grade? Fourth grade? Fifth grade? It's hard to find that rare combination of talented writer and knowledgeable teacher." A third requirement, he says, is "the ability to take an idea that started out as someone else's project, and craft your writing to those guidelines. You don't have complete artistic freedom."

Didax Educational Resources uses freelance writers, says Martin Kennedy, Vice President for Sales and Marketing. "We basically sell educational hands-on materials, math manipulatives, things like that. We began publishing books for teachers on how to work with these materials, and recently, we've entered into a joint venture with an Australian company to publish books for general classroom use. For our writers, an educational background is almost required. To have any credibility with the teachers who are the consumers, you almost have to have had it."

The Edcon Publishing Group is "strictly an educational publisher in reading and math," says President Philip Solimene. Edcon hires writers directly, looking for the right mix of experience and creativity. "This writing is very structured. The controls can be stifling, and for a creative person, it can be difficult. It takes a different kind of creativity to do this well, to write a story that has a beginning, a middle, and an end, where the vocabulary is enriching, but not overwhelming."

Marilyn Evans is the Acquisitions Editor for Evan-Moor Educational Publications. "We are a publisher of supplemental materials and teacher resources, for prekindergarten through sixth grade," she says. As parents become more active in their children's education, the company is also selling its educational materials directly to families. Evans says, "Today, teacher supply stores are becoming more parent/teacher supply stores. We have developed and will continue to develop more educational materials aimed at parents." Educational materials designed for parents tend to be "more straightforward and user-friendly," Evans notes. "We'll just give a couple of sentences of directions for parents, while a teacher might get a whole page."

Evan-Moor has in-house writers, Evans says, so "we probably don't use as many freelancers as some publishers. When we do, we tend to use people with teaching experience, but I can see that changing as we move into the parent market. Let's say we were developing materials on how to keep kids busy in summer vacation. Then, we might have a use for people who've been creative in other ways than the schools."

Creative Teaching Press also takes parents into account, says Carolea Williams, Director of Product Development. "We find parent involvement a growing part of the market, and consider parents in our product development plans," she says. Her press publishes a line of more than a hundred emergent-reader titles, geared for kindergarten and grade one. "Our emergent readers contain text that is repetitive and predictable. They're written with very natural language, and supportive illustrations. Our goal is to get children excited about reading. All the products we publish are developed by teachers. In considering writers for our resource materials, we first look at teaching experience."

"We're always looking for new writers," says Clair Hayes III, Publisher of Hayes School Publishing Co. "The people who have written for us have all been teachers, both published and unpublished. Foreign language is an important area for us, as are music education and early childhood materials." Hayes also looks for creative non-book ideas for classroom use, such as certificates and awards, progress reports, and other extras that teachers may appreciate.

At Amsco School Publications, which publishes materials for middle school and high school use, freelancers create review texts for state tests given at various grade levels, and work on many other projects. "You don't have to be a psychometrician to do this," says Ralph Hayashida, Publications Director. "But you do have to have knowledge of the instruction and the testing. A writer ought to know what kids at, say, the eleventh-grade level can understand. You have to pay attention to a readability level, so it isn't over their heads, yet not talk down to them. That's tough!"

Amsco works directly with freelancers, says Hayashida. "We have been employing writers on a regular basis. It's good if a writer knows what's current regarding the pedagogy, so that you know what the National Council of Social Studies might be projecting in a few years. If we talk about collaborative learning, you'll know what I mean without an explanation."

Whatever you write for school children, remember that what you're doing is important. "After all, what you're writing are the tools by which these kids will learn, and the teachers will teach," says Clifford. As Eaton puts it, "If you're not willing to access your best self and do your best work, don't do it! You have captive little children here. They're prisoners at their desks. They have to do whatever you create! I tell myself, if I can make school more fun for one kid, then it's worth it."

Magazines

New Panoramas in Parenting and Family

By Victoria Hambleton

OVERVIEWS

The millennium approaches, and the landscape of family life grows even fuller and more complicated. So must publications that aim to provide road maps through the complexities.

Janet Chan, Editor-in-Chief of *Parenting,* reflects on some of the changes the ten-year-old publication has witnessed. "When *Parenting* was born," she says, "it was conceived of as the baby book for baby boomers, and the assumption was that this was a generation that wanted information not just on the basics, like breast-feeding or potty training, but also on larger emotional issues, such as how to raise a child with a sense of community, with strong morals."

That basic premise, dealing with the larger "life" issues, hasn't changed, but the stakes have become higher. The balancing of work and family in dual-income families has become the norm, not the exception. Making that norm work, says Chan, will be a key issue for parenting publications in the next decade.

So will changing demographics. The parenting and family market overall will move toward more specialization, requiring greater focus and depth. Some titles already concentrate on particular aspects of family life, like education or recreation, while others define themselves by targeting segments of the family population: single parents, racial or ethnic groups, fathers, parents of teenagers, grandparents.

Parenting is big business. Family is hot. Publishers are looking both at growing populations, such as parents of teens, and at groups that are becoming more immediately involved in parenting, like grandparents and fathers.

Family and Parenting Magazines

Adoptalk
Adoptive Families
Alaska Parenting
American Baby
Atlanta Parent
Baby
Baby Talk
Baby's World
Bay Area Baby
Black Child
Child
Children Today
Child Times
Christian Home & School
Christian Parenting Today
City Parent
Cleveland/Akron Family
Colorado Parent
Connecticut Parent
Connecticut's County Kids
Dallas Child
Dallas Family
Dane County Kids
Early Childhood Today
Exceptional Parent
Family
Family Circle
The Family Digest
FamilyFun
Family Life
Family
FamilyPC
Family Pub. Group
Family Times (Delaware)
Family Times (Wisconsin)
Full-Time Dads
Genesee Valley Parent
Growing Parent
Guide for Expectant
  Parents
Hip Mama
Home Life

Hudson Valley Parent
Indy's Child
Island Family
Kansas City Family
Kansas City Parent
Kid Connection
Kid Konnection Family
  Resource
Kid's Directory
KIDS
Kids 'n Stuff
L.A. Parent
Lexington's Kids
Living with Teenagers
Long Island Parenting
  News
Mahoning Valley Parent
Manic Moms
Maryland Family
MetroKids
Metro Parent
Minnesota Parent
Modern Dad
Mothering
The Mother Is Me
Nashville Parent
New Jersey Family
The Nurturing Parent
On the Father Front
Our Children
Our Children, Our Selves
Our Family
Our Gifted Children
Our Kids & Teens
Parent & Preschooler
PARENTGUIDE News
Parenting
Parenting for Peace &
  Justice
Parenting New England
ParentLife
Parents & Children

Together Online
Parents' Choice
Parents Express
Parents' Monthly
Parents' Plus Family
  Travel & Leisure
Parents' Press
Parent Weekly
Pennsylvania's Child
Pentecostal Homelife
Pittsburgh's Child
St. Louis Parent
San Diego Family
San Francisco Peninsula
  Parent
Sesame Street Parents
Single-Parent Family
South Florida Parenting
Stepfamilies
Suburban Parent
Successful Black
  Parenting
Syracuse Parent
Tampa Bay Family
Texas Child Care
That's My Baby
Tidewater Parent
Toledo Area Parent
  News
Tulsa Kids
Twins
The Valley Family
Valleykids PARENT
  NEWS
Valley Parent
Welcome Home
Westcoast Families
Western New York
  Family
Working Mother
Your Child

This doesn't mean that *Parents,* for example, will suddenly devote huge amounts of editorial space to teenage girls or single fathers, but certainly those topics will increasingly become part of the editorial mix. There is, as yet, no publication targeting parents of teens, but that may change as teens continue to be the fastest growing sector of the population. The Meredith Corporation is the first to venture into the arena. It has acquired the rights to a magazine called *Raising Teens,* published by the Medill School of Journalism.

For freelancers, all this means that editors are hungry for writers who can either write to these niche groups, or who are able to tackle the more time-honored subjects with a new but solid perspective. Certainly there is no lack of work when it comes to writing about family in the 1990s.

A Better Job

When it was launched in 1983, *Working Mother* was a maverick among parenting magazines. Fifteen years ago, mothers who worked full-time were in the minority, and a focus on them was potentially risky. Guilt about leaving someone else to raise the kids was a primary concern. But *Working Mother* was like a life raft, something to hold onto that supported the dual careers of mother and breadwinner.

Today the guilt is lessened, despite high-profile nanny trials, but the issues of work and family and how to handle both remain. It's no longer a question of whether to work as much as where to work. "For us the big issues are scheduling and child care," says *Working Mother*'s Deputy Editor Deborah

Wilburn. "We are doing more articles on work/family benefits, benefits that enable a working mother to balance her time better. The issue could be parental leave, it could be flexible work schedules, or telecommuting. Today, we look at these not only in terms of how they will help the family, but how they will help the employer, too. More and more companies are coming to realize that a happy employee is more often a loyal employee."

Even *Working Mother* is addressing issues like paternity leave and fathers who are becoming more involved in the job of parenting. "When we talk about work/family issues our emphasis is certainly on mothers," says Wilburn, "but we are also beginning to look more closely at the father's role. Statistics show that men today are more interested in the raising of their children than they were eighteen years ago when we started, and we have to take that into account."

Nonetheless, Wilburn says, the goal remains the same: "to be at the forefront, the cutting edge when it comes to reporting on issues of concern to mothers who work." *Working Mother* continues to devote considerable editorial space to child care, an issue critical to many parenting publications, from nationals to regionals.

Liz White is the Publisher of *Atlanta Parent,* a fifteen-year-old regional magazine. "When I started this publication, I remember reading an article that proclaimed that parents spend more time choosing a new car than they do on child care, and that notion has stuck with me all these years and has kept me going."

White thinks today's parents are the first generation to look at parenting as a job they can learn to do better. Her concern is that this desire to "get it perfect" may create a generation of parents who are unsure about their abilities. "We all agree that being a parent is the most important job you will ever have in your life," she says. "But I also think there is a tendency today for parents not to trust their own judgment, to feel that they have to go to an expert, and that worries me."

White's concerns are echoed by Sandy Moeckel, Publisher of *Bay Area Parent,* one of the first regional publications. "I think everybody wants the one-minute manager, the one-minute solution. We are trained in the workplace to be quick, fast, and efficient. It's natural then to want parenting to work the same way."

Moeckel says that many of the basic issues of parenting remain the same today as they were a decade ago, but as parents become savvier, their ideas of what is acceptable and what is not have become more stringent. "We are more judgmental as parents than we were, say, ten to fifteen years ago, and that is reflected in the way we at *Bay Area Parent* cover stories. Today when we look at the issues of child care and divorce, we have the strength to say, for example, that it is not okay for an infant to be one of twelve in a day care center. It is not okay to put a thirteen-year-old, in the middle of adolescence, through a divorce."

Narrowing In

As parents pursue answers to the tougher but narrower questions of raising kids, not the basic how-to's, publications in niches that speak to specialized concerns are growing. Magazines targeting the black parent, single parent, fathers, parents of teens, and others are not replacements for basic parenting materials, but complements.

Black Child started in 1989 as an insert in *Interrace.* The need for such a publication was great enough for *Black Child* to stand on its own, and in 1995 it began publishing independently. Gabe Grosz, Associate Publisher, believes most of his readers pick up mainstream parenting publications, but then come to *Black Child* to deal with issues unique to the black parent. "We felt there was no publication addressing some of the very real issues that black parents today face—topics like sickle-cell anemia and how to develop self-esteem in a young black man. We cover these very serious issues and strive to present the black family in a positive way."

One of Grosz's primary concerns is the family headed by a single parent. "Two-thirds of black families today," he says, "are headed by single black women. I would hope that for the future, as we look seriously at the ways we define family, that there will come a realization that as a single parent you can do better, that you can, with help, raise

your children to be strong adults."

Focus on the Family, an organization that promotes Christian values, started *Single-Parent Family* in the mid-1990s in response to what Editor Lynda Hunter calls "the overwhelming need of our readers for a magazine that addressed the needs of the single parent." Says Hunter, "statistics indicate that 30 percent of all households with children under eighteen are headed by a single parent. That number is expected to jump another 4 percent by the year 2000."

The single parent is usually the mother, but sometimes the father. Growing numbers of single parents have never even married. Clearly the concept of what constitutes a family is fluid, not fixed.

One publication designed to address the variety of families is *Hip Mama*, now about six-years-old. Based in Oakland, California, the publication describes itself as "the parenting zine for progressive parents." Founder Ariel Gore says, "We try to look at the diversity of parenting experiences. Parents today are trying to find their own way but they need help. It's so easy to feel isolated and unsupported. The extended family that was once in place to help parents no longer exists and parents need to build their own networks, their own communities."

Gore has just finished the first *Hip Mama* book, which she describes as an alternative resource guide. It is to be published by Disney Press this year.

As the basic family unit takes on more shapes and sizes, Moeckel says parents in the next decade will have to get used to the idea that going it alone

isn't always the best solution. "With the majority of parents spending time in the workplace," she says, "I think parents are beginning to accept the idea of sharing the responsibility of rearing their children with other people, whether it's a husband or a child care provider or someone else in the community."

White concurs, but cautions that the final parenting decisions must come from the parents, not from other sources. "I see an awful lot of parents in my generation trying so hard to be a friend to their child that they leave the tough stuff or the boring stuff to someone else. But the bad guy role is part of being a parent too."

Opening Up

If there is one road sign that stands out as big as the golden arches on all the roads of nineties parenting, it is the one that cries out, "spend more time with your kids."

Baby boomers look to experts for answers. Two publications that address and provide expertise on these family needs are *Family Life,* and *Family Fun.* When *Family Fun* was started in 1991, explains Executive Editor Ann Hallock, "There were a lot of publications for parents, but there really wasn't one about enjoying time with your kids." Obviously the need was real: *Family Fun*'s circulation climbed to one million over six years.

Hallock thinks the magazine's success comes from parents' perception of goals. "Each generation looks at the job of parenting a little differently," she says. "I think this generation has been very determined to seek out whatever it is that is going to help them raise their kids." Quality family time is at the top of the list. "We've come to realize that, in many ways, having fun with your kids is one of the most important things you can do to forge positive memories and experiences" and that role is at "the core of a responsible adult."

Like *Family Fun*, *Family Life* was created to address the larger concept of family, rather than parenting. Both cover the fun subjects: leisure activities, travel, recreation. But *Family Life* also addresses more serious topics, including education and community service. Within that context, said *Family Life* Editor-in-Chief Peter Herbst, "the issues of adolescence are of utmost concern."

"When we did a piece on adolescence in a recent issue," says Herbst, "it was one of the highest scoring pieces we've ever done. I think to a parent, life for the child entering the teen years is so perilous, the issues are so serious, so weighty. I don't mean that issues of younger children are less important, but they don't tend to have the kind of edge that teen issues do."

Despite the steadily escalating teen demographics, the general interest parenting publications so far haven't run toward the niche. "I think teen issues are certainly an area we are going to revisit," says Herbst. "It's important to build that into the mix of our magazine, but our challenge remains to confront issues that will appeal to all our readers and the majority of those still have children under twelve. The other reality is that we don't have an ad base for teen editorial; we cover teen issues now because we feel it is the right way

to go, but there are no advertising dollars to support it."

Testing with Teens

As more and more children of baby boomers reach puberty in the next decade, that may have to change, and writers should be aware of the possibility. If it does, because teen issues can be particularly serious, the challenge for editors will be to find a way to offer practical information without scaring parents.

Living With Teenagers, published by the Baptist Sunday School Board, has covered the parenting of teens for more than twenty years. Editor-in-Chief Ellen Oldacre says her audience has grown steadily and that it will continue to grow as the teen population explodes.

"I think parents of teens are really screaming at us for information," says Oldacre. "We used to raise children in a way that when they reached twelve or thirteen we said, 'Phew! that's that!' Nowadays, you can't throw in the towel anymore. There's no towel to throw and if you stop at twelve or thirteen, you're really in trouble."

Of most concern to parents of teens, says Oldacre, is how to talk to their children, how to approach the tough topics like sex, drugs, AIDS, in a way that's not going to put them off. They are searching for a way to keep the lines of communication open.

While *Living With Teenagers* is currently the only national publication targeting parents of teens, regional publications are testing the waters. Some are adding teen panels to their publications; others are devoting more editorial space to regular features on adolescence. *Bay Area Parent,* the first regional publication to start a pregnancy and resource guide, was one of the first to enter the market.

"We started *Bay Area Teen* as a newsletter in October 1996," says Moeckel, "and we struggled mightily to sell it as a subscription publication, but parents wouldn't buy it." Instead, she says the decision was made to market it as a free publication supported by advertisers. By the fourth issue, distribution jumped to 65,000 from an original 20,000.

"I don't think parents of teens have a clue of how to deal with their kids," Moeckel says emphatically, "because the issues are so serious. There are some major issues for younger kids like finding the right preschool, or not letting a kid flail around for a year with the wrong teacher, but one look at the prevalence of crack-cocaine or heroin use and you realize that the teen world is not only complicated, but life-threatening at times."

A Problem of Perception

Kathy Mittler, Executive Director of Parenting Publications of America, (PPA), is not surprised that local publications are the first to address the issues of parenting teens. "Many of the women who started regional parenting publications started them because they had small children, and were hungry for more information and resources. Well, those toddlers are grown up now and those same women are finding the same dearth of information when it comes to how to parent teenagers."

"In general," says Moeckel, "regional parenting publications look to their area of greatest need first and to a large extent that area continues for now to be resource information and basic parenting information. *Bay Area Parent* has been around for a long time and we are financially more able to put our toe in the water and maybe lose a little money to see if a publication for teens will go or not. I think this would not be as easy to do on a national scale." Certainly there is an increased attention in the regional market towards the teen years and editors will be looking for freelancers that can write on teen issues.

Some in publishing aren't convinced that publications on the parenting of teens can work, however. The reasons may be twofold. *Parenting's* Chan is not sure there is a large enough audience to carry such a publication. "I don't think parents would turn to a parenting magazine for teens. I think they tend to look to other sources for advice, to their church, or school, or friends. But that may just be a problem of perception."

The September issue of *Atlanta Parent* focuses on the teenage years, but White feels her publication will stay primarily focused on the preteen and childhood years. "We plan our editorial to be a publication for all Atlanta parents, so our real goal is for everyone to find one thing that hits home with them." She questions whether there is a market for a publication that deals solely with teen issues. "I know some of the regionals are branching out with publications for parents of teen, but I honestly don't know if there is enough interest to support them or not. I'm taking a wait-and-see attitude."

Meredith Corporation, publisher of *Better Homes & Gardens,* is taking a stab at the market of parents of teens , however. They have acquired a magazine produced by the Medill School of Journalism at Northwestern University, *Raising Teens.*

Meredith has long been a corporate sponsor of Northwestern's editorial and marketing programs. David Abrahamson, Associate Professor at Medill, says that his students' research found that there is very strong evidence that the timing is right for a magazine targeting parents of teenagers.

The first finding is parents' greater need for help. While five or ten years ago, most people believed parents had very little effect on their children once they reached the teen years, Abrahamson says, "Our research showed that there is a new teenager and there is a new parent of a teenager out there. Being a teenager is not the same as it was ten years ago because they have to grow up much faster. The role of parenting a teenager may once have consisted of saying somewhere around puberty, 'Good luck, kid, you're on your own,' but now parents want to be much more involved in their teens lives."

The role taken by *Raising Teens,* therefore, was to face subjects "without taking a stand on any issue. It provides the information in a way that a wise and kind friend would," says Abrahamson. Also central to the magazine "is a sense of humor and fun, because we found that parents do have a sense of humor about their kids and they do in fact still have fun with them a lot of the time. The magazine targets ratio-nal, committed, loving parents who are involved in the upbringing of their teens and are convinced that they can make a difference and make their teens successful people."

Meredith says it is very excited about developing the magazine, but it remains on the drawing board without a definitive launch date.

Make Room for Dad, and Granddad

For niche publications in an increasingly crowded market, attracting a devoted audience to win advertiser dollars is essential. Most publishers agree that it is women who are the primary buyers of magazines. "Ninety percent of our audience is women," says *Family Life'*s Herbst. "We've been told that they do pass on relevant material to the men in the household, but men rarely are the original purchasers."

If this is true, then how do you market a magazine that targets fathers? The fact that men traditionally do not buy magazines has been a tough hurdle to clear for publications aimed at dads.

Full-Time Dads is a national newsletter started in 1991 that ceased print publication several years later because of difficulty maintaining an audience, but it was available on the Internet. James McLaughlin bought the publication, convinced that the time was right for "a serious publication focusing on fatherhood issues." Since that purchase, three issues of the bimonthly newsletter have appeared and subscription requests are coming in steadily. McLaughlin is looking for a distributor to help grow the publication.

"The honest truth," says McLaughlin, "is that men don't buy magazines.

Even *Sports Illustrated* is 90 percent purchased as a gift for men by women." Still, McLaughlin is counting on the notion that men will in fact buy, given the right product. "Men don't want fluff," he says. "They are not looking for the glossy come-on; they are looking for legitimate content."

Deborah Christensen, Managing Editor of *On the Father Front,* an evangelical newsletter distributed to members of the Christian Service Brigade, agrees. "We've been publishing our newsletter for ten years as part of our *Leadership* magazine and we have just decided to introduce it as a standalone publication. I see a real need for a publication on fathering, but I think it has to take just the right approach, and avoid the fluff."

She plans to offer shorter pieces, no more than 300 words, that are primarily practical or inspirational in content. Both McLaughlin and Christensen say they are actively looking for freelance writers who are fathers for their publications and agree that they are not finding enough.

Perhaps the shooting star of dad magazines was the national publication *Modern Dad*, which ceased publication after three issues. Publisher Shaun Budka, who conceived the magazine, says its demise resulted not from lack of positive response, but from financial problems.

Budka describes *Modern Dad* as "a lifestyle publication for fathers" rather than as a parenting magazine for men. From the first it was marketed to women as a gift-giving item. The problem was that not enough women knew about the magazine. The other problem was cash flow. Budka banked on the fact that he had a hot prospect that would quickly be picked up by a venture capitalist or publisher. The Meredith Corporation did show strong interest in the project, says Budka, but then backed off. In that period he decided to be conservative, "cut back. When the deal didn't go through, we frankly hadn't built a continuous sales base and our biggest problem was that we never enacted a proper circulation plan to get women aware of us."

Nevertheless Budka remains committed to publishing for fathers because he is convinced that the hunger for such a magazine is there and will continue to grow. The current plan is to start a publication called *First-Time Dad* in the next year, before trying to relaunch *Modern Dad*. The premier issue of *First-Time Dad* will be distributed free at childbirth classes nationwide, with subscription information. Initial distribution of the quarterly will be one million.

Budka compares the market for his projected publications to that of the women's sports magazines now coming on the market. "Gender roles are changing," he says, "and people are waking up to that." He also points out another critical fact: U.S. Census Bureau figures indicate that single-father families are growing at an annual rate of 10 percent, while the growth of single-mother households has leveled off. In 1996, 1.86 million households were headed by single dads as compared to 393,000 in 1970.

The senior population is growing as well, and they too are a potential audience for publications about family.

The first wave of baby boomers, like the Clintons, are sending children off to college. More and more will have a vested interest in grandchildren. PPA Executive Director Mittler says the market for grandparenting publications is one she expects to grow significantly in the next decade.

Mahoning Valley Parent, based in Ohio, has launched a grandparenting publication that now appears biannually. Editor Judy Shepard is very pleased with the response: She says the twenty-four-page publication is "snatched up as soon as it is printed." *Mahoning Valley Grandparent* offers "a mix of issues, from the light—cooking with grandma or intergenerational cruises—to the more serious," says Shepard. "We've covered the issues of grandparents as custodians of their grandchildren, as well as how to grandparent a disabled child."

Honey Hill Publishing, Inc., publishers of *Pittsburgh's Child,* also launched a grandparenting publication. Its premiere issue featured an article on grandparenting teenagers.

From generation to generation, the route continues to shift. If Moeckel is concerned that parents today are "drowning in information and thirsting for knowledge," Oldacre is optimistic that tomorrow's parents will do an even better job than preceding generations.

Parents today "are looking for answers, but ultimately the way to parent well comes not from do what I say, but do what I do," says Moeckel. "The morals have to come from inside the parent. I would hope that the next generation of parents will be better at filtering the knowledge they need from all the information they have available to them."

White says, you can read all the books and magazines you want, but ultimately, "they cannot tell you how to raise a responsible child, or a moral child. These are innate parenting skills that you have to mold on your own. No one can tell you how to do it."

"Our children are smarter than we are, and I think as parents they will be smarter than we were. The trick is staying up with what your children are exposed to at every age and being very aware of the danger zones," says Oldacre.

As complicated as the job of parenting is, the road maps are multiplying. It seems certain that in an expanding industry, niche publications will continue to appear around the turns and parents will be the ones who choose the destinations. For the writer who stays on course with these publications, the road could well be paved with gold.

Packagers
Making Books Happen

By Mark Haverstock

Y ou're a new writer with a great idea for a nonfiction book, but you're reluctant to go through the motions with traditional publishers. Why not try pitching your idea to a book packager? Book packagers, also known as book producers, are an often overlooked alternative to the publishing establishment. In some respects, they're becoming the next permutation of publishers.

A packager acts as a middleman between writers and publishers—part coach, part agent, and part publisher. The process of producing a book might be compared to a general contractor building a house. Instead of hiring carpenters, plumbers, and electricians, the packager contracts with writers, illustrators, and designers to build books for clients—who are often established publishing houses. Flexibility is the key

to their success; they do as much or as little as the publisher wants. Typically, packagers produce nonfiction, series fiction, and illustrated books.

Generally, packagers come to the business with a working knowledge of publishing. "Almost every packager was previously a writer, or editor, or graphic designer, or photo researcher," says David Rubel, President of Agincourt Press and also President of the American Book Producers Association (ABPA). "Some came from publishing houses and decided to run a small business creating books. Others have one or more of the component skills necessary to create books and decide they want to do the whole package."

According to Rubel, those from publishing houses tend to have managerial backgrounds, have larger operations with more staff, and use more freelancers. Those who are writers or graphic designers tend to be more like Rubel, working on a smaller scale, with two or three books a year.

Packager Advantages

The rise of packagers seems to stem from mergers and downsizing in the mainstream publishing industry. "As cost-conscious publishers find it necessary to trim their staff, they find it difficult to add books, to keep up their sales line," says Rubel. "Ironically in these times, book producers will do well because we offer the ability to add books to their list without adding editors or designers."

Publishers like Chelsea House enlist packagers to help fill the gaps. "The books that we generally have packaged are sports books for youth. The word count is relatively small and they follow a set formula," says Steve Reginald, Editor-in-Chief. "We just don't have the staff to do as many of those as we'd like." Packagers enable Chelsea House to double their output without great additional effort on their part.

According to Reginald, packagers handle everything connected with the inside of their books: They assign the manuscript, edit it, do picture research, pay usage fees, typeset, and produce it in a form available to the publisher, usually electronic media. The publisher will "generally handle the cover and the mechanical work," he says, and in some cases, provide a finished manuscript to a packager to do the layout, photos, or artwork.

A Great Place to Start

Author Jennifer Armstrong began her writing and editing career with one of the first packagers, Cloverdale Press. "I worked as an editorial assistant for a year, quit, and began writing for them instead." She wrote several books for Cloverdale Press, and followed partner Daniel Weiss when he established his own packaging firm.

"The pay was good, since I was highly productive and turned out a lot of work every year," says Armstrong. "I spent several years ghostwriting while I got my career off the ground, but also sold my own books to trade publishers." Eventually, she stopped writing for Daniel Weiss Associates and entered the trade market full-time.

Armstrong has since published numerous picture books and novels, and her current publisher is Alfred A. Knopf. But she still credits her success, in part, to early career opportunities with packagers. "The work I did for packagers over the years was an invaluable experience in the nature of an apprenticeship–I wrote a lot of books, and learned much about writing and publishing," she says. "I never hesitate to recommend working for a packager to a beginning writer. If you can do the work, it's a great place to start."

Packagers can relieve publishers of some of the headaches associated with producing books. "I think that publishers like the idea that most of their problems become the packager's problems. Packagers assume many of the financial and creative responsibilities," says Rubel. "Packagers can do books in a more effective way than publishers can, simply because there are fewer cooks making the stew." Rubel explains that there isn't as much of a consensus needed within the packaging company; only the publisher's agreement is needed.

In today's market, publishers are very reluctant to take on responsibilities for big, complicated, or expensive books. "Their staffs are overworked, each acquisitions editor has a lot on the plate, and to take on a labor-intensive project is just not in the cards," says Rubel. "Because editors are so busy, they don't have the time to micro manage, even if they have the inclination. They're dependent on the skill and expertise of the packager."

When it comes to complicated projects that involve interactive and novelty books, publishers such as Little Simon and Simon Spotlight also look at the cost-effectiveness of packagers. "These books are usually expensive to produce because pop-ups are extremely labor-intensive," says Editor Laura Hunt. "We'll often buy from packagers to get the cost benefits of their large, international co-editions."

Sometimes the service aspects attract publishers. "We handle the process from concept to bound book, or anything in-between," says Tom Hatch, President of Kent Publishing Services, "but often they come to us because they really like one of the services we provide, such as design."

From Idea to Book

Traditionally, book packagers conceived their own projects and then sold the ideas to publishers. But in today's market, it's as likely a publisher will assign a book project to a packager that is based on an idea generated in-house.

Once the project has been assigned, the packager begins the collaboration process with the publisher. "Typically, there will be one or more people from the publisher who will be responsible for working with us, usually an editor and someone representing the creative team," says Hatch, who mainly deals with educational materials. "We meet with them, and possibly someone from the marketing department, to plan the project. Sometimes that might involve creating prototypes, testing those prototypes with customers, and doing market research." Hatch works with the publisher to understand their editorial standards, to determine schedule and budget, and the flow of work.

"We subcontract to writers, illustrators, designers, photo researchers, and editors," says Hatch, "putting together a team for each project that suits the needs of the project." These are typically people who have worked with Kent Publishing on past projects.

The give-and-take process continues as the book develops. "Normally, our clients review the work that we do on a periodic basis—at the manuscript stage, at the page proof stage, and for layout and color," according to Hatch. "The amount of supervision varies according to the client; some are more busy than others."

What Hatch delivers to clients is the means to manufacture the book, in the form of electronic files. The client usually sends it to a jobber who prints the book, although some packagers arrange to do this step as well, and delivers bound books. From this point, the publisher, who has the marketing channels and the marketing expertise, handles the sales and publicity.

What's the total time involved from planning to a final book? "It varies from three to sixteen months," says Hatch.

Sell Yourself, Sell Your Ideas

Book packagers have different views on book proposals submitted by writers. Some don't consider them at all, preferring to develop them in-house or from publishing house requests. Others are open to proposals if they are marketable. The best way to find out is to check one of the many market guides available, or contact each book packager to learn about its policies. (See the sidebar, Finding a Packager, page 100.)

"About 25 percent of the projects we do come from ideas submitted to us," says Bruce Glassman, Editorial Director of Blackbirch Press. "For example, sometimes we get packages from photographers who have great nature or animal photographs along with a proposal. As for the other 75 percent, they are assigned from in-house needs to a network of freelancers Blackbirch has established over the years."

Glassman suggests a résumé or cover letter as the first step to indicate your interest. "Usually we can tell a lot from these, and if we're interested, we'll ask to see sample manuscripts. One thing that's helpful for us to see is a copy of an unedited manuscript that they submitted in the past." In this way, they get a better picture of a writer's capabilities minus the editor's influence.

Series books at Daniel Weiss Associates, such as Sweet Valley High and Bone Chillers, are handled in much the same way. "Writers should send samples of their published work," says Les Morgenstein, Associate Publisher. "But if they haven't been published before, it's best to write for guidelines and write a specific sample for the series." They will either buy ideas or work with an author to develop ideas and sell them together to a publisher. The latter is typically done with authors in their stable. Sometimes for the Love Stories novels, they'll acquire manuscripts through agents as well.

Hatch looks for expertise, as well as published samples. "Contact us with a résumé and a writing sample. Tell us what particular area of the school curriculum that you feel comfortable with and the age level you write for. Don't be afraid to contact us periodically. There are projects coming up all the time."

When pitching an idea, shorter is usually better, a query and an outline at the most. "We really don't like getting full manuscripts or sample chapters," says Glassman. The letter should explain the basic premise of the project: why it's special, or why it needs to be done. Writers should also explain their background and credentials. "Those are the two most important things we look at when considering a proposal."

Teamwork

One of the advantages of a writer working with a packager is the collaborative aspect, the opportunity to discuss a project and some editorial give-and-take. Author and former teacher Laurie Knowlton works on a regular basis with educational packager Tom Hatch.

"Usually, we brainstorm together over the phone," says Knowlton. "One time, Tom was doing an anthology for Modern Curriculum Press covering grades one to six. He was looking for unique ideas to help develop vocabulary for that age group. I shared some ideas, and he tried to see if they would fit into some of the general ideas they had for the anthology." Later, Hatch submitted a proposal incorporating Knowlton's suggestions.

On another occasion, Knowlton was asked by Hatch to do a Christian early-learner line for Frank Schaffer Publications. Having taught kindergarten, it was easy for her to come up with some ideas for teaching basic concepts. "Just like any writing, you write what you know. In this case, I put together a proposal for him for eight pieces, and then met with him. We polished the proposal until it was ready to submit to the publisher."

"Working with a packager is more like a magazine assignment," explains Knowlton, "you're not shooting in the dark. It's really an advantage if you can ask a packager: 'What exactly is your vision? What exactly would you like to see?'"

One piece of advice from Knowlton: "Really listen to what a packager wants, and try to produce it, staying in the realm of writing what you know and writing what you love."

At Kent Publishing, the process is a bit more informal. "It usually begins with a phone call or a letter," says Hatch. "Put together a proposal with a sample chapter or sample lesson plan."

Working With Packagers

Daniel Weiss Associates usually assigns a single title when working with an author for the first time. "For authors who are in our stable, we usually assign them multiple books under one con- tract," said Morgenstein. "Since most of our series are produced on a monthly schedule, it's easier for both us and the authors to plan their year this way."

The amount of direction given to an author varies with the book or series. "For the Sweet Valley series, authors always write from detailed outlines, which we provide," explains Morgenstein. "For all the other series, we may provide a plot description, then the au-

Finding a Packager

One excellent source for finding packagers is the *American Book Producers Association Directory,* available from ABPA, Suite 604, 160 5th Ave., New York, NY 10010. Another is *Literary Market Place,* published by R.R. Bowker. Listings in writers' market directories are also helpful, but they only list a sampling of packagers in the market.

Since a book producer's work is often hidden, the only credits, if any, will probably appear on the copyright page. You, as a prospective writer, will have to dig for information on what types of books specific packagers produce–many are specialists in certain areas. When you contact them, be sure to ask for their book lists or catalogues.

While they're checking your background, check theirs. Packagers who work with established publishers, like Bantam, Scholastic, etc., are most likely reputable. You may also want to contact an author or editor that has worked with the packager.

thor will do chapter outlines. We're very interactive and hands-on in the editorial process, much more so than a traditional publisher. But we may also ask for heavier revisions than a traditional publisher."

At Blackbirch Press, the amount of direction varies from project to project, depending on the complexity and the subject matter. There's always contact with the editors and some give-and-take in the process. "Sometimes the authors are responsible for developing the outlines, which they develop after detailed discussions with us about what we want and how much relative importance we want to give each of the major subjects or areas," says Glassman. "In other cases, we'll develop outlines here."

For the author, working with a packager can mean giving up some creative license. "When I write for packagers, there is plenty of brainstorming involved, especially in development of individual books in a series," says author Jennifer Armstrong. "However, there is much less control with a packager than with a traditional publisher. With Knopf, for example, I propose a book and write it as I like, and then it is edited. With the packager, there is often some degree of imposition from them or the publisher on the content, length, and other elements of the book. With a trade publisher, your book is whatever you want it to be."

Author Laurie Knowlton echoes similar sentiments about packagers versus trade publishers. "When you sell a book to a traditional publishing house, you're usually dealing with only one editor," she says. "But with a packager, you always have to deal with a third party."

The Package Deal
Book packagers are not traditional publishers, so writers will encounter busi-

ness practices that are different from the rest of the industry. "If they're hiring you as a freelancer, it's usually assumed that you'll get a flat fee or an hourly rate without profit participation," says Rubel. "The margins are small, so that's why most packagers use work-for-hire contracts."

Packagers also defend work-for-hire policies because the writer doesn't need to write a detailed proposal or hire an agent to sell it. Typically, packagers take a basic idea and expand it into a more detailed one, often presenting the writer with an outline or plan from which to work. They'll also work closely with the writer to organize the book.

But under some circumstances, writers can get a piece of the profits. "It depends on the situation. We both publish and package books," says Glassman.

"For the works Blackbirch publishes, we pay royalties 95 percent of the time. But when packaging, payment depends on the deal we struck with our client. Quite often, there are certain houses that don't pay us royalties, so in these cases we do projects strictly as a work-for-hire."

Typically, writers of Daniel Weiss's Sweet Valley series do not get a royalty. "With the newer series we pay royalties, but only one percent," says Morgenstein. "Any original work not from an outline is going to receive a royalty, and original material for the Love Stories series pays from one to four percent, and a percentage of the subrights as well."

Having a track record can also pay. "If the author is 'unknown,' it's a work-for-hire arrangement," says Dan Wood, Publisher and Chief Executive Officer of Ottenheimer Publishers. "If they

have done books before, and have established a name in publishing, we'll give an advance plus royalty."

Packager or Publisher?

Working with a book packager can be an attractive alternative for writers who are looking for a first book credit, but don't want to get involved in the long process of selling it to a traditional publishing house.

Packagers tend to hire experienced authors with expertise in a particular field and novices who will work for a flat fee or modest royalties.

"It's a great place for a new writer to learn how to write for this market," says Morgenstein. "There's an opportunity you have here that you don't have going to a traditional publisher. Not many people get their first novels published. But if you have talent, and can write to conform with a series, you can get the background you need. And a publisher is more likely to buy a series from us than from an individual author. We know how to package it and provide consistent quality. Someone with a great idea may not have the credibility going into a publisher, whereas they can partner with us, and we do."

"Working for a packager gives you exposure and it helps pay the bills, and anytime you get something published, it's one more thing you can add to your list of credentials," says Knowlton. "It can be one of the stepping stones to getting published in the trade market. Those who look down on packaging need to realize that this is one avenue a professional can use to earn a living and get into print."

THE BUSINESS SIDE

Part
4

Contracts

When Words Mean Business

By Catherine Frey Murphy

If you're like some creative people, the mere word *contract* might give you a headache. Plowing through pages of fine print may not seem closely connected to the artistic drives that led you to become a writer in the first place.

But whether it's long and complex, or short and uncomplicated, every contract is nothing more than an exchange of promises. Publishing contracts may cover many subjects, but the basic exchange is simple. The writer promises to provide the publisher with rights to use a certain piece of writing, by a certain date. In return, the publisher promises to publish the writing, and to pay the writer a certain amount of money.

A contract doesn't always have to be in writing to be valid, but writers know that the written word is important. By forcing everyone to think about the terms in advance, a written contract solves problems before they arise. It's a good idea to make sure every agreement you reach with a publisher is reduced to writing, even if your "contract" is nothing more than a letter confirming the terms you've established in a telephone conversation. It's also a good idea to make sure you understand the promises you and your publishers make to each other in your contracts. After all, that fine print is made up of nothing but words—and words are your business!

Contract Advisors

The first question to ask when you're evaluating a contract is, what kind is it? Magazine agreements are different from book contracts, and in the world of books, trade publishers offer differ-

Kinds of Book Publishers

■ **Trade publishers** produce books for retail sale in bookstores, libraries, and schools. Their lists include the more "up-market," literary titles, which are likely to earn good reviews and become candidates for prestigious awards.

■ **Mass-market publishers** are trade publishers who produce less expensive books, which may be sold in chain bookstores, supermarkets, and discount outlets, as well as bookstores. Mass-market titles may not be carried in the most exclusive bookstores, or purchased by libraries or schools. They reach a wide audience, and can sell in very large numbers.

■ **Small presses** are trade publishers that produce only a few books each year and often limit their lists to books dealing with a particular geographic region, or a specialized area of interest such as the environment. With these presses, payment is often lower. The shorter lists often allow small presses to give individualized attention to each author, and to publicize every book they publish.

■ **Textbook publishers** produce books for educational use in schools. **Religious publishers** produce books for religious bookstores, churches, and religious schools. These publishers may be divisions of large publishing companies, or small, independent houses. Payment is lower than with trade or mass-market titles. Religious and educational books may sell well for many years, however, and these publishers often provide writers with steady, income-producing work.

■ **Packagers** are usually not publishers themselves. Instead, they develop ideas for books or book series, sell the resulting book *package* to a publisher, and find authors and illustrators to create them. Packagers sometimes pay flat fees rather than royalties, and writers may not keep the copyright in the published work. Writing for a packager can be an excellent way to break into print, gain experience, and earn income.

ent provisions from small presses, educational publishers, or packagers.

With so much diversity, a writer must learn to tell if the terms of a contract are reasonable. Inform yourself, advises literary agent Sheldon Fogelman. "If you don't have experience, find out from other people's experience. You can network, ask questions, find out from people you know. Try to speak to people who've worked with at least two or three different publishing houses."

You can find seasoned writers in your critique group, Society of Children's Book Writers and Illustrators (SCBWI) chapter, or Internet mailing list or newsgroup. Author associations are also a good source of information. SCBWI offers its members a detailed pamphlet on book contracts for a stamped, self-addressed envelope, and the Authors' Guild and the National Writers' Union provide members with legal assistance and contract reviews. In addition, a number of excellent books are available on publishing contracts and negotiation.

A literary agent will help you understand your contracts, and negotiate them for you, too. A lawyer can also be helpful, as long as you remember that publishing law is a highly specialized field. A general practice attorney is unlikely to be familiar with publishing contracts. If you decide to use a lawyer, ask your writers' organization or state bar association to help you find a specialist in publishing law.

No matter whose contract advice you seek, remember that there's always a gap between the ideal and the real. "Nobody's contract is ideal," says Mary Flower, a publishing attorney who specializes in representing children's authors and illustrators. Flower, who wrote and self-published the book, *A Writers' Guide to a Children's Book Contract,* believes that authors negotiate more effectively if they understand the reasons for their contract terms. "I wanted my book to explain to authors why they should ask for changes," she says, "why it works the way it does."

Better Terms

Sometimes, new authors worry that if they ask for more money or try to change other contract terms, they will offend their editors. "That's silly," Fogelman says bluntly. "Obviously, if you're offensive, you'll offend. But there is a way of asking that's not offensive. I have an old philosophy: If you don't ask, you're not going to get it."

Flower agrees. "Contracts are meant to be negotiated," she says. "Even if the only thing you negotiate is fifteen author's copies instead of ten, you have to start somewhere."

That said, Fogelman and Flower agree that new authors probably have less negotiation success than those who have published several successful books. "Whether you're previously published or not is very important," says Fogelman. "The reason for this importance is the track record. Let's say you've had half a dozen books published, and each one sold 20,000 copies in hardcover. Your new contract will reflect that, because they'll expect your new book to sell like the previous ones. If you're an inexperienced writer and you're not agented, you can expect to be offered a minimum advance for your first book."

Flower has found that children's authors may not get contract advantages granted to authors of books for adults. "Children's books are viewed as the stepchild of the publishing business," she explains. "It's the adult stuff that garners the attention and the money. But we have that attitude in general in our society. If we thought that children were important, our schools would be better."

When the children's book boom slowed down in the mid-1990s, Flower says, "some of those little perks that used to come with later contracts when the first book did well became harder to get, though not impossible." For instance, she notes, "Many authors are finding it more difficult to get an increase in their book advances. Even after a successful book, publishers may say, 'Well, that was that book, and we don't know how this one will do.'"

Fogelman agrees that the children's publishing scene has changed in recent years, but he thinks that's good, not bad. He firmly believes that good children's books are still being published, and writers are still receiving good contracts. "There is not bad news out there," he says. "The editors in the United States, by and large, are the best editors in the world, because they *edit*. They're concerned. Children's book publishing is in a pretty healthy place right now."

Which publisher you're working with makes a difference, however. "You have to draw a distinction between first-line and second-line publishers," Fogelman says. "The first lines have more money, and will pay you more. There are many wonderful second-line publishers, but they can't afford to pay you as much."

Payment isn't the only contract issue, of course. Many writers care as much, or more, about whether their books are well designed and produced than about how much they'll be paid. Before you submit your manuscript, Fogelman advises, "Walk into a bookstore. Whose books do you like? Who is doing a good job with production? If you have an experienced eye, you can say, 'I love this book, but I hate the design.'"

When it's time to negotiate, some authors would rather give the job to an agent or a lawyer; others want to do it themselves. The choice depends on your personality, says Flower. "Some authors enjoy the negotiation process. But I'm not sure you're always the best person to negotiate on your own behalf. The whole idea of having to fight for something you think you deserve can be difficult."

For writers who choose to negotiate their own contracts, Flower recommends, "Be very professional about it. Writing or illustrating is your business. You have to do what makes business sense." First, she says, "distance yourself emotionally. Then read your contract and make a list. Decide what's really important, and write it down. A letter to your editor works much better than a two-hour phone conversation, especially in these days of fax machines."

Writing down your concerns before you talk will help you work them out in advance, Flower explains, so you don't have to think on your feet in the course of a conversation. Send the letter to your editor, and then call to talk it over. "You both have it in writing, so you can make notes on the letter as you discuss it. There's much less chance of misunderstanding that way, and it puts things on a less personal basis."

Book Contracts

Book contracts are the longest and most intricate publishing agreements. That's because, ideally, a children's book will last a long time, and so will the author's relationship with the publisher. A book contract is a little like a marriage. Like husbands and wives, both parties in a publishing contract must succeed if either side is to prosper over the long term. And like spouses, the partners in a publishing relationship have needs that must be met. But starting off with too adversarial an approach is unlikely to make for long-term happiness in the relationship.

As you review this explanation of some typical book contract clauses, remember that no contract is truly typical. Every publisher has its own preferences and procedures, and so does every author. There's no substitute for reading your contract carefully, asking your editor intelligent questions, and using every available resource to educate yourself.

Grant of Rights

You grant your publisher the right to publish your book, sell it, and license reprints. Unless you have an agent who is retaining subsidiary rights (discussed below), the contract will probably state that the publisher may do so in every language, in every country in the world. In most book contracts (except for work-for-hire contracts, discussed below, under Flat Fees), you'll keep the copyright, which is, essentially, ownership of the created work itself. Your publisher will register the copyright in your name with the Library of Congress.

Subsidiary Rights

This part of your contract covers sales of such other rights as book club sales, serialization in periodicals, British publication rights, translations, audio, television and dramatic versions, commercial, electronic, and merchandising rights. Most publishers insist on buying some subsidiary rights, such as serialization and paperback rights. But your agent, if you have one, may retain some rights to sell on your behalf, such as television, motion picture, or British publication rights. An agent may be able to get higher payment for these rights than publishers obtain. "We negotiate everything, and I do mean *everything*," says Fogelman. "We fight as if we're getting paid by the hour."

For authors without agents, it's standard to sell the rights to your publisher for a *split*, meaning that your publisher will receive part of the proceeds of any subsidiary sale, and you'll get the rest. Your contract will set out the percentages for each category, which vary among publishers and among the various subsidiary categories. Authors sometimes wonder if they should retain subsidiary rights, as agents do. But Fogelman asks, "What are they going to do with them? Authors usually don't know how to sell them, unless they used to be the subsidiary rights manager for a publisher."

In subsidiary rights, Flower says, "The real bone of contention now is electronic rights. Every person I've ever dealt with gets hot under the collar that the paragraphs are so all-inclusive—like 'throughout the universe' and 'everything ever invented.' The fears about this are strong, but it looks worse than it is."

Publishers must try to protect themselves from rapid change, Flower explains. But in truth, publishers don't have much more control over the future of electronic rights than authors do. "I don't know where electronic rights are going to go. Nobody knows where they're likely to go. There's no way we can control it entirely. You're just going to have to try to be sanguine."

Instead of mounting a futile fight to try to make your publisher remove this language from your contract, Flower recommends obtaining the right to approve, or at least be consulted, before a sale of electronic rights or any other commercial rights. "One would hope that the publisher would have the grace to consult authors anyway, but if it's not in the contract, they don't have to."

Promise to Publish

Here, your publisher makes its central promise: to publish your book at its own expense. Often, the publisher agrees to do this within a time limit of twelve to eighteen months after your manuscript has been accepted, or longer, if it's necessary to wait for illustrations. This provision keeps your publisher from postponing your book indefinitely, which can happen unfortunately, if the editor who originally signed your book moves to another house, or the publisher's marketing plans change.

Check your contract's provisions to see what happens if your publisher fails to meet the deadline. Unless the failure is due to circumstances beyond your publisher's control, you should be able to terminate the contract, keep your advance, and sell the book elsewhere.

Delivery

You promise to deliver a satisfactory manuscript to your publisher, on time. If this is your first book, you've probably met this requirement before signing the contract, since publishers rarely grant first-book contracts before they've seen a publishable manuscript. If you're signing the contract on the basis of a proposal or a few chapters, some publishing lawyers advise adding the words "in form and content" following "satisfactory." This helps to avoid the possibility that your publisher could reject your finished manuscript even though it meets the publisher's expectations, because, while you were writing, another house published a book on the same subject.

Royalties

The standard means of payment among trade publishers, royalties, are paid as a percent of the sales of your book. For trade hardcovers, the standard royalty ranges from 8 to 10 percent. For picture books, that percentage is usually divided equally between the author and illustrator. For trade paperbacks, royalties can range from 6 to 8 percent, although Flower says that 6 percent has become the standard in recent years. Mass-market publishers, small presses, and educational, and religious houses may pay lower percentages than these, and Fogelman says authors should expect a lower royalty rate for any "specialty book," by which he means board books, books accompanied by gimmicks like packaged toys, or "anything that does not look like a normal book."

Check your contract to see whether your royalty will be computed on *gross* (a percentage of your book's retail price) or on *net* (a percentage of the amount your publisher actually receives from booksellers). Gross royalties, paid by most leading trade publishers, are larger, but mass-market publishers, small presses, educational, and religious houses often compute royalties on net. If your contract provides for a net royalty, you can try asking for a larger royalty percentage, to make up for the less favorable formula.

Your contract will probably also include separate, lower royalty rates for book club sales, *deep discount* sales (sales of large numbers of books for a sharply lowered price), and other sales outside normal book-distribution outlets.

Your contract may also include an *escalation clause*, increasing your royalty percentage after the sale of a certain number of books—for example, from 10 percent to 12½ percent after the sale of 25,000 books. This gives you the opportunity to share in the profits if your book succeeds, but it also protects your publisher, who isn't required to pay anything extra unless the book sells well.

"If you have a good track record," says Fogelman, "you should always ask for an escalation." But Flower warns that escalation clauses have recently become more difficult to get. "Publishers absolutely don't want to give them," she reports, adding that when

they do agree to an escalation, they tend to require a higher number of books sold before escalating the royalty than they did in the past.

Advance

In a sense, an advance is a loan against your book's future royalty earnings— but you're not expected to pay it back, even if the book's earnings are disappointing. Advances are a standard part of trade book contracts, but many specialty houses and small presses don't pay them, instead relying entirely on royalties or flat fees. If your contract includes an advance, Fogelman says the publisher will determine the appropriate range of estimating your book's first year sales. If, for instance, your book is expected to sell 3,000 copies in the first year at ten dollars a copy, and your royalty is 10 percent, your first-year earnings would be $3,000. "Many publishers try to get you to sign for one-half of that potential," he says. "But you can get more if you're a good negotiator."

To figure out what your advance will be, Fogelman says, you need to know the printrun, or the number of copies the publisher expects to produce in the first printing. "They may say they don't know," he says. "But here's a clue. Every time a publisher is going to make an offer, they have to do a financial report, including a hypothetical printrun. You can ask, 'What printrun are you putting down on the financial report?'"

Don't expect an astronomical advance. In the children's book world, huge advances are reserved for a few star authors and illustrators. According to Flower, a typical advance for a first novel or nonfiction work may run from $3,000 to $5,000. A first picture book ranges from $1,500 to $5,000, if the author has written the text only, and twice that much for an author/illustrator who's creating the whole book. Fogelman observes that when an advance is divided between author and illustrator, it's common practice for the illustrator to receive a larger share.

Fogelman notes that most publishers allow some bargaining room with advances. He suggests asking politely, "Is that the highest you can possibly pay?" One picture book author reported that after her editor quoted an advance for her first book, she explained her own inexperience and asked meekly, "Is that amount fair?" The editor was silent for a moment—and then upped the offer!

Usually, half of your advance is paid when you sign the contract, the other half when you deliver a satisfactory manuscript. You should not have to pay back any of the advance unless you fail to provide the publisher with the promised manuscript in publishable shape by your deadline, or break your contract in some other significant fashion. Your contract's *termination* clause spells out what happens if you break the contract, or if you've complied with the contract, but the publisher decides not to publish the book after all.

Flat Fees

Mass-market publishers, packagers, small presses, educational, and religious publishers sometimes pay a flat fee instead of a royalty. That means you'll receive one payment and no more, no matter how successful your book may later become. For a first book, it's hard to change a flat-fee arrangement, although after publishing a few successful books with the same publisher, you may be able to insist on a shift to royalties.

Some flat-fee contracts are *work-for-hire* arrangements. A work-for-hire contract means that the publisher, not you, is the work's official creator and owns all rights in the work, including the copyright. That means the publisher can use your work more than once, or change it in whatever way it chooses, without consulting you or paying you anything more than the original fee. In spite of their obvious drawbacks, work-for-hire contracts are the standard in some areas of publishing. They may make sense if you're trying to break into print for the first time, or simply looking for steady income. But before you agree to sign such a contract, make sure you understand exactly what rights you're signing away.

Warranties and Indemnities

This part of a contract can be the most intimidating. You promise the publisher that your work is original, that you have the right to sell it, that you've obtained all necessary permissions, and that your book doesn't libel anyone or include any dangerous instructions that could cause injury. You'll probably also promise to protect your publisher from the cost of any lawsuits resulting from your book, including judgments, court costs, and lawyer fees.

Alarming as these provisions are, they're virtually impossible to change. It may be comforting to remember that these lawsuits are very rare in the children's book world.

If you have particular concerns about some aspect of your book (for instance, the *dangerous-instruction provision,* which may be quite important if you've written a book of science experiments or carpentry projects), you may want to bring it to the attention of your publisher's legal department. But in the long run, your best guarantee for avoiding problems with this clause is to make certain that all the promises you make are true.

Editing and Form
Although you may feel strongly about your book's editing, illustrations, or jacket art, almost all publishing contracts give the publisher the final right to edit the book, select its illustrator, and determine its appearance. In most situations, that's as it should be. Your publisher's editors, art directors, and marketing staff have professional expertise in producing attractive, marketable books.

Although your contract probably won't mention it, many publishers do allow authors to review copyediting, see illustration sketches before final art is created, and check jacket copy, as a matter of professional courtesy. Ask about your publisher's procedures, and if you have strong preferences about some aspect of your book, let your editor know. But in the end, remember that it's your job to write a good story. It's your publisher's job to figure out how to turn your story into a beautiful, successful book.

Option Clause
An option gives your publisher "first dibs" on your next book. It's flattering to know that your publisher's already interested in your future career—but be careful. If your relationship with this publisher works out unhappily, an option clause can be limiting. "I always ask to have option clauses taken out," says Fogelman. "But many publishers insist on it when they first take an author on." You may be able to get your publisher to limit its option to your next similar work, for instance your next middle-grade novel or science activity book.

You should also check the time periods in your option clause. "The ones I hate are the clauses where you can't even submit your second manuscript elsewhere, for a long period of time," says Fogelman. Check to see if your option requires the publisher to reach a decision on whether to publish your next work within a specific amount of time, say, four to six weeks. After that time, if you and the publisher are unable to negotiate an agreement in good faith, your contract should give you the freedom to submit the next work elsewhere.

Out-of-Print
It's sad but true: In today's competitive publishing climate, children's books don't stay in print as long as they used to. Your contract should define what *out-of-print* means: typically, when your book is no longer available for sale in an English-language version through bookstores in the U.S.

Once your book is declared out-of-print, you should be able to get back your rights, but your contract may require you to initiate this process, by sending a written demand to the publisher. Your publisher probably will reserve the right to sell off remaining copies at a *remainder* price when a book goes out-of-print, and you should have the right to buy some or all of those copies, as well as the plates and films from which the book was originally printed.

Author's Copies
Your contract will provide for you to receive a certain number of free copies of your book, and give you the right to buy more at a discount (generally 40 or 50 percent of list price). Ten free copies is the standard for large trade houses, but Fogelman says, "If you want twenty copies, you can get them." In fact, he says, it's so easy to get most publishers to agree to provide more free copies that, as a matter of negotiating practice, "that should be the last thing you ask for."

Joint Accounting
Some contracts provide that the publisher can deduct any indebtedness you may have to them on this book from your royalties on future books. This means that if this book doesn't *earn out* (that is, sell enough copies to cover your advance), the publisher can subtract the remainder from your earnings on more successful books in the future. Ask your publisher to remove this provision, or at least allow you to add a line specifying that the term *indebtedness* does not include unearned advances on this or any other book.

Miscellaneous Clauses
Your contract will probably include a number of paragraphs of legal boiler-plate, dealing with such matters as what happens if the publisher files for bankruptcy, which state laws govern any dispute that arises, and providing that the contract is the sum total of the agreement between you and the publisher.

That last provision is especially important. If the written contract differs from something you've agreed to orally, the written version will prevail. Make sure any variations are straightened out, and if you and your publisher decide to change some aspect of the contract after you've both signed it, make sure that the change is reduced to writing and signed by all parties.

Magazine Contracts

Although they're almost always shorter and simpler than book agreements, magazine agreements are as diverse as the magazines themselves. Your magazine contract may be a formal written contract, or a simple acceptance letter. Many smaller magazines use no contracts at all. With these publications, your first notification that a piece has been accepted may be the arrival of a check in the mail.

But most magazine agreements cover the basics: the nature of the work being purchased, the payment, what rights are being purchased, and sometimes, the publication date. At *Highlights for Children*, for instance, the magazine uses a formal contract that states a price and advises the author that the magazine purchases all rights, including copyright. Coordinating Editor Rich Wallace says, "We generally don't schedule a piece for publication at that point. Ordinarily, we're buying for an inventory, from which we may draw at any point."

Process Variations

As to payment, *Highlights* uses a database to track the articles it has bought from a particular author in the past, and the payment made for them. Since first-time authors aren't in the database, generally their payments fall into the ranges set out in the writers' guidelines.

Hopscotch uses a slightly less formal approach. "We're really pretty flexible here," reports Associate Editor Virginia Edwards, "but if we agree to publish a piece, we'll publish it, even though it may be five years down the road. We schedule articles far ahead, because we work around a theme for each issue. When we decide to use a piece, we send a letter to the author, saying, 'Your story is scheduled for such-and-such an issue.' Our guidelines state our payment schedule, so that's understood. We ask the writer to send back a letter confirming publication, and acknowledging that we buy first rights, or sometimes, second rights."

When the *Hopscotch* issue for which the piece is scheduled goes into production, the accounting department sends payment to the author.

At the Children's Better Health Institute's *Jack And Jill*, says Editor Daniel Lee, "What we have is an agreement. I suppose it amounts to a contract, but that's not what we call it. We have a holding system. If we like a piece, we'll send out a hold letter telling the author we'd like to use it, and if we do decide to use it, they'll be notified later on. That's definitely not a promise to publish, since a fair proportion of the pieces do not end up in the magazine."

When the CBHI editors decide to publish a piece, the author receives a notification letter, including the amount of payment, the publication date, and the transfer of all rights to *Jack And Jill*. "We always buy all rights," explains Lee. "If a manuscript comes to us marked first serial rights only, I'll include a note with the hold letter, saying we much prefer to buy all rights and asking if that's acceptable."

Pockets sends out an author card, to

be signed and returned by each writer whose work it purchases. The card lists the name of the piece, publication date, payment, and includes a statement acknowledging that the author owns rights to the material, and grants newspaper, periodical, electronic, and software-driven rights to *Pockets*. The card also advises the author that these rights can be regained one year after publication, by sending a written termination notice to *Pockets*.

Editorial staff member Patty McIntyre says, "We use this card for everything, whether it's an article, a story, or a poem." If an author is unwilling to grant all rights, which McIntyre says has happened with a poem or two, the editors note the author's objection on the card and do not reuse the material.

All Right to All Rights

The issue of whether authors should convey all rights in their manuscripts to publishers has recently become heated, as a result of the boom in republication of written work on the Internet and in computer databases. Magazines that buy all rights usually say they make up for the scale of their purchase in higher pay, and exposure to large circulations. But some writers object to this practice.

"The whole issue of the reuse of freelance writers' work on CD-ROMs, electronic databases, and other media that haven't been invented yet, but will be tomorrow, has mobilized writers," says Irwin Muchnik of the Publication Rights Clearinghouse (PRC). The National Writers' Union developed the PRC, which Muchnik calls "a model transaction-based royalty agreement" based on the workings of ASCAP, the organization that obtains payment for musicians and composers for the use of musical pieces. Writers who join the PRC are sent a list of *hits*, or citations of their work in the databases with which the PRC has agreements (currently only the fax delivery service UnCover, although arrangements with others are in progress). "Then we need a list of those other citations for which you are interested in licensing the secondary rights," says Muchnik. When the databases use the licensed materials, the PRC collects a royalty and passes it on to the author.

The Authors' Registry takes a different approach to the same problem. Founded by the Authors' Guild, the American Society of Journalists and Authors (ASJA), and several other groups, the Registry maintains a database listing individual Registry members, and the members of many of the largest writers' organizations. Instead of licensing material in advance, Terry King of the Registry says, "Our primary focus is to make deals with publishers, getting them to pay for uses they've already made." In the first two years of the program, the Registry has distributed more than $200,000 in royalties to participating writers.

Because of their differing approaches, writers can choose to sign up with both organizations. "Between the two of us," Muchnik says, "we're making a lot of progress in getting writers and illustrators to understand this very important issue."

But freelance writers were dealt a blow in August 1997, when a federal judge ruled that publishers may repro-

Which Rights Are Which?

Fledgling lawyers are taught that property rights are like a bundle of sticks. When you transfer rights in something you own to another person, you may hand over the whole bundle, representing all of your rights in that piece of property. Or you might give the other person just a few of your sticks, keep the rest, or give some of them to somebody else. Your contracts usually spell out exactly which rights you're being asked to convey in your writing, using terms like these:

■ **All rights:** This is the whole bundle of sticks. When you give up all rights in a piece of your writing, the publisher may reuse it any number of times, in more than one medium, and you no longer have any control over the piece. Sometimes publishers who insist on purchasing all rights will return them to you after a certain period of time and in all cases other than "work made for hire," you have the legal right to demand the return of your rights at the end of thirty-five years.

■ **First rights:** The publisher has the right to use your work once, with your guarantee that this is the first time the piece has been published. You keep all other rights.

■ **First serial rights:** The right to excerpt sections from a book, for use in a periodical or newspaper.

■ **First North American serial rights:** The right to publish your work for the first time, in the United States and Canada.

■ **One-time rights:** The right to publish the piece once, with no guarantee that somebody else hasn't published it before.

■ **Second serial rights:** The right to republish a work that has already been published somewhere else. In some publishing arrangements, these are also called reprint rights.

■ **Simultaneous rights:** The right to use your work once, granted to several publishers at the same time.

■ **Syndication rights:** The right for a syndicate to print your material in all the newspapers with which they have contracts. Syndicated rights may be first rights, second rights, or others.

duce purchased freelance materials in some electronic media without additional permission from, or payment to, the writers.

In a lawsuit brought by writers against The New York Times Company, Times Mirror, and others, the judge ruled that publishers have reproduction rights if the reused material appears in an electronic publication that is the same as, or a slightly revised version of, the original publication. The ruling compared reuse in newer technologies such as databases and CD-ROMs to microfiche or microfilm archiving. The ruling did not deal directly with publication on the Internet, specifically the World Wide Web, which has come to prominence since it was filed in 1993. It is clear that this case will not be the last word on electronic media and rights.

Contract Resources

Books

■ *A Writer's Guide to a Children's Book Contract,* by Mary Flower, Fern Hill Books, 600 West End Ave., Suite 10D, New York NY 10024.

■ *Every Writer's Guide to Copyright & Publishing Law*, by Ellen M. Kozack, Henry Holt and Company.

■ *Getting to Yes: Negotiating Agreement Without Giving In,* by Roger Fisher and William Ury, Houghton Mifflin, reprinted in paperback by Penguin Books.

■ *Negotiating a Book Contract: A Guide for Authors, Agents and Lawyers,* by Mark L. Levine, Moyer Bell Ltd., Colonial Hill, Mt. Kisco, NY 10549.

■ *The Writer's Law Primer,* by Linda F. Pinkerton, Lyons & Burford, Publishers, 31 W 21st St., New York NY 10010.

Professional Organizations:

■ *Society of Children's Book Writers and Illustrators:* 22736 Vanowen St., Suite 106, West Hills CA 91307. (310) 859-9887. Website: www.scbwi.org

■ *Publication Rights Clearinghouse:* 337 17th St. #101, Oakland, CA 94612. (510) 839-0110. Website: www.nwu.org/nwu/prc/prchome.htm

■ *The Authors' Registry, Inc.:* 330 West 42nd St., New York NY 10036. (212) 563-5363. Website: registry@interport.net

■ *National Writers' Union:* National Office East, 113 University Pl. 6th Fl., New York, NY 10003. (212) 254-0279. E-mail: nwu@nwu.org
National Office West: 337 17th St. #101, Oakland, CA 94612. (510) 839-0110. E-mail: nwu@nwu.org

■ *Authors' Guild:* 330 W. 42nd St., 29th Floor, New York, NY 10036. (212) 563-5904.

■ *Volunteer Lawyers for the Arts:* (515) 319-5787. Art Law Line: (quick answers to art-related legal questions); (515) 319-5910. Website: www.pictureframe.com/sps/business/lawyers.htm

Promotion

How Authors Sell

By Patricia Curtis Pfitsch

BUSINESS

Finally, the book is sold. The revisions are in. All you have to do now is bask in the glory of being an author with a published book. Right?

Wrong. "I think in this day and age, if you want to have a book published and have people know about it, you cannot rely on a publisher to do the job for you," says Walter Mayes, who travels the country for Bantam Doubleday Dell as Walter the Giant Storyteller. "Publishing no longer has the workforce and the time and the interest to promote every book properly—if it ever did. That's probably a myth."

"What you'd really love as an author is experienced, creative people being paid a lot to come up with original ideas of how to publicize your book," says Jane Kurtz, who has nine books out. Her latest, *Only a Pigeon,* was released in 1997. "I think that's every

author's dream and in the beginning I assumed that was close to reality. But the more I've gone along I've realized—no, that's not reality."

Publisher Standards

So what does a publisher do to promote the books on its list? "There are a whole bunch of things that publishers do automatically," says Stephen Roxburgh, President and Publisher of Front Street Books.

Libraries and schools make book-buying decisions based on reviews and awards, so publishers focus on review journals like *Publishers Weekly, Horn Book, School Library Journal*, and *Kirkus Reviews.* "Publishers submit books for awards," explains Stephanie Owens Lurie, Vice President, Associate Publisher, and Editorial Director of Simon & Schuster Books for Young Readers, "and they submit every book to the major review journals."

"If you're publishing a young adult novel, for example," says Roxburgh, "you need to know who the people are, the real supporters, and you need to be sure they get the book as early as possible. If I'm publishing a new writer, I will often send galleys to X number of people I know will respond, with a letter saying here's a new voice I want you to hear. I don't know what's going to come of that, but I know the chances are good they'll get it, they'll read it, and then it's in God's hands. It has to stand on its own. But if I didn't do that, the book could get lost."

Publishers distribute catalogues that list all their books. "Our catalogue is the biggest, the primary way the book is promoted to the industry," says Coy Batson, Marketing Director for Harcourt Brace Children's Book Division. "Every new book is included in the catalogue. Every book gets a full page. We include photographs and a short biography of the author and illustrator. We've found from the bookstores themselves that it's very important to know as much about the author and illustrator as possible. If it's a reissue from our list into paperback, no photo and no author 'bio,' and for picture books that are reissues, only two per page. But the jackets are fully illustrated. Everything is pictured in the catalogue." If publishers didn't do that, Batson adds, the book would never be known by people who don't go to conventions.

Most publishers take books to display at the yearly conventions held for the major book-related organizations: American Library Association (ALA), International Reading Association (IRA), National Council of Teachers of English, (NCTE), the American Booksellers Association (ABA), and the Association of Booksellers for Children (ABC). "If your publisher exhibits at those conventions," explains Mayes, "and you're part of the new list, chances are your book will be displayed in the booth."

Writers can usually count on these standard actions from their publisher. "The publisher has invested a fair amount of money in any book they publish," says Roxburgh. "They're not just going to leave it in the warehouse, so they do these standard, tried and proven useful things that need to be done to promote a book."

Special Promotions

"Beyond that," says Lurie, "it really depends on the book and the list it's on. We may decide that this author is so well spoken and has such a strong vision for this book and is so gregarious that we have to get him or her on the road. We'll actually develop a specific author tour for this one book."

Batson says that Harcourt often takes authors to national and state reading and library conferences. "They get to talk about their book; they get the educators excited, who in turn come back to us to find out how to get the book."

Occasionally publishers produce a postcard mailing for a book on the list. "We do postcards very selectively," says Batson. "They're expensive. If we do a postcard, we send it out to our contacts, whether it be media or publicity people or possible reviewers, or educators, but we don't do postcards for every book. In fact, we're only doing one postcard this fall."

Posters—an enlargement of the book cover to be handed out at conventions and used in displays—are even more expensive. "I happen to think posters are a colossal waste of time," says Roxburgh. "Every once in a while you'll have an image that is so striking that it's an art piece in and of itself. If you're at a convention it might actually draw people into the booth. But half the people don't walk into your booth; they simply take the poster. Most publishers even leave the things rolled up so you don't have to look at it—just grab it and keep going."

"We might decide this book is perfect for a poster or a postcard," explains Lurie, "but we really have to pick our shots because the money is tight and we have lots of books. Not every book's going to get a poster, maybe only one out of the forty that my imprint publishes, and maybe only one postcard will be done."

Brochures and flyers are also expensive for the publisher to produce. "For some of our authors we have author bios," explains Lurie. "Usually when they have three books published by us, we do an author bio, but if this is only their first or second book and they really need a flyer, we'll just do that. The editor puts it together on our computer and prints it up."

But there isn't enough money to do special promotions for all the books on a publisher's list. "We share the author's frustrations that there isn't enough money to make a huge impact, like there is in movie promotion," says Lurie. "Every author should know that we're all struggling with the current market for books, that the channels for distribution are changing all the time and we're trying to change along with them as quickly as possible. Publishers are trying to choose their shots wisely, and some books are going to go out there on their own and have to earn the reviews and awards that are going to help them."

Authors Who Promote

Given this reality, the author must take on some of the responsibility of marketing the book. "I wouldn't say we ever require people to promote their work," Lurie says, "but we encourage them to, especially in this market where it seems like exposure is everything."

"Any time authors want to work, we'll let them do that," Batson says. "I've had writers tell me, 'When I'm done with the book my work isn't done—I need to go out and promote the book.' That's a publisher's dream."

Kurtz recently asked an editor how much time a writer should spend on promotion. "I expected her to say: Do the promotion, but don't let it get in the way of the writing." Instead, the editor suggested that more time be spent on marketing. "I was shocked," Kurtz says. "It was a real wake-up call for me. Your editor may believe in you totally, but your editor is also going to meetings with the rest of the staff and trying to get them excited about your books. If your books aren't selling well, your editor ultimately faces a losing battle in trying to get more books under contract."

Mary Casanova has four books published. Her latest, *Wolf Shadows*, was re-

Hiring a Publicist

Since publishers don't have the time and money to plan an individual marketing strategy for every book they publish, would it make sense for an author to hire a publicist to market the book?

Opinions vary. Author Mary Casanova found that hiring a regional publicist was helpful. "My agent thought it was a brilliant move," Casanova says. "I really don't think *Moose Tracks* would have taken off as quickly. I'm guessing it's into the fifth printing. It has done unbelievably well."

Evelyn Gallardo, an author with a professional background in marketing, doesn't think it's necessary. "Publicists are for people who don't need them," she says. "They're very expensive and there are no guarantees that they will indeed get your name before the media."

Roland Smith's wife is his publicist. "I don't book the visits, I don't talk on the phone to people too much any more—she basically does the whole thing," says the author. I did it myself for a long time but it got to a level where we could afford to hire her. Spouses are probably number two as far as wanting to promote your books. You're number one. If they're good at it and they enjoy doing it, that's certainly something you can take advantage of."

Walter Mayes, who works as a storyteller to publicize Bantam Doubleday Dell, thinks it's a good idea "if you have a clear idea of what you want a publicist to achieve. So often, people hire a publicist and expect them to work miracles. A publicist can only expand on interest that is already potential. They can't create interest out of thin air."

Susan Raab, author of *An Author's Guide to Children's Book Promotion,* and owner of Raab Associates, a publicity agency for children's writers and illustrators, agrees with Mayes. "If someone's a fairly new author, I don't usually recommend that they bolt off and hire a publicist. Frankly, in that stage a publicist is going to have the same problem that you have. The amount of return on the time you're putting in is hard to gauge."

Raab believes that new authors without a proven track record are better off focusing on getting speaking engagements in schools. "You're local, and that's a big deal to them. You can use that. But to go out at that stage and hire a publicist—it may not be the right time. I would wait until they had a book that was particularly newsworthy, or you could talk not only about this book but about their backlist and about reviews they've gotten from different places."

Raab also finds it's more effective to work with people who understand marketing on a firsthand basis. "Then they'll know what they're getting when they pay for someone else to do the work. Many people feel that marketing is not their best

(continued on next page)

Hiring a Publicist *continued*

thing. But I think that to work effectively with someone who's doing your marketing, it's better if you understand what they're trying to do and how hard it is. Is it reasonable to think they'll get you on *The Rosie O'Donnell Show*? Maybe so, and maybe not. It's a long shot for most books. But the less someone understands about marketing, the more unrealistic their expectations are. What they imagine someone can do for them may be very different from what really can be done."

Raab likes to work with authors who understand and participate fully in the marketing. She discusses with the client what Raab Associates will do and in the meantime the author knows about other possible markets and is willing to talk to them. "They may ask who the best person to contact is, or how to approach them. We can have that kind of a dialogue, but they already understand what they're trying to do."

Mayes has some suggestions for authors who are thinking of hiring a publicist. "If you don't know what a publicist does, then you should talk to people who have used publicists before," he says. "Definitely interview the publicist. Find out what other children's authors they've handled and what they have achieved for children's authors."

Since promoting children's books is relatively new, there aren't many publicists who specialize in the field, but Mayes thinks, "It would certainly be worth your time to inquire of a publicist who has had experience promoting products of interest to children, someone in the children's music or children's video business. Ask, 'Is there anything you can do for me? Is this worth pursuing?' But you can't do it on the basis of one book—you need a body of work."

leased in 1997. She knew she wanted to do something to help her book sales when her first book came out. "My primary goal was to be able to keep writing and not have a publisher turn me away because my books hadn't sold enough copies. I felt that if I wanted to continue doing what I loved to do, which is write, I had to be somewhat realistic about the marketplace. I figured that as a first-time novelist, the odds were way against me to begin with. Whatever I did would be helpful. To do nothing would be irresponsible."

Jaguar, the latest work of fiction by accomplished fiction and nonfiction author Roland Smith, is the sequel to his first book, *Thunder Cave*. "What I usually tell people who are uncomfortable promoting their books is that it helps to think of them as their children. If you raise a kid, what will you do for it to get a leg up in life? Most parents would do anything."

"When I was doing it on my own," Smith says, "I would do one thing every day, seven days a week, to promote my books. Sometimes I'd make a phone call to a newspaper. Or I might talk to a reviewer who may not have seen my

What Not to Do in Marketing

Stephanie Owens Lurie, *Vice President, Associate Publisher, and Editorial Director of Simon & Schuster Books for Young Readers, on working with the publisher:* "We don't want to work at odds with the writer on marketing. For example, if a writer sets up a signing and hasn't kept us in the loop, we may not have bound books ready or the book may have just gone back to press for a second printing. We may be running low on copies. Don't go in blind to a bookstore and expect to set something up. Talk to us first and we'll help you. Keep us abreast of what appearances you've set up and what contacts you have."

Stephen Roxburgh, *President and Publisher, Front Street, on signing books:* "Writers should not walk into a bookstore and go over to the shelf, find their book and sign it. Theoretically, a bookseller has the right to return books whenever they want, but they're not supposed to return books that have been signed or altered. The point is, it's not the author's book. If the author wants to walk up to the desk and talk to the manager and say, 'I'm the author of that book. Would you like me to sign some copies for you?' and the manager says yes, then they can do it. Don't be offended if they say no thanks. But in most cases they'll be delighted."

Walter Mayes, *storyteller for Bantam Doubleday Dell, on marketing etiquette and professionalism:* "I watched an author walk up to a bookseller and say, 'Why don't you like my book?' She didn't even introduce herself. She just said, 'I'm so insulted. I went to your store and the staff said you didn't even have the book on

(continued on next page)

book. Or I would call a radio station."

Kurtz takes a somewhat different approach. "I have to tell myself over and over that I don't need to follow up on every good idea I have—it's really easy to make yourself crazy. Some authors just aren't suited to doing this, and everyone has time choices to make."

Casanova has had a similar experience. "You can only pick a few things at a time. I went nuts reading one book on a thousand ways to market your book. I was ready to give up. I just put that aside and thought, 'What can I do?'"

Distinguishing Author and Book

What are the basics for authors com-mitted to promoting their own books? "You do book promotion and you do author promotion," explains Roxburgh. "These are two separate things."

Publishers' efforts usually focus on promotion of the book itself, and there are things authors, too, can do to promote a particular book. "At the very least," Mayes says, "I would have a one-page, photocopied or professionally printed flyer about yourself and your most recent book. It can be nicely done in black-and-white, so we're not talking about spending a ton of money here. The flyer has a photo of the cover, the name of the book, your name, the name of the publisher, and the ISBN

What Not to Do in Marketing *continued*

the shelf.' She was just short of rude. The bookseller said, 'Oh, I'm terribly sorry; I'll check on that.' The author walked away thinking, 'Well, I put that bookseller in her place.' It is never your job to put someone who may carry your book in their store 'in their place.' Not only is that bookseller not going to go back and order the book, she's not going to order any other book by that author ever again. She'll tell the sales rep, and the sales rep will tell the publisher, and that author will begin to get a bad reputation. That's not what you want. When you market your book, you do it with some class and some respect, and you treat people the way you'd want them to treat you."

Coy Batson, *Marketing Director for Harcourt Brace Children's Books, on fees for speaking engagements:* "New writers shouldn't gouge: They won't get any gigs. I don't think anyone expects them to do it for free. But there are a few times I would even encourage them to offer their services for free—to their children's school, for example, and their local library."

Bruce Balan, *author of the Cyber.kdz series and Technology Advisor to the Society of Children's Book Writers and Illustrators, on the Internet:* "The thing about listservs and newsgroups is that you don't want to post blindly. There's a feeling of community on the Internet, so you don't want to just come on, post something, and leave. It's better to be a participant for a while and then say,'Hey, I'd like to tell everybody....' People will respond much more positively."

BUSINESS

number. If there have been any reviews, you can excerpt those for the flyer. One page, two-sided, that tells a little bit about you and your book."

Mayes suggests giving a copy of that flyer to booksellers, librarians, and teachers you meet, and to newspaper and media people in your area, "with a personal note from you saying, 'Hi, I want to introduce myself. This is my book. I'd love you to carry it or support it or use it. I'm available for signings or interviews or whatever and please contact me at this number.'"

Batson agrees. "Promote yourself. If you're willing to do presentations to schools, that information should be on the flyer, with an accurate address. Many times you'll see flyers that say, 'contact me for presentations' and there's no means of contact."

Evelyn Gallardo comes to children's writing from a marketing background. She's the author of *Among the Orangutans,* and her latest book is *How to Promote Your Children's Book: A Survival Guide.* She takes the concept of a flyer a step further. "One of the key sales pieces is a brochure," she says, "a well-written, trifold brochure. With desktop publishing anybody can do it. I run them by the thousands and I leave them everywhere."

Although bookstore signings are

Promoting Books on the Internet

"Promoting your book on the Internet is good for support, not initial promotion," says Bruce Balan, author of the Cyber.kdz series and Technology Advisor to the Society of Children's Book Writers and Illustrators. "If people know about you, they have a place they can go and get more information. You're not necessarily going to attract hundreds of thousands of readers by putting a website up—in fact, I can guarantee you won't."

Because there are millions of websites on the Internet, it's unlikely that people are going to discover your site by 'surfing' randomly on the Web. "People aren't going to come to your page unless it's really something of interest to them or gets publicity in some other way," Balan says.

An author's website, or home page, can be very useful for teachers and librarians. "If a school is looking at two different authors and one has a website so they can download information, maybe they'll go with that author," says Balan, "because they don't have to make a phone call or wait for things in the mail. I think it's a great way of distributing information to people who know about you already."

Before beginning to set up a web page, authors should ask themselves two questions:

Am I interested in creating a web page? "It's a lot of work," Balan says. "Many writers don't like technical things, or they may not have a good sense of layout. You want to have a page that looks good."

How much time and money am I willing to invest? "There are three types of money you'll be investing," Balan says. "You will invest in the creation of the page," which may include tools or paying a graphics artist or even a web design company, and you must invest in "the maintenance of the page, and the ongoing fee for someone to host it. There may not be a fee, but certainly if you want a domain name, you will have one." (The domain name, or address, will include your name: for example, www.janbrett.com). Balan also points out that it's important to keep adding information to your page so people will want to come back again and again.

Authors who hire someone to put the page together still have to develop the content of the page, the third cost. "You need a vision for your page," Balan explains. "Is it to advertise your book? Is it to advertise you? Is it to offer information to teachers, or help get school kids interested? A good starting point is: what is it about you or your book that attracts people? It's nice when a page has a personality."

Balan's home page (http://cyber.kdz.com/balan) was the first one in North America created by a children's author himself rather than a publisher. "I wanted it to be fun—that's why you get all that clickable stuff. But I also wanted to provide a
(continued on next page)

Promoting Books on the Internet *continued*

lot of information." He also has a page that extends his Cyber.kdz series (http://cyber.kdz.com). "It's an extension of the books. It's there to make the kids who are reading the books like them even more."

Once your page is created, the next step is listing it in as many places as possible on the Web. "There's a site called Submit-it.com," Balan says. "It helps you submit your site to a lot of search engines without having to go to all of them. It's very easy." Balan also recommends notifying as many children's sites as you can find, starting with the Children's Literature Web Guide. This site lists children's author's websites as well as links to journals and book reviews, resources for teachers, parents and writers, organizations, and other related sites. From there you can visit each site and list your page.

A website is only one way of using the Internet for promotion. There are other less expensive things an author can do. "E-mail is very valuable," Balan says. "You can put a sig file—short for signature file—at the end of your E-mail messages that advertises your latest book. Then every time you send an E-mail message, the name of your book is going out into the world."

Joining listservs and newsgroups can also lead to promotion. Listservs and newsgroups are like electronic bulletin boards organized around different subjects. Members post messages and everyone on the list can read them. An author whose book is about eclipses might join a newsgroup on science for kids and post something.

Jane Kurtz finds that one problem with these groups is the number of messages they generate. "You have to decide if it's worth it to devote the time. I delete and ignore stuff I'm not interested in. On one listserv I got a lot of messages about using the computer in the classroom and I'd delete those. But then, here are some asking about multicultural books, and I'd join into the discussion."

Even if you don't have a web page, Balan thinks it's worth visiting the many online bookstore sites and letting them know about your book. "There are also sites that do children's book reviews. Let them know about your book, too." Lists of online bookstores can be found by using Yahoo or another search engine.

BUSINESS

Internet Sites of Interest

■ Children's Literature Web Guide
http://www.ucalgary.ca/~dkbrown

■ Submit-it
http://www.submit-it.com

■ The Writer's Net
http://www.writers.net

■ Bruce Balan's Office
http://cyber.kdz.com/balan

■ Mary Casanova
http://www.marycasanova.com

■ Cyber.kdz
http://cyber.kdz.com

■ Jane Kurtz's Web Page
http://www.geocities.com/Athens/5232/

■ Roland Smith's Web Page
http://www.comet.net/writersc/RSMITH/

■ Evelyn Gallardo's Web Page
http://www.evegallardo.com

■ Raab Associates Web Page
http://www.raabassociates.com

to your store, would you be kind enough to host a signing for me?' I can't imagine a bookstore that wouldn't be interested in that. And may I add that I hope in most of these instances you do that with your locally owned independent bookstore? Wherever possible, it is best to support your locally owned businesses because you're a local author and therefore you want that kind of homegrown symbiosis. The chains don't really have any interest in you as a local author."

"A major mistake that many authors make," adds Gallardo, "is that they go through the time and effort to convince a bookseller to hold a signing and then they just show up on the day at the appointed hour. I send mailers to anyone I know in the area and ask them to bring friends and family. I also leave extra flyers announcing my visit at local libraries."

Getting media attention can help sell books. Casanova took advantage of a service offered by Minnesota Press Service. "For $99, they send out 400 press releases to editors of small and large newspapers in Minnesota. So I wrote my own news release and sent a photo. Each state might have something similar. It would be worth looking into."

often unsuccessful for most new writers, Mayes suggests a way of increasing your chances for a successful bookstore signing: "You go into the bookstore and introduce yourself nicely to the owner, manager, or children's buyer. You say, 'Hi, I'm Sally Smith and I live in the neighborhood. If I gave you a list of mailing addresses of fifty friends of mine whom I thought would come

Get Media Attention
Roland Smith builds himself a media packet. "It's a promotional packet that has all sorts of stuff in it—my brochure and my card and any kind of newspaper article that has ever been written about me. If you want to get an article in the newspaper and you have articles that have already appeared, it gives them ideas. 'Hey,' they say, 'we could

do something like that. Other people are interested in this person; therefore we should be interested.'"

"Very often," Gallardo says, "people don't think about children's authors attracting the media, but there's really a formula to get articles written about you." She devoted a chapter of her book on promotion to media attention. "You can get local media and use that to springboard to regional media," she says.

"Your own local paper, even if it's a free throwaway paper, is an opportunity you don't throw away." Her press kit might include a copy of the book and a press release, a bio and a photo. "Your bio isn't like a résumé," Gallardo says. Instead, it should "read like an interesting story." She always suggests authors "get a head shot because the media are more likely to run a story on you if they have a photo to go with it. The whole idea of getting media attention is to make their job as easy on them as possible. Your press materials should introduce you to the media, so they could almost write the story without even talking to you."

Gallardo makes up three lists. "List A is my priority list: These are the people who are most likely to do a story. Have you ever met a reporter at a conference? Does your mother's neighbor write for a newspaper? You check with everybody you know. The B list is nice if you can get them, and the C list is the people you probably won't get in a gazillion years, but try anyway. I send a copy of the book and a press kit."

Hired Help?
In some cases it pays to hire someone to help get media attention. Casanova decided to hire a regional publicist to help publicize her first book. "I am up here on the Minnesota-Canadian border, hours away from any city, and for me to do it all by driving around was impossible. So I hired a publicist, somebody who works only in the region—this wasn't a national publicist. He was already in place and had all the contacts. I thought if I could build regionally first, that would make sense."

The publicist set up radio and TV interviews and book signings. "From his efforts over the last few years I've been on Minnesota Public Radio a couple of times. It goes out to about four states. He put me on Channel 11 twice in the Twin Cities; they're a *Today* show affiliate. The first time, I talked about seasonal children's books. I did a quick promotion of eight or nine other children's books and at the beginning and end of that interview they did a little highlight on my first book, *Moose Tracks*. For the other one, I talked about breaking into print and what people could do to get started."

Casanova has been on *Radio AHHS,* a radio program for kids by kids, three times now, once with each novel. "It's live and nationwide. I didn't realize the impact of it until one of my daughter's friends said he'd heard me on the radio in Arizona."

She admits that doing interviews on television and radio was scary at first. "I was prepared in my answers somewhat. I didn't have anything memorized, but on each book I'll write up 'twenty questions to ask Mary Casanova.' My new book, *Wolf Shadows,* is about wolf issues in Northern

Minnesota, so I came up with twenty questions I thought the media might be interested in asking me. They may not ask any of those questions, but at least I know what I want to talk about."

Her publicist also suggested that no matter what the questions asked, Casanova should have in mind what she wants to say and find a way to say it early in the interview. "So you take charge of the interview in a way, and not get done with a half-hour interview and realize you never got a chance to make your point. I try to tune out all the viewers and listeners out there. I focus on the interviewer and simply talk to them as I would to any other person or friend."

Casanova realizes that hiring a publicist is not something every writer could do. "It probably cost me about $1,500 out of my own pocket, which seemed like a sizable investment. Looking back, however, I'd almost say it would be worth going to the bank and borrowing the money. Ultimately, the book itself has to succeed with readers, but if you never get it to the reader, then it doesn't stand a chance."

Tie It In

In promoting a specific book, it helps to explore niche markets. "An author who has written a book that has some sort of subject area often knows more about specific potential markets than the publisher does," Roxburgh says.

"I think the publisher expects the author to come up with some of those ideas," Casanova points out. She explains that the main character in *Moose Tracks* is home schooled. "I asked, 'Shouldn't this get out to some of those homeschoolers?' And because of my initiating that, it eventually led to an interview on Christian radio—a home school segment that went out nation-wide."

"If you can tie your book into some kind of nonprofit organization," Gallardo says, "they might include your book in their gift catalogue." Gallardo's book is about apes, and she's connected with the International Primate Protection League, the Orangutan Foundation International, and the Great Ape Project. She has spoken and signed books at their conferences, and they carry her book in their catalogue.

Front Street recently published a book told from the point of view of a deaf girl. "The author herself is dealing with deteriorating hearing," Roxburgh explains. "She was able to put us in touch with a whole block of specialized journals. There's one very cool one called *HIP*; it stands for hearing impaired person. So I sent off a copy of the book. They ran a review. I don't know what it sold, but as far as I'm concerned that particular copy was an enormously cheap way to get a book in exactly the right place. Those are the kinds of things the publisher just wouldn't know about."

Gallardo believes any author can find a niche for a book. "If there's not one there you've got to claw one out. That's part of promotion and marketing. You've got to find that little angle. What is it that's different about my book? It often takes showing someone how your book relates to them."

Authors Talk

Another way authors can promote

themselves rather than a specific title is to speak at schools and conferences. "We do a lot of this in children's books," explains Roxburgh, "because children's book publishing is still a backlist publishing exercise. If you can get invited to speak at a school anywhere near you, use any contact you've got. Some schools have no budget and maybe all they're going to offer you is bus fare and a tuna fish sandwich. Do it."

Smith recommends that authors become comfortable speaking in front of groups even before they publish a book. "When I was a biologist, I got sick of being scared to death, so I put out the word that I would talk to any group, anytime, anywhere. I talked at the weirdest places you can imagine. I ate a lot of really bad lunches, got a lot of really poor pens in presentations after the talk. I did it to the point where I got comfortable doing it. The more you do it, the better you get."

Gallardo suggests attending talks by other authors. "Go watch some friends and see what they do. At conferences, use the keen scientific observer's eye when you're watching the speaker. Notice how they move and how they interact with the audience. You can learn from other speakers."

Most publishers have author promotion coordinators, people who set up speaking engagements for their authors.

"We work hard to get our authors into schools where they can talk to kids," says Roxburgh. He explains that schools often call the publishing companies to schedule author events. They're usually looking for well-known authors who command high speaking fees. But the publisher can sometimes schedule an event for an unknown writer. "What we find out after we talk to them for three seconds," says Roxburgh, "is that they really don't need Madeleine L'Engle. They need a warm body to talk to the kids. Often we'll have some new writer who's passionate about her book and will do the job just fine."

But most school and library visits are scheduled by authors themselves. "When I am interviewed by the newspaper," Gallardo explains, "I'll also mention the school visit I did last week. If it's mentioned in the story, then all the educators in the area know I'm available for school visits. When I'm at a bookstore signing books, and people come up with children, I ask them what school they go to and I let the parent know I love to do school visits. I hand them my brochure and tell them to feel free to pass it on to the principal."

Gallardo reminds authors not to limit themselves to literary and education conferences. She speaks at conferences on orangutans and primates. "We're going beyond the obvious of literary conferences and writers conferences and children's conferences and reading council conferences."

"But speaking at librarian groups and reading associations are the best things you can do," says Smith, "because those are the people who decide what books the kids are going to read. You want to introduce yourself to them so they consider your book."

He points out that getting invitations to speak at conferences is a matter of networking. "You find out who's in charge. You send them a packet, and you say I'd really like to speak at this event. Sometimes you fail and sometimes you get an invitation. If you're speaking at one event and somebody sees you who's in charge of another event, they may come up and say, 'We'd really like to have you speak at our event.'"

Maximizing Contacts

Speaking engagements often result from contacts the author has made over the years. "I've been active on e-mail," Kurtz explains. "It's a way to stay connected without leaving the house."

She's an active participant on several Internet listservs related to children's literature. (A 'listserv' is a group of people who don't necessarily know each other but who exchange e-mail about a specific topic.) "When I was at ALA (the American Library Association), as they introduced the members of the Newbery and Caldecott committees, those names were familiar to me. The people who have influence in the library and teacher world hang out on many of these lists. And for me, living in an isolated place, it's enjoyable and it's something I've made a conscious decision to devote some time to."

Kurtz has met people on the listservs who have been helpful in promoting her books. She struck up one conversation with a library aid in California. "I told her I had this idea of putting together a box of things you can touch and feel that are related to Ethiopia, where many of my books are set. She said she'd really like to do that with me. She was my guinea pig: I sent her a box of stuff and she introduced my books to the kids using my materials to help interpret and give more depth to the experience."

Kurtz also attends conventions. "She doesn't just go to a convention," explains Lurie, who's published several of Kurtz's books. "She talks to people. She's not shy about introducing herself and talking about what she does. She is very interested in what other people are doing, too, so she asks questions; she's not self-serving. Then those people refer her to someone else and she follows up. She does this at IRA (the International Reading Association)—a teacher's convention, and ALA—a librarian's convention—and she often pays her own way to go to them, just to walk around and talk to people."

Kurtz considers herself an introverted person, but she likes speaking at schools and conferences. "There's something very protected about getting up in front of a lot of people and giving a talk. I grew up watching my father preach and do a lot of storytelling: It came through to me very naturally how to do that." When she had only one book out, she told the kids how she got the story for the book. "The book came from a real-life incident that happened to one of my kids. There's even some dialogue that's a direct quote from real life. I use it to show kids the difference between fiction and nonfiction. I ask them the difference and they always see it in very clear-cut categories, and I use the book to show them it's not really as clear-cut as all that."

When Kurtz goes into a school, she knows there will be only a few kids with the same kind of passion for writing she has. "For these kids, I can be a role model. But I also recognize I have something to offer all the kids. I can give them a sense of the process of writing and a connection to my books so they can get excited about my books and about reading in general."

Kurtz and Casanova both limit themselves to one out-of-town promotional trip a month, whether it's three days or a full week. "The big word is balance," Casanova says. "Though I love kids and have come to enjoy public speaking, if I go too much into promoting, I get sick of hearing my own voice. The remedy is to go back to my desk and back to the writing."

Smith, on the other hand, is experimenting with adding more school visits to his schedule. In this last year, Smith has done 100 talks. "I don't think I'd be able to keep that pace up, but I just wanted to see what it felt like to do that. I'm not recommending that, but it's a possibility. It depends on you and what you want to do and what your schedule's like."

Book One, Book Two

Despite the extraordinarily expensive and public media campaigns surrounding some famous writers, for most people, promotion is a long, slow process. "The best thing you can do for book one is to have book two," Lurie says. "The really big successes in our industry have kept publishing. They don't overpublish, they don't have two books in the same season from different publishers competing with each other. They try to publish wisely and then follow up with their contacts as much as possible. I think that's how the big guys have become successful: consistent delivery, watch their career, make sure they're not crowding themselves, and try to build their fan base."

"What authors have to understand," says Roxburgh, "is that this is not about immediate gratification. It's really got to do with common sense, economic constraints, and patience. This is how you have to approach it. Unfortunately, people tend to see where lightning strikes, so they think this is what it's all about. No, that's not what it's all about at all, and the people who chase that are endlessly disappointed. It's the people who keep reaching for the stars—and I'm not talking about in their writing, I'm talking about in their expectations—who are constantly disappointed. Especially in the children's book business, it's a long-term commitment. The people who can approach it that way are often pleased; they're pleased by modest achievements that are real and important and in fact, work."

Promotion Bibliography

■ **Bruce Balan**
The Cyber.kdz Series
  In Search of Scum (Avon, 1997)
  A Picture's Worth (Avon, 1997)
  The Great NASA Flu (Avon, 1997)
  Blackout in the Amazon (Avon, 1997)
  In Pursuit of Picasso (Avon, 1998)
  When the Chips Are Down (Avon, 1998)
Buoy—Home at Sea (Bantam, 1998)
The Cherry Migration (Green Tiger, 1988)
Jeremy Quacks (Picture Book Studios, 1989)
The Moose in the Dress (ABC ,1991)
Pie in the Sky (ABC, 1993)
What I Saw At Sea (ABC, 1991)

■ **Mary Casanova**
The Golden Retriever (Crestwood House/Macmillan, 1990)
Moose Tracks (Hyperion, 1995)
One Dog Canoe (DK Ink, 1997)
Riot (Hyperion, 1996)
Stealing Thunder (Hyperion, scheduled for 1999)
Wolf Shadows (Hyperion, 1997)

■ **Evelyn Gallardo**
Among the Orangutans (Chronicle, 1993)
Endangered Wildlife (GINN)
How to Promote Your Children's Book: A Survival Guide (Primate Productions,1997. Order through Gallardo's web page.)

■ **Jane Kurtz**
Fire on the Mountain (Simon & Schuster, 1994)
I'm Calling Molly (out of print)
Miro and the Kingdom of the Sun (Houghton Mifflin, 1996)
Only A Pigeon (Simon & Schuster, 1997)
Pulling the Lion's Tale (Simon & Schuster, 1995)
Trouble (Harcourt Brace, 1997)

■ **Susan Raab**
An Author's Guide to Children's Book Promotion (Raab Associates, 1996. Order through Raab Associates web page.)

■ **Roland Smith**
African Elephants (Lerner, 1995)
Amy's Missing (YS Press, 1996)
Cats In the Zoo (Millbrook, 1994)
Inside the Zoo Nursery (Cobblehill, 1993)
Jaguar (Hyperion, 1997)
Journey of the Red Wolf (Cobblehill, 1996)
Primates in the Zoo (Millbrook, 1992)
Sea Otter Rescue (Cobblehill, 1990)
Snakes in the Zoo (Millbrook, 1992)
Thunder Cave (Hyperion, 1995)
Whales, Dolphins, and Porpoises in the Zoo (Millbrook, 1994)

Books

Show Writers the Money

By Dorothy K. Mock

BUSINESS

"*If anything is certain, it's change.*" While that aphorism applies as much to publishing as to any field, one aspect of the business remains constant: Writing for a living is not, and never has been, easy.

At the same time, most writers write because they are almost inextricably drawn to it. That may even be more true for many committed to writing for children. Yet children's writers need to balance their aesthetic and even emotional compulsions with the practicalities of earning a living.

The last nationwide "census reflects a noticeable difference between the incomes of men and women" who write, says Kirby G. Posey, Statistician at the Income Statistics Branch of the Housing Household Economics Statistics Division of the U.S. Census Bureau. "28,482 full-time, year-round male au-

thors made average earnings of $44,558, and 20,351 full-time, year-round female authors pulled in average earnings of $32,751, while 21,497 part-time male authors made average earnings of $29,928 and 28,536 part-time female authors made average earnings of $14,378."

Payment problems in the publishing industry are as old as the industry itself. Authors, male and female, have often published for little or no pay at some point in their careers. Flat-fee sales and profit sharing were common in the nineteenth century, until some writers developed business savvy. Ralph Waldo Emerson paid for the manufacturing of his books and gave his publisher a commission on their sales. Henry Wadsworth Longfellow bought the printer's plates to eight of his books and sold printing rights to

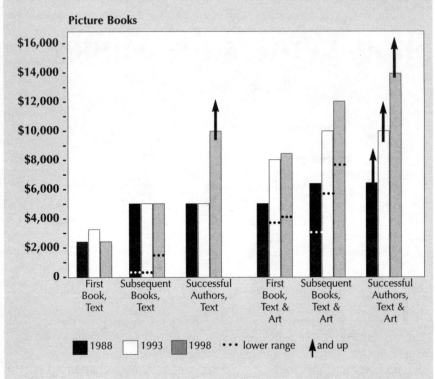

Representative Trade Publisher Advances

Picture Books

Legend: ■ 1988　□ 1993　▨ 1998　••• lower range　↑ and up

Categories: First Book, Text; Subsequent Books, Text; Successful Authors, Text; First Book, Text & Art; Subsequent Books, Text & Art; Successful Authors, Text & Art

Source: Graph based on information provided by publishers and Mary Flower.

the publishers. As the number of successful writers rejecting flat-fee and profit-sharing agreements grew, publishers desperate to sign big names developed the royalty system, by which 10 to 20 percent of the retail selling price of marketed copies goes to the author.

At the turn of the century, however, beginning writers were still at the mercy of publishers. In 1896, the Reverend Charles Monroe Sheldon wrote and sold America's first nonfiction bestseller, *In His Steps, or What Would Jesus Do?*, to the Chicago Advance for $75. In 1903, Jack London sold *The Call of the Wild* to a New York publisher for a flat fee of $2,000. Many authors needed someone who could negotiate better financial terms. That's when agents and advances entered the scene.

The Beginning Advance

As a rule, children's books have not been a priority for publishers. Well into the twentieth century, children's book

Representative Trade Publisher Advances

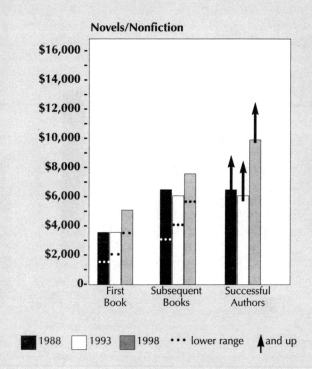

Novels/Nonfiction

Legend: ■ 1988 □ 1993 ■ 1998 ••• lower range ▲ and up

Source: Graph based on information provided by publishers and Mary Flower.

budgets were small and advances and royalties, when paid at all, were too slight to attract an agent's interest.

"In 1962, I was a children's book editor for Lothrop, Lee & Shepard," says long-time children's book editor and author James Cross Giblin. "Our advances started at $500 for a picture book text and $1,000 for a novel. Few literary agents had ventured into the children's book field."

Eleven years later, author Pat Windsor wasn't thinking about advances when she landed an unagented contract with Harper & Row for her first book. "At that time, an advance was not as important as getting published," she says about the $1,500 advance and 10 percent royalty for *A Summer Before.* "But Harper & Row continued with their low advances, even after I got an agent," says Windsor, who received identical terms for her second book, *Something's Waiting for You, Baker, D.* When Windsor's agent "finally managed to get $2,000 or so, she made it sound as if she'd done me a favor. I eventually fired her, and my new

Representative Trade Publisher Royalties

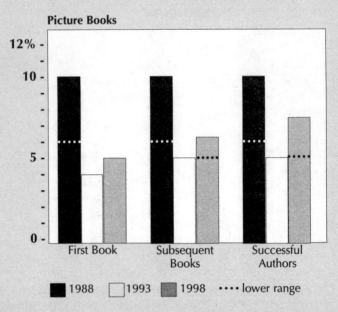

Picture Books

Source: Graph based on information provided by publishers and Mary Flower.

agent—to whom I sent *The Sandman's Eyes*—really catapulted me onto a new financial plateau. She sent the manuscript to George Nicholson at Delacorte Press and he offered $15,000. Suddenly, I was an author who could possibly make a living from writing. That's what a good agent can do."

Sandy Asher's first young adult novel, *Summer Begins,* was published in hardcover in 1980 by Elsevier/Nelson, which is now Dutton, and as a Bantam paperback in 1982. A second Bantam edition of that book, *Summer Smith Begins,* was released in 1986. "My original advance was $1,500," says Asher, "but the paperback rights sold for

$23,000," split with Elsevier/Nelson. "It was an agented sale, advance/royalty, and as a first novel, was reviewed everywhere imaginable."

Daughters of the Law, Asher's second book, was also an agented YA novel, but it was actually her first attempt at a novel. In the ten years of rewriting and gathering seventeen rejections for *Daughters of the Law,* Asher says, *Summer Begins* sort of wrote and sold itself. "When *Daughters of the Law* finally sold, my editor at Elsevier/Nelson went off to start a new company, Beaufort Books, and took me with her," says Asher. "Then she was 'let go.' So *Daughters of the Law* was back to about a

Representative Trade Publisher Royalties

Novels/Nonfiction Books

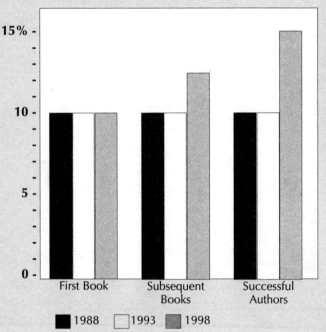

Source: Graph based on information provided by publishers and Mary Flower.

BUSINESS

$2,000 advance, and eventually sold to Dell in paperback for maybe $5,000 or $6,000."

Then there was the incredible roller coaster ride between Asher's second and last books. "After that editor left Beaufort, there was an auction for my third book, *Just Like Jenny,* and I accepted a two-book, hardcover and paperback contract from Delacorte/Dell for $45,000. My run with Delacorte/Dell generally brought $15,000 single-book advances for hard and soft rights,

and a run of YA titles that were Junior Library Guild selections, state award nominees, overseas reprints, etc. Then Delacorte/Dell was bought up by Bantam, my books went out of print one after another, and every editor I'd known at Dell disappeared! Now I have one book at Dutton, two at Walker, and one at Harcourt Brace."

Current Numbers

According to the findings of Mary Flower, lawyer, contract consultant,

Representative Religious Publisher Advances

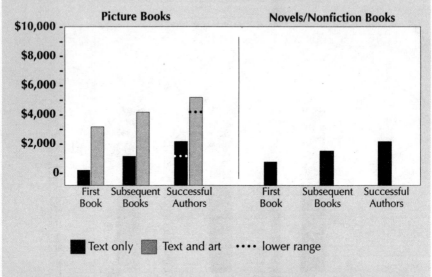

Picture Books   **Novels/Nonfiction Books**

$10,000 –
$8,000 –
$6,000 –
$4,000 –
$2,000 –
0–

First Book | Subsequent Books | Successful Authors | First Book | Subsequent Books | Successful Authors

■ Text only   ■ Text and art   •••• lower range

Source: Graph based on information provided by publishers and Mary Flower.

and author of *A Writer's Guide to a Children's Book Contract* (See more on contracts, and Flower's perspectives, in "Contracts, When Words Mean Business," pages 105), high figures were exceptions to the rule when Windsor and Asher began their writing careers.

"Typical hardcover advances on a first novel at that time ranged from $2,000 to $3,500 or $2,000 to $3,000 for paperbacks," says Flower, "while authors with stature were commanding $6,500 and up for hardcover and $5,000 and up for paperback." The advance on a first picture book, for text only, ranged from $2,000 to $2,500. The advance was $5,000 and up for

well-established authors."Educational and religious houses gave very small advances or often no advance on first books, and for subsequent books advances also remained well below the norm."

The numbers haven't changed all that much. Today, some educational houses are giving $1,000 to $2,000 advances, and with or without an agent, most trade book publishers and religious houses publishing more than fifty books a year offer authors an advance payment against a royalty on sales of the book. According to Giblin, "In recent years, the typical hardcover advance on a picture book text by a

Representative Religious Publisher Royalties

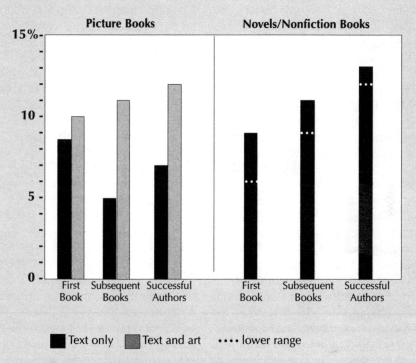

Picture Books — Novels/Nonfiction Books

Categories: First Book, Subsequent Books, Successful Authors

Legend: ■ Text only ■ Text and art •••• lower range

Source: Graph based on information provided by publishers and Mary Flower.

new author ranged from $2,000 to $3,000, while the typical hardcover advance on a first novel or nonfiction project ranged from $3,000 to $5,000, depending on the publisher's estimated rate of sales for the project."

Other sources list a typical picture book advance at about $2,000 for a new author and $5,000 for an experienced writer. The advance on a first novel or nonfiction book ranges from $4,000 to $5,000 for hardcover or $2,000 to $3,500 for an original paperback. The advance on a novel or nonfiction hardcover for experienced writers is $8,500 to $10,000, and sometimes higher, and $4,000 for original paperbacks.

Flower says that her "prosperous" picture book authors or illustrators receive "about $25,000 for writing and illustrating, about $20,000 for just illustrating, and about $10,000 for just writing. Paperback royalties have generally fallen from 8 percent to 6 percent at most houses, and escalators are almost impossible to get unless you've become successful." Escalators, or a sliding scale, are royalty clauses that agree to increase the royalty percentage once a certain number of books—10,000, say, then 15,000—have sold.

Taking an Interest

"Most publishers compute and pay royalties twice a year on sales in the preceding six months, which is why I often say to authors that books are like bonds, and royalty checks like interest payments," says Giblin.

According to data collected from publishers in a survey for this article, interest rates look good. Ten percent remains the typical royalty rate for a first-time novel or nonfiction book, while 6 percent is the going rate for first-time, original paperbacks, unless the book contains pictures. In that case, the artist or photographer might receive 2 or 3 percent of that royalty. Established authors typically receive a sliding scale for hardcovers of 10 to 12 ½ percent and apparently sometimes 15 percent (Flower says she has never seen an escalation to 15 percent, however), and 6-8-10 percent for original paperbacks. Religious publishers' royalties on first paperback novels or nonfiction projects range from 7 to 9 percent for first-time authors, and 12 to 13 percent for experienced writers.

For mainstream and religious publishers, the royalty on a picture book text by a new author is 5 percent, split with the artist or photographer. Expe-rienced picture book authors get 7 percent from religious publishers and a sliding scale in the range of 5–6¼–7½ percent from secular publishers.

Nonetheless, there are still some publishers paying in the range of 3 to 5 percent. In these instances, as volume levels of sales are reached, royalty percentages become retroactive. For instance, an author may receive 3 percent for sales to 9,999 books, 4 percent for 10,000 to 49,999, and 5 percent for sales over 50,000 copies. When the book sells copy 10,000, the royalty increases to 4 percent and payment for retroactive royalties on the first 9,999 copies is made with the next royalty statement. An increase occurs again when the 50,000 mark is reached.

Small or no advances and low royalty rates almost always mean small printruns—copies of a title the publisher prints at one time. Printrun numbers are often hard to pin down, but currently the average printrun on a picture book by a new author is 8,500 to 10,000 copies, and by an established author, 15,000 to 20,000 copies. Printruns on first hardcovers are 6,500 to 7,500, and for more published authors, 10,000 to 15,000. Religious publishers' printruns of picture books by new authors are about 12,000 copies, and 15,000 to 20,000 copies for published authors; on first hardcovers, the numbers are 7,500 and 12,000.

Good News

While of course the financial figures for first authors are consistently lower than those for established authors, Asher says, "The good news is that first-time authors will always be courted.

The bad news is that corporate takeovers of publishing houses and bookstores will continue to limit the publishing of midlist books and send books out of print with increasing speed."

Windsor sees hope for writers in the current trend toward *merchandising*—selling books with themes, trendy packaging, and related gimmicks. "Publishers also seem interested more in series possibilities, for all books," says Windsor. "And some publishers, like Stephen Roxburgh, formerly of Farrar, Straus, & Giroux, have started their own small companies," like Front Street.

Although most writers agree the growth of the small publishing industry holds promise, nothing in the writing and publishing business is guaranteed. "Everything changes: No one can really predict the future," says Asher. "So write because you love it, write because you can't not write, but keep in mind that only 5 percent of published freelance authors in the United States actually support themselves on a regular basis by writing alone."

Magazines

The Profit in Market Research

By Elaine Marie Alphin

Writers invest in submitting manuscripts: the cost of supplies, the cost of postage, the value of their writing time, and the emotional investment of hoping that this one will be a sale. Yet editors constantly complain how many writers, new and published, apparently do not commit to up-front research to ensure that the manuscript matches the targeted magazine.

It's such familiar editorial advice: "Study guidelines," says Christine Walske, former Editor with the Cricket Group. "And read the magazines. Read back issues, and get a feel for the tone, the philosophy, and the topics. The editor can tell if you're not familiar with the magazine." They really can, and the more expertise you develop in researching markets compatible with your writing interests, style, and career needs, the more that professionalism will pay back.

Initial Approach

Writers should think about market research the moment an idea strikes, before actually writing the manuscript, and they must move beyond the obvious choices in markets, beyond superficial judgments about what the editors want. Knowing your target markets well enables you to write the piece to suit a particular editor's needs. Start with easy matches, perhaps, but look more deeply into their current requirements. If you haven't sent for sample copies or editorial guidelines recently, do it again. Read several copies of the magazine, if possible, either at the library or, if you can afford it, off the newsstand. Look also at alternative possibilities. The Children's Better

Focus Your Idea: Fiction

■ What's your theme?

■ What's the subject?

■ What's the conflict?

■ Who is your protagonist? Age, gender, personality traits?

■ Who are your important secondary characters?

■ What's the setting?

■ Are you aiming for boys or girls or both?

■ Are you planning a secular approach or a religious approach? Would you be comfortable writing the article either way, based on the market needs?

■ What age is your target readership?

■ List five possible magazines that match your subject and readership. Indicate why they might be interested in your theme or slant:

1.

2.

3.

4.

5.

Focus Your Idea: Nonfiction

■ What's your topic?

■ What's your slant?

■ How much research is needed? What are your sources?

■ What experts will you interview, or what is your expertise?

■ Can you provide photos? What are the subjects and sources of the photos?

■ Are you aiming for boys or girls or both?

■ Are you planning a secular approach or a religious approach? Would you be comfortable writing the article either way, based on the market needs?

■ What age is your target readership?

■ List five possible magazines that match your subject and readership. Indicate why they might be interested in your theme or slant:
   1.

   2.

   3.

   4.

   5.

BUSINESS

What the Editor Wants

What the Editor Wants

- Magazine Mission:
- Readership:
- Special Considerations of Readership:
- Fiction:
    - Genres:
    - Length:
    - Original or reprints?
    - Query first or complete manuscript?
- Articles:
    - Categories/Subjects:
    - Length:
    - Query first or complete manuscript?
- Columns, Departments, Puzzles, Filler:
    - Categories/Subjects:
    - Length:
    - Query first or complete manuscript?
- Special Needs:
- Themes (by issue, along with deadline):
- Seasonal Material Advance Time:
- Hard Copy Format:
- Computer Disk Format:

What the Editor Offers

- Response Time:
- Willing to consider simultaneous submissions?
- Rights Purchased:
- Payment:
- Payment on acceptance or on publication?
- Provides contributor copies and/or tear sheets?

Health Institute publications, for instance, might seem the perfect choice for that wrestling story, but they may have run something similar recently. Look for other general interest or niche magazines whose editors are interested in sports stories, but may receive fewer.

This process is arguably even more necessary for nonfiction than fiction. Your idea about handbell choirs may seem a natural for *Young Musicians,* but they've probably already thought of it. Include them on your list of possible markets, of course, but don't pin all your hopes on them. Consider your idea more closely: What is it about handbell choirs that really fascinates you? If it's their history, general interest magazines may be curious, and may not have seen anything on the topic. If you want to profile a real child in a handbell choir, look for magazines who request profiles. With nonfiction, your slant on the topic makes all the difference. (See the Focus Your Idea forms, pages 146-147.)

Close Analysis

Another step in improving the return on your market research investment is to really "work" the guidelines. Editors do their best to tell writers what they want in their guidelines. Analyze them, paying particular attention to the editor's explanation of specifications like word count. For example, if overall length ranges from 300 to 900 words and the magazine is marketed to readers from six to twelve, the editor may specify 300 to 500 words for primary graders, and 500 to 900 words for middle graders. If your primary grade article runs 750 words, you'd have to cut it

---

Sample Copy Requests

Regularly send away for sample copies and editorial guidelines. The request should consist of a brief note—three sentences should cover everything:

Please send me your guidelines and a recent sample copy of your magazine. I enclose an SASE and payment [if required]. Thank you.

Market directory listings will tell you whether to enclose payment and how much, and also what size SASE to enclose. These sample copies and guidelines are a small investment up front. They cost less than postage and paper to send your manuscript to half a dozen markets where it doesn't stand a chance.

---

for this magazine. (See What the Editor Wants, page 148.)

Editorial guidelines may include theme lists. These range from specific themes for upcoming issues, along with deadlines for each issue, to a more general mission statement, and comments on the sorts of themes they're always looking for but don't see often enough, or fundamental themes that are basic to every manuscript they purchase. Not every story in *Turtle* has to be solely about health or fitness, for instance, but a kid shouldn't act in unhealthy ways unless it's a character flaw that will cost him in the end.

Also look at the less quantifiable information the editor gives you about special requirements of a magazine's readership. Certain religious magazines won't accept manuscripts that show characters dancing or going to the movies, for instance. In some, girls can't wear jeans, or characters shouldn't eat meat. Writers often include casual descriptive details that would make their manuscript inappropriate for these magazines. If you know the editorial restrictions before you write the story, however, you may be comfortable using details that fit such requirements. If not, save your postage in submitting to that magazine, and find other markets.

In addition to explaining what goes inside your manuscript, guidelines also cover the submission format the editor prefers. All editors expect to see a typed, double-spaced manuscript in black ink on white paper with ragged right margins, but some editors have more specific requirements that make scanning (computerized input system) or typesetting (manual input system) easier. Some require sixty characters per line, while others merely want wide margins. Some ask for an exact word count, while others find the nearest twenty-five or fifty words sufficient. Some editors prefer a computer disk submission in a certain word processing format, others prefer hard copy, and some request both a disk and a printout. Certainly any submissions editor will read a neatly typed manuscript, but you can increase your chances for acceptance by giving the editor the material asked for in the format that's easiest to use.

Business Sense

Guidelines aren't only about what an editor wants from you. They also tell you what the editor offers in return. Your goal is to succeed at the business of being a writer by selling your material—realistically, you want to sell it quickly for the best possible price. So note the response time and the payment terms the editor offers. While it's desirable to sell one-time rights for top dollar, magazines that pay top dollar are usually difficult for freelancers to

Match the Masthead to the Contents

■ Do editors' names appear as bylines for regular features, departments, or columns? Or do activities, puzzles, or features appear without bylines? If so, these are probably staff-written and not open to freelancers.

■ What is the ratio of fiction to nonfiction? Is nonfiction written by staff members or freelanced? Based on the ratio and the freelance opportunity, does fiction or nonfiction offer the best chance of breaking in?

■ Are the photo credits institutions or individuals? If they are individuals, do the names match the writers' names? If so, submissions may stand a better chance of acceptance if the writer can provide photos.

■ Does the Editor-in-Chief publish an editorial or mission statement on the masthead? Can you see how this is expressed in the published contents? Use this to get a feel for the publisher's intended purpose.

Match the Guidelines to the Magazine

■ Do the lengths of the articles and stories match the length specified in the guidelines? Are actual sales shorter or longer?

■ Are the themes the editor particularly requested in the guidelines among the themes in the stories? If not, are any of them themes you could write about?

■ Does the magazine feature timely, news-like articles and features? Check the guidelines for a fax number or e-mail address—the editor may be willing to consider speedy electronic queries to stay on top of breaking ideas.

■ Do charts, sidebars, graphs, or maps accompany articles? Whether or not the guidelines specifically request these extras, include them to show your familiarity with the publication's needs.

■ What is the target readership shown in the guidelines? Reading the stories and articles, do you find that most of them fit your expectations for the reading ability of that age group, or is the reading level higher or lower? Be sure to match the reading level of the actual contents in your own manuscript.

break into until they have a substantial list of credits. They also tend to buy more on assignment and less on speculation, and to want first or all rights.

Look for markets that are best suited to your idea, even if they pay less and buy different rights than you'd considered selling. (See the sidebar, Which Rights Are Which, page 117.) Selling rights is a trade-off. Many writers are so concerned about keeping future rights that they refuse to consider a market that's perfectly suited to their manuscript but buys all rights. You have to ask: Is the possibility of future reprint sales great enough that it outweighs the payment a more prestigious magazine is willing to offer now to purchase all rights? Will that single credit actually mean more on your résumé than multiple credits with smaller magazines, spread out over several years?

Or is this a timely piece that will see print once? If so, sell it where you can get the largest payment, regardless of the rights. Particularly if a piece is timely, note whether or not the editor will consider simultaneous submissions, and get the manuscript to as many potential markets as possible. See also if an editor welcomes fax or e-mail queries on a time-sensitive subject.

Finally, pay attention to whether a magazine pays on acceptance or on publication. If the magazine pays on publication, note whether or not they will sign a contract for the work. Otherwise, you may find your manuscript sitting in publishing limbo—you don't want to sell it elsewhere on the chance the editor will, indeed, print it, but years may pass without your words seeing print and your having tear sheets (the pages that contain your published story or article). Because other editors may request clips of your published work to help them evaluate future proposals, it's important to be sure that the magazine sends contributor copies (the complete issue in which your work appears) or at least tear sheets. If they don't offer to send them, be sure to ask. If you have to pay for copies that contain your work, you may realize less of a profit on the sale than you anticipated.

Evaluate Everything

"Caution: Reading our editorial guidelines is not enough! Careful study of current issues will acquaint writers with each title's 'personality,' various departments, and regular features, nearly all of which are open to freelancers."

This caveat appears in the Children's Better Health Institute guidelines and is a fair warning. Guidelines are a skeletal introduction to the magazine. They give you the bare bones of what an editor is looking for. Reading a sample copy will let you know whether this is a magazine you'd like to write for or not. If you don't like what you read, or can't imagine your manuscript in that magazine, then set the copy and guidelines aside to share with other writers who might be more interested. But if you like the magazine, don't settle for one issue. Go to the library, and see if you can read back issues. Consider subscribing to magazines you see yourself submitting to often. Read the magazine for pleasure, but also read it professionally. Start with the masthead.

The masthead gives you the latest information on the address of editorial offices and the names of specific editors to contact. Because magazines relocate and editors move from publisher to publisher, you must stay up-to-date. A manuscript sent to an old address could take weeks to be forwarded, and a new editor may feel insulted to see a former editor's name on a cover letter—at the very least, she'll know the writer hasn't a clue what's happening at the magazine. Make a good impression by being on top of changes.

Some magazines have a table of contents, either on the same page as the masthead or on an adjacent page. If the publication is only four or eight pages long and doesn't include a contents page, make your own. Use the What the Editor Wants form on page 148 to list the stories, articles, departments, features, columns, poems, and other activities or fillers you see in the magazine. Analyze each for length, purpose, development, and readership. Now dig deeper—compare masthead and contents. Use the Match the Masthead to the Contents sidebar, page 150, to see where the greatest freelance potential lies for this magazine, and how to make your manuscript stand out by embodying the editor's mission.

Now go back to the guidelines, and evaluate the contents in light of what the editor specified. What an editor publishes, in contrast to what she requests, can help you polish your own manuscript. If the guidelines allow manuscripts up to 1,000 words but the maximum length of a published piece is 800 words, you can expect that shorter pieces stand a better chance of acceptance. On the other hand, if an editor wistfully requests certain themes or stories aimed at girls in the guidelines and you can't find anything like that in the magazine, you might make a sale by granting the editor's wish. Use the Match the Guidelines to the Magazine sidebar, page 151, to help you compare and contrast the published product with the bare bones introduction.

Analysis Pays Off

Denise Jordan, a writer from Indiana, listened to Christine Walske's advice to writers that began this article. She set a goal to sell something to *Spider*, and noted that they were specifically looking for Kwanza stories. "I went to the library," she explains, "and checked out six to ten issues and read all the fiction in each issue. I analyzed each story to see exactly what happened in it." Even though every story was different, she found they had certain things in common in terms of plot structure and tone. "I also looked at my own writing to see what kind of story I liked to write, and then at the stories in *Spider* to decide which ones of those I could see myself writing."

Her analysis paid off—Walske accepted "Sugar's Kwanza Surprise" for *Spider*. "A writer needs to get a feel for a magazine," says Jordan. "The only way to get that feel is to immerse yourself in a magazine's stories and analyze them before you start writing." Based on her successful analysis, Jordan has sold a second story to *Spider*. Let these forms lead you to the same publishing success.

Children's Book Agents

BUSINESS

Alp Arts Co.
221 Fox Rd., Suite 7
Golden, CO 80403
Established: 1994
Contact: Sandy Ferguson Fuller, Agent.
Current Clients: Robert Baldwin, Holly Huth, and Bo Flood.
Submissions: Queries for middle-grade and YA fiction and nonfiction; manuscripts for easy-to-read and picture books. Accepts simultaneous and multiple submissions.
Client Requirements: Published and unpublished.
Fees: Reading fee, $60 for easy-to-read and picture books; $80 for middle-grade and YA fiction and nonfiction.
Services: Editorial services for clients and nonclients included in reading fee.
Contract: Commission, 15%, published authors; 10%, nonpublished.
Categories: Fiction and nonfiction: concept, toddler books, and early picture books (0-4 years); easy-to-read (4-7); story picture books (4-10); chapter books (5-10); middle-grade (8-12); YA (12-18); bilingual; hi-lo; novelty; series. Nonfiction only: how-to, general interest, photoessays.
1998 Needs: Any children's genre through YA, including multimedia projects and licensed characters. Not interested in teachers' resource materials.
Comments: The current market is an incredibly creative outlet for authors and offers exciting opportunities. Research competition; be different!

Joseph Anthony Agency
15 Locust Court, R.D. 20
Mays Landing, NJ 08330
Established: 1964
Contact: Joseph Anthony, President.
Submissions: Complete manuscripts

with SASE. Accepts simultaneous submissions.

Client Requirements: Published and unpublished.

Fees: Reading Fee, $85.

Contract: One-year term. 15% domestic; 20% foreign.

Categories: Fiction: toddler books, early picture books (0-4 years); easy-to-read (4-7); story picture books (4-10); chapter books (5-10); middle-grade (8-12); YA (12-18); adult.

1998 Needs: All genres—the children's market is open to any type of book.

Comments: Remember that all manuscripts must be in the standard format: double-spaced, grammatically correct, and neatly typed.

Authentic Creations Literary Agency

875 Lawrenceville-Suwanee Rd.
Suite 310-306
Lawrenceville, GA 30043
Established: 1995
Contact: Mary Lee Laitsch, Agent.
Current Clients: *The Royal Bee, My Freedom Trip,* Frances and Ginger Park.
Submissions: Queries with SASE; complete manuscripts with SASE. Accepts simultaneous and multiple submissions.
Client Requirements: Published and unpublished.
Fees: None.
Services: Some editorial services at the client's request; fee based on project. No manuscript critique for nonclients.
Contract: One-year contract for each title; 15% commission.
Categories: Fiction and nonfiction: concept, toddler books, and early picture books (0-4 years); easy-to-read (4-7); story picture books (4-10); chapter

books (5-10); middle-grade (8-12); YA (12-18); adult; activity books; bilingual; novelty; series. Nonfiction only: educational, how-to, general interest, photoessays, reference.

1998 Needs: We believe the children's market is open to any well-crafted book, regardless of the genre.

Comments: Those authors who rely on innovative ways to tell their story, even if the theme is basically traditional, are much more likely to be offered a publishing contract.

Author Author Literary Agency Ltd.

P. O. Box 34051, 1200-37 St. SW
Calgary, Alberta T3C 3W2 Canada
Established: 1991
Contact: Joan Rickard, President.
Submissions: Queries with sample chapters for novels, nonfiction. Complete manuscripts for picture and chapter books. Accepts simultaneous and multiple submissions. Please enclose adequate postage.
Client Requirements: Published and unpublished.
Fees: None.
Services: Clients receive some editorial services within moderation, no fee. No manuscript critiques for nonclients.
Contract: Usually a two- to three- year contract; 15% domestic (Canadian), 20% foreign (non-Canadian).
Categories: Fiction and nonfiction: early picture books (0-4 years); easy-to-read (4-7); story picture books (4-10); chapter books (5-10); middle-grade (8-12); YA (12-18); adult; hi-lo; novelty; series. Nonfiction only: how-to and general interest.
1998 Needs: Our agency is open to writers of all genres.

Comments: Due to a tight economy, high printing costs, and the number of established authors, the children's market is a very difficult one for new writers to crack, with or without an agent. But don't give up—persevere!

Curtis Brown, Ltd.
10 Astor Place
New York, NY 10003
Established: 1914
Contact: Ginger Knowlton, Agent.
Submissions: Queries with SASE and first chapter for novels, nonfiction; complete manuscripts with SASE for picture books. No simultaneous or multiple submissions.
Client Requirements: Published and unpublished.
Fees: None.
Contract: Commission, 15% domestic.
Categories: Fiction and nonfiction: concept, toddler books, and early picture books (0-4 years); easy-to-read (4-7); story picture books (4-10); chapter books (5-10); middle-grade (8-12); YA (12-18); adult; series.

Pema Browne Ltd.
Pine Rd., HCR Box 104B
Neversink, NY 12765
Established: 1966
Contact: Pema Browne, President.
Current Clients: The Kwanzaa Contest, Miriam Moore and Penny Taylor; School Spirit, Linda Cargill.
Submissions: Queries with bio and SASE. Accepts multiple submissions. Does not review manuscripts that have been sent to publishers.
Client Requirements: Published and unpublished.
Fees: None.

Contract: Commission on advance and royalties even after agent and author have terminated. 30-60 days written termination. 15% domestic; 20% foreign.
Categories: Fiction and nonfiction: concept, toddler books, and early picture books (0-4 years); easy-to-read (4-7); story picture books (4-10); chapter books (5-10); middle-grade (8-12); YA (12-18); adult; activity books; novelty; series. Nonfiction only: how-to, general interest, reference.
1998 Needs: We are interested in seeing manuscripts in every category, especially novelty and picture books. We're looking for strong writing and new approaches in the YA market.
Comments: There's still a demand for children's books all the way through middle-grade. Horror and YA romances are still soft.

Cambridge Literary Agency
150 Merrimack St., Suite 301
Newburyport, MA 01950
Established: 1990
Contact: Michael Valentino, President.
Submissions: Complete manuscripts with SASE. Accepts multiple submissions.
Client Requirements: Published and unpublished.
Fees: None.
Services: Some editorial services for clients as needed, no fee; no manuscript critiques for nonclients.
Contract: 15% domestic; 20% foreign.
Categories: Fiction and nonfiction: toddler books (0-4 years); easy-to-read (4-7); story picture books (4-10); chapter books (5-10); middle-grade (8-12); YA (12-18); series. Nonfiction only: concept books (0-4 years); educational.

Fiction only: adult, series.

1998 Needs: We're looking primarily for YA fiction and nonfiction.

Comments: We don't mind seeing books with talking animals. But authors should remember our motto: Make every word count!

Ciske & Dietz Literary Agency

P.O. Box 163
Greenleaf, WI 54126
Established: 1981
Contact: Patricia Dietz, Partner.
Submissions: Queries with synopsis and sample chapters for novels; formal proposal for nonfiction. Accepts simultaneous queries and partial manuscripts but complete manuscript is always on exclusive.
Client Requirements: Published and unpublished.
Fees: None.
Services: Manuscript critique for clients and nonclients, $35 for first 50 pages.
Contract: Non-binding, per project agreement. Commission, 15% domestic; 20% foreign.
Categories: Nonfiction only: easy-to-read (4-7); story picture books (4-10); chapter books (5-10); educational; how-to; general interest; photoessays; reference. Fiction and nonfiction: middle-grade (8-12); YA (12-18); adult; activity books; bilingual; hi-lo; novelty; series.
1998 Needs: Strong, unique characters for middle-grade and YA fiction. Not interested in the occult or New Age material.
Comments: There's a lot of interest in female athlete books that avoid the "jock" image. Fiction featuring teens with future career goals is always in demand. Visit our home page: http://members.aol.com/evrgren39/index/html/ or e-mail us with questions at evrgren39@aol.com. Please, no e-mail queries.

SJ Clark Literary Agency

56 Glenwood
Hercules, CA 94547
Established: 1982
Contact: Sue Clark.
Current Clients: Tatiana Strelkoff, D. B. Borton.
Submissions: Queries with SASE or complete manuscripts with bio. Accepts simultaneous and multiple submissions.
Client Requirements: Unpublished.
Fees: Reading and critique fee, $50 for clients and nonclients.
Services: Fees vary for other editorial services.
Contract: We specialize in working with unpublished writers so our commission is 20%. Fee often reduced to 15% once client is published.
Categories: Fiction: story picture books (4-10); chapter books (5-10); middle-grade (8-12); YA (12-18); adult; series. Nonfiction: how-to.
1998 Needs: Picture books, mysteries, and animal stories.

Hy Cohen Literary Agency Ltd.

P.O. Box 43770
Upper Montclair, NJ 07043
Established: 1975
Contact: Hy Cohen, President.
Current Clients: Daniel Hayes, Dean Gabbert.
Submissions: Send complete manuscripts with SASE. Accepts simultane-

ous and multiple submissions.

Client Requirements: Published and unpublished.

Fees: None.

Contract: 10% commission.

Categories: Fiction and nonfiction: easy-to-read (4-7); story picture books (4-10); chapter books (5-10); middle-grade (8-12); YA (12-18); adult. Nonfiction only: educational, how-to, general interest, photoessays, reference.

1998 Needs: Looking for good, thoughtful, well-written, and imaginative work in all categories.

Ruth Cohen, Inc.

P.O. Box 7626

Menlo Park, CA 94025

Established: 1982

Contact: Ruth Cohen, President.

Submissions: Queries with first 10 pages and SASE. No simultaneous or multiple submissions.

Client Requirements: Published and unpublished.

Contract: 15% commission. Contract for each individual project; 30-day cancellation notice.

Categories: Fiction and nonfiction: easy-to-read (4-7); story picture books (4-10); chapter books (5-10); middle-grade (8-12); YA (12-18).

1998 Needs: We're in the market for carefully-characterized books that change the way young children perceive themselves and the world around them. No poetry or film scripts.

Comments: It's a tough market out there, so we want to see quality writing.

Dwyer & O'Grady, Inc.

P.O. Box 239

East Lempster, NH 03605

Established: 1990

Contact: Elizabeth O'Grady, President.

Submissions: Accepts queries; complete manuscripts with SASE. Accepts simultaneous and multiple submissions.

Client Requirements: Published and unpublished.

Fees: None.

Services: Some editorial services for clients and nonclients.

Contract: Exclusive contract. 15% domestic; 20% foreign.

Categories: Fiction and nonfiction: early picture books (0-4 years); easy-to-read (4-7); story picture books (4-10); chapter books (5-10); middle-grade (8-12); YA (12-18); series. Nonfiction only: how-to, general interest, photoessays.

1998 Needs: Picture book and middle-grade manuscripts.

Educational Design Services, Inc.

P.O. Box 253

Wantaugh, NY 11793-0253

Established: 1981

Contact: Bertram Linder or Edwin Selzer.

Submissions: Queries with content outline, sample chapter, and SASE. Complete manuscripts with SASE.

Client Requirements: Published and unpublished.

Services: Some editorial services for clients.

Contract: 15%, domestic.

Categories: Nonfiction only: bilingual; hi-lo; educational material for kindergarten through twelfth grade.

1998 Needs: K-12 text materials only. We don't handle fiction or supplementary materials.

Ethan Ellenberg Literary Agency
548 Broadway, Suite 5E
New York, NY 10012
Established: 1984
Contact: Ethan Ellenberg, President.
Current Clients: Eric Rohmann, Julian Noonan, Ruth Krauss, Sara Banks.
Submissions: Queries or complete manuscripts with SASE; also accepts writing samples. Simultaneous and multiple submissions accepted.
Client Requirements: Published and unpublished.
Fees: None.
Services: Editorial services for clients. No fee.
Contract: Flexible-term agreement for each individual book; 15% domestic; 20% foreign sales.
Categories: Fiction and nonfiction: concept, toddler books, and early picture books (0-4 years); easy-to-read (4-7); story picture books (4-10); chapter books (5-10); middle-grade (8-12); YA (12-18); adult; activity books; bilingual; hi-lo; novelty; series.
1998 Needs: Mainly fiction, all ages and areas.
Comments: We're always looking for talented writers.

Flannery Literary Agency
1140 Wickfield
Naperville, IL 60563
Established: 1992
Contact: Jennifer Flannery, President.
Submissions: Queries with SASE. Complete manuscripts with SASE. Accepts multiple submissions. No faxes or phone queries.
Client Requirements: Published and unpublished.

Fees: None.
Services: Editorial services for clients, as requested; no fee.
Contract: Standard, author-friendly agreement: 15% of earnings; 10%-10% split with sub-agents.
Categories: Fiction and nonfiction: concept, toddler books, and early picture books (0-4 years); easy-to-read (4-7); story picture books (4-10); chapter books (5-10); middle-grade (8-12); YA (12-18).
1998 Needs: Good writing of all kinds. I want to hear from new writers with a unique perspective.
Comments: I hope there will always be a home for good books written by passionate authors who care about children and what they read.

FRAN Literary Agency
7235 Split Creek
San Antonio, TX 78238-3627
Established: 1992
Contact: Fran Rathmann, Agent.
Current Clients: *The Sea Gooches,* Addie Stewart.
Submissions: Queries with SASE; complete manuscripts with outline and SASE. Accepts simultaneous and multiple submissions.
Client Requirements: Published and unpublished.
Fees: Processing Fee, $25; no reading fee.
Services: Minor editing for clients, no charge. Critique for full-length manuscript for nonclients, $150.
Contract: Two-year exclusive contract; 15% commission.
Categories: Fiction and nonfiction: concept, toddler books, and early picture books (0-4 years); easy-to-read (4-

7); story picture books (4-10); chapter books (5-10); middle-grade (8-12); adult; activity books; bilingual; series. Nonfiction only: educational, how-to, general interest, YA (12-18).

1998 Needs: Nonfiction; unique fiction; juvenile westerns. No stories about fairies or goblins.

Comments: The current market is tough, but we're eager to see new work so send us something special! You'll get an answer in two months.

Gem Literary Agency
4717 Poe Rd.
Medina, OH 44256
Established: 1989
Contact: Darla Pfenninger, President.
Current Clients: *Strange Goings On at Kniny-Knoll*, Anna O'Sullivan; *Immovable Animals,* Erica Stux.
Submissions: Queries with synopsis or summary. Accepts simultaneous and multiple submissions.
Client Requirements: Published and unpublished.
Fees: None.
Contract: Six-month agreement. Any fees charged for supplies will be returned after placement. Commission: 15% domestic; 20% foreign, film rights.
Categories: Fiction and nonfiction: early picture books (0-4 years); easy-to-read (4-7); story picture books (4-10); chapter books (5-10); middle-grade (8-12); YA (12-18); adult. Fiction only: activity books, novelty, series. Nonfiction only: educational, how-to, general interest, photoessays, reference.
1998 Needs: Well thought-out stories. We want to see more educational and multicultural nonfiction, as well as YA

fiction and science fiction series. No alphabet books.
Comments: Educational and multicultural manuscripts are in demand.

Andrew Hamilton Literary Agency
P.O. Box 604118
Cleveland, OH 44104-0118
E-mail: Clevetown@msn.com
Established: 1991
Submissions: Queries with SASE.
Client Requirements: Published and unpublished.
Fees: Depends on word count. Marketing fee, $250.
Contract: One-year agreement with option for two years; 15% commission.
Categories: Fiction and nonfiction: concept, toddler books, and early picture books (0-4 years); easy-to-read (4-7); story picture books (4-10); chapter books (5-10); middle-grade (8-12); YA (12-18); adult. Nonfiction only: educational, how-to, general interest, reference.
1998 Needs: Good books in all genres.

Heacock Literary Agency
1523 6th St., Suite 14
Santa Monica, CA 90401
Established: 1978
Contact: Rosalie Heacock, Author's Representative.
Current Clients: Audrey and Don Wood, Larry Dane Brimmer, Ann Wagner.
Submissions: Queries with SASE. No multiple or simultaneous submissions.
Client Requirements: Published and unpublished.
Fees: None.
Contract: One-year agreement; 15% commission.
Categories: Fiction and nonfiction:

BUSINESS

story picture books (4-10); adult. Non-fiction only: general interest.

1998 Needs: We want to represent authors who wish to grow in their craft.

Eddy Howard Agency
37 Bernard St.
Eatontown, NJ 07724-1906
Established: 1981
Contact: Dr. Eddy H. Pevovar.
Submissions: Queries with sample chapters and SASE; complete manuscripts with résumé and SASE. Accepts simultaneous and multiple submissions.
Client Requirements: Published and unpublished, but prefers previously published.
Fees: None.
Services: Editorial services for clients and nonclients; fees vary.
Contract: Each agreement is drawn up individually; 10% commission.
Categories: Fiction and nonfiction: toddler books (0-4 years); easy-to-read (4-7); story picture books (4-10); YA (12-18); adult; hi-lo; novelty; series. Nonfiction only: concept books, early picture books (0-4 years); chapter books (5-10 years); middle-grade (8-12 years); activity books; educational; how-to; general interest; photoessays; reference.
1998 Needs: Nonfiction; education. Not interested in cartoons.
Comments: The current market is very progressive and adapts easily. It keeps getting better all the time.

Barbara S. Kouts, Literary Agent
P.O. Box 560
Bellport, NY 11713
Established: 1980
Contact: Barbara S. Kouts.

Current Clients: Robert San Souci, Joseph Bruchac, Jonathan London.
Submissions: Queries only, SASE. Accepts multiple submissions.
Client Requirements: Published and unpublished.
Fees: None.
Services: Editorial services for clients, no fee.
Contract: Letter of agreement; 10% commission.
Categories: Fiction and nonfiction: concept, toddler books, and early picture books (0-4 years); easy-to-read (4-7); story picture books (4-10); chapter books (5-10); middle-grade (8-12); YA (12-18); adult. Nonfiction only: photoessays; series.
1998 Needs: Middle-grade and YA fiction.

Barbara Markowitz Agency
117 N. Mansfield Ave.
Los Angeles, CA 90036
Established: 1980
Contact: Barbara Markowitz.
Current Clients: Valerie Hobbs, Barbara O'Connor, Kristiana Gregory.
Submissions: Queries with the first two chapters and SASE. Must have U.S. stamps on return envelopes. Accepts simultaneous and multiple submissions.
Client Requirements: Published and unpublished.
Fees: None.
Contract: One-year agreement. Commission: 15% for all rights.
Categories: Fiction and nonfiction: middle-grade (8-12); YA (12-16).
1998 Needs: Wants to see historical and contemporary fiction, mysteries, sports, and nature themes. No fantasy, fables, fairy tales, or poetry.

Comments: 1998 marks our eighteenth year in the business.

McIntosh and Otis, Inc.
310 Madison Ave.
New York, NY 10017
Established: 1928
Contact: Reneé Cho, Dorothy Markinko.
Submissions: Queries with sample chapters for novels and nonfiction; SASE. Complete manuscripts with SASE for picture books.
Client Requirements: Published and unpublished.
Fees: None.
Contract: 15% commission.
Categories: Fiction and nonfiction: concept, toddler books, and early picture books (0-4 years); easy-to-read (4-7); story picture books (4-10); chapter books (5-10); middle-grade (8-12); YA (12-18); activity books; novelty; series. Nonfiction only: how-to, photoessays, reference.
Comments: We look for good stories that are meaningful without being didactic. Please, no simultaneous or multiple submissions.

McLean Literary Agency
14206 110th Ave. NE
Kirkland, WA 98034
E-mail: donnam@mcleanlit.com
Established: 1985
Contact: Donna McLean.
Submissions: Queries with SASE; complete manuscripts with fee and SASE. Accepts simultaneous submissions.
Client Requirements: Published and unpublished.
Fees: Reading fee, $50 for concept, toddler, and early picture books; $100 for easy-to-read and chapter books; $125

for middle-grade and YA. For adult fiction, $200; adult nonfiction, $250.
Services: Editorial services for clients, fees vary; manuscript critique for non-clients, $100 fee, refunded from commission.
Contract: One-year agreement with automatic renewal; 30 days written termination notice. 15%, domestic; 20% foreign.
Categories: Story picture books (4-10); chapter books (5-10); middle-grade (8-12); YA (12-18); adult; activity books; novelty; series.
1998 Needs: YA and juvenile fiction and nonfiction. We want to see fresh, unique stories. No poetry or rhyming texts.
Comments: This market is tough for new writers to break into.

Mews Books Ltd.
20 Bluewater Hill
Westport, CT 06880
Established: 1965
Contact: Sidney B. Kramer, President.
Submissions: Queries with plot outline, sample chapter, and résumé for novels, nonfiction. Complete manuscripts for picture books.
Client Requirements: Published and unpublished.
Contract: Commission, 15%; 20% foreign.
Categories: Fiction and nonfiction: concept, toddler books, and early picture books (0-4 years); easy-to-read (4-7); story picture books (4-10); chapter books (5-10); middle-grade (8-12); YA (12-18); adult; series. Nonfiction only: educational, how-to, general interest, photoessays, reference.
1998 Needs: Professional quality ma-

terial in all categories.

Comments: Mr. Kramer is an attorney who reviews contracts and problems with publishers on a fee basis.

New Age World Services & Books
62091 Valley View Circle #2
Joshua Tree, CA 92252
Established: 1957
Contact: Victoria E. Vandertuin.
Current Clients: Frank Nicoletti, Peter Hall.
Submissions: Queries only with outline, author bio, sample chapters, and SASE. No unsolicited manuscripts. Accepts simultaneous submissions.
Client Requirements: Unpublished.
Fees: Rates vary, depending on services.
Contract: Representation fees based on length and nature of work.
Categories: Fiction and nonfiction: concept, toddler books, and early picture books (0-4 years); easy-to-read (4-7); story picture books (4-10); middle-grade (8-12); YA (12-18); adult; activity books. Nonfiction only: educational, how-to, general interest.
Comments: We work with new, unpublished writers in the fiction and nonfiction fields. We also handle poetry manuscripts.

Nordhaus-Wolcott Literary Agency
P.O. Box 7493
Shawnee Mission, KS 66207
Established: 1996
Contact: Chris Wolcott.
Submissions: Queries with sample chapters. Accepts simultaneous submissions.
Client Requirements: Published and unpublished.
Fees: Reading fee, $150.
Services: Editorial services for clients included in reading fee.
Contract: One-year exclusive contract. Commission, 10% domestic; 20% foreign.
Categories: Fiction only: chapter books (5-10); middle-grade (8-12); YA (12-18); adult; activity books; novelty; series. Fiction and nonfiction: early picture books (0-4 years); easy-to-read (4-7); story picture books (4-10). Nonfiction only: concept and toddler books (0-4 years); educational, how-to, general interest, photoessays, reference.
1998 Needs: Open to all genres.
Comments: We want quality writing. We're here to help unpublished writers.

Norma-Lewis Agency
360 W. 53rd St., Suite B-A
New York, NY 10019-5270
Established: 1980
Contact: Norma Liebert.
Submissions: Queries only.
Client Requirements: Published and unpublished.
Contract: Sole representation for a minimum of eight months. Commission: 15% domestic and Canadian; 20% foreign.
Categories: Fiction and nonfiction: concept, toddler books, and early picture books (0-4 years); easy-to-read (4-7); story picture books (4-10); chapter books (5-10); middle-grade (8-12); YA (12-18); adult; activity books; novelty; series. Nonfiction only: educational, how-to, general, photoessays, reference.

Northwest Literary Services
2699 Decca Road
Shawnigan Lake, B.C. V0R 2W0
Canada
Established: 1986

Contact: Brent Laughren, Agent.
Current Clients: Ruth Dickson, Julie Flowers, Doris Hart.
Submissions: Queries with first three sample chapters. Accepts simultaneous submissions.
Client Requirements: Published and unpublished.
Fees: Reading fee for unpublished writers: $50, picture books; $75 for YA (synopsis and first three chapters).
Services: For clients, copyediting at $1.00 per page; for nonclients, $100 for the first 20,000 words and $1.00 per page thereafter.
Contract: Basic agreement. A clause can be added, altered, or deleted by mutual consent. Termination by written notice. 15% domestic; 20% foreign.
Categories: Fiction and nonfiction: easy-to-read (4-7); story picture books (4-10); chapter books (5-10); middle-grade (8-12); YA (12-18); adult; bilingual (English/French); series. Nonfiction only: educational, how-to, general interest, photoessays, reference.
1998 Needs: Concentrating on older readers, especially YA.
Comments: Writers must research intended readers. Use age-appropriate language and never talk down to your audience. We are extremely interested in developing new, unpublished talent.

Pacific Literary Services
1220 Club Court
Richmond, CA 94803
Established: 1991
Contact: Victor West, Agent.
Current Clients: Maria Mathis, Scott Lewis.
Submissions: Queries with synopsis and SASE. Send SASE for a list of editorial services and submission guidelines. Accepts simultaneous and multiple submissions.
Client Requirements: Published and unpublished.
Fees: Rates vary.
Services: Editorial services for clients and nonclients available for a fee. Postage costs extra.
Contract: One-year contract; 10% commission.
Categories: Fiction and nonfiction: concept, toddler books, and early picture books (0-4 years); easy-to-read (4-7); story picture books (4-10); chapter books (5-10); middle-grade (8-12); YA (12-18); adult; activity books; bilingual; hi-lo; novelty; series. Nonfiction only: educational, how-to, general interest, photoessays, reference.
1998 Needs: Open to anything.
Comments: Market is strong yet flexible. We only submit professionally executed manuscripts to publishers.

Pocono Literary Agency, Inc.
P.O. Box 759
Saylorsburg, PA 18353
Established: 1993
Contact: Carolyn Hopwood Blick, President.
Current Clients: Edmund Plante, Andrea Nagy, Daniel Berenson.
Submissions: Queries with synopsis and or writing samples, and SASE. Accepts multiple submissions, if identified. No unsolicited manuscripts.
Client Requirements: Published and unpublished.
Fees: None.
Services: Editorial services for clients at no charge.
Contract: One-year agreement with

BUSINESS

written termination notice. Commission: 15% domestic; 20% foreign.

Categories: Fiction and nonfiction: concept, toddler books, and early picture books (0-4 years); easy-to-read (4-7); story picture books (4-10); chapter books (5-10); middle-grade (8-12); YA (12-18); adult; activity books; bilingual; hi-lo; novelty; series. Nonfiction only: educational, how-to, general interest, photoessays, reference.

1998 Needs: Middle-grade books; picture books; and books that can be used in a classroom.

Comments: The historical fiction market is hot, but markets for horror and suspense books are fading fast. Fiction with a school setting is popular. Avoid rhyming texts.

Remington Literary Associates, Inc.
10131 Coors Rd. NW, Suite I 2-886
Albuquerque, NM 87114
Established: 1995
Contact: Kay Lewis Shaw, President.
Current Clients: Caroline Garrett, Heiko-Roberto Kiera, Jackie J. Schaefer.
Submissions: Queries with SASE only. Accepts simultaneous and multiple submissions.
Client Requirements: Published and unpublished.
Fees: Reading Fees: $25, picture books; $50, middle-grade and YA; $75, adult. Annual marketing fee, $150.
Contract: One-year contract with renewal option. 15% domestic; 20% foreign; 20% dramatic, audio, electronic.
Categories: Fiction and nonfiction: concept, toddler books, and early picture books (0-4 years); easy-to-read (4-7); story picture books (4-10); chapter books (5-10); middle-grade (8-12); YA

(12-18); adult; activity books; bilingual; hi-lo; novelty and series. Nonfiction only: how-to, general interest, photoessays; some educational, reference.

1998 Needs: Primarily interested in work by previously published writers and illustrators—or those who do both.

Comments: We set very high standards and are very selective. Enroll in a class for children's writing; subscribe to a writer's newsletter.

Rhodes Literary Agency
P.O. Box 89133
Honolulu, Hawaii 96830-9133
Established: 1971
Contact: Fred C. Pugarelli, Director.
Current Clients: More than 50 writers.
Submissions: Queries or manuscripts with synopsis and bio; accepts first two chapters, poem selections, and résumés.
Client Requirements: Published and unpublished.
Fees: Reading fee, $125, children's; $165-$175, novels and nonfiction.
Services: Some editing done for clients at no charge.
Contract: No contract offered. Terms include reading fee and 10% commission; 20% foreign, electronic sales.
1998 Needs: Any type of manuscript from picture book to novel or play; juvenile to adult age range.
Comments: The market for children's books is a tough, competitive one. However, we have sold more than 120 manuscripts of all genres to a number of publishers. We are a Writers Guild agency.

Rose Agency, Inc.
P.O. Box 11826
Fort Wayne, IN 46861
Established: 1993

Contact: Lynn Clough, President.
Current Clients: Stephen Burke, Marcey Jones.
Submissions: Query first with SASE; complete manuscripts with SASE.
Client Requirements: Published and unpublished.
Contract: One-year exclusive. Commission: 15% domestic; 20% foreign.
Categories: Fiction and nonfiction: chapter books (5-10); middle-grade (8-12); YA (12-18); adult. Nonfiction only: educational, how-to, general interest.
1998 Needs: Not interested in poetry.
Comments: We're very open to queries, and accept about 90% of those we receive. Tell us about your best work, and present it in a fresh, unique way.

Pesha Rubinstein Literary Agency

1392 Rugby Rd.
Teaneck, NJ 07666
Established: 1990
Contact: Pesha Rubinstein, President.
Current Clients: Jane Kurtz, Linda Joy Singleton, Amy Littlesugar.
Submissions: Send brief letter, first 10 pages of manuscript, and SASE. Accepts simultaneous and multiple submissions.
Client Requirements: Published and unpublished.
Contract: Mutual agreement between client and agent; 15% domestic; 20% foreign.
Categories: Fiction only: story picture books (4-10); chapter books (5-10); middle-grade (8-12); adult.
1998 Needs: We focus on excellent storytelling. We're interested in fiction that lends itself to the commercial market, à la The Golden Compass.

Susan Schulman

454 West 44th St.
New York, NY 10036
Established: 1979
Contact: Susan Schulman.
Submissions: Queries with résumé and SASE. Accepts simultaneous and multiple submissions.
Client Requirements: Published and unpublished.
Fees: None.
Contract: One-year, one-project contract. 10%-15% domestic; 20% foreign.
Categories: Fiction and nonfiction: story picture books (4-10); middle-grade (8-12); YA (12-18); adult.
Comments: The current children's market is very limited.

Laurens R. Schwartz, Esq.

Literary, Film, and Art Representative
5 East 22nd St., Suite 15D
New York, NY 10010-5315
Established: 1981
Contact: Laurens R. Schwartz.
Submissions: Query first with SASE; complete manuscripts with SASE. Five-week right of first refusal.
Client Requirements: Published and unpublished.
Fees: None.
Services: Editorial services for clients as needed, no fee; occasional manuscript critiques for nonclients at no charge.
Contract: Commission: 15% domestic; 20% foreign.
Categories: Fiction and nonfiction: concept, toddler books, and early picture books (0-4 years); easy-to-read (4-7); story picture books (4-10); chapter books (5-10); middle-grade (8-12); YA (12-18); adult; activity books; novelty; series.

Nonfiction only: educational, how-to, general interest, photoessays, reference.
Comments: We have handled 15 juvenile/YA bestsellers.

The Snyder Literary Agency
7123 East Jan Ave.
Mesa, AZ 85208
Established: 1996
Contact: Dawn M. Snyder, Agent.
Submissions: Queries first with SASE; manuscripts under 20 pages with SASE. For manuscripts over 20 pages, enclose reading fee and SASE. Accepts simultaneous and multiple submissions, if identified.
Client Requirements: Published and unpublished.
Fees: Reading fee: $50 for manuscripts over twenty pages.
Services: Editorial services available for clients upon request; no fee. Manuscript critique for nonclients, $50.
Contract: One-year agreement. 15% domestic, 20% on foreign, TV, film.
Categories: Open to most genres and age ranges.
1998 Needs: Middle-grade to YA. Wants to see scripts for all ages.
Comments: We enjoy working with children's authors. Anything with a positive message for children catches our eye.

Sandra Watt & Associates
8033 Sunset Blvd. #4053
Hollywood, CA 90046
Established: 1977
Contact: Priscilla Palmer.
Current Clients: Cynthia Chin-Lee, *A is for Asia;* Mindy Dwyer, *Coyote in Love;* Ramin Jaleshgari, *Nefersat's Dream.*
Submissions: Queries only with SASE.

Accepts simultaneous submissions, if identified.
Client Requirements: Published and unpublished.
Contract: Standard agreement with 15% commission.
Categories: Fiction and nonfiction: easy-to-read (4-7); story picture books (4-10); chapter books (5-10); middle-grade (8-12); YA (12-18); adult. Nonfiction only: educational, how-to, general interest, photoessays, reference.
1998 Needs: Middle-grade and YA fiction.
Comments: Research the market. Know your competition. Make sure you can write a book proposal. Most importantly, be patient.

Writers' Productions
P.O. Box 630
Westport, CT 06881
Established: 1977
Contact: David L. Meth, President.
Submissions: Queries only, with SASE. Keeps exclusive submissions for one month.
Client Requirements: Published and unpublished.
Services: Editorial services provided only for clients working on a project.
Contract: Standard project agreement, includes exclusive representation and termination clause. 15% domestic, 25% foreign, drama, multimedia.
1998 Needs: We're interested in seeing work that creates a whole new landscape and universe of characters. We'd like to see original characters and settings—a cross between Hobbits and Smurfs™ with a challenging, inventive use of language.

STYLE & TECHNIQUE

Part 5

Editors on Plot

What Makes for Story?

By Catherine Frey Murphy

STYLE

"A good plot is like Velcro. It catches the reader and keeps him reading," says Daniel Lee, Editor of *Jack And Jill*. At *Highlights for Children*, Senior Editor Marileta Robinson concurred, through a different metaphor. "What makes a good plot is if the reader cares how the story turns out. Keep in mind that you're doing a dance with your readers. You're trying to draw them along."

Editors surveyed agree that fine plotting is central to fine stories. But every editor has individual ideas about what makes a plot work. "Nobody uses the word the same way," says Stephen Roxburgh, President and Publisher of Front Street Books. When asked about plot, some editors nonetheless emphasize character. Others say they look for dramatic action. And still others say that plotting is a seamless web, in which all parts of the story work together to add up to a compelling whole.

A Beginning, Middle, and End

"Writers need to learn the difference between situation and plot," says Robinson. By situation, she means the story's basic problem—for example, being the last child in first grade to lose a baby tooth. That problem alone doesn't create a plot, Robinson says. "There needs to be a progression. Maybe the child tries various ways to get the tooth out. And maybe, through that process, the child learns something."

The secret to making a situation into a plot, Robinson says, is told in three familiar words: beginning, middle, and end. The beginning introduces the story's problem, and Robinson says that the sooner that's accomplished, the better. "For a magazine story, try to introduce your conflict in the very first sentence." Marilyn Edwards, Editor-in-Chief of *Hopscotch,* agrees that a story's beginning can make it or break it. "The beginning is so important. Kids are less patient than adults, and if you don't hook them right off the bat, they'll turn the page."

Then comes the middle, or dramatic exposition, in which the story's conflict develops to its crisis point. In the middle, Robinson recommends, "Don't be afraid of conflict. Often, we like our characters and we don't want to make life too hard for them, but that's a mistake. I once had a writing teacher who said, 'Introduce complications. Then complicate the complications!'"

"The ending of the story has to answer the question that was asked in the beginning, in such a way that you can't predict how it will turn out," says Robinson. "Look for a resolution that makes your reader feel they've covered some territory, that they've gotten somewhere," adds Lee. "There has to be something at the end to make the reader glad he read the story, instead of spending the time staring out the window."

Try for surprise, suggests Harcourt Brace Editorial Assistant Hilary Achauer. "Too often, plots are resolved in a way that's too predictable. It's all tied up very neatly, but it just doesn't feel right."

"A good plot needs to have a good conclusion," says Paula Morrow, Editor of *Ladybug* and *Babybug* at the Cricket Magazine Group. "There needs to be surprise and satisfaction. The child's development affects the surprise, of course. 'Look in the mirror and see yourself: An infant will be surprised!'—that's all the plot a baby needs. But put that story in *Spider*, for older children, and it won't work."

"We all want closure," says Roxburgh. "I may be sophisticated enough to accept that, in real life, there is no closure—but I still want it. As writers, we're making order out of chaos all the time. Readers want their expectations, which you've set up, to be fulfilled."

Lee says that every good plot has a number of essential elements, all of which must fall into place if the story is to succeed. "If the characters aren't interesting or realistic, or the situation isn't interesting or believable, or the solution is either unbelievable, or not there at all, then you haven't got a plot. Too many pieces are 'slice-of-life' stories, minus some or all of these essential elements. A good plot is supposed to tell an interesting, believable story, with a beginning, a middle, and something of a payoff at the end."

"Narrowing down your plot's focus is most important." The strongest element, says Erica Jacobs, Editor at Chronicle Books, "is having a simple story to tell." But, she adds, that's not easy. "Taking the simplest action and describing it so that all the elements are in place is a complicated task that few accomplish. Ask yourself, what is it in particular that means your story has to be told? In this competitive market, with all the books already out there, why should this particular story be on the shelves? Once you've figured that out, develop your characters and plot with that specific focus in mind."

When he defines *plot*, Roxburgh

looks all the way back to Aristotle. "Loosely paraphrasing, he said a plot is a beginning, a middle, and an end. The beginning is that which nothing needs to precede, but something must follow. In the middle, something must precede, and something must follow. And the ending is that which something must precede, and nothing can follow."

Story and Plot: Synonymous?

Quoting Robert Louis Stevenson, Roxburgh adds that in a good plot, the reader is "caught up on the wave of incident, and tumbled forward." But great plots aren't made of incident alone. "What drives action is tension," he says. "You have to think not just in terms of incident, but of feelings. If a character we're sympathetic to is out in the frozen night, we want that character brought into the warmth. We all want tension resolved."

Consider the difference between story and plot, Roxburgh suggests. "E.M. Forster said that this is story: The king died, and then the queen died. This is plot: The king died, and then the queen died of grief."

Why does knowing about the queen's grief change our response? We wonder why she grieved so deeply for the king. But to answer that question, we need to find out who the queen was. Maybe she was a timid person who depended on the king, and wasted away after his death because she wasn't strong enough to survive alone. Or maybe she was intensely passionate, loving the king so fiercely that she threw herself over a parapet after the state funeral. Or, possibly, she didn't love the king at all. Maybe she poisoned him to get rid of him, only to be consumed by remorse after his death. Forster's plot sketch suggests countless story possibilities—and every possibility begins with the character of the queen.

Tested in Fire

"Character is at the base of plot," says Patricia Gauch, Editorial Director of Philomel Books. "The stories that matter begin with a character who is going someplace, a character who wants something. There's a void that needs to be filled." For Gauch, plot comes about when that needy character interacts with a situation. "The character is like a pinball. How does it react to what it hits? If you don't have anything for the pinball to bump into, you can't find out who the character will be."

Look at *I Am Regina*, by Sally M. Keehn, Gauch suggests. "On the surface, it's a historical tale about a girl taken captive by a Native American tribe in the seventeenth century. But in fact, it's about Regina. What does it feel like when you are captured, taken away from your home and everything you know? How does it feel when you begin to like the Native Americans you're living with?" When she returns, utterly changed by ten years of captivity, Regina finds her mother by reaching into her own dimly remembered past, to sing a song she recalls from her babyhood. "Where has she been in all that time?" Gauch asks. "She's been fired, like a piece of pottery in a kiln. Plot is the firing of character. It's almost as if the story is there to test the character."

STYLE

If the character is to be truly tested, the kiln has to be truly hot, Gauch adds. "Too many people write in a safe area, in the middle ground, and then they can't figure out why nobody's buying their work," she says. "What's at stake? If there's a character we care about, we recognize ourselves. Then our humanity is at stake. We're at stake."

"Plot is dependent on character," agrees Susan Hirschman, Editor-in-Chief of Greenwillow. "It's contrived characters and cardboard plots that hold back story. A strong plot is a three-dimensional, believable character, moving through the action of the story. And the action comes out of who the character is."

Hirschman suggests that writers study Mary, in Frances Hodgson Burnett's *The Secret Garden*. "Look at how she changes." Or for a more modern example, she says, read *The Cuckoo's Child*, by Suzanne Freeman, about an American girl who has grown up in the Middle East, but moves to a small Southern town in the United States after her parents are killed. "Not that much happens in the book, really," says Hirschman. "It's who the character is, and the impact she has on that small community, that makes the story extraordinary."

"The most important element of plot is whether the characters have touched you, so you feel concern," says Robinson. "If you don't have lifelike characters, then the plot is happening in a vacuum. There's not much to care about." Achauer says, "Often, beginning writers focus too much on the plot. The characters are being pulled along by the plot, rather than moving it along themselves."

Shannon Lowry, Associate Editor at *Boys' Life,* says that a character's growth is at the heart of plotting. "When the character doesn't go through some kind of dramatic tension, and arrive at a new understanding, it leaves the plot rather flat."

Active and Concrete

"Characters are important," acknowledges Deborah Churchman, Senior Editor for *Ranger Rick*. "But wonderful characters aren't enough. Something has to happen. You have to get some action in."

Christie Ottaviano, Senior Editor at Henry Holt and Company Books for Young Readers, looks for a plot that takes a purposeful narrative direction. "I often find manuscripts that have strong characterization, but lack plot direction. Developing a plot that will carry a character forward is just as important as creating a wonderful character. A plot needs to follow a natural progression, moving toward the climax from the beginning."

Roxburgh observes that many of the most popular children's books have entirely action-based plots. "Look at the Nancy Drew books," he suggests. "The characters never change at all, and that's why kids like them!" Roxburgh notes that the first novels ever written had picaresque, or action-based, plots. "Since Cervantes, modern fiction has focused more on character, and the children's books that win the awards emphasize character development." Roxburgh adds that even a coming-of-age novel, in which the plot is built

Plot Prescriptions: A Writer's Rx

Children's editors have helped to improve so many plots that they have stored up some fine advice for writers. Here are a few suggestions they shared:

Mary Lou Carney, Editor-in-Chief, *Guideposts for Kids:* Don't think about plot first. Get yourself a marvelous character, then get her into a perilous situation—and plot happens!

Shannon Lowry, *Boys' Life:* Read! I think the way most writers learn their craft is to study other writers who are similar in style, and whom they want to emulate. Write daily. And if you're not sure your stories are working, try them on kids. See if their little antennae come up!

Paula Morrow, The Cricket Magazine Group: Go to the library, and ask for a stack of the most popular books at the age level you want to write for. Read them all. If you have to outline every one, do that, until you figure out what you're missing.

Christie Ottaviano, Holt: Do a really detailed outline so you can chart the progression of the plot before you hit the keys. Once you have the skeleton for the plot, you can work on fleshing out the story.

Hilary Achauer, Harcourt Brace: Take a step back from your story, and think everything out from beginning to end. Make sure the characters fit into the plot, make sure all the elements are there, make sure all the parts work together as a whole. The whole story should flow naturally.

Marilyn Edwards, *Hopscotch:* Read our June 1994 issue, where we published an article for children on how to write an adventure story. In between each paragraph of the story, there's an explanation in italics of how the story was put together. Thinking of all the manuscripts that come in here—and I only see the best ones—I think this would be helpful for many adult writers to read!

Erica Jacobs, Chronicle Books: Take accountability and responsibility for your work. Read it over six times before you send it in. Reread, reread! Revise, revise!

Deborah Churchman, *Ranger Rick:* Watch cartoons! I'm being facetious, of course, but you have to admit, they have plot down. Something always happens!

around a character's discovery of himself, can't neglect action. "The best children's fiction is action-driven."

Mary Lou Carney, Editor-in-Chief at *Guideposts for Kids,* says that strong plots are built around growth in a character's understanding, as the character comes to realize some central truth. "But don't get too cerebral," she warns. "To provide the turning point, get a concrete object involved in your plot, like a lunchbox, or a fishing pole. At *Guideposts,* we call that object the *vehicle.* When there's an actual object associated with the come-to-realize moment, all that cerebral stuff goes out the window—which is where it belongs!"

In "Rocks in My Head," for instance, a lunchbox becomes the vehicle for a character's growth. When a boy's mother buys him a lunchbox that he hates, he doesn't want to carry it to school, but he doesn't want to hurt his mother's feelings, either. "In the end, the boy figures out a way to solve his problem and use the lunchbox, without any adult assistance," Carney says.

Adventure of the Spirit

That absence of benevolent adult aid is crucial to a successful children's plot, Carney believes. "I tell authors to 'put the adults in the well,' to get rid of them. The adults in a children's story should be like those adults in the Charlie Brown TV shows. When they talk to the kids, you can't even understand them. All you can hear is 'mwah mwah mwah!'"

"I often get manuscripts that are okay, but the adults have all the power," agrees Churchman. "Maybe the kid listens to a grandparent and learns something. But that's total fantasy! Kids don't want this. They get enough of it at school. The action has to be child-centered."

"The child should solve the problem," agrees Edwards. In "Sophie and the Christmas Crib," for instance, Sophie spills flour on the floor when she visits her grandfather's bakery. Flour is scarce, and Sophie's upset at having wasted it, until she realizes she can mix it with salt and use it for dough to make a Nativity scene as a Christmas gift for her family. "When a child is faced with a problem, and solves it in the right way, that's a story about someone who has made a choice," Edwards says. "That's my favorite story to read. It's still fiction, and it's entertaining, but it leaves the reader with something more."

The complexity and subtlety of your plot depends on the age of your readers. "In picture books," says Gauch, "the story is an adventure that engages the character. It's the most basic idea of adventure: things happen. In a novel for older children, there's really more than that. It's an adventure of the spirit." Morrow says, "Be sure that your problem or conflict is appropriate to the target age of your audience. Know children's developmental stages. If your story is appropriate for an eight-year-old, don't send it to a magazine for two- to four-year-olds!"

For any age, Robinson says, a plot must engage a character in conflict. "But for younger children, those conflicts are much simpler, and less scary," she says. "Kids have verbal experience, but not that much life experience," says Roxburgh. "As they develop a more complex worldview, they're more open to complexity in their reading. There's a point where they start to bring more to books, and want more from them."

Then there's originality. "A plot really needs to be fresh," says Carney. "In one day, I might see three stories about the mean old lady who lives next door, and when your ball goes in her yard, you find out she's nice after all. Give kids a break! Even if, somehow, they haven't seen that plot before, they deserve more than that."

"It starts with originality," agrees Gauch. "The books that become classics are originals. Look at *The Giver*. Look at *The Midwife's Apprentice*. It must be obvious that originality is at the root of their success. What is a writer, after all? A writer is someone who thinks and feels. It starts from a deep place, not a shallow place. Who are you? Why are you writing? It starts with you."

But originality isn't just thinking up a new plot gimmick. Sometimes, its essence is in the author's voice. "A good writer has a rhythm and a style in their writing that is all their own," says Lowry. "You need strong character development, and a plot that's believable, but in the best stories, the tone and the language feed into whether that plot's going to hold up." Ottaviano agrees. "I've seen familiar plots cleverly executed."

Plot is made up of so many diverse elements that plot-building may seem, at first, to be a fragmented, impossible task. But when those pieces come to-

gether, magic can happen—that particularly human form of magic that we call story. "As humans, we're addicted to story," said Robinson. "When you write, that's what you're doing. You're spinning out a web to catch your reader, to pull your reader along, to make him want to keep reading."

At best, says Roxburgh, the writer who masters plot can become what he calls "a lantern-bearer. You bring light into darkness."

In *What Jamie Saw*, by Carolyn Coman, for example, a small boy learns how to survive an act of terrifying abuse. "Jamie achieved a fairly precarious balance of comfort and security," Roxburgh says. "He made one step further in the dark. That's all. He didn't climb Mount Olympus—he just took one step. It's great writing, because it sheds light. It's that light, that resonance, that brings us back to great literature, over and over again."

HOW TO BREAK STUFF

Submissions

Proposing In Style

By Ginger Roberts Brackett

For most people, the word *proposal* evokes images of bended knee, diamonds, perhaps roses and candlelight. For writers and publishers, *proposal* carries a different connotation. Surprisingly, these two types of proposals have qualities in common: mutual attraction, an offer, commitment, and a long-term relationship.

A publisher is attracted when a writer's research reveals a particular writer fulfills that publisher's needs. After attraction comes the offer that convinces an editor that yours is a union made in heaven. A clear, concise and, yes, exciting proposal will touch that editor's heart.

Proposals, like engagement rings, differ in shape and size, varying from simple queries to lengthy book outlines. For nonfiction, magazines often request query letters proposing future projects, rather than the finished projects themselves. Some want accompanying support materials, such as proposed sources, a résumé or compilation of publishing credits, perhaps clips.

Marcia Preston of *ByLine* magazine describes the "ideal" query as one in which the writer "generally sums up the subject," then elaborates, adding "one or two specific details." A query to *ByLine* proposing an article on setting in fiction might note that, while plot and character receive much attention, the importance of setting is often overlooked. To prove that importance, the article might focus on the Southern novel, *To Kill a Mockingbird* and the Spanish Civil War novel, *For Whom the Bell Tolls,* arguing that both depend totally on setting for plot.

Preston stresses that writers should

also always propose a length that falls within *ByLine*'s guidelines. Preston does not want to hear "the reasons your mother loves the idea, or any sales job telling me why this subject is perfect for *ByLine*." She also advises, "Don't tell an editor his job. Just sound excited about your idea." For Preston, commitment begins with a brief, general proposal, bolstered by specific examples, and is best accompanied by a dollop of enthusiasm.

While Preston may not like the sound of a sales job, other editors do want to hear why your article is perfect for their publication. Most editors who want proposals in the form of a query letter also want writers to confine queries to one page, and to mention any personal expertise related to your subject: Volunteer work at the local zoo could be important to writing a feature on exotic animals, for instance. While such experience isn't essential, it makes you a more credible writer. Attach a proposed source list, consulting a handbook for proper bibliographic form. Your one or two publishing credits deserve mention in the query itself, while lengthy credentials should appear on a separate sheet.

An editor's agreement to see your completed project represents the second step toward mutual commitment. Remember, however, that proposal acceptance rarely guarantees a finished project acceptance.

Book Proposals

Book proposals involve a somewhat similar, but greatly expanded, plan that depends on the publisher's needs. First, you must read guidelines, advice

---

Nonfiction Magazine Proposal Package

- Query letter
  - Specific statement of idea.
  - One or two supporting details.
  - Projected length (within guideline specifications).
  - Indication of personal expertise.
  - One or two publishing credits.
- Proposed source list, in proper bibliographic form.
- List of publishing credentials.
- Clips, if available.

---

echoed repeatedly by editors. That is critical because the proposal and development process of nonfiction—and even historical fiction—book publishers can vary greatly in the specific approach.

Publisher 1: Filling in the Blanks

For some projects, it is the publisher, not the author, who provides the proposal. ABC-Clio, a Denver-based publisher specializing in contemporary world issues and reference books for the high school library, supplies authors with a proposal outline on disk as well as in hard copy.

A blurb in a writer's newsletter motivated me to contact the then Senior Acquisitions Editor. After guidelines and information on published ABC-Clio single-edition literature encyclopedias arrived, the editor and I discussed subjects in which I might be interested and how to proceed with research. High school and college students, as well as librarians, use the encyclopedias, which focus on novel-length works read in the classroom. I

Nonfiction Book Proposal Types

- Author-generated idea, outline, bibliography, sample chapters, proposed sources, estimated length, audience.
- Publisher-initiated ideas, with the author following a precise formula.
- Publisher-initiated ideas, with room for the author's participation in development.

agreed to compile a list of the most widely read works in the area I was interested in. The editor then mailed the proposal. A fill-in-the-blank type of document, it requires no challenge to design on the part of the writer. The writer's work takes place before filling those blanks.

As part of my proposal for a column on literature of love and romance, I supplied *headword lists* for the titles, authors, characters, and subjects to be included in the 600-page project. The proposal that the editor presented to his publisher contained my lists of hundreds of topics, estimated submission deadlines, and additions before my final presentation was accepted. In this instance, my part in the proposal included no burden of convincing the publisher of the value of my idea. Rather, it acted as a working document explaining exactly what I promised to deliver, and when. ABC-Clio depends on their writers' expertise on their subjects to shape content. The editor works with writers to shape presentation.

Asked why he supplies his own proposal, the editor explains that he knows what he wants, and writers don't. When he receives a query letter, he doesn't want to read about how many libraries exist in the U.S. "It's my job to know such things," he says. "I need the writer to tell me something I don't know, like why he believes an idea will fit our encyclopedia series." Because ABC-Clio serves a specific, stated audience, an author's query needs to convince editors the audience will find the subject attractive and helpful.

Publisher 2: Proposing Plot

Becky Durost Fish, Editor of Barbour & Company's American Adventure series, confirms the need to follow guidelines: "I'm always surprised by how many writers neglect this important point." She adds that she "really appreciates" those proposals that speak to the needs of her endeavor.

Barbour's procedure is to provide authors with a specific, one-page summary of their needs. The American Adventure series is actually historical fiction, but shares the qualities of historical nonfiction in following different generations of the same family.

The editors can't depend on disparate writers working on their own for the required consistency. Instead, the conflict and character description are supplied to prospective writers. The author proposes plot development, which Fish closely examines. "We do understand that plots may alter somewhat, because characters do things we don't expect. We can be flexible, but writers need to consider carefully issues involved in the conflict. The story

STYLE

must move at a rapid pace, and a good proposal will show this movement. This is absolutely critical to writing for children," she emphasizes. Her guidelines reflect her philosophy that "history should be exciting and real." Any proposal seriously considered demonstrates that the writer shares that philosophy.

Publisher 3: Expanding Horizons
Sometimes a proposal of one project may lead to the completion of another. I read a newsletter request by Morgan Reynolds Press for young adult materials, particularly biographies and histories. The editor wanted "queries, partial manuscripts with an outline or synopsis, and finished projects," and "sample consecutive chapters." His needs matched my desire to write a collection of chapter-length biographies on little-known women writers who lived in the seventeenth to nineteenth centuries.

So in a twelve-page proposal, I described works by each woman, supplied brief quotations from her writing, mentioned attributes making her worthy of discussion, and described my anticipated approach to that discussion. It included two chapter-length biographies, one on Elizabeth Cary, an English Renaissance playwright and historian whose inspiring life had become a favorite project for me.

When Publisher, John Riley, called, imagine my delight when he asked, "Could you write a full-length biography of Cary?" He said that of the two women, I "just seemed more passionate" about Cary. Upon hearing that story, a fellow writer commented, "What a perceptive editor!" She was right; I couldn't let this one get away. The real work began with his request for a chapter-by-chapter outline to demonstrate how I would flesh out Cary's life in 25,000 words.

Expansion of a single chapter into ten or twelve seemed daunting, but I focused on the adage that "every journey begins with one step." I mentally divided my imagined book into three units by dates that covered Cary's childhood, youth, and adulthood, to establish a rough timeline and provide a skeleton outline. I committed those dates to paper, then added the names and effects on her life of other individuals and of historic events. I next added details about her life and works, and noted the relationships among those key factors.

Also important was the recording of every source used. Updating a bibliography during research is much simpler than trying later to recall sources. The outline proposal allowed me to complete most of the required research and organization; it proved invaluable when I actually wrote the book, *Elizabeth Cary: Writer of Conscience*.

Asked about his ideal proposal, Riley comments that he likes lots of detail, showing the proposed project "meets our needs" and "high quality of writing." "I see the same ideas consistently," he adds. "In my field, the two poles are originality and need. The best work for my purposes is supported by these two forces." He agrees with other editors that the biggest problem with "a high number of proposals," is that they simply "do not fit my needs." His best advice to proposal writers: Do your homework, and "make sure the publisher is interested in the proposal."

As romantic relationships differ, so do writing relationships. Every writer won't form a perfect match with every editor; even the best-written proposal may not catch the imagination of your target. But if your vision regarding your project remains clear and focused, and you study guidelines and market needs, you'll find that perfect publisher match. Just remember, your proposal marks only the beginning of a long-term relationship. Planning, purpose, effort, and enthusiasm will result in a satisfying investment for both you and your publisher.

STYLE

Sidebars

Snagging Sales on the Side

By Norma Jean Lutz

STYLE

"I love sidebars!" came the bright, bubbly voice over the telephone line. "Sidebars are one of my very favorite things." I was talking to Mary Lou Carney, Editor of *Guideposts for Kids*, who made no secret of her enthusiasm on the subject. When any facet of writing elicits such a lively response from an editor, writers do well to listen up.

You may wonder, "What's a sidebar?" You see them all the time: They're the shaded areas on the magazine page containing information related to (but not part of) an adjacent article. A sidebar may contain lists, instructions, statistics, resources, and even quizzes. Sidebars round out and add dimension to the major story.

They're found in virtually every magazine—whether for children, teens, or adults—because readers love them as much as editors do. Let's look at some of the reasons why sidebars are such a hit.

Why Editors Love Them

"Our preteen readers like to process information in chunks as opposed to a long drawn out piece," says Karen Bokram, Editor-in-Chief of *Girls' Life*. Sidebars provide that accessible "chunk" to which Bokram refers.

Carney likes to think of them as "entry points." *Guideposts for Kids,* she explains, is committed to providing multiple entry points for their readers. "If the young reader doesn't want to launch into the large block of text, the smaller entry point becomes inviting." Carney adds, "When sidebars are well done, they draw the reader back into the major piece."

Which brings us to the next point.

Not only do sidebars present neat capsules of information, they also grab reader attention through the use of bullets, font variations, bold borders, and sharp colors. Today's youngsters are highly visual due to a daily diet of video games, television shows, and computers. They respond to this type of lively graphic art. Study copies of your target publications to see the wild splashes of color and art in sidebars. The eye is automatically pulled to it.

"If the information were in the article," rather than a sidebar, explains Daniel Lee, Editor of *Jack And Jill*, "it might disappear. But in a sidebar the reader's attention is drawn to it." Becoming aware of layout helps a writer to envision an article enhanced by supportive sidebars. This means writers must train themselves to think not only of the text, but of the graphics as well.

Another benefit: Sidebars can solve an editor's nitty-gritty space problems. "Sidebars help us work in extra details that we'd have trouble finding space for in an article," Lee says.

While an article demands smooth transitions from one point to the next, information in a sidebar does not. Bulleted points can be almost choppy, using incomplete sentences, thus making it possible to squeeze more information into less space. Lee tells of a *Jack And Jill* article on lightning safety that contained a sidebar of barely a hundred words explaining how to count down from "flash to boom" to determine the location of a storm. "A sidebar," he continues, "segments the -information into portions, which allows it to be more organized and there-fore more efficiently presented."'

Rachel Buchholz, Special Features Editor of *Boys' Life* agrees. "If you have information that doesn't quite jive with your focus, but is still pertinent," she says, "this information may fit perfectly into a sidebar."

Seeing how beneficial these nifty blocks of information can be, writers should be eager to know more about how to write them.

How Writers Provide Them

Early Planning. The key to writing winning sidebars is to be aware of them during the crafting process of the article. Early planning allows for them to be "discovered" as research progresses. Whether you're conducting an interview or library research, keep an eye out for possibilities. Advance planning allows specific sidebar suggestions to be presented in the query letter, which definitely gives the writer a professional edge. Carney cites the example of a sidebar that accompanied an article on immigration. The sidebar listed successful business, political, and sports figures who were immigrants to this country. Considering the research involved, this was obviously not an afterthought on the part of the writer.

Variety. If you plan to submit two sidebars with an article, try not to make them similar in form or subject. In other words, if one is a bulleted list, make the other a narrative. "We ran an article in *Jack And Jill* on meteorite showers," says Lee. "One sidebar listed dates of upcoming meteorite showers, the other told about the Hale-Bopp comet. These were related items, but not the same subject, which worked

Formatting a Sidebar

- Set up the sidebar on a separate page from the article.
- Use a standard heading, as though the sidebar were an article. In case it is inadvertently separated from the article, this information makes it identifiable.
- Beneath the title, place in parentheses: (Possible use as a sidebar).
- Give the sidebar word count.
- When submitting two sidebars, use a separate page for each.
- Do not paper clip the sidebar to the article. Give it its own clip.
- Place sidebars behind the main article in the envelope.
- If you sent no query letter and this is an unsolicited submission, mention the sidebars in the cover letter so the editor will know what is in the package.

well for us." In a parenting article, "Creative Playtime," I offered the editor two sidebars: one a list of books for further reading on the subject, and the second a recipe for homemade play dough. Both were used.

Imaginative. The possibilities for attention-getting sidebars are virtually limitless. In my own parenting articles, I like to present the reader with additional resources. A parenting article for *SingleLife,* "Big Fat Fibs and Little White Lies," was accompanied by a list of five readaloud books for children on the subject of lies and lying.

Carney noted that the subject may even be a counterpoint to the article. For an article discussing vegetarianism, she used a sidebar entitled "Make Mine Meat!"

In addition to how-to's and lists, you may want to search out background information pertaining to your subject. An article about a certain holiday could be supported by a sidebar explaining the history of that holiday. Short quizzes relating to the article subject are always popular with the younger set. And don't forget the ever important "where you can get more information" box. In this day and age, websites are common in children's articles.

Word Count Watch. Since editors are word-count minded, writers must be also. Be aware that sidebars increase word count. While a sidebar for an adult publication may be as many as 500 words, sidebars for children's magazines are much shorter. Lee suggests that instead of sending an 800-word article, "send a 500-word article along with a couple of short sidebars."

Carney echoes this strategy. "If you know *Guideposts for Kids* uses articles of 1,400 words, consider writing a 1,000-word article with two sidebars of 200 words each. Even though the sidebar may be an integral part of the article, the article should not require the sidebar to carry it."

"If we run out of room," Bokram reminds writers, "out it goes!"—and *it* is the sidebar.

Not only do sidebars call attention to the information contained in an article, but a tidy professional package of sidebars will call attention to you, the writer. Well-written, appropriate sidebars are the mark of a professional. "When I see sidebars," says Lee, "it tells

STYLE

me the writer knows the subject well."
Clearly, it also tells editors the writer
knows the ins and outs of publishing a
magazine well, too.

While the editors interviewed stated
they wouldn't turn down an article due
to a lack of sidebars, each agreed that
sidebars were a clear plus. The sidebar-
savvy writer pleases both reader and
editor when pertinent sidebars are
tucked into a nonfiction package.
When your professional package snags
a sale for you, you'll be the most
pleased one of all.

Language

The Descriptive Zone: Beyond Adjectives & Adverbs

By Pegi Deitz Shea

STYLE

Forget the names of colors. Just forget them. Or imagine you have landed in a new world where Crayola doesn't exist, and the words *sky blue* have no meaning. Now, you can start fresh by describing with simile, metaphor, analogy, *and* verbs.

Those of you who still remember these figures of speech from junior high may skip this paragraph. *Simile* (which I still want to pronounce *smile)* uses *like* or *as* to compare one thing to another. *Metaphor* doesn't need these valley girl-appropriated words; it compares by implication. *Analogy,* a point-for-point alignment of one thing to another, works best when you want to make a new concept or entity familiar to your audience. Verbs help all these figures of speech to accomplish comparison. Action verbs have the power by themselves to evoke the five senses.

Although purists may disagree, simile, metaphor, analogy, and action verbs all exercise in the brain lobe reserved for metaphoric language. The prefix *meta* expresses the notion of "sharing, action in common," says the *Oxford English Dictionary* (OED). *Phor* means "bearing." Therefore, I consider metaphor to be the Nautilus machine of description, figures of speech the lifting stations, and words, the weights. So let's get pumping.

Appropriate Imagery

Some metaphors work. Some don't. Why? While comparisons between two different objects or sensations need to excite the reader's imagination, they shouldn't divert the reader's attention away from the story to your fabulous craftsmanship. Metaphors must be appropriate.

Creative Connections

These exercises can help you see past the obvious comparisons. Use your own world of metaphor, and try them through the eyes of different characters and in different plot situations.

■ Add "the color of ..." to each of these nouns. Write two new comparisons. Extra credit: Try "the shape of ... "

	the color of		the shape of
dog's nose	Kingsford charcoal	a roof shingle	baseball field
rotten teeth			
autumn leaf			
minivan			
necktie			
blonde hair			
fingernails			
hamburger			
noodle			
socks			
cherub			

■ Add "as if ... " or "the way ... " to the following neutral action verbs, and write two new comparisons that cause widely different effects. Again, picture several different characters and situations. And use action verbs.

	as if	the way
bending	crumbling after a punch	a road hugs a mountain
chewing		
tapping		
mumbling		
sticking		
chewing		
sitting		
listening		
scratching		
singing		
staring		

Character: Metaphoric language needs to fit the uniqueness of your character—her world of experience, his age, her personality. For instance, I recently tried to describe a refugee's first impression of the Pacific Ocean as she flew over it in a plane. The first image that came to my mind was "the water sparkled like diamonds." That phrasing is as fresh as the pocked summer squash in my fridge.

I needed to dive deeper into my character to find the appropriate simile. The refugee, Mai, had never seen diamonds in her fourteen-year-old life, much of which she had spent in a Thai refugee camp. What could she have possibly seen sparkle in a hot, filthy, overcrowded camp? My mind's eye toured the camp I had visited eight years ago, and found the perfect image: brand new corrugated metal. I then ditched *sparkled* (as used as my '84 Oldsmobile). I thought again of the simile I'd chosen, and wrote "rippled and shined like new metal roofing," to convey the roof's and the sea's similarity of movement, as well as appearance.

Stay true to your character's world of experience. Select standards of comparison he would know. A computer whiz's cat could purr like a hard drive. To a shortstop, Grandpa's skin could feel as scruffy as her glove.

Plot Situation: Your metaphors need to fit plot specifics as well. Let's take the color red. We're not going to use it now. Remember: no color labels. If your character sees an enemy wearing a red shirt, you could write: "Butch's shirt was the color of my baby brother's diaper rash." If your character sees a friend wearing a red shirt, you could try: "the color of my dog's tongue when he drops me the tennis ball for more more more." Same color. Two totally different impressions.

Switching Senses

We've all read of music (something you primarily hear) described in terms of color (something you see): bluesy, red hot jazz. Why not try the same? Reach for comparisons of two different senses: "His words scraped like tree bark," or, "The factory air stuck in my windpipe like a funeral procession."

Challenge your readers. Surprise them! But don't blind them with five images in one paragraph. As a brilliant gem needs a strong, yet unobtrusive setting, your image needs space to dazzle readers.

Action Verbs Describe

A university professor of mine once underlined nearly ninety verbs of being (is, was, were, etc.) in my seven-page paper. Ouch! She transformed me into a *Was* Cop. Relying on verbs of being indicates that you're telling instead of showing. Ditch the was's and adverbs and use onomatopoetic verbs—clatter, stomp, whip—and metaphoric verbs—steamroll, twist, fork.

Again, match these descriptive verbs to the uniqueness of your character and plot situation. And use these verbs in surprising ways. "Her mind forked: 'Should I or shouldn't I snatch that last piece of cheesecake?'" Yes!

Catch the Zone

Sometimes, I find that same *zone* top athletes talk about when they've scored forty points in a basketball champi-

STYLE

Switching Senses

A switched sense metaphor works best when you have few other images to compete with it. Its complexity needs room to settle, then resonate. Take each neutral phrase below and use the five senses to evoke different interpretations of the phrase.

■ **sight:**   Ellen's dress looked
   hearing:
   smell:
   touch:
   taste:

■ **sight:**   The clerk hunched
   hearing:
   smell:
   touch:
   taste:

■ **sight:**
   hearing: The dog's bark sounded
   smell:
   touch:
   taste:

■ **sight:**
   hearing:
   smell: Breakfast on the farm smelled
   touch:
   taste:

■ **sight:**
   hearing:
   smell:
   touch: The book felt
   taste:

■ **sight:**
   hearing:
   smell:
   touch:
   taste: The water tasted

onship. I see everything through metaphor-tinted lenses. My eyes, ears, nose, taste buds, fingertips transform every sensation into something else.

But don't wait for that zone to arrive. You must invite it. When you see an object, don't take the easy way out and label it with a color. Instead, say it's "the color of … " and imagine another object within the grasp of a child's world (depending on which age group you're writing for, of course). When you see an action, ask yourself "as if …?" or "the way …?" For example, "a leaf tumbling as if late for a train" conveys speed. The same leaf tumbling "as if out for a Sunday stroll" conveys the opposite. A child lowering his eyelids "the way petals sag after a storm" shows a burden. Lowering his eyelids "the way a tiger sinks before a pounce" shows mischief or malevolence.

Reach into your own experience, your own world of metaphor, to find these fresh images. What do you like to do? (Besides write, romance, and eat chocolate, I mean.) If you garden, make creative connections to the way slugs burrow into your tomatoes, the folds of your begonias, the texture of the caked mud you track into the kitchen. If you play the guitar, find your imagery in the frayed end of a broken string, the squeak of a tuning screw, the lingering vibration of a C chord (the furthest I got in lessons).

Feed your insatiable world of metaphor by attending symphonies, art exhibits, and live performances; trying new activities with your own or borrowed kids; and by reading the best literature, especially poetry.

Poetry uses more daring metaphor on more occasions than prose. Read poetry written for adults as well as for children. My favorite poets include Robert Frost, Seamus Heaney, Marilyn Nelson (Waniek), Alicia Ostriker, and Margaret Atwood for adults, Valerie Worth, Arnold Adolf, Doug Florian, and Myra Cohn Livingston for children.

In my "In and Out of Context" writing workshop, I use the following Valerie Worth analogy:

Roaming these
Furry prairies,
Daring every so
Often to stop
And sink a well
In the soft pink
Soil, hoping
To draw up a
Hasty drop, and
Drink and survive…
(from *Small Poems Again*)

In "Song for the Old Ones," Maya Angelou writes about her African-American "Fathers" sitting on park benches: "They nod like broken candles/all waxed and burnt profound." Can't you just see the bit of wick—neck—scarcely holding the two pieces of candle together? Can't you picture the men's raggy limbs dripping off them? The "burnt profound" not only refers to the color of the extinguished wick and the fathers' skins; it also evokes the depth to which the candle, hence the fathers, have shrunk, their flames having been diminished physically and spiritually.

Study how experts use metaphor to share creative energy with readers. Then sprint, drive, shop, kick back in your metaphor-tinted lenses, and you'll soon find yourself in the descriptive zone.

Editing and Revision

Anyone for Rigor?

By Donald R. Gordon

STYLE

Unbridled enthusiasm and an overactive mind can sabotage good writing. These qualities are blessings so far as ideas, energy, and inspiration at the front end of the writing process are concerned, but they interfere with the rigor you need to edit your prose and come up with an error-free manuscript that an editor will like.

Keep in mind always that editors get blamed for errors, omissions, and all other shortcomings that slip through into print. If you send in a manuscript containing such blemishes, you put yourself at serious risk.

Rigor is definitely the key. That's the way you can catch your mistakes before they do you damage. That's the way you can make sure that your mechanics of grammar, spelling, and punctuation are flawless. That's the way you can be sure that you have cov-ered all the bases so far as content and characters are concerned.

"I think rigor is essential to (1) being a good writer and producing good writing, and (2) getting published," notes writer Becky Bradway of Illinois State University. "Rigor is what makes us refine our work until it's the best it can possibly be and rigor is what makes us work on the business part of it until the piece sees print. It's craft, the part that pushes talent into something that's real and tangible."

So what do you do? How can you organize and discipline yourself to slog through repeated checks and dreary reviews of the kind needed to polish your prose to perfection?

Use a checklist, and reward yourself afterwards. Tick it off as you go, carefully and thoroughly, through a step-at-a-time review and revision.

Revision Checklist

■ **First Rereading: Central Substance**
 ❑ Content check: Is it credible, engaging, coherent?
 ❑ Character check: Are they worth caring about? Are they true to themselves?
 ❑ Dialogue/quotes check: Have I shown, not told? Does dialogue enrich the characters? Do quotes draw in the reader, arouse interest?
 ❑ Imagery check: Are images vivid, but appropriate?

■ **Second Rereading: Opening**
 ❑ Title check: Does it hint at the theme?
 ❑ Lead check: Does it plant questions in the readers' minds? Is it true to the theme?

■ **Third Rereading: Words**
 ❑ Spelling check.
 ❑ Typo check.
 ❑ Word choice check: Are there any instances where the word chosen could be improved, meaning clarified?

■ **Fourth Rereading: Sentences**
 ❑ Fragment check: Do all sentences have subjects and verbs? If fragments are being used for effect, are they necessary? Do they do the job well?
 ❑ Run-on check: Are the commas, semicolons, colons, conjunctives used in the right way?
 ❑ Verbiage check: Are there unnecessary phrases (in order to, there is…), empty words (things, a lot), or words used too often—like a verbal tick?

■ **Fifth Rereading: Punctuation**
 ❑ Punctuation check: commas, hyphens, exclamation points, question marks.

■ **Sixth Rereading:**
 ❑ Digressions check
 ❑ Unsubstantiated statement/motivation check
 ❑ Do you depend too much on rhetorical questions?

Here's one based on almost fifty years of trial and error and the encouragement provided by many successful sales:

1. Reread and Review

Read your manuscript carefully to check on content, character descriptions, and what you have *shown* (not told) in the form of quotes or dialogue, imagery and other literary touches.

Content has to be credible, engaging, coherent and carefully organized. So, look at your content and ask yourself these questions about it:

- Is it believable? Why?
- Does it catch a reader's attention and interest? How?
- Can it be understood? Prove it.
- Does it flow readily from one point to another?

Characters have to become real for your audience. Readers have to be persuaded to care about them and about what happens to them—positively or negatively. If readers do not care about the people in your prose, they will seldom care about your story or article.

Quotes or dialogue help moderate the nag-nag flavor of all *tell* writing. *Show* writing instead enriches character descriptions by demonstrating to readers how your people speak and think and what their personalities are like. They add to the impact and the reader's sense of involvement by allowing readers to go right into your prose to hear and sense for themselves.

Look at the vivid *images* and impressions you have in your own mind: If they are not vivid and dramatic in your own mind, make them so. List the ingredients that make them vivid and

real for you. Then make sure those ingredients are included in your prose—basics such as age-height-weight-dress-color-sex and so on; brief personal histories and backgrounds; striking traits, gestures, and mannerisms.

Imagery helps readers to relate what you are writing to experiences and circumstances they are familiar with. This helps them form clearer and more compelling images and impressions. This helps them understand what is going on in your prose. It helps them *feel* with your prose, too.

"Writing is like building fences to keep sheep penned in," Canadian author and teacher John Oughton notes. "Every time you leave a fence out, or down, you'll lose some of your sheep—your readers. A dangling modifier, errant commas, or unintended double entendres and you have lost some of them. They're no longer where you want them. One of the jobs of writing definitely is controlling ambiguity. When you want it, know how to create it. When you don't want it, know the conventions and implications and connotations stirred up."

Be aware of your other literary touches too. If you opt for dialect in dialogue, make sure it's there for a reason. If you use alliteration or rhyme or any other tool of the writing trade, make sure they serve definite purposes. Otherwise readers will be puzzled and distracted.

2. Open Well

Carefully check the combination of your title and opening paragraph, or lead, to make sure that it hints at the interesting basic theme of your short story or article. Make sure that it plants questions in readers' minds, questions that will persuade readers to go further into your prose to find answers.

Always refer your opening, and your writing in general, to two basic questions:

- What is this article or story really about?
- Why should a reader care?

Then use the answers to guide you to your best opening. For example, you might end up with answers like: "This is the story of a young woman who stands up to her stern father and marries her childhood sweetheart. Readers are interested in the drama of standing up to the father and in the excitement of the woman's new-found freedom."

Such answers, in turn, can help you find an opening along these lines:

Free At Last

Hannah knew she had to do something. If she didn't stand up to her father, she and Tom would never get married.

"Your first responsibility," thundered Silas Quincy, "is to me and your mother!"

Poet and Professor Katharine Coles of Westminster College in Salt Lake City, Utah, puts it this way: "As in dance, it's the disciplining of the body of a piece of writing that releases it into its dreams of movement and freedom. It is the ongoing disciplining of the mind of the writer that releases it into the dream out of which the individual work rises."

3. Avoid Unwanted Distraction

Read your manuscript again to catch spelling errors and typos. *This is very important.*

Editors hate spelling errors and typos because they slip past them into print much too easily. (And, it is the editors who usually get blamed when they do.) If editors spot even one such error, editors are presented with a terrible temptation: "I've got more than a dozen error-free manuscripts on that pile," they muse. "Why not turn to them instead?" Then, the only sound heard is the rustle of your prose as it lands on the reject pile.

"I try to be as accurate as I can," affirms writer Pat Valdata of the University of Delaware Parallel Program. "Nothing is more irritating to editors than being distracted by spelling and other technical errors. It's something I work hard to avoid in my books and articles. Reviewers note this with relief."

4. Remove Fragments and Run-ons

Read your manuscript a fourth time to ferret out sentence fragments and run-on sentences.

Sentence fragments are sentences that lack a subject or verb. Something like this, for example. Run-on sentences are those in which two or more sentences are bundled in together without colons or semicolons or any other indications that such bundling has occurred.

"Sentence fragments and run-on sentences are best avoided," concludes novelist Colin Morton, author of *Oceans Apart* (Quarry Press, 1995). "While sentence fragments are okay in dialogue—since people often speak that way—you risk condemnation for ignorance or laziness when you use them in regular prose. For their part, run-on sentences are simply tiring and confusing and usually too long."

Reread also for proper word choice and for unnecessary verbiage or words used as filler or too often. Use *infer* the right way, for example (it doesn't mean *to imply*), and cut out largely extraneous phrases like *in order to*. Be like Gustave Flaubert, most well known as the author of *Madame Bovary*, and weigh each word.

5. Punctuation Pointers

Read your manuscript a fifth time, slowly and deliberately, to check for missing commas and hyphens, incorrect dialogue punctuation, too many exclamation marks, and numbers that should be spelled out (usually, one to nine) or presented in figures (ten and up, except at the start of a sentence).

These are all too common errors that often wait until you get tired (or bored) before sneaking into your prose. In point of fact, they appear frequently enough to merit a separate check for each variety.

Be especially aware of problems with excessive exclamation marks. Most of the time, they make your prose look like the excited excesses of a teenager's diary.

6. Simple and Good

Read your manuscript a sixth and final time to discover and root out pointless digressions, fuzzy asides, unsubstantiated general statements, or assertions and instances where overwriting has kicked in.

Colette, the famous French writer, heartily supported this kind of checking: "An author is one who can judge his own stuff's worth, without pity, and destroy most of it." Somerset Maugham, saw it in these terms: "To write simply is as difficult as to be good."

7. In the End

Reward yourself for your efforts. You might allow yourself a coffee break, a walk in a park, a movie, lunch with a friend, or even a glass of something. Whatever your preference may be, indulge it. You've earned it.

Rigor may take extra time, but it is worth every second that you invest in it.

STYLE

REFERENCE & RESEARCH

Part
6

Photo Research

Detectives Nonpareil

By Carolyn Yoder

To be a photo researcher or not to be? That is the question. Full-time photo researchers work freelance or are affiliated part-time with magazines, book publishers, or stock picture agencies. But for some reason, the answer to the question can be agonizing for an individual interested in publishing.

Magazine and book editors and authors acknowledge that they are part-time picture researchers: Finding photographs is one of many tasks they perform! Many say that the responsibilities of photo researchers make for fun and exciting detective work.

Authors as Photo Researchers

Author Alexis O'Neill writes children's books and magazine articles, develops slide presentations for museums, and teaches in the UCLA Extension Writers' Program. For her, the search for photos has two levels.

The first is the simple identification of images that help illustrate an article or chapter. "When I'm doing research for an article, I'm always on the lookout for good illustrations. I photocopy any interesting photos, lithographs, maps, drawings, paintings, etc., and then immediately write the source directly on the photocopy. If I find the illustration in a secondary source—a textbook, for example—I note the picture's source as well as the book in which I found it. (Picture credits are usually lumped together in the front or back of the book. I'm very grateful when they are printed right beside the illustration.) I usually attach some samples with my article to give the editor some inspiration if the editor is the one who has to obtain permission for use."

The Makings of a Good Photo

How can the author or editor who is not a trained photographer or an expert in the field determine what is a good photograph—one that will also appeal to children? For Valerie Vogel, a freelance photographer and picture researcher, a good photo is editorially and stylistically appropriate. The image must have a strong design and meet certain technical criteria, including lighting, exposure, and focus. Also taken into consideration is how the photo is being used, whether as a cover of a book or magazine, a unit opener, or for inside use.

Elizabeth Lindstrom, Senior Editor of *Odyssey*, says, "Kids like many different images, especially images that include other kids and animals. I think bright color is important. Kids like gory images, but use of them has to be weighed very carefully with an editor's purpose. Challenging picture puzzles are also fun. But there are kids who like very technical images too. Photo houses are best for these because they use interesting angles." Lindstrom advises that "the best rule is, if you think kids will find an image boring, don't use it."

Author Alexis O'Neill agrees that kids like to see kids, people, and animals, and adds, "Kids like to enter the picture and be part of it, but they also like curiosities—magnifications, interesting angles, and strong designs."

Freelance picture researcher Francelle Carapetyan thinks you should throw the reader a curveball. "Don't be willing to accept what falls into your lap. Stretch the direction of the article. Offer something that might not be in the article."

If an editor or writer is trying to decide between a photograph or an illustration, O'Neill suggests that "photography allows the viewer to enter into a scene.
(continued on next page)

O'Neill also reflects on level one as it relates to the query. "Research is research. When I begin to investigate a topic, I gather bunches of information, visual and written. I throw photocopies, brochures, clippings, and notes into a folder. If, when I write the query, I feel a picture will visualize my idea better, I include it. It can't hurt. Most people like pictures. Editors are people. Therefore, I assume editors must appreciate some visuals in the slush pile."

For O'Neill, the second level of photo research is not much fun. It involves the dreaded paperwork! "If you are responsible for providing pictures for your article," says O'Neill, "then you have to track them down (still fun), find out what the usage fees are, get written permission to use the images, pay the fee, wait for the reproductions to arrive, and turn the pictures over to your editor. The process always takes much longer than you expect. You might also find a perfect picture that carries a huge price tag, so you have to settle for a less than ideal picture in its place."

On a Budget

Laurence Pringle, author of more than

The Makings of a Good Photo *continued*

Although more sophisticated folks know that a photographer can create reality (focusing on one dirty spot in a very tidy room) and set a tone through their images, the image still inspires awe: 'That's the way it really was.' When I look at historical photographs, I spend lots of time looking at faces and clothing and landscapes, thinking about lives and loves and places, wondering about all the unanswered questions they raise."

For Carapetyan, "magazines are now driven by the electronic media and are forced to be more action-packed. Photos are more 'real' than engravings and illustration." Vogel adds that "children today are more visually sophisticated and literate than ever before. They live in a world full of visual stimulation and are bombarded with images from television, movies, computers, and digitally enhanced material. Photographs offer children a sense of reality. The images capture their attention more immediately. Also, children relate to and identify with photos of children their own age. The value of illustrations is that they can portray fiction. Some capture subjects too complicated to photograph, too expensive to photograph, or too far from reality. But illustrations can give a more dated look to a product."

Lindstrom thinks that the most important aspects of illustration are age-appropriateness and a fresh look. In science, readers definitely prefer photos to illustration. She opts for computer-generated images for her science publication. But even when the illustration is superb, science readers definitely prefer the real thing—photos.

eighty children's books, almost always does all the photo research for his nonfiction books. That means he is responsible for obtaining prints, sometimes paying the print and reproduction fees, handling all of the paperwork.

"Sometimes the publisher allots a certain amount of money for photographs and the challenge is to come in under budget." Most nonfiction book contracts stipulate that authors provide photographs, or illustrations or cartoons. For his recent title, *Animal Monsters: The Truth About Scary Animals,* however, the publisher found and bought the rights for all the photographs. In a case like this, the nonfiction writer should make sure to review all photographs so mistakes are averted—make sure the bat depicted really is a vampire bat. According to Pringle, "even if magazine or book publishers have photo researchers, they appreciate the author getting the photographs or helping with research." Pringle adds that "publishers have rejected some of the photographs gathered because of quality and sometimes for editorial reasons. But, I have fought for certain photographs."

Among Pringle's photo research tips are to "pay attention to photographs by reading the photo/picture credits in books—you might discover new sources" and to "beware of the overused photograph." For some subjects, Pringle spends considerable time at the New York Public Library Picture Collection, where, he says, "You can actually check images out. But before you use them, try to find out if they are still under copyright. The library's collection is valuable for an artist who needs references for illustrations."

Pringle's work begins as he researches and writes a manuscript. He makes up an illustration and photograph hunt list. Organized by his manuscript page numbers, the list includes photographs and illustrations and their likely sources. Pringle uses many photos from state and federal government agencies whose archives are open to the public. His work has taken him to the Department of Defense; National Park Service; U.S. Forest Service, a division of the Department of Agriculture; the National Archives; NASA; and the Library of Congress.

Researcher and Editor: Through the Same Lens

Elizabeth Lindstrom, Senior Editor of the middle-school science magazine, *Odyssey*, and a former photojournalist, has tackled photo research on many levels. She first started working with a photo researcher, went on to do the research on her own, and now works directly with an associate editor who handles photo research.

Lindstrom, who is visually oriented, admits to placing equal importance on text and image, which represents a fact perhaps unknown to many readers and authors: editors are equally serious about editorial and design.

Lindstrom says, "I have for periods of time done all the photo research myself, but have found that even when I have a photo researcher, I spend at least six hours on each issue getting involved in the research and selection process. Photo research is hard work, but it is more fun than editing. It's sort of like detective work. You follow a trail that can lead to the ultimate image or to absolutely nothing. When you find the perfect cover shot, the reward is immediate."

When photo researchers and editors work together, says Lindstrom, "It's important for both the editor and the researcher to see the issue through the same focal lens. A researcher has to understand the subject matter of an issue and interpret its focus and tone through a selection of pictures with a minimum of direction from the editor. The most important quality a good researcher can have is persistence. Mediocre images are not acceptable. You have to go for the gold, especially when sprinting to find a cover shot. The bold, simple, colorful image that tells the story makes the best cover."

For editors and photo researchers, the author can play an active role in photo selection. O'Neill offers the following pep talk: "Start early, collect photocopies, document everything very clearly, and think 'words and images coming together.'" She points out that "not all magazines expect the au-

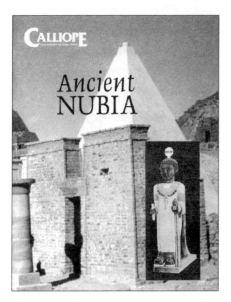

CALLIOPE

Ancient
NUBIA

thor to do picture research, but it helps if they do. In general, editors appreciate the suggestions, but ultimately they find the pictures that they think will work best."

O'Neill warns that "all parties need to be clear about responsibilities, quality, budgets, and timelines. In terms of book publishing, some fine nonfiction writing has been sunk for a picture-poor production. Too often, book publishers tie the picture allowance into the author's royalty advance instead of giving them a separate allowance, so essentially the author ends up footing the bill for illustrations, instead of the publisher. On one of my books, I worked with three art directors. (High turnover!) I submitted photos and slides along with each chapter. The art director chose the placement and wrote the captions—and didn't let me read galley proofs of the captions. Of course, a snowshoe label landed on cross-country skis and a reader faulted

me." One is reminded of Pringle and his bats.

When It's a Career

Francelle Carapetyan, now a freelance picture researcher, started her career at Cobblestone Publishing working on the magazines *Cobblestone, Calliope, Faces,* and *Odyssey* as a detective with difficult cases to solve. Photo research was part of the job for many at Cobblestone, not just one person's concern. Carapetyan's job was to improve the look of the magazines—jazz them up. "With an emphasis on the role of children and history, more photographs of children were encouraged," Carapetyan says. "The cover, the only four-color element, needed to say 'read me' and be eye-catching."

"For *Calliope,* a magazine devoted to ancient and world history, the aim of the cover was to show a contemporary action shot of an ancient subject. For *Faces,* a magazine about people around the world, we wanted a blend of old and new history—what, how, or why people did and do certain things. *Faces* offers more of an opportunity to juxtapose history and the contemporary."

In her search for picture clues—sources—and because of the focus of the magazines, Carapetyan's work led her to foreign photo sources. It helps that she came to the profession from a broad-based background: She speaks four languages, travels often, loves museums, and has a strong interest in art history. She has taught languages to undergraduates and for eleven years was a secondary schoolteacher.

Valerie Vogel, a freelance photographer and picture researcher, who stud-

REFERENCE

ied photography in California and started her career at a New York City picture agency, also comes to photo research with a valuable background. Vogel has photo research in her blood: Her mother is a photo researcher for Associated Press (AP).

As a photographer, Vogel knows how to take and compose a photograph. Work at the picture agency taught her how to edit photos, understand what makes a good photo, and determine what it takes to meet a client's needs. A picture researcher for more than eighteen years, Vogel specializes in children's publishing—textbooks, trade, and magazines. For her, the picture researcher knows where the collections are, is the detective who is given clues by the author and editor.

Taking the Pictures Yourself

For Carapetyan, an enormous number of the *Faces'* photographs come from the authors. "In regard to field work," she explains, the authors "sometimes were the only people studying the featured subject. Authors knew where the historical photos were because they were the experts in the field. They would write the captions. The ideal *Faces* photographer was trained as an anthropologist. With a 'sympathetic' eye, he was steeped in many cultures. The photographs have a sense of not being manufactured or posed, not slick travelogues."

Vogel relies on authors to provide accurate research. "It is a waste of time and money if authors don't help out." It is up to the picture researcher to take what the author has provided and come up with good resources.

For Pringle, the ideal situation is when the author handles photo research, reviews all photographs, and writes the captions. He recommends the author as photographer only when the author is serious, talented, and prolific enough to justify the cost of photographic equipment.

Lindstrom agrees that some authors are really helpful in finding or taking great images to illustrate their articles and activities. "I certainly use this option whenever I can, but only if I know an author will deliver high-quality material. A couple of authors come to mind who have developed into good photographers. They gather kids from the neighborhood and click away to illustrate activities, submitting the images in slide format with model releases and great captions."

Need to Know

Recognizing a good photo, and one that will add to the writing, is essential, but knowing about costs, collections, organizations, rights, and the latest technology is also important.

One misconception is that all great photos are costly. Photos from small museums, historical societies, government agencies, libraries, and archives can be inexpensive or free. Free photographs can be obtained from corporations (refer to the *Standard & Poor's Index*), chambers of commerce (especially for general themes), tourist boards, associations, universities, and organizations. But Vogel warns that "some free sources are diminishing. They are fighting cutbacks and layoffs and cannot offer fast turnarounds and top-quality photographs. Sometimes they adhere restrictions to the photographs. Sometimes their images are only available in black and white, an unattractive offer in this world of four-color images. And, sometimes, they are not the copyright holders." Some free images are in the public domain, but many carry copyrights.

Carapetyan spends time educating herself. She reads the *Christian Science Monitor* and the *Boston Globe* to review photography openings as well as the *Art Bulletin* (published by the College Art Association), *Art in America, Art-News, Civilization, Natural History, Smithsonian,* and *Doubletake* (Center for Documentary Studies at Duke University). She belongs to the American Society of Picture Professionals (ASPP), and the Educational Press of America (EDPress). While she currently works most on college textbooks, she still reads kids' magazines such as *Kids Discover, ZooBooks, Cricket, Muse,* and *Odyssey.*

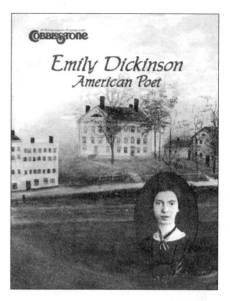

According to Vogel, "rates are based on what rights you would like to license. All of the following must be taken into account: the type of product, the size of the printed photograph, the printrun or circulation, distribution, the languages the product will be published in, the copyright date. Most likely you will be granted standard, one-time, North American rights."

The researcher must also consider liability; copyright is complicated but essential. A picture researcher must be detail-oriented. Certain original film can be valued at $1,500 to $2,000 each (replacement cost), so accurate record-keeping is essential. Many times, the picture researcher or author can negotiate each purchase. Some sources offer bulk rates. Right now, electronic rates for picture use vary widely. There has not been a rate structure guideline established industrywide, as there has been in the print media.

Photo researchers must also be

aware of the latest sources. Lindstrom notes that "the Web can be an excellent source for obtaining images, but the resolution of images and downloading can cause problems." As far as anticipated changes in photo research are concerned, Vogel states that the industry is currently in flux, due to electronic/digital transmission, use, and storage of images, whether downloading from online, or CD-ROM.

O'Neill is uneasy about the quality of images being downloaded. "The good part about locating photo sources online is that hard-to-reach collections are becoming more accessible. The bad part is that institutions and libraries do not have the resources or the staff to enter all their collections onto a website. Most likely, they will choose to put up their most popular images and those images will be used over and over again. It's the auxiliary photos—family, friends, pets, landscapes, etc.—that might not be found unless the researcher does some serious digging."

Sources for Photo Research

Organizations
- American Society of Media Photographers
  14 Washington Road, Suite 502, Princeton Junction, NJ 08550
  phone: 609-799-8300   *online:* info@asmp.org
- American Society of Picture Professionals
  2025 Pennsylvania Avenue, Washington, DC 20006
  phone: 202-955-5578   *online:* www.aspp.com
- Picture Agency Council of America (PACA)
  phone: 1-800-457-PACA (7222)
  fax: 507-645-7066   *online:* www.pacaoffice.org
- Special Libraries Association
  1700 Eighteenth Street, N.W., Washington , DC 20009-2514
  phone: 202-234-4700

Books, Directories, Pamphlets, Magazines
- *American Library Association Guide to Information Access: A Complete Research Handbook and Directory*
  Sandy Whiteley, Random House
- *American Library Directory*
  R.R. Bowker, Reed Elsevier, New York
- *Art in America Annual Guide to Galleries, Museums, Artists*
  Brant Art Publications, New York
  phone: 212-941-0981
- *Blue Book, The Directory of Geographic, Travel, and Destination Stock Photography*
  Green Book, The Directory of Natural History and General Stock Photography
  A.G. Editions, New York
  phone: 212-929-0959   *fax:* 212-924-4796   *online:*www.ag-editions.com
- *Dictionary of American Portraits.*
  Hayward Cirker and Blanche Cirker, Dover Publications
- *Directory of Archives and Manuscripts Repositories in the United States,* 2nd ed.
  National Historical Publications and Records Commission, The Oryx Press, Phoenix, AZ (out of print, but may be available at your local library)
- *Directory of Historical Organizations in the United States and Canada*
  Mary Bray Wheeler, Editor, American Association for State and Local History
  (out of print, but may be available at your local library)
- *DoubleTake*
  P.O. Box 56070, Boulder, CO 80322-6070   *phone:* 1-800-234-0981, ext. 5705

(continued on next page)

REFERENCE

Sources for Photo Research *continued*

- *Finding Images Online*
  Pamela Berinstein, Pemberton Press, Wilton, CT 06897
- *Foundation Directory*
  Michael N. Tuller, Editor, The Foundation Center, New York
- *Gale Encyclopedia of Associations*
  Gale Research, Detroit
  phone: 1-800-347-4253
- *Illustration Index IV–Illustration Index VII*, 4th ed.
  Marsha C. Appel, Scarecrow Press, Lanham, MD
  phone: 301-459-3366
- *Image Directory (Online Visual Image Bank)*
  Academic Press, San Diego, CA 92101
  online: www.imagedir.com
- *Index to American Photographic Collections*, 3rd ed.
  Andrew H. Eskind, Editor, G.K. Hall
- *International Directory of the Arts*
  R.R. Bowker, Reed Elsevier, New York
  phone: 1-800-521-8110
- *Literary Market Place (LMP)* and *International Literary Market Place (ILMP)*
  R.R. Bowker, Reed Elsevier, New York
- *Men: A Pictorial Archive from Nineteenth-Century Sources* and *Women: A Pictorial Archive from Nineteenth-Century Sources*
  Jim Harter, Dover Publications, Mineola, NY (copyright-free illustrations)
- *The Metropolitan Museum of Art Guide*
  The Metropolitan Museum of Art, New York
- *Museums of the World*
  R.R. Bowker, Reed Elsevier, New York
- *The New York Public Library Book of How and Where to Look It Up*, revised
  Sherwood Harris, Editor, Macmillan Publishing
- *The Official Museum Directory*
  R.R. Bowker, Reed Elsevier, New York
- *Photographer's Market 1998*
  Michael Willins, Editor, Writers Digest Books, Cincinnati, OH
- *Photography Index: A Guide to Reproductions*
  Pamela Jeffcott Parry, Greenwood Press, Westport, CT

(continued on next page)

Sources for Photo Research *continued*

- *Picture Agency Council of America Directory, 1997*
  PACA, P.O. Box 308, Northfield, MN 55057-0308
  phone: 1-800-457-PACA (7222)   *online:* www.pacaoffice.org
- *Picture Researcher's Handbook: An International Guide to Picture Sources and How to Use Them,* 6th ed.
  Hilary Evans and Mary Evans, Routledge, London, New York
- *Picture Sources,* 4th ed.
  Ernest H. Robl, Editor, Special Libraries Association, New York
- *Practical Picture Research: A Guide to Current Practice, Procedure, Techniques and Resources*
  Hilary Evans, Routledge, London, New York
- *Stock Photo Deskbook*
  The Exeter Company, 767 Winthrop Road, Teaneck, NJ 07666
  phone: 201-692-1743   *online:* www.stockphotodeskbook.com
- *Subject Collections,* 7th ed., 2 vols.
  Lee Ash and William G. Miller, compilers, R.R. Bowker, Reed Elsevier, New York
- *World Chamber of Commerce Directory*
  Jan Pierce, Editor, World Chamber of Commerce Directory
- *World Guide to Special Libraries*
  R.R. Bowker, Reed Elsevier, New York

Library of Congress
  Washington, DC 20540
  online: www.lcweb.loc.gov/homepage/lc
- *The National Union Catalog of Manuscript Collections*
- *Prints and Photographs: An Illustrated Guide,* Bernard F. Reilly, Jr.
- *European Collections: An Illustrated Guide*

National Archives
  National Archives and Records Administration (NARA)
  Washington, DC 20408
  phone: 202-501-5455
- *The American Image: Photographs from the National Archives, 1860-1960*
  Pantheon Books, NY
- *Guide to the Holdings of the Still Picture Branch of the National Archives*
  Compiled by Barbara L. Burger

(continued on next page)

REFERENCE

Sources for Photo Research *continued*

- *The National Archives of the United States*
  Abrams, New York
- *War and Conflict: Selected Images from the National Archives, 1765-1970*

CD-ROMS
- *Associations Unlimited: A CD-ROM from Gale Research*
  Mary Allen Bates, Gale Research, Detroit, MI
  phone: 1-800-347-4253
- *Publishing Market Place Reference Plus*
  R.R. Bowker, Reed Elsevier, New York

Collections/Stock Agencies
- Archive Photos
  530 West 25th Street, New York, NY 10001
  phone: 1-800-688-5656   *online:* archivephotos.com
- Archives of American Art
  Balcony 331, Eighth and F Streets, N.W., Washington, DC 20560
  phone: 202-357-2781
- Art Resource
  65 Bleeker Street, New York, NY 10012
  phone: 212-505-8700   *online:* www.artres.com
- ArchivesUSA
  Chadwyck-Healey, Suite 380, 1101 King Street, Alexandria, VA 22314
  (research purposes)
  phone: 1-800-752-0515   *online:* www.chadwyck.com
- The Associated Press (AP)
  50 Rockefeller Plaza, New York, NY 10020
  phone: 212-621-1500
- Brown Brothers
  P.O. Box 50, Sterling, PA 18463
  phone: 717-689-9688   *online:* www.brownbrothersusa.com
- Center for the Humanities, The Miriam and Ira D. Wallach Division of Art,
  Prints, and Photographs
  Photography Collection, Room 308, The New York Public Library, Fifth Avenue
  and 42nd Street, New York, NY 10018
  phone: 212-930-0837
  (continued on next page)

Sources for Photo Research *continued*

- Comstock
  30 Irving Place, New York, NY 10003
  phone: 1-800-225-2727
- Corbis/Bettmann
  902 Broadway, New York, NY 10010
  phone: 212-777-6200
- Corbis Corporation
  15395 SE 30th Place, Suite 300, Bellevue, WA 98007
  phone: 206-649-3363
- Culver Pictures
  150 W. 22nd Street, New York, NY 10011
- George Eastman House/International Museum of Photography and Film
  Photography Collection
  900 East Avenue, Rochester, NY 14607
  phone: 716-271-3361   *online:* www.eastman.org
- The Getty Information Institute
  401 Wilshire Boulevard, Suite 1100, Santa Monica, CA 90401
  online: www.gii.getty.edu
- The Image Bank
  2777 Stemmons Freeway, Suite 600, Dallas, TX 75207
  phone: 214-863-4900
- The Image Works
  P.O. Box 443, Woodstock, NY 12498
  phone: 1-800-475-8801   *online:* www.theimageworks.com
- Liaison International
  11 East 26th Street, New York, NY 10010
  phone: 1-800-488-0484   *online:* www.liaisonintl.com
- The Museum of Modern Art, Film Stills Archive
  11 West 53rd Street, New York, NY 10019
  phone: 212-708-9830   *online:* www.moma.org/filmvideo.html
- NASA Photo Gallery/NASA Image Exchange
  online: www.nasa.gov/gallery/photo/index.html
- Northwind Picture Archives
  165 Federal Street, Alfred, ME 04002
  phone: 1-800-952-0703

(continued on next page)

REFERENCE

Sources for Photo Research *continued*

- Photo Researchers
  60 East 56th Street, 6th floor, New York, NY 10022
  phone: 1-800-833-9033
- Prints and Photographs Division
  Library of Congress, Washington, DC 20540
  online: www.lcweb.loc.gov/homepage/lc
- Schomburg Center for Research in Black Culture
  515 Malcolm X Boulevard, New York, NY 10037
  phone: 212-491-2200
- Smithsonian's Office of Printing and Photographic Services
  Smithsonian Institution, Washington, DC 20560
- Tony Stone Images
  122 S. Michigan Avenue, Suite 900, Chicago, IL 60302
  1-800-234-7880
- United Press International (UPI)
  1510 H Street, N.W., Washington, DC 20005
  phone: 202-898-8000   *online:* www.upi.com
- Visuals Unlimited
  P.O. Box 10246, Swanzey, NH 03446-0246
  phone: 603-352-6436   *online:* visualsunlimited@top.monad.net

Interviews

An Expert Voice to Bring Nonfiction to Life

By Elaine Marie Alphin

Nonfiction research once meant time in the library reading encyclopedias, reference books, and dipping cautiously into periodicals and professional journals. Then the first writers to navigate the growing Internet discovered access to a vast cyberspace reference "library." As more writers learned to be good researchers, however, so did students. Kids now surf the Web in search of information for school assignments. If a writer uses the same sources kids use, a youngster probably won't want to read a rewritten simplification—and an editor won't want to publish it.

To give readers more than they can find for themselves, you need to go beyond what someone else has written. You need to get in touch with someone who's living your topic: You need to speak with an expert in the field. "Many authors get notes back from editors that say, 'This is a good topic, but there's no life here,' or 'We really don't get to know this person,' or 'The piece lacks focus'," says Andy Boyles, Science Editor at *Highlights for Children*. "One way to satisfy those criteria is to talk to someone."

Writers often shy away from hands-on research. They don't know any experts. Where could they find someone to interview? Perhaps they feel shy about approaching a complete stranger to ask for time to explain their specialty for a children's article. A struggling writer may even feel inadequate to speak with a successful scientist or artist or athlete. It's true that some professionals are too busy to give interviews, but most enjoy talking about their work, and like the idea of having kids read about them and admire their accomplishments.

REFERENCE

Experts Online

If you know the expert you're looking for, but don't know how to contact them, online research can help you click your way to their doorstep.

Contacting a Designated Expert

Research may show that your expert teaches at Pomona College. Go to a listing of American universities at www.clas.ufl.edu/CLAS/american-universities.html and find Pomona College. Click on it, and you'll be transported to their web page. From there, go to the listing of faculty and staff and search for the expert's name by department. You'll find a phone number and, most often, an e-mail address and a postal address. Send them an e-mail or a letter requesting the interview.

If your expert is farther away, say, teaching at Oxford University in England, the Web stretches wide enough to find him. Go to a listing of international universities at: www.mit.edu:8001/people/cdemello/univ.html and click on Oxford. If your expert is affiliated with a museum, you could track him down by getting a listing of museums at: www.icom.org/vlmp/index.html*museums and clicking on the appropriate museum to jump to its web page.

Locating an Expert

Sometimes you don't know the name of an expert to contact, and are searching for someone in a particular field. A good way to locate an interview source is to join an electronic newsgroup or mailing list. See the sidebar, Mailing List and Newsgroup Websites, page 220, which lists URLs (Uniform Resource Locator) addresses, to help you find one in your field. There's no charge for an electronic subscription; mailings from the group will automatically be deposited in your electronic mailbox. Read the postings for a few weeks, and you'll probably see one or two people who are

(continued on next page)

Fred Bortz, author of five books and more than forty magazine articles, finds inspiration for children's nonfiction in science books he reviews for adults and in scientific talks he hears. "I see an angle I like, and turn it around to write it for kids," he explains. "The theme and angle is right for kids, but it wasn't aimed at kids originally. I say, 'Hey, I can do that!'"

Hearing an expert speak gives you a good opportunity to introduce yourself and ask if you might get in touch later about an interview. Usually, however, you want to find an expert for a topic you've read about. You can write the article without interviewing, but chances are you'll get the manuscript back. If it shows enough promise, the editor may specifically ask for an interview. According to John D. Allen, Associate Editor of *Cricket*, "It works out sometimes to send things back and ask authors to research more deeply. In that situation,

Experts Online *continued*

articulate, explain things well, and look like good candidates. Members of professional mailing lists and newsgroups usually sign their posts with their academic or professional titles, so you have an idea of who you are considering, and you can e-mail them a request for an interview. Universities provide students with academic accounts, however, so check the academic faculty listing to be sure that this "professor" exists, and when you carry out the interview, phone the department and ask to be put through to the professor, to be sure that a student or teaching assistant isn't borrowing someone's identity online.

Engineering a Search

In case your research and your online eavesdropping fails to connect you with the right expert, don't give up. Try a search engine. The main ones are listed in the article in this section, "The Tools You Need to Find What You Want," page 235.

Suppose you're looking for an expert on architecture. You can type in *architecture* to start with and search—but chances are you'll get far too many listings. Narrow your field by using the topics provided. For example, in Yahoo you might scroll down to arts and humanities, then choose architecture. From there you could jump to architects, and from there choose commercial firms or personal exhibits and click on web pages with phone, fax, or e-mail connections.

If you draw a complete blank, you can always search for a recommendation. Go to: www.askanexpert.com/ and enter your topic or search by categories. This URL provides links to web pages where you can ask an expert any question—but be sure to do the background research to ensure that your "expert" is really an expert! Another source is ProfNet at: www.profnet.com/.

This search engine allows you to send questions to nearly 4,000 public information officers around the world.

REFERENCE

---

the manuscript is something shy of a complete article. With a little extra direction, the authors can find what they need in a particular spot to flesh out the article."

What they need is personal input from someone in the field. According to Boyles, "The things you get from an interview that you can't get from book research are direct quotations, lively anecdotes, firsthand impressions, and some insight into the subject that may not come through in other venues; in other words, an entryway into the article, something that will crystallize your focus."

"This can be much more important in magazine writing than in books," Melissa Stewart, Senior Science Editor at Grolier, points out. "Most books don't have direct quotes unless we're trying to get very current information, as discoveries are being made. In some series, of course, interviews are essential. Our series, To the Young..., consists entirely of interviews with professionals in certain fields, and a social studies series consists of diary entries from historical periods."

Stewart notes that "interviews are important and a good research source, but it doesn't mean that a writer has to use direct quotes in a book." Whether to do so or not is somewhat dependent on the age for which you're writing. "We almost never use direct quotes for younger kids," Stewart explains. "At the young adult level, however, it can be nice to throw in a few quotes to get the flavor of the topic."

Finding the Elusive Expert

The first challenge is finding an expert to interview. "In some cases," says Bortz, "I know enough about the field that I can identify a whole bunch of potential experts. In that case, the hard part is trying to deduce who's going to be a good interview. If they've tried to write for the popular market, it shows their willingness to get away from the stereotypical test tube and talk to people."

Mailing List and Newsgroup Websites

These URLs will link you to directories of mailing lists and newsgroups in fields ranging from agriculture and the arts to sports, politics, science, and even writing, and give you instructions for subscribing.

- America Online's Mailing List Directory
  www.idot.aol.com/mld/production/mld-master-index.html
  For AOL members: Keyword: Mailing Lists
- Directory of Scholarly and Professional E-Conference
  n2h2.com/KOVACS/
- Lists Available as Newsgroups
  info.lib.uh.edu/liblists/newsgrp.htm
- The List Server Page
  www.cuc.edu/cgi-bin/listservform.pl
- Liszt: Directory of E-Mail Discussion Groups
  www.lizst.com/
- Mailing Lists
  lc.ust.hk/maillist.html
- Newsgroups Available Under Bit.Listserv
  drake.ee.washington.edu/news/bit.listserv.html
- Post Office Central
  ourworld.compuserve.com/homepages/djessop
  For CompuServe members: inettforum

If you don't know anyone in the field, a recommendation from a friend can help. For example, Bortz was looking for a scientist to interview about the chemistry of buckminsterfullerene (buckyballs) and related molecules for *To the Young Scientist*. He heard from a former colleague that Richard Smalley of Rice University was very forthcoming when he spoke to college undergraduates. "Based on that," explains Bortz, "I knew going in that he would understand enough about my audience that he would give the right balance between the technical details and the human side."

Writers can also turn to the Internet for help. (See the sidebars on online research and on websites for ideas to start your search.) Bortz also recommends putting a posting on an Internet bulletin board asking readers, "Who would you like to interview?" and "What would you like to ask them?" He explains, "Obviously, if you have friends, you ask them, and these days your friends are on the Internet." But not just any expert will do. "I always have some criteria in mind when I do the search," Bortz says. "It's not just that the science is good and interesting, but also that the subject is human and genuine."

Boyles agrees that it is important to get input on potential interview subjects. "If you want to write about science," he advises, "you need to develop a cadre of friends who are willing to accept a phone call, some confidants who will help you find your way when you're trying to decide whether or not this is a topic to pursue."

There are also book sources, such as *Who's Who* directories, that will help you locate an expert. *Dial-An-Expert, The National Directory of Quotable Experts*, by Marc McCutcheon, comes out with a new edition annually. One advantage of this source is that the professionals listed have agreed to be included, which means they're willing to be interviewed.

Sometimes your reading points you toward a specific interview source from the beginning, but that individual doesn't respond or simply refuses an interview. "Sometimes it would just kill an article if you can't reach a person," Bortz admits. "It goes into your file of good ideas that just didn't quite work."

Or the person you originally wanted to interview may have another idea. "I really wanted to interview one scientist who courteously said no," Bortz recalls. "But he also said he was no longer active in the field and recommended another scientist. I was disappointed, but the contact he recommended turned out to be exactly right. You just have to be prepared to redirect. You have to know what your goals are so you can understand when redirection will be appropriate."

If you've worked with an editor before and the article is an assignment, the editor may well suggest an interview source. But watch out for sending a proposal to an editor who doesn't know you, and asking for a recommendation for a source.

"When a person sets out to write an article," says Allen, "they should have a strong enough interest and background in the topic to know who they're looking for. If a person came and asked me, 'Whom should I inter-

Phone, Online or In Person?

Once you're ready to do the interview, you have to decide whether to do it from a distance or up close. E-mailing questions and receiving answers can work for distant subjects (given the time difference, it could be awkward to interview someone in China otherwise), but e-mail replies tend to be stilted. Phone interviews work better if you can't travel to meet with your subject. "It's always better to do it in person," advises science writer Fred Bortz. "You see the person in the work environment and can talk to other people associated with your main interview. In a phone interview, you aim for thirty to forty-five minutes, an hour at the most. In person, you start at an hour and go from there."

The real issue, however, is the added expense of a face-to-face interview. "For an article, it's not really justified," Bortz admits. "The questions are much more focused on a single topic—you try to ask questions that have the interviewee talk a lot. In a magazine interview, I have them talking to me and I reinterpret. In a book interview, those questions are still the heart, but I can set them up with shorter questions to get them thinking more along the lines of what my audience might want—they're talking to the kids themselves. It gives them a chance to size you up and connect themselves more directly to your readers and not see you as an intermediary."

view?' it would make me think they really hadn't done much work. If you send me a strong article that is missing an aspect, I may well suggest an interview and recommend a source if I can, but that's different than coming to me in the beginning and asking for a source."

Preparing for the Interview

Once you zero in on your topic and select an expert, it's time to plan how you intend to conduct the interview. This is where techniques diverge. There are as many ways to run a successful interview as there are writers. Most interviewers believe that it's important to refine your work and become familiar with the topic before you contact any potential interview subject, but not all.

"Some writers advocate going in cold, open as a babe," says Boyles. While this can certainly make the interviewer more receptive to the wonder of the subject, Boyles cautions, "It's easy to miss important ideas because you're trying to understand the basics. They're trying to talk about Shakespeare, and you're still on the ABCs."

Instead, Boyles advocates researching the individual you plan to interview, as well as the subject matter and terminology, in advance. "If you're serious about presenting yourself as a professional, you need to have a good handle on the topic before you go in," he says, and points out that you need to go beyond an introduction in the encyclopedia. "Ask them to have someone on their staff give you references to some of their recent papers, and read them."

Writers also have different views on how to contact the source to schedule the interview. Some like to phone the subject as their first contact. This lets you explain in person what you plan to do in this article and why you want to interview them. Particularly if your enthusiasm spills over into your voice, this can make a good impression and sway a decision toward giving you the interview: Many people are susceptible to impulse buys.

Bortz warns, however, "On the phone they may say, 'Oh, no, not another interview.' I prefer to contact them in writing with some details about the project and give them time to reflect." He points out, "The hard thing is knowing whether or not you've actually reached them, and how long to wait. You must pursue them courteously. When you follow up, you hope to get their secretary because you don't want to interrupt them at work." It's important to remember that experts are busy people. You have to impress them with your professionalism, and be willing to work around their schedule.

If an editor has assigned the article, it's easier for the writer to show the expert that this is worth the investment of time. Most articles, however, are written on speculation. "*Muse,* our newest magazine, does commission articles," says Allen, "so they give people what documentation they need to pursue interviews. We don't commission articles at *Cricket,* but occasionally we give a writer a letter of interest to show the interviewee. We have to be careful about this, because we don't want to mislead the author into thinking that it's an acceptance of the piece in advance. If it doesn't get published, things can get ugly."

Not only the author can suffer from an interview-based article that doesn't pan out. Boyles says, "I'm reluctant to give a firm go-ahead to a beginning author. Experts control the interviews they give because they hold their time to be valuable. The same person won't want to grant multiple interviews for the same magazine, so *Highlights* has something at stake." If the first article doesn't work out and the author said it was a definite piece for a specific magazine, another writer may have trouble interviewing the expert by saying the piece is aimed for the same magazine. The writer should always be honest with the subject by making it clear whether the piece is an assignment or on spec. That honesty is the first step in establishing a relationship that will lead to a successful interview.

Connecting with the Subject

"You need to earn the subject's trust for this sort of 'one-hour friendship' by recognizing where the subject is coming from," says Boyles. "You're each doing something for each other. You're getting an article; they have to get something too."

Often, the subject is happy to get a willing listener. This is where your advance re-

search in the field pays off. "A scientist goes to picnics or family reunions," explains Boyles, "and can't talk to people. They ask him what he does, he tries to tell them, and their eyes glaze over. He has maybe three friends in the world who understand what he's saying. If you can make yourself that fourth friend for an hour, you can have a great interview."

Once you've made that connection with your subject, you get them talking. You should have an idea of the direction you would like to take with the article before you start, and should prepare a list of questions that will focus your subject on the aspect of the topic that interests you.

One of the most important factors in making a connection with your subject, says Bortz, "is having a well-designed interview protocol when you go in, but knowing when to deviate based on what they say. Being able to make that decision on the fly is a very important skill." It's a good idea to have those questions prepared before you phone or write, to make the initial contact to schedule the interview. Often you'll catch the subject at just the right moment, and they'll suggest doing it immediately, rather than scheduling it for later.

After the Interview

When transcribing quotes from the interview, you're faced with two concerns. The first is the question of accuracy: Just because your expert said it doesn't make it true.

"I'm a scientist," Bortz says. "You always have to look at your evidence

Take Notes or Tape-Record?

Some writers like to take notes during the interview, while others opt for tape-recording. The advantage to taking notes is that it takes longer to write the quotes than the instantaneous recording of a machine. People are uncomfortable with silence, and often the subject will inject comments into the silence that prove wonderfully illuminating.

The disadvantage, of course, is the danger of missing something. That can also be a disadvantage of relying on technology, however. A bad tape or a recorder that's low on batteries can leave you without a record of your interview, so doublecheck. Despite the risks, science writer Fred Bortz advises taping. "You can be so focused on getting the words down on paper that you miss the meaning. I can't get all the nuances of the conversation if I take notes, and to me the essence is often in the nuances. So I take the somewhat risky step of relying on technology for the words while I make notes and listen for the nuances. I use two tapes of different lengths so I don't become so entranced in the interview that the tape runs out and I have to ask the person to repeat. There's also the possibility that words can be garbled on tape; the second tape may be clearer."

with a healthy skepticism. It's not that I don't trust them, but people don't always remember things perfectly. If there's a significant fact, I'll doublecheck. If there's anything that sends up a red flag, I'll follow it up."

Allen agrees. "If an expert tells the author anything that conflicts with what the author thinks he knows, the author might check with a third source to be sure he understood the interviewee originally, and also to be sure that the interviewee hasn't made a mistake."

This doesn't mean that a writer must get multiple confirmations for commonly accepted facts. "For most children's articles, people aren't really getting into a contested spot," Allen points out. "One interview may be enough, depending on how deeply the topic is explored or whether it's on the cutting edge." Boyles adds, "You're also working with your editor, and the editor should have a sense of whether a new development is going to be upsetting apple carts."

The second concern is how the subject sounds. "People tend to hem and haw," warns Stewart. "They're not always articulate, and we emphasize proper English in our books for young people." Allen agrees. "You want your authorities to speak grammatically, which people do not. You want your quotes to sound as polished as the rest of the article. If they're not, it makes the expert look like less of an authority."

Boyles adds, "Writers can leave out the ahs and the stammering. That's just making the subject sound good. Who could complain? You get into trouble when you've misunderstood something. A subject may give you the same idea three times, and say the first part clearly once, the end clearly later on, and the middle most clearly the third time. You go through the interview and put the parts together so they read smoothly. That's fine as long as you don't violate the spirit of what they were trying to say, so it's a good idea to call back and read such quotes aloud, or fax so they can read their quotes." This practice is called "cooking the quotes," and writers must be careful to fact-check any changes with the subject, because misrepresenting what the subject says and putting wrong ideas into his mouth will spoil a good writer-subject relationship and could even leave the writer open to libel.

Some editors who are used to the newspaper business might disagree with checking the quotes with the source. But very few interviews for children's magazines lead to dramatic exposés that the interviewee would be unwilling to confirm. "It's very important to get back to the source to check the quotes," says Allen. "You don't want to leave the interviewee with the feeling that the author is out to take advantage of them. The author should want to represent the subject accurately."

After finishing the article, be sure to thank your subject for giving you their time. Most writers send a copy of the published piece to their source, or ask their publisher to do so. "I almost always try to follow up," says Bortz, "especially if they've given me an indication they care about seeing it. In fact, I'd be disappointed if they didn't. I guess I'd think I'd found the wrong person." Following through on a successful interview lays the groundwork for you to return to that subject for a related interview in the future, or to ask their help in referring you to a good source for an article about a different topic.

Well Worth the Work

Interviews do take considerable effort. "Interviews are more work than spending hours reading," Allen admits, "and it's hard because you have to find the person and break through the ice. Probably for this reason, interviews are the one thing in nonfiction that aren't done enough. Book research is wonderful, but finding an authority to interview is what elevates a common article to an exceptional one."

Exceptional articles and books sell—the next time you get a quirky nonfiction idea with sure-fire kid appeal, bring it to life by augmenting your research with an expert interview. In addition to making a friend who'll enhance your enthusiasm for your topic, you'll increase your chances of seeing your work in print.

Research

Steps on the Research Road

By Joan Broerman

Who said death and taxes are the only sure things in life? Mark Twain or Will Rogers? To find out takes research. Writers add research to that list of sure things. Whether you write books, magazine stories or articles, fiction or nonfiction, for toddlers, teens, or adults, expect to hear "How do you know?" from a thorough editor, a vigilant librarian or teacher, a sharp-eyed reviewer, or a savvy young reader. If you've researched well and documented carefully, you will have an answer.

Editor Karen Grove, of Harcourt Brace, says the smallest inaccuracy in one writer's work erodes the reader's confidence in both writer and publisher and could impact other writers at a house. "Anything that comes into question reflects on everybody. At Harcourt Brace we want to keep the best interest of all writers under our umbrella in mind."

Under such pressure to be accurate, how can a writer create? Author Eve Bunting recommends, "Be yourself. That's the only way you can be anyhow. Find the system that works for you." Begin by finding what you care about. Bunting, who has sold 167 books for young people, advises: "Love the subject before you write about it. You won't work up to your potential if you don't."

Step Out

Research begins with an identification of a subject that interests you. Your own attic might be a good place to start. Letters, diaries, and journals are primary material prized by historians and biographers. Read voraciously to find ideas. Natalie Bober, a biographer, urges writers to read the sources and find a focus. "Find something you can relate to your own passion." She quotes one of her subjects, Robert Frost: "No tears in the writer, no tears in the reader." Or take a notebook on vacation. Bunting visits historical museums whether she intends to write about the particular area or not. Who knows what ideas will find her?

The critical link of research and true interest exists for writers of both fiction and nonfiction. "You have to have passion or your work will be as dry as the history book. What will stoke the fire?" asks Han Nolan. Nolan's young adult novel, *Dancing on the Edge*, received the latest National Book Award; her *Send Me Down a Miracle* was nominated the preceding year. Writer Sandra Markle considers herself an information detective who loves science. In following leads on the latest scientific discoveries, she finds and welcomes new topics as a fresh chance to do detective work.

While editors and writers uniformly warn that writing directed solely at filling a market niche usually fails, publishers' catalogues offer ideas, too. Nonfiction educational publishers offer series that provide a framework in which a writer may be inspired to expand or create. What series have piqued your interest? What ideas does an existing line of books bring to mind?

Reference books, for adults and children, can also be of use before you're actually looking up details and facts, too. (Use the Idea Generation section of this *Children's Writer Guide to 1998*,

How One Writer Keeps Track

For sorting and stacking, writers use a variety of containers from color coordinated tubs and labeled boxes to filing cabinets filled with color-coded folders. Index cards of all sizes are popular, but the three-by-five-inch cards fit a standard shoe box. Whatever the method, a writer must be able to return to references and back-up facts. Other writers are sophisticated enough technologically to use databases or other computer resources.

Tracy Barrett uses three-by-five cards in white and colors. For example, when she wrote her book on Nat Turner, she had heading cards on "Background," "Who is Nat Turner," and "Conditions in Virginia." All the heading cards were the same color, pink, and eventually denoted the beginning of chapters. Her subheadings were blue. She wrote facts on white cards (one fact per page!) and filed the white data cards behind her pink heading and blue subheading cards. As the file grew, she could see whether her chapters were about the same length. She also identified subheadings within her larger subheadings. "The outline almost wrote itself." For her bibliography, Barrett keyed her cards to a list of sources. She numbered the first Source #1 and put that number on her data card along with the page number in the source. On a separate sheet, she listed information about Source #1: title, author, library, even the section of the library. She alphabetized her bibliography later.

Snares to Beware

■ **Invented Dialogue**
Natalie Bober, author of *Abigail Adams, Witness to a Revolution,* winner of the 1995
Golden Kite for nonfiction, says the biographer must not invent dialogue. The words
of her subjects come from primary material: letters, diaries, journals, manuscripts,
and (living subjects) direct quotes.

■ **Words Before Their Time**
The fiction writer must also watch what characters say. Were the words a character
speaks used during the time she lived? Could a Civil War era character invite friends
to a picnic? Cheryl Zach, author of a young adult romance series set during the
1860s, depends on a recent edition of *Webster's Collegiate Dictionary* to be sure.
The *Oxford English Dictionary* is another source for the history and origin of words
and is found in most public libraries. Figurative speech must also be matched with
the right time period.

■ **Misplaced Value Systems**
Harcourt Brace Editor Karen Grove warns writers to avoid imposing the value
systems of one period on another.

---

and the listing of annotated references, to spark thoughts, find information, and brainstorm.)

Paths Taken
Once inspired about their subjects, writers take different research paths, but often tread in the same general direction.

Tracy Barrett, who has written about events as well as people, looks first for a general book on the period or topic she has selected, to help her set up a framework. What are the important events, facts, qualities? Next, she makes a rough outline of how to approach her subject, but even as she skims and roughs out, Barrett looks for first-person anecdotes to add important dimension and detail.

"Skim, outline, concentrate," says Jo Kittinger, a science writer. Her routine is to read until an outline takes shape in her mind. Then she takes the broad reading she has done and begins to concentrate her research.

Bober begins by reading several fine, scholarly biographies to get a sense of other writers' impressions of her subject and a jumpstart on places to look for more sources. She browses in old bookstores and follows a trail from one book to another. Seeking to show how a person's accomplishments were an outgrowth of the life the subject lived, Bober reads newspapers from that individual's lifetime. What was he seeing every day? What was happening in the society around her? "Find the details that give the past a pulse," she advises.

REFERENCE

After Bober has read widely, she "walks the territory." For her biography of Thomas Jefferson, she went to Monticello and Paris. Bunting does the same. "Nothing beats being there and absorbing the sensory details. Even if a century has passed, you still get a sense of the place, part of the character's particular corner of the world" she says.

How does the writer prepare to visit and research a setting? Often, a day or two is all time or money will allow. "Keep your objective in mind: atmosphere, time period, or special event in history," says Cheryl Zach, writer of mystery and historical fiction series. Tour books and work by other authors give her ideas for places she plans to visit on behalf of her characters. When she arrives, Zach looks for local interest books that often cannot be found anyplace else. Writers can fill shopping bags with this kind of material!

When Zach returns from a trip, she sorts her notes, photocopies, and anything else that might be helpful into files such as animal life, geography, or local customs. "Don't skip this step" in the research, Zach says. "Common knowledge isn't always accurate. If you mention a particular bird in your story, be sure the bird lives in that setting!"

Zach's research spurs her imagination, giving her ideas for future plots. Kittinger, who recently completed a series on rocks and minerals, expands her research beyond the original subject and works on several projects at the same time.

Markle says that in this research process, information builds. "It will feed into another book." Because information is expensive in time, she determines at least three other uses for it in magazines, newspapers, or conference workshops and talks.

Stops on the Way

That information-building can get out of hand unless writers develop organizing skills, however. Barrett offers this tip to all researchers: "Keep track scrupulously, on cards or computer, of where your references come from, including the actual library branch. It's Murphy's Law. The very fact you need to recheck will be in a library book, and you'll run to the wrong library!"

Such organization eases the way for other reasons, too. Sometimes, Barrett says, the research trail can go cold. A return to the reference will help the writer see the larger context. In Nolan's work on a book about the Holocaust, her notes felt dry. She read her sources a second time to recapture what she felt the first time through.

When help is needed, record-keeping helps librarians help you. Barrett, like many writers, believes librarians are probably writers' best resources. "They love a challenge!" They also appreciate specifics. The writer armed with names, dates, and places will be prepared to seek help efficiently.

Archivists, like librarians, can best help the writer who has already done some digging. Peter Wilkerson, Senior

Ten Tips for a Trip to the Archives

1. You can bring only pencils and paper into the reading room. Purses, bags, and briefcases are not allowed for security reasons. They may be stored in lockers.
2. Laptop computers with charged batteries may be used. Outlets for computer adaptors may be limited.
3. The reference staff is there to help, but must help other researchers, too. The staff will orient you to policies and procedures designed to provide accessibility and protect archival material.
4. Browsing the stacks is usually not allowed in a special library.
5. Be prepared to explain to the reference staff how you know what you already know and what you want to know. (Note: a letter with this information can be sent ahead of time.)
6. Plan to take notes. Don't plan on photocopying entire collections. It may take weeks to process a photocopy order.
7. Take careful notes about where you find documents or images (call numbers, containers, files). This will be important to you and the archivist in a variety of ways.
8. Fill out any forms requested by the staff. These aid in planning for the future.
9. Learn how to use the catalogue and find aids to request material more efficiently.
10. Letters of appreciation for good help are always appropriate and appreciated.
    (With thanks to Peter L. Wilkerson, Senior Archivist, South Carolina Historical Society.)

REFERENCE

Archivist at the South Carolina Historical Society, cautions, "There is a fine line between doing your homework—knowing what you are looking for—and thinking you have all the answers."

What is your topic and what specifically do you want to know about it? Write the archivist and make your question the subject of your first paragraph. What have you already explored? Attach a list. Ask about fees and whether you must make an appointment with the archivist or reserve work space.

Both librarians and archivists appreciate thank you notes from the writers they've helped. Archivists may ask the writer to complete a form to help them plan for the future. These letters and papers indicate the impact of a research facility and can be useful at funding time.

Wilkerson recommends a preliminary meeting between the archivist and writer. During a question-and-answer interview, the archivist listens and thinks, "Which collection? What research strategy?" Every institution has a different set of collections, and the archivist's special knowledge can lead to a writer's exciting discovery.

Model Letter to an Archivist

January 1, 1998

Peter L. Wilkerson, Archivist
South Carolina Historical Society
100 Meeting Street
Charleston, S.C. 29401-2299

Dear Mr. Wilkerson:
For a children's book I am writing about John C. Calhoun and his daughter, Anne Calhoun Clemson, I'm looking for letters the two exchanged during the years 1830 to 1850. I'm also interested in knowing what Charleston was like during the years Anne was growing up, before she attended boarding school in Columbia (1831), and would like to find letters or diaries of some of the people the Calhouns knew in their everyday lives in Charleston.

I've read Ann Russell's article in *The Carologue,* Autumn 1996, page 14 and have noted her sources. A list of other sources is attached.

My trip to Charleston is planned for the week of May 15, 1998. Should I make an appointment to see an archivist or to reserve space? Please tell me what fees to expect. I'd like to arrive at the Archives around 10 a.m. on the 16th. An SASE is enclosed for your response.

Thank you for your help. I look forward to meeting you.

Sincerely,

Joan Broerman
Address
E-mail address
Phone and fax numbers

In addition to librarians and archivists, Kittinger recommends, "Talk with professionals, professors, and hobbyists. Go to museums and clubs. Do field research yourself if the subject allows." Interviews with contacts such as these can be the heart of a piece of writing, and they, too, demand good record keeping. (See "An Expert Voice to Bring Nonfiction to Life," page 217.)

Markle, who has more than forty nonfiction books plus a new interactive CD-ROM series about cyberspace aliens to her credit, enlists help throughout her research process. She nurtures a worldwide community of experts in many fields.

Because information in a science book could be four years old before it appears in print, Markle goes where breakthroughs are made. She reads professional journals, searches the Internet, notes credentials, and builds a community of contacts. "Who can you refer me to?" Markle asks. She taps the genius behind the discovery and shares with kids her involvement in what is happening on the cutting edge. Markle says oversimplification can cause mistakes, so she depends on expert readers to keep her work on target.

Destinations

When is it time to stop researching and get down to the business of writing? "You never feel finished with research," says Nolan. "As soon as you have a story or picture in your head and the fire is in you to write, begin!" She does much of her writing and research at the same time, letting each feed the other. "I like the interplay of the two. The work stays fresh and exciting because I'm getting to the point I want to be, which is the writing."

Then there is the eternal question, with its own demands on research: "What does an editor want?" Patra Sevastiades, Editorial Director of The Rosen Publishing Group, a nonfiction house that does series for teens and for kindergarten to grade four, says, "We love writers and want new ideas all the time." But Sevastiades also demands precision. The writer must be certain facts are rock solid.

In series writing, in particular, a writer builds a relationship with the editor that research can bolster. Once the writer learns style and format, "You could do six books at a pop," says Sevastiades, who likes to see an outline and the first chapter with a query letter.

Successful series writers find freedom within the formula. Research can give writers the breadth necessary for a series, and the depth to give overworked editors good ideas in a form they can grasp quickly and easily.

Bonnie Szumski, Editorial Director of Lucent Books, which publishes for schools and libraries, sees nonfiction as an area of opportunity because publishers are pressured for more books and must look for more writers. She is open to new series, but Szumski expects writers to fact-check their research and writing and advises them to take two steps before writing a query letter: to look at the publisher's catalogue and at the publisher's books. "It's endearing if you can reveal you know something about the publisher in your query letter."

As a fiction editor, Grove admittedly

reads a manuscript searching first for a good story, and then for strong characters. The importance of research is third, but it is still important to "make it real. Bring the period to life," she says. Grove doesn't question accuracy unless something jumps out. Anachronisms can jar the reader out of the writer's time period. If, after the initial editing process, an editor feels comfortable with the manuscript, it goes to the copy editor to check facts. A question could be a flag to the editor to go back to the author.

Magazines are excellent markets, and a source of clips, for a writer who can research well and write in a reader-friendly voice that connects. Writing articles also truly can lead to books, as Carolyn Yoder, now Senior Editor, History, at *Highlights for Children,* attests. (See Yoder's article on photo research, "Detectives Nonpareil," page 203.)

At children's nonfiction magazines today, documentation is expected and guidelines are explicit. *Muse,* from the publishers of *Cricket* and *Smithsonian* magazines, requests a bibliography listing all resource material, including names, addresses, and telephone numbers of key people interviewed for an article. *Muse* also requires that "authors should always go to primary sources" before submitting a story.

Love your subject, read widely, find your focus, outline, choose your style of keeping track, ask for expert help, and free yourself to write when the sparks fly. Both Mark Twain and Will Rogers may have said, "In this world nothing is certain but death and taxes," but they were quoting Benjamin Franklin from a letter he wrote to M. Leroy in 1789. (Bartlett, John. 1901. *Familiar Quotations.*)

Electronic Research

The Tools You Need to Find What You Want

By Mark Haverstock

Many writers buy computers solely as word processors, and some may even dabble in e-mail or computer games. But few ever learn their computers' other talents. It's like having a Ferrari in your garage, and only driving it to the market for an occasional load of groceries.

Besides acting as your high-tech typewriter and mailbox, your home computer can also be a high-powered research assistant. Although it won't entirely eliminate trips to the library, it can cut your research time considerably, and can provide you with some new resources you never knew existed.

CD-ROM References

Your computer already has two built-in references—a spell checker and the thesaurus—but you'll probably want more. Practically any general reference

you have or want in hardcover is available in some electronic form. One advantage of electronic CD-ROM references is the ability to sift quickly though massive amounts of information using keywords or short phrases you supply. Electronic media is also cheaper than print versions, so having a complete reference library at your fingertips is more affordable than it's ever been. You can compile a basic reference collection for a little more than a hundred dollars, and that takes up less than an inch of shelf space.

The first shelf of your electronic library should include a variety of commonly used references. *Microsoft Bookshelf* integrates eight reference works: *Encarta World Atlas, The American Heritage Dictionary, Roget's Thesaurus, The World Almanac, The Concise Columbia Encyclopedia, The Columbia Dictionary of*

REFERENCE

Search Managers

Wouldn't it be great if you could send someone else out to do your research, organize it, and return an organized list of results within minutes? Search managers are programs that can handle these chores. Two of the best are WebCompass and Internet Fast Find.

Typically, you define a search for the program and tell it what search engines you want to include. The program logs onto the Internet and works in the background, while you continue working with your word processor or do other computer chores. When the search manager is done, the results are compiled, duplicates removed, and the best prospects are put at the top of the list. WebCompass also offers an option that will save the results of your searches so you can view them offline at your convenience.

Quotations, *The People's Chronology,* and the *National Five-Digit ZIP Code and Post Office Directory.* Internet users will appreciate two bonuses, an Internet directory of more than 5,000 sites and the latest release of Internet Explorer.

Infopedia also squeezes an entire bookshelf of information into CD-ROM format. You get instant access to the twenty-nine volume *Funk and Wagnall's Encyclopedia, Merriam-Webster's Dictionary of Quotations, Merriam-Webster's Dictionary of English Usage, Webster's New Biographical Dictionary, Hammond World Atlas, Roget's 21st Century The-*saurus, *The World Almanac,* and *Merriam-Webster's Dictionary.*

Next, consider a CD-ROM encyclopedia. They combine the text of traditional encyclopedias, but they're much easier to use and generally much less expensive. You can search for specific information using keywords or phrases, or browse using built-in guided tours, timelines, or topic lists. Most include more pictures than their print counterparts, and a selection of sounds and video clips. Microsoft's *Encarta Deluxe Edition* is the best-selling multimedia reference, containing more information than a traditional twenty-nine volume encyclopedia. Jump text, a series of 300,000 cross-references, lets you move quickly to related articles. *Encarta* also goes beyond the basic CD-ROM by linking with more than 5,000 World Wide Web sites for additional, updated information.

World Book and *Grolier's* take a similar approach, linking articles to current information accessible on the Web. They contain all the text of the print versions, while incorporating multimedia sight and sound. Both include an atlas, and *World Book* goes one better with a 225,000-word dictionary.

If you're looking for in-depth information and can forego the multimedia features, *Britannica CD* is the ultimate CD-ROM encyclopedia It contains the complete text of the *Encyclopedia Britannica,* all thirty-two volumes. A bargain compared to the print version, it's still pricey compared to other electronic encyclopedias.

Internet Reference Sources

You'll find an assortment of references

on the Internet, most of which are free. They're good alternatives to purchasing your own resource books, especially those you use infrequently. To reach these sites, type the URL (the Internet address enclosed in parentheses) into your Web browser.

Billed as a one-stop reference desk, *Research-It* (www.itools.com/research-it) provides a combination of quick-search tools in the areas of language, library reference, geography, finance, mailing, and the Internet. Some of the more interesting features include a universal translator that translates a word in any language to a large list of other languages; computer, anagram, and acronym dictionaries; and a variety of sources for on-screen maps. This site also contains more conventional references, such as a standard dictionary.

The CIA is usually associated with covert operations, but one that isn't very secret is CIA Publications (www.odci.gov/cia/publications/pubs.html). Here, you'll find searchable copies of their popular *CIA World Factbook, Handbook of International Economic Statistics,* and other publications available to researchers without a security clearance.

Looking for a phrase, but can't remember in what book or play you found it? Wisdomquest (www.websonar.com/websonar/sonar.html) is a huge library containing everything from the classics to video transcripts. If "to be or not to be" is the question, enter the phrase. Before you can say *Hamlet,* Act III, you've got the source.

Bartlett's Familiar Quotations (www.columbia.edu/acis/bartleby/bartlett) has become a standard reference for authors and speech writers. The ninth edition is online with search by keyword and browse-by-author functions.

The WWW Virtual Library (www.w3.org/vl) has the distinction of being the Web's first distributed subject catalogue. Although its list of categories is limited, each item provides links to some of the best Web pages available. Some of the notables include African Studies and the History of Science, Technology, and Medicine.

Global Internet Searches

The Internet is the largest repository of knowledge on earth. It's grown to the point where it can provide virtually any type or format of information. In addition to text, it offers archives of graphic materials such as maps, charts, illustrations and photos. There's good, useful information out there, but finding exactly what you need efficiently is the key.

A common scenario with a Web search engine is that it brings up too many sites to cope with—sometimes hundreds, or even thousands, ranked by someone else's definition of relevance. Looking at each possibility is time-consuming. Frustrated, you try to narrow your search, or in desperation, try another search engine only to come up with the same result.

One web page that's a must read is *Using the Internet for Research* (www.purefiction.com/pages/res1.htm). This guide was compiled especially for writers to give no-nonsense tips and answers to frequently asked questions (FAQs) about finding information on the Internet. Be sure to check this page

REFERENCE

Save Time/Save a Trip

■ Websites

Why spend hours at your local public or university library looking for print materials? Let your mouse do the walking by doing a preliminary search on their online card catalogue. Many libraries have online catalogues you can access using your Internet browser. Check out these indexes of websites for hundreds of libraries that are connected to the Internet:

Libweb (www.sunsite.berkeley.edu/libweb) provides links to public, university, state, regional, and special libraries in the U.S., as well as foreign countries.

Bookwire (www.bookwire.com/index/libraries.html) furnishes quick access to more than 500 U.S. and foreign libraries.

The Library of Congress (www.lcweb.loc.gov/homepage/lchp.html) is the Mother of all libraries, containing its own extensive catalog and links to other libraries, databases, and resources for researchers. Be sure to tour the entire site for a wealth of sources.

If your library isn't on the World Wide Web, chances are it still has a local dial-up connection. Contact your local library for more specific information about online access.

■ Pay Database Services

CARLweb. (www.carl.org/carlweb, 303-758-3030) Carl Corp; Open Access document retrieval, $10 plus any applicable copyright fees.

Electric Library (1-800-247-7644) for computers equipped with Netscape or Internet Explorer. Infonautics Corp.; $9.95/month, $59.95/year, free 30-day trial offer.

(continued on next page)

---

out before cranking up one of the popular search engines on the Internet.

There are dozens of search engines on the Internet, but these select few will routinely deliver the most relevant hits. Along with each, you'll find some search tips listed to help you make the most of each one.

AltaVista (www.altavista.digital.com) is still the best site to use when you're looking for obscure topics—a needle in a haystack. It also does well with more common topics if you narrow your search parameters from the start. One

way to do this is to put quotation marks around names. "Grover Cleveland" produced about 1,000 responses, almost all of the top twenty about the former president. Typing Grover Cleveland without quotes produced about 30,000 Web pages containing that word combination, including subjects further from the target, like presidential memorabilia or Grover Cleveland Williams.

Excite (www.excite.com) has one of the most complete and up-to-date catalogues of the Web. Using the Sort by

Save Time/Save a Trip *continued*

Pathfinder Personal Edition (www.pathfinder.com) for computers equipped with Netscape or Internet Explorer. Time New Media, Inc.; $4.95/month, $29.95/year, free two-month trial offer.

■ **Product List:**

CD-ROMS

Britannica CD, Windows 95, Macintosh. Encyclopaedia Britannica; $299.

Encarta Deluxe Edition, Windows 95, Macintosh. Microsoft; $55.

Grolier's Multimedia Encyclopedia, Windows 95, Macintosh. Grolier Electronic Publishing; $50.

Infopedia, Windows 95, Macintosh. The Learning Company; $46.

Internet Fast Find, Windows 95. Symantec Corp.; $50

Microsoft Bookshelf, Windows 95, Macintosh. Microsoft; $70.

World Book Multimedia Encyclopedia, Windows 95.

IBM/World Book; $50.

WebCompass, Windows 95. Quarterdeck Corp.; $50

Author's note: You may find that some Internet sites have moved since this chapter was written. One of the search engines, such as AltaVista or Infoseek, will often help you find a site's new location.

REFERENCE

Site function can sometimes help improve the relevancy of responses. If you find a particularly useful site, choose "Click here for a list of documents like this one" to find additional related sites.

Infoseek (www.infoseek.com) provides a great variety of sources, and provides advanced search techniques similar to those found in AltaVista. It also has a unique image search function that displays thumbnail images, rather than just shuffling you off to a website. Be sure to check out Related Topics, above the list of search results. They'll usually give you some helpful suggestions for expanding your search.

Yahoo! (www.yahoo.com) is an entirely different animal. Built like an index, it's a directory to the Web that's compiled and classified by a group of people. Yahoo's human intervention has its strengths and weaknesses. The half-million listings are categorized more relevantly than a computer search engine could ever do. But other search engines find websites automatically that Yahoo! may not know about, and the listings will be more up-to-date.

Ask a Researcher

Sometimes a computer search engine isn't the best way to get to specific information. If you're tired of wading through the hundreds of document summaries returned by computerized search engines, HumanSearch (www.humansearch.com) serves up information the old-fashioned way, with the human touch.

The first step is to log in on their home page with your name and e-mail address. When you submit the question, don't use keywords; phrase your question as if you were asking a reference librarian for help. From there, your question is sent to a distributor who assigns it to a qualified searcher. The searcher then retrieves all the information that he can find, in the form of answers and websites. These answers are read by an inspector to verify that the answers are relevant, and the inspector then sends it back to you via e-mail. This service is free, and turnaround time is about forty-eight hours or less.

Another free service is Pitsco's Ask an Expert (www.askanexpert.com/askanexpert). Ask an expert is made up of twelve categories, ranging from the arts to science and technology. More than 300 websites and e-mail addresses are provided to help you find the right expert, one of many who have volunteered their time to provide answers.

One of the oldest and best-known research companies, Find/SVP, sponsors Findout (www.findout.com), a service which promises free answers to specific questions and guidance to the best sources of information. Their "Ask Us" service promises a turnaround time of two business days. If you want to do a little exploring on your own, their researchers have compiled a library of sources covering several categories.

The Newsstand

Many newspapers, periodicals, and newswire services now have sites that are easily accessible on the Web. Some, such as *USA Today* (www.usatoday.com) feature current headline news, and keep limited back issues. Others keep more extensive searchable archives that date back several years. Though all offer some free text, some may ask you to register on the site and charge modest fees for premium services or downloading articles. For example, the *Boston Globe* (www.globe.com) charges $1.25 to download an article at off-peak hours (6:00 P.M. to 6:00 A.M.).

One stellar starting point for periodicals is the *American Journalism Review* (AJR) NewsLink (www.newslink.org/menu.html). They've assembled a comprehensive collection of more than 4,000 worldwide links to newspapers, magazines, TV and radio networks, news wires, and news services on the Web. Make your first stop the Starting Point for Journalists list.

Reuters (www.yahoo.com/headlines/current/news/summary.html) in conjunction with the Yahoo! Search Index provides hourly news summaries, as well as search capabilities though Reuters' extensive news story archives.

The Electronic Newsstand (www.enews.com) is home to 200 magazine sites, and has comprehensive links to 2,000 other magazine-related sites. At the least, there are sample articles of various magazines but they've also compiled an archive of articles from their clients' publications, which you can search by topic. Note that this electronic news site also serves as a promotional site for some magazines and their subscription services.

Pathfinder (www.pathfinder.com) is the home page for Time Warner's group of periodicals including *Time, People, Sports Illustrated* and others. Choose a particular magazine, or search the entire Pathfinder site for full-text articles. You don't have to always search for the news. Instead, the news can come to you through Pathfinder's Personal Edition. This pay news clipping service searches and retrieves topics you want from the entire Time Warner magazine group and news wires, such as AP, UPI, and Reuters, putting the articles it finds into a personal newspaper format.

Television news giant CNN (www.cnn. com/SEARCH) provides text and pictures of current news events on its home page, and a search feature to find full-text articles in the news archives. The free Custom News is CNN's version of Personal Edition, drawing from CNN and more than 100 magazines and news outlets. It can keep a constant lookout for articles on a particular subject, or you can look for yourself with an interesting feature that lets you search for news article themes.

Another freebie, Crayon (www. crayon.net), lets you create your own customized news page from several hundred different print and broadcast sources. It's especially helpful if you have upcoming writing projects in a specific area. For example, if you're writing on health topics, you might subscribe to *USA Today*'s Healthline and Reuters' Health Info Services to get a steady supply of background articles and ideas.

Online Databases

Serving up the best bibliography for the buck is Electric Library (www.elibrary.com). At this site, you'll find more than 150 full-text newspapers, several wire services, hundreds of full-text magazines, and references like *Collier's Encyclopedia* and *World Fact Book*. Though it's advertised as a general reference source for school and home users, it's also a viable and inexpensive resource for writers.

Rather than calling up a specific reference, you type in key words or a question or phrase relating to your topic on the Electric Library Home Page. After entering your search, results are returned to you ranked in order of relevance, listing source, author, and date of publication. A built-in intelligent search technology assures most of the results will be on target.

Choose the documents you want, then print or save on disk. There's no limit or per-document charge. Best of all, there's a thirty-day free trial.

CARLweb (www.carl.org) is a web-based search interface for searching Knight-Ridder's huge inventory of articles, and it also acts as a link to other commercial databases. Their open access service provides free searches, which list the source, publication date, and a short summary of the content. You can order the full text from CARL for a nominal fee, or you can take the search results and look up the article yourself for free at the library.

Finding phone numbers and addresses of people and organizations can sometimes be a hassle, but there are several free databases that can help. If they're listed in any phone book, you'll find them at one of the following sites:

Database America (www.database america.com) gives one of the more comprehensive listings of residential phone numbers and addresses. You can search by either name, address, or phone number.

WhoWhere (www.whowhere.com) provides links to international phone directories of more than 50 countries.

Big Yellow (www.bigyellow.com) is the Internet's business yellow pages. You can search their 16.5 million business listings by category, or by specific names and addresses.

WorldPages (www.worldpages.com) combines white page and yellow page listings, government listings, and links to 200 directories worldwide.

So how do you find who's who? The A&E cable network sponsors Biography (www.biography.com). This spin-off of the popular TV program offers a searchable database of more than 15,000 people worth knowing, both past and present.

Expert Sources
Once you've done the basic research, an expert can help confirm facts and add authority to your article or book. Sometimes good sources are hard to find, but these websites can help.

ProfNet (www.profnet.com) can help you locate the expert you need. This "virtual Rolodex" puts you in contact with 2,700 public information officers (PIOs) from colleges and universities, corporations, government agencies, and nonprofit organizations. In turn, you'll receive biographical information, contact information, and help from PIOs who can often facilitate interviews. There's also a professional experts database (www.profnet.com /ped) you can search, containing more than 2,000 experts at hundreds of colleges and universities.

Another site, experts.com (www.experts.com), also provides a searchable database of experts, and consultants complete with brief information about the individuals. Though many fields of expertise are covered, they tend to favor legal and political sources.

Yearbook News (www.yearbook news.com) is an online version of Yearbook of Experts, Authorities, & Spokespersons. They specialize in providing interview sources and contacts to journalists in print, broadcast, and online media. All participants have been reviewed regarding their qualifications, and have expressed an interest in being available for interviews.

Writers and Writing Tools
The Internet has dozens of pages that cater to writers and journalists. Many provide research tips and sources, as well as specific information about the writing craft and the business of writing.

One of the best writers' sites on the Web is Inkspot (www.inskpot.com). Here, you'll find a comprehensive source of links, from references to the craft of writing. Their electronic newsletter, *Inklings,* provides a collection of timely tips and market information. Inkspot also cosponsors writers' forums and chat with The Writer's BBS (www.writersbbs.com), a place where you can post questions or discuss writing issues with other authors.

Several individuals have spent numerous hours compiling lists of writers' resource links to various websites. Their content ranges from lists of reference resources on the web to online writers' workshops. Since these lists can change frequently, be sure to visit any or all of these sites on a regular basis. They include Writer's Resources (www.arcana.com/ shannon/writing. html), Writer's Resource Page (www. comet.chv.va.us/writersr/index1.htm), Great Links for Writers (members. aol.com/writewkshp/page4.html) and Writer Resources (www.webwitch.com/ writers/writers1.html).

Is it okay to join independent clauses with a comma? How do I write tight sentences? Strunk's *Elements of Style* (www.columbia.edu/acis/bartelby/strunk) teaches beginners the tricks of clear and simple writing and it's not a bad reference for experienced writers as well. This timeless 1918 version is still the standard for English usage.

The Home Researcher
"Don't leave home without it" was a catch phrase of the 1980s that applied to a major credit card and applies equally as well to a researcher's library card. With the electronic research tools of the 1990s, you may not have to leave home at all. Instead, you can save precious time and effort gathering hard-to-find facts by using a computer as a research tool. For nearly the same cost as a year's worth of cable television service, you can have unlimited Internet access for 1998, and a home CD-ROM reference library.

REFERENCE

References

Annotated Research Primer

General References

Here you can begin your search for books or periodicals on any topic. You can also check to see if an idea you have for a book has already been done and, if so, how long ago.

Books in Print

New York, NY: R.R. Bowker, 1948- , annual. Listings from more than 49,000 publishers of their books currently in print. The multivolume set can be searched by author or title.

Also in the *Books in Print* family:

Forthcoming Books

(bimonthly, 1966 -), Paperbound Books in Print, and Books in Series.

Subject Guide to Books in Print

Books listed in *Books in Print* are assigned topical headings in this companion set. Contains nonfiction only. After your public library's catalogue,

this is usually the next stop in an initial search for information. Indispensable for the writer.

Children's Books in Print

New York, NY: R.R. Bowker, 1969- , annual. Following the same format as *Books in Print*, this reference lists over 88,000 books for children by author, title, and illustrator. It also contains information on fifty children's book awards: qualifications, past winners and when the award was established. A companion publication is the *Subject Guide to Children's Books in Print*. All of the *Books in Print* publications can be searched through online databases such as DIALOG and BRS; ask if your library subscribes to these services.

Children's Catalog

New York: H.W. Wilson, 1909- , annual supplements, cumulated. Lists books by Dewey number, with a bibliographic citation (including price, grade level, description, and evaluation). Includes indexes and directory of publishers.

Cumulative Book Index
New York: H.W. Wilson, 1898- , monthly except August, cumulated. English language books by author, title, subject. Especially helpful for writers who want to find books on any given subject, including fiction titles on that topic.

Ulrich's International Periodicals Directory
New York, NY: R.R. Bowker, 1932- , annual (with updates 2/year). Provides bibliographic information on over 165,000 periodicals classified under 969 subjects, with subject cross-referencing and index. Includes serials available on CD-ROM and online, cessations, refereed serials (reviewed by an expert in the field). Ulrich's Hotline helps subscribers in solving research problems.

Readers Guide to Periodical Literature
New York: H. W. Wilson, 1901- , monthly with annual cumulation. An author and subject index to approximately 250 selected general interest periodicals. For specialized research, try some of the other Wilson guides, such as *Art Index, Social Sciences Index, Applied Science,* and *Technology Index.* Ask at the reference desk for these and many other specific subject indexes.

Databases
Librarians at university and large public libraries can search national online services, which are collections of databases, saving you hundreds of hours of research time. Ask for what is available, as there is usually a charge. Many libraries also now have databases for searching periodical information; a popular one is *InfoTrac.* Yours may also have CD-ROM encyclopedias and other research tools (many of the titles in this chapter are available on CD-ROM). For more information on databases and CD-ROMs, see *Gale Directory of Databases* (Detroit: Gale Research, every 6 months) and *CD-ROMs in Print* (Westport, CT: Meckler, annual).

Trade and Market Information
With these books you can target your article and book submissions, find an agent or a publisher, and keep up-to-date on children's books and news in the publishing world. Check your library, too, for specialty market guides (for example, *Religious Writers Marketplace*) by subject or region.

Writer's Market
Cincinnati: Writer's Digest Books, annual. A practical, comprehensive guide to the business side of writing. Lists book and magazine publishers with editor's names, what they are looking for, intended audience, submission guidelines, and how to obtain sample copies and writer's guidelines. Script, syndicate, and greeting card markets are also covered, as well as basic information on queries, manuscript format, rights, taxes.

Children's Writer's & Illustrator's Market
Cincinnati: Writer's Digest Books, annual. Follows same format as *Writer's Market,* including articles specifically aimed to inform and inspire the writer for children.

The Writer's Handbook
Edited by Sylvia K. Burack. Boston: The Writer, annual. First half: articles by authors about writing; second half: list of markets, how to contact, what they publish, number of words, pay, more. Lists a variety of magazines, book publishers, theaters, conferences, writers' colonies.

Literary Market Place (LMP)
New York, NY: R.R. Bowker, annual. Contains a wealth of information about the publishing industry. Check this if you need to find a certain type of publisher, help with photo research, public relations and promotion, an agent, proofreader, consultant, or contest. More than 2,000 pages of the names and addresses of anyone having anything to do with books.

International Literary Marketplace
New Providence, MJ: R.R. Bowker, 1983- , annual. (Also available on CD-ROM.) This publication provides information similar to that provided in Bowker's *Literary Market Place,* but on an international scale. It lists publishers in more than 160 countries, identifies major international booksellers and libraries, and provides other international publishing information.

The Insider's Guide to Book Editors, Publishers, & Literary Agents, 1997-1998
Jeff Herman. Rocklin, CA: Prima, 1995. Lists publishers' addresses, phone numbers, contact names, and what they publish. Also includes articles on writing and lists of organizations.

Publishers' Trade List Annual
New York, NY: R. R. Bowker, annual. A collection of publishers' catalogues, alphabetical by publisher's name, with index.

International Directory of Little Magazines and Small Presses
Len Fulton, ed. Paradise, CA: Dustbooks, annual. A listing of alternative, literary, and small press offerings. Companion volume: *Directory of Small Press & Magazine Editors & Publishers,* the name index to above title.

Publishers Weekly
New York: R.R. Bowker, 1872- , weekly. The magazine to read for information on the publishing world. See especially spring and fall children's book announcement issues.

Reviews
The following contain reviews of new children's books and are well-regarded in the field:

Booklist
Chicago: American Library Association, 1905- , 22/year.

The Horn Book Guide
Boston: Horn Book Magazine, 1989- , semi-annual.

School Library Journal
New York: School Library Journal, 1954- , monthly.

Biography
People are usually the makers of history and libraries are full of biographical sources. Whether all you need are birth and death dates or a whole book about a famous person, this area will guide you to your needed information. Much overlap exists between historical and present-day sources, although some are specifically about one or the other.

Biography and Genealogy Master Index

2nd ed. Detroit: Gale Research, 1980. 8 volumes. With annual updates, cumulated every 5 years. Original set contains 3.2 million citations to articles in standard works of collective biography; updates add thousands more each year. Biographical sources fill many shelves; start here to save time. Arranged by person's last name, followed by biographical source(s) person appears in. Sources are abbreviated, but a key appears in the front of each volume.

Biography Index
New York: H. W. Wilson, 1947- , quarterly, cumulated (now annually). Indexes biographical material, whether magazine, book, or chapter in a book, by name of subject.

Who's Who
New York, NY: Marquis Who's Who. Publishes many titles, including *Who's Who* (1849- , annual), *Who's Who in America* (1899- , annual), *Who Was Who* (1897-), *Who Was Who in America* (1897-), *Who Was Who in America Historical Volume 1607-1896, Marquis Who's Who Publications: Index to all Books* (1974- , biennial).

The International Who's Who
London: Europa Publications, 1935- , annual. Short biographies of almost 20,000 living persons with dates, career, publications, interests, address, and phone.

Almanac of Famous People
5th ed. Detroit: Gale Research, 1994. Brief biographical sketches of 27,000 persons, living and dead. Alphabetical by name, with indexes.

Current Biography Yearbook
New York: H.W. Wilson 1940- , monthly except December, cumulated annually. Long articles (several pages)

of current persons of note, with biographical references at end.

Newsmakers [date]
Detroit: Gale Research, 1988- , quarterly, with annual cumulation. (Supersedes Contemporary Newsmakers, 1985-87) Up-to-date biographical and career profiles of people in the news. Covering all fields, from business and international affairs to literature and the arts.

The Dictionary of National Biography
Founded in 1882 by George Smith. London: Oxford University, 1908-9. 22 volumes and 9 supplements to cover the twentieth century. Covers Britain's citizens from "earliest times" to 1900, including noteworthy colonial American. Evaluative and factual information.

Dictionary of American Biography
American Council of Learned Societies. New York: Charles Scribner's Sons, 1928-36, ongoing. 20 volumes, index volume, and supplement volumes with comprehensive index. Similar to the *Dictionary of National Biography*; presents lives of now-dead Americans through essays by people who knew them.

The National Cyclopaedia of American Biography
New York: James T. White, 1898- . Biographies of living and dead Americans. Not in alphabetical order, so must use index (one in each volume and a cumulative index published in 1984).

Notable Americans: What They Did, from 1620 to the Present
4th ed. Edited by Linda S. Hubbard. Detroit: Gale Research, 1988. Listing of names only. Includes candidates in presidential elections, members of Congress (including Confederacy), mayors, association executives, award winners, more.

Research Guide to American Historical Biography
Edited by Robert Muccigrosso. Washington, DC: Beacham, 1988-91. 3 volumes. Biographies of 278 famous Americans, followed by a listing of primary sources, fiction, juvenile biographies, archives, museums, societies devoted to the person.

Biographical Directory of the American Congress 1774-1971
Washington, DC: U.S. Government Printing Office, 1971. First part arranged chronologically by each Congress, including Continental; lists senators and representatives from each state and territory. Second part arranged alphabetically by name; short biography.

Notable American Women 1607-1950: A Biographical Dictionary
Edited by Edward T. James. Cambridge, MA: Belknap Press of Harvard University Press, 1971. 3 volumes. Encyclopedia-type articles, with further reference sources at end.

Notable American Women, the Modern Period
Edited by Barbara Sicherman and Carol Hurd Green. Cambridge, MA: Belknap Press of Harvard University Press, 1980. 442 biographies, covering late nineteenth to mid-twentieth centuries.

Contemporary Black Biography
Detroit: Gale Research, 1992- . 9 volumes as of 1995. Includes biographical and interview information, photographs, writings, awards, and sources. Most of the subjects are modern, although some are from earlier in twentieth century.

Encyclopedia of Frontier Biography
Dan L. Thrapp. Lincoln: University of Nebraska/ Spokane, WA: Arthur H. Clark, 1988. 3 volumes. Short bios of explorers, Indians, soldiers, outlaws, scouts, hunters, artists, and more; with references to further reading under each entry.

American Historical Images on File: The Faces of America
New York: Facts on File, 1990. Portrait (large photo, drawing, engraving, painting) of subject with short bio. All areas—artists, statesmen, musicians, sports figures, explorers, industrialists, journalists, many more. See also others in this series: The Black Experience, Colonial and Revolutionary America, The Native American Experience, more.

Eponyms Dictionaries Index
Detroit: Gale Research, 1977, with 1984 supplement. Where did Graham crackers, Ferris wheel, and the Taft-Hartley Act get their names? Find out here. Identifies biographical sources and dictionaries for 33,000 eponymous terms and the people upon whom they are based.

History
Read a newspaper article from the 1800s, or a speech delivered in 1961, or an eyewitness account of a Colonial event. For writers of historical fiction and nonfiction, this is your guide to an exciting trip back in time. Included here are general works, chronologies, and historical indexes; check out your library's reference works for histories of specific ethnic groups, countries, and fields of knowledge.

World History: A Dictionary of Important People, Places, and Events, from Ancient Times to the Present

REFERENCE

Bruce Wetterau. New York: Henry Holt, 1994. Short entries on almost 10,000 subjects, plus chronologies.

The Encyclopedia of World Facts and Dates
Gorton Carruth. New York: Harper-Collins, 1993. In chronological order, from the Big Bang 18 billion years ago to 1992. Covers all areas.

The New York Public Library Book of Chronologies
Bruce Wetterau. New York: Prentice-Hall, 1990. Differs from other books of this type in its arrangement by subject (more than 250 separate chronologies).

The Timetables of History
3rd rev. Bernard Grun. New York: Simon & Schuster, 1991. Follow tables from 5000 B.C. to the present to see what events occurred at the same time in history/politics, literature/theater, religion/philosophy, visual arts, music, science/technology, and daily life.

Day by Day: the Eighties
Edited by Ellen Metzler, Marc Aronson. New York: Facts on File, 1995. World events, U.S. politics and economy, science/technology, culture/leisure is listed for each month and day of the decade. See also volumes on the Forties, Fifties, Sixties, Seventies.

Chronicle of the 20th Century
Liberty, MO: JL International Publishing, 1992. Each page represents one month of each year from 1900 on; short articles on what happened in all areas. See also *Chronicle of the World, America, French Revolution, Second World War,* and other titles by same publisher.

Monarchs, Rulers, Dynasties, and Kingdoms of the World
Compiled by R.F. Tapsell. New York: Facts on File, 1983. Lists over 13,000 rulers and dynasties by country in chronological order.

International Dictionary of Historic Places
Chicago: Fitzroy Dearborn, 1995. 5 volumes: Americas, Northern Europe, Southern Europe, Middle East and Africa, Asia and Oceania. Several pages for each place, such as Boston's Freedom Trail, Hollywood, Santiago.

Dictionary of Historic Documents
George C. Kohn. New York: Facts on File, 1991. Short explanations of more than 2,200 documents, including Code of Hammurabi, Ten Commandments, U.S. Pledge of Allegiance, Treaty of Paris, Cuban Constitution; with dates.

The Annals of America
Chicago: Encyclopaedia Britannica, 1976. 20 volumes plus supplement volume 21(1987). Speeches, letters, diaries, poems, songs, excerpts from books and magazines addressing important issues in American life by famous and little-known authors. Pictures and background information interspersed throughout.

Documents of American History
10th ed. Edited by Henry Steele Commager and Milton Cantor. Englewood Cliffs, NJ: Prentice-Hall, 1988. 2 volumes. Includes proclamations, acts, decrees, decisions, speeches from 1492 to the present; collected by noted historian.

Historical Statistics of the United States: Colonial Times to 1970
White Plains, NY: Kraus International Publications, prepared by Bureau of the Census, 1989. 2 volumes. Need to know the population in 1790? Immigrants in 1820? Exports in the 1600s? This reference has those numbers and much more.

Famous First Facts
4th ed. Joseph Nathan Kane. New York: H.W. Wilson, 1981. Lists more than 9,000 first happenings in American history from 1007 A.D. to 1980. Alphabetical by fact, with extensive indexing.

This Day in American History
Ernie Gross. New York: Neal-Schuman, 1990. 11,000 entries under day of the year that they happened.

The Negro Almanac: A Reference Work on the African American
5th ed. Compiled and edited by Harry A. Ploski and James Williams. Detroit: Gale Research, 1989. Comprehensive overview of black culture, including statistics, biographies, chronologies, and articles on legal, historic, labor, political, artistic, religious areas. 1,600+ pages.

The Writer's Guide to Everyday Life in the 1800's
Marc McCutcheon. Cincinnati: Writer's Digest Books, 1993. Covers clothing, language, transportation, furniture, money, medicine, dances, foods, crime, war. Includes chronologies of events, books, magazines, innovations, songs. See also *The Writer's Guide to Everyday Life: Prohibition to World War II* by the same author (1995) and *The Writer's Guide to Everyday Life in the Middle Ages* by Sherrilyn Kenyon (1995) and *The Writer's Guide to Everyday Life in the Renaissance*, by Kathy Lynn Emerson.

Poole's Index to Periodical Literature, 1802-1906
William Frederick Poole. Boston: Houghton Mifflin, 1882-1908. 2 volumes plus supplements. Helpful for writer who wants to examine style of writing or read original texts from pre-vious century. Author Index, compiled by C. Edward Wall. Michigan: Pierian Press. Cumulative, 1971.

Famous First Facts About the States
David Stienecker. Woodbridge, CT: Blackbirch Press, 1995. Gives information on state birds, flowers, and trees, for all 50 states, along with notes on famous people born in each state and important dates in state history.

Local History Sources
To find out how the people of your community lived in the past and what events affected their lives, look for old newspapers, genealogies, and local history books of the era. Ask your librarian how to access these sources; some major libraries have sizable genealogy and local history collections.

United States Local Histories in the Library of Congress: A Bibliography
Edited by Marion J. Kaminkow. Baltimore: Magna Carta, 1975. 4 volumes plus 1 supplement (1986) with index. Arranged by region, then state. Includes city, title, place, publisher, date, number of pages. After you find the titles, you may be able to find these locally or through interlibrary loan.

News Sources
From current events reporting comes story ideas, people to contact for information and interviews, and the very latest in what's happening in any field. Back issues and volumes can be handy, too, for historical perspective.

Facts on File: World News Digest with Index

REFERENCE

New York: Facts on File, 1941- , weekly with bound annual cumulation. Cumulative index issued every 2 months. Condenses the news of the week from more than 70 newspapers and newsmagazines from around the world. Includes fact boxes, page references to earlier articles, maps, and tables. Covers government/politics, health, economy/finance, the arts, sports, environment, national/international events, business, science. Includes a color world atlas with index.

The CQ Researcher
(Formerly *Editorial Research Reports*). Washington, DC: Congressional Quarterly, 1923- , weekly. Each volume addresses one topic, such as organ transplants. Includes background, current views, the future, sources for more information, and subject and title indexes.

Newspapers in Microform, United States and
Newspapers in Microform, Foreign Countries
Washington, DC: Library of Congress, 1984. Covers 1948-1983. By state, city, with title index. Lists hundreds of libraries. Dates of publication and title changes helpful for researcher.

NewsBank
New Canaan, CT: NewsBank, 1981- , monthly, with quarterly and annual cumulations. Provides subject access to articles from newspapers of over 450 U.S. cities. Full text is on microfiche, index is printed. Has directions for use on each page.

Major Newspaper Indexes
The following newspaper indexes are in most large public libraries and are also available on CD-ROM:

The New York Times Index
1851- , semi-monthly.
Wall Street Journal Index
1955- , monthly.
Washington Post Index
1971- , monthly.

Literature and Legend
Literature in general and children's literature in particular are topics with a good number of reference books for the writer. Specialized indexes abound to find poetry, essays, fairy tales, plays, songs, short stories, speeches, and book reviews.

The Oxford Companion to Children's Literature
Humphrey Carpenter and Mari Prichard. Oxford: Oxford University Press, 1984. Alphabetical listing of authors, characters, categories of children's literature, titles, and geographical areas (children's literature in various countries).

Characters from Young Adult Literature
Mary Ellen Snodgrass. Englewood, CO: Libraries Unlimited, 1991. Settings, synopsis, major and minor characters for each work, with author and character indexes.

Oxford Dictionary of Nursery Rhymes
Edited by Iona and Peter Opie. London: Oxford University Press, 1984. Arranged alphabetically by most prominent word (cat, father, London Bridge, for example); gives origin and explanation.

Calendar of Literary Facts
Edited by Samuel J. Rogal. Detroit: Gale Research, 1991. Day-by-day: births and deaths of famous authors, publishers. By year: births, deaths, publications, events.

Pseudonyms and Nicknames Dictionary

Edited by Jennifer Mossman. Detroit: Gale Research, 1987. 2 volumes. 80,000 aliases, pen names, code names, stage names, etc., of 55,000 persons; provides real name, basic biographical information, and sources. Covers many fields.

Brewer's Dictionary of Names

Adrian Room. New York: Cassell, 1992. Defines people, places, and things in mythology, the Bible, history, politics, business, languages, literature, astronomy.

Children's Writer's Word Book

Alijandra Mogilner. Cincinnati, OH: Writer's Digest Books, 1992. Word lists by grade and a thesaurus using graded words.

The Macmillan Visual Dictionary

New York: Macmillan, 1995. Labels parts of objects such as tape measure, bulldozer, camera, baseball field, snake; names and shows types of glassware, tools, road signs, dresses, furniture. 25,000 terms in 600 subjects. Also available: multilingual edition.

The Oxford English Dictionary

2nd ed. Oxford: Clarendon, 1989. 20 volumes. First choice for looking up pronunciation, meaning, and historical origin of any word. For writers: Find out if an object, phrase, or word was used in the year you are writing about.

Random House Historical Dictionary of American Slang

Volume 1, A-G. Edited by J.E. Lighter. New York: Random House, 1994. Well-received first volume of proposed multivolume set. Includes when slang was first used, with year, author, and reference (can be book, magazine, television show, film). Usually several examples of usage under each word.

The Macmillan Book of Proverbs, Maxims, and Famous Phrases

Selected and arranged by Burton Stevenson. New York: Macmillan, 1987. Nearly 3,000 pages; traces sources (title, author, date). Arranged by subject, with index.

A Dictionary of American Proverbs

Edited by Stewart A. Kingsbury and Kelsie B. Harder. New York: Oxford University Press, 1992. Organized according to word; reveals the proverb source (first use and in the twentieth century) and distribution (by state).

Bartlett's Familiar Quotations

16th ed. Edited by Justin Kaplan. Boston: Little, Brown, and Company, 1992. Arranged in chronological order, with indexes by author and quote.

A Dictionary of Common Fallacies

Philip Ward. Buffalo, NY: Prometheus, 1988. 2 volumes. Find out why mermaids don't exist, whales don't spout water, and the Declaration of Independence was not signed on July 4, 1776—and why many people believe it was.

Bulfinch's Mythology

Edited by Richard P. Martin. New York: Modern Library, 1991. The classic in its field. Includes gods and goddesses (including Hindu and Norse), King Arthur and knights, other British hero tales, Charlemagne legends.

Funk and Wagnalls Standard Dictionary of Folklore, Mythology and Legend

Edited by Maria Leach. San Francisco: Harper & Row, 1984. More than 8,000 articles (some long, some short) on folk heroes, beliefs, spells, rhymes, festivals, dances, more.

REFERENCE

Science

Information about science and technology comes in a variety of difficulty levels. Investigate until you find the ones with which you are most comfortable. Not everyone can be an atomic physicist, but writers can read to understand basic principles and explain concepts to children.

McGraw-Hill Encyclopedia of Science & Technology
7th ed. New York: McGraw-Hill, 1992. 20 volumes. 7,500 entries with 13,000 illustrations, analytical index, topical index, cross references, study guides, list of contributing authors.

McGraw-Hill Dictionary of Scientific and Technical Terms
5th ed. Edited by Sybil P. Parker. New York: McGraw-Hill, 1994. Includes pronunciation, field or subject, short definition. Handy appendices.

Dictionary of Scientific Literacy
Richard P. Brennan. New York: John Wiley & Sons, 1992. Short explanation of words and phrases the average adult needs to know, from absolute zero to zygote with Doppler effect, global warming, radio telescope, much more.

Chemical Formulary
New York: Chemical Publishing, 1933- Ongoing multivolume set contains formulas for foods, drugs, cosmetics, cleaners, fabrics, adhesives, more. Good especially for historical research. Cumulative Index to volumes 1-25. Harry Bennett. New York: Chemical Publishing, 1987.

Milestones in Science and Technology: The Ready Reference Guide to Discoveries, Inventions, and Facts
2nd ed. Ellis Mount and Barbara A. List. Phoenix, AZ: Oryx, 1994. 1,250 topics, such as gasoline, rocket, porcelain, cable TV, zipper; includes explanation, field, and suggested additional reading.

Asimov's Chronology of Science & Discovery
Isaac Asimov. New York: HarperCollins, 1994. Even though Asimov died in 1992, his name lives on in this updated version of one of his many books. From 4,000,000 B.C. to 1993 — what was happening in math, medicine, technology, astronomy, agriculture, exploration, and more. Easy to understand.

The Timetables of Technology
Bryan Bunch and Alexander Hellemans. New York: Simon & Schuster, 1993. Follow the advance of invention, discovery, publications, construction from 2,400,000 B.C. to the present in tables. See also *The Timetables of Science* by the same authors.

McGraw-Hill Yearbook of Science & Technology
New York: McGraw-Hill, 1962- , annual. Supplement to the *McGraw-Hill Encyclopedia of Science and Technology.* Articles from AIDS to zeolite on the achievements in science and engineering, with charts, diagrams, graphs, photos.

Yearbook of Science and the Future
Chicago: Encyclopaedia Britannica, 1975- , annual. Science update in the familiar *Encyclopaedia Brittanica* format, to revise certain sections of that work; year in review takes in all scientific fields; more.

Field Guides

Field guides cover all areas of science. They are very helpful for identification, geographical location, and description. Some examples:

National Audubon Society Field
Guide to African Wildlife
Peter C. Alden. New York: Alfred A.
Knopf, 1995.
**Simon & Schuster's Guide to Salt-
water Fish and Fishing**
Angelo Mojetta. New York: Simon &
Schuster, 1992.

Almanacs
Almanacs include retrospective information and basic standard information, and are generally more up-to-date
than encyclopedias. This list includes
general American almanacs, international, and specialized subject almanacs. General almanacs contain
look-it-up-fast info: yearly data such as
members of Congress, current events,
and sports statistics, and general information such as maps, text of the Constitution, facts on nations and states,
outline of history, and so on. The following are some of the most popular.

Information Please Almanac.
Boston: Houghton Mifflin, 1947- , annual.
The Universal Almanac
Kansas City: Andrews and McMeel,
1989- , annual.
**The World Almanac and Book
of Facts**
Mahwah, NJ: World Almanac Books,
1868-1876, 1886- annual.
Canadian Almanac & Directory
Toronto: Canadian Almanac & Directory Publishing, 1847- , annual. Provides geographical and political
information. Lists hospitals, unions,
organizations, television stations, magazines, publishers, libraries, museums.
The Annual Register World Events:

A Review of the Year
New York: Stockton: 1758- , annual.
Published in the U.K., copublished in
U.S. and Canada. Country-by-country
events and almanac-type information,
international bodies (UN, NATO,
African conferences, etc.), fields of religion, science, environment, architecture, arts, law, sports, more.
Statesman's Year Book
London: Macmillan/New York: St. Martin's, 1864- , annual. Bulk of the book
is current information on countries
(politics, economics, statistics, weather);
small section on international organizations.
Europa World Year Book
London: Europa Publications, 1926- ,
annual since 1960. Provides detailed
statistical and historical information
about every country in the world.
Demographic Yearbook
New York: United Nations, 1948- , annual. Compilations of statistics for over
200 countries, such as population, life
expectancy, marriage, divorce, deaths.
**Almanac of the 50 States: Basic
Data Profiles with Comparative
Tables**
Edited by Edith R. Hornor. Palo Alto,
CA: Information Publications, 1985- .
State-by-state statistics: geography, demographics, vital statistics, education,
government, economics, communications. Tables ranking states in area,
population, education, labor force, income, more.
The Old Farmer's Almanac
Dublin, NH: Yankee Publishing, 1792-
, annual. Astronomy, farmer's calendar, weather predictions, entertaining
articles and useful information.
The Weather Almanac

REFERENCE

7th ed. Detroit: Gale Research, 1996. Historical and current U.S. information. Lots of statistics for each city, plus articles on weather, air, storms, with charts, maps, photographs.

Atlases

For a standard geographical/political atlas, look for a recent copyright date. Changes have been too fast the past few years to trust an old one. Beyond that, there are atlases on just about any area—sports, caves, railroads, politics, women, etc.—so browse your reference section! Historical atlases concentrate on the past and can be general or specific for countries or events. Gazetteers are dictionaries of geographical place names.

The International Atlas
Chicago: Rand McNally, 1993. Views of the world, from regions, countries, down to individual cities. Multilingual.

Hammond New Century World Atlas
Maplewood, NJ: Hammond, 1996. Contains political, physical, topical maps.

Atlas of the World
Washington, DC: National Geographic Society, 1992, revised 6th edition. Includes infrared and satellite photos; the moon, the solar system, and a brief statistical overview of each country.

The Times Atlas of the World
9th ed. London: Times Books, 1992. Plates contain all types of maps, with easy-to-read key. Lists 210,000 place names in index.

The Dorling-Kindersley World Reference Atlas
London: Dorling Kindersley, 1994. Col-

orful, country-by-country coverage. Maps, charts, graphs, statistics, world ranking, chronology, many facts.

The Economist Atlas of the New Europe
New York: Henry Holt, 1992. Arranged by subject: history, communications, business, finance, politics, international relations, war, environment, people and culture, and, within each, by a country analysis. Big, colorful use of maps and charts.

Atlas of Contemporary America: Portrait of a Nation
Rodger Doyle. New York: Facts on File, 1994. Includes population density, ethnic dispersion, weather, taxes, political climate, much more.

Atlas of United States Environmental Issues
Robert J. Mason and Mark T. Mattson. New York: Macmillan, 1990. Maps, charts, and text used to illustrate water, waste, air, forest, energy, and other topics affecting the environment.

The Rand-McNally Commercial Atlas and Marketing Guide
Chicago: Rand McNally, annual. Need a map of railroads, military installations, or college population? This huge book is filled with statistics and maps. Provides population, economic, and geographical data for more than 128,000 U.S. places, with detailed maps.

Ancient History Atlas
Michael Grant. New York: Macmillan, 1971. By the acclaimed historian. 87 very clear, easy-to-read maps cover 1700 B.C. to 500 A.D. in the ancient Greek and Roman world.

The Times Atlas of World History
Edited by Geoffrey Barraclough. Maplewood, NJ: Hammond, 1993. A visual

and written narrative of world history from earliest times to the present. Detailed maps.

Chambers World Gazetteer: An A-Z of Geographical Information
5th ed. Edited by Dr. David Munro. Cambridge: Chambers, 1988. Placewords (cities, countries, states, geographical sites) with pronunciation, location, information, sometimes a map.

Omni Gazetteer of the United States of America
Detroit: Omnigraphics, 1991. 11 volumes. Contains 1.5 million place names in the U.S. and its territories. Arranged by region, then by state, with an alphabetical list of places and information about each. Includes indexes.

The Map Catalog.
Edited by Joel Makower. 3rd ed. New York, Vintage, 1992. Sourcebook of maps to purchase (historical, county, wildlife, weather, and others) plus aerial photographs, educational materials, anything connected to maps or geography.

Encyclopedias
Encyclopedias can be a good place to start a search, but they are almost never the place to end when writing for children. Editors of books and magazines alike today demand broader and deeper research for their readers. Encyclopedias—sources of "all knowledge" —can be just one book or a multivolume set.

For a review of various encyclopedias, see Kister's *Best Encyclopedias* (Phoenix: Oryx, 1994), where Kenneth Kister compares and evaluates general and specialized encyclopedias.

Academic American Encyclopedia.
Danbury, CT: Grolier
Collier's Encyclopedia.
New York: P.F. Collier
Compton's Encyclopedia.
Chicago: Compton's Learning/Encyclopaedia Britannica
Encyclopedia Americana.
Danbury, CT: Grolier
The New Book of Knowledge.
Danbury, CT: Grolier
New Encyclopaedia Britannica.
Chicago: Encyclopaedia Britannica
World Book Encyclopedia.
Chicago: World Book

CD-ROM Encyclopedias:
Academic American
Britannica
Compton's
Concise Columbia
Grolier (Academic American Encyclopedia)
Information Finder (World Book Encyclopedia)
Microsoft Encarta
Random House

Subject encyclopedias:
Choose from dozens available at your local library. Just a quick scan of the shelves can lead you to encyclopedias on computer science, comics, crime, cities, states, science fiction, mammals, medicine, music, art, antiques, espionage, extraterrestrials, the Renaissance, any religion, Western lawmen, and world coins. The following are examples of two multivolume sets that are worth checking.

Oxford Illustrated Encyclopedia
New York: Oxford University Press,

1993. 8 volumes: 1. The Physical World. 2. The Natural World. 3. World History from Earliest Times to 1800. 4. World History from 1800 to the Present Day. 5. The Arts. 6. Invention and Technology. 7. The Universe. 8. Peoples and Culture. Edited by experts in each field; sumptuous illustrations.

World Geographical Encyclopedia

New York: McGraw-Hill, 1995. 5 volumes: 1. Africa. 2. The Americas. 3. Asia. 4. Europe. 5. Oceania and index. Geography, history, economics, and the politics of each country, plus beautiful color photos.

Government Documents

The U.S. government, the largest publisher in the world, is a source of information that all writers should keep in mind when beginning their research. If you can think of a subject, the government has probably published a book, pamphlet, periodical, or statistic about it.

Monthly Catalog of U.S. Government Publications

Washington, DC: U.S. Government Printing Office, 1895- , monthly, with supplements, cumulations, and indexes. All branches, agencies, and departments are represented in this up-to-date list.

Statistical Abstract of the United States

Washington, DC: U.S. Department of Commerce, Bureau of the Census, 1878- , annual. More than just population numbers; for example, attendance for various arts activities by sex, race, age, education level, and income, or average annual expenditure on consumer goods by region and size of household. If you need numbers, look here first.

The United States Government Manual

Washington, DC: Office of the Federal Register, National Archives and Administration, General Services, annual. Lists names and addresses of government offices and their head people.

PROFILES

Part
7

Joanna Cole

A Simple, Natural Progression

By Victoria Hambleton

An imaginary day in a science classroom. Everyone looks hot and sticky as the sun beats through an open window. Everyone that is, except the teacher, who looks cool as an ocean breeze, outfitted in a dress patterned in fans and ice cubes, thermometer earrings, and shoes that sport miniature snowmen. She is the unflappable Ms. Frizzle, or the Friz, as she is known to her class and she is probably the most famous science teacher in America.

Ms. Frizzle is the creation of author Joanna Cole who, along with illustrator Bruce Degen, has penned the wildly successful Magic School Bus series for children. The books have made Cole's a household name to parents, teachers, and children literally around the world. Spin-offs from the books (nine have been published in the past eleven years) include a Public Broadcasting System (PBS) television program, a Sega game, clothing, stationery, and in 1998, School Bus toys. To date, more than twenty million copies have been sold. As if that weren't enough, Cole has authored dozens of other well-received books, including a child development series, an animal body series, and numerous works of fiction, including a new series called The Gator Girls in collaboration with Stephanie Calmenson.

Although she has been writing for nearly thirty years, the incredible success of the Magic School Bus still astounds Cole, in part because she has always written exactly what she wanted to write about. Fortunately for the rest of us, what she wanted to write about most was science for children. She has a unique gift for making scientific subjects accessible and fun at the same time.

"I've always written books for myself and I have always had a desire to explain complicated concepts in a simple way. Even when I was in grade school, if the teacher was explaining something and some of the kids couldn't follow what she was saying, I remember I'd have my hand raised 'Ooh, ooh, let me!' and I would explain it and they would know what she meant. I guess I have that sort of talent."

Good Beginnings

As for the fun part, Cole says she has always liked science and can't imagine why anyone would find it boring. Born and raised in East Orange, New Jersey, she attributes part of her love for the subject to her school district's science program and to her teachers. Although none were a Ms. Frizzle, the germs of her inspiration came from Cole's early positive introduction to science.

After college she went to work in New York as a library teacher, when she realized how few easy-to-read science books existed for children. "Kids would come to the library and say, 'I want a book on dinosaurs or sharks,' and we'd go to the shelves and there would be books, but they would be too difficult for that child."

Her first book was about cockroaches, and she never looked back. "I guess when I started writing," she recalls, "it was just a natural progression. I knew what I wanted to say, and that I wanted to make my explanations as simple as possible. The Magic School Bus is an example of this: The text is simple but focuses on relatively sophisticated concepts."

The ninth Magic School Bus book is *The Magic School Bus and the Electric Field Trip.* Cole admitted to being very proud of this book in particular because, as she puts it, "Electricity is such a complex topic. It's so difficult to make it simple without deforming it, you know, making it untrue. As Einstein said in another context, it has to be simple enough but not too simple. I'd be writing, and feeling pretty good about the way it was going and then all of a sudden I'd have to say something about alternating current—a difficult concept to spell, much less explain, especially when you have only an inch and a half of space for text!"

A Partnership

Cole says the book could never have happened without the talent of illustrator Bruce Degen, whom she describes as "incredibly brilliant."

"For example, we'd be talking about how a turbine in an electrical power plant is going to look, and he'd figure out a way to make it most accessible and fun, too."

All the Magic School Bus books take

a tremendous amount of work to create. "Our aim," says Cole, "is to do one a year, which we are doing. They take a long time, not just because of the research—all science books take research. The trick is tying together the story, the humor, and the science to make every part of it clear and funny, all on each two-page spread. Now that's a challenge."

Asked if she will ever tire of doing the series, Cole says she doubts it, as long as there are topics that interest her. A tenth book about the senses is in the works. And considering she reads at least five science magazines a week, it's doubtful that she will ever run out of subject matter.

A New Balance

When she's not working on Ms. Frizzle's adventures these days, Cole is likely to be at work on The Gator Girls, about two good friends who happen to be alligators. She is co-writing the books, three so far, with longtime associate Stephanie Calmenson. Cole says the two of them have as much fun writing the books as the fictional Allie and Amy have in the stories.

"You know the characters live next door to each other and are always on the phone. And when Stephanie and I write the books, we do it over the phone. Each of us has a headset and we have our computers on modem so that we are each looking at the same page. First one of us writes a paragraph and then the other takes over with an idea. We have a great time."

With all her varied talents as a writer, Cole says there is one project she won't be taking on: an adult book.

Joanna Cole, Selected Titles

- *Anna Banana: One Hundred One Jump-Rope Rhymes.* Morrow Junior, 1989.
- *Bony Legs,* Simon & Schuster, 1984.
- *Bug in a Rug,* with Stephanie Calmenson, Morrow Junior, 1996.
- *The Clown-Arounds Go on Vacation.* Parents Magazine Press, 1984.
- *Don't Tell the Whole World.* HarperTrophy, 1992.
- *Evolution.* HarperTrophy, 1989.
- *The Gator Girls,* with Stephanie Calmenson, Morrow Junior, 1995.
- *I'm a Big Sister.* Morrow Junior, 1997.
- *Hungry, Hungry Sharks.* Random House, 1986.
- *Monster Manners.* Cartwheel, 1995.
- *A Pocketful of Laughs,* with Stephanie Calmenson, Doubleday, 1994.
- *Six Sick Sheep: One Hundred One Tongue Twisters,* with Stephanie Calmenson, Morrow Junior, 1993.
- *Magic School Bus* titles, with Bruce Degen, Scholastic:
  - *The Magic School Bus in the Human Body,* 1993.
  - *The Magic School Bus in the Time of the Dinosaurs,* 1994.
  - *The Magic School Bus All Dried Up: A Book About Deserts,* 1996.
  - *The Magic School Bus Lost in the Solar System,* 1995.
  - *The Magic School Bus: Inside a Beehive,* 1996.
  - *The Magic School Bus Inside a Hurricane,* 1996.
  - *The Magic School Bus Meets the Rot Squad: A Book About Decomposition,* 1996.

PROFILES

"I have written parenting books and articles for adults, but I don't find it very interesting. I prefer the challenge of writing for children." But she does plan to try to slow down a little bit.

"In the past thirty years," she says, "I've worked very, very hard, sometimes doing ten books a year, as well as magazine articles. I did everything. I like the idea of the new experience of juggling only two or three books. Who knows where that will lead me? I may have time to think of new things I want to write about. That's what's wonderful about being a writer; you never know what's going to come next."

Whatever it is, another field trip with the Friz or a wacky day with Allie and Amy, you can be sure that it will be opened with joy and the thrill of discovery by Cole's fans, young and old alike.

Barbara Cooney
The Chain of Story

By Catherine Frey Murphy

"I always thought I'd be an artist," says Barbara Cooney. "At first, I just wanted to illustrate, but there weren't enough good stories, so I began to write my own." For more than fifty years, Cooney has been writing and illustrating picture books, and her work has won the American Book Award, the *Boston Globe-Horn Book* Award, Maine's Lupine Award, and—not once, but twice—the Caldecott Medal.

"I love to write," Cooney says. "But it wasn't always like that. At first, writing was just a vehicle for the pictures, and a pretty awkward one, too, let me tell you! But over time, through doing it, I came to love writing. It's just like doing a jigsaw puzzle. You put a piece in place, you take it out, you try it someplace else, and bit by bit, you figure it out. It's always a struggle. But it's fun!"

PROFILES

Art was a family tradition for Cooney, who grew up on Long Island and spent her childhood summers in Maine. "My mother was an artist, and she always had paints and brushes around. She never stopped me from using them, as long as I cleaned up after myself." Cooney studied art at Smith College, and by the time she graduated, she knew she wanted to create children's books. In 1940, she illustrated her first book, *Ake and His World.* A year later, she followed it with *King of Wreck Island,* which she both wrote and illustrated. Since then, she has published more than a hundred books, many with her own text and pictures, and many more illustrating texts by others.

A Playful Process

Today, Cooney lives in a house she designed and built with one of her sons, in Walpole, Maine, where she can watch the sea as she works.

She loves to paint, but when she creates a book, she says, "The story comes first. Once in a while, there's a picture in my mind as I start. But the story holds it together. I compare it to a necklace. There's a chain that holds the whole thing together." The story is that chain, she explains, and the illustrations are the beads. "The beads may be very beautiful, they may be pearls—but they can't stand on their own."

Over the years, Cooney has watched her own creative process change. "Things have evolved." she says. "I'm different now. I used to be a joker!" Playfulness is still a constant characteristic of her work, but Cooney says her later stories draw more deeply on her own experiences and family history.

Her artwork has changed, too. Today, she creates her full-color paintings in acrylic with Prismacolor pencil accents, but that wasn't always so. Because of the expense of color printing, art directors used to urge Cooney "to learn to think in black and white," she says. "And everybody goes through a

mouse stage, drawing sweet, furry little mice. I used to do scratchboard, and that makes very nice fur, so I got lots of animals. But technology has advanced. We used to have to separate the colors, but now I can just paint pictures!"

The Perfect Book

For inspiration, Cooney draws on the events and settings of her life. Her four children, now grown, appeared as models in many of her early illustrations. "I don't know how many of my children were the Christ child, at one time or another," she says. "I was getting a lot of Nativity books at that time, and I used my children over and over."

Places Cooney loves appear everywhere in her work. Her stories and paintings about Long Island's ocean shore, the rocky coast of Maine, and the hills and valleys of New England are all drawn from places she has lived. To illustrate Donald Hall's *Ox-Cart Man,* for instance, which won the Caldecott Medal in 1979, Cooney simply looked out the window at the fields, forests, and winding roads of Pepperell, Massachusetts, where she and her physician husband raised their family.

Presently, Cooney is illustrating a picture book about a clan of basket makers, called *Basket Moon,* by Mary Lyn Ray, to be published by Little, Brown. "I always make a fairly complete dummy, blocking out the whole story all the way to the end," she says. "I break up the text and block out the idea for each picture. Often, the finished illustration is very much the same as the drawing in the dummy.

With *Basket Moon,* the dummy's done, but I'm not!"

Although she has written and illustrated so many beautiful books, Cooney says she's still working toward a lifelong goal: "I haven't ever made a perfect book. Maybe other people don't notice the faults, but I do. I know what could be better." She pauses to reflect. "Well, sometimes they're almost perfect. *Island Boy* might be pretty close to perfect. That's my favorite book, because it's my childhood."

An Artist Awakens

Island Boy tells the story of a man who creates a home for his family on a Maine island. "It's my hymn to Maine," says Cooney. "I spent all my summers in Miscongus Bay, near Waldoboro, where my grandmother lived. There were fifteen cousins who came every summer. We spent our lives in boats, visiting islands. We had two islands in the family then, owned by relatives of mine. Children never forget their summers in Maine. At least, I never did."

Island Boy is one of three books that, taken together, make up her autobiography. The others are *Miss Rumphius* and *Hattie and the Wild Waves.* The settings of all three are based on Cooney's childhood homes, and the spirit of each story's protagonist is Cooney's own. "You write what you know," she explains. "You can't help but be autobiographical."

Hattie and the Wild Waves tells the story of a young Victorian girl who discovers her calling as an artist as she grows up in a wealthy German family on Long Island. "The story is based on

Barbara Cooney, Selected Titles
■ *Eleanor.* Viking Penguin, 1996.
■ *Hattie & the Wild Waves.* Viking, 1990.
■ *Island Boy.* Puffin, 1988.
■ *King of Wreck Island* (out of print).
■ *Miss Rumphius.* Puffin, 1985.
■ *The Story of Christmas,* rev., Harper-Collins, 1995.

As Illustrator:
■ *Ake and His World.*
■ *Basket Moon,* by Mary Lyn Ray, Little Brown.
■ *Ox-Cart Man,* by Donald Hall.

my mother's life," Cooney says. "Many of the grandchildren had never even known my mother, and I wanted to change that." The hotel that Hattie's family owns in the story is based on Cooney's parents' Hotel Bossert, where Cooney herself was born in room 1127. As she wanders on the Long Island shore before she enters art school, young Hattie asks herself, "What are the wild waves saying?" The story's setting is her mother's, but Cooney says that Hattie's answer to the waves' questions comes from her own heart. "The part about Hattie's awakening as an artist is mine."

A World More Beautiful

Cooney's lifelong love of Maine inspired *Miss Rumphius,* winner of the American Book Award and the first recipient of the State of Maine's Lupine Award, honoring outstanding children's books by Maine residents.

"When I was building my house in

Maine," she says, "I asked one of the carpenters why there were so many lupines around the Damariscotta River. He explained, 'There's a woman down in Christmas Cove who collects the seeds every summer and throws them around.'" That real life woman became the fictional Alice Rumphius, who settles down in a little Maine house by the sea after a lifetime of travel. There, she discovers a way to meet her grandfather's childhood challenge to "make the world more beautiful," by scattering lupine seeds everywhere she goes.

Cooney loves lupines, too. "You find them all over the world. They're in Patagonia and New Zealand. The Texas bluebonnets are lupines, and there are little ones on the slopes of Mount Rainier." But the lupine paintings of Miss Rumphius turned out to be unexpectedly challenging. "As the blossoms go up the stalks, they change," says Cooney. "Each little layer is a slightly different color. I'm not sure I'd ever have done this book if I'd known how difficult lupines are to draw!"

Miss Rumphius and Cooney are alike in other ways as well: Neither backs away from challenges, and before she settled down in her own house by the sea in Maine, Cooney loved travelling as much as her character. "If I'd had my way, the travelling part of the book would have been much longer," she says. "I wanted to put in more of the places Miss Rumphius travelled to, but in picture books, you can't go over a certain number of pages. My editor decided three visits were enough."

The challenge to make the world more beautiful is Cooney's own. "That's what one is meant to do," she says. "I may not say it, but I feel that that's what you're meant to do in the world: something unselfish, beautiful, and good."

Christina Ferrari
In the Big Arena

By Victoria Hambleton

PROFILES

"**P**ressure? Oh yes, yes," says Christina Ferrari, with a laugh. She is Editor of a new magazine for young adults by one of the nation's leading companies. "We're talking Time, Inc., we're talking *People* Magazine. They don't like failure, and they certainly don't like public failure. But you know, *Teen People* is everyone's baby and they want to see it survive and win, and they've given me tremendous support."

Ferrari's determination to succeed in the big arena is not surprising given her rapid rise in the field. At the ripe old age of thirty-two, she is at the helm of a magazine that conceivably has the potential to reach millions of readers.

Start-up Work

Magazine publishing and working in New York have been two of Ferrari's goals since she finished college in 1986. Born and raised in California, she graduated Phi Beta Kappa from the University of California at Berkeley with a degree in English and French. She went on to Harvard to attend the Radcliffe publishing course, a six-week, intensive program on book and magazine publishing. While there she met Robin Wolaner, who hired Ferrari as her assistant on a new magazine she was starting up, *Parenting*.

"I wanted to be in New York," recalls Ferrari, "but when this job came up, even though it was back in California, in San Francisco, I knew it was an opportunity I couldn't pass up. I'd always wanted to work on a start-up, to do that from the ground up—and it was literally from the ground up. The day I started was the day we moved the magazine from Robin's house to its first office space. And now, here I am doing it all again, only this time I'm in charge." She says this with a sense of acknowledgement and appreciation, but not one of awe.

After *Parenting*, Ferrari went on to work at several top women's magazines—*Self, McCall's,* and *Redbook*—before moving into the top spot at *YM*, a position that got her recognized by the top brass at *People*. No wonder. Under her leadership as Editor-in-Chief, *YM's* newsstand sales soared, reaching an all-time record high in August 1996.

People's Managing Editor Landon Y. Jones, Jr. has described Ferrari as "the hottest young editor in a hot field." While her modesty keeps her from taking this too seriously, clearly she knows how to get the job done and has found a road map to what appeals to teens. And she has strong opinions about what makes a good editor.

"One of the most important qualities in an editor," she says, "is the ability to empathize with your reader, not to *be* your reader. Before *YM*, I spent my whole career working on magazines that were for women older than I was, and I didn't find that to be a problem. So when people ask, what

makes you a teen expert, well, I'm not. But I can tap into those emotions and that's what matters—that you have the heart, that you remember what it was like to fight with your best friend, to have your first crush, or to see your parents divorce. And I'm excited by the challenge of creating a new teen magazine because I really feel I can deliver something new."

On the Bandwagon

If this explanation sounds too easy, it is not. Market researchers have burned the midnight oil for nearly a year to fine-tune the editorial direction of the new magazine.

"Obviously what's hot in music and fashion changes, but those are surface things you can keep up with, especially if you hire a great young staff," she says. "We were going to launch in September, and looking back I'm glad we waited and took the time to really talk to a lot of young people and get a grasp of the issues that are really important to them."

The majority of those teens are, as one would suspect, girls. "We are aiming for a breakdown of 85 percent girls, 15 percent boys," Ferrari says. "But I think there will be enough material to appeal to both genders. Boys are hard to reach with a magazine but *Teen People* could be the magazine to change that."

Ferrari and *People* are not the only ones to jump on the teen bandwagon. In fact, it is one of the fastest growing markets in magazine publishing. And why not? Statistics from the U.S. Census Bureau indicate that the teen population, ages twelve to nineteen, already numbers twenty-nine million and is expected to swell to a whopping thirty-four million by 2010! All of which has publishers and potential advertisers anxious for a piece of the pie that is the teen-aged consumer's disposable income.

"It's certainly a very competitive group," admits Ferrari, "and nobody wants to be last of the field. There are a lot of new magazines all coming out at the same time and I don't think they can all survive. But I do think that with the strength of *People*, and the knowledge of Time Inc. about the magazine industry, that we'll succeed." It doesn't hurt that *People* estimates that 4.6 million of its readers are teenagers.

Ferrari also expects to come out on top because, she claims, her magazine's editorial content and point of view will be radically different from anything else on the market. "I can honestly say that *Teen People* is going to be different. We're not going to be a traditional fashion and beauty book for girls. We are more of a lifestyle and pop culture magazine for teenagers and that just doesn't exist."

Plans for the new magazine include reincarnations of several of *People*'s most popular features, including Star Tracks, Style Watch, and Chatter. "Our design will be similar to *People*'s," says Ferrari. "We'll emphasize photographs like they do, but we'll have more color, bolder graphics, and more interactive pieces. For example, within a story we may throw a quiz or a side bar."

An Irreplaceable Confidante

Come February, the decision of how good *Teen People* really is will be determined by the teen consumer. And while anyone in publishing will tell you that the buying public can be fickle, Ferrari doesn't seem worried. Part of her calm stems from her outlook on the bigger picture and she is convinced that the magazine format is here to stay.

"I'm one of those people who think that magazines will never die," she says with conviction. "They will always be part of the entertainment landscape. I think they are going to evolve and I think that the Internet will force them to get better and that's good. But I do think they are unique. For one thing, the sheer variety of a magazine is special. You can come away with the feeling that you've really gotten a taste of everything you are interested in."

For the impressionable teen-aged girl, this specialness is even more important. "Reading a magazine is a social activity for a teen girl," says Ferrari, "and magazines are things to be shared and looked at over and over again."

It is just this kind of appeal that Ferrari, and likely the other new magazines as well, are counting on to take them all the way to the bank.

"Girls really look at a magazine as a friend, a confidante, something you can take into your room and pore over, something you can read aloud with your best friend."

Too soon to tell, but it's a safe bet that across America many teen-aged girls' bedside tables will have a well-thumbed copy of *Teen People* lying by the lamp. And Christina Ferrari will be the first to say, I told you so.

E.L. Konigsburg
Starting with Water

By Ellen Macauley

The novels and picture books of Elaine Lobl Konigsburg (the initials were adopted in tribute to *Charlotte's Web* creator, E.B. White) have generated acclaim the world over. But this particular author/illustrator's standing in the annals of children's literature awards gives her yet another level of fame.

E.L. Konigsburg is a two-time Newbery Award winner, one of only five repeat winners since the award was first given in 1922. She received the medal in 1968 for *From the Mixed-up Files of Mrs. Basil E. Frankweiler,* and made history that year when her first published novel, *Jennifer, Hecate, Macbeth, William McKinley, and Me, Elizabeth,* was also named a Newbery Honor book. This was the only time in the history of the award that an author has had two books so honored in the same

PROFILES

year. Nearly thirty years later, in 1997, Konigsburg won the Newbery again, for *The View from Saturday.*

Both Newbery medal winners were dedicated to her psychologist husband and apparent lucky charm, David. Both experiences, she says, further spirited the author with pride, joy, and courage. Courage? Konigsburg explains: "After I won, children all over the world let me know that they liked books that take them to unusual places where they meet unusual people. That gave me the courage to write more such books. Readers then let me know that they like books that have more to them than meets the eye. Had they not let me know that, I never would have written *The View from Saturday*."

The Unconventional

Reviewers often describe Konigsburg's work as offbeat, even quirky, something the soft spoken, intelligent author considers a compliment. "I think that's probably the way my head works. That's how I communicate. I'm glad it reaches children."

Both Newbery books could be considered unconventional children's writing. Into the standard third-person perspective of *From the Mixed-up Files of Mrs. Basil E. Frankweiler*, the author merged a running narrative from the point of view of a character who doesn't even appear until near the end of the book.

The View from Saturday interspersed four, short, first-person stories, united by a theme, into its basic plot: a very special academic team coached by one very special teacher. Konigsburg found that fitting all the stories together into the whole appealed to readers' spirit of adventure, enhancing the appeal of the characters. As one fan wrote, "I was completely surprised. In your book you wrote about who I wish were my four best friends. If any of these four kids really exist, please give them my address."

No one could ever accuse Konigsburg of talking down to her readers. The vocabulary is challenging, the topics sophisticated. And, a rarity in chil-

E. L. Konigsburg Titles

- *About the B'Nai Bagels*. Atheneum, 1971.
- *Altogether, One at a Time*. Atheneum, 1971.
- *Amy Elizabeth Explores Bloomingdales*. Atheneum, 1991.
- *Father's Arcane Daughter*. Atheneum, 1976.
- *From the Mixed-up Files of Mrs. Basil E. Frankweiler*. Atheneum, 1970.
- *(George)*. Bantam Doubleday Dell, 1985.
- *Jennifer, Hecate, Macbeth, William McKinley, and Me, Elizabeth*. Atheneum, 1985.
- *Journey to an 800 Number*. Atheneum, 1982.
- *A Proud Taste for Scarlet and Miniver*. Atheneum, 1973.
- *Samuel Todd's Book of Great Colors*. Atheneum, 1990.
- *Samuel Todd's Book of Great Inventions*. Atheneum, 1991.
- *The Second Mrs. Giaconda*. Atheneum, 1978.
- *TalkTalk: A Children's Book Author Speaks to Grown-Ups*. Atheneum, 1995.
- *T-Backs, T-Shirts, Coat, and Suit*. Atheneum, 1993.
- *Throwing Shadows*, reprint, Macmillan, 1988.
- *Up from Jericho Tel*. Atheneum, 1986.
- *The View from Saturday*. Atheneum, 1996.

dren's writing, the author often rounds out various situations by focusing on an adult's perspective.

Deeper, Richer

Konigsburg's books often seamlessly weave themes into the narrative. These "lessons" are a bonus, not an intent. "I have a story I want to tell. I think that that's paramount. All this other stuff has to ride in the backseat. I think kids relate to character and kids relate to narration and when you write for children you owe them a good story. As I said in my first Newbery address, it's like licking chocolate ripple ice cream. You keep licking vanilla and every now and then you come to something with a deeper, richer, and darker flavor."

Konigsburg's writing was influenced by her early years as an upper-level science teacher at a private girls' school. "The headmistress was Miss Olga Pratt. Upon my being hired, she asked to see my first lesson plan. I had prepared a lesson outlining the history and methods of science. Miss Pratt looked it over, closed the folder, and said, 'No. I think you should start with water.' She was right. I started with water. There was no way those kids could learn about water without also learning about the scientific method, and the history of science."

"That lesson," continues Konigsburg, "translated into a writing lesson for me: Go from the specific to the general. Do not talk about all fourth graders or sixth graders; talk about *a* fourth grader or *a* sixth grader."

Respect and Inspiration

Konigsburg started her writing career when the youngest of her three children began school. "I always got up, got dressed, and went to work. I found I had to respect my own time. I had to create the time to allow myself to use mornings for writing."

Her story ideas spring from "people I've met, places I've been, things I've read" or her own extensive mixed-up files of various items of interest. A newspaper article about a bargain purchase by New York's Metropolitan Museum of Art led to the premise of *From the Mixed-up Files of Mrs. Basil E. Frankweiler.* Her artistic side may be triggered by a single image. Prior to the writing of *The View from Saturday,* she recalls being struck by the unexpected sight of four teenagers quietly taking tea at the Plaza Hotel in New York.

"A book unfolds like a movie in my head," Konigsburg says. "It differs with each book. Sometimes the revisions go hard and sometimes they don't. I think I have sent in two manuscripts that went directly from typescript to typesetter and I believe that was the equivalent of getting an A+."

One constant in the process has been the support of longtime editor Jean E. Karl, founder of Atheneum Books for Young Readers, author of *How to Write and Sell Children's Picture Books,* and *Children's Writer* columnist.

Konigsburg has a message for aspiring writers: "I would like to tell them that this is the most fortunate of careers. I wish anyone who tries persistence, and I wish them well."

Thirty-plus years ago, Konigsburg started with water. It has been smooth sailing ever since. Her admirers look forward to thirty-plus more years of exceptional literature for children.

PROFILES

Ursula K. Le Guin

Cultivating a Fantastic Garden

By Cheryl Bowlan

PROFILES

Ursula K. Le Guin lives in a bookish home behind a jungle of flowers and a front door painted Chinese red. She is an avid gardener—of tender lettuce sprouting from a plot on the porch side of her Victorian home in Portland, Oregon, but also of richly imaginative stories.

She comes by her storytelling naturally. Her father, noted anthropologist Alfred Kroeber, told campfire tales he collected from Northern Californian Native Americans. Her mother, writer Theodora Kroeber, especially loved myths and legends from around the world.

Le Guin, sixty-eight, has produced forty-five books and relishes her freedom to write whatever she likes. Best known as a science fiction writer and essayist for adults, she has earned five Hugo Awards, five Nebulas, a National Book Award, and a Pushcart Prize. But she has also written ten children's books, and sometimes the border between her audiences blurs.

The Earthsea Quartet, Le Guin's classic fantasy series, was originally written for young adults. *The Tombs of Atuan,* second of the set, won a 1972 Newbery Honor. A check of library and bookstore shelves, however, shows adults read these novels, too. And many young Earthsea fans graduate to Le Guin's science fiction.

Whatever the age, readers who have followed Ged, the series' main character, from brash boyhood as an apprentice wizard to middle age and hard-earned wisdom, will be happy to know a fifth book is being published. In *Tales from Earthsea*, Le Guin fills in the history of her magical land to the time of Ged.

She is also adding a fourth volume to her popular Catwings series of beginning chapter books. *Jane on Her Own* continues the winged feline adventures.

CWG98: You wrote your first children's book, *A Wizard of Earthsea*, at the request of an editor. You've said that at the time, the idea scared you. You were already a successful adult writer. Why did you continue writing for children?

Once I realized the main difference between a children's novel and an adult novel is a protagonist under the age of twenty, I was fine. I was so happy to find out I could write for children. It's like writing poetry. Kids read and respond so intensely. Every word has to be right. My example is Beatrix Potter. I just read her books to my little granddaughter. Every word is right—the nuance, the rhythm of the sentences, the sound of the words. With Beatrix Potter, it's beautiful; it's perfect.

CWG98: You move fluidly between writing for adults and children, as well as across genres.

I do a lot of hedge-hopping—science fiction, fantasy, poetry, essays, children's lit. Writers are not supposed to do all those things. Writers are not supposed to write both literature and children's books. Why not? I've been a kid. I've raised kids.

One reason I write YA science fiction and fantasy is I don't have to meet conventional expectations. Critics have burdened realistic fiction with these expectations. Writing in the genres, you can do things the critics get all upset about, including making people cry. That's just not done now. There's definitely a freedom in the genres, including in romance. I haven't written romance, but it would be fun to try. Those writers get away with outrageous things.

CWG98: *Tehanu*, the final novel of the Earthsea Quartet, was published in 1990, more than two decades after *A Wizard of Earthsea*. Its story is darker and more adult than that of the other books. The main character is a middle-aged woman who eventually finds a deep, mature love. In your books, where do you draw the line between young adult and adult subject matter?

Both subject matter and age in *Tehanu* have nothing to do with conventional young adult structure. I perhaps wrongly feel this freedom in fantasy. I feel that my readers don't mind. Even young readers don't need a young protagonist to identify with; they'll read whatever you give them. That's the great thing about kids. They bring their own interpretations to books.

I don't feel with a YA book you have to pull punches on subject matter at all. For children under eleven, there are things they can't handle. Some kids are ready for more serious things at nine and some not until later. I can't dump a lot of adult problems on an eight-year-old. That's not fair and it's not right.

CWG98: What quality in your YA books creates loyal readers all the way from eleven-year-olds to eighty-year-olds?

Fantasy has that capacity. Look at Tolkien. He wrote *The Hobbit* for nine-year-olds, but adults read it over and over again. His work doesn't deepen the way Dickens's writing does, but it is *there*. It does not exhaust itself. I don't know why. I guess because his books deal with timeless subjects.

I grew up with Kipling. He tells a story on four or five levels, all with a wink of the eye, but a good wink. He's probably the greatest children's writer I've ever read. *Kim* is a remarkable book. There's a spiritual element, especially when Kim connects with the Tibetan monk. That part is an introduction to Buddhism, and it's pure gold. I read the book every ten years or so.

CWG98: *Tehanu*'s ending could easily lead to a sequel. Will there be another Earthsea book?

Ursula K. Le Guin, Children's Titles

- *A Wizard of Earthsea*. Parnassus, 1968.
- *The Tombs of Atuan*. Atheneum, 1971.
- *The Farthest Shore*. Atheneum, 1971.
- *Very Far Away from Anywhere Else*. Atheneum, 1976.
- *Solomon Leviathan's Nine Hundred Thirty-First Trip Around the World*. Puffin, 1976.
- *Leese Webster*. Atheneum, 1979.
- *The Beginning Place*. Harper,1980.
- *A Visit from Dr. Katz*. Atheneum, 1987.
- *Catwings*. Orchard, 1988.
- *Catwings Return*. Orchard, 1989.
- *Tehanu: The Last Book of Earthsea*. Atheneum,1990.
- *Fish Soup*. Atheneum,1992.
- *A Ride on the Red Mare's Back*. Orchard, 1992.
- *Wonderful Alexander & the Catwings*. Orchard, 1994.

I was trying to leave the door wide open, not for another book but, in a sense, for another generation. When I finished *Tehanu*, I really couldn't take it any further. Obviously, there's going to be a big change in Earthsea. The dragons are going to re-enter that world and redefine their relationship with human beings. But how it will work itself out, I don't know.

The book wrote itself. When you let a book do that, when you entrust yourself to the story and the people in it, you give up control and, possibly, closure. I felt it should stay open. We're not used to that in children's literature.

PROFILES

Kids want closure and quite rightly. It was a chancy thing to do. But my readers are really gallant. They'll follow me into all kinds of crazy places.

I have this feeling that maybe it will take a young person to go forward, that in *Tehanu* I was verging on a future that really isn't mine. That kind of future belongs to the young, at least to make a novel out of it.

Arthur A. Levine
The Books that Matter

By Donna Freedman

PROFILES

A rthur A. Levine saw something very gratifying recently: an adolescent boy at a school book fair with a stack of books—a *big* stack. The boy could have been playing video games, renting movies, or cruising the Internet. Instead, he was perusing books like *Woman Hollering Creek and Other Stories,* and *The Watsons Go to Birmingham—1963.* It was "quality literary fiction," says Levine, "and he wasn't a geek."

The sight proved what Levine already knew from his fifteen years in children's publishing: Kids will read great books if given the opportunity.

They'll be getting more chances than ever with the debut of Arthur A. Levine Books, his imprint at Scholastic. Its first book, Norma Fox Mazer's *When She Was Good,* was released in fall 1997. Although the book is formally directed at teens, Levine says it should also appeal to grown-up readers because its topic—mental illness and physical abuse in a family—is sophisticated, and its writing is "accessible and beautiful." Coming this spring are a middle-grade novel, *Jonah, the Whale,* by Susan Shreve, and two picture books, *Beautiful Warrior: The Legend of the Nun's Kung Fu,* by Caldecott winner Emily Arnold

McCully (*Mirette on the High Wire*), and *Badger's Bad Mood,* by Hiawyn Oram, with illustrations by Susan Varley.

Levine cannot accept unsolicited manuscripts because, he says, "It's a physical impossibility to get to them all," but he vows to consider every query that comes across his desk and at least once or twice a week, he requests a manuscript from that query pile. "I'm selecting books I love," says Levine. "I'm a reader, and I'm a person who buys books. I think there are many people like that, and I'm publishing for them. What I'm hoping for is that each book will be a beautifully written and beautifully produced enterprise. I hope people will look back and say, 'Those books really mattered.'"

Levine's first job was as an assistant to Margaret Frith, who was at the time Editor-in-Chief and Publisher of Putnam & Grosset. He became an editor himself, moved to Dial as Senior Editor, and returned to Putnam, where he eventually was named Editor-in-Chief. He held the same title later at Alfred A. Knopf Books for Young Children.

Levine has been the editor of several award-winning books, including the 1993 and 1995 Caldecott Medal winners, McCully's *Mirette on the High Wire,* and Peggy Rathmann's *Officer Buckle and Gloria,* and last year's Carnegie Award winner, *The Golden Compass,* by Philip Pullman.

Levine has written books of his own, including *All the Lights in the Night,* and *Pearl Moskowitz's Last Stand.* Understanding publishing as both an editor and a writer, he is realistic about the business side, and idealistic about the creative.

CWG98: What is the current state of children's writing and publishing?

It's a tremendously exciting time for children's literature. Really great things are being written. I see a lot of wonderful writing, much more than I can publish myself. I see other things being published from other publishers and editors I admire very much.

CWG98: But aren't there numerous series out there?

That's always been true. It's two very different kinds of publishing. They're not competitive and they're not mutually exclusive. Look at the adult side. Knopf is not publishing genre series fiction, they're publishing literature, but Bantam can certainly continue to churn out romance novels. The presence of a rack full of popular romance fiction doesn't indicate an absence of Toni Morrisons or Anne Tylers.

Within Scholastic, we're delighted to be publishing Goosebumps and other series that are a lot of fun for kids to read. Craig Walker's group continues to produce exciting popular fiction for a very broad audience. On the other hand, they hired me to do a literary hardcover list of fine fiction and picture books and translations. That's within the same publishing house. It's two completely different things.

CWG98: Some people believe that series fiction isn't a good thing. Others say that it gets kids into libraries and bookstores. What do you think?

I'm not interested in publishing series fiction, but that doesn't mean I think it shouldn't be published. In fact, another part of my company does it, and does it well. It doesn't help anyone to be snobbish about reading.

On the other hand, I think it's important not to underestimate or ignore the presence of a discerning and sophisticated group of teenagers who appreciate fine writing. You can't talk about "what kids read" as if they were a monolithic group. So I think there is both room and need for a full spectrum of publishing for children and young adults.

CWG98: There's a common belief that stores stock series at the expense of individual novels.

That may well be the case. But here's my challenge to your readers: If everybody who felt that way went to their local booksellers and demanded to buy more hardcover literary fiction, then those bookstores would fill those shelves with hardcover fiction.

CWG98: So people shouldn't try to write to what they perceive as the market?

Well, to me that seems backward. It would be like putting a vase of flowers in front of a painter and then suggesting, "Don't paint what you see. Paint what you think others will want to see."

In my opinion, writing is very difficult. If you're going to do it, and persist in doing it, you have to do something you have a real passion for. If the kind of book you love to read and have a great time writing is a series kind of book, you should write that. On the other hand, if you have a beautiful literary novel in you, my goodness, you should write that. It may be tough to sell a literary young adult novel. So

---

Arthur Levine Titles

- *All the Lights in the Night.* Tambourine Books, 1992.
- *The Boardwalk Princess.* Tambourine Books, 1993.
- *Bono and Nono.* Tambourine Books, 1995.
- *The Boy Who Drew Cats: A Japanese Folktale.* Dial, 1994.
- *Pearl Moskowitz's Last Stand.* Tambourine Books, 1993.

---

your novel had better be so great that nobody can resist it, not the editor you're trying to get to publish it, not the bookseller you're trying to get to make space for it on their shelves, and not the reader.

CWG98: How is a great book made? What role does the editor play?

Primarily, a great book is made by a great author and a great illustrator. My job is to see that all of that work comes through in its most clear and best presentation. It's as if I were the director of a play, and the author and illustrator were the actors. How good the performance is depends on the actors, and the actors' talent. I can't make the actors be any more talented than they are. What I can do is say, "You're not giving me all that you have at this point. What are you thinking when you're saying those words?" I can try to call out their best performance, but it's still their performance. My mission is to create a body of work that will have made a difference to children's literature as a whole. That's what I would like to do. And I'd like to do it book by book.

PROFILES

Lois Lowry

Playing with Words

By Donna Freedman

Publishers Weekly prints a bestseller list every month. *The Giver,* published in 1993, is still on it. To author Lois Lowry, that can mean only one thing: "People are still picking it up and getting pissed off over the ending," she says.

The ambiguous conclusion of this Newbery-winning novel has made for a steady stream of correspondence. Yet even if the denouement had been clear-cut, Lowry's mailbox would probably still overflow. Quite simply, *The Giver* is unlike anything else ever written for children. It tells of a futuristic society whose "precision of language" and endless regulations have freed its members from hatred, pain and conflict—and robbed them of love, ecstasy, and intellectual freedom.

Lowry's own precision of language has won her fans worldwide. She writes

PROFILES

powerfully of subjects like oppression and loss, courage and hope. Her other Newbery winner, *Number the Stars,* has made the lessons of the Holocaust accessible to younger readers. Still, some readers know Lowry as the author of more amusing fare, particularly the Anastasia Krupnik books. That series came to Lowry quite by accident, as an antidote for melancholy. Recently divorced and quite broke, and in the middle of writing her third "serious and sad" novel in a row, Lowry took an intellectual time-out to write "a silly little book" about a spirited young girl. The response was so intense that Lowry stayed with the character. Recently, she created a second series for younger readers, about Anastasia's little brother, Sam. While not every writer feels comfortable writing both humor and drama, Lowry finds "great satisfaction" in either genre.

That gratification is her reason for writing. At age 60, with so many bestsellers on the shelf, she doesn't need to keep to her writing career. But she does need to write. "I don't have any plans to retire, as long as I love doing it— and I can't imagine not loving it," Lowry says. The author, who lives in Massachusetts, took time out from her daily writing schedule to talk about her craft, and about *The Giver.*

CWG98: Why do people still argue about the meaning of *The Giver?*

I think everybody brings their own beliefs and passions to a book, and therefore everybody is going to read into the end of *The Giver* what they bring to it. I don't want to ruin that by making it more explicit, even though everyone would like me to. I'm not going to tell you what happened, because I don't know. The ending is what you think it is.

CWG98: Some adults reacted negatively to the book.

There's been a lot of protest. It's kind of a surprising thing, because at the same time a lot of churches and religious organizations have taken the book as theologically important, and used it for their needs. Sometimes I think teachers have used it for children who are too young. If it's used, for example, in third or fourth grade, the kids just don't get it. They don't get deeper meanings from it. When it's used in seventh or eighth grade, it evokes tremendous discussions.

CWG98: Do discussions and protests mean that people aren't just reading, but thinking?

I think it works both ways. I'm certainly delighted when people find implications in it that provoke them to thought and discussion and debate. What more can a writer hope for? But at the same time, on occasion, there are people who blindly take offense at the book. It bothers me when people take things out of context. That happens often. When a book is called into question by parents, often they're taking things out of context. There's no way you can combat that.

CWG98: In your Newbery speech, you said life would be more comfortable if we could forget the painful. Books won't let us forget?

"Those who don't learn from history are doomed to repeat it." I guess that's the simplest way of saying it. We just can't ignore history, or our own history, as painful as it may be.

CWG98: You also said, "Each time a child opens a book, he pushes open the gate that separates him from Elsewhere. It gives him choices. It gives him freedom." Is your job

opening the gate, or giving kids the freedom to open it themselves?

That's semantic, I think, that question! Every child has that gate to push open. It's the role of many people to help. A book writer like myself is only one of many. The others are parents, librarians, and teachers—all those people who create the village that allows a child to grow.

CWG98: What do you think of the current state of children's writing and publishing?

I think there's always going to be a love for fine literature. There will always be publishers for it, and always readers for it. What bothers me about current publishing is the amount of awful literature out there.

What I particularly loathe is that Hollywood, in the broadest sense, makes a movie, then makes a book out of the movie. *Mary Poppins* is an example. It became a movie, and none of my children read *Mary Poppins* because they saw the movie. A whole generation of children has lost the original book. I think kids can, and do, make their way through hard books. I really hate those Disneyesque things that purport to be books. The cartoons have nothing to do with a piece of literature. I just wish they wouldn't ruin good books.

CWG98: What about series fiction?

The series don't bother me as much. My grandchild, who is fourteen now, worked his way through Goosebumps and then outgrew them. I have a couple of step-granddaughters and they're working their way through The Baby-

Sitters Club. I don't think it will hurt them. It gets them in the habit of holding a book. They take up space in the bookstore, but they get kids into the bookstore. That's not a bad place to be.

CWG98: Any advice for would-be writers?

I often find myself speaking to

Lois Lowry Titles

- *All About Sam*. Houghton Mifflin, 1988.
- *Attaboy, Sam!* Publisher, 1992.
- *Anastasia, Absolutely*. Houghton Mifflin, 1992.
- *Autumn Street*. Houghton Mifflin, 1980.
- *The Giver*. Houghton Mifflin, 1993.
- *Number the Stars*. Houghton Mifflin, 1989.
- *The One Hundredth Thing About Caroline*. Houghton Mifflin, 1983.
- *See You Around, Sam!* Houghton Mifflin, 1996.
- *A Summer to Die*. Houghton Mifflin, 1984.
- *Taking Care of Terrific*. Houghton Mifflin, 1983.
- *Your Move, J.P.!* Houghton Mifflin, 1990.

Selected *Anastasia* books, Houghton Mifflin:
Anastasia, Absolutely
Anastasia Again
Anastasia at This Address
Anastasia at Your Service
Anastasia's Chosen Career
Anastasia Has the Answer
Anastasia on Her Own

PROFILES

groups of people who want to be writers. What distresses me sometimes is they want to "be writers," but what they should be wanting to do is to write. It's a very different thing. They like the thought of being a writer, but perhaps they don't realize or appreciate the joy that comes from sitting alone in a room and writing. I don't see how anybody can be a successful writer without experiencing the immense satisfaction that comes from the act of writing. That, to me, is the important thing: the writing. Not the publishing: That's a nice thing that happens later. If you don't have the desire to sit there alone and play with words, it isn't going to happen.

CWG98: You still vary the serious and sad books with fun ones. Does this keep you intellectually limber, or just cheerful?

I like to cook, but I don't like to cook the same meal every night, or even the same style of cooking. I like to knit, but I don't make the same sweater over and over. For me, it's very comfortable to go back and forth. I think probably my style is much the same whether I write serious or fun. There's always a lot of attention paid to characterization. There's always a lot of dialogue. And interspersed throughout there will be certain descriptive elements. People sometimes ask me if I think about the audience, who a book is directed toward. I don't even think about that when I'm writing. I guess I'm writing for myself.

Eloise Jarvis McGraw

Inventing Other Times, Other Worlds

By Cheryl Bowlan

PROFILES

Eloise Jarvis McGraw has an itch in need of a scratch. This eighty-two-year-old author of eighteen children's books is waiting for an idea—one idea that digs deep under her skin, takes hold, and launches another story.

The last one led to *The Moorchild,* a novel about a half-fairy changeling struggling to find her place among humans, and it led to several awards: a third Newbery Honor, a *Boston Globe-Horn Book* Honor, a Parent's Choice Silver Honor, and the Society of Children's Book Writers and Illustrators' Golden Kite.

"I haven't had a dry spell in quite a long time," says McGraw. "I don't like it. Takes me long enough to write a book, so I at least have to get the idea going pretty soon. But you can't hurry it, and you can't even encourage it very much. Sometimes what you'd like to get is not what you get."

McGraw, who is best known as a young adult novelist, has always felt an urge to write. Except for the decade following college, when she married, began a family, and focused on art, she has always written, starting at age eight with her first story, "The Cedar Pencil Boys," inspired by a set of pencils with little hat-like erasers.

These days she sometimes combines the passions of writing and art by creating her book jacket illustrations in the basement studio of her Oregon home, and her novels in the upstairs office she shares with her husband, children's author William Corbin McGraw. "I can either write or do art," she says. "But I have to do one or the other, or I pace around and feel empty."

Her career has spanned nearly half a century, and much has changed since she published her first book, *Sawdust in His Shoes,* in 1950. That novel, about a boy raised in a circus, and the never published manuscript that preceded it, took shape on a table turned toward the wall of her children's playroom while her young son and daughter kept busy with their toys.

"I started writing," she says, "because paints and little kids don't work. I had to do something that was non-smeary."

Growing Through

Back in those early years, there were many small publishers with good reputations who would take a chance on a first book with promise, then publish something "bound to be popular and take up the slack," McGraw says. "You could join the slush pile any time you wanted to and get discovered. That's what I did. Now it's all business and publicity."

McGraw is concerned about trends in adult publishing shifting to the juvenile side of the industry. "The children's field seems to be trying to ape the adult field, where it's entirely star-oriented," she says. "The same people

Eloise Jarvis McGraw Titles

- *Sawdust in His Shoes.* Coward-McCann, 1950.
- *Crown Fire.* Coward-McCann, 1951.
- *Moccasin Trail.* Coward-McCann, 1952.
- *Mara, Daughter of the Nile.* Coward-McCann, 1953.
- *Pharoah,* Coward-McCann, 1958.
- *Techniques of Writing Fiction,* The Writer, Inc., 1959.
- *The Golden Goblet.* Coward-McCann, 1961.
- *Merry Go Round in Oz.* (with Lauren McGraw). Reilly & Lee, 1961; reprinted, Books of Wonder, 1989.
- *Greensleeves.* Harcourt, 1968.
- *Master Cornhill.* Atheneum, 1973.
- *A Really Weird Summer.* Atheneum, 1977.
- *Joel and the Great Merlini.* Pantheon, 1979.
- *The Forbidden Fountain of Oz.* (with Lauren McGraw). The International Wizard of Oz Club, 1980.
- *The Money Room.* Atheneum, 1981.
- *Hideaway.* Margaret K. McElderry Books, 1983.
- *The Seventeenth Swap.* Margaret K. McElderry Books, 1986.
- *The Trouble with Jacob.* Margaret K. McElderry Books, 1988.
- *The Striped Ships.* Margaret K. McElderry Books, 1991.
- *Tangled Web.* Margaret K. McElderry Books, 1993
- *The Moorchild.* McElderry, 1996

get 'squillions' in advance, and their books sell like mad. I think it's a poor trend. I'd rather there were more publishers and more different kinds of books and more attention paid to non-bestsellers."

Even the fuss around the Newberys didn't exist back when McGraw won her first two Honor awards, for *Moccasin Trail* in 1952 and *The Golden Goblet* in 1962. "I got the word from my editor as a kind of casual announcement," says McGraw. "She said congratulations, and that was about it. Nobody asked you to speak. There were no newspaper articles. When you worked in children's writing, you got used to being private. Nobody else ever heard of you."

After *The Golden Goblet,* a novel about a young Egyptian goldsmith of the Old Kingdom, says McGraw, "I made myself stop writing historicals, because they were in disrepute, or at least they were unpopular. *Young adult* was just entering the language. You were supposed to come to the party and be part of the present world, not go on daydreaming. I got all this through magazine articles and the general atmosphere in the business. I couldn't write the sort of thing I read other people writing. I didn't know how to do that. I didn't want to. But I insisted to myself and had a traumatic couple of years."

Because her own son and daughter were grown by that time, McGraw saw herself as out of touch with children and their perceptions. "I solved that problem by remembering how I felt about things—how your character feels, how people felt in ancient Egypt, how I felt in my childhood, and how I feel today have a lot in common. I wrote *Greensleeves,* which has far too complicated a plot. But after that I wasn't so scared of the present tense."

Better than Anything

She returned to historical novels with the 1973 publication of *Master Cornhill,* a novel set during the English plague of 1665 and the Great Fire of London. By then she was comfortable travelling across eras, from ancient or imagined to modern. She went on to write mysteries, fantasy (including two with her daughter Lauren McGraw), contemporary novels, and more historicals.

Looking back on her long career, she says, "I thought I was doing a good job to write those modern novels. Now it seems the historicals are the ones that have really lived in my work."

Today McGraw claims to play no favorites with genre. For her next book, she would like to come up with an idea for a fantasy, a kind of story she describes as a "natural gesture" for her. "I loved fantasy when I was a child—fairy tales, Oz books, pretend," she says. "It didn't occur to me to write any for a long time because I thought it would be considered very unsophisticated. Fantasy has become much more popular now than when I first started publishing."

At this time of her life, nothing will deter McGraw from writing what she enjoys and what plants itself in

PROFILES

her imagination. "I love to invent, better than anything. I'm just poking around, waiting for something to hit me."

Joan Lowery Nixon

Kids Love a Mystery

By Donna Freedman

PROFILES

The wildflowers were lovely along the road to San Antonio last spring. But they were more than just scenery to Joan Lowery Nixon. They were a potential clue for an as yet unwritten mystery. Roadside blossoms, newspaper stories, TV shows, chance remarks: It's all grist for the idea mill. By her own estimate, if Nixon used up every clue in her file, she'd still be writing at age 150. "I find things every day, practically," says Nixon. "It's like having a bank account of ideas."

Keeping her eyes and ears open is one of the secrets to her success. Another secret is the habit of asking herself, "What if ... ?" She has asked it often, and she always gets an answer. Not right away, mind you; it took her three months to puzzle out a way to solve *The Kidnapping of Christina Lattimore*. But sharp eyes and ears and an inquisitive nature have resulted in more than 100 books in 34 years.

Nixon is perhaps best known for her mysteries; she has won four Edgar Allan Poe awards. Her dedication to the genre stood her in good stead last year, when she served as president of the Mystery Writers of America. That organization encourages its leaders to do a personal "presidential project." Nixon planned not one, but two. The first was to inaugurate a series of mysteries for adults learning to read, since literacy programs find it tough to get grown-up students interested in elementary education books. Written in reading levels from fourth to eighth grades, the books will feature adult characters and plots. They'll be published by NTC Publishing Group.

The second project, Kids Love A Mystery Week, is tailor-made for her loyal fans. Nixon works with Barnes & Noble on this special event; the 1998 date is February 23-28. Stores nationwide invite mystery authors and stage mysterious goings-on to celebrate the fact that kids have always liked a good puzzler. And always will, in Nixon's opinion.

"I think juvenile mysteries are going to become even more popular," she says. "There are so many teachers who write to me and say, 'Kids who won't read anything else will read a mystery.' I get letters from kids who say the same thing: 'I never liked to read, but my teacher gave me your book and I loved it.'"

No Pigeonholes

Nixon may be renowned for mysteries, but she hasn't allowed herself to be pigeonholed. She has done picture books, young adult novels, juvenile Westerns, and a hybrid genre she calls history-mystery. Her recent Orphan Train and Ellis Island historical series have won over a new generation of readers.

She has even tried her hand at horror: a short story called "There's a Tomb Waiting for You," published in an an-thology, *Short Circuit.* The story was one of those what-ifs. On a visit to New Orleans, she met a woman who told her that a neighborhood had "adopted" and cared for tombs in a local cemetery. Nixon thought about that for a while. "What if I were a kid and adopted a tomb," she mused, "and whoever was in it followed me home?"

It's not a big leap from mysteries to scary stories, since many whodunits have fearful underpinnings. The protagonist in *The Kidnapping of Christina Lattimore* fears for her life as she languishes in a dark, rodent-infested basement. In *The Other Side of Dark,* a girl wakes from a coma unable to recall the face of the man who murdered her mother. *The Seance* includes an element of the supernatural, since one character claims to be able to contact the dead.

No Fudging

Nixon stresses the need in children's writing for absolute accuracy on everything from cooking utensils to weather patterns to the inner workings of police departments. Research is the key to a good mystery—or a good anything, for that matter.

"I'm not going to say, 'They're just kids, what do they know?' I want them to trust me, to trust that I'm going to give them the right facts," she says. "If you put something in a book that you just fudged, they're through with you."

In the age of publishing conglomerates, writers have to work harder than ever to reach young audiences. Nixon fears that editors are relying heavily on best-selling series. That means some midlist authors are ban-

Joan Lowery Nixon Titles

- *Backstage with a Ghost*. Disney Press, 1995.
- *Before You Were Born*. Our Sunday Visitor, 1980.
- *Beware of the Pirate Ghost*. Disney Press, 1996.
- *Catch a Crooked Clown*. Disney Press, 1995.
- *A Dangerous Promise*. The Orphan Train Adventures. Delcacorte, 1994.
- *Deadly Promise*. Bantam Doubleday Dell, 1993.
- *The Happy Birthday Mystery*. Albert Whitman, 1980.
- *Haunted Island*. Scholastic, 1987.
- *If You Were a Reader*. Simon & Schuster, 1988.
- *Keeping Secrets*. The Orphan Train Adventures. Delcacorte, 1996.
- *The Kidnapping of Christina Lattimore*. Bantam Doubleday Dell, 1992.
- *Murdered, My Sweet*. Delacorte, 1997.
- *A Place to Belong*. The Orphan Train Adventures. Delcacorte, 1996.
- *Sabotage on the Set*. Disney Press, 1996.
- *Search for the Shadowman*. Delacorte, 1996.
- *Valentine Mystery*. Albert Whitman, 1979.
- *When I Am Eight*. Dial, 1994.
- *Will You Give Me a Dream?* Four Winds, 1994.

ished when they don't bring in the big bucks. The same is happening in the adult mystery field, she notes. "Some authors are dropped because their series didn't make any money. They have to go off looking for another publisher."

How can writers fight back? By recognizing that publishing is a business, she says, and adopting a businesslike work ethic. The only way to turn out top-notch writing is to work at it, and then to work diligently at finding the right publisher.

When Nixon taught writing classes, some of her students would plead a too-busy schedule as an excuse for not turning in assignments. This rationalization did not sit well with their teacher. It's her feeling that if you really want to write, you simply have to carve a piece of time out of your schedule. Neither day jobs, spouses, nor children should keep you from your work. "Writing is definitely a business. It is not a hobby," Nixon says.

She remains optimistic about the publishing of juvenile and young adult genres. Even when the bottom line is the dollar sign, the editors still tend to stay very involved with their authors. "A book is teamwork," says Nixon. In fact, she believes that editors' names should be in books along with the writers'.

She doesn't buy into the notion that today's kids are too media-savvy to want to flip pages. "Kids love to read," says Nixon. "Granted, there are a lot of distractions, but they love to read. You can't go to bed with a computer; you take a book and a flashlight. There's only so many hours you can play Nin-

PROFILES

tendo. When television was invented, movie producers thought they'd all go out of business, but they didn't. People still like to get out of the house. And people still love reading books."

J.D. Owen
Moving Through the Ranks
By Mark Haverstock

What does an Eagle Scout do when he grows up? Gerald Ford became the thirty-eighth President. Steven Spielberg earned recognition as one of the outstanding film directors and producers of this century. Neil Armstrong took mankind's first step on the moon. J.D. Owen became Editor-in-Chief for the Boy Scouts of America's three periodicals: *Boys' Life, Exploring,* and *Scouting.*

Early Start
The young J.D.Owen never anticipated that his participation in scouting would eventually lead to a career with the Boy Scouts of America (BSA). He joined the Cub Scouts in his hometown of Abilene, Texas, and later graduated to Scout Troop 8, where he attained Scouting's highest rank. "Scouting was a big deal to me," says Owen. "I really enjoyed the activities, especially camping every month."

Besides Scouting activities, Owen was active in journalism at both high school and college levels. "I worked on the Cooper High School *Cooper Crest* and the *SMU Daily Campus* at Southern Methodist University," says Owen. "I also interned for the *Abilene Reporter News,* writing obituaries."

Owen graduated from SMU with a Bachelor of Fine Arts degree, majoring in journalism. His first job was as an editor with a suburban newspaper in the Dallas area, the *De Soto News*. "At a small newspaper like that, I did it all, from covering sports to fires and the police, the courthouse, feature articles, and taking pictures," says Owen. During his tenure as editor, his paper won several awards from the Texas Press Association.

Getting with the Program

Owen answered an advertisement in another Dallas newspaper that eventually led to his association with BSA publications in 1982. Starting with the Boy Scouts in their book publishing division, he worked with merit badge handbooks. "I did general editing and dealt with freelancers—contributors to the merit badge series. Since there were more than 100 merit badge books, it was a constant fight to keep these books up-to-date. We were constantly on the lookout for qualified people to help us revise them."

Although it's not a well-known fact outside scouting circles, the BSA is a prolific publisher with more than 2,000 titles on their list, including *Scoutmaster Handbook* and *The Field Book*. Their bestseller, *The Boy Scout Handbook,* has sold more than 35 million copies since 1910. During his tenure with the book division, Owen served as editor of the tenth edition of this Boy Scout classic.

Owen calls working for BSA publications very rewarding. "You reach a large audience with the *Handbook* and merit badge booklets. It has a real im-

pact on the lives of young people."

Moving through the ranks, Owens became Editor of *Boys' Life* in April 1995. This promotion put him at the helm of one of the top ten magazines in the children's market. "The Magazine for All Boys," boasts a circulation of more than 1.3 million.

A Long Tradition

Owen is quick to point out that *Boys' Life* takes pride in its traditions. "There's a lot that you build on. You don't come into this organization and start from scratch, or try to change things immediately," he explains. Over the years, *Boys' Life* has published some of America's best writers, including Jack Schaefer, Issac Asimov, and Gary Paulsen. "It's a legacy that we intend to continue—to present some of the best writing around for young people."

The basic formula has worked for eighty-eight continuous years: Make it a fun-filled, adventurous, upbeat, and exciting publication. "Over the years, our readers have enjoyed the same kinds of things in the magazine—jokes, sports, true stories of scouts in action, cartoons, and the variety of columns and articles in the magazine," says Owen. Sports stories are favorites, and feature major league athletes who exemplify good sportsmanship and integrity. "We try to present strong male role models for our readers in any field we cover, especially in sports."

Who are *Boys' Life* readers? "Most of our subscribers are scouts, but it's a magazine intended for all boys, and that's the way we try to make it," says Owen. "There are scouting elements in the magazine. For instance, we have a scouting-program feature in every issue. One of our purposes is to reinforce scouting values. But our main goal is to foster literacy and the enjoyment of reading for everyone."

Blazing New Trails

While the traditional formulas still work well, Owen and his editorial staff continue seeking ways to fine-tune for success. "Two years ago, we began to publish demographic editions of the magazine. We're swapping out up to a dozen pages per issue, with certain pages being geared for younger readers. Those are primarily cartoons, word games, puzzles, and some Cub Scout features. For our older readers, we usually include more feature articles."

So far, the response to the demographic versions has been good, "but it will take awhile to get an accurate read on that," explains Owen. "Subscriptions are up and are growing at a higher percentage than scout membership, especially among our younger readers. It could be that younger boys feel that there's more in the magazine for them."

Owen notes that gender boundaries are fading fast. Sisters of scouts read the magazine too. "We receive a lot of correspondence from girls about the magazine. The general interest features seem to have a universal appeal to all young people."

The Competition

The struggle to grab kids' attention in a world of video games, television, and computers has also affected the *Boys' Life* format. "You'll see that our articles have gotten shorter, and there are more photographs and illustrations—a trend I've seen in my two years with the magazine. We'll continue to pare down our article size." Owen says it's rare to see a 1500-word article in *Boys' Life* any more. "They're no more than 1200 words. You want to give kids as much information as you can in fewer pages, and much of it is going to be done graphically."

For years, *Boys' Life* had no real competition in the magazine market. Now they've been joined by newer publications such as *Disney Adventures, Sports Illustrated For Kids, National Geographic World,* and *Nickelodeon.* "Those are publications that have some deep pockets behind them, and they've been doing quite well," says Owen. "They cover different market niches than we do; we're general interest, while they're more specific interest." He notes that many *Boys' Life* readers read these other publications as well. "It's not that they necessarily pick one over the other, they just read more, which is great."

Leader of the Pack

Owen's 1997 promotion to Editor-in-Chief of the BSA's magazine group now puts him in charge of editorial content, budgets, and scheduling for three magazines. He intends to carry on the traditions of *Boys' Life,* seeking the best for his readers.

"Writing for children is one of the toughest things to do and do well," says Owen. "Patronizing attitudes just don't cut it. You want to speak right to them in an intelligent, forthright, and interesting way and give them information they can use, whether in their personal lives, just for fun, or to stimulate their imaginations. I think it is difficult to do well. The writers that we publish on a regular basis are the ones who can come up with the good story and write it in a way that's going to appeal to a younger reader."

Katherine Paterson

Building Characters and Miracles

By Ellen Macauley

Katherine Paterson is best known as the author of *Bridge to Terabithia*, winner of the 1978 Newbery Award. The phenomenal success of the heart-tugging novel tends to overshadow this prolific author's many other accomplishments. In fact, all of her published works—twenty, in as many years—have received accolades, including the 1977 National Book Award for *The Master Puppeteer*, another Newbery for *Jacob Have I Loved* (1981), and the Scott O'Dell Award and American Library Association Best Book for *Jip, His Story* (1996).

Paterson's books are treasured for the depth and richness of her characters. There's the unforgettable Jesse Aarons of *Bridge to Terabithia*, a lonely country boy who reaches out to a fearless girl for validation. The spunky Louise of *Jacob Have I Loved* copes with living in her perfect twin's shadow. There are many, many more. The reader comes to know these protagonists heart and soul, so deeply drawn are Paterson's creations.

In a recent interview, Paterson, a warm woman with a down-home accent and frequent, gentle laugh, says, "I don't write about people I don't deeply care about because I can't understand why anybody would want to read about them. I certainly don't want to live with such a character for the year or two it takes to complete the book."

No labored, preliminary character sketches are made by this author. "I know a little bit about him or her when I start a book, but not nearly as well as I'm going to know them when I finish the first draft. Each rewriting is a getting to know these people better."

Discipline and Subconscious

Paterson has lived around the world. Her family moved eighteen times before her eighteenth birthday. As a young woman, she fell in love with Japan, prompting a lifelong interest in the country, as well as her first three books.

In 1962, she married the Reverend John Paterson ("my first editor and greatest booster"). She recalls this "before-playing-famous" period in her life when her four children were small and in need of constant attention as the most productive of her writing career, despite "publishing practically nothing."

That is because, she says, "I learned that, with discipline, I could write without long, sustained periods in which to do so. I also learned that your subconscious is always working for you and the book is growing underneath."

Paterson "shed a lot of guff" upon winning a bout with cancer. Her gypsy soul has settled in Vermont in the midst of family and friends. "Writers need other people to nourish our souls and activities that nourish our imaginations."

A key member of her support team is Virginia Buckley, her editor since 1971. (Buckley was at Lodestar until that imprint was closed in late 1997). Appreciative of the increasing rarity of a long-term editorial relationship, Paterson is sympathetic to the obstacles facing new writers. "There's hope in the small publishers, who seem to be more willing to take risks than the big ones. I'm not sure my first book would be published now. It's a hard time for people who write books out of the mainstream and those are usually the best."

No Greater Compliment

A former teacher, Paterson is particularly gratified to reach the "reluctant" reader. One experience that touched her heart greatly was a book report on *The Great Gilly Hopkins* written by a stereotyped "bad kid in class": It read, "This book is a miracle. Mrs. Paterson. knows exactly how children feel."

"There can't be any greater compliment than when a child whose life does not include books suddenly finds himself in the world of a book," says Paterson. "That's why we need a lot of books. It's a great feeling to know yours was pivotal in a reader's life. Children are loyal. They want your book to be the best book they've ever read. I don't think a writer can ask for more than that."

An adult reader of Paterson's books relates not only to her characters' childlike emotions, but *remembers* feeling the same way. "I think I have a good emotional memory," Paterson says. "I'm writing to that child I once was."

While certainly not perfect, her characters are consistently hard working, often noble, and seemingly the antithesis of the perception of modern children. Yet these are the very kids for whom her books hold the greatest appeal. "It's a little bit of a mystery to me why children love my books. But for the texture of the book, if you describe a person who's not deeply involved in something other than their own egos, you have a very thin book. The play of the outer and inner world of the character and some element of the adventure is part of what makes a true novel."

Paterson finds that the hardest part of the writing process is starting a new book. "I finish a book and I think that's the end of my career. It's not that I don't have any ideas, it's just that they never seem worthy. I think about all the trees that are going to have to give their lives for this book. I'm my own worst enemy, I suppose."

However painful, the outcome is always terrific for the reader and cathartic for the author, and fortunately, 1998 brings the release of three new books. "You're always finding part of yourself in characters. I don't write about people that aren't somehow deeply kin to me."

Jip gave some thought to what he liked in a book in *Jip, His Story:*

> Now Jip was just an ignorant boy and it wasn't his business, he knew, to try to tell a writer how to write a book, but it stood to reason that if you want to catch a reader tight, the trap needs to be plain and strong with no smell of the trapper lingering in it.

It seems that what Jip was looking for is what millions of fans have already discovered—a book by the inspirational Katherine Paterson.

Katherine Paterson Titles

- *Angels and Other Strangers.* HarperCollins, 1979.
- *Bridge to Terabithia.* HarperCollins, 1977.
- *Come Sing, Jimmy Jo.* Dutton, 1985.
- *Flip-Flop Girl.* Dutton, 1994.
- *The Great Gilly Hopkins.* HarperCollins, 1978.
- *Jacob Have I Loved.* Avon, 1981.
- *Jip, His Story.* Dutton, 1996.
- *The King's Equal.* HarperCollins, 1996.
- *Lyddie.* Dutton, 1991.
- *The Master Puppeteer.* Avon, 1981.
- *A Midnight Clear, Twelve Family Stories for the Christmas Season.* Dutton, 1995.
- *Of Nightingales that Weep.* HarperCollins, 1974.
- *Park's Quest.* Puffin, 1989.
- *Rebels of the Heavenly Kingdom.* Dutton, 1983.
- *The Sign of the Chrysanthemum.* HarperCollins, 1988.
- *The Smallest Cow in the World.* HarperCollins, 1991.
- *The Tale of the Mandarin Ducks.* Dutton, 1990.
- *Who Am I?* Eerdmans, 1992.

1998 Publication:
- *Parzival.* Penguin, 1998.
- *Celia and the Sweet, Sweet Water.* Clarion, 1998.
- *Images of God,* with John Paterson. Clarion, 1998.

PROFILES

E. Russell Primm III
A Constant Devotion

By Victoria Hambleton

One of the first things you learn about E. Russell Primm III is that he loves books. He always has. It is this passion and devotion that have helped lead him to his position today: In late 1997, he started his own writing, consulting, and book packaging corporation, called Editorial Directions, Inc.

Before that, he was Editorial Director of Children's Press and Franklin Watts, two the top names in publishing for the school and library markets. Primm successfully managed to unite the two companies while also allowing each to keep its own identity. He was responsible for bringing their books into the age of technology. Not bad for someone who is only thirty-eight. Asked if he is young for this level of success, Primm laughs and answers, "I guess so, but I feel very old."

Primm grew up in the Midwest—all over the Midwest. His father works in retailing and the family moved fourteen times before Primm entered high school. Despite the many relocations, books were a constant part of his life.

"My mother read to me from the time I was born," he recalls. "And I've always loved books. I catalogued my book collection when I was six years old! As kids we were allowed to buy a book a week. It might have been a Peanuts comic strip book or a Dennis the Menace book, but we had books and we were encouraged to read. And I always knew I wanted to be either an editor or a librarian."

Primm's book collection has since grown considerably: Today he admits to owning more than 4,000 volumes.

Up the Ladder

By the time he was in high school, Primm's family had settled in the Chicago area and he went to college at Loyola University, majoring in English. After a brief stint in banking, he landed a position in his chosen field, publishing. The company was J G Ferguson, a small publisher specializing in reference materials, and the job was secretary to the Editorial Director.

Primm remembers being amazed that he actually got the job. "I had absolutely no experience—none. I had never edited, never written in college. I knew nothing. But I convinced this guy with my enthusiasm to hire me, and he gave me the job over people who had years of experience." At the end of his first day on the job, the Editorial Director called Primm into his office and told him he should quit, that there was "no future in publishing."

"He told me I was too smart for the business," laughs Primm, "and that I ought to go become a doctor or a lawyer. I looked at him and said, 'You know my mother isn't going to like this, so if it's all the same to you I'm going to come back tomorrow.'"

Within two months, Primm's secretarial duties took a backseat to editorial

responsibilities as he was given more and more book projects of his own. After three years of learning the basics at minimal pay ("I started at $9,900 and only got up to $11,000") Primm left Ferguson for a job that offered twice the money and excellent benefits. He worked on accreditation manuals and newsletters on risk management. While the work was sometimes "a little bit boring," the experience was invaluable. "I really learned production," Primm recalls. "Page make-up, dummying, proofreading, copyediting: They were all things that when I left the job, I felt I really knew well."

In addition to the experience, the job turned out to be a good decision because, once he was gone, the Editorial Director at Ferguson realized he had lost a talent. A year later, Primm was back with the publisher, this time for more money and with the title, Editor. He stayed for three more years and then decided it was time to go back to school. He applied to the University of Chicago's Graduate Library School and was accepted and given a scholarship. It was a hectic time. Primm continued to work part-time at Ferguson, while attending school full-time, and took on yet another part-time job. "I was asked if I wanted to work as an Editorial Assistant for the Journals Division of the University of Chicago Press. The job came with an office, my own key to the library school, and my own computer, so I said yes, I want this! I was very busy but also very happy."

While still in school, Primm was offered the position of Editorial Director at J G Ferguson after the man who originally hired him quit. He was determined to finish school, but also knew he'd have to do both, since it was a job he couldn't turn down. He was twenty-nine. The next year, he completed his degree in children's literature.

Up and Running
It was a time in his life when Primm says he sometimes felt young for the job. "I was fine over the phone because I guess I didn't sound twenty-nine, but one-on-one was sometimes a problem. I had one freelancer who, when he met me, told me I was too young and he planned to do exactly what he thought was right. I learned, because I had to, how to handle people."

Juggling people and personalities is part and parcel of being an Editorial Director. "When you are in a position of authority," says Primm, "you tend to make enemies and you disappoint many people, but that comes with the territory. I have a responsibility to my company but also to publishing in general, because what I do says something. It's my job to publish the best quality books I can, and along the way there are some editors and writers who may disagree with me, but I have to go with what I think is right."

In 1989, having learned all he felt he could at Ferguson, Primm accepted a job with Children's Press as a Project Editor, developing books and educational materials for use in the classroom. Two years later, Grolier decided to consolidate the back offices of Children's Press and Franklin Watts and, in 1995, when the consolidation was complete, Primm was named Editorial Director of both houses.

The first task at hand was the re-making of Children's Press. It was a tall order. When the company moved to its new headquarters in Danbury, Connecticut, only four staff members made the move. "We had no editors," recalls Primm. "We had to outsource nearly everything and keep it all going while we hired a completely new staff. I'm proud to say we didn't lose a single season." The years of juggling paid off and gave Primm the skills to carry through the first year.

Today, Primm and his new company are consulting for J G Ferguson on career guidance materials, and helping them form library boards and move into new markets. Primm is also writing twenty-eight books for a company in Minnesota, and at press time was contracting with Grolier to handle its geography publishing program, a sixty-eight book deal that includes the relaunching of two series, America the Beautiful and Enchantment of the World.

Keeping Up with the Times
Another challenge Primm has had to face, one the publishing industry as a whole has had to meet, is how to keep books an integral part of a society that is increasingly relying on technology. Nowhere has the impact of technology been more profound than in the arena of children's publishing.

"The market is very different from what it was in the eighties," explains Primm. "For one thing, library book budgets are smaller, and so we are competing for a smaller piece of the pie when it comes to the school and library markets. For another, we have new competition in the form of Nick-

PROFILES

elodeon, the Internet, computers, and magazines. We need to make books as interactive as we can in a static format."

"I think in many ways we've made our books look *magaziney,* if you will, in that we try to find typefaces that while they are still readable, have a more fun feel to them. If you look at Children's Press books prior to 1995, they were very, very formatted, with pictures at either the top or the bottom of the page, most of them black-and-white. But to change that in terms of page format and layout, and to use color pictures, all costs a lot of money. But we had no choice if we were going to compete."

The response to the new look of the Children's Press was favorable. In particular, a series on the states, From Sea to Shining Sea, is very popular. Another innovation that received accolades from librarians and reviewers was the reference material now included in the back of both Franklin Watts' and Children's Press books. "We included print resources and multimedia resources as well, whether a video, an appropriate movie, a picture book, and we include relevant Internet addresses. It was a way of extending the life of the books, of making them more dynamic," says Primm.

Transported

Given all the competition, will books survive? For Primm the answer is an absolute yes.

"Nobody wants to sit and read books on a computer. But more than that, there is an intimate relationship between the reader and the book as an object. It's the feel of the book, its weight, the feel of the paper, its smell and texture that are evocative of all sorts of things. A book connotes a sense of safety and transports you to a place of joy."

"I see teachers more and more showing their students that books are objects, that they are more than just the information they contain. And I think that's going to continue. As to what books will look like, say, ten years from now, or how they'll be made, who knows?"

For the future, Primm believes the greatest challenge is one that sounds simple: making sure all children can read. "It's a challenge that the President of the United States has given us," he says, "and we are a part of that. Every kid in the third grade should be able to read at the third-grade level. But they don't."

Success, he feels, will come only through a joint effort among parents, educators, children's book publishers, and librarians. No one is more committed to producing quality than E. Russell Primm. "I really do think that publishing educational books for children is important and that's very important to my quality of life. The books we publish make a difference in children's lives and for me, that's what it's all about."

Anita Silvey

A Circle of Books

By Patricia Curtis Pfitsch

Anita Silvey, Vice President and Publisher of Children's Books, Trade and Reference Division of Houghton Mifflin, has had the unusual distinction of coming around full circle twice in her publishing career. She spent five years at the *Horn Book* as Assistant Editor, then went to Houghton Mifflin. After eight years at Houghton, she went back to the *Horn Book* as Editor, and after eleven years, assumed her current position as Publisher at Houghton.

"When that happens," Silvey says, "you hope you bring something better when you come back. That's what I'm able to do: Bring an inside knowledge that I didn't have before."

Silvey trained in education and had planned to be a teacher. But when she graduated from college in 1970, teaching jobs were nonexistent. Instead, she took a position at Little, Brown and

PROFILES

Company and began her training in children's book publishing. "As assistant to the head of the department, you do everything," Silvey explains.

From there she went to the *Horn Book*. "As far as I was concerned, the job was heaven itself," Silvey says. Every afternoon she would have tea with Editor Paul Hines, who would ask her what books she had read and what she thought about them. "I got an education you can never get at a single publishing house. At a house, you know your own books very well and everyone else's at somewhat of a distance. As a reviewer, I read all the books and thought about them with equal weight."

Two Worlds

Of editing and reviewing, Silvey says, "I'm drawn to both worlds. The moment I'm in one, I find I'm in love with the other." When she was asked to come to Houghton Mifflin as head of Marketing for children's books, she took the job. "I worked for Walter Lorraine," Silvey says. "I was very interested to see how books sold and what you could do to sell books of quality."

Eight years later, she was offered the editorship at the *Horn Book*. "There is no equal to that job anywhere," Silvey says. "You have the chance not only to read, but to meet everyone in the field, to travel widely, to travel internationally. I had no intentions of leaving."

Except that in 1995 the position of Publisher came up at Houghton. "I heard the siren call again," she says. She wanted "to have the ability to publish, to make those decisions yourself rather than to have someone else make them for you. As Editor of the *Horn Book* I found a hundred books, maybe even three hundred books every year that were just wonderful, that were everything I wanted. But as publisher, if I'm looking at a problem with a book, I can still do something about it."

The Long Term

Although she had spent time at Houghton before, when Silvey became

Publisher, the job was full of new challenges. But her knowledge of the house and its authors has been a definite advantage. Her goal is "to continue to do well what we've always done well."

Pointing out that Houghton has one of the "finest backlists in publishing," she puts primary emphasis on commitment. "I believe," Silvey says, "that the best long-term economic rationale is to publish books of quality. We ask, 'Will it still be in print in fifty years?' rather than 'Can we make a good five dollars on it now and then let it go into oblivion?'"

Silvey believes in creating lists "book by book, author by author. My contribution is keeping that vision. We sign on authors: It's a creative person we are interested in. Our job is to support that person in that creative effort."

She has not made major changes in the publishing program, but Silvey is able to bring her vast knowledge of the children's book industry to bear when making decisions about what Houghton should publish. "I read 5,000 books a year at the *Horn Book*. I can tell my editors, 'I've seen a hundred books like that; we don't need to publish the one hundred and first.'"

On the other hand, her experience at the *Horn Book* has also made her aware of needs that should be filled. "As a reviewer I saw that there was very little good middle-grade fiction published, so I'd love to publish some." She also saw that many wonderful books have gone out of print. "As publisher, I'm starting to bring some of those back into print."

Sufficient Unto the Day

Because her role as publisher requires

her to oversee the entire publishing process, she rarely has time to work on specific projects. "Sometimes people will send me work that I'm very excited about, but I usually try to find an editor here to handle the project and give it all the attention the author deserves. Given what I believe I need to do, it's not the wisest choice to spend an enormous amount of time editing."

Since each of Silvey's jobs in publishing has made her uniquely qualified for the next, one might assume she has an overarching plan for her total publishing career. The opposite is actually true. "My career is entirely based on one principle," Silvey says. "I never think about the future. I always think about the day I'm in, and I do the best job I can on that particular day. My jobs have always led to other things that have surprised me more than anyone."

She pointed to her own book, *Children's Books and Their Creators*, published in 1995 as an example. "I did an 800-page reference book—certainly one of the most satisfying things I've ever done, and I had no intention of ever writing a book." Among her recent work as editor is *Help Wanted: Short Stories About Young People Working*.

Although Silvey would be the first to admit that the children's publishing industry has its ups and downs, her enthusiasm and pleasure in her work shine through everything she says. "The wonderful thing about a job in publishing is that it's always exciting; it's always changing. That's part of what keeps it fresh."

She has a clear vision of the importance of children's publishing. "Any of us who get to work with children's books in whatever capacity, writers, illustrators, reviewers, teachers, librarians, parents, the person who puts the book in children's hands: There's so much satisfaction in that. All I have to do is see my authors working with kids and I remember how important this is. We have reason to feel good about what we do. I think we're all very fortunate."

PROFILES

Judy Wilson
From the Ground Up

By Victoria Hambleton

PROFILES

The tall, graceful art deco building looms high above its neighbors on lower Madison Avenue in New York City, a few short blocks from the venerable Morgan Library. Despite the vacancy signs that fill its huge ground floor windows, the building commands attention. Several floors up, tucked away down a winding, narrow hallway are the editorial offices of Orchard Books, an imprint of Grolier Inc. Like the building, Orchard has continued to remain strong despite its vacancies.

In 1996, Orchard's three top editors, Neal Porter, Richard Jackson, and Melanie Kroupa left to launch their own trade imprint with DK Publishing, a company that ironically has its offices in the very same building. Grolier filed a lawsuit against the three and DK Publishing, saying that the former Orchard Book executives conspired, to quote *Publishers Weekly*, "to expropriate the entire Orchard Children's list and to destroy its business." Ultimately, the suit was settled with an undisclosed amount being paid by DK Publishers to Grolier, and a statement from the three editors that they "regret any harm that may have occurred through our actions."

Meanwhile Orchard continued to produce, and the credit is due to one determined and remarkable woman: Judy V. Wilson. Appointed President of Orchard Books in late November 1996, her job was to rebuild from the ground up a company that had no editorial staff, and had lost many of its authors. Asked why she would want to take on such a seemingly impossible task, Wilson gave a deep, throaty laugh and answers, "Well, truthfully, I thought about it long and hard and it was, and is, certainly a challenge. But I thought, this is a wonderful, wonderful imprint and it's not going to go under if I have anything to say about it!"

Becoming Grounded

Wilson is someone who clearly likes a challenge and has faced and won many in a publishing career that has lasted nearly three decades. Yet despite the considerable name she has earned in the arena of children's publishing, she did not begin in the field.

"I always wanted, from childhood, to be a teacher," she recalls. Born in Tennessee, Wilson lived in Iowa and then Richmond, Virginia, as a child before attending Smith College in Northampton, Massachusetts. "After I left school, I realized that I didn't have the patience to be a teacher. In the long run though, I guess children's publishing isn't so far afield. You have to have an understanding of children to be in this business, but you don't have to deal with twenty of them in a classroom!"

Wilson majored in philosophy and minored in English at college. Afterwards, Wilson and several friends decided on a lark to up and move west, to

San Francisco. Her first job was with the Britannica Center for Studies in Learning and Motivation. "I was teaching teachers and graduate students how to write materials in programmed instruction." But after a couple of years, Wilson decided that the West was not for her, and she moved back East, to New York. If nothing else, that first job in California gave her an interest in publishing, and she was determined to find work in the field.

Her first job in New York was with the well-known trade publisher John Wiley & Sons. Although it does have a children's imprint now, it did not while Wilson was there. She stayed with the company for almost twenty years and says she was fortunate because during that time she worked in many different areas of publishing and "really got grounded in the business."

"I jumped around a lot and got a chance to work in a number of different divisions. I started in trade and then launched Wiley's software division and their training materials group. It was a wonderful experience, a wonderful place to work."

An Immersion

Her varied experience at Wiley led Wilson to her next job, with Macmillan, where she first went to work with children's books.

"Macmillan had recently bought Atheneum, Margaret K. McElderry Books, and Scribner, and they were merging these with their own three hardcover children's imprints, Macmillan, Four Winds Press, and Bradbury, and needed someone to manage the group. A friend of mine who had worked in children's publishing called me and said, 'You don't want to do that; let me tell you how difficult that is going to be.' But he did not dissuade me and I loved every minute of it."

Wilson recalls that she started at Macmillan on December 6, 1985, and spent her first day of work on a plane on her way to a sales conference in Puerto Rico, reading the catalogue on the flight. The next year was chaotic. It was Wilson's job to bring the six imprints together in a way that didn't bruise any egos and also kept the editorial voice of each line unique.

"I don't think I read an adult book for that first year at Macmillan." Wilson says. "I just immersed myself in children's books. I wanted to read the best backlist titles of every imprint so that I would know what was important to that imprint. And I thoroughly enjoyed it, even if I did get behind in my adult reading."

"I wanted to keep each editorial line autonomous. We had certain rules, which were that you couldn't steal authors from other imprints within the group. And we'd meet every week to discuss problems other than authors and illustrators, and that worked pretty well. I set up a marketing department that would service each of the imprints. Each imprint had an editorial director and maybe one or two editors and their own art director that reported directly to the editorial director. It worked well."

Although she makes it sound simple, in truth Wilson was dealing with some of the top editors in children's books including Margaret McElderry and Norma Jean Sawicki, as well as

Richard Jackson and Neal Porter, late of Orchard Books.

The Jewel

Wilson stayed with Macmillan for eight years until the company was bought by Simon & Schuster. It is a time and a job that she looks back on with great pride.

"The last two years I was there we were mainly selling the company. It was very sad. Those years were filled with presentations to bankers and investors. But I think the Macmillan Children's Book group thrived while I was there. When the company was up for sale, the *Wall Street Journal* called the children's group 'the jewel of Macmillan's assets.'"

After her years at Macmillan, Wilson decided to take a couple of years off to "have some fun consulting in the children's book industry," which she did for three years. During that time she worked extensively with Lerner Publications in Minnesota, which produces materials for the school and library markets. She also developed a five-year-plan for an adult publisher entering children's publishing for the first time, and consulted at Scholastic.

It was her consulting work that prompted Grolier to ask Wilson to come to Orchard in August of 1996 after Jackson, Porter, and Kroupa had left. By the middle of November, Wilson was named President and Publisher of Orchard. She concedes that the job of putting together a new team has been tough, but not perhaps as grim as some would imagine.

"When I came on board, we had no editorial staff, that's true," she says.

"But the Director of Subsidiary Rights was here, and the Managing Editor. The Marketing Manager unfortunately had planned to leave before the editorial staff left, and with no editorial or marketing staff, that was truly difficult. I must say I'm sometimes here until eight or nine at night. I do need to hire another editor, and we did lose some authors, who felt they wanted to follow their editors, but others have stayed and we have discovered some new authors that we are very excited about." While she is still not fully staffed, the pieces are beginning to fall into place.

Judy Wilson's message to the world is, "Orchard is alive and well and going to be here for a long time to come. Our spring 1997 list was down a couple of books from previous years to twenty-eight books and our fall list is twenty-two, but we will, for sure, recover."

Last fall Orchard celebrated its tenth anniversary. With Wilson at the helm, there's a good chance it's just the beginning of another good decade.

CONTESTS & CONFERENCES

Part
8

CONTESTS

Children's Writing Contests and Awards

Jane Addams Children's Book Award

Eurydice Kelley, Contest Coordinator
Jane Addams Peace Association, Inc.
Sixth Floor, 777 United Nations Plaza
New York, NY 10017

Description: Presented annually for more than forty years, the Jane Addams Children's Book Award honors a book that most effectively promotes the causes of peace, social justice, world community, and the equality of the sexes and all races.

Fiction or nonfiction books of any length, suitable for readers ages two to fourteen, are eligible. Themes may include nonviolent problem-solving, responsibility for the future of all peoples, overcoming prejudice, or compassionate understanding of human needs. The author, illustrator, or publisher may submit two review copies.

Deadline: April 1.

Announcements: Winners announced, September 6.

Representative Winners: *The Well: David's Story*, Mildred Taylor; honor book: *From the Notebooks of Melinan Sun*, Jacqueline Woodson.

Award: Winner receives a certificate and a seal for the winning book, presented at an awards ceremony in New York, NY.

AIM Magazine Short Story Contest

Ruth Apilado, Editor
AIM, America's Intercultural Magazine
7308 S. Eberhart
Chicago, IL 60619

Description: *AIM* Magazine seeks to "purge racism from the human bloodstream by way of the written word" and its annual contest is an extension of this message.

New writers are welcome to submit

compelling, well-written short stories, to 4,000 words. Submissions must be unpublished. No multiple submissions; no entry fee. Send SASE for contest guidelines.

Deadline: August 15.
Announcements: Winners announced in the autumn.
Representative Winner: *The Number 60 Bus*, Deb Carrenti.
Award: Publication in AIM and a $100 monetary award.

Alcuin Society Citation Awards

Richard Hopkins, Director
The Alcuin Society
P.O. Box 3216
Vancouver, BC V6B 3X8, Canada
Description: This annual award is the only Canadian contest to honor excellence in book design. Winners are selected from books published in Canada in the previous year. Judges look for a sound marriage of design and content, appropriate cover design, page layout, typography, and, where applicable, a balance of illustration and text. Books must be published in Canada or co-published with a company in another country, but must represent the work of a Canadian book designer.

Awards are presented in four categories: general trade books, limited editions, text and reference books, and books for juveniles. Books, short stories, short nonfiction, and poetry are eligible. Entry fee, $10. Multiple submissions accepted. Send SASE for contest guidelines.
Deadline: March 15.
Announcements: Contest announced in January; winners are announced at the annual general meeting in May.

Representative Winner: *The Very Hungry Lion*, Annick Press.
Award: An awards certificate is presented at the annual meeting.

America and Me Essay Contest

Lisa Fedewa, Advertising Assistant
Farm Bureau Insurance
Box 30400, 7373 Saginaw Highway
Lansing, MI 48909
Description: The purpose of this contest, now in its twenty-ninth year, is to give Michigan students the opportunity to express their thoughts on their roles in America. The contest centers on a different theme each year. It is open only to eighth graders living in Michigan. Essays of no more than 500 words should follow the contest theme.
Deadline: December 31.
Announcements: Winners announced in April.
Representative Winners: *Mickey Harte Was Here*, Barbara Park; *Time for Andrew*, Mary Downing Hahn.
Award: Winner receives a scroll illustrated by a Vermont artist, presented at a ceremony in May or June.

American Association of University Women Award for Juvenile Literature

Dr. Jerry C. Cashion, Awards Coordinator
North Carolina Literary and Historical Association
Room 305, 109 East Jones Street
Raleigh, NC 27601-2807
Description: Held annually to stimulate and reward the writing of literature for young people, this award is open only to North Carolina residents. Winners are selected for creative and imaginative quality, excellence of style, and

relevance to North Carolina and its people.

To be eligible, books must have been published during the twelve months ending June 30 of the year for which the award is given. Submit three copies of each entry. No entry fee; three entries maximum per participant allowed. **Deadline:** July 15.

Announcements: Contest announced every spring. Winners announced at the annual meeting, held in November in Raleigh, NC.

Representative Winner: *Ashpet*, Kenn and Joanne Compton.

Award: Engraved cup presented at annual meeting; winning title and author are inscribed on a permanent plaque.

Américas Award for Children's and Young Adult Literature

Julie Kline, Award Coordinator
Consortium of Latin American Studies
c/o Center for Latin America
University of Wisconsin, Milwaukee
P.O. Box 413
Milwaukee, WI 53201

Description: This contest is designed to encourage and commend authors and publishers who produce quality children's and young adult books that portray Latin America, the Caribbean, or Latinos in the U.S., and to provide teachers with recommendations for classroom use. The award recognizes a work of fiction, poetry, or folklore (from picture books to works for young adults) published in the U.S. in Spanish or English that "authentically and engagingly presents the experience of individuals" in any of the three regions. Books are judged on quality of story, cultural authenticity/sensitivity, and potential for classroom use.

Books published during the calendar year preceding the contest are eligible, and authors must be nominated in writing. Nominations are accepted from anyone with an interest in children's and young adult literature. One copy of the nominating letter and a review copy of the book should be sent to the Award Coordinator, and a review copy of the book should be sent to each of the five members on the Review Committee.

Deadline: January 15.

Announcements: Award/commended list announced in the spring for books published the previous year.

Representative Winners: *Tonight, By Sea*, Frances Temple; *The Mermaid's Twin Sister*, Lynn Joseph; *Vejigante Masquerader*, Lulu Delacre.

Award: Cash prize of $200 for the author, and a letter of citation to the author and publisher; presentation held at the Library of Congress.

Hans Christian Andersen Award

Leena Maissen, Executive Director
International Board on Books for Young People
Nonnenweg 12, Postfach, 4003 Basel
Switzerland

Description: Named after Denmark's famous storyteller, the Hans Christian Andersen Award is given to an author and an illustrator every two years. The author's award originated in 1956, the illustrator's award in 1966. A distinguished international jury of ten children's literature specialists chooses the winners based on literary and artistic criteria.

Deadline: August.

CONTESTS

Announcements: Winners announced at the Children's Book Fair in Bologna. **Representative Winners:** Author Uri Orlev from Israel; illustrator Klaus Ensikat from Germany. **Award:** Winners receive a gold medal and a diploma at an awards dinner.

Annual Writing Competition

June Rabin
South Florida Chapter, National Writers
   Association
P.O. Box 570415
Miami, FL 33257
Description: Open to all writers, this sixth annual competition accepts quality writing of short stories, short nonfiction, and poetry. Photocopies are accepted. Entry fee, $10.
Deadline: January 15.
Announcements: Contest announced in the fall; winners are named in April.
Award: Winner receives $100 at an awards luncheon on the first Saturday in April.

Arizona Young Readers' Award

Arizona Library Association
9451 North 33rd Way
Phoenix, AZ 85028
Description: Sponsored by the Arizona Library Association, the Arizona Young Readers' Award is given annually to familiarize young readers with recently published high-quality books, and to honor favorite books and authors. Young readers in Arizona vote annually for the best picture book, chapter book, and middle school/YA book.

   Titles are nominated by young readers, their teachers, and librarians. After receiving nominations, the award committee prepares a master voting list of ten titles for each category. Then the list is sent back to schools and libraries for the children's votes.
Deadline: March 14.
Announcements: Winners announced at the annual conference.
Representative Winners: Picture book, *The Toll Bridge Troll*, Patricia Rae Wolff; chapter book, *Mick Harte Was Here*, Barbara Park; middle school/YA book, *The Name of the Game Was Murder*, Joan Lowery Nixon.
Award: Winning authors receive their awards at the Arizona Young Readers' Award luncheon.

Arkansas Diamond Primary Book Award

James A. Hester, Secretary/Treasurer
Arkansas Elementary School Council
Arkansas Department of Education
4 Capitol Mall, Room 302-B
Little Rock, AR 72201
Description: The Arkansas Diamond Primary Book Award promotes quality children's literature and reading for students in kindergarten through grade three. The award was established to promote literacy and interest in books. Winners are based on the voting of children in kindergarten to grade three.

   Published short stories, short nonfiction, books, and poetry are eligible. Send SASE for contest guidelines.
Deadline: Write for 1998 date.
Announcements: Contest, March 15. Winners, in May.
Award: Medallion awarded to winning author at a banquet presentation.

ARTS Award

Wendy Paige Wheeler, Programs
   Associate

National Foundation for Advancement in the Arts
Suite 500, 800 Brickell Avenue
Miami, FL 33131
Description: ARTS, the Arts Recognition and Talent Search Award, is a national program to identify and encourage high school seniors who demonstrate excellence in writing, theater, photography, dance, music, voice, jazz, and visual arts. Judges select as many as twenty candidates in each category, who go to Florida for further evaluation in the talent search, as well as workshops and discussion sessions.

Short stories, short nonfiction, books, and poetry are eligible for consideration in the writing category. Judges consider language, originality, imagination, and overall excellence. Entry fee: $25 for entries received by June 1; $35 for entries received between June 2 and October 1. Send SASE for guidelines and application packet.
Deadline: June 1 and October 1.
Announcements: Winners notified by mail in late December. Awards announced in January.
Award: Cash awards of $100–$3,000; opportunities for college and presidential scholarships. Honorable mentions receive a $100 cash award. All awards are issued in June.

Atlantic Writing Competition
Joanne Merriam, Contest Coordinator
Writers' Federation of Nova Scotia
Suite 901, 1809 Barrington Street
Halifax, Nova Scotia B3J 3K8
Canada
Description: This competition is unique in Canada in offering constructive feedback to each entrant. Open only to unpublished writers living in Canada's Atlantic Provinces, the contest encourages new and unpublished writers to explore their talents. Included among the contest's five categories is the Joyce Barkhouse Writing for Children Prize, awarded for fiction or nonfiction (to 20,000 words), poetry, or stage plays.

Contestants may send only one entry for each category. Entry fee is $10 for Writer's Federation members, senior citizens, and students, and $15 for nonmembers.
Deadline: August 1.
Announcements: Contest announced in April. Winners announced at the Federation's gala, held in February.
Representative Winner: Joyce Barkhouse Prize: Gary Castle.
Award: Cash prizes, from $50 to $200, awarded at the annual gala.

The Margaret Bartle Annual Playwriting Award
Blanche Sellens, Chairman
Community Children's Theatre of Kansas City
8021 East 129th Terrace
Grandview, MO 64030
Description: One of the purposes of the Community Children's Theatre of Kansas City is to teach children to appreciate live theater. Winning plays in this annual competition are performed for school audiences by the group's three trouping units, which are comprised of women volunteers.

Only unpublished plays are eligible. Plays should be written for an elementary school audience, have fewer than eight characters, be sixty minutes long, and have relatively simple technical requirements. Original ideas, legends, folklore, biographies, and adaptations of children's classics usually provide good plays. Slang, cursing, violence, or seasonal plays are not accepted.

Deadline: January 31.

Announcements: Winner(s) named in April or May at the annual meeting.

Representative Winners: James Ploss, Cheryl Christmas, Judy Wolfman, Steven Otjinoski.

Award: $500.

Bay Area Book Reviewers Association Award

Jon Sharp, Contest Coordinator
c/o Chandler & Sharp Publishing
110 Commercial Boulevard
Novato, CA 94949

Description: This annual award was created in 1981 by the Bay Area Book Reviewers Association (BABRA) to consider and honor the work of local writers. It recognizes the best fiction, nonfiction, poetry, and children's literature. BABRA also gives the Fred Cody Award to honor literary figures committed to bettering their community.

Only published books are considered. No fees, no entry form. Send three copies of each title.

Deadline: December 1.

Announcements: Winners announced at an awards ceremony.

Representative Winners: *A Girl Named Disaster*, Nancy Farmer; *Officer Buckle and Gloria*, Peggy Rathmann.

Award: $100 award presented at ceremony, held in March or early April.

The John and Patricia Beatty Award

California Library Association
Suite 300, 717 K Street
Sacramento, CA 95814-3477

Description: First presented in 1989, this award is given to encourage the writing of quality children's books that highlight California and its culture, heritage, or future. Any children's or young adult book, fiction or nonfiction, set in California and published in the preceding calendar year is eligible. The setting must be depicted authentically and must be an integral focus. Entries are evaluated based on quality of writing, relationship of text to illustration, and total presentation.

Submit review books to each of the six members of the Beatty Committee. Contact the California Library Association for guidelines.

Deadline: Write for 1998 deadline.

Announcements: Winners announced during National Library Week.

Representative Winner: *Cat Running*, Zilpha Keatley Snyder.

Award: An engraved plaque and $500 is presented at the California Library Association's annual conference.

Geoffrey Bilson Award for Historical Fiction for Young People

Jeffrey Canton, Program Coordinator
The Canadian Children's Book Centre
35 Spadina Road
Toronto, Ontario M5R 2S9
Canada

Description: This award is given to works of historical fiction for young people published in the preceding calendar year. Candidates are selected from the *Our Choice* catalogue, produced annually by the Centre. The winner is chosen by a jury appointed by the Centre. Send SASE for more information.

Deadline: Ongoing.

Announcements: Presented in the fall.
Representative Winner: *The Lights Go On Again*, Kit Pearson.
Award: Cash award of $1,000.

Irma Simonton and James H. Black Award for Excellence in Children's Literature

Linda Greengrass, Coordinator of School Services
Bank Street College of Education
610 West 112th Street
New York, NY 10025
Description: This prize is given each spring to a book for young children published in the previous calendar year that demonstrates excellence in text and illustration. A group of writers, librarians, and educators choose about thirty-five books they consider to be the best candidates for the award. These books are sent to eight-to-ten-year-olds at schools throughout the U.S., and the children select the winning book.

Authors should ask their publishers to submit one copy of their books. Multiple submissions are permitted; no entry fee.
Deadline: Books should be submitted no later than the first week of January.
Announcements: Contest announced in October; winners announced May.
Representative Winners: *Jojofu*, Michael Waite and Yoriko Ito; *Wicked Jack*, Connie N. Wooldridge and Will Hillenbrand.
Award: A scroll, designed by Maurice Sendak, inscribed with the winner's name and a gold seal, that can be affixed to the winning book.

Waldo M. and Grace C. Bonderman National Youth Theatre Playwriting Workshop

Indiana University-Purdue University at Indianapolis
W. Mark McCreary, Literary Manager
525 North Blackford Street
Indianapolis, IN 46202
Description: Playwrights are encouraged to create scripts for audiences in grades three to twelve for this biennial competition. Winners must be willing to travel to Indianapolis for development of their scripts; transportation and lodging are provided.

Plays should run approximately forty-five minutes. Musicals or previously produced, professional plays are not eligible. If the play is an adaptation or dramatization, submit written proof that the source or original work is in the public domain. Author's name must not appear on the typed manuscript. Submit three copies, one entry form, SASE for return of manuscript. No entry fee.
Deadline: September 1.
Announcements: Competition announced in the spring of even years; winners announced in January.
Representative Winners: Colleen Neuman, Ric Averill, Ellen Cooper.
Award: Top four winners receive $1,000 each and staged readings.

The *Boston Globe/Horn Book* Awards

Stephanie Loer, Children's Book Editor
11 Beacon Street, Suite 1000
Boston, MA 02108
Description: This prestigious award has been cosponsored by the *Boston Globe* and the *Horn Book* since 1967. A committee of three professionals from the field of children's literature evalu-

CONTESTS

ates submissions from publishers to select winners in three categories: picture book, nonfiction, and fiction. Judges may also designate honor books in each category.

To be eligible, books must be published in the U.S.; authors do not have to be U.S. citizens. Any juvenile book is eligible, but textbooks are not considered. The committee evaluates the quality of each book as a whole, and text and illustrative material are appraised for how they work together. Publishers may submit up to eight books.

Deadline: May 15.

Announcements: Competition is announced in October. Winners announced the following year at the award luncheon of the New England Library Association's fall conference.

Representative Winners: Fiction and poetry: *The Friends*, Kazumi Yumoto; nonfiction: *A Drop of Water: A Book of Science and Wonder*, Walter Wick; picture book: *The Adventures of Sparrowboy*, Brian Pinkney.

Award: Cash award of $500 and a silver bowl; winners' speeches are printed in the *Horn Book*.

Ann Connor Brimer Award

Noreen Smiley, Coordinator
Nova Scotia Library Association
3770 Kempt Road
Halifax, Nova Scotia B3K 4X8
Canada

Description: The Ann Connor Brimer Award, given to a resident of Atlantic Canada, recognizes excellence in children's writing in books intended for a readers to the age of fifteen. Fiction and nonfiction published in Canada between May of the preceding year and

April 30 of the contest year are eligible.

Deadline: April 30.

Announcements: Winner announced in September.

Representative Winner: *Of Things Not Seen*, Don Aker.

Award: Winner receives a $1,000 prize at an award ceremony in November at the Maritime Museum of the Atlantic.

Buckeye Children's Book Award

Ruth Metcalf
State Library of Ohio
65 South Front Street
Columbus, OH 43215-4163

Description: This award, given every two years, is designed to encourage Ohio children to read literature critically, promote teacher and librarian involvement in children's literature programs, and award authors. Ohio students in kindergarten to grade eight nominate and vote for their favorite books. From nominations, the contest board selects a master voting list.

To be nominated, books must have been published by a U.S. author no more than three years before the nomination year. Nominations may be made in fiction and nonfiction for three levels: kindergarten to grade two, grades three to five, and grades six to eight. Guidelines are available at www.winslo.ohio.gov/buckhist.html.

Announcements: Winners announced in April.

Deadline: Write for 1999 deadline.

Representative Winners: Kindergarten to grade two: *Dogzilla*, Dav Pilkey; grades three to five: *The Haunted Mask II*, R.L. Stine; grades six to eight: *The Giver*, Lois Lowry.

Award: Winning books become part of

the Buckeye Children's Book Award Hall of Fame, housed in the Columbus Metropolitan Library.

ByLine Magazine Contests

Marcia Preston, Publisher
P.O. Box 130596
Edmond, OK 73013-0001
Description: *ByLine* conducts monthly contests to inspire writers and to challenge them with deadlines and competition. Nearly fifty categories are represented, including children's story or picture book, juvenile short story, children's poem, and children's fiction.

ByLine also sponsors an annual Literary Award, given for poetry (any length, theme, or style), and short story (on any subject, to 5,000 words). Unlike the monthly contests, the award is open only to subscribers.

Contest entries must be unpublished. Multiple entries are permitted; each must be accompanied by the appropriate entry fee, which varies. Literary Award entry fee, $3 per poem, $5 per story. Manuscripts are not returned. Send SASE for guidelines.
Deadline: Literary Award, November 1. Monthly contest deadlines vary.
Announcements: Literary Award winners announced in the February *ByLine*. Contest winners announced in *ByLine* four months after the contest deadline.
Award: Literary award winners receive $250 and publication in *ByLine*. Contest winners receive varying cash prizes.

Randolph Caldecott Award

Stephanie Anton, Program Officer
Association for Library Service to Children, American Library Association
50 East Huron Street

Chicago, IL 60611
Description: The American Library Association (ALA) bestows this award on "the artist of the most distinguished American picture book for children published in the U.S. during the preceding year." The ALA defines "distinguished" as marked by conspicuous eminence, distinction, and excellence in quality.

The award places no limitations on the picture book except that the illustrations be original work. The contest is open only to U.S. citizens. The criteria include excellence of execution of the artistic technique and of pictorial interpretation of the story, theme, or concept, and appropriateness of illustration style to the story, theme, or concept. The book must be a self-contained entity, not dependent on other media. Guidelines available for SASE.
Deadline: December 1.
Announcements: Winners are announced at the ALA's Midwinter Meeting, in January or February.
Representative Winner: David Wiesniewski, *Golem*.
Award: Caldecott Medal presented at awards banquet.

California Book Awards

Jim Coplan, Senior Director
Commonwealth Club of California
595 Market Street
San Francisco, CA 94105
Description: Established in 1931, the Commonwealth Club's Book Awards Program has recognized both new and established California authors. The purpose of these awards is to encourage literature in the state and honor California's contribution to the nation's

scholarship. Published works in the areas of fiction, nonfiction, poetry, first work of fiction, and children's literature are eligible; there is no limit on submissions.

Deadline: January 31.

Announcements: Competition announced in the fall; winners contacted in June or July, and a press release sent to book editors.

Representative Winners: Children's literature, to age ten: *Minty: A Story of Young Harriet Tubman*, Alan Schroeder; children's literature, ages eleven to sixteen: *A Girl Named Disaster,* Nancy Farmer.

Award: Gold and silver medals; awards reception at the Commonwealth Club.

California Writers' Club Contest

Willie Rose, Contest Coordinator
4913 Marlborough Way
Carmichael, CA 95608

Description: This contest is held every two years in conjunction with the biennial conference of the California Writers' Club (CWC). Awards are presented for stories, novels, nonfiction, juvenile picture books, and juvenile fiction or nonfiction for readers age seven and older.

Books are judged by writers and literary agents. Only unpublished material is eligible, and a contestant may send only one entry for each category. Manuscripts are not returned and critiques are not offered. The entry fee is $10. Send SASE for guidelines.

Deadline: Contact for 1999 deadline.

Announcements: Contest announced every other January. Winners announced prior to the conference.

Representative Winners: Juvenile picture book: *Baby Danced the Polka*, Karen

Beaumont Alarcón; juvenile fiction and nonfiction: *What's in a Name?,* Marisa Montes.

Award: Winners receive prizes from $75 to $150 and certificates; honorable mentions receive certificates. Awards presented at a conference dinner.

California Young Playwrights Contest

Candis Paule, Marketing Director
Playwrights Project
450 B Street, Suite 480
San Diego, CA 92101-8002

Description: This contest, open to Californians under the age of nineteen, accepts plays and stages winning scripts in association with the Old Globe Theatre. Scripts must be original, in any style, on any subject. Collaborations or group plays are also eligible.

Plays must be ten pages or longer. Scripts should be typed, bound securely, and have numbered pages; on the title page, enter name, address, phone number, and date of birth. Playwrights should include a brief cover letter about themselves. Scripts will not be returned; photocopies are acceptable. There is no entry fee and no limit on entries. Each submission is professionally evaluated and every entrant is mailed an evaluation of their work.

Deadline: April 1.

Announcements: Contest announced in the fall; winners announced in August by press release.

Award: Honorarium; professional production of the play at the Old Globe Theatre in San Diego.

Calliope Fiction Contest

Sandy Raschke, Fiction Editor

P.O. Box 466
Moraga, CA 94556-0466

Description: This annual contest, based on a different theme each year, is sponsored by the Writers' Special Interest Group (SIG) of American Mensa. SIG members and nonmembers are eligible. The winning entry is published in *Calliope*.

Submit unpublished fiction, to a maximum of 2,500 words. Do not submit works with graphic sex, extreme horror, or violence. On a separate cover sheet, list author's name, address, phone number, and the title of the story. Each writer is allowed five entries. SIG members receive one free entry and must pay a $2 fee for each additional entry; fee for nonmembers is $2 per entry. Manuscripts are not returned. Guidelines available for SASE.

Deadline: September 15.

Announcements: Competition announced in the March/April *Calliope*. Winners announced in November/December issue.

Representative Winner: *Ruby and the Nighttime Visitor,* Andy Entwistle.

Award: Cash prize of $10 for first place, $7.50 for second place, and $5 for third place; winners and honorable mentions receive certificates; winning entry published in *Calliope*.

Canadian Authors Association Awards

Alec McEachern, Administrator
Box 419
Cambellford, Ontario K0L 1L0
Canada

Description: The Canadian Authors Association (CAA) sponsors the Vicky Metcalf Awards, given "solely to stimulate writing for children by Canadian authors." The Metcalf awards include the major prize for a body of work in fiction, nonfiction, poetry, or picture books, and a prize for a short story published in an English language periodical or anthology.

Nominations for the award may be made by an individual, publisher, or association. For the major prize, the nomination letter should list the nominee's published works and biography. For the short story prize, submit four tearsheets or photocopies of the published work, along with a biography of the writer and the name of the editor. Contact the CAA for guidelines and nomination forms.

Deadline: Nominations must be received by December 31.

Announcements: Contest announced in September. Winners announced in April.

Representative Winners: 1996 Body of Work award: Margaret Buffie; short story award: Bernice Friesen.

Award: Body of Work award: $10,000 cash prize; short story award: $3,000 cash prize. Presented at awards dinner.

Canadian Library Association Book Awards

Awards Committee
CLA Membership Services
Suite 602, 200 Elgin Street
Ottawa, Ontario K2P 1L5
Canada

Description: Literary and graphic excellence in books for children and young adults is promoted through the Canadian Library Association's (CLA) book awards program, which consists of three annual awards.

The award for Book of the Year for Children goes to the author of an outstanding children's book, and the Amelia Frances Howard-Gibbon Award to the illustrator of an outstanding children's book. Eligible books must have been published during the previous year, and books should be suitable for readers up to age fourteen. The Young Adult Canadian Book Award recognizes the author of an outstanding Canadian book aimed at readers ages thirteen to eighteen. Only published fiction or short stories are eligible.

For all three awards, authors must be Canadian citizens or permanent residents, and all books must have been published in Canada in the previous calendar year. Books can be nominated for any of the awards by CLA members and the publishing community. Contact the CLA for contest guidelines.
Deadline: Write for 1998 deadline.
Representative Winners: Book of the Year for Children: *The Tiny Kite of Eddie Wing*, Maxine Trottier; Howard-Gibbon Award: *Just Like New*, Karen Reczuch; Young Adult Canadian Book Award: *The Maestro*, Tim Wynne-Jones.
Award: Winners of the Book of the Year for Children and Howard-Gibbon awards receive a medal, and the winner of the Young Adult award receives a leather-bound book with the Award seal embossed on the cover. All are presented at the CLA's annual conference.

Raymond Carver Short Story Contest
Lorraine Michaels, Contest Coordinator
Humboldt State University
English Department
Arcata, CA 95521
Description: This contest is held to encourage unpublished short story writers. 1998 marks the fifteenth year of the contest, named in honor of award-winning writer and Humboldt State University alumnus Raymond Carver. Winners are published in *TOYON*, the university's literary magazine.

Open to writers living in the U.S. or U.S. citizens living abroad. Stories must be in English, previously unpublished, and not accepted for publication elsewhere. Rights to the winning story revert to the author upon publication in *TOYON*. Send two double-spaced copies of each story. Maximum length, 6,000 words (roughly twenty-five double-spaced pages). Manuscripts are not returned. Multiple entries permitted. Entry fee, $10 per story. Contest guidelines available with SASE.
Deadline: November 1.
Announcements: Winners are announced in May.
Representative Winners: First place: *Paper Horses*, Angela Tung; second place: *Lightning Rod*, Daniel M. Davis; third place: *Down by the Salley Gardens*, Marjorie Kennedy.
Award: First place: $500 and publication in *TOYON*; second place: $250 and honorable mention; third place: honorable mention.

Rebecca Caudill Young Readers' Book Award
Contest Chair
P.O. Box 871
Arlington Heights, IL 60006-0871
Description: The threefold purpose of this award, given in honor of Illinois author Rebecca Caudill, is to encourage children to read, to develop a statewide awareness of outstanding lit-

erature for young readers, and to foster cooperation among state agencies that provide educational services.

The annual award is given to the book voted most outstanding by readers in grades four to eight in participating Illinois schools. Students, teachers, school library media specialists, and public librarians nominate titles for a master list of twenty books, which is finalized by the Awards Committee. To be nominated, books must be in print, published in the U.S. within the last five years, and can be nonfiction, poetry, or fiction. Textbooks, anthologies, and translations are not eligible.

Deadline: Nominations for the 1999 award must be submitted by May 15, 1998. Ballots must be returned by February 28. The 1999 contest brochures will be mailed in April.

Announcements: Winners are announced in March 1998.

Representative Winner: *Flight Number 116 Is Down*, Caroline Cooney.

Award: A $500 honorarium and a plaque are presented to the winner at an awards dinner.

Children's Writer Contests

95 Long Ridge Road
West Redding, CT 06896-1124

Description: Three annual contests for unpublished fiction and nonfiction are sponsored by the publishers of *Children's Writer*. Faculty and editorial staff from the Institute of Children's Literature judge the entries on publishability, originality, plot, characterization, quality of writing, and adherence to age range.

Themes and target age ranges vary for each contest; length runs from 350 to 1,000 words. No entry fee for subscribers to *Children's Writer*; nonsubscribers pay a $10 reading fee for each submission, which entitles them to an eight-month trial subscription. Guidelines available for an SASE.

Deadline: February, June, and October.

Announcements: Contests and winners announced in *Children's Writer*.

Representative Winners: Early reader science: "When Dragons Conquer the Air," Kate Carr; fairy or folktale: "Prince Otto Ecnirp," Thomas W. Cruger.

Award: Cash prize of $250–$1,000; publication in *Children's Writer*.

Mr. Christie's Book Award Program

Marlene Yustin, Program Coordinator
2150 Lakeshore Boulevard West
Toronto, Ontario M8V 1A3
Canada

Description: Since 1989, Christie Brown & Company has sponsored this annual award for writing and illustrating excellence in Canadian children's literature. The award program is designed to further the development and publishing of quality children's books.

Submissions are judged on their ability to inspire imagination, recognize the importance of play, represent the highest standard of integrity, bring delight, and help children understand the world intellectually and emotionally. Prizes are awarded for best books for children seven and younger, eight to eleven, and twelve to sixteen.

Entrants must be Canadian citizens; books must have been published in Canada from January 1 to December 31 of the preceding year.

Deadline: January 31.

Announcements: Competition announced each fall, winners in May.

Representative Winners: Seven years and younger: *The Fabulous Song*, Don Gillmor; eight to eleven: *Discovering the Iceman*, Shelley Tanaka; twelve to sixteen: *Uncle Ronald*, Brian Doyle.

Award: $7,500.

Christopher Award

Peggy Flanagan, Awards Coordinator
The Christophers
12 East 48th Street
New York, NY 10017

Description: This award is given to those whose works "affirm the highest values of the human spirit." Awards are given in several categories, including books for young people, books, motion pictures, and television specials. A lifetime achievement award is also given.

Books must be original titles, submitted during the calendar year in which they are first published. No entry fee; no entry form. Submissions are reviewed year-round, and participants should send two copies of nominated books as soon as they are published (do not send galleys). Contest guidelines available with SASE.

Deadline: December.

Announcements: Winners announced in February in the *New York Times*.

Representative Winners: *The Log Cabin Quilt*, Ellen Howard; *Minty: A Story of Young Harriet Tubman*, Alan Schroeder; *Irrepressible Spirit: Conversations with Human Rights Activists*, Susan Kuklin.

Award: Bronze medallion given at an awards ceremony held in February.

CNW/FFWA Florida State Writing Competition

Florida Freelance Writing Association
P.O. Box A
North Stratford, NH 03590

Description: This competition is open to all writers. Awards are given in several categories, including children's literature, adult nonfiction, feature article, and essay/column. All entries are judged on presentation, suitability, and structure. Nonfiction entries are also judged on logic and statistics, and fiction is judged on characterization, dialogue, and plotting.

Submissions can be any length (except for short-short fiction, which must be under 1,000 words). Author's name cannot appear on any manuscript; a completed entry form must accompany each submission. For manuscripts under 3,000 words, entry fee is $5 for current members and $10 for nonmembers. For submissions longer than 3,000 words, entry fee is $10 for members and $20 for nonmembers. Manuscripts are not be returned. Send an SASE for guidelines.

Deadline: March 15.

Announcements: Competition announced in the fall, winners in May.

Award: $75 and certificate for winners; other prizes vary.

Colorado Book Awards

Megan Maguire, Program Director
Colorado Center for the Book
2133 Downing Street
Denver, CO 80205

Description: The Colorado Book Award, a project of the Colorado Center for the Book, is given annually to Colorado authors who exemplify the best writing in the state in a given year.

Any book on any subject matter can

be submitted. Any book with a 1998 publication date or certification that it was published in November or December 1997 is eligible. Authors must have been a Colorado resident for three of the last twelve months prior to December 31, 1998. Multiple entries permitted; entry fee, $30. Entries should include six copies of the book or manuscript. Entries are not returned.
Deadline: December 1.
Announcements: Winners announced in April.
Representative Winner: *Tops and Bottoms*, Janet Stephens.
Award: $500, awarded at a banquet.

Marguerite de Angeli Contest
Wendy Lamb, Executive Editor
Bantam Doubleday Dell BFYR
1540 Broadway
New York, NY 10036
Description: Established to foster the writing of contemporary children's fiction set in North America, this contest offers the winner a standard book contract, an advance, and royalties. It was created to honor children's book author and illustrator Marguerite de Angeli.

U.S. and Canadian writers who have not previously published a novel for middle-grade readers are eligible, and can submit a maximum of two manuscripts. Manuscripts sent for this contest cannot be submitted to any other publisher while under consideration at Bantam Doubleday Dell. Submissions should be contemporary or historical fiction set in North America, for readers seven to ten, and between 40 and 144 pages long. Include a brief plot summary with a cover letter. Submit a SASE if you want your manuscript returned—please, no manuscript boxes.
Deadline: Submissions must be postmarked between April 1 and June 30.
Announcements: Contest results will be announced no later than October 31 in *School Library Journal*, *Publishers Weekly*, and other trade publications.
Representative Winner: *Beastle* (tentative title), Vickie Winslow Wolfinger.
Award: $1,500 a book contract for hardcover and paperback editions, and $3,500 advance against royalties.

Delacorte Press Prize for a First Young Adult Novel
Wendy Lamb, Executive Editor
Bantam Doubleday Dell BFYR
1540 Broadway
New York, NY 10036
Description: The winner of this annual contest, held to stimulate the writing of contemporary young adult fiction, receives a book contract, including an advance and royalties. The contest is open to U.S. and Canadian writers who have not previously published a young adult novel.

Submissions should consist of a book-length manuscript (100 to 224 pages) with a contemporary setting, suitable for readers ages twelve to eighteen. Manuscripts submitted for the contest may not be sent to other publishers while under consideration for the Delacorte prize. Authors may not submit more than two manuscripts to the contest. Send a SASE for guidelines.
Deadline: Entries must be postmarked between October 1 and December 31.
Announcements: Contest results will be announced no later than April 30 in *Publishers Weekly*, *Book Links*, and other trade publications.

Representative Winners: *Breaking Boxes*, A.M. Jenkins; honor book: *For Mike*, Shelley Sykes.

Award: Winner receives a book contract for hardcover and paperback edition, a cash award of $1,500, and a $6,000 advance against royalties.

Arthur Ellis Award

Crime Writers of Canada
3007 Kingston Road, Box 113
Scarborough, ON M1M 1P1
Canada

Description: The Crime Writers of Canada award the Arthur Ellis Award for the best in crime fiction in a given calendar year. Open to writers living in Canada, or Canadian authors residing in another country, this competition defines crime as detective, espionage, intrigue, crime, mystery, suspense, and thriller fiction; and factual accounts of criminal doings. Established in 1984, the Arthur Ellis Award is given for published works in the categories of crime novel, first crime novel, short story, true crime, juvenile crime novel, genre criticism/reference, and play.

Deadline: January 31 of the year following publication.

Announcements: Winners announced at the end of May at an awards dinner.

Representative Winner: Best juvenile crime novel: *How Can a Frozen Detective Stay Hot on the Trail?*, Linda Bailey.

Award: Winner receives an "Arthur" statuette.

Emphasis on Reading Children's Choice Book Award

Dr. Jane Bandy Smith, Education
   Administrator
Alabama Department of Education
50 North Ripley Street
Montgomery, AL 36130

Description: Established nearly twenty years ago, this award is designed to motivate students to read quality literature. Children in Alabama schools select winners in the categories of kindergarten to grade two, grades three to five, and grades six to eight.

Books are chosen from the starred reviews in the *School Library Journal*. Books by Alabama authors that do not appear in the journal can be nominated for voting. Contest guidelines available with SASE.

Deadline: Ballots must be returned in March.

Announcements: Contest announcement made in August. Winners named in April at the Alabama Library Association conference.

Representative Winners: Kindergarten to grade two: *Bamboozled*, David Legge; grades three to five: *Mick Harte Was Here*, Barbara Park; grades six to eight: *What Jamie Saw*, Carolyn Coman.

Award: The winner in each category receives a paperweight bearing the Emphasis on Reading logo.

Empire State Award

Carol Dratch-Kovler, Youth Services
   Consultant
New York Library Association Youth
   Services, Upper Hudson Library
   System
28 Essex Street
Albany, NY 12206

Description: This award, presented for excellence in literature for young people, was first given in 1990 to honor a New York State author or illustrator.

Nominated by librarians, the recipient of this award must have made a significant contribution to children's or young adult literature.

Deadline: November 30.

Announcements: Winner announced at the spring conference of the New York Library Association.

Representative Winner: Richard Peck.

Award: Engraved medallion presented to the winner at the New York Library Association's award luncheon.

Dorothy Canfield Fisher Children's Book Award

Grace W. Greene, Children's Services
  Consultant
DCF, c/o Northeast Regional Library
R.D. 2, Box 244
St. Johnsbury, VT 05819

Description: This child-selected book award is cosponsored by the Vermont Department of Libraries and the Vermont PTA. It inspires Vermont children to become enthusiastic and discriminating readers by providing them with books of excellent quality. Children read books from a master list of thirty titles selected by the award committee, and choose their favorite.

All forms of writing are considered, including fiction, nonfiction, short stories, and poetry. Books must have been written by a living author who is a U.S. citizen, and must have been published in the preceding calendar year. Send SASE for contest guidelines. Contact Grace Greene (ggreene@dol.state.vt.us) with questions about the process.

Deadline: December 31.

Announcements: Winners announced in April.

Representative Winners: *Mick Harte Was Here*, Barbara Park; *Time for Andrew*, Mary Downing Hahn.

Award: Winner receives a scroll illustrated by a Vermont artist; presented at an awards ceremony in May or June.

FOCAL Award

Friends of Children and Literature
Renny Day, President
Los Angeles Public Library
630 West Fifth Street
Los Angeles, CA 90071

Description: This annual award is presented to a published author or illustrator for excellence in a work that enriches a child's appreciation and understanding of California. Sponsored by the Friends of Children and Literature, FOCAL was founded in 1979 by teachers, librarians, parents, authors, and illustrators to support and enrich the programs and resources of the children's literature department of the Los Angeles Public Library.

Deadline: December 31.

Announcements: Winner announced in mid-January.

Representative Winner: *California Blue*, David Klass.

Award: Winner is invited to an award luncheon in Los Angeles; puppet resembling main character in book is presented to winning author.

Folktales Contest

Lee-Perry Belleau, Artistic Director
For A Good Time Theatre Company
P.O. Box 5421
Saginaw, MI 48603-5421

Description: For A Good Time Theatre Company, offering this contest for the first time in 1998, is a professional children's touring company that performs entertaining and educational plays and musicals in schools in the Great Lakes Region. The winning play in the contest will be produced as part of the troupe's 1998 season.

The theme of the contest is "Folktales from Around the World." Entries should be original, unpublished plays that include—but are not limited to—tales from Africa, Mexico, the Middle East, and Europe. Multiple entries are permitted. Entries must be fifty minutes long, written to be performed by three adults, and suitable for children in kindergarten through sixth grade. Include costumes, characters, and properties, as well as a scene synopsis. Entries must include a signed release. Guidelines and release available with SASE. Entry fee, $10.

Deadline: September 15.
Announcements: Winners announced to the media and notified by mail no later than November 1.
Award: First prize, $1,000 cash award and a videotape of the produced script.

Foster City Writers' Contest
Foster City Art & Culture Committee
Ted Lance, Contest Chairman
650 Shell Boulevard
Foster City, CA 94404
Description: Foster City Writers' Contest seeks to encourage and recognize new writers of fiction, humor, children's story, rhymed verse, and blank verse.

Fiction, to 3,000 words; children's story, to 2,000 words; verse, two double-spaced pages. Entries must be unpublished, typed, and carry only the title of the work and the category. Each submission should be accompanied by an index card with author's name, address, phone number, entry title, and category. Entry fee, $10. Manuscripts are not returned.
Deadline: November 30.
Announcements: Competition announced on May 1; winners announced the following January.
Award: First-place prize is $250; and honorable mentions receive $125.

H.E. Francis Short Story Contest
The Department of English
University of Alabama in Huntsville
Huntsville, AL 35899
Description: The Ruth Hindman Foundation and the English department of the University of Alabama in Huntsville sponsor this contest, named after a retired English professor. Unpublished manuscripts, to 5,000 words, may be submitted; multiple submissions acceptable. Author's name must not appear on the manuscript—an accompanying cover sheet should contain the story title, name and address of the author, and word count.

Entry fee, $15 per submission and made out to the Ruth Hindman Foundation, is tax-deductible and goes toward scholarships for undergraduate and graduate students.
Deadline: December 1.
Announcements: Winners announced in March.
Representative Winner: Roberta Carter.
Award: Winner receives $1,000 and possible publication in *Hometown Press*.

Georgia Children's Book Award
Georgia Children's Picture Storybook Award

Department of Language Education
125 Aderhold Hall
University of Georgia
Athens, GA 30602

Description: The purpose of these awards is to promote reading for pleasure. After receiving nominations, a selection committee of teachers and librarians prepares a list of twenty titles for each award and the list is sent to schools for the children's vote. Eligible books must be works of fiction and published in the last five years. The storybook award must be appropriate for students in kindergarten to grade four and the children's book award is directed at grades four to eight. Nominees must have literary merit, and be free of stereotypes; picture storybook award nominees must have both visual and literary merit. Authors must be residents of the U.S. or Canada.

Deadline: December.

Announcements: Winners are announced in May.

Representative Winners: Children's Book Award: *Mick Harte Was Here,* Barbara Park; Picture Storybook Award: *The Stinky Cheese Man and Other Fairly Stupid Tales,* Jon Scieszka.

Award: $1,000 and a plaque presented at the University of Georgia Children's Literature Conference.

Gold Medallion Book Awards
Doug Ross, President
Evangelical Christian Publishers
    Association
1969 East Broadway Road, Suite 2
Tempe, AZ 85282

Description: The Gold Medallion Award is presented annually by the Evangelical Christian Publishers Association (ECPA) in recognition of excellence in evangelical Christian literature. To be eligible, books must give an overtly Christian message, and have explicit Christian content or a distinctively Christian worldview. Judges evaluate entries based on content, literary quality, design, and significance of contribution.

Among the twenty-two categories of awards are three children's groupings: fiction and nonfiction for preschool children, through age six; fiction and nonfiction for elementary children, ages seven to twelve; and fiction, nonfiction, Bible study or social/moral issues for junior high or senior high youth, ages twelve to eighteen. All entries must have been published in the year preceding the contest. Books should be submitted by publishers. Publishers need not be ECPA members, but must meet the qualifications for voting membership. The entry fee is $100 per title for ECPA members and $250 per title for nonmembers.

Deadline: December 1.

Announcements: Contest entry forms mailed October 14. Winners announced each summer.

Representative Winners: Preschool: *Just in Case You Ever Wonder,* Max Lucado; elementary: *The Treasure Tree,* Gary and Norma Smalley and John and Cindy Trent; young adult: *Don't Check Your Brains at the Door,* Josh McDowell and Bob Hostetler.

Award: Plaque awarded at the Gold Medallion Awards Banquet.

Golden Archer Award
Nancy Roozen, Committee Chair
Wisconsin Educational Media
    Association (WEMA)

1300 Industrial Drive
Fennimore, WI 53809

Description: The goal of this children's choice award is to encourage young readers to become better acquainted with quality literature, and to honor favorite books and their authors. Elementary and junior-high students select winners in three categories: primary, intermediate, and middle/junior high. All titles published in the previous ten years are eligible. Send SASE for contest guidelines.

Deadline: October 15.

Announcements: Winners announced at the annual spring conference.

Recent Winners: Primary: *Officer Buckle and Gloria*, Peggy Rathmann; intermediate: *The Stinky Cheese Man and Other Fairly Stupid Tales*, Jon Scieszka; middle/junior high: *Harris and Me*, Gary Paulsen.

Award: Bronze medal and certificate awarded at annual conference.

Golden Kite Awards

Sue Alexander, Contest Coordinator
Society of Children's Book Writers
    and Illustrators
22736 Vanowen Street, Suite 106
West Hills, CA 91307

Description: Four Golden Kite statuettes, one each for fiction, nonfiction, picture book text, and picture book illustration, are awarded annually to the most outstanding children's book written or illustrated by a member of the Society of Children's Book Writers and Illustrators (SCBWI).

Every book by any SCBWI member is eligible during the year of original publication; for co-authored books, both authors must be SCBWI members. Books may be submitted between February 1 and December 15. Authors should submit three review copies, six review copies if the book is to be considered for the picture book text award and the picture book illustration award. Galleys are not accepted. Contact SCBWI for more information.

Deadline: December 15.

Announcements: Winners announced in the spring in the *SCBWI Bulletin* and in press releases.

Representative Winners: Fiction: *The Watsons Go to Birmingham—1963*, Christopher Curtis; nonfiction: *Abigail Adams*, Natalie S. Bober; picture-book illustration: *Fairy Wings*, Dennis Nolan and Lauren Mills.

Award: Statuette presented at SCBWI events, plaques for honor books.

Governor General's Literary Awards

The Canada Council for the Arts
P.O. Box 1047
Ottawa, Ontario K1P 5V8
Canada

Description: Publishers may submit books for these annual awards given to the best English-language and best French-language work in each of seven categories: fiction; literary nonfiction; drama; poetry; translation; children's literature, text; and children's literature, illustration.

Submissions must be first edition trade books written, translated, or illustrated by Canadians or permanent residents of Canada. Books with more than two authors, or whose author was deceased at time of publication, are not eligible; self-published books are not accepted. Submissions must be at least forty-eight pages, except for children's titles, which must be a minimum of twenty-four pages. Books must be available in Canadian bookstores.

Peer assessment committees, composed of writers, critics, or independent book professionals, examine all the nominees for artistic and literary merit and then select the winners.
Deadline: Books published between September 1 and April 30 of the award year have a May 15 deadline. Books published between May 1 and September 30 of the award year must be submitted by August 15.
Announcements: Winners announced in mid-November.
Representative Winners: Children's literature, text: *Ghost Train,* Paul Yee; children's literature, illustration: *The Rooster's Gift,* Eric Beddows.
Award: At an awards ceremony, each winner receives $10,000 and a specially bound copy of their book. They are honored at a reception and dinner.

Hackney Literary Awards
Birmingham-Southern College
P.O. Box 549003
Birmingham, AL 35254
Description: The Hackney Literary Awards competition recognizes excellence in writing in three categories: short story (to 5,000 words); novel; and poetry (to 50 lines). Only original, unpublished manuscripts are acceptable; each entry must have two cover sheets listing title of entry, author's name, address, phone number, and category; author's name must not appear on manuscript. Unless specified for the national competition, poetry and short story entries from Alabama will be entered in the state contest; entries can only be judged in one category—either state or national. For novels, include a $25 fee per entry; for short stories and poetry, enclose a $10 fee per entry. Manuscripts will not be returned.
Deadline: Novel, September 30. Short story and poetry, December 31.
Announcements: Winners announced at the Birmingham-Southern College Writing Today Conference in March.
Representative Winners: Novel: Frederick Reiken; national short story: Patricia Traxler; state short story: Eric Smith; national poetry: Liliane Richman; state poetry: Rosemary McMahan.
Award: $2,000, novel; $2,000 in prizes for poetry and short stories.

Highlights for Children Annual Fiction Contest
Marileta Robinson, Senior Editor
803 Church Street
Honesdale, PA 18431
Description: *Highlights for Children's* annual contest designates a new theme each year; the most recent was stories that break the mold. New writers are urged to submit unpublished stories to 900 words, or stories for beginning readers, to 500 words.

Entry envelopes should be labeled "Fiction Contest" and the word count should be indicated in the upper right-hand corner of the manuscript. Include a SASE with each submission. No entry form or fee is required. Contest stories not chosen as winners have a chance of being purchased for publication by *Highlights for Children.*
Deadline: Entries must be postmarked between January 1 and February 28.
Announcements: Contest announced in September. Winners are notified by

CONTESTS

phone in June and list of winners is mailed to 120 top newspapers, and to writers' magazines.

Representative Winners: "The Strange Disappearance of Sir John," Christina Ashton; "Dust Pictures," Lee Eble; and "Elf Tracks," Susan Krawitz.

Award: Three winners receive $1,000, an engraved pewter bowl, and publication of their stories in *Highlights*.

IBBY Honour List

Leena Maissen, Executive Director
International Board on Books for
Young People
Nonnenweg 12
Postfach, 4003 Basel
Switzerland

Description: The IBBY Honour List recognizes the creativity and commitment of outstanding children's book writers, illustrators, and translators. Presented every two years, the contest furthers IBBY's aim of promoting international understanding through children's books.

Entries are selected by the national sections of IBBY, and each member country can submit three entries: one each for excellence in writing, illustration, and translation. To be eligible, books must have been published no earlier than three years before the awards are presented.

Deadline: October 15.

Announcements: Winners announced every other September, at the IBBY Congress.

Representative Winners: For the U.S., Writing: *Catherine, Called Birdy*, Karen Cushman; illustration: *The Creation*, James Ransome.

Award: Honour List diplomas are pre-

sented at the IBBY Congress, and winning books are shown at travelling exhibitions worldwide.

Insight Writing Contest

Michelle Sturm, Editorial Assistant
55 West Oak Ridge Drive
Hagerstown, MD 21740

Description: *Insight*, a weekly Christian magazine for teenagers, developed this contest to honor the best true short stories and poems written by teens. Winners are selected based on standard of writing, originality, and showing rather than telling a moral lesson.

Submit unpublished short stories (eight-page maximum) and poems (one-page maximum). No entry fee; multiple submissions permitted. Entries can be e-mailed to insight@ rhpa.org. *Insight* acquires first rights for works in the contest.

Deadline: May 31.

Award: Winning entries published in a special issue of *Insight*, roughly six months after the contest deadline.

Inspirational Writers Alive! Open Writing Competition

Maxine Holder, Director
Route 4, Box 81-H
Rusk, TX 75785-9410

Description: This competition looks for submissions that have an inspirational appeal and a Christian perspective. Writers may enter their works in: short story fiction (2,500 words); nonfiction article (1,500 words); devotional (300 words); poetry (48 lines); children's and teens' short story (750 words); and short story (750 words), article (1,000 words), and poetry (48 lines) submitted by children and teen writers only, ages twelve to seventeen.

Submissions must be unpublished and only one entry is allowed in a category. Author's name should not appear on manuscript; include a cover sheet with name, address, phone number, and title of submission. Entry fees are $4 each for IWA members; $5 for nonmembers. Manuscripts will not be returned. Guidelines available for SASE.
Deadline: April 1.
Announcements: Competition announced in November; winners announced in May or June at a banquet.
Representative Winner: Jan Payne-Pierce.
Award: Cash prizes for the three top winners in each category; award certificates to all winners; publication in *Timbrels of God* anthology.

Island Literary Awards

Lucy Maud Montgomery Children's
Literature Award
PEI Council of the Arts
115 Richmond Street
Charlottetown, PE C1A 1H7
Canada
Description: The Island Literary Awards, sponsored by the Prince Edward Island Council of the Arts, invites submissions to competitions for poetry, adult short fiction, children's literature, feature article, and creative writing for young people. For the Lucy Maud Montgomery Children's Literature Award, submissions of unpublished children's stories for readers aged five through twelve are accepted; maximum length, sixty pages.

Enclose a cover sheet with name, address, phone number, title of entry,
and category; author's name must not appear on any part of the manuscript. Entry fees are $8 per submission; no fee required for the creative writing contest. No limit on number of entries but include SASE for return of submissions. Entrants must be residents of Prince Edward Island for at least six months before the contest deadline date.
Deadline: February 15.
Announcements: Winners announced in April.
Representative Winners: Lucy Maud Montgomery Children's Writing Award: *The Ferry Boy,* Nancy Russell.
Award: Lucy Maud Montgomery Writing Award: $500, first place; $200, second place; $100 third place. Other competitions, prizes vary.

Jefferson Cup Award

Rachael Dehaven, Chairperson
Children's and Young Adult Round-
table of the Virginia Library
Association
P.O. Box 8277
Norfolk, VA 23503-8277
Description: Established in 1982, the Jefferson Cup honors the best book published for children and young adults in American history, biography, or historical fiction.

Original short nonfiction, books, and collections published in the year prior to the selection may be submitted. Entries must be about U.S. history or an American from 1492 to the present, or fiction that highlights the U.S. past. All submissions must be suitable for young people. Multiple submissions accepted.
Deadline: March 1998.
Announcements: Contest announced

in September. Winning author announced and notified in June.
Representative Winner: *The Ornament Tree*, Jean Thesman.
Award: $500 award presented at Virginia Library Association conference.

Keats/Kerlan Collection Memorial Fellowship
Contest Coordinator
109 Walter Library
117 Pleasant Street SE
Minneapolis, MN 55455
Description: This award, from the Ezra Jack Keats Foundation, provides $1,500 to a "talented writer and/or illustrator of children's books who wishes to use the Kerlan Collection for the furtherance of his or her artistic development." Special consideration is given to an entrant who would find it difficult to finance the visit to the Collection. SASE for application packet and guidelines.
Deadline: May 1.
Announcements: Contest announced in fall or winter newsletter. Winners announced in June.
Representative Winner: David Pelletier, illustrator, *The Graphic Alphabet*.
Award: Fellowship winner receives transportation costs and a per diem allotment.

Kentucky Bluegrass Award
Jenny Smith, Contest Coordinator
Northern Kentucky University,
    Steely Library
Highland Heights, KY 41099
Description: This annual award, first presented in 1983, honors the authors of quality children's and young adult literature. The goal of the award is to encourage children to read and enjoy a variety of books: Kids select their favorites from a master list of thirty to fifty recently published works that have been nominated by librarians and teachers in Kentucky.

Awards are given for kindergarten to grade three (short picture books and beginner readers), and grades four to eight (junior novels and longer picture books). Send SASE for guidelines.
Deadline: April 1.
Announcements: Winners announced in the spring.
Representative Winners: Kindergarten to grade three: *Officer Buckle and Gloria*, Peggy Rathmann; four to eight: *Piggie Pie*, Margie Palatini and Howard Fine.
Award: Award presented at the Kentucky Bluegrass Award Conference on Children's Literature.

Kerlan Award
Children's Literature Research
    Collections
109 Walter Library
117 Pleasant St. SE
Minneapolis, MN 55455
Description: This award is open only to children's authors and illustrators who have donated to the collection of the University of Minnesota's Kerlan Library. Given annually, the award was created to honor their contribution to children's literature and in appreciation of their donation of resources to the collection. Manuscripts, illustrations, and books are judged.
Deadline: Contest announced in the fall. Call for nominations runs from September 1 to November 1.
Announcements: Winner announced

in the winter issue of the newsletter.
Representative Winner: Author, 1997:
Theodore Taylor.
Award: Certificate presented at an
awards dinner.

Janusz Korczak Literary Awards
Anti-Defamation League
823 United Nations Plaza
New York, NY 10017
Description: Janusz Korczak was a
champion of children, a director of or-
phanages in Warsaw, and an acclaimed
educator and author. During the Holocaust, he refused to abandon his or-
phans and died with them in the gas
chambers of Treblinka. This biennial
award, to be presented in 1998, is named
in his honor, and recognizes outstanding books for and about children.

Awards are given in two categories:
for children: published fiction or nonfiction for elementary or secondary
school readers, and published books
about children, their welfare and nurturing, written for parents and educators. Entries must have been published
two years before the award year. Five
copies of each book must be submitted; there is no entry fee.
Deadline: Fall.
Announcements: Winners announced
in the spring.
Representative Winners: Books for
children: *The Frozen Waterfall*, Gaye Hi-
cyilmaz; books about children: *Did the
Children Cry?*, Richard C. Lukas.
Award: For each category, winner receives $1,000 and a plaque.

Magazine Merit Awards
Society of Children's Book Writers
and Illustrators
22736 Vanowen Street, Suite 106
West Hills, CA 91307
Description: Any member of SCBWI
may submit a magazine article published in the current year. The work
must be youth-centered but may be fiction, nonfiction, or illustrated by a
SCBWI member. Send four copies of
the published work; illustrators may
send color photocopies or tearsheets.
Enclose proof of publication, either the
contents page or a verification from the
editor, and a cover sheet containing
member's name, address, phone number, name of entry, category, and publication name and issue date.
Submissions will not be returned.
Deadline: Submit entries between January 31 and December 15 of the year of
publication.
Announcements: Contest announced
in January; winners announced in April.
Representative Winners: Fiction:
Vicki Grove, *American Girl*; nonfiction:
Alyce Jenkins, *Guideposts for Children*;
illustration: Pamela Levy, *Cricket*.
Award: Winners receive a plaque at an
awards dinner; honor certificates
awarded in each category.

Majestic Books Writing Contest
Cindy MacDonald
P.O. Box 19097-CW
Johnston, RI 02919
Description: Majestic Books created its
contest, open to students in all grades,
to encourage students in all grade levels to write. Judges look for creativity
and orginality. Winning entries are
published in a Majestic Books anthology.

Students in grades one and twelve
enrolled in any Rhode Island school

CONTESTS

are eligible. Submit short stories (2,000 words maximum), either published or unpublished. Send SASE for guidelines. **Deadline:** October 14. **Announcements:** Contest announced in September. Winners are announced in November and are notified by mail. **Award:** Copy of the anthology, presented at an awards ceremony.

Massachusetts Children's Book Award

Diane E. Bushner, Chairperson
Salem State College
352 Lafayette Street
Salem, MA 01970-5353
Description: Sponsored by the Education Department at Salem State College, this award encourages reading in grades four to six. Teachers and librarians may nominate books for consideration. The books must have been published in the past seven years and still be available in hardcover and paperback.

Children from Massachusetts can participate in the voting if they have read five of the books from the master list of nominees. The book that receives the most votes is declared the winner. Guidelines are available for teachers. **Deadline:** December 12. **Announcements:** Competition announced in June, winners in April. **Representative Winner:** *Wayside School Gets a Little Stranger,* Louis Sachar. **Award:** Certificate. Author is asked to write a letter to Massachusetts' children.

David McCord Children's Literature Citation

Mary Pat Craig, Curriculum Librarian
Framingham State College
100 State Street
Framingham, MA 01701
Description: In honor of David McCord's long and enduring contribution to children's literature, this award is given to an author or illustrator whose work has contributed significantly to the field of children's books. A committee of four professional librarians and teachers select the annual winner. **Deadline:** Committee selects the award recipient eighteen months in advance of the announcement. **Announcements:** Winners are announced in November. **Representative Winner:** Patricia Polacco. **Award:** Winner is honored at the David McCord Children's Literature Festival, held in November at Framingham State College.

Society of Midland Authors Book Awards

P.O. Box 10419
Chicago, IL 60610-0419
Description: This annual award, open to published authors living in the Midwest, honors literary achievement. Qualifying authors should send copies of their published work for consideration. Books should be at least 2,000 words long. Multiple submissions permitted; no entry fee. **Deadline:** January 30. **Announcements:** Contest announced each fall. Winners announced in April. **Representative Winners:** *Would My Fortune Cookie Lie?*, Stella Pevsner; *Orphan Train*, Andrea Warren. **Award:** $350, at awards dinner in May.

Midwest Radio Theatre Workshop Script Competition

Sue Zizza, Executive Director
115 Dikeman Street
Hempstead, NY 11550
Description: This award is sponsored annually by the Midwest Radio Theatre Workshop to solicit radio scripts from established and emerging writers. Plays are evaluated on dialogue and an understanding of how sound can amplify emotional content and set a scene in the listener's mind. Of particular interest are stories that "deserve to be told because they enlighten, intrigue, or simply make us laugh out loud." Contemporary scripts with strong female roles, multicultural casting, and diverse viewpoints will be favorably received.

Scripts should be twenty-five to thirty minutes in length. Submit three copies of the original radio play and $15 entry fee. No stage plays, monologues, short stories, or screen plays. Only one entry per writer. For contest guidelines, send SASE.
Deadline: November 15 of each year.
Announcements: Winners announced in May.
Award: Winners divide $800 and participate in a production workshop.

Milkweed Prize for Children's Literature

Children's Book Reader
Milkweed Editions
430 First Avenue North, Suite 400
Minneapolis, MN 55401-1743
Description: All middle-grade manuscripts submitted to Milkweed Editions are automatically considered for this prize. Milkweed is looking for manuscripts of "high literary quality that embody humane values and contribute to cultural understanding."

All manuscripts an author submits in a given year are considered, if they have not been published in the U.S. or by Milkweed. Stories should be written for ages eight to twelve. Collections of short stories are not eligible, nor is the retelling of a legend or folktale. Send SASE for submission guidelines.
Deadline: Ongoing.
Announcements: Winner announced when the book is published.
Representative Winners: *Behind the Bedroom Wall*, Laura E. Williams; *The Summer of the Bonepile Monster*, Aileen Kilgore Henderson.
Award: Publication of the submitted manuscript and a $2,000 cash advance on any royalties.

Minnesota Book Awards

Roger Sween, Coordinator
Suite 116
2324 University Avenue
St. Paul, MN 55114
Description: The intent of this award is to strengthen the links between Minnesota's community of authors, illustrators, publishers, booksellers, librarians, educators, and readers. It recognizes, promotes, and celebrates Minnesota authors and illustrators who contribute to the state's quality of life. Awards are given in several categories, including picture books (author and illustrator awards), children's nonfiction, and young adult fiction.

Published books by authors, illustrators, designers, editors, and translators who have a major responsibility for creation of the work and who live in Minnesota are eligible. Contest guidelines available with SASE.
Deadline: December 31.

Announcements: Winners announced in January, prior to National Library Week.

Representative Winners: Picture books (author): *Aunt Nancy and Old Man Trouble*, Phyllis Root; picture book (illustrator): *Mud*, Lauren Stringer; children's nonfiction: *Snapshot: America Discovers the Camera*, Kenneth P. Czech; young adult fiction: *Sees Behind Trees*, Michael Dorris.

Award: $100 and certificate awarded at reception.

Mary Molloy Fellowship for Juvenile Novel in Progress

Deirdre Heekin, Director
Children's Literature Division
Heekin Group Foundation
P.O. Box 209
Middlebury, VT 05753

Description: Now in its third year, this award is given to new and unpublished writers to enable them to complete fiction projects in progress. It is awarded annually to a beginning writer whose work exhibits literary merit and perception, and is rich in imagination.

The contest is open to any writer who has not published a juvenile novel. Submit the first thirty-five to fifty pages (8,750–12,500 words) of the work in progress for readers ages nine to fourteen. Send SASE for guidelines.

Deadline: December 1.

Announcements: Contest announced in July. Winners announced in June.

Representative Winner: *Dance Over the Mountain*, Laura Schlivek.

Award: Cash award of $2,000.

Mountains and Plains Booksellers Association Regional Book Awards

Lisa Knudsen, Executive Director
805 LaPorte Avenue
Ft. Collins, CO 80521

Description: This annual award is given to honor books set in the Mountains and Plains regions of Colorado, Wyoming, New Mexico, Utah, Idaho, Texas, Montana, Kansas, Arizona, Nebraska, and South Dakota. The Spirit of the West award goes to an author whose books embody the region's essence.

To be eligible, books must have been published in the year prior to the deadline and must be set in the region. Publishers and authors can submit books for consideration. Prizes are awarded to one children's book and three adult books. Nominations are *not* solicited for the Spirit of the West award.

Deadline: November 1.

Announcements: Contest announced in late summer. Winners announced in January.

Representative Winner: *Bill Pickett, Rodeo-Ridin' Cowboy*, Brian and Andrea Pinkney.

Award: A framed copy of the awards poster and a $500 cash award is presented at the Author Banquet, held each March in Santa Fe, NM.

National Association of Parenting Publications Award

John Kearns, Marketing Assistant
443 East Irving Drive
Burbank, CA 91504

Description: Children's books, videos, software, and storytelling media can be submitted in this contest, which spotlights products that enrich the educational and entertainment experiences of young children. Supported by forty-four regional parenting magazines, the

National Association of Parenting Publications (NAPP) award is the largest consumer awards program for children's media and toys.

Book awards are divided into four categories: preschool (one to five years); and for ages five and up, picture story books; nonfiction; and folklore, poetry, and song. Entry fee is $60 to $80, depending on the number of entries. Send SASE for contest guidelines.
Deadline: July 31.
Announcements: Competition announced each May. Winners notified in September; editorial write-ups appear in the November or December issues of the sponsoring publications.
Representative Winners: Preschool: *Where, Oh Where Is Kipper's Bear?*; picture story book: *Bear at the Beach*; nonfiction: *The Season's Sewn*; folklore, poetry, and song: *Animal Crackers*.
Award: Gold-prize winners receive an editorial write-up, certificate, and award letter. Honor winners receive a certificate and award letter.

National Book Award for Young People's Literature

Sherrie Young, Program Associate
The National Book Foundation
Room 904, 260 Fifth Avenue
New York, NY 10001
Description: The National Book Foundation seeks to raise the cultural value of great writing in the U.S., and this award recognizes American literature of exceptional merit. Awards are given in the categories of young people's literature, fiction, nonfiction, and poetry.

The contest is open only to books submitted by publishers. All genres of children's literature are accepted. Entry fee, $100. SASE for contest guidelines.
Deadline: July 15.
Announcements: Competition announced in June. Finalists announced in October, and the winner in November.
Representative Winner: *Parrot in the Oven: Mi Vida*, Victor Martinez.
Award: $10,000. Other finalists, $1,000. Prizes presented at an awards ceremony in November.

National Written & Illustrated By... Awards Contest for Students

Teresa Melton, Contest Director
Landmark Editions, Inc.
P. O. Box 270169
Kansas City, MO 64127
Description: Celebrating creativity, this contest encourages elementary and high school students to submit their short stories, poetry, plays, and novels. Students can enter one of three age categories: six to nine; ten to thirteen; or fourteen to nineteen.

Text and illustrations should run between sixteen and twenty-four pages. No limit on submissions, but each entry requires a one dollar fee and entry form, signed by a teacher or librarian. Books are judged by a panel of judges—editors, writers, illustrators, teachers, and school librarians—who base their selections on originality, writing, and illustration. Enclose SASE for return of manuscript.
Deadline: May 1.
Announcements: Winners announced in October.
Representative Winners: Six to nine: *Mouse Surprise*, Alexandra Whitney; ten to thirteen: *Don't Bug Me!*, Gillian McHale; and fourteen to nineteen: *The*

Incredible Jellybean Day, Taylor Maw.
Award: Winning writers receive a publishing contract.

National Council of Teachers of English Award for Excellence in Poetry for Children

Karen Smith, Associate Executive
  Director
1111 West Kenyon Road
Urbana, IL 61801

Description: This award honors the lifetime work of a living American poet, and is given every three years. The next winner will be announced in 2000. A committee meets regularly for three years to select the winner. Judges evaluate the literary merit of a poet's work, the poet's contributions, evolution of the work, and its appeal to children.

Letters of recommendation may be sent to the committee chair. SASE for guidelines.
Deadline: Ongoing.
Announcements: Winner announced every three years at the council's spring conference.
Representative Winner: Eloise Greenfield.
Award: Medallion presented at the Books for Children Luncheon, at a November conference.

Nevada Young Readers' Award

Nevada Department of Education
700 East 5th Street
Capitol Complex
Carson City, NV 89701-5096

Description: The Nevada Young Readers' Award, sponsored by the Nevada Library Association and the Nevada Department of Education, encourages Nevada students to improve skills by reading the best in modern children's literature. Primary, young reader, intermediate, and young adult awards are given The winning book in each category is nominated by Nevada's young readers, read by them, and then voted on. Only students who have read or been read the required number of titles in a particular category are allowed to vote; each student can vote only once in each category.

Readers submit nominations through their librarians and teachers. Books must appeal to the age group for which the nomination is made and must have been published in the last three years.
Deadline: Nominations due January 15.
Announcements: Schools and libraries receive ballots in May; they are returned by the following April 15; winners are announced that May.
Representative Winners: Primary: *Harvey Potter's Balloon Farm,* Jerdine Nolen; young reader: *Shape Changer,* Bill Brittain; intermediate: *Loch,* Paul Zindel; young adult*: Shadow,* Joyce Sweeney.
Award: Plaque awarded at a dinner.

The John Newbery Award

Stephanie Anton, Program Officer
Association for Library Service to
  Children
American Library Association
50 East Huron Street
Chicago, IL 60611

Description: This award, the most distinguished in the field, is named in honor of London publisher and bookseller John Newbery. It is given annually to "the author of the most distinguished contribution to American literature for children published in the U.S. during the previous year." Honor books may also be named. The award committee considers plot development, character delineation, appropriateness of style, and excellence of presentation for a child audience.

The contest is open only to U.S. residents, and only published works are eligible. Authors may submit an unlimited amount of published work, and there is no entry fee. All forms of writing—fiction, nonfiction, and poetry—are considered, but reprints and compilations are not eligible.
Deadline: December 1.
Announcements: Winners are announced at the ALA's Midwinter Meeting in January or February.
Representative Winner: E.L. Konigsburg, *The View from Saturday*.
Award: Newbery Medal presented at awards banquet.

New England Book Award
New England Booksellers Association
847 Massachusetts Avenue
Cambridge, MA 02139
Description: Established in 1990 by the New England Booksellers Association, the largest regional bookselling organization nationwide, the New England Book Award recognizes excellence in fiction, nonfiction, children's, and publishing. The Award helps promote New England authors and publishers whose body of work have made a significant contribution to New England's culture, and who deserve wider recognition.

Nominations are sought from more than 600 New England bookstores and publishers. A committee of booksellers,

chosen by the association, then selects the winners. Previous winners are ineligible.
Deadline: October 31.
Announcements: Winners announced in January.
Representative Winner: Children's: Natalie Kinsey-Warnock.
Award: Winners honored at a ceremony at the Boston Public Library in April; each receives a framed poster.

Scott O'Dell Award
Zena Sutherland, Chairperson
1418 East 57th Street
Chicago, IL 60637
Description: This annual award was established to honor quality writing in historical fiction. To be eligible, books must be written by an American citizen, published by a U.S. publisher, and set in North or South America. Entries are usually submitted by publishers.
Deadline: December 31.
Representative Winner: *Under the Blood Red Sun*, Graham Salisbury.
Award: $5,000.

Ohioana Awards
Linda Hengst, Director
Ohioana Library Association
65 South Front Street, Suite 1105
Columbus, OH 43215-4163
Description: These annual awards honor authors, poets, musicians, artists, and performers from Ohio who have made outstanding contributions to the arts and humanities. The Ohioana Book Award is presented to the author of an outstanding book published each year. The award is given in six categories, including juvenile books. The Alice Wood Memorial

Award is given to an author of children's literature for a body of work, or a lifetime of contributions to children's literature.

To be eligible for either award, authors must have been born in Ohio or lived in that state for five years. Books considered for the Ohioana Book Award must be received by the Ohioana Library during the calendar year and must have a copyright date within the last two years. Guidelines available with SASE.

Deadline: December 31.

Announcements: Winning author and publisher notified in May; public announcement made in late summer.

Representative Winners: Alice Wood Award: Michael Rosen; Ohioana Book Award: *Her Stories*, Virginia Hamilton.

Award: Alice Wood Award recipient receives $1,000 cash award; Ohioana Book Award recipient receives glass artwork and a certificate.

Oklahoma Book Award

Glenda Carlile, Executive Director
Oklahoma Center for the Book
200 N.E. Eighteenth
Oklahoma City, OK 73105

Description: A panel of judges selects the winner of this contest, held annually to recognize the best works by Oklahoma authors and illustrators. Awards are given in the categories of fiction, nonfiction, children's/young adult, poetry, and design/illustration.

Fiction, nonfiction, and poetry are considered in the children's/young adult category. To be eligible, a book must have been written by an author who resides or has resided in Oklahoma, or must have an Oklahoma-based theme. Eligible books must have been published in the year preceding the contest. Send SASE for guidelines.

Deadline: Contact contest sponsors for 1998 deadline.

Announcements: Finalists notified in February and announced at an awards ceremony in March.

Representative Winner: Children's/ young adult: *Stone Water*, Barbara Snow Gilbert.

Award: Medal presented at awards ceremony.

Once Upon a World Book Award

Janet Garfinkle, Museum Education
    Coordinator
Museum of Tolerance
9786 West Pico Boulevard
Los Angeles, CA 90035

Description: This award, given annually by the Simon Wiesenthal Center/Museum of Tolerance, is designed to encourage tolerance and diversity in books for readers six to ten.

Picture books, fiction, nonfiction, or poetry are eligible, provided they are written in English. Books are judged on relevance to the themes of tolerance, social justice, dignity, and equality of people, and the success in presenting the theme in nondidactic, artistic terms. Literary quality, originality of text and illustration, clarity of style and language, and excellence in design, format, and illustration are also considered. Multiple submissions accepted. Send SASE for contest guidelines.

Deadline: June 1.

Announcements: Winners announced in September.

Representative Winner: *A School for Pompey Walker*, Michael Rosen.

Orbis Pictus Award for Outstanding Nonfiction for Children

Karen Smith, Associate Executive
  Director
National Council of Teachers of
  English
1111 West Kenyon Road
Urbana, IL 61801
Description: Designed to promote and recognize excellence in nonfiction for children, this award is given annually by the National Council for Teachers of English (NCTE). It commemorates J.A. Comenius's *Orbis Pictus*, published in 1657 and believed to be the first book planned for children.

Books, short nonfiction, and collections are eligible, and can be nominated by NCTE members or the educational community at large. No textbooks, historical fiction, folklore, or poetry is eligible. The award committee considers accuracy, design, organization, writing style, and the book's usefulness for teaching in kindergarten through eighth grade.
Deadline: November 30.
Announcements: Competition anoun - ced in March or April. Winners announced at the spring conference of the National Council of Teachers of English.
Representative Winner: *Leonardo da Vinci*, Diane Stanley.
Award: Plaque awarded at NCTE annual convention, held in November.

Helen Keating Ott Award

Contest Coordinator
Church and Synagogue Library
  Association
P.O. Box 19357
Portland, OR 97280-0357
Description: This award, one of four sponsored by the Church and Synagogue Library Association (CSLA), honors a person or organization for a significant contribution in promoting high moral and ethical values through children's literature. Nominees include authors, illustrators, editors, publishers, librarians, editors, and clergy.

Anyone may make a nomination for the award (no self-nominations permitted) and anyone can be nominated. Nominations should include a detailed description of the reasons for the nomination, accompanied by documentary evidence of accomplishment. Contact CSLA for more information.
Deadline: Contact CSLA.
Award: Certificate of recognition and a one-year membership in CSLA, awarded at the annual conference.

Panhandle Professional Writers Contest

PPW Contest Chairman
1908 South Goliad
Amarillo, TX 79106
Description: This annual contest awards literary excellence in ten categories, including writing for children and juvenile or young adult novel.

Entries must not have been accepted for publication prior to the contest deadline, and writers can submit two entries per category. For the writing for children award, submit short stories, articles, or picture book text (1,500 words maximum). Identify the target age group on a cover sheet and first page. Juvenile or young adult novel entries should target readers ages eight to eighteen. Submit first chapter and complete synopsis; the complete entry should not exceed twenty pages.

Entry fee is $7.50–$15 for PPW members; $10–$25 for nonmembers.
Deadline: Write for 1999 deadline.
Announcements: Winners announced at Frontiers in Writing Conference.
Award: Prizes range from $20 to $75.

Paterson Prize for Books for Young People

Maria Mazziotti Gillan, Director
Poetry Center
Passaic County Community College
One College Boulevard
Paterson, NJ 07505-1179
Description: Short stories, short nonfiction, books, poetry, and collections are considered in this contest, in which judges select the most outstanding book for young people published in the previous year. The award is given in the categories of prekindergarten to grade three, grades four to six, and grades seven to twelve.

Books must be submitted by publishers; three copies of each entry should be submitted. Books entered in the competition are donated to the Poetry Center Library at Passaic County Community College.
Deadline: March 15.
Announcements: Contest announced in September. Winners announced in July.
Representative Winners: Prekindergarten to grade three: *The Carousel*, Liz Rosenberg; grades four to six: *Dog People: Native Dog Stories*, Joseph Bruchac; grades seven to twelve: *One Bird*, Kyoko Mori.
Award: $500 for each category.

PEN Center USA West 1998 Literary Awards

Justin Chan, Awards Coordinator
PEN Center USA West
Suite 41
672 South Lafayette Park Place
Los Angeles, CA 90057
Description: Established in 1982, this contest was created to recognize outstanding works produced or published by writers who live west of the Mississippi River. Winners are selected in ten categories, including fiction, nonfiction, children's literature, poetry, and translation. A panel of judges, comprised of writers, editors, critics, and booksellers, selects the winner.

Any book published in the previous year is eligible, and works may be submitted by authors, their publishers, agents, or publicists. Submit entry form, four copies of submission, and $10 entry fee for each submission. Multiple entries are accepted. Send an SASE for guidelines.
Deadline: December 31.
Announcements: Competition announced in July. Winners announced in May.
Representative Winner: Children's literature: *Small Steps: The Year I Got Polio*, Peg Kehret.
Award: $1,000, given at an awards ceremony in Los Angeles.

PEN/Norma Klein Award

Pen American Center
568 Broadway
New York, NY 10012
Description: This biennial prize, established in 1990 in memory of the late PEN member and children's author, recognizes an emerging voice of literary merit in children's fiction. Candidates are new authors whose books for

elementary to young adult readers demonstrate the spirit of Norma Klein's own works, although they do not necessarily emulate her style.

The judges welcome nominations from authors and editors of children's books. Nominating letters should describe the author's work and list their publications; do not send books at this time. Three distinguished children's book authors judge this award.
Deadline: December 15.
Announcements: Winners announced in May.
Representative Winner: Rita Williams-Garcia.
Award: $3,000, given at an awards dinner in May.

Pennsylvania Young Reader's Choice Award
Jean Bellavance, Contest Coordinator
Pennsylvania School Librarian's
    Association (PSLA)
148 S. Bethlehem Pike
Ambler, PA 19002-5822
Description: The winner of this award is selected by students in Pennsylvania from a master list of books finalized by a PSLA committee. Students in kindergarten through eighth grade read books from the list from September through March, and then select their favorites.

To be eligible, a book must be written for readers in kindergarten through eighth grade, and its author must currently be living in the U.S. Books can be nominated for the master list by students, teachers, parents, and librarians. Send an SASE for contest guidelines.
Deadline: September.
Announcements: Contest announced

in March; winners announced in the spring at a PSLA conference.
Representative Winners: *Officer Buckle and Gloria*, Peggy Rathmann; *Swamp Angel*, Anne Isaacs; *Heart of a Champion*, Carl Deuker.
Award: Certificate presented at PSLA conference in Hershey, PA.

Please Touch Museum Book Award
Katie Gorman, Competition Coordinator
210 North 21st Street
Philadelphia, PA 19103
Description: The Please Touch Museum Book Award recognizes and encourages the publication of children's books of the highest quality. To be eligible for consideration, a book must explore and clarify an idea for children, be distinguished in text and illustration, have been a first book by an American author, and must have been published in the last calendar year. Publishers must nominate books.
Deadline: May 19.
Announcements: Competition announced in January. Winners announced in October.
Representative Winners: *Follow the Leader*, Miela Ford; *Baboon*, Kate Banks.
Award: Book signings; guest of honor at a presentation at the Please Touch Museum; plaque.

Pockets Fiction-Writing Contest
Lynn W. Gilliam, Associate Editor
P.O. Box 189
Nashville, TN 37202-0189
Description: *Pockets* is a devotional magazine for children in grades one to six. It sponsors this annual competition as a way to discover new writing talent for its publication.

CONTESTS

Unpublished submissions, 1,000 to 1,600 words, are eligible; no historical fiction; photocopies and computer printouts accepted. Label the envelope and cover sheet "Fiction Contest," and note the word count on the cover sheet. Enclose an SASE for return of your manuscript. No entry fee.
Deadline: August 15.
Announcements: Competition announced in January. Winners announced in late October.
Representative Winner: *Get Real*, Betty Tesh Davenport.
Award: $1,000 and publication in *Pockets*.

Edgar Allan Poe Award
Priscilla Ridgway, Executive Director
Mystery Writers of America
Sixth Floor, 17 East 47th Street
New York, NY 10017
Description: Honoring the best in published works in mystery fiction, nonfiction, television, and film, the Edgars are presented annually by the Mystery Writers of America at the group's annual banquet in New York. Awards are given in sixteen categories, including young adult and juvenile works.

All books, short stories, television shows, and films in the mystery, crime, suspense, and intrigue fields are eligible, as long as they were published or produced for the first time in the U.S. during the calendar year. Multiple submissions permitted. A copy of the manuscript must be submitted to each of five committee members and to the Mystery Writers of America; be sure to identify entries as an Edgar submission. Guidelines available with SASE,

or at www.mysterywriters.org.
Deadline: December 1.
Announcements: Nominations announced in February, and winners announced in April.
Representative Winners: Best young adult: *Twisted Summer*, Willo Davis Roberts; best juvenile: *The Clearing*, Dorothy Reynolds Miller.
Award: Ceramic bust of Edgar Allan Poe, presented at awards banquet.

Quill & Scroll International Writing/Photography Contest
Quill and Scroll Society
School of Journalism and Mass Communication
The University of Iowa
Iowa City, IA 52242
Description: This competition, open to enrolled high school students, recognizes and rewards student journalists for their writing, reporting, and photojournalism skills. Students may enter any of the ten divisions: editorial, editorial cartoon, news story, feature story, in-depth reporting (individual or team), advertisement, sports story, photography/news feature, or photography/sports. Entries must have been published in a high school or professional newspaper. Each participating school is entitled to two entries for each division; one student may submit all of the school's allotted entries. Fee, $2 per entry, to a maximum of $40.
Deadline: Early February.
Announcements: Competition announced in December; announcements of winners sent to the journalism advisors at the participating schools in mid-March.
Award: Gold Key Charm. Winners can

apply for one of the Edward J. Nell Memorial Scholarships in Journalism.

Regina Medal

Jean R. Bostley, SSJ, Executive Director
Catholic Library Association
Suite 224, 100 North Street
Pittsfield, MA 01201-5109

Description: The Regina Medal recognizes lifetime achievement in children's literature. The sole criterion is excellence in writing for children. Recipients of this annual award are selected by a committee.

Announcements: Winners announced in the fall in *Catholic Library World*. The medal is awarded in the spring.

Representative Winners: Eve Bunting; Russell Freedman; Gary Paulsen.

Award: Silver medal presented at an awards luncheon.

Rip Van Winkle Award

Ellen Rubin, Immediate Past President
School Library Media Specialists of
    Southeastern NY
29 Queen Anne Lane
Wappingers Falls, NY 12590

Description: School Library Media Specialists of Southeastern New York presents this award annually to an author or illustrator who has made outstanding contributions to the field of children's literature.

Nominees must live in the seven-county area represented by the group, which includes Orange, Ulster, Rockland, Dutchess, Sullivan, Putnam, and Westchester counties. SASE for more information.

Announcements: Winners announced in the spring.

Representative Winners: Lee Bennett

Hopkins; Betty Miles.

Award: Engraved bowl presented at the spring conference, held in West Point.

Rochester Playwright Festival Contest

Joan Sween, Executive Director
Midwest Theatre Network
5031 Tongen Avenue NW
Rochester, MN 55901

Description: This contest is held every two years and is aimed at discovering and promoting new works for the theatre and supporting emerging playwrights. The finalists are selected by the Midwest Theatre Network, which includes five theaters and a production company. Each theater selects its own winner from the finalists, and the winning plays are performed at the biennial Rochester Theatre Festival.

Any full-length script (roughly one-hour for a children's play) that has never been published or produced by a professional theater is eligible. Adaptations of children's scripts or musicals are also eligible. No entry fee for the first entry; $10 reading fee for each successive entry. SASE for guidelines.

Deadline: November 30.

Announcements: Winners announced every two years in March.

Representative Finalists: *Maria's Loom*, Jane R. Howard; *The Snow Queen*, Charlotte Samples and Steven Moore; *A Tale from the North Woods*, Lynn-Steven Johanson.

Award: Honorarium of $1,000 presented at awards dinner.

Ana Davidson Rosenberg Award

Paula Friedman, Award Director
Judah Magnes Museum

2911 Russell Street
Berkeley, CA 94705

Description: This contest is designed to honor poetry on the Jewish experience. Prizes are given in three categories: youth commendation (for poets younger than nineteen), senior award (for poets sixty-five and older), and new and emerging poets.

Entries should be unpublished, original poems, written in English, on the Jewish experience. A total of eight double-spaced pages consisting of one to three poems may be submitted. Submit four copies of each poem. Entries are not returned. Entry fee, $2.

Deadline: August 15, 1998.

Announcements: Competition announced in April, winners in December.

Representative Winners: Senior award: Inge Israel and Harry Waitzman; new/emerging poet: Diana Ben-Merre.

Award: Cash prizes of varying amounts presented at awards ceremony; poems read at the Magnes Museum during Hanukkah.

Eliot Rosewater Indiana High School Book Award

Association for Indiana Media Educators
Administrative Office
1908 East 64th Street
Indianapolis, IN 46220-2186

Description: Students in grades nine to twelve help select the recipient of this award, given to an author who receives the most votes in Indiana.

Named from Kurt Vonnegut's *God Bless You, Mr. Rosewater*, this award encourages recreational reading. A Book Award Committee selects twenty titles based on age-appropriateness, and par-ticipating schools must make available to their students at least twelve of the twenty titles. Students who have read five or more titles are eligible to participate in the voting.

Deadline: Schools must be enrolled by December 1.

Announcements: Students vote in April and winners are announced by April 30.

Representative Winner: *The Giver*, Lois Lowry.

Award: Winner receives an appropriate award, decided on by the Book Award Committee. Award is presented at the annual AIME Conference.

Carl Sandburg Literary Arts Award

Tina Garepis, Program Manager
Friends of the Chicago Public Library
400 South State Street
Chicago, IL 60605

Description: This award is presented annually to Chicago-based authors to reward excellence in fiction, poetry, nonfiction, and children's literature. Contest is open to authors who are current residents or natives of Cook, Lake, DuPage, McHenry, Kane, or Will counties. Submit two copies of published books only. Entry fee, $25. SASE for contest guidelines. Information available at www.cpl.lib.uic.edu/cpl.html.

Deadline: August 1.

Announcements: Winners announced in mid-October.

Recent Winner: *Shadow Catcher: The Life and Work of Edward S. Curtis*, Laurie Lawlor.

Award: $1,000, at awards banquet.

SCBWI Grants

Society of Children's Book Writers

and Illustrators
Suite 106, 22736 Vanowen Street
West Hills, CA 91307

Description: SCBWI instituted its grant program to encourage continuing excellence in the creation of children's literature. It includes work-in-progress grants, Don Freeman Memorial Grant-in-Aid, and the Barbara Karlin Grant.

Work-in-progress grants are divided into four categories: a general work-in-progress grant, a grant for a contemporary novel for young people, a nonfiction research grant, and a grant for work whose author has never had a book published. SCBWI members may apply for any of the first three grants; the fourth is chosen by the SCBWI from all entries.

The Don Freeman Grant is given to the SCBWI member who intends to make picture books their chief contribution to children's literature. Applicants should submit a rough book dummy and two finished illustrations, or ten finished illustrations suitable for picture book portfolio presentation.

Established to recognize and encourage the work of aspiring picture book writers, the Barbara Karlin Grant is for writers who have never had a picture book published. Applicants should submit one picture book, the text of which can be an original story, a nonfiction work, or a retelling/adaptation of a fairy tale, folktale, or legend.

Deadline: Work-in-progress applications must be postmarked between February 1 and March 1. Don Freeman Grant applications must be postmarked January 10 to February 10, and applications for the Karlin Grant should be postmarked April 1 to May 15.

Announcements: Requests for work-in-progress and Karlin Grant applications may be made beginning October 1; grant recipients are announced in the October/November *SCBWI Bulletin*. Freeman applications may be requested on June 1, and awards are announced the following June. For all contests, instructions for sending completed applications and written material will be sent with the application.

Award: First-place winners receive a grant of $1,000; runners-up receive a $500 grant.

Seventeen Magazine Annual Fiction Contest
850 Third Avenue
New York, NY 10022

Description: Unpublished writers between the ages of thirteen and twenty-one may enter this annual competition sponsored by *Seventeen*. Multiple entries are acceptable. Entries should be no more than 4,000 words in length (approximately sixteen pages). Include name, address, telephone number, birth date, and signature in the top right corner of the first page of each story. No entry fee; manuscripts not returned.

Deadline: April 30.

Announcements: Contest announced in *Seventeen* in the November issue. Winners notified by mail.

Award: First prize, $1,000; second prize, $500; third prize, $250; and five honorable mentions of $50 each. Winning entries published in *Seventeen*.

Charlie May Simon Book Award
James A. Hester, Secretary/Treasurer

Arkansas Elementary School Council of Arkansas Department of Education
4 Capitol Mall, Room 302-B
Little Rock, AR 72201
Description: This award was established in 1970 to honor Arkansas children's writer Charlie May Simon and to promote quality children's literature. The annual award is decided by fourth-, fifth-, and sixth-grade students statewide, who select their favorite from a list of twelve to twenty books. A winning book and an honor book are selected.

Published works only. Short stories, short nonfiction, books, and original poetry are eligible, as long as they are suitable for grades four to six. SASE for contest guidelines.
Announcements: Contest announced March 15 for the next school year. Winners announced in May.
Representative Winners: *The Best School Year Ever*, Barbara Robinson; *The Secret Funeral of Slim Jim the Snake*, Elvira Woodruff.
Award: A medallion for the winning book and a plaque for the honor book, awarded at an annual banquet.

Skipping Stones Honor Awards
Arun N. Toké, Executive Editor
P.O. Box 3939
Eugene, OR 97403-0939
Description: *Skipping Stones* Honor Awards recognize exceptional contributions to multicultural and nature education. Books, magazines, and educational videos are considered in two categories. The multicultural and international category features books that include the themes of cultural and ethnic diversity within a country and sustainable relationships between different cultures. Submissions in the ecology and nature category should promote an awareness of the natural world, environmental protection, and conservation of resources.

Books, magazines, and videos published between April 1996 and April 1998 are eligible. Send four copies of books and magazines, and two copies of educational videos. Entry fee, $50 (50 percent discount for small nonprofit publishers).
Deadline: January 10.
Announcements: Winners announced in April.
Representative Winners: *Muskrat Will Be Swimming*, Cheryl Savaqueau; *Necessary Roughness*, Marie G. Lee.
Award: Books are reviewed in the spring issue of *Skipping Stones*; honor award certificates are presented to authors, illustrators, and publishers.

Kay Snow Writing Awards
Willamette Writers
9045 SW Barbur Boulevard, Suite 5A
Portland, OR 97219-4027
Description: The purpose of this annual contest is to help unpublished writers reach their professional goals. Categories include: adult short story (2,500 words); adult nonfiction (2,500 words); poetry (maximum, five pages); scriptwriting (ten pages); and juvenile short story or article (1,500 words). There is a special student writers division for those eighteen-years-old and under who wish to enter any of the categories.

No limit on submissions as long as they are unpublished; no manuscripts returned. Submit three copies of each entry accompanied by a registration form and entry fee of $10 each for members, $15 each for nonmembers, $5 each for students.

Deadline: May 15.

Announcements: Contest announced in January; winners notified by mail in late July.

Award: $200 for first place, $100 for second, and $50 for third, in each category. Awards presented at the Willamette Writers banquet dinner and winning entries appear in *The Willamette Writer* newsletter.

South Carolina Children's Book Awards

South Carolina Association of School
  Librarians
Shirley Harris, Book Award Board
  Representative
P.O. Box 2442
Columbia, SC 29202

Description: The purpose of the South Carolina Children's Book Awards is to encourage students to read quality, contemporary literature. The awards are given in three divisions: children's, junior, and young adult. Each year, the SCASL selects 100 to 150 books. Of these, all must have at least two favorable reviews to recommend them. A judging committee then reads all these titles and chooses the twenty best. These nominees are then read by students across the state of South Carolina who vote for their favorite.

All nominees are published titles with a copyright date within the last three years; publishers send the SCASL copies of their books for consideration.

Deadline: Ongoing.

Announcements: Winners announced in the spring.

Representative Winners: Children's: *The Best/Worst School Year Ever,* Barbara Robinson; junior: *Phoenix Rising,* Karen Hesse; young adult: *Harris and Me,* Gary Paulsen.

Award: Medal presented at a luncheon at the SCASL Conference in March.

Southwest Book Awards

Border Regional Library Association
c/o El Paso Public Library
501 North Oregon Street
El Paso, TX 79901

Description: Books about the Southwestern U.S. and northern Mexico are eligible for the Southwest Book Awards. Published titles in any genre (fiction, poetry, nonfiction, reference) and directed toward any audience (scholarly, popular, children) are acceptable. Titles should be high quality; related to the Southwest, defined as West Texas, New Mexico, Arizona, and northern Mexico; and published between August 1 and July 31 of the current year. Books are usually nominated by publishers but authors are free to submit titles.

Deadline: September 30.

Announcements: Competition announced in July. Winners notified in January or February.

Award: Certificate presented to winner at the annual BRLA Awards Banquet.

Southwest Writers Workshop Contest

Suzanne Spletzer, Contest Chair
Southwest Writers Workshop
1338-B Wyoming Boulevard NE
Albuquerque, NM 87112

Description: In addition to helping

CONTESTS

new writers become published, this contest encourages writers and honors excellence. Prizes are awarded in eighteen categories, including children's picture book, children's/young adult short story, and middle-grade or young adult novel. Editors and agents critique the top three entries in each category, and a published author or professional gives a written critique of other entries.

SASE for contest guidelines (or e-mail questions to spletzer@swcp.com). Entries should include a synopsis and the manuscript's first twenty to thirty pages, and should indicate the age range of the intended reader. SASE for return of manuscript and critique. Entry fee, which includes critique, is $34 for nonmembers and $24 for SWW members. Multiple entries accepted.
Deadline: May 1.
Announcements: Contest announced every January. Announcements of winners in the fall.
Representative Winners: Children's picture book: *A Mighty Sad Tale*, Ivon Cecil; children's/young adult short story: *Self Help*, Carolyn Flynn; middle grade/young adult novel: *Song of the Caravans*, Grace J. Cooley.
Award: $50 to $100. Best of Show receives the Storyteller Award and $500. All awards presented at the annual SWW conference.

Spring Fantasy Contests
Women in the Arts
P.O. Box 2907
Decatur, IL 62524
Description: *Spring Fantasy* is an annual anthology published by Women in the Arts. Published and unpublished writers may submit entries to these cat-

egories: fiction, to 1,500 words; juvenile fiction, to 1,500 words; rhymed poetry, or unrhymed poetry, thirty-two lines each.

No names should appear on the entries. Indicate name, address, phone number, title of entry, category, and word count for fiction on a cover sheet for each entry. On poems, type title of poem in upper left corner; on fiction, page numbers belong in the upper right corner and title belongs in the upper left corner of each page. $2 fee per entry; limit of five submissions per entrant. Photocopies and computer printouts acceptable. No entries returned.
Deadline: November 15.
Announcements: Winners announced March 15.
Representative Winners: Juvenile fiction: *Hildy's Big Nose*, Melissa Russell; Fiction: *What Happened to Charlie?*, Jill Lynne Ness; rhymed poetry: *Sweet Memories*, Linda V. Nelson; unrhymed poetry: *Note to Red Riding Hood's Mother*, Susan Landgraf.
Award: Varying cash awards and publication in *Spring Fantasy*.

Spurs
W. C. Jameson, Spur Director
Western Writers of America
1012 Fair Street
Franklin, TN 37064
Description: Sponsored by the Western Writers of America, the purpose of Spurs is to reward excellence in Western writing. The competition is open to all writers and accepts children's books, as well as picture books.

Guidelines are available after August 15 of each year. Writers are allowed one submission for each contest year. Entries should be in book format. Submit four copies of the book. There is an entry fee of $10.

Deadline: November 30.

Announcements: Competition announced in July. Winners announced in *ROUNDUP* Magazine and in a press release in the spring.

Award: Plaque given at award dinner.

The Stanley Drama Award

Wagner College
Department of Theatre and Speech
631 Howard Avenue
Staten Island, NY 10301

Description: This annual award is open to all original full-length stage plays, musicals, or one-act play sequences that have not been professionally produced or received trade book publication. Writers of musicals are urged to submit music on cassette tapes as well as book and lyrics. The Stanley Drama Award is presented as a memorial to Alma Timolat Stanley.

All scripts must be typed or word-processed, bound, and accompanied by a completed application form. Include SASPC for notification of manuscript receipt and SASE for notification of contest winner. There is a reading fee of $15, payable to Wagner College. One submission is allowed for each entrant. Plays submitted previously and former Stanley Award winners are not eligible to compete.

Deadline: December 1.

Announcements: Winners announced in April.

Award: Winner receives $2,000.

George C. Stone Center for Children's Books Recognition of Merit

Doty Hale, Director
Stone Center
Claremont Graduate School
131 East 10th Street
Claremont, CA 91711-6188

Description: This contest honors a book or body of work for its power to please and heighten the awareness of children and teachers that have shared the work in the classroom. Judges look for books of superior quality that can be used effectively and extensively by teachers and students.

Any genre of children's or young adult literature from any period or any country is eligible for consideration. Multiple submissions permitted. Recommendations from students, school teachers, university professors, and librarians are considered by the awards committee. SASE for guidelines.

Deadline: July 1.

Announcements: Winners announced in March at Claremont Reading Conference.

Representative Winners: Myra Cohn Livingston.

Award: Scroll, presented at a session of the annual conference.

Sugarman Family Award for Jewish Children's Literature

Director, Judaics and Library Programs
District of Columbia Jewish
   Community Center
1529 Sixteenth Street NW
Washington, DC 20036

Description: Previously awarded annually, this biennial award was created by noted author Joan Sugarman to thank, encourage, and inspire other writers and illustrators for Jewish children. The goal of the award is to enrich

CONTESTS

all children's appreciation for Jewish culture and literature. The award offers a monetary award for the best Jewish children's book published in the previous calendar year.

Fiction and nonfiction books are eligible, and entries should be geared to readers fifteen and under. Works are judged on the basis of written language, knowledge of the subject, and interest to a particular age group. Originality and universal appeal are also taken into consideration.
Deadline: December 31, every two years.
Announcements: Winners announced at a spring awards ceremony.
Representative Winners: *When I Left My Village*, Maxine Rose Schur; honorable mention: *The Hand-Me-Down Horse*, Marion Hess Pomeranc; *A Prayer for the Earth: The Story of Naamah, Noah's Wife*, Sandy Eisenberg Sasso.
Award: $750, presented at an awards ceremony in Washington, DC.

Sunshine State Young Reader's Award
Sandy Ulm, Supervisor, School Library Media Services
Florida Association for Media in Education
Florida Department of Education
522 Florida Education Center
Tallahassee, FL 32308
Description: The Sunshine State Young Reader's Award is presented to the author of a book judged most outstanding by students in grades three to eight in participating Florida schools. The purpose for this award is to stimulate students to read for personal satisfaction and to help them understand, relate to, and enjoy life through positive experiences with literature.

Nominations come from school library media specialists, who consult with teachers and students before making their final choices. The master list for grades three to five and the master list of titles for grades six to eight each include fifteen books. These lists are then sent to participating schools; those children who have read at least three of the titles are eligible to vote.
Deadline: Ballots must be returned the following spring.
Announcements: Winners announced at the annual FAME Conference.
Representative Winners: Grades three to five and six to eight: *Nasty, Stinky Sneakers*, Eve Bunting.
Award: Bookends engraved with the award seal are given to the winner at the annual FAME Conference.

Sydney Taylor Manuscript Competition
Paula Sandfelder, Coordinator
Association of Jewish Libraries
1327 Wyntercreek Lane
Dunwoody, GA 30338
Description: The Sydney Taylor Manuscript Competition aims to encourage fiction writers whose work has not yet been published. Manuscripts should be fiction with Jewish content and universal appeal for readers ages eight to eleven. Works should serve to deepen the understanding of Judaism for all children, and should reveal positive aspects of Jewish life.

Open to unpublished authors only. No multiple submissions. Submit two copies of a double-spaced, typewritten manuscript that is between 64 and 200 pages in length. Signed release form

must accompany all submissions. Manuscripts are not returned. SASE for contest guidelines and release form.
Deadline: January 15.
Announcements: Winners announced in June at an annual banquet.
Representative Winner: *Passover Promise*, Donna Agins.
Award: $1,000 and certificate.

Marvin Taylor Playwriting Award
Sierra Repertory Theatre
P.O. Box 3030
Sonora, CA 95370
Description: The Sierra Repertory Theatre, founded in 1980, sponsors the Marvin Taylor Playwriting Award. Plays are judged on merit, the ability to perform the production at the Sierra Repertory Theater, and the potential for growth the play offers the cast. Past winners have included comedies, dramas, and a musical. Plays with a cast of eight or fewer performers are preferred.

Entries must be full-length, typed, and either a new play or a play that has been produced no more than two times. No application form is necessary; no entry fee. Photocopies and computer printouts accepted; enclose an SASE for return of the entry.
Deadline: August 31.
Announcements: Winners announced in the spring of the following year.
Award: $500, against royalties and production at the Sierra Repertory Theatre.

Texas Bluebonnet Award
Annette Nall, Coordinator
Texas Library Association
3355 Bee Cave Road, Suite 401
Austin, TX 78746
Description: This award, established in 1979 to encourage Texas children to read more books and identify their favorites, is part of a statewide reading program for children in grades three to six. Students who have read at least five of the books on the master list are eligible to vote. The Texas Bluebonnet Committee creates the master list that is sent to participating elementary schools in Texas, but students are free to suggest additions to this list.

The committee considers literary quality, favorable reviews, and reading level. The author must be a living U.S. citizen and the book must have been published in the U.S. in the previous three years. Fiction and nonfiction are eligible.
Deadline: August 1.
Announcements: Contest announced in April. In August, promotional material is sent to registrants. Master list and voting forms sent on January 1. Winners announced to schools on March 1.
Representative Winner: *Math Curse*, Jon Scieszka.
Award: Engraved medallion presented to the winner at annual award luncheon.

Book Publishers of Texas Award
Judy Alter, Secretary
Texas Institute of Letters
P.O. Box 298300
Fort Worth, TX 76129
Description: The purpose of this annual award is to honor the author of the best book for children or young people published during the previous year. To be eligible, the author must have a connection with Texas—either born there, lived in Texas for two years or more, or the book should be associated with Texas.

Submit three copies of published books. No multiple entries; no entry fee. Guidelines available with SASE.

Deadline: January 2.

Announcements: Winner notified in March; official announcement in April at awards banquet.

Representative Winners: *Uncle Comanche*, J.A. Benner; *Liza's Blue Moon*, Diane Stevens; *Breathing Room*, Barbara Elmer.

Award: $250 honorarium presented at an awards banquet in April.

Treasure State Award

Bette Ammon, Library Director
301 East Main Street
Missoula, MT 59802

Description: Children in kindergarten through third grade select the winner of this annual contest by choosing their favorite picture book from a list of five books. The contest is designed to increase exposure to great books and to build critical evaluation skills. It is sponsored by the Missoula Public Library, Missoula County Schools, and the Montana Library Association.

Fiction and nonfiction picture books published in the preceding five years and still in print are eligible. SASE for guidelines.

Deadline: March 20.

Announcements: Winners announced in April.

Representative Winners: *Three Cheers for Tacky*, Helen Lester; *Zomo*, Gerald McDermott.

Award: Varies.

Vegetarian Essay Contest

Debra Wasserman, Co-Director
Vegetarian Resource Group
P.O. Box 1463
Baltimore, MD 21203

Description: This annual essay contest, sponsored by the Vegetarian Resource Group, is open to children ages eight to eighteen and is designed to value young people's commitment to vegetarianism. Entrants need not be vegetarians to enter.

Students should submit a two-to-three-page essay on any aspect of vegetarianism. Entries will be divided into three categories: eight years and under, nine to thirteen, and fourteen to eighteen. Essays should be based on personal opinion, interviewing, or research, and should include the author's age, grade, school, and teacher's name.

Deadline: May 1.

Announcements: Winners announced in late summer.

Award: $50 savings bond; winning essays published in *Vegetarian Journal*.

Volunteer State Book Award

Dr. Beverly Youree
Tennessee Library Association
P.O. Box 184
Murfreesboro, TN 37132

Description: This award is sponsored by the Tennessee Library Association in an effort to promote good reading among students in kindergarten through twelfth grade. Students select the winner from three master lists of twenty titles each: kindergarten to grade three, grades four to six, and young adult. Participating schools nominate books for the master lists, which are finalized by librarians and educators.

To be placed on the master list,

books must be by American authors and copyrighted within five years prior to voting. Textbooks, anthologies, translations, and books from foreign publishers are not eligible. No entry fee. Send SASE for contest guidelines.
Deadline: Write for 1998 deadline.
Announcements: Winners are announced in April at Tennessee Library Association Spring Conference.
Representative Winners: Kindergarten to grade three: *Dogzilla*, Dav Pilkey; grades four to six: *The Best/Worst School Year Ever*, Barbara Robinson; young adult: *Deadly Deception*, Betsy Haynes.
Award: Winners honored at an awards banquet.

Stella Wade Children's Fiction Award
Amelia Magazine
329 E Street
Bakersfield, CA 93304-2031
Description: In children's fiction, *Amelia* looks for knowledge of genre, plot, and interest. Unpublished short stories for children, primarily those meant to be read aloud, are eligible for this annual fiction contest.

Entries are limited to 1,500 words and there is a submission fee of $7.50 per entry; no limit on entries. Photocopies and computer printouts acceptable. SASE for return of manuscript. Writers under seventeen must have entry signed by parent, teacher, or guardian to verify originality. Contest guidelines available for an SASE.
Deadline: August 15.
Announcements: Winners notified by mail eight to ten weeks after contest closes.
Award: $125; publication in *Amelia*.

Washington Children's Choice Picture Book Award
Rebecca Miller, Contest Coordinator
P.O. Box 1413
Bothell, WA 98041

Description: Children in kindergarten to grade three in the state of Washington select the winner of this annual award. Selections are made from a list of twenty books provided by a committee of librarians. Books are chosen from children's works published three to four years before the award year.
Deadline: December 31.
Announcements: Winners announced in April.
Representative Winner: *Harvey Potter's Balloon Farm*, Jerdine Nolen.
Award: Winner receives a scroll illustrated by a Vermont artist; presented at an awards ceremony in May or June.

Wellspring Magazine
Meg Miller, Chief Editor
Castalia Bookmakers, Inc.
4080 83rd Avenue N., Suite A
Brooklyn Park, MN 55443
Description: This biannual contest is open to unpublished fiction writers ages thirteen to eighteen. Creative short stories to 2,000 words are eligible for consideration. Photocopies, computer printouts, and disk submissions (Word or WordPerfect) are accepted.

Send SASE for contest guidelines. There is no limit on the number of submissions allowed for each entrant. The fee is $5 for each submission. First-time North American and one-time rights are acquired when writers submit work for the competition.
Deadline: January 1 and July 1.

CONTESTS

Announcements: Winners receive notification by mail.

Award: Winners are published in *Wellspring*. First-place winner receives $50, second-place winner receives $30, third-place winner receives $20, and honorable mentions receive $3 each.

Western Heritage Awards

M. J. Van Deventer, Director of
Publications
National Cowboy Hall of Fame
1700 NE 63rd Street
Oklahoma City, OK 73111

Description: These awards honor writers whose works preserve the legends and myths of the West in books, movies, film, and television. Literary categories include Western novel, nonfiction book, juvenile book, art book, short story, magazine article, and poetry. Nonfiction entries are judged on scholarship, organization, interpretation, presentation, and quality of writing. Fiction and poetry are evaluated on originality, creativity, and quality of writing.

Five copies of each published work must be submitted, along with an entry form; these cannot be returned. For short stories and nonfiction articles published in a periodical, send five copies of the magazine. Tear sheets or photocopies are not acceptable. $35 entry fee per submission; no limit on entries.

Deadline: November 30.

Announcements: Competition is announced on September 1. Winners are announced in mid-March at a gala awards banquet at the National Cowboy Hall of Fame in Oklahoma City.

Award: Wrangler trophies (original bronze sculptures) given at an awards ceremony.

Jackie White Memorial Children's Playwriting Contest

Betsy Phillips, Director
Columbia Entertainment Co.
309 Parkade Boulevard
Columbia, MO 65202

Description: The winning play in this annual contest is performed by the CEC's Children's Theatre School. The goal of the contest, now in its tenth year, is to find top-notch scripts that challenge and expand the talents of the school's ten-to-fifteen-year-old students.

Submit unpublished, original full-length (one to one-and-a-half hours) plays with speaking roles for twenty to thirty characters, with at least ten characters developed in some detail. Plays should be enjoyable for audiences of all ages, especially for middle-school students and up. Do not send plays with only a few roles, or roles in which children play animal parts. Previously produced plays are accepted. Entry fee, $10; multiple submissions accepted. Send SASE for contest guidelines.

Deadline: June 1.

Announcements: Winners are announced in August.

Representative Winners: 1996: *Hauncho's Xellent Xmas*, Ned Campbell; 1995: *John Lennon and Me*, Cherie Bennett.

Award: $250 and production of the play; travel stipend.

Laura Ingalls Wilder Award

American Library Association
50 East Huron Street

Chicago, IL 60611

Description: The Laura Ingalls Wilder Award was first presented in 1954. Since then, it has been awarded every five years between 1960 and 1980, and now is given every three years. This award is presented to an author or illustrator whose books are published in the U.S. and who has made an outstanding contribution to children's literature.

Members can present their nominations to the award committee. Books are judged on literary and artistic merit, as well as whether they have established a new trend in children's publishing; they must be exceptionally notable, and leading examples of a particular genre.

Deadline: Ongoing.

Announcements: The contest is announced every three years: 1998 will be the next award year.

Representative Winner: Virginia Hamilton.

Award: Winner receives a medal at an award presentation.

Thomas Wolfe Fiction Prize

Bobbie Collins-Perry, Program and
    Services Director
North Carolina Writers' Network
(NCWN)
3501 Highway 54 West, Studio C
Chapel Hill, NC 27516

Description: Established in 1994, this annual fiction contest honors internationally acclaimed North Carolina author Thomas Wolfe. Open to all writers, unpublished short stories or novel excerpts are eligible for this contest.

Contest guidelines are available by sending SASE to the above address.

Submit two copies of a previously unpublished fiction manuscript and a cover sheet with name, address, phone numbers, and title of piece. Manuscripts can not exceed twelve double-spaced pages. Names should not appear on any of the manuscript pages. No manuscripts will be returned. There is an entry fee of $7.00. Simultaneous submissions are allowed but the NCWN should be notified if the entry is accepted elsewhere. Send SASE for list of contest winners. E-mail address of NCWN is ncwn@sunsite.unc.edu and website: http://sunsite.unc.edu//ncwriters.

Deadline: August 31.

Representative Winners: *Mine*, Andrea Blumenfeld.

Award: $500, and NCWN will seek publication of the manuscript.

Carter G. Woodson Book Award

Rose-Kathryn Young Chaisson
Communications & Recognition
    Programs, National Council for
    the Social Studies
3501 Newark Street, NW
Washington, DC 20016

Description: This award goes to the most distinguished social science books, appropriate for young readers, that depict ethnicity in the U.S. Established in 1974 by the National Council for the Social Studies (NCSS), the award is intended to encourage publication of outstanding social studies books that treat topics related to ethnic minorities and race relations sensitively and accurately.

To be eligible, a book should be an informational or nonfiction trade or supplementary book (not primarily a

textbook) published in the U.S. in the year preceding the award. The book must deal with the experiences of one or more racial/ethnic minority groups in the U.S. and accurately reflect the perspectives, cultures, and values of the particular group or groups. No entry fee; multiple entries permitted. Contact NCSS for contest guidelines.

Deadline: Mid-February. Contact NCSS for 1998 deadline.

Announcements: Competition announced in December or January. Winner announced in the summer.

Award: Winning books are reviewed in the NCSS journal *Social Education*, and a certificate is presented at the NCSS annual conference in November. Winning authors can also participate in a discussion group and a book signing at the conference.

Writer's Block Contest

Shaun Donnelly, Editor
Box 32
9944-33 Avenue
Edmonton, Alberta T6N 1E8
Canada

Description: Sponsored by *Writer's Block Magazine*, the aim of this twice-yearly contest is to promote outstanding genre fiction, especially by unpublished writers. *Writer's Block* spotlights exceptional stories in several genres, including mystery, science fiction/fantasy, humor, and romance.

Contest guidelines are similar to the magazine's guidelines for writers, with two additions: stories must be accompanied by a $5 entry fee, and multiple submissions (to a maximum of three stories) are permitted. Stories should not exceed 5,000 words.

Deadline: March 1 and December 1.

Announcements: Winning entries are published in the issue following the contest deadline.

Representative Winners: "Penelope's Revenge," Gwen Lariviere; "The Breakers," J.A.H. Rice.

Award: Publication of winning story in *Writer's Block*, $50 cash award (in addition to payment of $.05 per word for published work), and hardcover books in the winner's genre.

1998 Writers' Competition

Eileen Roggenthen, Chairman
National League of American Pen
    Women
P.O. Box 692
Keystone, SD 57751

Description: This annual competition, designed to encourage writers to become published authors, accepts original, unpublished submissions in a variety of categories, including children's fiction (ages five to eight); children's fiction (ages nine to twelve); adult non-fiction; and adult fiction. Winning entries must hold the readers' attention. Fiction should teach a lesson, solve a problem, or be informative.

Entry fee is $2 per manuscript; multiple submissions accepted. Accepts original, unpublished work. Include a cover sheet listing titles, categories, author's name, address and phone number. Writer's name should not appear on any submission. Entries are not returned.

Deadline: February 15.

Announcements: Competition announced in July; winners and local press notified in March.

Representative Winners: Vera Bakker,

Jane Allen.
Award: Prizes range from $5 to $50 in each category.

Writer's Digest Annual Writing Competition
Competition Coordinator
1507 Dana Avenue
Cincinnati, OH 45207
Description: In 1997, two new categories were added to this competition: Children's Fiction and Children's Nonfiction. All original, unpublished manuscripts are eligible. Other categories include personal essay, feature article, literary and mainstream/genre short story, rhyming poetry, non-rhyming poetry, stage play, and television/movie script.

Competition accepts photocopies and computer printouts. Manuscripts can be up to 2,000 words; scripts, to fifteen pages of the standard format; and poems, up to thirty-two lines. Writers may submit an unlimited number of manuscripts; however, there is a reading fee of $10 for each submission. For grand-prize and first-place winners, *Writer's Digest* uses first-time serial rights for one-time use. Send SASE to Department PR at the above address for official rules and entry form.
Deadline: May 29.
Announcements: Competition announced in the January *Writer's Digest*. Winners announced in the November issue.
Award: Grand-prize winner wins an expense-paid trip to New York to meet with four editors or agents. First-, second-, and third-place winners in each category receive $500, $250, and $100 respectively, and $100 worth of

Writer's Digest books. Fourth- and fifth-place winners receive $50 and $25 respectively, and a copy of the *1999 Writer's Market* with CD-ROM and a one-year subscription or renewal to *Writer's Digest* magazine.

Writing Conference Writing Contest
John H. Bushman, Director
The Writing Conference, Inc.
P.O. Box 664
Ottawa, KS 66067
Description: The Writing Conference, Inc. sponsors annual writing contests for students in three age levels: elementary, junior high/middle grade, and high school. The goal of the contests is to increase student writing. Winning entries are published in the *Writer's Slate*, a magazine whose audience is comprised of students and teachers in elementary, middle, and secondary schools.

Submissions must be original and unpublished. Students can submit a poem, essay, or narrative on a topic specified by the Writing Conference. Guidelines available with SASE or on the Internet at www.scrtec.rtec.org/writing.
Deadline: January 6.
Announcements: Contest announced in February. Winners announced in March at annual conference on writing and literature.
Award: All winning entries are published in the *Writer's Slate*; first-place winners are invited to annual conference on writing and literature; second- and third-place winners receive certificates.

Young Hoosier Book Awards

Association for Indiana Media Educators
1908 East 64th Street, South Drive
Indianapolis, IN 46220-2186

Description: The primary purpose of the Young Hoosier Awards is to encourage recreational reading among elementary and junior high students. The Book Award Committee, composed of AIME members, selects twenty books for each age division from suggestions by teachers, students, parents, and media specialists. Books must meet these standards: Author must be living and a resident of the U.S.; the book must have been published within the last five years; and the author is restricted to one submission a year.

The list of twenty top selections are sent to participating schools, where students may vote.

Deadline: New schools must be enrolled in the program by December 1. Voting results are due before April 15.

Announcements: Winners are announced in April at the annual spring meeting of AIME.

Representative Winners: Picture book: *Harvey Potter's Balloon Farm,* Jerdine Nolen; grades four to six: *Wayside School Gets a Little Stranger,* Louis Sacher; and grades six to eight: *Nightjohn,* Gary Paulsen.

Award: At the AIME Spring Conference, the division winners each receive a commemorative plaque.

Young Reader's Choice Award
University of Washington
Graduate School of Library & Information Science
Box 352930
Seattle, WA 98195-2930

Description: The Young Reader's Choice Award was established in 1940 to promote reading for enjoyment, and to honor books that reflect quality children's literature. This annual award is the oldest children's choice award in the U.S. and Canada, and the only regional award that is selected by children of two countries.

Nominated titles, which must have been published three years prior to the voting year, are suggested by teachers, librarians, and students. The target reading age for the two divisions of the award is grades four to eight (junior division) and grades nine to twelve (senior division). Nominations should reflect the reading interests, abilities, maturity levels, and developmental stages of these age levels. Children who have read at least two of the nominated books in each division may vote in both.

Voting takes place in schools and public libraries in Alberta and British Columbia, Canada, and in the states of Washington, Montana, Idaho, Oregon, and Alaska.

Deadline: Book nominations must be received by February 1. Tallied votes for nominated titles are due by March 15.

Announcements: Winners are announced in April; announcements also made through library journals.

Representative Winners: Junior division: *Nasty, Stinky Sneakers,* Eve Bunting; Senior division: *Driver's Ed,* Caroline Cooney.

Award: A silver medal is presented to each division winner at the annual Pacific Northwest Library Association Conference.

Writers' Conferences

Conferences Devoted to Writing for Children
General Conferences

Celebration of Children's Literature
Montgomery College Continuing Education
51 Mannakee Street
Rockville, MD 20850
Description: This annual, one-day conference, sponsored by Montgomery County's public schools, community college, and public libraries, brings together those interested in children's literature. Participants may register for one morning and one afternoon session; continuing education credits are available through attendance at this conference.
Date: Late spring.
Subjects: Some of last year's topics included oral tradition and folklore; creating a series; getting started in writing for children; historical fiction for the middle grades; reviewing books for children; and why children love horror stories.
Speakers: In 1997, featured speakers included authors Laua Melmed, Valerie Tripp, and Lulu Delacre; photographer/illustrator Jennifer Ashabranner; *Horn Book* columnist Kristi Thomas Beavin; and Trev Jones from *School Library Journal*.
Location: Montgomery College, Germantown, MD campus.
Costs: $60 for Maryland residents; $84 for out-of-state attendees.
Contact: Sandra Sonner, Senior Program Director.

Children's Book Seminar: The

Creation of Books that Entertain—and Teach

Rhode Island School of Design
Summer Programs/Continuing
    Education
Two College Street
Providence, RI 02903-2787

Description: Rhode Island School of Design's Continuing Education department sponsors this two-day seminar for writers and illustrators. Now in its third year, this seminar brings together a panel of notable professionals from the field of children's literature to discuss the writing/illustrating concept. An open portfolio review is also scheduled the last day of the seminar.

Date: Summer.

Subjects: Last year's topics included what makes a children's book timeless; editorial submission; and learning through stories, illustrations, and visual models.

Speakers: In 1997, author/illustrator Tomie dePaola, editor Megan Tingley, and a professor of illustration at Rhode Island School of Design were among the seminar faculty.

Location: To be announced. 1997 program took place in Boston at the Museum of Fine Arts.

Costs: $275 for the children's book seminar; $75 for dinner with guest speaker; and $30 for registration. Hotel accommodations are extra.

In Celebration of Children's Literature

Professional Development Center
University of Southern Maine
305 Bailey Hall
Gorham, ME 04038

Description: Since 1981, the University of Southern Maine has celebrated children's literature in this 3-day institute given for teachers, librarians, parents, media specialists, and those who care about children and books. In workshops and idea sessions, award-winning authors and illustrators share their ideas on everything from exploring picture books to ways in which to expand middle-grade and young adult literature. Workshops are also geared to different grade curriculums and explore themes, teaching strategies, hands-on activities, and different literary genres. On the last day, there is a discussion panel and workshop session in which attendees can meet and learn from various children's book artists.

Dates: Second or third week in July.

Subjects: Language Concepts & Children's Books; Book Review; The Personal Art of Illustration; Life Stories: Women Who Made a Difference; and A Teacher/Storyteller's Journey.

Speakers: In 1997, featured faculty included authors Phyllis Reynolds Naylor and Russell Freedman; author/illustrator Gail Gibbons; artists Melissa Sweet and Peter Catalanotto; and agent Edite Kroll.

Location: University of Southern Maine in Gorham.

Costs: In 1997, the cost for the 3-day program was $180. Overnight accommodations on campus or at nearby motels are available at an extra charge.

Contact: Joyce Martin, Program Coordinator.

Institute of Publishing and Writing: Children's Books in the Marketplace

Vassar College
124 Raymond Avenue

Poughkeepsie, NY 12604

Description: For fifteen years, the Institute has been bringing together top professionals from the publishing industry to share their experience and expertise with those interested in children's writing and illustrating. This six-day intensive conference gives students a behind-the-scenes look into writing, editing, marketing, and working with an agent. Students are housed in a Vassar residence hall, with meals provided.

Date: Mid-June.

Subjects: The Editorial Process, Writing Fiction, Writing Nonfiction, Creating the Picture Book, and Marketing Your Work.

Speakers: To be announced. In 1997, Jean Van Leeuwen, Margery Facklam, and Judith Whipple were among the guest faculty.

Location: Vassar College.

Costs: $800 includes tuition, room and board; students pay $750.

Contact: Maryann Bruno, Associate Director of College Relations.

Ohio Kentucky Indiana Children's Literature Conference

The Greater Cincinnati Library Consortium
3333 Vine Street
Suite 605
Cincinnati, OH 45220-2214

Description: Promoting children's literature in the tri-state area is the aim of the Ohio Kentucky Indiana (OKI) conference. This one-day program, organized in 1996, brings together writers, illustrators, teachers, librarians, and parents in order to share information and ideas about linking children, books, and reading. Book-signing sessions with the featured authors are scheduled.

Date: November 7.

Subjects: A variety of programs on writing and illustrating children's books are offered.

Speakers: Some of last year's speakers included Louise Borden, Issac Olaleye, and Chris Soentpiet.

Location: College of Mt. St. Joseph, Cincinnati, OH.

Costs: 1997 registration fee was $25—lunch included.

Contact: Ron Frommeyer, Staff Development Coordinator, 513-751-4422.

Once Upon a Time: Children's Literature in the Late Twentieth Century

Key West Literary Seminar
419 Petronia Street
Key West, FL 33040

Description: Now in its sixteenth year, this annual seminar explores the field of contemporary children's literature and features some of the most famous names in children's publishing today. Four days are devoted to workshops on writing and illustrating.

Date: January 5-11, 1998.

Subjects: Storytelling; children's fiction; illustration; fantasy; and writing.

Speakers: Judy Blume, Jerry Pinkney, Nancy Willard, Bruce Coville, Joseph Bruchac, Jane Yolen, Richard Peck.

Location: San Carlos Institute in Key West, FL.

Costs: $400 for the workshops; $295 for the seminar alone.

Contact: Miles Frieden, Executive Director.

Perspectives in Children's Literature

School of Education
226 Furcolo Hall #2-22639
University of Massachusetts
Amherst, MA 01003-3035
Description: Writers, illustrators, teachers, librarians, parents, and students have been attending this culturally diverse conference for the past 28 years. A wide range of topics are covered which touch on such subjects as poetry, illustration, developing a story, and what an editor looks for in submissions. Academic credit is available. There is also a publishers' exhibit featuring educational materials and the latest books.
Date: April 4.
Subjects: 1997 topics: A Writer's Sense of Place, Illustrating a Story That Isn't Your Writing, and Retelling Fairy Tales.
Speakers: Gary Paulsen, Patricia Lee Gauch, Barry Moser, and Sheila Hamanaka were among last year's guests.
Location: University of Massachusetts.
Costs: $55—includes lunch.
Contact: Dr. Masha K. Rudman, Director, 413-545-1116.

Robert Quackenbush's Children's Book Writing & Illustrating Workshops
460 East 79th Street
New York, NY 10021
Description: Beginning and professional artists and writers attend these five-day workshops to learn how to produce books for children. Working with author/illustrator Robert Quackenbush, in classes limited to ten, students will create either a manuscript or a dummy book by the end of the workshop. Occasionally, a visiting editor will give a talk or the class may take a field trip to visit a publisher; students receive daily feedback on their work.
Date: July 13-17.
Subjects: New directions and outlets for children's books; how to develop projects for today's children's market; writing, editing, illustration, and design.
Speakers: Robert Quackenbush.
Location: Robert Quackenbush Studios in New York City.
Costs: 1997: $650 tuition. Lodging and meals not included. On request, a list of nearby hotels will be sent.
Contact: Robert Quackenbush, Director, 212-744-3822.

Wildacres Children's Writers Workshop
233 South Elm Street
Greensboro, NC 27401
Description: While the adult writing workshop has been in existence for 15 years, 1998 is only the second year for a separate children's program. Writers will submit either 15 pages of a young adult or middle-grade manuscript or the entire manuscript of a picture book. The manuscript will be submitted to only one workshop, but attendees may audit other workshops.
Date: Early July or late August.
Subjects: Workshops focus on writing picture books, middle-grade and young adult fiction; illustration; and information on finding an agent.
Speakers: To be announced. Last year's faculty included Cheryl Zack, Belinda Hurmence, Donna Jakob, Virginia Wright-Frierson, and agent Dorothy Markinko.
Location: Wildacres Retreat in Little Switzerland, NC.

Costs: In 1997, $350—this includes room, board, workshop fees, and the cost of manuscript critique.
Contact: Judi Hill, Director.

Write for Success Workshop: Children's Books

3748 Harbor Heights Drive
Largo, FL 33774
Description: Since 1988, the Write for Success Workshops have been a yearly event. A full-day seminar is offered as well as a three-day evening course. Topics covered include what editors are looking for, how to revise a manuscript, the principles of good writing, and what the publishing industry is all about. Manuscript critiquing is also available.
Date: The workshops are usually held in February or March.
Subjects: Picture book writing, the middle-grade chapter book, writing dialogue, creating characters, finding ideas, plotting, developing conflict, and revision.
Speakers: Theo Carroll and others.
Location: Clearwater, FL.
Costs: 1997 fee was $85.
Contact: Theo Carroll, Program Coordinator, 813-581-2484.

The Writers Center at Chautauqua

P.O. Box 406
Chautauqua, NY 14722
Description: Since 1988, week-long writing workshops and classes for adults and children have been held every summer at Chautauqua. Most of the classes and workshops mix students of all levels of experience, from beginners to published writers. Classes focus on the teacher's presentation and discussion. Workshops focus on critiques of students' submitted work and are limited to 12 students.
Date: Begins in late June.
Subjects: Classes are given in poetry, nonfiction, creative nonfiction, novel and short story, humor, mystery, fiction, and journalism. A young writers workshop is scheduled for ages 7 to 17 as well as a workshop on writing for children. A special Writers' Day and Young Writers' Day are held once each summer during July.
Speakers: Past faculty members have included Susan Rowan Masters, Margery Facklam, and Carol H. Behrman.
Location: The CLSC Alumni Hall in Chautauqua.
Costs: Registration fees for 1997 ranged from $60 to $70 per week. Students must make their own room reservations.
Contact: Clara Silverstein, Assistant Director.

Conferences Devoted to Writing for Children
Society of Children's Book Writers & Illustrators

Alabama

SpringMingle '98
Southern Breeze Region SCBWI
1616 Kestwick Drive
Birmingham, AL 35226
Description: Held every year in Alabama, Georgia, or Mississippi since 1993, this conference offers a professional focus for writers and illustrators of children's books and encourages the production of quality children's literature. Writers and illustrators from all levels of professional experience benefit from group sessions. The conference also provides a preliminary supper for all participants, a forum for book sales, an autograph party, and a banquet.
Date: March 1998.
Subjects: 1998 has scheduled a tour of the DeGrummond Collection which includes a talk on Children's Literature Research led by curator Dee Jones. Last year's conference included the following lectures: Celebrating Courage...Taking Risks; Publishing on the Fringe; Creating Complete, Accurate, and Exciting Nonfiction for Magazines; Risky Business; Drawing a Fine Line; The Publisher's Almanac; and Celebrating Courage...Reaping the Rewards.
Speakers: Last year's faculty included Stephen Roxburgh, Carolyn Yoder, Jody Taylor, Kent Brown, and Han Nolan.
Location: Hattiesburg, MS.
Costs: Members, $60–$80; nonmembers, $75–$100. Manuscript critiques and portfolio reviews, $35.

Contact: Joan Broerman, Regional Advisor; Linda Ratto, Spring Conference Coordinator; and Rita Herron, Special Events Coordinator.

Writing and Illustrating for Kids
Southern Breeze Region
1616 Kestwick Drive
Birmingham, AL 35226
Description: The Southern Breeze Region's first conference was held in 1992. Each year since, this conference has offered more than 20 different workshops from entry level to professional track, as well as numerous lectures on the craft of writing and illustrating from early picture books through young adult novels. Its purpose is to support the production of quality children's literature.
Date: The third Saturday in October.
Subjects: Nuts and Bolts, How to Avoid Unscrupulous Publishers, Writing Plays for Children to Perform and See, Writing Picture Books, Characterization—Hands On!, Who Needs an Agent and Why?, From an Editor's Perspective, Career Opportunities for Illustrators, and more.
Speakers: To be announced. At the last conference were Ted Rand, Meridee Stein, Liz Van Doren, Betty Strand, Evelyn Coleman, Jim Bass, Faye Gibbons, and many more.
Location: To be announced. Last year's conference was held at an elementary school in Birmingham, AL.
Costs: Members, $50–$60; nonmembers, $65–$75. Critiques and portfolio reviews, $35. Room accommodations

are available at a local inn, SCBWI rate of $51.06 (tax included), reserve by October 1.

Contact: Joan Broerman, Regional Advisor.

California

North Central March Modesto Conference
8931 Montezuma
Jamestown, CA 95327
Description: For six years, this one-day informative gathering tries to broadly cover all genres of children's literature. Open to all those interested in writing and/or illustrating books for children, the conference sometimes offers a written manuscript evaluation.
Date: Around March 18–23, 1998 (one-day conference).
Subjects: Among the topics scheduled to be covered for the 1998 conference: picture books, nonfiction, middle-grade novels, illustration, agents, and the market.
Speakers: Deborah Hopkenson, Jane Kurtz, Susan Campbell Bartoletti, Lee Wardlaw, and Elizabeth Law.
Location: Modesto, CA.
Costs: Approximate fees. Members, $50; nonmembers, $55. Motel accommodations, $60 per night. $15 for manuscript evaluation if available (first 15 registrants to include critique fee will receive the evaluation).
Contact: Tricia Gardella, Regional Advisor.

SCBWI National Conference on Writing and Illustrating for Children
Membership Office
Suite 106
22736 Vanowen Street
West Hills, CA 91307
Description: This four-day extravaganza offers an accomplished faculty of children's book authors and illustrators who host workshops and give lectures that are designed to inspire and educate writers and illustrators about children's literature. Established in 1972, popularity of this conference grows every year, it attracts a diverse audience of writers and illustrators representing 30 states and several foreign countries. A luncheon for the winning authors of the Golden Kite Awards followed by a book signing are also included in the conference festivities.
Date: August 1998.
Subjects: To be announced. Last year covered such topics as A Failure to Imagine Will Make Us Die, Writing Picture Books That Endure, The Use of Subconscious in Fiction, Publishing on the Lunatic Fringe, Warts and All: Creating a Character to Love, Beginnings: The First Page, Writing Nonfiction that Kids Want to Read, The Visual Side of Nonfiction...to name a few.
Speakers: Last year's staff included: Craig Walker, Jack Gantos, S. E. Hinton, Paula Danziger, Connie C. Epstein, Eloise McGraw, Barry Moser, Lynn Reid Banks, Holly Berry, and many more.
Location: To be announced. Last year's conference was held at the Century Plaza Hotel in Los Angeles, CA.
Costs: Members, early registration, $295 (receipt of registration form and tuition fees before July 9), after July 9, $320; for nonmembers, $340. Consultation on manuscripts or portfolios is an additional $40; they must be received by July 21 for critique. Univer-

sity credit is available through UCLA Extension for an additional fee of $60 (to be included with the registration form).
Contact: Lin Oliver, Conference Director.

Kansas

Writing For Children in the Heart of America
Johnson County Community College
12345 College Boulevard
Overland Park, KS 66210
Description: Sponsored by JCCC for the second year, this one- to two-day conference provides networking and instructional opportunities to writers and illustrators of children's books. A manuscript critique is provided to participants by local writers.
Date: October 1998.
Subjects: Picture books, young adult and children's books, the magazine market, nonfiction, and editor's viewpoint.
Speakers: To be announced.
Location: Johnson County Community College in Overland Park, KS.
Costs: Members, $55; nonmembers, $60. Accommodations are extra.
Contact: Judith Choice, Program Director, Community Services; and Lisa Hardraker, Kansas Representative.

Michigan

Working Writers' and Illustrators' Retreat
5859 124th Avenue
Fennville, MI 49408
Description: This weekend retreat, open to all authors and illustrators of

children's books, offers critique groups, workshops, and personal evaluations from editors. The purpose of this retreat is to hone the craft of writing and illustrating children's books, to establish new contacts, and to nurture creativity in all participants.
Date: October 1998.
Subjects: All subjects related to children's books.
Speakers: Elaine Marie Alphin, John Allen, and Margaret Garrou.
Location: To be announced. Last year's conference was held at a retreat center in Almont, MI.
Costs: $160, usually an early-bird discount is offered. Critiques are an extra $30.
Contact: Joan Donaldson, Coordinator.

New York

Conference for Children's Book Illustrators & Author/Illustrators
% 32 Hillside Avenue
Monsey, NY 10952
Description: Established in 1986, this one-day conference gives published and unpublished authors and illustrators a chance to exhibit their portfolios to prospective buyers in the publishing and allied fields; it also informs participants of current trends. Registration is limited to 125, and only 80 portfolios will be accepted for exhibition. Portfolio and book-dummy evaluations with experienced professionals are available to all participants.
Date: May 1998.
Subjects: Slide presentations from published authors/illustrators and a Q & A panel.
Speakers: Last year's conference in-

cluded slide presentations from Anita Lobel and Floyd Cooper. Q & A session included the following: Robert Warren of HarperCollins, Elizabeth Voees of Kirchoff/Wohlberg, Inc., and Ava Weiss of Greenwillow Books.

Location: Society of Illustrators, 128 East 63rd Street, New York, NY 10021.

Costs: Members showing portfolios $75; nonmembers $90. Without portfolios, members $45 and nonmembers $55. Portfolio evaluation is $50 for a 30-minute session and book-dummy evaluation is $25 for a 15-minute session.

Contact: Frieda Gates.

Conference in Children's Literature

P.O. Box 20233
Park West Finance Station
New York, NY 10025-1511

Description: This one-day conference offers a choice of workshops and a wide variety of lectures designed to aid writers and illustrators with improving their craft. The faculty consists of 21 distinguished speakers that are experienced professionals in the realm of children's literature. The Golden Kite Awards are presented during the conference. There is also a book signing so participants can network and socialize.

Date: Early November.

Subjects: Creating Books for the Very Young, Writing Historical Nonfiction, Breaking Into Magazines, Making Nonfiction Come Alive, Writing the Middle Grade Novel, Writing and Illustrating Picture Books, Creating a Web Page, Analyzing the P & L Statement, The Current Market for Children's Books, 6 Mistakes that Sink Submissions, Creating a Professional Press Packet, A Talk

with an Editor, Working with a Packager, Professionals: Ask an Agent, and more.

Speakers: Sue Alexander, Tom Arma, Eileen Charbonneau, Connie Epstein, Lila Perl, Andrea Davis Pinkney, and many more.

Location: To be announced. Last year's conference was held at Union Theological Seminary, 90 Claremont Street (between 120th & 122nd Streets), New York City.

Costs: Members, $70; nonmembers, $75; same-day registration, add $15.

Contact: Kimberly Colen, Chair; Nancy Lewis; and Frieda Gates.

Hofstra University Children's Literature Conference

UCCE Hofstra University
Hempstead, NY 11550-1090

Description: Established in 1984, this one-day conference offers the opportunity for both published and aspiring writers to gather and meet with librarians, educators, editors, and others interested in creating and sharing good children's literature. Each year, the program features two general session speakers, five special interest groups (participants choose two), and a panel of two children's book editors who randomly select manuscripts submitted by registrants for critique.

Date: April 1998.

Subjects: To be announced. Last year's conference covered: Picture Books, Fiction, Nonfiction, Mystery Books, Submission Procedures, and Panel: Does It Make Me Want to Read More?

Speakers: To be announced. Last year's faculty included Diane Roback, Kay Chorao, Gordon Korman, Ann Mc-

CONTESTS

Govern, Joanna Cole, Carol Barkin, Betsy James, and Margery Cuyler.
Location: Hofstra University campus, Long Island, NY.
Costs: Fee for the conference is approximately $65, dorm rooms are available as overnight housing for approximately $35.
Contact: Lewis Shena, Assistant Dean.

North and South Carolina

SCBWI: Carolinas Annual Conference
104 Barnhill Place
Chapel Hill, NC 27514
Description: This conference is geared toward writers and illustrators, librarians, and others interested in children's literature; its goal is to provide information about children's books and magazines and encouragement to aspiring authors and illustrators. A social is hosted for all participants the night preceding the conference. Other activities include a book sale with special discounts on selected books, an illustrator's display, and the presentation of the SCBWI–Carolinas Service Award.
Date: To be announced. In October or early November.
Subjects: Conference usually covers the following: picture books, middle-grade and young adult novels, fiction and nonfiction, and publishing and marketing.
Speakers: Barbara Seuling and Marileta Robinson.
Location: To be announced. Last year's conference was held at Bryan Park Enrichment Center in Greensboro, NC.
Costs: Members, about $55; nonmembers, about $65. Manuscript critique is

approximately $20. Rooming accommodations are available at the Hilton Hotel.
Contact: Frances A. Davis, Regional Advisor.

North Dakota

Writers Conference in Children's Literature
University of North Dakota
English Department
Grand Forks, ND 58202-7209
Description: Now in its eighteenth year, this one-day conference sponsored by the regional SCBWI and hosted by the University of North Dakota provides a forum for children's authors, editors, and agents to exchange ideas with prospective writers. The conference also sponsors the Emily Award which is a cash prize of $250 given to the most promising manuscript submitted by a registered participant.
Date: To be announced. Fall 1998.
Subjects: Topics scheduled for the 1998 conference are writing, marketing, and promoting children's literature.
Speakers: To be announced. Last year's faculty included Dian Curtis Regan, Christy Ottaviano, Ginger Knowlton, and Emily Rhoads Johnson.
Location: Chester Fritz Library, University of North Dakota.
Costs: Members, $55; nonmembers, $60. Written and oral critique by author, editor, or agent is an additional $25.
Contact: Faythe Thureen and Ursula Hovet.

Tell Me a Story
SCBWI North Central Texas
University of Dallas

1845 East Northgate Drive
Irving, TX 75062

Description: This annual one-day conference held in the Fort Worth/Dallas, Texas area, offers an educational program and networking opportunities for beginning and professional illustrators and writers. The conference also includes a lunch by genre, writers' displays, and an illustrators' roundtable where work will be viewed by art directors and professional illustrators.

Date: In the fall.

Subjects: Members of the conference faculty give lectures on what editors are looking for in children's books and magazines, on the necessity of an agent, and on how to write and sell picture books and young adult and middle-grade novels.

Speakers: Laura Hornik, William Joyce, Anna Myers, Sarah Maizes, Deborah Vetter, and Don Whittington participated in last year's faculty.

Location: To be announced. Last year's conference was held at the University of Dallas in Irving, TX.

Costs: Members, $55; nonmembers $60. After September 27, add $5 for late registration. Manuscript and art consultations are an additional $25 to be included with the initial conference fee.

Contact: Registration through Marilyn Yates, 3909 Allendale, Colleyville, TX 76034; other conference contacts are Kathryn Lay; Karen Ferrell; and Sally Roberts, Public Relations.

Tennessee

SCBWI Midsouth Spring Conference
P.O. Box 3342

Clarksville, TN 37043-3342

Description: This conference is a one-day program that provides information and support to writers and illustrators who work for children, this conference hosts workshops on topics from writing a query letter or a book proposal to magazine writing to book contracts. It also provides an autograph and book-signing session, special entertainment during the lunch break, and a question-and-answer panel with the faculty.

Date: Usually the last Saturday in April.

Subjects: Topics covered last year were An Editor's Perspective, Writing Query Letters and Book Proposals, Mining History for Ideas, What Books Do Librarians Want to See?, Whodunit? Writing Children's Mysteries, Writing about Koalas and Quantum Physics or the Birds in Your Backyard, Successful School Visits, Book Contracts, and Writing for *Pockets* Magazine.

Speakers: Tracy Barrett, Geraldine Gutfreund, Elise Howard, Susan Johnston, Janice Knight, Robin Rector Krupp, Mary LaFleur, Mike Milom, and Cheryl Zach made up last year's faculty.

Location: Nashville, TN. Last year's conference was held at University School, Vanderbilt Campus.

Costs: Members, $60; nonmembers, $65. Manuscript and portfolio consultations are an additional $35 to be included with the registration fee. For out-of-town participants, rooming accommodations are available for approximately $63.95 per night at a special conference rate.

Contact: Cheryl Zach, Regional Advisor; and Tracy Barrett, 2802 Acklen Avenue, Nashville, TN 37212.

CONFERENCES

Washington

Writing and Illustrating for Children
Washington State Chapter
4037-56th Avenue, SW
Seattle, WA 98116
Description: Now in its ninth year, the goal of this conference is to inform, inspire, and offer a network for all individuals interested in children's literature. Only illustration critique sessions are offered to participants.
Date: April 1998.
Subjects: Among the topics scheduled to be covered for the 1998 conference: novels, picture books, nonfiction, poetry, marketing, and writing techniques.
Speakers: To be announced. Art directors, authors, and illustrators are always included in the faculty.
Location: Seattle, WA. Last year's conference was held at Seattle Pacific University.
Costs: Approximately $55 (members get a discount). Motel/hotel accommodations available at a variety of costs.
Contact: Donna Bergman, Regional Advisor.

Wisconsin

SCBWI Fall Retreat
Route 1, Box 137
Gays Mills, WI 54631
Description: This three-day retreat offers a great gathering for Wisconsin writers to network, provide advice on the writing process, and to connect with editors/writers from both coasts and the larger community. The conference tries to cover various topics for people who aspire to write for children from birth through the teenage years. An optional open mike is scheduled for Saturday night; participants are encouraged to share five minutes of a manuscript with the faculty members and attendees. There is also a Book Sharing Table for registrants to display their latest published books or book jackets. Books written or illustrated by the faculty will be on sale.
Date: October or November 1998.
Subjects: Among the topics scheduled to be covered for the 1998 conference: picture books, chapter books, and middle-grade and young adult literature.
Speakers: To be announced. Linda Zuckerman, Simone Kaplan, Rich Wallace, and Ava Weiss participated in last year's faculty.
Location: To be announced. Held in Madison or Racine, WI. Last year's conference was held at the Siena Center in Racine, WI.
Costs: To be announced. Last year's conference, early bird rates (registration before July 15): members, $215; nonmembers, $235. After July 15, add an additional $20. Fee includes room and board for three days. Individual critique session is an additional $30.
Contact: Patty Pfitsch and Pam Kuck, Co-regional Advisors.

Conferences with Sessions on Writing for Children
University or Regional Writing Conferences

California Writers' Club Conference at Asilomar
3975 Kim Court
Sebastopol, CA 95472
Description: The California Writers' Club, founded in 1909 by Jack London, has been holding writing conferences for members and nonmembers since 1943. A non-profit corporation with ten branches throughout California, the club encourages beginning and professional authors who want to perfect their craft and successfully market their work. Over ninety workshops are available covering writing in 14 fiction and nonfiction genres.
Date: June 26-28.
Subjects: Targeting the YA Reader; The Children's Hour Nightowl; Developmental Children's Fiction; Literary Magazines Are What You Need; Writing for the Craft Market; Family Stories to Novel to Screenplay to Movie were some of last year's topics.
Speakers: Ginger Wadsworth, Liz Koehler-Pentacoff, and Susan Wooldridge presented workshops at the 1997 Conference.
Location: Asilomar Conference Center in Pacific Grove, CA.
Costs: In 1997, tuition fee of $435 included conference workshops, room and board; $285 included conference fees and meals.
Contact: Gilbert Mansergh, Conference Director, 707-823-8128.

Cape Cod Writers' Summer Conference

Cape Cod Writers' Center, Inc.
P. O. Box 186
Barnstable, MA 02630
Description: Week-long courses in young adult and children's writing, fiction, poetry, humor, mystery, and screenwriting are part of the thirty-sixth annual Cape Cod Writers' Conference. Aspiring writers, as well as published authors, can schedule a thirty-minute personal conference with a resident editor or agent for an additional charge. Manuscripts can be critiqued for a fee.
Date: August.
Subjects: Classes were held last year in all genres of fiction, as well as nonfiction; young adult fiction and writing for children.
Speakers: Margery Facklam, M.J. Auch, and Deborah Savage were featured faculty in 1997.
Location: Craigville Beach Conference Center, MA.
Costs: 1997 fees: Registration, $60 nonmembers; $50, members. One-day registration, $15. Tuition costs: $85 per course, or $30 per day per course. Personal conference, $30; manuscript evaluation, $60.
Contact: Don Ellis, President, 508-375-0516.

Cleveland Heights/University Heights Mini Writers Conference
Cleveland Heights/University Heights Community Service
34200 Ridge Road #110
Willoughby, OH 44094
Description: The aim of this annual

conference is to help writers get published. Topics covered include all genres of fiction and there is usually one children's session offered.

Dates: October.

Subjects: Short stories, nonfiction articles, and how to sell your book are topics that have been covered in past years.

Location: Cleveland Heights, OH.

Costs: To be announced. Last year's registration fee was $29.

Contact: Lea Leever Oldham, Program Coordinator, 800-653-4261.

The College of New Jersey Writers' Conference

Department of English
Hillwood Lakes, CN4700
Trenton, NJ 08650-4700

Description: This annual one-day conference, now in its seventeenth year, offers workshops in all writing genres including a session on children's literature. Panel leaders give readings from their works and participants are invited to register for an open reading. A short story and poetry contest is open to those who are registered for a workshop; cash prizes are awarded.

Date: April.

Subjects: Past workshops have included Play, Television, and Screenwriting; Breaking Writer's Block; How to Begin Publishing Poetry and Prose; and Literature for the Young.

Speakers: Margery Cuyler, Ray Bradbury, and Charles Simic were among last year's faculty.

Location: The College of New Jersey.

Costs: 1997 fees: $40 registration; workshops, $10 each; additional cost for special presentations by keynote speakers.

Contact: Jean Hollander, Director, 609-771-3254.

DownEast Maine Writers' Workshops

P.O. Box 446
Stockton Springs, ME 04981

Description: Located in a historic writer's studio on the mid-Maine coast, the DownEast Workshops teach unpublished writers the essentials of writing and publishing their work. Classes are limited to 15 students and take place in summer and fall. Topics include fiction, nonfiction, creative writing, and writing for the children's market. A special Windjammer writing workshop aboard a schooner is available in September.

Date: July through October.

Subjects: Workshops deal with nonfiction, getting your work published, the writing process, creative fiction, and the children's market.

Speakers: Janet J. Barron.

Location: A historic writer's studio in Stockton Springs. The Sampler Windjammer writing workshop takes place aboard the sloop *Roseway*.

Costs: In 1997, daily tuition cost $115; a three-day workshop cost $295; the Windjammer workshop, $499. Lodging accommodations are available at an extra charge.

Contact: Janet J. Barron, Director, 207-567-4317.

Florida Suncoast Writers' Conference

Department of English
University of South Florida
4202 East Fowler Avenue
Tampa, FL 33620

Now in its twenty-sixth year, the Florida Suncoast Conference continues to promote its aim—to provide those interested with information on the art, craft, and business of writing. For three days the conference sponsors workshops on all areas of writing and different aspects of the publishing industry. For an additional fee, manuscripts will be critiqued.
Date: February 5-7, 1998.
Subjects: Fiction, nonfiction, poetry, screenwriting, storytelling for children, marketing.
Speakers: To be announced.
Location: University of South Florida, St. Petersburg campus.
Costs: Last year, tuition costs were $120. Local lodging is available for an extra fee.
Contact: Steve Rubin, Director, 813-974-1711.

Heartland Writers Conference
Heartland Writers Guild
P. O. Box 5
Cape Girardeau, MO 63701
Description: Published and unpublished writers have the opportunity to meet with top editors and agents in this three-day conference. Out of 26 workshops, usually 1 or 2 are devoted to children's topics; the rest focus on the changing markets, self-publishing, screen writing, and the mechanics of a novel. A writing competition for novels, nonfiction, poetry, and children's picture books is available to those who attend. Conference is limited to 140 participants.
Date: June 4-6.
Subjects: Workshops cover as many genres as possible; past topics in children's publishing included concept to marketing strategies for picture books. Group appointments, limited to 7 people per group, are available so that attendees can meet with agents and editors.
Speakers: To be announced. Past speakers have included editors, agents, and writers.
Location: Sikeston, MO.
Costs: Registration: $175, until March 21; $185, until May 15; and $200+, thereafter. Lodging is extra.
Contact: Pat Dunlap, Attendee Liaison, 573-297-3325.

The Heights Writers Conference
Writer's World Press
P.O. Box 24684
Cleveland, OH 44124-0684
Description: In 1992, this conference began as a small, limited gathering but it has grown into an all-day event. Writer's World Press, which sponsors this conference, is the publisher of a series of writing books and is committed to helping writers succeed. Conference programs include finding and working with agents, marketing and promoting nonfiction books, and writing for children, as well as author book signings.
Date: First Saturday in May.
Subjects: Some of last year's topics covered self-promotion of nonfiction books, approaching editors and publishers, and a workshop on writing for children.
Speakers: Tracey E. Dils, Mary Emma Allen, and Nancy Christie were featured speakers last year.
Location: At the Cleveland Marriott East, Beachwood, OH.
Costs: In 1997, registration was $75 if

CONTESTS

paid before April 25; after that date, the fee was $85. Fee includes meals, choice of seminars, and all activities.
Contact: Lavern Hall, Conference Director, 216-481-1974.

Hofstra University Summer Writers' Conference
UCCE
Hofstra University
Hempstead, NY 11550-1090
Description: For ten days, attendees participate in a choice of five daily workshops led by a master. Readings by guest authors, and visits by a publisher, editor, or agent round out this annual conference. Students receive individual feedback on manuscripts from mentoring authors. An opening reception is held as well as a conference dinner at the conclusion. Graduate or undergraduate credit is available.
Date: July 6-17.
Subjects: Last year's conference featured a writing for children workshop, along with fiction, nonfiction, poetry, and performance writing classes.
Speakers: Marilyn Levinson gave a workshop on children's writing in 1997.
Location: Hofstra University.
Costs: In 1997, tuition cost $350 plus $26 for registration per workshop. Students taking courses for credit paid a higher rate. Dorm rooms, $350.
Contact: Lewis Shena, Assistant Dean, UCCE, 516-463-5016.

Jack London Writers' Conference
Peninsula Branch
California Writers' Club
135 Clark Drive
San Mateo, CA 94402-1002
Description: In 1909, Jack London,

George Sterling, Austin Lewis, and Herman Whitaker founded the California Writers' Club. Today, the club has a membership of over 1,000 professional and aspiring writers. The Peninsula Branch, which sponsors this conference, was one of the first branches of the club. This one-day conference provides an opportunity for writers to expand their knowledge of their craft. Workshops are given by authors, agents, editors, and writing teachers. Continuing education credits are available and there is a manuscript contest that participants can enter.
Date: March 7, 1998.
Subjects: Topics cover different aspects of nonfiction, short story, novel, and poetry writing. This year, writing for young adults will be featured.
Speakers: To be announced.
Location: Holiday Inn at San Francisco International Airport North.
Costs: 1997's costs ranged from $65 to $80. Hotel accommodations available.
Contact: Marlo Faulkner, Coordinator, 415-615-8331.

Manhattanville's Summer Writers' Week
Manhattanville College
2900 Purchase Street
Purchase, NY 10577
Description: This program offers the opportunity to spend an intensive week of writing and working closely with some of the best writers and writing teachers in the country. Beginners to advanced writers participate in morning workshops and in private conferences; teachers of writing spend afternoons in a methods workshop that will help them use their own writings to develop

an effective writing curriculum. For beginning writers, there is a special workshop entitled "The Writers' Craft," which introduces the elements of creative writing. Classes are offered in fiction, short fiction, creative nonfiction, poetry, and children's and young adult literature. Manhattanville also offers a 32-credit Master of Arts in Writing degree.

Date: Late June.

Subjects: Workshops are offered in seven genres including one devoted exclusively to the craft of writing for children. A special short story editing workshop is also part of the program.

Speakers: Odds Bodkin, C. Drew Lamm, Sheri Reynolds, and Honor Moore were 1997 speakers.

Location: Manhattanville College.

Costs: $560, noncredit; for graduate credit, $780 to $1,170; registration fee, $25.

Contact: Ruth Dowd, Dean of Adult & Special Programs, 914-694-3425.

Maritime Writers' Workshop

University of New Brunswick
Dept. of Extension & Summer Session
P. O. Box 4400
Fredericton N.B. E3B 5A3
Canada

Description: This workshop has been offering instruction in fiction, creative nonfiction, poetry, and children's writing since 1976. Participants can choose one out of four workshop categories; each workshop is limited to ten writers. The week-long session begins with an informal social and ends with readings, followed by a banquet. Participants must be eighteen or over and are requested to submit short manuscripts of ten to twenty pages with their applications.

Date: Early July.

Subjects: In addition to daily group workshops, there are lectures, discussions, public readings, and special events.

Speakers: Juvenile author Barbara Greenwood was on the faculty in 1997.

Location: University of New Brunswick.

Costs: Tuition in 1997, $300; room and board at the university, $585 to $610.

Contact: Glenda Turner, Coordinator, 506-454-9153.

Midland Writers' Conference

Grace A. Dow Memorial Library
1710 West Saint Andrews Road
Midland, MI 48640-2698

Description: This annual one-day conference brings beginners and established writers together with professional writers, agents, and editors for an exchange of ideas. A keynote address by a noted speaker begins this conference; in 1997, film critic Roger Ebert gave the address. Sessions range from finding a literary agent to writing poetry and one session is always devoted to the children's market.

Date: June 13, 1998.

Subjects: Topics change every year and cover different genres. Last year's children's workshop discussed historical fiction including reference resources, markets, and the increasing use of historical fiction in the school curriculum.

Speakers: Gloria Whelan, Terry Wooten, and Roseanne Bittner were among the 1997 faculty.

Location: Grace A. Dow Memorial Library.

Costs: In 1997, $50, early registration fee; $40 for senior citizens, students, or

those who are handicapped; $10, late registration fee. Tickets for keynote address are extra.

Contact: Katherine Redwine, Coordinator, 517-835-7151.

North Carolina Writers' Network Spring Gathering

North Carolina Writers' Network
P.O. Box 954
Carrboro, NC 27510

Description: NCWN is a nonprofit literary service organization which encourages and serves writers through workshops, conferences, and literary competitions. This annual 1-day conference was started in 1990 to celebrate the literary arts. Last year, one of the four workshops in the spring gathering was on children's literature; the rest was on writing for adults. Since children's literature may not be included in each year's conference, it is best to check.

Date: June 6.

Subjects: Past children's writing workshops have included topics on writing for children in the middle years; and the changing field of children's literature.

Speakers: Jackie Ogburn hosted the 1997 children's writing workshop.

Location: North Carolina Resource Center and Library in Chapel Hill.

Costs: 1997 prices ranged from $25 to $35, depending on whether you are a member of NCWN. Lunch, $7 in advance. Hotel accommodations at an additional charge.

Contact: Bobbie Collins-Perry, Program and Services Director.

Pima Writers Workshop

Pima Community College

2202 West Anklam Road
Tucson, AZ 85709

Description: Anyone interested in writing is welcome at this annual three-day conference. Ample opportunity is available for participants to meet and talk with professional writers, editors, and agents. Manuscript conferences with an author or agent are available to those who submit their manuscript in advance.

Date: May.

Subjects: Topics include fiction, nonfiction, poetry, and writing for children. Last year, workshops involved finding an agent, developing a personal essay, and small press opportunities.

Speakers: Maia Wojciechowska Rodman and Peter Meinke spoke last year.

Location: Pima Community College, Tucson.

Costs: Credit and non-credit fees ranged from $65 to $121 in 1997.

Contact: Meg Files, Director, 520-884-6974.

Skyline Writers' Conference

Skyline Writers' Club
P. O. Box 33343
North Royalton, OH 44133

Description: Now in its fifteenth year, the Skyline Writers' Club holds this one-day conference featuring topics ranging from children's writing to survival tips for writers. Participants can also enter the club's literary contest and submit manuscripts to any two of the following categories: Fiction, Nonfiction, Poetry, and Children's Literature. These entries are critiqued by professional writers and winners are announced at the conference luncheon, where cash prizes are awarded.

Date: August.

Subjects: Fiction, poetry, inspirational writing, children's literature, and editorial needs.

Speakers: Laura Williams conducted two workshops on children's writing last year.

Location: North Royalton.

Costs: 1997 fees: $40, Skyline member; $50, non-member; $35, half-day attendance.

Contact: Mildred Claus, conference Director, 216-884-1284.

Southeastern Writers Conference
P.O. Box 102, Route 1
Cuthbert, GA 31740

Description: Founded in 1975, this six-day conference helps beginning and advanced writers achieve publication. To insure hands-on help, enrollment is limited to 100. Topics covered include romance writing, short stories, juvenile fiction, nonfiction, and poetry. Plot, dialogue, viewpoint, style, and pace are also a part of the program offerings. Manuscript evaluation is available.

Date: Third week in June.

Subjects: 1997 topics included juvenile writing, nonfiction, poetry, romance, playwriting, and songwriting.

Speakers: Last year's faculty included Max Childers, Doris Buchanan Smith, and Paula Wall, among others.

Location: Epworth-by-the-Sea Conference Center in St. Simons Island, GA.

Costs: Tuition costs range from $200 to $245, including a one-year membership in SWA. Accommodations are available for an additional charge.

Contact: Patricia Laye, Co-Director, 912-679-5445.

Southwest Writers' Workshop Conference
Suite B, 1338 Wyoming Blvd. NE
Albuquerque, NM 87112

Description: Adult writing as well as writing for children are featured topics at this three-day conference, in existence for sixteen years. Attendees may register for a 10-minute session with a featured editor or agent. An awards banquet honoring the winners of the SWW contests is held the first night.

Date: August.

Subjects: 1997 workshops: 18 Articles Editors Buy; The Art of Research; How To Write a Nonfiction Book Proposal; How To Craft a Picture Book; and Developing Characters For Children's Novels.

Speakers: Penny Durant, Kersten Hamilton, Elsie Kreischer, and Madge Harrah were among the 1997 guest faculty.

Location: Hilton Hotel, Albuquerque.

Costs: Tuition costs in 1997 ranged from $215 to $320 depending on SWW membership. Lodging, meals, and the awards banquet are all extra.

Contact: Carol Bruce-Fritz, Executive Director, 505-293-0303.

Split Rock Arts Program
University of Minnesota
306 Wesbrook Hall
77 Pleasant Street SE
Minneapolis, MN 55455

Description: This summer arts program, in existence since 1984, offers courses in creative writing, creativity enhancement, and the visual arts. A renowned faculty of writers and artists are able to provide one-on-one contact

with students due to the small size of the workshops. Most classes are held at the University of Minnesota's Duluth campus, which overlooks Lake Superior. Continuing education credits are available to participating students.

Date: July and August.

Subjects: Topics from last year included Writing for Children and Writing Fiction for Young Adults.

Speakers: From 1997, Jane Resh Thomas and Will Weaver.

Location: University of Minnesota at Duluth.

Costs: In 1997, tuition cost $375; housing ranged from $162 to $246 weekly for on-campus rooms and apartments.

Contact: Andrea Gilats, Program Director, 612-624-6800.

State of Maine Writers' Conference

P.O. Box 7146

47 Winona Avenue

Ocean Park, ME 04063-7146

Description: Celebrating its 57th year, the State of Maine Writers' Conference is one of the oldest of its kind in the country. Each year, the program differs in theme and faculty. The aim of this three-day conference is to create a sense of community among its attendees so they will feel free to communicate with each other, thus fostering a sense of growth in their writing endeavors.

Date: Held two weeks before Labor Day.

Subjects: All genres of fiction, poetry, history, and children's writing.

Speakers: Authors, writing teachers, publishers, editors, and poets.

Location: Porter Hall in Ocean Park.

Costs: 1997 prices: tuition, $85; room and board extra.

Contact: Richard F. Burns, Chairman, 207-934-9806.

Summer Writing Program

University of Vermont

322 South Prospect Street

Burlington, VT 05401

Description: Begun in 1994, the Summer Writing Program is a two-week intensive workshop that brings together those interested in writing for adults and children. College credit is available; a writing sample is requested with the application.

Date: July.

Subjects: Fiction and nonfiction, poetry, journalism, illustration, children's picture books and chapter books.

Speakers: Jean Marzollo and Karen Hesse have been guest speakers.

Location: University of Vermont.

Costs: 1997 prices included a $25 application fee and tuition costs of $790 to $1682. Meals and housing costs are an additional fee.

Contact: Daniel Lusk, Director, 802-656-5796.

Taos Institute of Arts Workshops

Taos Institute of Arts

P.O. Box 5280 NDCBU

Taos, NM 87571

Description: The Taos Institute of Arts, a nonprofit school offering college-accredited courses dealing with the arts, encourages and nurtures individual creativity in an atmosphere that respects the peoples and cultures of the past. Though the majority of its workshops are on the cultures and arts of the Southwest, three courses dealing with children's publishing were offered in 1997. Workshops usually last three to five

days. Continuing education credits are available.
Date: Summer.
Subjects: Past workshops included: Book Writing for Children; and Illustration and Writing of Children's Books.
Speakers: Toni Knapp, Karen Kelly, and Craig Brown taught 1997 workshops.
Location: Taos, New Mexico.
Costs: In 1997, children's publishing workshops ranged from $240 to $345; registration fee, $20.
Contact: Judith Krull, Associate Director, 505-758-2793.

Western Reserve Writers & Freelance Conference
Lakeland Community College
Suite 110, 34200 Ridge Road
Willoughby, OH 44094
Description: All types of writing are covered at this 16th annual conference for novice and published writers. The one-day program highlights a variety of writing genres as well as marketing, self-publishing, and financial help. Several area writing groups and Lakeland Community College sponsor this event.
Date: First Saturday after Labor Day.
Subjects: Nonfiction, researching, poetry, and children's fiction.
Speakers: Last year's faculty included Laura Williams and Robert James.
Location: Lakeland Community College.
Costs: 1997 prices: $49; $6, lunch.
Contact: Lea Leever Oldham, Conference Coordinator, 1-800-653-4261.◆

The Write People Annual Literary Conference
The Write People, Inc.

P. O. Box 188
Scottville, MI 49454-0188
Description: This conference, which serves the rural west Michigan communities on Lake Michigan, is open to those who take writing seriously as an art, and who want to improve their writing skills. A one-day conference is planned for 1998. Both children's and adult authors will be on hand and the program will include lectures and workshops on various aspects of writing.
Date: To be announced.
Subjects: Poetry, editing, plot and character development, and illustration are some of the areas covered.
Speakers: To be announced.
Location: West Michigan.
Costs: To be announced.
Contact: Jean Stickney or Jacky Jeter, Conference Coordinators, 616-757-9432.

Writing Children's Books
New York University School of Continuing Education
48 Cooper Square, Room 203
New York, NY 10003
Description: Each semester, NYU offers several courses on writing children's books taught by recognized names in children's publishing. In most classes, a guest editor, author, or literary agent is invited to speak at one of the sessions. Two of the seminars meet for one full Saturday while one course runs for ten evening sessions.
Date: To be announced.
Subjects: How To Get a Children's Book Published; Writing for Children; and Children's Book Manuscript Critique were seminars offered in 1997.
Speakers: Authors Kate McMullan, Is-

abelle Holland, and editor Susan Lurie were part of the 1997 guest faculty.

Location: New York City.

Costs: Last year, tuition costs ranged from $135 to $430.

Contact: Janet Zelner, Program Coordinator, 212-998-7130.

Conferences with Sessions on Writing for Children
Religious Writing Conferences

American Christian Writers
P.O. Box 110390
Nashville, TN 37222
Description: American Christian Writers conferences generally cover all aspects of Christian literature for the adult through children's market. Conferences are held nationwide in such cities as Ft. Lauderdale, Atlanta, Houston, Phoenix, San Diego, Los Angeles, Seattle, St. Louis, Detroit, Chicago, Memphis, and Nashville. Each one- to seven-day conference has guest speakers that specialize in Christian literature. Scheduled programs offer from 25 to 36 workshops and sessions. Usually, there is an awards banquet planned during the conference.
Date: Conferences are held in different cities all over the United States throughout the year. In November, there is a Carribean Writers Cruise and two retreats scheduled in Nashville, TN, one in August and the other in September.
Subjects: All conferences have at least one workshop on writing for children.
Speakers: To be announced.
Location: 32 conferences with locations all over the United States, usually held at local hotels.
Costs: Conference tuition approximately, $149. Room accommodations are extra. The Christian Carribean cruise costs between $949–$1,049 without port tax ($115.50).
Contact: Reg A. Forder, Director.

Florida Christian Writers Conference

Park Avenue Retreat Center
2600 Park Avenue
Titusville, FL 32780
Description: This conference offers 48 workshops that cover all genres of adult literature as well as writing for children. It provides a retreat for Christians and offers instruction, inspiration, and a time for reflection, as well as information on marketing opportunities. Attendees should submit 4 manuscripts for editorial evaluation and marketing purposes. Awards are given to registered participants in several different categories.
Date: January 29–February 2, 1998.
Subjects: Children's Literature, Nonfiction for Kids, CD-ROM Interactive Books, and Devotionals.
Speakers: Melody Carson, Dr. Wally Metts, Rachel Hoyer, and Nancy Otto Boffo.
Location: PABC Retreat Center.
Costs: Tuition includes food, $295. Rooming accommodations are $180 for a single- and $105 for a double-occupancy room.
Contact: Billie Wilson, Conference Director.

Green Lake Writers Conference
Green Lake Conference Center
American Baptist Assembly
W2511 State Highway 23
Green Lake, WI 54941-9300
Description: Green Lake Conference is a place for renewal of the mind, body, and spirit. This is the conference's fiftieth year in existence. The purpose of

this week-long retreat is to offer encouragement, training, and critique to new and experienced writers, the beautiful surroundings offer a focal point of inspiration to participants. Faculty leaders are available to critique manuscripts written during the conference at no additional cost.

Date: First week of July.

Subjects: Seven workshops are offered: Writing for Children, Essay Writing, Poetry, Article Writing, Devotional/Inspirational, Fiction, and Exploring the Writer in You; and one seminary presentation, Spiritual Values in Children's Literature.

Speakers: To be announced. Last year's faculty included Emily Auerbach and Jacquelyn Mitchard.

Location: Green Lake Conference Center.

Costs: Program fee, $80. Room and board are an additional $262–$434 depending on facility and location.

Contact: Jan De Witt, Vice President of Program.

Montrose Christian Writers' Conference

Montrose Bible Conference
5 Locust Street
Montrose, PA 18801

Description: This conference's aim is to sharpen skills and rejuvenate the spirits of participants. Many activities are scheduled throughout the day during this week-long conference, the daily program includes Plenary Sessions, Editorial Presentations, Continuing Seminars, Workshop Potpourri, Circle of Sharing, and Writers' Theatre where conferees share their writing. The conference also offers professional critiques,

critique groups, appointments with editors, drama productions, and an autograph party.

Date: July 5–10, 1998.

Subjects: 1997 Conference theme was Equipping for Excellence. The 1998 conference will cover Interactive Books for Children.

Speakers: To be announced. Last year's conference included Shirley Brinkerhoff, Athena Dean, David Fessenden, Theresa Hayes, Dr. James Russell, Sally Stuart, and Carol Wedeven.

Location: Montrose Bible Conference.

Costs: Early bird tuition, $90. After June 6, $100. Room and board range from $37–$53 per day and $195–$285 per week, add an additional $30 for single occupancy. RV grounds available from $10–$17 per day and $54–$90 per week, meals not included.

Contact: Patti Souder, Program Coordinator; and Jill Meyers.

St. Davids Christian Writers Conference

St. Davids Christian Writers Association
87 Pines Road East
Hadley, PA 16130

Description: Founded in 1957 at Eastern College in St. Davids, PA, this five-day conference's goal is to establish and encourage Christian writers. Editors, publishers, and theatrical producers attend the conference to meet and discuss works in progress with the attendees. Tutorials, market consultations, and meetings with the editors are also scheduled as part of the program. All registered, attending conferees are eligible to compete for cash prizes and certificates in contests sponsored by the conference; categories include short fiction, short nonfiction, children's fiction, character sketch, humor, and poetry.

Date: Mid to late June.

Subjects: Covers all types of writing: fiction, nonfiction, poetry, juvenile, and scripts for beginning to advanced writers. Last year's conference included Interactive Books for Children and Storytelling.

Speakers: To be announced. Last year's workshop leaders were Kermit Jackson, Susan Wright, Scott Kirk, Evelyn Minshull, and Virginia Muir.

Location: Geneva College, Beaver Falls, Pennsylvania.

Costs: Tuition, $225. (Dorm) room and board, $220 for double and $225 for single.

Contact: Susan Swan, Program Coordinator and Audrey Stallsmith, Registrar.

IDEA GENERATION

Part
9

Idea Generation

Let Inspiration Lead

By Sandy Fox

I deas swarm around some writers like pesky flies, distracting them from focusing on one writing project at a time. For other writers, just when you need an idea, your mind goes blank. You stare at an empty screen that echoes the void in your brain. Where is the muse when you need her?

Here are twenty-one ways to jump start your creativity—and a demonstration of how to turn ideas into finished stories, articles, or books.

1. Remember, your brain wants to help. It will seek for whatever you tell it to. Train yourself to look for ideas in every place, situation, and event. Humor writer Tanya Kelly always has an ear for a story. Share an event with her and she'll pull out the funny parts. "There's a story in that," she says.

Ask: Is there a story in this? How can I turn this information into an article? Where is the slant or focus to this idea that will make it a saleable project?

2. Read the newspaper. Find stories in the news: profiles of kids doing interesting things, settings for stories, conflicts for plots. Emily Rhoads Johnson read about a boy finding a letter in a bottle. The result: "Sending a Letter by Bottle Post," sold to *Jack And Jill*.

3. Books. Can you take information from a book for adults and slant it for children? What is the essential information? What about this person or event would appeal to a child or teen? Are there scenes in the book that conjure up ideas for a setting for a children's story or book?

4. Journals and letters. See the Civil War, cross the ocean, or struggle during the Great Depression through the eyes of the person experiencing it.

IDEAS

Some of the writers were children. *The Boys' War* by Jim Murphy and *Letters from a Slave Girl* by Mary E. Lyons came from journals of kids. Find journals from your own history, from ancestors or friends, or from archives, libraries, and university collections.

5. Eavesdropping. Well, call it listening to kids and adults. As you listen you can hear conflict, character, and dialogue that spark ideas.

"Well, I finally have a girlfriend, but I don't know what to do with her."

"Why does everybody I love live so far away?" Cindy Rogers heard a child lament. That problem of loneliness and missing loved family became the basis for her book: *A Family for Casey*, published by Standard Publishing.

6. Research. As you delve into information for your current story or article, you often find more material than you can use. What else can you do with these enticing facts or anecdotes?

As Pamela Greenwood researched information for her historical fiction, she found material on time balls—balls dropped at noon to standardize time around the country. It became an article for *Highlights for Children*. It could have become a story about a boy responsible for dropping the ball each day. Look at articles and stories you or others have already written. Do you have research that could trigger new stories or articles?

7. What if? These two words are the greatest springboard to idea generation. Take a character: What if this happened to that child? Take a situation: What if a protagonist had to deal with that? Newspaper articles, conversations, your children's actions all offer events that can spring into a story with just supposing.

8. Develop a character. Interview your character to find out more about him or her. What does he like? Fear? Want? Get to know your character well, and he will create his own story. Throw road blocks in the way of a goal and watch the character solve the problem.

9. Find a scene. A haunted mansion, a Southwestern ranch, Disney World. What characters might live or visit here? What kind of story could happen here?

10. Theme. Often magazines ask you to write to a theme, perhaps a *Pockets* theme, such as hope, laughter, or cooperation in the family. Who might need hope? How could they get it? What do you have to say about laughter? What do the experts say? Could you profile someone with these attributes? What stands in the way of getting these things? Themes can serve a purpose beyond the editorial organizing of a magazine. They are chosen in part because of what they might inspire from writers.

11. Conflicts. Everyone has learned in English class at one time or another the standard conflicts in fiction, here adapted to children:

■ Child vs. child, exemplified in Judy Blume's *Tales of a Fourth Grade Nothing*.

■ Child vs. nature, as in *Hatchet*, by Gary Paulsen.

■ Child vs. society, a theme in Lois Lowry's *The Giver*.

■ Child vs. himself, a problem (death, divorce, drugs), a moral or inner conflict. *Dear Mr. Henshaw,* by Beverly Cleary, is an example.

Ask yourself: What conflict does my story have? What kind of character would have this conflict?

12. Pictures. Look at pictures in magazines, yearbooks, *National Geographic,* books, or greeting cards. Imagine a scene, character, conflict, or emotion.

13. Lists. Look at the list of names from the program of a graduation, band program, elementary school play, or dance or piano recital. What kinds of images do the names generate? What kind of character would have a particular name? Are any of these remarkable kids who could be profiled for their accomplishments?

14. Make your own lists. What things make you happy? Sad? Angry? Disappointed? Could you give a character one of these situations or problems? When you write from your deepest emotions, you'll write with power!

List all the places you've ever lived or dreamed of living. Let them inspire you. List interests and careers you or friends and family pursued or dreamed of.

15. Remember. Set yourself back in your fourth-grade (or second- or ninth-grade) classroom. Recall the faces and names of your classmates. Think of their characteristics. What were their problems? What funny things happened? What sad things happened? What unjust things happened?

16. Create Titles. Good titles create questions and can be springboards to whole stories:

Dance for the Dead

The Day the Skunk Came to Town
Blue Moon
No Tomorrow
The Mystery of the Green Cow

Toss title ideas into the air. See what stories they spark.

17. Read listings in market directories. Concentrate on any comments from the editors themselves. Editor's Comments. Can you write the book, article, or story they are looking for?

18. Thesaurus, Dictionary, Pictionary, Descriptionary. Look at odd words, odd things, unusual people or places. Would someone else be curious about these things?

19. Maps, travel guides, tourist brochures. Look at the odd names some places have. Could your character live there? Is there a history behind the name?

One town in Arkansas is called Ink. Why? Because when it came time to vote, the postmistress, wanting to be able to read the names clearly, asked people to "Please write in ink."

Look at brochures to call up a place kids want to know about, a history begging to be told, a setting for a new book.

20. Look at the Milestones Lists in the *Children's Writer's Guide.* Science and Technology; Government, Politics, and History; News and Lifestyle; Sports and Games; Arts and the Media; Deaths. People, places, and events parade before your eyes. Think of profiles. Where are they now? What if a child watched or participated in this event? What part of this event would a kid be interested in? Use free thinking— word associations to call up similar topics or ideas to run with.

IDEAS

21. Music. Listen to music without words. Imagine the story the music is trying to tell. Now that you've come up with all these great ideas, what will you do with them? As you listen to the music, create an idea book. Each time you get an idea, sketch out the outline, or synopsis. Jot down two or three markets that might work for the idea. Set a goal of one to three ideas a day, and soon you will be overflowing with the beginnings of your next stories, articles, and books!

The Idea Book

When you need an idea, pluck it from your ongoing idea book and set to work fashioning it into a polished manuscript. Let's take three different ideas and turn them into a story, an article, and a book.

A Story

Suppose you skim through a list of names at your child's graduation. "Mississippi Breeze Johnson." What a name! Think about conflict. What would happen to a kid with a name like that? What would happen if a character had a name she hated, that everyone giggled at whenever the teacher first read her name at the beginning of the school year? Say she couldn't change it because she was named for both grandmothers and her mother loved the name.

What could Victory Bell do? She might shorten it to Vicky and try to let the teachers know ahead of time of her nickname. But school and business forms always require real names. She might learn more about her grandmothers and come to respect the courage and bravery they had and realize her name is valuable. She might take up martial arts and intimidate anyone who laughs at her. She might laugh it off and be such a nice person people don't want to tease her.

Consider character. Her character will influence her decisions. So what kind of person can she be? You decide these solutions fit a middle-grade reader and put her at age twelve. You like the nice person who can laugh at herself. So you make this the final goal. Maybe she's zany and generous.

Now let's make the problem worse. Suppose, she's just moved to a new school and no one knows who she is. She has no friends. She has an oddball name.

> She scudded around the corner of the imposing brick building and flipped her red hair out of her eyes. "New school," she thought. "New kids." She eyed the door to the sixth-grade room. Could she get to the teacher before she called roll? What would happen if everyone learned her name was Victory Bell?

Victory fails to get to the teacher. Everyone laughs at her name. She complains, again, to her mother about her absurd name. Her mother reminds her she was named after her two grandmothers who love her very much. Victory decides to call her grandmothers and ask how they dealt with the teasing.

One grandma, born on V-Day, says she remembers her father's courage. And whenever someone teased her about her name, she just remembered how glad she was her dad lived to come home from the war. So she became proud of her name. Victory calls the other and discovers Grandma Bell's sense of humor saved the day when they called her a "ding-a-ling." "I just laughed along with them."

(continued on next page)

IDEAS

The Idea Book *continued*

Victory comes to realize her name is unique, different, one-of-a-kind. Like she is. She decides she doesn't really want to change her name. Instead she'll live up to it. She'll be victorious, proud, and willing to laugh with the teasing. She discovers that everybody remembers her because of her unusual name, and soon she has lots of friends at the new school.

You've created a story with a believable character who solves her own problems. The story shows intergenerational relationships and a theme about appreciating differences. This story could be placed in a general interest magazine like *Highlights for Children,* a girl-specific magazine like *Hopscotch,* or a religious values magazine like *Pockets*. And you've discovered how to take a name idea and make it into a story.

An Article

As you read the local paper, you see sixteen-year-old Justin won state championships in a number of states and is going on to the International Bowhunter's Organization (IBO) World Competition in New York. Wow! A kid that's really done something. Who would like to know about him?

You pull out your market directory and check the listings. You skim the index under Nature/Environment and Profiles to find markets. Is he a Boy Scout? Would *Boys' Life* be interested? Is it enough of a sport to spark the interest of *Sports Illustrated For Kids*? Is there a regional magazine that likes to profile successful kids? It's a hunting event, would *Field and Stream* be interested?

You check the listing for *Field and Stream*. It no longer has a separate insert targeted to children, but it still takes articles of interest to kids. Justin's 16, maybe a little old for a kid's profile, and too young for an adult profile. And no profiles are listed. Okay. It does list how-to articles, though. Articles to 450 words. Could Justin explain a facet of bow hunting that would interest a twelve-year-old? The article says Justin began bow shooting when he was five, so he should have an idea of what a twelve-year-old would like to know about bow hunting. It talks about him shooting at life-like animal targets and the importance of knowing the "kill zone" for each animal. Maybe young hunters would like tips on that.

You call him and arrange an interview. You have an idea for the slant of the article and ask questions about "kill zones" but also listen for other skills young hunters need to know. You discover that judging the distance to the target was the most difficult thing for Justin, but he figured out a way to tell how far away a target is. Ahah! You have your topic and slant.

(continued on next page)

The Idea Book *continued*

International Bowhunter's Organization Champion, Justin, spent eleven of his sixteen years practicing both target shooting and hunting. "One of the hardest parts of successful bow hunting is to estimate the distance to the target," Justin says. "But about three years ago, I finally got the knack of it." Learn how you, too, can judge distance accurately and hit your target every time.

The article then continues with a step-by-step plan to estimate various distances, using Justin's actual quotes as often as possible. So you started with an idea from the newspaper. Then, based on marketing research and further information about the topic, you turned that idea into an article.

A Book

Say you looked at the Milestones section of this *Children's Writer Guide,* which begins on page 423 and see that an entry for 1975 reads, "The inventor of the X-ray tube, William Coolidge, dies at age 100." Inventions, you think. There have been so many of them recently. Do kids know about modern inventors? Who invented Netscape, hair blow dryers, cellular phones, supersonic jets, fax machines, and modems? Sounds exciting. Exciting enough to spend months researching and writing? Yes. You want kids to see inventors as role models, someone to emulate, a goal to strive for.

Okay. Research. You hit the library and look at *Children's Books in Print.* You find several books about inventors written for kids: *American Inventors of the 20th Century; Inventions and Discoveries; Brainstorm! The Stories of Twenty American Kid Inventors; Girls & Young Women Inventing: Twenty True Stories about Inventors.* You check out the ones your library has and request the others through interlibrary loan. So is there a niche for a book? Yes, if you slant it correctly.

What kind of slant or focus do you want to take? Do you want to focus on the person or the invention? How the invention made this person rich and famous? Or how the invention benefitted people? Major inventions or little inventions? What kinds of categories? You decide to focus on inventors in America who were born after 1950 and invented something that kids could recognize that has changed their lives somehow. You decide each chapter will focus on one inventor and you'd like to have at least ten, maybe fifteen or twenty, if you can find that many. And you decide to target the young adult.

Back to the library to view the *Readers Guide to Periodic Literature.* Under inventors you find all kinds of inventions: flat screen TV, card games, sun-proof clothing, rubber toys, Velcro. You find resources and people to contact. You

(continued on next page)

IDEAS

The Idea Book *continued*

check the Internet for more sources. You come up with a list of inventors and inventions.

Now you need to market. Which publishers want this kind of book? You check the publishers of existing books. They might like another one. Review a market directory. Ask at writers' conferences. Make a list of possible publishers and their requested submissions methods.

Most likely you will need to research one inventor (choose the most interesting one), write a sample chapter, and submit that with your synopsis. You believe in this book. Keep researching and writing while you wait for responses. You've turned your idea into a well-formed and well-developed book. You know it will sell.

So find those ideas. Write them down. Then transform them into stories, articles, and books that reflect your interests, research, and creativity. What a great idea!

Idea Development
From Seed to Full Bloom

By Sandy Fox

U se the facts in this section to begin a brainstorming process, for inspiration for an entire article, story, or book, or to help develop a character, scene, conflict, or point of view.

Picture Book = PB
Early Reader = ER
Middle-Grade = MG
Young Adult = YA
Parenting = P

1999 Anniversaries

Example 1

5th Anniversary - 1994
The U.S. Senate falls four votes short of passing an amendment to the Constitution that would require a balanced budget.

Nonfiction Books:
- *How Our Government Works*. Takes young readers through the inner workings of the three branches of government. (ER)
- *Should This Constitution be Changed?* Proposed and successful amendments to the U.S. Constitution and what it takes to make an amendment. The basic principles behind Constitutional law and government. (MG, YA)
- *A Penny Spent*. Basic economic principles of how money and the economy work. (MG, YA)

Magazine Nonfiction:
- "Where the Money Goes." The range of government spending—important and silly government spending. (ER, MG)
- "The Purse Strings." An age-targeted review of how federal, state, or local

government spends money—the agencies that monitor and control spending and the processes that they go through. (ER, MG, YA)

- "A Balancing Act." The current state of the budget and what it would take to balance it. What is truly balanced, and what is creative financing (i.e., "proposed" cuts that come in future years). Relate to a child's use of allowance. (MG, YA)

- "Profile of a Senate Page." What a page does, where, for whom, with a sidebar on what it takes to become one. (MG, YA)

Fiction, Books or Magazines:

- *Mickey's Trip to Capitol Hill.* See the Senate and House of Representatives through the eyes of a young tourist. (PB, ER)

- *The Mystery of the Wedgwood Files.* Gary, an amateur sleuth, learns that friends of his father are altering figures to throw off the budget calculations at their business. How can he let the truth be known without hurting his father? (MG, YA)

Example 2
10th Anniversary - 1989

Former President Ronald Reagan receives an honorary knighthood from Queen Elizabeth II of England.

Nonfiction Books:

- *How to Knight a Knight.* Show the pomp and ceremony of the event. Who gets knighted? Why? How? Photoessay. (PB, ER)

- *Famous British Knights.* Profiles of ten of the most dramatic or influential knights in history. (MG, YA)

- President Reagan: a look at his ten greatest presidential achievements. (MG, YA)

- President Reagan is now suffering from Alzheimer's disease: What is it? Who gets it? Cures? (ER, MG, YA)

Magazine Nonfiction:

- How did knighthood begin? (ER, MG)

- Profile of a current knight. (ER, MG, YA)

- President Reagan: What did he do for kids as president? (ER, MG, YA)

Fiction, Books or Magazines:

- Sarah learns to understand and accept Alzheimer's disease in her grandmother. (ER, MG)

- Gerald performs a heroic feat and is knighted by the king or queen. Choose any time period from the middle ages to World War II. (MG, YA)

Example 3
10th Anniversary - 1989

Mel Blanc, the cartoon voice of Bugs Bunny, Daffy Duck, and many others, dies.

Nonfiction Books:

- *History of Bugs Bunny. History of Daffy Duck.* How the cartoon characters came to be. How they were drawn, about their qualities as characters, the cartooning art itself, the spin-offs, etc. (Photo Essay, ER, MG)

- *Cartoons, What makes them work?* A look at traditional and/or computer generated cartooning. (ER, MG, YA)

Magazine Nonfiction:

- Who thinks up cartoons? A look at

the creative process of a current cartoonist—Power Rangers, etc. (ER, MG, YA)

■ Profile of Mel Blanc. How he came to be a cartoon voice. (MG, YA)

■ "So You Want to Become a Cartoon Voice." What it takes to make a career in cartoon voices. (YA)

Fiction, Books or Magazines:

■ Karen gets a pet duck and discovers it can talk. (PB, ER, MG)

■ Matt accidentally "sucks" Bugs Bunny out of the TV and now Bugs Bunny follows him everywhere. (ER, MG)

■ Taylor has a gift for mimicry. A story built on the conflict of talent and its effect on others. (ER, MG)

Example 4

15th Anniversary - 1984

Two Soviet cosmonauts in the orbiting space station Salyut 6 return to Earth after a record-breaking 175 days in space.

Nonfiction Books:

■ How does a space station work? (PB, ER, MG)

■ *Space Station Mir, A Photoessay.* What does it look like? (ER)

■ *Exploring Space.* A look at the science behind the ways men and women have tried to learn more about space. (MG, YA)

Magazine Nonfiction:

■ Profile of the youngest astronaut to go to a space station. (ER, MG, YA)

■ How does the space station Salyut 6 compare with Mir? (MG, YA)

■ The difficulties Mir has experienced and the effects on Russian-American

scientific cooperation. (MG, YA)

■ "First Trip into Space." Recount the differences between man's first trip into space and current trips. (MG, YA)

Fiction, Books or Magazines

■ George wins the science fair and is chosen to be the first boy to go into space. (ER, MG, YA)

■ Kids in an astronaut school on Mars long for a trip back to Earth to see if their families are safe. Should they try to stow away? (MG, YA)

■ Soviet and American competitors become friends as they work to enter the space program. (MG, YA)

Example 5

25th Anniversary - 1974

In the U.S., the National Transportation Safety Board and The Nuclear Regulatory Commission are created.

Nonfiction Books:

■ Trucks. Photoessay on different kinds of trucks (PB, ER)

■ Bridges. Different kinds of bridges and how they are made. (PB, ER)

■ *Source of Energy.* Where does it come from? Discusses energy supplies and where and how they are used. For older readers, a look at cost effectiveness, environmental effects. (PB, ER, MG, YA)

Magazine Nonfiction:

■ How are roads built? (ER, MG)

■ How does nuclear power work? (ER, MG)

■ What is a regulatory board? Why should you care? (MG, YA)

■ "Is Nuclear Energy Safe?" Show pros and cons. How it compares to other kinds of energy. (MG, YA)

Fiction, Books or Magazines:

- Kevin's backyard road building gets out of control! (ER)
- Jessica thinks she can solve all her problems when she runs away by stowing away in a truck. (MG, YA)
- Nick learns to deal with his truck driver dad who is never home. (MG, YA)

Example 6
25th Anniversary - 1974

West Germany wins the tenth World Cup Soccer Tournament.

Nonfiction Books:

- *So You Want to Play Soccer.* The basic rules of the game. Playing field, positions and what they do. Simple drills to improve skills. (ER, MG)
- *Soccer's Best.* Photoessay of best players, best plays, dramatic moments in World Cup soccer. (ER, MG, YA)

Magazine Nonfiction:

- How soccer came to the United States. (ER, MG, YA)
- The origins of soccer. (MG)
- Germany's best soccer player: A Profile and tips for the younger player. (MG, YA)
- "How to Play World Cup." A game or training drill for few to many players. (MG, YA)
- "Help for Soccer Moms and Dads." A parents' guide to the rules, or how to coach a soccer team, or how to handle the social end of soccer leagues: the too demanding coach, aggressive parents on the sidelines, lack of team play or spirit. (P)

Fiction, Books or Magazines:

- Sean lives and dreams of soccer. Then his family moves to a town without a soccer team. (ER, MG, YA)
- Karen's soccer team's field is being used to build a high-rise building. What can she do? (ER, MG, YA)
- The coach's son dominates the team and ruins some of the plays. How can Keith, the goalie, do his job of directing the team without alienating the coach or his son? (MG, YA)

Example 7
25th Anniversary - 1974

Amy Vanderbilt, longtime author of a column on etiquette, dies.

Nonfiction Books:

- *When She Was Good....* A picture book depicting appropriate and inappropriate behavior with family, friends, schoolmates. (PB)
- *Classroom and Playground Etiquette.* Skill-building for elementary and middle-school kids on interaction with others. (ER, MG)
- *Dating Etiquette for the Nineties.* (YA)

Magazine Nonfiction:

- "Manners? Who Needs Them?" Places and times you need good manners. What happens if you don't have them. (ER, MG, YA)
- "Profile of a Proper Person: Amy Vanderbilt." How she came to write etiquette columns. (Or what life was like when she was a child.) (MG, YA)
- "How to Eat a Formal Dinner Without Making a Fool of Yourself." (YA)

Fiction, Books or Magazines:

- Backcountry child moves to New York City and has to deal with the cultural and etiquette changes. (ER, MG, YA)

- Set a story in another decade of this century. Show a problem uniquely associated with behavioral standards of that era (the Great Depression, WWII), and the child's actions and dealings with the problem. (MG, YA)

Example 8
75th Anniversary - 1924
Anthropologist Raymond Dart discovers a species he names Australopithecus africanus, or Australopithecinea, a fossilized skull that belongs to neither apes nor humans.

Nonfiction Books:
- Photoessay of a current dig or recent discovery, such as the burial ground from the sixth century discovered on an American airbase in Britain. Show what an anthropologist does. (PB, ER)

Magazine Nonfiction:
- "An Everyday Evolution." Photo essay of the life cycle of a seed. (PB, ER)
- What is evolution? What do we know about human development over the centuries. Age-targeted exploration of facts and theories. (ER, MG, YA)
- How modern forensic experts recreate faces from skulls to help solve murders, discover victims' identities, etc. (MG, YA)
- Where does Australopithecus africanus fit in our current understanding of the development of primates? Have more recent discoveries found their place in nature? (MG, YA)

Fiction, Books or Magazines:
- Burt eats a mutant cabbage and dis-

covers he is evolving into a different life form. (ER, MG, YA)
- Jessica finds a charm that stops her at sweet sixteen. She stays the same but watches her friends continue to evolve and grow. (YA)

Example 9
100th Anniversary - 1899
Ragtime becomes popular.

Nonfiction Books:
- *Scott Joplin: Ragtime Composer.* Biography or a profile of the music and times, through the compositions of one man. (MG, YA)
- Ragtime music. What it is, what it came from and led to musically, and how it came to be popular. (ER, MG)

Magazine Nonfiction:
- What is ragtime? (ER)
- "The Beginnings of Ragtime." (MG, YA)
- Show how the "Maple Leaf Rag" came to be. (MG, YA)
- Show ragtime's influence today. Trace a piece of music throughout the years showing where it might have been played. Or be more clinical and show the elements of ragtime music in other types of popular music. (MG, YA)

Fiction, Books or Magazines:
- A poor child loves music. How can he afford piano lessons? (ER, MG)
- A young woman musician chafes under the tutelage of strict masters who want Mozart and Bach pieces played perfectly. The young person longs for the freedom to create music of her own. (MG, YA)

IDEAS

Example 10

500th Anniversary - 1499

Spices like those brought back by da Gama (cloves, nutmeg, and pepper) are used to preserve meat and disguise the flavor of spoiled meat, which comprised the bulk of the diet in late winter and early spring.

Nonfiction Books:

■ *Paths of the Early Explorers.* Where they went, what they discovered. (ER, MG)
■ *Photo Essay: Spices.* What they look like when cultivated, different ways they are used and preserved. (ER, MG, YA)
■ *Spice History.* The economic role spices have played over centuries. (MG)

Magazine Nonfiction:

■ "How Meat Spoils, and How to Prevent it." (ER, MG)
■ "You Think Your Food Tastes Nasty?" A look at the diet of fifteenth-century kids. (MG)
■ "The Beginning Cook's Guide to Spices." (MG, YA)

Fiction, Books or Magazines:

■ Henry works in the castle kitchens. He overcomes his fear of "poison" spices and learns how to use them. (MG, YA)
■ The cabin boy on da Gama's ship explores the world (or a part of it) with his famous captain. (MG, YA)

2000 Anniversaries

Example 1

5th Anniversary - 1995

Egyptian archaeologists discover a mausoleum with at least sixty-seven chambers, believed to be the burial place of the royal sons of Ramses II, one of Egypt's greatest pharaohs.

Nonfiction Books:

■ *Photo Essay: Egyptian Mausoleums.* Show the chambers and tell about the use of each. (ER, MG.)
■ Biography: Ramses II (ER, MG, YA)

Fiction, Books or Magazines:

■ Mummy/Ghost story. Could the sons of Ramses II haunt the mausoleum and appear to the son of the archaeologist? (ER, MG, YA)
■ Time travel of a girl who goes back in time to Ancient Egypt. (ER, MG, YA)
■ Story of a servant boy and how he helped the sons of the Pharaoh. (ER, MG, YA)

Magazine Nonfiction:

■ "Egyptian Burials—Religion and Science." The rituals and processes involved. (ER, MG, YA)
■ Interview and profile of an archaeologist. (MG, YA)
■ "Careers in Archaeology." (YA)
■ Accomplishments of Ramses II (MG)

Example 2

5th Anniversary - 1995

The Nobel Prize in Chemistry is awarded to Drs. E. S. Rowland, M. Molina, and P. Crutzen for explaining the chemical processes that deplete the ozone shield.

Nonfiction Books:
- *The Air.* Pictures and text about what makes up our atmosphere, the actions of air. (PB, ER)
- *Chemistry and Current Events.* How modern chemistry is changing our lives. (MG, YA)

Fiction, Books or Magazines:
- Silvia takes a balloon ride high in the sky. What does she see? (ER)
- Mike discovers alien forces are the cause of ozone disruption. It's up to him to get help or to get the aliens to leave. (MG)
- Zoltag's colony is in danger of extinction. Cause: unknown pollutants that attack the adults first. Will he be able to discover the cause and cure before the effects hit him? (YA)

Magazine Nonfiction:
- What is ozone? Why do we care about it? (ER)
- "A Shield for the Ozone." An update on the ozone shield: laws passed, their effects. (MG, YA)
- "Out of Control Pollution Control?" Is it? What effects have our environmental efforts made? Are we winning the war? (MG, YA)
- "The Ten Dirtiest Cities in the World." Informational article on environmental problems around the world. (MG, YA)
- Using chemistry to solve today's problems in textile manufacturing, the space program, computers, foods, medicine, etc. (MG, YA)

Example 3

5th Anniversary - 1995
Baltimore Orioles shortstop Cal Ripken, Jr., plays his 2,131st consecutive game, breaking a fifty-six-year record established by Lou Gehrig, and thought to be unbreakable.

Nonfiction Books:
- An introduction to baseball. Photo essay about the sport (ER)
- Sports records. Motivational profiles of the best baseball players and what made them great. (ER, MG, YA)
- How-to hints: Professional players on secrets of sports success. (MG, YA)
- The virtues and requirements of longevity and endurance. Profiles of record holders in a variety of endeavors or careers. (MG, YA)

Magazine Nonfiction:
- So you want to play baseball. An introduction to the game, how to get started, playing in leagues. (ER)
- Profile of Lou Gehrig. (ER, MG, YA)
- What to look for when buying baseball equipment. (ER, MG, YA)
- Who are the next greats? A look at those poised to break records. (MG, YA)
- How medicine and medical improvements are expanding athletic careers. (MG, YA)
- Lou Gehrig's disease. What it is, how it got its name, current treatment. (MG, YA)
- Cal Ripken, Jr., tells secrets of great batting. (MG, YA)
- High school baseball players signing into the big leagues. Who they are, their promising talents, or what it takes to make a career in baseball. (YA)

Fiction, Books or Magazines:
- A young baseball fan dreams of meet-

IDEAS

ing baseball greats, and how he does it. (ER, MG, YA)

- A kid named after baseball greats Lou or Cal by sports fanatic parents finds his own identity. (MG)
- No one in Ashley's family has any interest in sports at all. They're into museums, music, and art. But Ashley longs to chuck his piano lessons to play on the local baseball team with his best friend. (ER, MG)

Example 4
5th Anniversary - 1995

Explorers discover an underground cave in the Ardeche region of France that contains well-preserved paintings from the Stone Age, perhaps as long as 20,000 years ago.

Nonfiction Books:

- *Photo Essay: Cave Drawings.* Who drew them. What they mean. (PB, ER, MG)
- *Spelunking: How to Explore Caves.* Safety, equipment, kinds of caves. (MG, YA)
- *Preservation Science.* The techniques behind maintaining ancient, antique, contemporary works of art or documents, etc. (MG, YA)

Magazine Nonfiction:

- "Telling Stories with Pictures: Pictographs." Combine with the next item for a possible book. (ER, MG)
- "How to make a Modern Pictograph." Can you tell a story or create your own language with pictures? (ER, MG)
- Other written forms of communication—runes, ideographs. (ER, MG, YA)
- Who lived here before you did? Re-

gional article looking at the remains of earlier inhabitants (dinosaurs, indigenous peoples). (ER, MG, YA, P)
- Local caves to explore spelunking. Regional (YA, P)

Fiction, Books or Magazines:

- Jeff discovers ancient drawings in a cave that is about to be destroyed to make way for his family's dream house. (MG, YA)
- Misty and Greg go exploring and get lost in a cave. Ancient pictographs help them find their way out. (MG, YA)

Example 5
10th Anniversary - 1990

A Missouri Court rules that after eight years in an irreversible coma, Nancy Cruzan has the right to die. Life support systems are stopped, and she dies twelve days later.

Nonfiction Books:

- *A Book of Courage.* Profiles of children with potentially terminal diseases. How do they cope? Give courage to other kids going through serious illnesses. (MG)
- *The Nancy Cruzan Story: Profile of a Right-to-die Movement.* (YA)

Magazine Nonfiction:

- "What is Death?" Religious/spiritual approach. (ER, MG, YA)
- "A Breathing Machine." The development of the iron lung and contemporary medical care. (ER)
- Murder? Death? Is the gap shrinking? Recent legislation on abortion and the right to die, and a current news story of a mother accused of murder for abandoning her newborn. (YA)

- Living wills. What are they? Do you need one? Family issues. (P)

Fiction, Books or Magazines:
- Child with leukemia faces the conflicts of painful treatments and the possibilities of death. (MG, YA)
- Grandmother is on life support and the family must decide what to do. (MG, YA)

Example 6

20th Anniversary - 1980

A severe summer heat wave in the southern U.S. is blamed for 1,117 deaths in twenty states, and forces Missouri to declare a state of emergency.

Nonfiction Books:
- *Heat Waves: The Greatest Natural Disaster.* Responsible for more deaths than any other natural disaster. (ER, MG, YA)
- *Meteorology.* An inexact science that can still save lives. (ER, MG, YA)

Magazine Nonfiction:
- What makes summer so hot? (ER)
- What's a heat wave? What causes one. Heat stroke and exhaustion—what they are, prevention and first aid. (ER, MG, YA)
- Find people who lived through the 1980 heat wave, and others, and have them compare them. (MG)
- Phone a friend program: Taking care of the elderly in the community during a heat wave. Introduce readers to the program. Invite them to help set it up or participate in it. (MG, YA)

Fiction, Books or Magazines:
- Three zany twelve-year-olds try different ways to stay cool in the heat. (ER, MG)
- Becky befriends an elderly neighbor who has no air conditioning. When a heat wave comes, Becky visits the neighbor, discovers her ill condition, and saves her life. (ER, MG)
- Teen working a manual labor job in the scorching heat meets an older mentor who helps him learn the ropes and stay cool. (YA)

Example 7

20th Anniversary - 1980

Colonel Harlan Sanders, founder of Kentucky Fried Chicken, dies.

Nonfiction Books:
- *The Harlan Sanders Story.* His work toward success. How he never gave up. (ER, MG, YA)

Magazine Nonfiction:
- "The First Fast-Food Franchise and How It Worked." (ER, MG, YA)
- How to make great fried chicken. (MG, YA)
- Qualities of an entrepreneur. (YA)
- So you're going to get a job in the fast-food industry. Tips to get a job and keep you employed. (YA)

Fiction, Books or Magazines
- Russell decides to raise chickens to become rich. But he didn't count on foxes, competition, heat, and other complications. (ER, MG)
- Wheeler-dealer teen discovers he's been out-conned. (YA)

Example 8

25th Anniversary - 1975

Margaret Thatcher succeeds Edward

Heath as the leader of the British Conservative Party.

Nonfiction Books:
■ *A Woman's Rise to Power: Biography of Margaret Thatcher.* (ER, MG, YA)
■ A queen and a parliament? How British politics works. (MG, YA)

Magazine Nonfiction:
■ Margaret Thatcher as a girl: elements in her life that led to her political career and her rise to power. (ER, MG, YA)
■ How parliament selects its leader. (ER, MG)
■ What Margaret Thatcher has to say to girls of the 1990s. Selections from speeches, research material, or interviews. (MG, YA)

Fiction, Books or Magazines:
■ Shy girl listens to boys at her table denigrate girls. She finally gets the courage to speak up and defend herself and women. (ER, MG, YA)
■ Jennifer wants to play hockey on an all-boys team. After reading about Margaret Thatcher's life, she figures out how to make it happen. (MG, YA)
■ Child dreams of politics— of becoming president. He/she ends up organizing the classmates in a political rally to save the friendly custodian's job (ER, MG), save a local park (MG, YA) or elect a local political leader (YA).

Example 9

50th Anniversary - 1950

Horse racing establishes the Triple Crown Trophy to signify past and future winners of the Triple Crown series of races: the Kentucky Derby, the Belmont Stakes, and the Preakness.

Nonfiction Books:
■ *The Making of a Racehorse.* The story of a horse from foal to winner's circle. (ER, MG)
■ *Photo Essay: Winners of the Triple Crown.* Information about winning horses. (All ages.)

Magazine Nonfiction:
■ "A Day at the Races." Profile of a race track, or a look at a race horse. The parts of horse, equipment, or a track. (ER)
■ Profile a young jockey or exercise boy or girl. What's it like to ride race horses and work on the track? (ER, MG, YA)
■ "The Last Triple Crown Winner." The horse and his career. (MG)
■ "To be a Jockey." What it takes to be one. (MG, YA)

Fiction, Books or Magazines:
■ *The Race Track Mystery.* Kim and Jim's grandfather takes them to the races. He gives them clues and they search the race track with grandfather until they finally solve the mystery and discover grandfather's new young race horse is named after them (or becomes theirs). (ER, MG)
■ Kelly gets an ex-race horse and struggles to calm it down enough to turn it into a winning jumper. (ER, MG, YA)
■ Jack, a stable boy, learns that his favorite race horse is being drugged to lose races. (MG, YA)
■ Ed sees his compulsive gambler dad bet everything on the horse who won the Belmont, but loses the Preakness. (MG, YA)

Example 10
100th Anniversary - 1900

The United States Library of Congress is established.

Nonfiction Books:
- Photo Essay: ten or fifteen of the most important documents in the Library of Congress. (ER, MG)
- How we got our Library of Congress: The story behind the nation's largest library. (MG, YA)

Magazine Nonfiction:
- Why Congress needed a library: What it is, what it does. (ER, MG)
- So you want to find out something? Look in the Library of Congress. What it has, what it doesn't. How to use it. (MG, YA)
- How to use the Dewey Decimal System (ER, MG) and how to use the Library of Congress filing system. (MG, YA)

Fiction, Books or Magazines:
- An eccentric researcher dies and leaves a string of clues in his will for his young nephew and niece to find money. The two kids traipse through the Library of Congress, unraveling the researcher's clues. They learn about the library and finally find their inheritance: money and knowledge. (MG, YA)
- Orphaned Naomi sees an old picture of a girl who looks just like her. After searching the archives, she discovers a great-grandfather and aunts and cousins she never knew about. (MG, YA)

2001 Anniversaries

Example 1
20th Anniversary - 1981

IBM launches the first "home" or "personal" computer.

Nonfiction Books:
- The inventors of the first PC. How did it happen? (ER, MG)
- Using computers to do homework. How to make it look great. Graphics, word processing, etc. (MG, YA)

Magazine Nonfiction:
- What is IBM? What does it do? How does it affect your life? (ER, MG)
- How does a computer work? (ER, MG)
- How have computers changed our lives? Show the effects of computers and computer chips in all walks of life: scanners, watches, cars, etc. What would life be like without them? (ER, MG, YA)
- Using an if-then flow chart to solve your problems. A logical approach to problem solving. (YA)
- Computer games: Do they make you smart or stupid? A look at new research on the effects of long-term computer game playing. (MG, YA)
- Best software choices for non-readers. Best software choices for learning. Focus on a particular age level and write to that group. Reading, SAT prep, etc. (P)

Fiction, Books or Magazines:
- Kid inventor comes up with the next step beyond the PC but no one will believe him! (ER, MG, YA)
- While Edwin tries to fix his computer

(or explores the innards of his computer) (ER) the computer gets absorbed into him and he becomes a walking computer, a super intelligent person... with few logical drawbacks. (MG, YA)

■ Carol discovers the "Chat Rooms" on the Internet and gets more than she bargained for. (MG, YA)

■ Sandy and Allan find clues to a murder mystery on the Internet. They track down the murderer from the safety of their home. Or is it so safe? (ER, MG, YA)

Example 2
25th Anniversary - 1976
Fourteen people are killed as Idaho's Teton River Dam collapses.

Nonfiction Books:
■ Nature's Dams: a look at beavers and other dam builders. (ER, MG)

■ Photo Essay: Images of the tragedy and survival at the Teton Dam disaster, relief efforts, and the Teton Valley today. Focus on children at the disaster, helping, and now. (ER, MG)

Magazine Nonfiction:
■ Kids at the Teton Dam disaster: profile three kids who survived the dam disaster. (ER, MG, YA)

■ How safe is your dam? A regional piece on the construction of a local dam. What would it take to make it break? What would happen? (MG, YA)

Fiction, Books or Magazines:
■ Beth sees everything she owns washed away in the flood. How she learns to deal with her losses. (ER, MG, YA)

■ Race to high ground. Ben and Tara struggle to outrun the rising waters. (ER, MG)

■ A river is overflowing with the steady rains. Jason's dad had asked him to keep everything safe while he was gone. Should Jason try to save the animals? What about old blind Jerry? Who would help him? (MG, YA)

Example 3
40th Anniversary - 1961
The Berlin Wall is constructed. Vice President Lyndon Johnson tours Berlin.

Nonfiction Books:
■ True story of a family's escape to freedom from a dictatorial country, told from the child's point of view. (ER, MG, YA)

■ *The Wall That Made Time Stand Still.* As the Berlin wall came down, the West had prospered, but the East still had bomb-shattered buildings and rubble. How efforts continue to put the pieces back together. (MG, YA)

Magazine Nonfiction:
■ "The Candy Bomber." True story of an Air Force pilot who dropped candy to Berlin children during the Berlin airlift. (ER, MG)

■ Do you have a piece of the wall? The story of how pieces of the Berlin wall were sold when the wall finally came down. (ER, MG, YA)

Fiction, Books or Magazines:
■ Ernest sees the Berlin wall go up, dividing not only his city and his nation, but his family. When will he see his father again? Can he devise a cunning plan to smuggle him out of the East? Must he wait, hope, pray, and

work for the day when the wall comes down and the family can be reunited? If you show the long-term event, maybe it can be seen through a series of children—the boy, his son, and his grandson finally see the wall come down. (ER, MG, YA)

Example 4
50th Anniversary - 1951
The King and I, a musical by Rodgers and Hammerstein, premiers in New York.

Nonfiction Books:
- Photoessay on the play's staging. (ER, MG)
- *Photo Essay: Palaces of the Kings of Siam* (now Thailand)—Ayutthya, Summer Palace, Grand Palace. (ER, MG, YA)

Magazine Nonfiction:
- Profiles of Rodgers and Hammerstein. How did they come to work together? How did they make music together? (ER, MG, YA)
- So you want to be on stage: How to try out for Broadway parts. (MG, YA)
- True story: Boaters were taking the family of Thailand's king to the summer palace. On the trip up the river, two of the king's children fell into the river. They drowned because it was against the law (on penalty of death) to touch a member of the royal family. (MG)
- The story behind one of the actual kings of Siam, and the education of his children. (ER,MG)

Fiction, Books or Magazines:
- Young servant boy longs to be worthy to serve the child king. (ER, MG)

- Although white elephants are sacred to the king, marauders from Burma (now Myanmar) don't care. How will the king's elephant boy protect his animals from this danger? (MG)
- Katie longs to sing and dance on the stage. A production of *The King and I* is coming to town and auditioning children. Can she make it? (MG, YA)

Example 5
75th Anniversary - 1926
Magician Harry Houdini dies from peritonitis, caused by a blow to the stomach. The anniversary of his death is celebrated as National Magic Day.

Nonfiction Books:
- *Six Famous Magicians.* Who they were, their most famous tricks, how they came to be magicians. (ER, MG, YA)

Magazine Nonfiction:
- Adaptations of a few of Houdini's tricks, or those of a contemporary magician, such as David Copperfield. (ER, MG)
- National Magic Day: What it is, how it came about. (ER, MG, YA)
- How Harry Houdini became a magician. If a child followed those steps could he become one too? The special gifts of Harry Houdini, the elements that made him uniquely suitable to be a magician. (ER, MG, YA)
- Houdini's death: How a blow to the stomach can kill you. How to be careful so it won't happen to you. (ER, MG, YA)
- A show business career, in magic. (YA)

Fiction, Books or Magazines:
- Pat longs to be a magician despite the

IDEAS

ridicule of his family (ER) and the disapproval of his best friend who thinks it's evil. (MG, YA)

■ Sean, a fledgling magician, discovers a new use for his tricks when he fools a burglar. (MG)

■ A child gets more than he bargained for when a mail order magic trick takes on a life of its own. (ER, MG, YA)

Example 6
100th Anniversary - 1901
The first American Bowling Club tournament is held in Chicago.

Nonfiction Books:

■ A child's history of bowling: How the sport came to be. Variations on the bowling sport. Some of bowling's greats. (ER, MG, YA)

■ A collection of the funniest stories about bowling. (MG, YA)

Magazine Nonfiction:

■ What was Chicago like a hundred years ago: Picture essay, glimpse into life in that era. (ER, MG)

■ How to make a strike. (ER, MG, YA)

■ The beginner's guide to scoring a bowling game. (ER, MG, YA)

■ Profile of a young bowler who has won some tournaments. (ER, MG, YA)

■ How to organize a tournament. (MG, YA)

Fiction, Books or Magazines:

■ Fable about why a bowling ball has three holes. (ER, MG)

■ A child who feels like a failure at sports finds out she has a knack for bowling, but her friends think it's an "uncool" sport. (ER, MG)

■ Jessica organizes a tournament to

honor her grandfather, who taught her how to bowl. Is it fair for her to play in it? If she wins, will other kids think she rigged the tournament? (MG, YA)

Example 7
200th Anniversary - 1801
The first system to identify and organize animals without backbones is created by Jean-Baptiste de Lamark, a French naturalist who also created the science of invertebrate zoology and coined the terms "invertebrate" and "vertebrate."

Nonfiction Books:

■ *Photo Essay: World's Weirdest Bugs.* (ER, MG)

■ *The Man who Loved Bugs, Beetles, Worms, and Other Creepy-Crawlies.* A biography of Jean-Baptiste de Lamark. (ER, MG, YA)

Magazine Nonfiction:

■ What's a backbone? Who has one, who doesn't? How can you tell? (ER, MG)

■ "Behind the Zoo Scenes." What does a zoologist do? (ER, MG)

■ "Bugs You Can Eat." A look at edible bugs and maybe a recipe or two. (ER, MG)

■ "Bug Order." How Jean-Baptiste de Lamark organized invertebrates. (MG, YA)

■ "Career Choices: Invertebrate Zoology." What do you do with a degree in zoology? (YA)

Fiction, Books or Magazines:

■ A small child overcomes his fear of bugs. (ER)

■ John trains his tarantulas (worms,

beetles) to climb a ladder (or some other kind of trick) but when he takes them to school for show and tell, they get loose in the classroom. (ER, MG)

- "You don't have any backbone," Casey's mother says. And when Casey wakes up the next morning, he (she) finds himself literally without a backbone. (ER, MG)

Example 8

300th Anniversary - 1701

Yale College is founded in Killingworth, Connecticut, as the Collegiate School. It's relocated to New Haven and renamed Yale in 1745.

Fiction, Books or Magazines:

- A poor, black kid from a cotton picking family struggles to go to Yale. (YA)
- Anna's father, grandfather, and generations of Smythes have all gone to Yale. Anna has a learning disability. She's the only child in the family. How can she uphold the family tradition when she can't read? (YA)

Magazine Nonfiction:

- What's an Ivy League school? Include famous people who went to one of them. (ER, MG)
- America's first colleges: What was taught there? Kinds of students who went—ages, occupations. A glimpse at a segment of an earlier era. (ER, MG, YA)
- The first college in America: How it was founded. (MG, YA)
- "So You Want to Go to Yale." What it takes to get in. How to prepare yourself. (YA)
- "A Guide to College Towns." Exhibits, activities for children on the college campuses: museums, libraries, sporting events, etc. (P)

Example 9

400th Anniversary - 1601

East India Company's James Lancaster gives his crew lemon juice at the Cape of Good Hope, before traveling to Madagascar to take on more citrus fruit. His crew of 200 is the only crew not decimated by scurvy.

Nonfiction Books:

- The East India Company: where it went, what it did. Famous explorers of the company. (MG, YA)
- *Journal of a Voyage to ....* Show the voyage of an early trading ship through the journals of a young person (if possible) or a trader. (MG, YA)

Magazine Nonfiction:

- Early boat trips around the Cape of Good Hope. Map out the travels of early spice traders. (ER, MG)
- Citrus fruits: Where did they come from? When were they first introduced to the West? (ER, MG)
- Tell about scurvy and its effects through the story of James Lancaster's trip. (ER, MG, YA)
- Madagascar. Cut off from Africa by water, many plants and animals evolved differently. Tell about the different kinds or variations of life found there. (MG, YA)

Fiction, Books or Magazines:

- Take the journey of James Lancaster through the eyes of his cabin boy. (MG, YA)
- Master Charles, son of a British East India Company employee, becomes

IDEAS

friends with Kim, an Indian boy, in spite of the disapproval of his family. They go adventuring together. (ER, MG, YA)

■ Poor British boy leaves home to make his way upon the high seas and earn his fortune in India. (MG)

Example 10
500th Anniversary - 1501
Card games, first introduced 100 years earlier, gain great popularity throughout Europe.

Nonfiction Books:
■ Simple card games for travel or fun. (ER, MG, YA)
■ *A Child's History of Cards.* Show card games from around the world to illustrate the history and different kinds of card games. (ER, MG, YA)

Magazine Nonfiction:
■ Two easy card games, and how to play them. (ER. MG)
■ How cards got their faces. Different kinds of faces cards can have. (ER, MG, YA)

■ Early English card games and who played them. (MG, YA)
■ "Gambling: A Costly Addiction." How much gambling costs the U.S. in lost time, lost money, broken families. (MG, YA)
■ Is there a compulsive gambler in your house? Ten signs to look for. (MG, YA)

Fiction, Books or Magazines:
■ Kerry thinks she can read the future in her playing cards. (MG, YA)
■ Samantha uses computer-generated greeting cards secretly to befriend the cranky owner of the lot her team wants to use to play. (ER, MG)
■ Gary tries to stop his friend's compulsive gambling before it lands him in deep trouble. (YA)

Milestones

1999 Anniversaries

5th Anniversary ...1994

Science and Technology

■ Space shuttle astronauts repair the $1.6 billion Hubble space telescope and prepare it for its next mission: looking for black holes.

■ A federal study finds that the drug AZT reduces the transmission of HIV (the virus that causes AIDS) from mothers to their newborn babies.

■ The first skull of Australopithecus afarensis, the earliest human ancestor since the species split off from the great apes, is found in Africa.

Government, Politics, and History

■ The U.S. Senate falls four votes short of passing an Amendment to the Constitution that would require a balanced budget.

■ Despite an earlier refusal, President Bill Clinton grants a U.S. visa to Sinn Fein leader Gerry Adams so Adams can attend a conference in New York.

■ U.S. Attorney General Janet Reno appoints former U.S. Attorney Robert Fiske as special prosecutor to investigate President Clinton's Whitewater holdings and their relation to the failed Morgan Guaranty Savings & Loan.

■ Human rights investigators in Mexico report that government troops in the southern state of Chiapas are abusing suspected members of the Zapatista National Liberation Army.

■ The Ukraine signs an agreement with the U.S. and Russia to destroy 175 long-range missiles and more than 1,800 warheads.

News and Lifestyle

■ More than 800 people are killed when a ferry from Estonia capsizes in

IDEAS

the Baltic Sea off Finland.

■ A U.S. judge rules that the Citadel's exclusion of women is unconstitutional and orders the military college to accept a woman who had sought admission, nineteen-year-old Shannon Faulkner.

■ The Walt Disney Co. abandons plans to create a historic theme park on the site of Civil War battlefields in northern Virginia.

■ In the largest software deal in history, Microsoft announces plans to acquire Intuit, the makers of Quicken personal financial software, in a deal reportedly worth $1.5 billion.

Sports and Games

■ Golfer Nick Price wins the British Open and Professional Golf Association championships.

■ The National Football League adopts a two-point conversion rule and moves the kickoff to the 30-yard line, considered by some to be the most sweeping changes to the game in 20 years.

■ U.S. skier Tommy Moe wins the men's Olympic downhill, becoming the first American to win a gold medal at the Winter Olympics in Lillehammer, Norway, and the second American ever to win the event.

Arts and the Media

■ Edvard Munch's painting *The Scream* is stolen from the National Art Museum in Oslo, Norway.

■ Tony Kushner's *Angels in America* wins a Tony award for best play.

■ E. Annie Proulx wins the Pulitzer Prize for fiction for *The Shipping News*.

■ Steven Spielberg joins with David Geffen and Jeffrey Katzenberg to form a new movie studio, Dreamworks SKG. The venture is said to be the biggest combination of talent since a group of actors formed the United Artists Studio in 1919.

Deaths

■ U.S. singer and talk-show host Dinah Shore dies at age 76.

■ Burt Lancaster, an American film actor famous for his roles in *From Here to Eternity* and *Elmer Gantry*, dies at age 80.

■ Linus Pauling, winner of the 1954 Nobel Prize for Chemistry and 1962 Nobel Prize for Peace, dies at 93.

■ Britain's Anthony Burgess, author of *A Clockwork Orange*, dies.

■ Experimental playwright Eugène Ionesco dies.

10th Anniversary ...1989

Science and Technology

■ Florida and Virginia allow DNA "fingerprinting" as admissible evidence in some rape cases.

■ Voyager 2 reaches Neptune, currently the furthest planet from the Sun, and its satellite Triton.

■ Viruses infect computer networks worldwide, and Lloyd's of London creates a new policy to cover losses caused by computer viruses. The policy is available everywhere but in the U.S., due to the proliferation of viruses there.

■ Meteorologists pronounce 1989 the warmest year on record, possibly a sign of the greenhouse effect.

■ Mathematicians discover the largest known prime number, which is 65,087 digits long.

Government, Politics, and History

■ In the U.K., television stations begin to broadcast the proceedings of the House of Commons.
■ Soviet President Mikhail Gorbachev meets Pope John Paul II, becoming the first Soviet leader to meet a Pope.
■ Gen. Colin Powell is the first black American to become the Chairman of the Joint Chiefs of Staff.
■ Gorbachev meets with U.S. President George Bush at a two-day summit in Malta.
■ France celebrates the bicentenary of the French Revolution.
■ Chinese leader Deng Xiaoping retires from politics due to age.
■ The Romanian government is overthrown by anti-Communist protesters, and President Nikolae Ceausescu and his wife are swiftly tried and executed.
■ Japan has three prime ministers in 1989: Noboru Takeshita resigns after admitting links to a recruit bribery scandal; Sosoku Uno's credibility is weakened by involvement with a geisha; Toshiki Kaifu is named as Uno's replacement.

News and Lifestyle

■ Eighty nations adopt a declaration to stop producing chlorofluorocarbons—thought to damage the world's ozone layer—by 2000.
■ Mysterious "crop circles" appear in cornfields in the United Kingdom.
■ The United Nations Population Fund predicts that world population will reach 14.2 billion by 2100 A.D. (from the 1989 level of more than 5 million).
■ Japan's Mitsubishi buys Rockefeller Center in New York.

■ American televangelist Jim Bakker is convicted of fraud and is sentenced to forty-five years in jail.
■ Former President Ronald Reagan receives an honorary knighthood from Queen Elizabeth.

Sports and Games

■ Cuba's Javier Sotomayer becomes the first high jumper to clear eight feet.
■ Pete Rose is banned from baseball for life after admitting that he bet on games.
■ The Detroit Pistons win the National Basketball Association championship, and the Calgary Flames win hockey's Stanley Cup.

Arts and the Media

■ A controversial glass pyramid designed by architect I.M. Pei is erected outside the Louvre in Paris.
■ Mikhail Baryshnikov leaves the American Ballet Theatre.
■ The new Bastille Opera House, due to open one year later, stages special concerts to commemorate the French Revolution.

Deaths

■ Mel Blanc, the cartoon voice of Bugs Bunny and Daffy Duck, dies.
■ American boxer "Sugar" Ray Robinson dies.
■ American poet and U.S. poet laureate Robert Penn Warren dies.
■ British aeronautical engineer Sir Thomas Sopwith dies.

20th Anniversary ...1979

Science and Technology

■ Two Soviet cosmonauts in the orbit-

IDEAS

ing space station Salyut 6 return to Earth after a record-breaking 175 days in space.

- The Nobel Prize for Physics is awarded to two Americans, Sheldon Glashow and Steven Weinberg, and Pakistan's Abdus Salem.
- French oceanographer Phillipe Cousteau dies.

Government, Politics, and History

- U.S. President Jimmy Carter and Soviet President Leonid Brezhnev sign a second strategic arms limitation treaty (SALT-2) in Vienna, despite opposition from the U.S. Congress.
- U.S. General Alexander Haig, chief of Allied Forces in Europe, survives a terrorist assassination attempt.
- Direct elections to the European Parliament are held for the first time.
- The Vietnamese Army invades Cambodia and installs a new government under Heng Samrin.
- Chinese forces attack Vietnam and discover mass graves of as many as 3 million victims of the Khmer Rouge.
- South Korean President Park Chung Hee is killed—allegedly by accident—by his Chief of Intelligence.
- St. Lucia, St. Vincent, and the Grenadines win independence from Britain.

News and Lifestyle

- Ayatollah Khomeini issues a ban on music and reaffirms bans on most Western movies, alcoholic drinks, and singing by women, and prohibits men and women to swim in the same pool or at the same beaches.
- Pope John Paul II becomes the first Pope to visit a Communist country

when he returns to his native Poland. He later tóurs the U.S. and, with President Carter, calls for universal peace.

- The Ku Klux Klan stages a 50-mile "white rights" march from Selma to Montgomery, Ala.
- More than 270 people are killed in the worst airplane disaster in the U.S., when an engine falls off a DC-10 on take-off at Chicago Airport.
- Karen Silkwood is posthumously awarded approximately $10 million in damages for negligent exposure to atomic contamination in 1974.
- Mother Teresa wins the Nobel Peace Prize.

Sports and Games

- Fourteen people are killed when the Fastnet International yacht race between Cornwall and Ireland is hit by an Atlantic storm.
- The Montreal Canadiens defeat the New York Rangers to win their fourth consecutive Stanley Cup.
- Norway's Grete Waitz becomes the first woman to break the 2½ hour mark while running the New York Marathon.

Arts and the Media

- English art historian Anthony Blunt is discovered to be the "fourth man" in the Burgess, Maclean, and Philby spy scandal, and is stripped of his knighthood by Queen Elizabeth II.
- *The Elephant Man*, a play by Bernard Pomerance, wins the New York Drama Critics Award and a Tony Award.
- French composer Oliver Messiaen's seventieth birthday is marked by the renaming of a peak in Utah as Mount Messiaen.

- Sam Shepard wins the Pulitzer Prize for drama for his play, *Buried Child*.

Deaths

- Jazz composer and bassist Charlie Mingus, born in 1923, dies.
- Jack Haley, a stage and screen actor best known for his role as the Tin Man in *The Wizard of Oz*, dies.
- American actor John Wayne dies.
- English punk rock singer Sid Vicious dies of a drug overdose.

25th Anniversary ...1974

Science and Technology

- Tandem Computers is founded in Cupertino, Calif. by James Treybig. The company produces its first computer one year later.
- Skylab 3 astronauts spend 84 days in space, surpassing the Skylab 2 record of 59 days.
- American scientists discover a new subatomic particle, called the psi or J meson, interpreted as a state composed of a charmed quark and a charmed antiquark.
- A Soviet space probe lands on Mars and detects more water vapor than scientists predicted.

Government, Politics, and History

- In the U.S., the National Transportation Safety Board and the Nuclear Regulatory Commission are created.
- Worldwide inflation prompts dramatic increases in the cost of fuel, food, and materials. Oil-producing nations increase prices, heightening inflation, and economic growth slows almost to zero in most industrialized nations.
- Yitzhak Rabin is named to head the Israeli Cabinet after Premier Golda Meir steps down.
- U.S. Secretary of State Henry Kissinger persuades Syria and Israel to agree to a cease-fire on the Golan Heights.
- Juan Perón, President of Argentina in 1946-1955 and again in 1973, dies, and is succeeded in office by Vice President Maria Estela Perón, his wife.
- The U.S. establishes formal diplomatic ties with East Germany, twenty-five years after the creation of that country.
- Haile Selassie, Emperor of Ethiopia since 1916, is peacefully deposed.

News and Lifestyle

- The Dow Jones index falls to its lowest level since the recession of 1970.
- Patty Hearst, the daughter of publisher Randolph Hearst, is kidnapped in Berkeley, California, by the Symbionese Liberation Army, which demands public food give-aways as part of its ransom.
- Charles Schwab founds a brokerage house in San Francisco to take advantage of a ruling by the Securities and Exchange Commission that eliminates fixed commissions on stock transactions. By charging a lower commission than his competitors, Schwab quickly becomes one of the major companies in the field.
- Floods kill at least 2,500 in Bangladesh; a drought-induced famine threatens millions in Africa.

Sports and Games

- South African golfer Gary Player wins his third British Open and his second Masters championship.

IDEAS

■ Little Current wins the Preakness and Belmont Stakes.
■ The Oakland A's win baseball's World Series by beating the Los Angeles Dodgers four games to one.
■ West Germany wins the tenth World Cup soccer tournament.

Arts and Media

■ *People* and *The Star* are among the magazines and newspapers first published in 1974.
■ Aleksandr I. Solzhenitsyn publishes *The Gulag Archipelago*.
■ The Pulitzer prizes for drama and literature are not awarded this year.
■ Russian ballet dancers Valery and Galina Panov are granted permission to emigrate to Israel.

Deaths

■ American comedian and actor Jack Benny, born in 1914, dies.
■ Amy Vanderbilt, etiquette expert, dies.
■ Famed jazz musician Duke Ellington dies.
■ Pulitzer prize-winning poet Anne Sexton, born in 1928, dies.

40th Anniversary ...1959

Science and Technology

■ Luna 2, launched by the Soviet Union, becomes the first spacecraft to land on the moon.
■ The First International Conference of Oceanography is held in New York.
■ *Savanna,* the first nuclear-powered merchant vessel, is launched.
■ A rocket carrying two monkeys is launched by the Soviet Union.

Government, Politics, and History

■ President Dwight D. Eisenhower in-vokes the Taft-Hartley Act to stop a 116-day strike by steelworkers.
■ Soviet leader Nikita Khruschev travels to the U.S., and later visits Albania.
■ Britain and the United Arab Republic resume diplomatic relations.
■ The New York City Council appoints a commission to study the possibility of becoming the fifty-first state.

News and Lifestyle

■ The Barbie doll, developed by Ruth Handler, first appears.
■ The auto accident death toll reaches 1.25 million in the U.S., a figure that exceeds the number of people who died in all U.S. wars combined.
■ Anti-semitism flares in Cologne, West Germany.
■ Pope John XXIII announces the first calling of the Ecumenical Council since 1870.

Arts and the Media

■ U.S. Postmaster General Summerfield bans D.H. Lawrence's *Lady Chatterley's Lover* from the mails on grounds of obscenity, but his ban is reversed one year later by a court of appeals.
■ Bill Mauldin wins his second Pulitzer prize for his cartoons.
■ The anniversaries of Henry Purcell (b. 1659), George Frederic Handel (d. 1759), and Franz Joseph Haydn (d. 1809), are celebrated.
■ Popular songs include "The Sound of Music," "Everything's Coming up Roses," and "He's Got the Whole World in His Hands."

Sports and Games

■ Heinz Wichmann catches a 92-pound Chinook salmon at Sheena

River, British Columbia, and Alfred Dean lands a 2,664-pound shark at Ceduna, South Australia.

■ Jack Nicklaus wins the U.S. Golf Association Amateur Championship.

■ Ingemar Johansson defeats Floyd Patterson to win the world heavyweight boxing title.

Deaths

■ American tenor Mario Lanza dies.

■ Blues musician Billie Holliday, born in 1915, dies.

■ American statesmen John Foster Dulles and George C. Marshall die.

50th Anniversary ...1949

Science and Technology

■ Cape Canaveral, Florida, is opened by the U.S. military as a testing ground for rockets.

■ The U.S. launches a guided missile 250 miles, the highest altitude ever reached by man.

■ U.S. researcher Selman Waksman isolates neomycin, an antibiotic that can be used to treat infections.

■ American Phillip Hench discovers cortisone, used in the treatment of rheumatoid arthritis.

Government, Politics, and History

■ The arms race begins with President Harry Truman's announcement that the Soviet Union has developed atomic weapons. (The Soviets detonated their first atom bomb on September 22.)

■ Congress establishes the General Services Administration to manage property and records.

■ Dean Acheson is appointed U.S. Secretary of State.

■ The U.S. Foreign Assistance Bill grants $5.43 billion in aid to Europe.

■ The U.S. completes the withdrawal of its occupying forces in South Korea.

■ Pandit Nehru becomes Prime Minister of India.

■ A democratic republic is established in East Germany, headed by Wilhelm Pieck as President.

News and Lifestyle

■ The term "cold war" is first used in October by Bernard Baruch in a speech to a U.S. Senate committee.

■ Eleven U.S. communists are found guilty of conspiracy to overthrow the government.

■ The samba comes into fashion.

■ Cartoon character Mr. (Quincy) Magoo (featuring the voice of Jim Backus) first appears, in "Ragtime Bear."

■ Roughly 135 million paperback books are sold in the U.S. during this year.

Arts and the Media

■ Rodgers and Hammerstein's *South Pacific* debuts April 7 in New York.

■ The Natural Trust for Historic Preservation is established in Washington, D.C.

■ William Faulkner wins the Nobel prize for literature.

Sports and Games

■ After defeating "Jersey" Joe Walcott, Ezzard Charles is named the world heavyweight boxing champion.

■ Golfer Cary Middlecoff wins the U.S. Open tournament.

■ Richard A. "Pancho" Gonzales wins the U.S. Lawn Tennis Association's Men's Singles championship, and Mrs.

IDEAS

Margaret O. duPont wins the Women's Singles title.

■ New York wins the World Series by defeating Brooklyn, 4-1.

75th Anniversary ...1924

Science and Technology

■ Anthropologist Raymond Dart discovers a species he names *Australopithecus africanus*, or *australopithecinea*, a fossilized skull that belongs to neither apes nor humans.

■ Bell Laboratories is established in New Jersey.

■ Explorers F.M. Bailey, H.T. Morsehead, and F.K. Ward find the source of the Brahmputra-Tsangpo River in Tibet.

■ English astronomer Arthur Eddington discovers that the luminosity of a star is related to its mass.

Government, Politics, and History

■ An act of Congress grants U.S. citizenship to Native Americans.

■ A U.S. bill limits immigration, and prohibits all Japanese from emigrating to America.

■ The Pan-American Treaty is signed to prevent conflicts between states.

■ Gaston Doumerque is elected President of France.

■ The Republic of Albania is founded.

■ Hitler, sentenced to five years in prison, is released after serving eight months.

News and Lifestyle

■ The Wrigley Building is constructed in Chicago.

■ Allan and Samuel Bronfman establish The Seagram Company, a liquor distillery in Montreal, Quebec.

■ British Imperial Airways begins operations.

■ The game of Mah-jong becomes a world craze.

Arts and the Media

■ American comedian Will Rogers is at the height of his career.

■ George Gershwin's Rhapsody in Blue is performed for the first time on February 12 in New York.

■ Jules Stein, an ophthalmologist with a hobby of playing music in clubs and managing musicians, establishes the Music Corporation of America in Chicago. Now known as MCI and located in California, the company became one of the biggest talent agencies by the end of World War II.

■ Three companies form Metro-Goldwyn-Mayer (MGM) Studios, which goes on to produce such films as *Gone with the Wind* and *The Wizard of Oz*.

Sports and Games

■ The World Chess League is established in The Hague.

■ In a game starring the "Four Horsemen," Notre Dame upsets Army at the Polo Grounds in New York.

■ The first Winter Olympic Games are held at Chamonix, France. Sixteen nations (293 participants) took part in the Games, which featured 16 events from eight sports.

Deaths

■ Italian composer Giacomo Puccini dies November 29 at age 65.

■ American legislator Henry Cabot Lodge dies.

■ Woodrow Wilson, twenty-eighth President of the U.S., dies at age 67.

■ Samuel Gompers, American Labor unionist and president of the American Federation of Labor, dies.

100th Anniversary ...1899

Science and Technology

■ The first national physics association, the American Physical Society, is formed in New York, N.Y. on May 20.
■ The first magnetic recording of sound is made.
■ A.T. Marshall of Brockton, Mass. receives a patent for a refrigerator designed to be used in the home.
■ The first radio broadcast—a yacht race—is made in Sandy Hook, N.J.

Government, Politics, and History

■ The first juvenile court in the U.S. is established in Chicago, thanks in part to the efforts of Jane Addams and Julia Lathrop.
■ The Philippines demand independence from the United States.
■ The First Peace Conference is held at The Hague.
■ In France, the *cour de cassation* annuls the judgement against army officer Alfred Dreyfus (found guilty of treason in 1894) and orders a retrial. Dreyfus is later pardoned by presidential decree.

News and Lifestyle

■ The first mail collection by automobile is tested in Cleveland, where a mail truck takes 2 hours and 27 minutes to make 126 stops along a 22-mile route. While the trip takes less than half the time of a horse-drawn wagon, the Post Office waits 15 years before establishing a motor vehicle division.

■ President William McKinley becomes the first U.S. president to ride in a car, taking a trip in a Stanley Steemer.
■ Henry Bliss, 68, is the first pedestrian killed by an automobile in the U.S. A car driven by Arthur Smith hit Mr. Bliss as he stepped off a streetcar at the corner of 74th St. and Central Park West in New York.
■ American Telephone & Telegraph is established after a reorganization of Bell Telephone Company. In its earliest days, it is controlled by banker J.P. Morgan.
■ The first automobile parade is held on September 7 in Newport, R.I.
■ Federal elections held February 14 mark the first use of voting machines in the U.S.
■ Carry Nation, one of the founders of the women's temperance movement, begins her anti-saloon drive in Medicine Lodge and Kiowa, Kansas.
■ Henry Ford forms the Detroit Automobile Co.

Arts and the Media

■ Ragtime music becomes popular.
■ Oscar Wilde completes *The Importance of Being Earnest*.
■ Jean Sibelius' Symphony No. 1 in E Minor is performed for the first time on April 26 in Helsingfors, Finland.
■ The word *automobile* is first used—in an editorial in the *New York Times*.

Sports and Games

■ Boston's G.F. Grant receives a patent for the first golf tee.

200th Anniversary ...1799

Science and Technology

■ Italian physicist Alessandro Volta

IDEAS

produces an electrical current from a chemical cell, a container with zinc and copper plates.

■ The Egyptian Institute is founded at Cairo.

■ Explorer Mungo Park publishes *Travels in the Interior of Africa*.

■ Benjamin Waterhouse, a Cambridge, Mass. researcher, devises the first American vaccine against smallpox.

Government, Politics, and History

■ A taxpayers' rebellion, led by John Fries in eastern Pennsylvania, ends peacefully with Fries' arrest. The group tried to stop the U.S. from collecting taxes used to support a war with France. Fries was convicted of treason and sentenced to death, but was later pardoned by President John Adams.

■ Austria declares war on France, and defeats the French Army at Stockach, Magnano, and Zurich, but loses at Bergenop-Zoom.

■ Britain joins the Russo-Turkish Alliance.

■ The Kingdom of Mysore is divided between Britain and Hyderabad.

■ The Russian government grants the monopoly of trade in Alaska to the Russia-American Company.

News and Lifestyle

■ According to a Spanish census, roughly 42,300 people live in settlements in southern Louisiana.

■ Swiss educator Johann Pestalozzi opens a school in Burgdorf, Switzerland.

■ Aaron Burr and Alexander Hamilton establish the Manhattan Company. The company, designed to supply water to New York, is one of the firms that later forms Chase Manhattan Bank.

■ The term *scab*—workers hired to cross picket lines during a strike—is used for the first time during a strike in Philadelphia by the Federal Society of Cordwainers (shoemakers).

Arts and the Media

■ Painter Jean-Louis David completes *The Rape of the Women of Sabine*.

■ *The Baltimore American*, the first newspaper outside of Washington, D.C. to provide verbatim accounts of Congressional debates, is founded.

■ Gracie Mansion, an example of the country mansions built in the eighteenth century in upper Manhattan, is built. The mansion is acquired as a home for the mayor of New York City in 1924.

■ Editor Charles Brockder Brown publishes *American Review and Literary Journal*, the first quarterly review in the U.S.

Deaths

■ Joasaph Bolotov, consecrated as the first Russian Orthodox bishop in the New World, drowns in the Bering Strait on his way to Alaska.

300th Anniversary ...1699

Government, Politics, and History

■ Changes to the voting laws in the colony of Virginia give voting rights only to those who own land.

■ Denmark and Russia sign a mutual defense pact.

■ The partition of Sweden is outlined in the Treaty of Preobrazhenskoe, signed by Denmark, Russia, Poland, and Saxony.

■ Denmark's King Christian V dies and is succeeded by Frederick IV.

■ The colonies of Maryland and Virginia restrict Irish Catholic immigration.

News and Lifestyle

■ The first epidemic of Yellow Fever strikes the American colonies, killing one-sixth of the population.

■ Some 4,500 convicts have chosen to relocate to the American colonies from England since 1655, rather than face the death penalty.

■ In Casco Bay, Maine, Abenaki Indians and Massachusetts colonists sign a treaty ending conflict in New England.

■ William Penn returns to Pennsylvania as governor after fifteen years in England.

Arts and the Media

■ George Farquhar completes his comedy *Love and a Bottle*.

■ Chimes and bells are first manufactured in the Colonies, by Benjamin Hanks in Plymouth, Massachusetts.

■ Jonathan Dickinson's adventure story, *God's Protecting Providence*, is a best seller in the Colonies, and is later reprinted in German and Dutch.

400th Anniversary ...1599

Government, Politics, and History

■ The Earl of Essex, Lord Lieutenant of Ireland, signs a truce with Irish rebel Lord Tyrone, and is arrested on his return to England. He is tried for misdemeanors in Ireland one year later, and loses his offices at court.

■ The Duke of Sully, the French superintendent of taxes, reforms taxation, economic policy, overseas trade, and agriculture.

■ The Swedish Diet deposes Sisigmund III, and proclaims Charles of Södermanland ruler, as Charles IX.

■ James VI of Scotland publishes *Basilikon doron*, a treatise on the divine right of kings.

■ San Gabriel Gov. Juan de Onate seizes the settlement of New Mexico for the King of Spain after invading it with 500 soldiers, servants, and Spanish settlers.

■ Four Dutch vessels return from India with pepper, cloves, cinnamon, and nutmeg to establish Holland's control of the Asian spice trade. The Dutch raise the price of pepper from three shillings a pound to six-to-eight shillings, prompting eighty London merchants to establish the East India Company.

News and Lifestyle

■ Two Franciscan priests in the Florida colonies are killed as Native Americans ravage coastal missions. The murders were sparked by another priest, who reprimanded Chief Don Juanillo for having more than one wife.

■ Prices in western Europe are six times higher than in the previous century. Much of the nobility is impoverished, and in some cases forced to sell land to the middle class.

■ Black death takes a heavy toll in the Hanseatic city of Essen, one of Europe's largest cities (population roughly 5,000). Plague and famine will decimate other areas, including Andalusia and Castile, over the next two years.

Arts and the Media

■ The first known book auction is held in the Netherlands.

■ William Shakespeare completes *Much Ado About Nothing* and *Henry V*.

IDEAS

500th Anniversary ...1499

Science and Technology

■ Antimony, produced in Hungary, is exported to neighboring countries.

Government, Politics, and History

■ Amerigo Vespucci and Alonso de Ojeda leave Spain on a voyage to explore South America.

■ The Peace of Basel is signed by the Swiss and King Maximilian I of Germany to end the Swabian war. The treaty effectively makes Switzerland independent, although the country is not considered a separate state until 1648.

■ Louis XII of France marries Anne of Brittany, widow of Charles VIII, to retain the duchy of Brittany for the French crown.

■ Portuguese explorer Vasco da Gama opens a sea route to India during a two-year trip around the Cape of Good Hope.

■ War erupts between the Turks and Venice. The Venetian fleet is defeated at Sapienza, and Lepanto surrenders to the Sultan.

News and Lifestyle

■ Another outbreak of the black death strikes London.

■ Spices like those brought back by da Gama (cloves, nutmeg, pepper) are used to preserve meat and disguise the flavor of spoiled meat that comprises the bulk of diets in late winter and early spring.

Arts and the Media

■ Fernando de Rojas completes *Celestina*, one of the first Spanish comedies.

■ Italian painter Luca Signorelli begins work on the frescoes at the Cathedral at Orvieto, a task that will take him five years to complete.

■ Venice's *campanile*, or clock tower, is completed in the Piazza San Marco after three years of construction.

Deaths

■ Explorer John Cabot dies at sea.

2000 Anniversaries

5th Anniversary ...1995

Science and Technology

■ Researchers in Pennsylvania develop a set of tests that may enable doctors to predict heart disease and stroke and pinpoint patients who need therapy.

■ National Institute of Health researchers identify a virus believed to cause a new type of hepatitis.

■ Egyptian archaeologists discover a mausoleum with at least 67 chambers, believed to be the burial place of the royal sons of Ramses II, one of Egypt's greatest pharaohs.

■ The Nobel Prize in Chemistry is awarded to Drs. F.S. Rowland, M. Molina, and P. Crutzen for their work in explaining the chemical processes that deplete the ozone shield.

Government, Politics, and History

■ Voters in Quebec narrowly defeat a provision that would have enabled the province to secede from Canada.

■ Leaders from around the world come to New York to commemorate the 50th anniversary of the United Nations.

■ Roh Tae Woo, South Korea's president from 1988 to 1993, is arrested on charges that he accepted nearly $650 million in illegal campaign donations while in office.

■ The Yugoslav War Crimes Tribunal, meeting in The Hague, issues indictments against civilian and military leaders of the Bosnian Serbs for their treatment of Muslim civilians during and after the capture of Srebenica.

■ The House Committee on Ethics unanimously approves an independent counsel investigation of allegations that Speaker Newt Gingrich (R-Ga.) violated tax laws in a college course he taught in Georgia and televised via satellite.

News and Lifestyle

■ Ending months of speculation, General Colin Powell, the first black to serve as the chairman of the Joint Chiefs of Staff, announces that he will not seek the Republican nomination for President.

■ Five Americans are among the seven people killed when bombs explode at a military training and communications center in Riyadh, Saudi Arabia.

■ A bomb explodes on an underground train in Paris, injuring twenty-nine people. The incident was the eighth in a series of bombings believed to be the work of Algerian terrorists.

■ President Bill Clinton repeals the federal speed limit of 55 miles per hour, enacted in 1974 to conserve fuel during an international oil embargo.

Sports and Games

■ The Atlanta Braves complete a four-game sweep of the Cincinnati Reds, and win the first World Series in the team's history.

■ Baltimore Orioles shortstop Cal Ripken, Jr. plays in his 2,131st consecutive game, breaking a 56-year record established by Lou Gehrig and thought to be unbreakable.

■ Thunder Gulch wins two of horseracing's Triple Crown events, taking first at the Kentucky Derby and the Belmont Stakes.

Arts and the Media

■ Explorers discover an underground cave in the Ardeche region of France that contains well-preserved paintings from the Stone Age—perhaps as long as 20,000 years ago.

■ Corbis Corp., owned by Microsoft founder Bill Gates, purchases the Bettman Archive (containing millions of photos that chronicle the twentieth century) from Kraus Corp.

■ Irish poet Seamus Haney wins the Nobel Prize for Literature, and Pulitzer prizes in Fiction and History are awarded to Carol Shields and Doris Kearns Goodwin, respectively.

Deaths

■ Viveca Lindfors, Swedish stage and film actress, dies in Upsala, Sweden at age 74.

■ James "Scotty" Reston, a *New York Times* editor and prize-winning journalist, dies at age 86.

■ Terry Southern, a novelist and screenwriter whose works included *Easy Rider* and *Dr. Strangelove*, dies at 71.

■ Louis Malle, French director of such

IDEAS

films as *Pretty Baby* and *Au Revoir les Enfants*, dies at 63.

10th Anniversary ...1990

Science and Technology

■ The U.S. Food and Drug Administration approves the first low-calorie fat substitute.

■ A four-year-old girl becomes the first human to receive gene therapy. It is hoped that the adenosine deaminase gene that she lacks can be replaced by this treatment.

■ American Elias J. Corey wins the Nobel Prize for Chemistry for his research in the synthesis of complex molecules.

Government, Politics, and History

■ Despite widespread opposition, England adopts the community charge or "poll tax."

■ Japan's Emperor Akihito is formally proclaimed that country's 125th Emperor.

■ Edouard Shevardnadze resigns as Soviet Foreign Minister.

■ North Korean Premier Yon Hyong Muk makes an unprecedented journey to South Korea.

■ Yitzhak Shamir forms a right-wing coalition government in Israel.

■ Iraq arrests and executes Observer reporter Farzad Barzoft for espionage.

News and Lifestyle

■ "Junk bond" pioneer Michael Milken is found guilty of fraud and fined $600 million.

■ Three major U.S. companies announce they will no longer buy tuna caught in nets that also trap dolphins.

■ Perrier withdraws its water supply worldwide after traces of benzene are found in some bottles.

■ The first Anglican female priests in the United Kingdom are ordained at St. Anne's Cathedral in Belfast, Ireland.

Sports and Games

■ West Germany wins soccer's World Cup championship.

■ The Detroit Pistons win basketball's national championship, and the Edmonton Oilers take hockey's Stanley Cup.

■ James "Buster" Douglas defeats Mike Tyson to become the world heavyweight boxing champion.

Arts and the Media

■ Twelve works of art worth $100 million are stolen from Boston's Isabella Stewart Gardner Museum, the largest art theft in the world.

■ The director of Cincinnati's Contemporary Arts Center is indicted for obscenity for exhibiting photographs by the late Robert Mapplethorpe, some of which show homoerotic or sadomasochistic acts. He is later found not guilty.

■ Titian's paintings are exhibited in Venice, and the exhibition later moves to Washington, D.C.

■ Van Gogh's Portrait of Dr. Gachet sells in New York for $82.5 million, and Monet's At the Moulin de la Galette is sold for $78.1 million.

Deaths

■ A Missouri court rules that after eight years in an irreversible coma, Nancy Cruzan has the right to die. Life support is stopped, and she dies 12 days later.

- Psychologist B.F. Skinner, born in 1904, dies.
- Film actress Ava Gardner dies.
- Pearl Bailey, a jazz and popular singer, dies.
- An Wang, founder of Wang Laboratories, dies.

20th Anniversary ...1980

Science and Technology

- The World Health Organization announces the worldwide eradication of smallpox.
- Soviet cosmonauts return to Earth after spending a record-setting 185 days aboard the Salyut 6 space station.
- U.S. researcher Walter Alvarez and his colleagues discover a worldwide layer of irridium-enriched clay that may be the residue of a gigantic meteorite that struck the Earth and eradicated the dinosaurs.
- The Voyager I space probe sends back pictures of Saturn, its rings and moons including six newly discovered moons.

Government, Politics, and History

- Soviet forces clash with Mujaheddin guerrillas in Afghanistan. The United Nations General Assembly calls for Soviet troop withdrawal from Afghanistan, and President Jimmy Carter restricts grain sales to the U.S.S.R. to protest the Soviet presence there.
- President Carter breaks off diplomatic relations with Iran and announces a trade ban as Iran continues to detain hostages from the U.S. Embassy.
- Vigdis Finnbogadottir becomes Iceland's first female president.
- In the U.S.S.R., Andrei Sakharov, dissident and Nobel laureate, is stripped of honors and sent into internal exile in Gorky.
- Canada's Pierre Trudeau defeats Joe Clark to regain the office of Prime Minister.

News and Lifestyle

- Pope John Paul II visits six African countries, and travels later that year to Brazil, France, and West Germany.
- A priceless eighth-century gold chalice and other gold and silver treasures are found in Tipperary, Ireland, by a tourist with a metal detector.
- A severe summer heat wave in the southern U.S. is blamed for 1,117 deaths in twenty states, and forces Missouri to declare a state of emergency.

Sports and Games

- Spain's Severiano Ballesteros becomes the youngest golfer ever to win the Master's Tournament.
- Anne Myers is the first woman drafted by the National Basketball Association, but fails to make the Indiana Pacers team.
- National League's Philadelphia Phillies win the World Series, beating the Kansas City Royals of the American League, 4–2.
- In hockey, the New York Islanders defeat the Philadelphia Flyers to take the Stanley Cup.
- Rollerblades first appear.

Arts and the Media

- More than one million people visit New York's Museum of Modern Art to see a Picasso retrospective exhibition featuring 1,000 of his works.
- *Camelot*, a musical starring Richard Burton, is revived on Broadway.

IDEAS

■ Jasper John's *Three Flags* is sold for $1 million, setting a record for a work of a living American painter. *Juliet and Her Nurse* by J.M.W. Turner is sold in New York for $4 million, a world record for a painting.

Deaths

■ Colonel Harlan Sanders, founder of Kentucky Fried Chicken, dies.
■ American actress Mae West dies.
■ Oscar Romero, Archbishop of San Salvador in El Salvador, is assassinated while celebrating Mass.
■ Comedian Jimmy Durante, born in 1893, dies.
■ Mohammed Reza Pahlavi, deposed Shah of Iran, dies in Cairo.

25th Anniversary ...1975

Science and Technology

■ The U.S.S.R.'s Tupolev-144 becomes the first supersonic airplane used on a regularly scheduled mail-and-freight flight.
■ Andrei Sakharov, the Russian physicist who developed the Soviet Union's hydrogen bomb, receives the Nobel Peace Prize.
■ Linus Pauling receives the U.S. National Medal of Honor from President Gerald Ford.

Government, Politics, and History

■ President Gerald Ford signs legislation to provide equal educational opportunities for children with disabilities.
■ Former U.S. Secretary of Commerce Maurice Stans pleads guilty to five misdemeanor charges of violating campaign laws during the 1972 Nixon re-election campaign, becoming the third Nixon cabinet member convicted.
■ A ruling by the Supreme Court ends the practice of locking up mental patients who are not a danger to society.
■ Margaret Thatcher succeeds Edward Heath as the leader of the British Conservative Party.
■ Saudi Arabia's King Faisal is assassinated by a nephew, who is later beheaded. Faisal's brother Khalid assumes the throne.
■ Spanish Chief of State Generalissimo Francisco Franco dies, and Prince Juan Carlos I is sworn in as King Juan Carlos I, the first king of Spain in 44 years.

News and Lifestyle

■ The *Mayaguez*, an American-owned merchant ship, is captured by Cambodian forces, who claim that the crew was spying and the ship illegally sailed within Cambodia's 12-mile coastal zone. U.S. Navy and Marine forces staged a rescue in which the 39 crew members were freed but 16 American lives were lost.
■ Patricia Hearst, missing since February 1974, is caught by the FBI in San Francisco with kidnappers William and Emily Harris, former members of the Symbionese Liberation Army.
■ Justice William O. Douglas retires from the Supreme Court after serving nearly 37 years. John Paul Stevens takes Douglas' seat on the Court.
■ The cost of mailing a first-class letter increases from 10¢ to 13¢.

Sports and Games

■ The New Orleans Superdome is dedicated on August 1.
■ The Cincinnati Reds defeat the Boston Red Sox, 4–3, to win the World Series.

■ Jack Nicklaus wins his fifth Masters tournament and his fourth Professional Golfers' Association championship.

■ Billie Jean King wins Wimbledon's women's singles tennis championship for the sixth time, and Chris Evert wins the U.S. Open women's singles tennis championship.

Arts and Media

■ Unpublished work by James Joyce is found at the University of Padua.

■ Six thousand life-sized pottery figures from the third century BC are found in northwest China.

■ Sara Caldwell becomes the first woman to conduct the Metropolitan Opera in New York.

■ A musicians' strike closes 12 Broadway musicals for 25 days.

Deaths

■ Lionel Trilling, American writer and professor, dies at age 70.

■ American painter Thomas Hart Benton, born in 1889, dies.

■ Elijah Muhammad (born Elijah Poole), leader of the Black Muslims, dies, and is succeeded by his son, Wallace Muhammad.

■ Chicago Mob boss Sam Giancana, born in 1910, dies.

■ The inventor of the x-ray tube, William D. Coolidge, dies at age 100.

40th Anniversary ...1960

Science and Technology

■ The American Heart Association issues a report attributing higher death rates among middle-aged men to heavy cigarette smoking.

■ An experimental U.S. rocket-powered airplane travels at nearly 2,200 miles per hour.

■ D.A. Glaser, a U.S. researcher, wins the Nobel Prize in Physics for his work in constructing a bubble-chamber to study subatomic particles.

■ The first weather satellite is launched and can transmit television images of cloud cover around the world.

Government, Politics, and History

■ Cyprus declares its independence, and names Archbishop Makarios as its president.

■ West German Chancellor Konrad Adenauer visits the U.S.

■ Leonid Brezhnev becomes President of the U.S.S.R.

■ Summit talks held in Paris between Charles de Gaulle, Nikita Khrushchev, Harold Macmillan, and Dwight Eisenhower fail to produce any agreements.

■ Neo-Nazi political groups are banned in Germany.

■ Cuba signs a major trade agreement involving the sale of sugar to the People's Republic of China.

News and Lifestyle

■ The first televised Presidential debates are broadcast, featuring Republican Richard Nixon and Democrat John F. Kennedy.

■ Prince Andrew is born to Elizabeth II and Prince Phillip, the first birth to a reigning monarch since 1857.

■ Convicted rapist Caryl Chessman is executed after spending 12 years on Death Row appealing his case.

Sports and Games

■ At the Olympic Games in Rome, Aus-

tralia's Herb Elliott runs 1,500 meters in 3 minutes and 35.6 seconds.

■ A 410-pound blue shark is caught by R.C. Webster off Rockport, Mass., and Dr. A. Cordeiro lands a 296-pound yellowfin tuna off Mexico.

■ Sixteen-year-old Bobby Fischer successfully defends his U.S. chess title.

■ Paul Pender defeats "Sugar" Ray Robinson to win the middleweight boxing championship.

Deaths

■ American civil rights leader W.E.B. duBois dies.

■ Russian author Boris Pasternak, born in 1891, dies.

■ Zora Neale Hurston, American author and folklorist, dies.

■ Composer Oscar Hammerstein II, born in 1895, dies.

50th Anniversary ...1950

Science and Technology

■ The National Science Foundation is established in Washington, D.C.

■ The radioactive elements californium and berkelium are discovered.

■ Albert Einstein publishes *General Field Theory*, an attempt to expand his *Theory of Relativity*.

■ The xerographic copy machine is first introduced for commercial use.

Government, Politics, and History

■ Two Puerto Rican nationalists attempt to assassinate President Harry Truman. One is killed and the other is sentenced to death. (That sentence was later commuted to life imprisonment.)

■ Klaus Fuchs is found guilty of betraying British atomic secrets to the U.S.S.R. and sent to prison. Harry Gold, his American confederate, is sentenced to 30 years in prison.

■ Indonesia is admitted to the United Nations.

■ King Leopold III of Belgium returns after six years in exile and is met by Socialist demonstrations that force his abdication one year later.

News and Lifestyle

■ President Truman dedicates the Grand Coulee Dam, located on Washington's Columbia River.

■ The Brooklyn Battery Tunnel opens in New York.

■ Cyclamate, the first artificial sweetener, is offered to consumers.

■ The world population reaches 2.3 billion, and the U.S. population about 150 million. There are 1.5 million television sets in the U.S., and that figure will reach 15 million by 1951.

■ The United Nations building in New York is completed.

Arts and the Media

■ The Library of Congress, established 50 years earlier, holds 8.6 million books, 11 million manuscripts, 2 million musical scores, and 128,000 yearly newspaper volumes.

■ Margaret Mead's work *Social Anthropology* is published.

■ Benny Goodman and the NBC Symphony Orchestra premiere Clarinet Concerto by Aaron Copland.

■ A.B. Guthrie's novel, *The Way West*, wins the Pulitzer Prize for fiction.

Sports and Games

■ Horse racing establishes the Triple

Crown Trophy to signify past and future winners of the Triple Crown series races: the Kentucky Derby, the Belmont Stakes and the Preakness.

■ The automatic pin-setting machines are installed in bowling alleys in the U.S., and for the first time, the American Bowling Congress allows nonwhite males to participate in professional competition.

■ Joe Sobek of Greenwich, Conn., a former professional tennis player, creates the game of racquetball (originally called paddle rackets), which combines elements of handball and squash.

■ A record crowd of nearly 200,000 watches Brazil take on Uruguay in a World Cup soccer game in Rio de Janeiro.

75th Anniversary ...1925

Science and Technology

■ Scottish inventor John Logie Baird transmits recognizable human features by television.

■ Dry ice is commercially available.

■ Oskar Barnack builds the first Leica camera.

■ New York experiences a solar eclipse, the first in three hundred years.

Government, Politics, and History

■ In the U.S., Calvin Coolidge is sworn in on March 4 for his second term as President.

■ Norway changes the name of its capital from Christiania to Oslo.

■ Japan introduces general suffrage for men.

■ Hitler reorganizes the 27,000-member Nazi Party and publishes volume one of *Mein Kampf.*

■ Britain enacts the Unemployment Insurance Act.

News and Lifestyle

■ The first motel, a motor inn in Monterey, Calif. called the Milestone Motel, opens for business.

■ Walter Chrysler establishes the Maxwell Motor Company, which will eventually become the Chrysler Company.

■ W.M. Davis founds Winn-Dixie Stores in Lemon City, Fla.

■ Madison Square Garden opens in New York, N.Y.

Arts and the Media

■ The first Guggenheim Fellowship is awarded to Aaron Copland.

■ Dmitri Shostakovich finishes Symphony No. 1.

■ Bennett Cerf establishes Modern Library, a publishing company in New York that will be renamed Random House (based on the way Cerf and his partner, Donald Klopfer, select some of their first authors).

■ Professor A.O. Rankine predicts in a lecture (entitled "Hearing by Light") that talking motion pictures are possible in the not-too-distant future.

Sports and Games

■ Grantland Rice begins his selection of All-American teams in *Collier's Weekly*.

■ American Harold Vanderbilt develops the game of contract bridge during a Caribbean trip.

■ Walter Camp, a football player who threw the first forward pass and went on to pick the All-American teams from 1889 to 1924, dies.

IDEAS

- Pittsburgh (NL) defeats Washington (AL) to win the World Series.

Deaths

- Sun Yat-sen dies on March 12.
- William Jennings Bryan, American politician, dies.
- First Viscount Leverhulme, English soap manufacturer and founder of Lever Brothers, Ltd., dies.

100th Anniversary ...1900

Science and Technology

- The Otis Elevator Co. registers a trademark for its invention, the escalator. The first escalator is installed in a Philadelphia building one year later.
- Count Ferdinand von Zeppelin flies the first rigid airship, which could be steered in any direction. The dirigible was made possible by the development of low-cost supplies of aluminum, which Zeppelin used to build a frame that was streamlined to minimize wind direction.
- The first Daisy air rifles, the creation of Clarence Hamilton, hit the market.
- Offshore oil wells are first drilled near Santa Barbara, Calif.
- U.S. inventor Benjamin Holt develops the first modern tractor.

Government, Politics, and History

- The U.S. Navy buys its first submarine, the U.S.S. Holland.
- The Boxer Rebellion begins in China, as one Chinese faction tries to rid the nation of foreign control.
- Congress creates a gold reserve for U.S. currency by passing the Gold Standard Act.
- Italy's King Umberto I is assassinated by an anarchist, and is succeeded to the throne by his son, Victor Emmanuel III.
- The Tongo Islands become a British protectorate.

News and Lifestyle

- Plywood is made available for the first time.
- The Eatery, located in New Haven, Connecticut, is credited with making the first hamburger.
- Milton Hershey establishes Hershey Foods Company to manufacture candy, and builds the first factory in Derry Church, Pa. (The town later renamed itself after its major employer.)
- Paris hosts the World Exhibition.
- H.J. Heinz & Co. is incorporated in Pennsylvania.

Arts and the Media

- The United States Library of Congress is established.
- The Associated Press is founded.
- Frank Doubleday and Nelson Page found Doubleday, Page & Co., a book-publishing business that will be renamed Doubleday & Co. in 1946.
- Claude Debussy's Nocturnes I and II is performed for the first time, on December 9 in Paris.

Sports and Games

- Britain's W.G. Grace ends his cricket career with a lifetime total of 54,000 runs.
- William Muldoon is proclaimed the first professional wrestling champion.

Deaths

- Author Stephen Crane dies.
- Friedrich Nietzsche, a German philosopher born in 1844, dies.

200th Anniversary ...1800

Science and Technology

■ The process of electrolysis is first used to separate water into hydrogen and oxygen.
■ Water purification using chlorine is conducted for the first time.
■ Marie François Xavier Bichat publishes *The Treatise on Membranes*, the first medical book to describe types of living tissue. The book marks the development of the science of histology.

Government, Politics, and History

■ Napoleon establishes himself as First Consul in the Tuileries; a plot to assassinate him is uncovered later in the year.
■ British forces capture Malta.
■ U.S. federal offices are relocated from Philadelphia to Washington, D.C., a city with a population of 3,087 people.
■ The City of Ottawa is founded in the Province of Ontario, Canada.
■ Letter post is introduced in Berlin.

News and Lifestyle

■ The population in New York reaches 60,000, and the total population in the U.S. is estimated at 5,308,483.
■ Grossglockner is the first mountain in the Austrian Alps to be scaled successfully.
■ The first canal in the U.S. is completed; it runs from the Santee River to Charleston Harbor in Charleston, S.C.
■ English social reformer Robert Owen takes over New Lanark Mills and institutes social reforms.
■ Philadelphia shoemaker William Young is the first to make separate shoes for the left and right feet.

■ Four-tined forks come into use, replacing two- and three-tined models.

Arts and the Media

■ Ludwig van Beethoven's Piano Concerto No. 1 and Symphony No. 1 in C Major are performed in Vienna.
■ Goya completes *Portrait of a Woman*.
■ Middlebury College is chartered in Vermont on November 1, and awards its first degrees two years later.

Sports and Games

■ Gouging, a frontier sport in which the ultimate goal is to gouge out an opponent's eye with a thumbnail, becomes popular in the Ohio Valley.

300th Anniversary ...1700

Science and Technology

■ The Berlin Academy of Science is founded, and Gottfried von Liebniz is elected as its president.
■ England's Jethro Tull invents the seed drill.
■ The first commercial distillery for making rum opens in Boston.

Government, Politics, and History

■ The Great Northern War begins with the Saxon invasion of Livonia.
■ The Duke of Gloucester, the only surviving child of Princess Anne, dies. Succession to the English throne passes to the Electress Sophia of Hanover, mother of the electoral prince, the future George I.
■ Under a crown treaty between the Emperor Leopold I and Elector Frederick III of Brandenberg, the Elector is recognized as Frederick I, King in Prussia.

IDEAS

■ Charles XII of Sweden defeats Peter the Great at Narva.

■ An enactment in Massachusetts gives Roman Catholic priests three months to leave the colony. Those who choose to stay will be considered "incendiary and a disturber of the public peace . . . and an enemy to the true Christian religion."

News and Lifestyle

■ European population figures: France, 19 million; England and Scotland, 7.5 million; Hapsburg Dominions, 7.5 million; Spain, 6 million.

■ Pope Innocent XII dies, and Gian Francesco Albani becomes Pope Clement XI.

Arts and the Media

■ Joseph Saveur measures and explains vibrations of musical tones.

■ The first pipe organs are imported into the U.S., to the Episcopal Church in Port Royal and Gloria Dei Swedish Lutheran Church in Philadelphia.

■ Kabuki theater is developed in Japan.

■ The Earl of Bellomont, governor of New York, establishes a reading room that will eventually become the New York Society Library.

400th Anniversary ...1600

Science and Technology

■ Astronomers Tycho Brahe (from Denmark) and Johann Kepler (Germany) work together at Prague.

■ Caspar Lehmann, a jewel cutter to Emperor Rudolph II, begins the cut-glass process.

■ Spaniards in Barbados make rum by refining molasses.

Government, Politics, and History

■ Ieyasu defeats his rivals at Sekigahara, declares himself as unquestioned ruler of Japan, and moves the capital from Kyoto to Yedo (Tokyo).

■ Maurice of Nassau defeats Archduke Albert's Army at Nieuport.

■ Henry IV marries Maria de'Medici.

■ English navigator William Adams, the first Englishman to visit Japan, becomes Ieyasu's adviser on shipbuilding.

News and Lifestyle

■ Roughly one million Indians are living in North America as European exploration there begins.

■ The Amsterdam Bank is founded.

■ The population of Germany reaches 14.5 million; Poland, 11 million; and Holland, 3 million.

■ Italian philosopher Giordano Bruno is burned as a heretic in Rome.

■ Sweden, under Charles IX, begins persecuting Catholics.

Arts and the Media

■ William Shakespeare completes three plays: *As You Like It, Twelfth Night,* and *Julius Caesar.*

■ The Fortune Theatre opens in London.

■ Italian violin maker Andrea Amati, born in 1530, dies.

■ The recorder, known also as the flute-à-bec, becomes popular in England.

500th Anniversary ...1500

Science and Technology

■ Drawings by Leonardo da Vinci introduce the concept of the helicopter, which will not become reality for another 400 years, and one of the first-known versions of a musket, a hand-held firearm.

■ Hieronymus Brunschwig produces the first herbal medicine.

Government, Politics, and History

■ After a representative of Queen Isabella arrives in Hispaniola and finds seven Spaniards hanged in the town square, Christopher Columbus is arrested, put in leg irons, and brought to Spain. Columbus says he was forced to take action after a revolt against the Queen.

■ Ferdinand of Aragon suppresses a Moorish revolt in Granada.

■ Lodovico Sforza recovers Milan from the French. The town is reconquered two months later, and Sforza is captured and imprisoned in France.

■ The Diet of Augsburg establishes the Council of Regency for administering the Holy Roman Empire, and divides Germany into six "circles," or regions.

■ Pope Alexander VI proclaims a Year of Jubilee, and imposes a tithe for a crusade against the Turks.

■ Portuguese explorer Gaspar Corte-Real charts the eastern coast of Greenland, the first to complete the task since Leif Ericson in 1000.

News and Lifestyle

■ Silver guilders are introduced in Germany (and will remain in use until 1892).

■ The first regular postal connection between Vienna and Brussels is established.

■ Two types of earthenware to remain well-known for centuries—faience and majolica—are manufactured for the first time in Faenza and Majorca.

■ Juan de la Cosa publishes a map of the New World.

Arts and the Media

■ Hieronymus Bosch completes the painting *Ship of Fools*, and Michelangelo completes *Madonna and Child*.

■ Aldus Manutius of Venice establishes an academy for the study of Greek classics and invents italics.

Sports and Games

■ The first horserace meetings are held at Chester.

Deaths

■ Portuguese navigator Bartolomeo Diaz drowns near the Cape of Good Hope.

IDEAS

2001 Anniversaries

5th Anniversary ...1996

Science and Technology

■ Comet Hyakutake is discovered by a Japanese astronomer in late January, roughly two months before the comet comes closer to Earth than any other comet since 1983.

■ U.S. astronaut Shannon Lucid becomes the first woman to work aboard Russia's Mir space station, and her 188 days in orbit set an American record for longevity in space.

Government, Politics, and History

■ President Bill Clinton and Vice President Al Gore carry 31 states and the District of Columbia to defeat Republicans Bob Dole and Jack Kemp and win re-election to a second term. Clinton becomes the first Democrat since Franklin D. Roosevelt to be re-elected to a second term.

■ A plane crash near Dubrovnik, Croatia on April 3 takes the life of U.S. Commerce Secretary Ronald Brown.

■ Overcoming poor health and doubts about the economy, Boris Yeltsin is re-elected President of Russia in a runoff against Communist Party candidate Gennadi Zyuganov.

■ The Arab-Israeli peace process is stalled in February and early March by a series of terrorist bombings in Israel that claim 60 lives. In May, Benjamin Netanyahu defeats Shimon Peres in the election for Israeli Prime Minister.

■ Troops from the U.S. and other countries monitor the implementation of a peace accord between the three warring factions in Bosnia and Herzegovina that includes elections for a new collective presidency and legislators.

■ In the U.S., the 108-year-old Interstate Commerce Commission is abolished, and its remaining responsibilities are transferred to the Department of Transportation.

News and Lifestyle

■ Theodore Kaczynski is arrested in April and is thought to be the Unabomber, sought for more than 17 years in connection with a series of mail bombs that killed three people and injured more than twenty.

■ More than 5,900 items owned by the late Jacqueline Kennedy Onassis and her husband, President John F. Kennedy, are auctioned off at Sotheby's.

■ The first McDonald's restaurant opens in India in late 1996, and, in keeping with Hindu religious beliefs, is the only McDonald's that does not serve beef. (The Indian equivalent of a Big Mac is the Maharajah Mac, made of mutton.)

■ A TWA flight en route from New York to Paris explodes over Long Island, killing all 230 people aboard.

■ Britain's Prince Charles and Princess Diana are officially divorced on August 28, ending their fifteen-year marriage.

Sports and Games

■ The New York Yankees defeat the Atlanta Braves, 4–2, in the World Series.

■ The Summer Olympic Games, held in Atlanta, Ga., are marred by a bombing at Centennial Olympic Park that kills one person. The games continue despite the bombing.

■ Tiger Woods becomes the first golfer to win three consecutive U.S. Amateur championships (1994-1996), and announces that he will leave college to join the Professional Golf Association tour. He wins his first professional tournament two months after turning pro.

■ Steffi Graff wins the women's singles title in the U.S. Open, the French Open, and at Wimbledon.

Deaths

■ Mel Allen, longtime "Voice of the Yankees," and one of the first announcers inducted into the Baseball Hall of Fame, dies at age 83.

■ Spiro T. Agnew, former Maryland governor and Richard Nixon's vice president from 1969 until his resignation in 1973 after pleading guilty of tax evasion, dies at 77.

■ Mary Thompson, daughter of slaves who was thought to be the oldest living American, dies in Florida at age 120.

■ Electrical engineer and father of the "supercomputer" Seymour Cray dies.

■ Roger Tory Peterson, ornithologist and author of the classic *Field Guide to the Birds*, dies at the age of 87.

10th Anniversary ...1991

Science and Technology

■ Scientists find the ozone shield to be weakened over the U.S. and other temperate climates in the summer, when the sun's ultraviolet rays are at their strongest and pose the greatest damage to people and crops.

■ Studies indicate that doctors treat women with heart disease less aggressively than they treat men with the same illness.

Government, Politics, and History

■ U.S. and allied forces open war in the Persian Gulf in January to drive Iraq from Kuwait. The occupation of Iraq ends in May, when United Nations forces take over a nine-mile demilitarized zone as well as thousands of refugees.

■ Iraq admits to running three secret programs to produce enriched uranium that could be used to produce an atomic bomb.

News and Lifestyle

■ A drought in California forces the cut-off of water to the major farm regions in that state's central valley.

■ An Australian air liner carrying some 220 people explodes over Thailand, killing everyone aboard.

■ One year after an accident at the Chernobyl nuclear reactor, the plant is entombed in a giant concrete sarcophagus, and residents of the "Forbidden Zone" begin returning to their homes.

■ Financial regulators in seven countries seize control of the Bank of Credit and Commerce International, whose $20 million in assets were regulated in Great Britain and Europe. Two of the bank's leaders are indicted in the U.S. on charges of fraud, theft, and money laundering.

Sports and Games

■ The U.S. Olympic Committee lifts a

IDEAS

twenty-one-year ban on South Africa, allowing athletes in that country to participate in the 1992 Olympic Games in Barcelona.

■ Calumet Farm, whose thoroughbreds won eight Kentucky Derby crowns over fifty years, files for bankruptcy to pay off debts of $70 million.

■ The New York Giants defeat the Buffalo Bills to win football's Superbowl.

■ Golfer Corey Pavin is the leading money winner on the PGA tour, taking home $979,430 in prize money.

Arts and the Media

■ Walter H. Annenberg announces plans to bequeath approximately $1 billion in Impressionist and Post-Impressionist works to the Metropolitan Museum of Art.

■ Some Japanese purchases of multimillion dollar western paintings are now said to have been intended to conceal the transfer of millions of dollars in cash or to evade taxes.

Deaths

■ Movie director Frank Capra, 94, dies.

20th Anniversary ... 1981

Science and Technology

■ IBM launches the first *home* or *personal* computer.

■ U.S. pilot Stephen Ptacek makes the first solar-powered flight across the English Channel, making the 180-mile trip from Paris to Kent in 5½ hours.

■ Scientists identify Acquired Immune Deficiency Syndrome (AIDS).

■ Columbia, the first U.S. space shuttle, completes its maiden flight, with astronauts John Young and Robert Crippen.

Government, Politics, and History

■ Socialist François Mitterand is elected President of France, narrowly defeating incumbent Giscard d'Estaing.

■ Sandra Day O'Connor is the first woman named to the U.S. Supreme Court.

■ Egyptian President Anwar Sadat is assassinated by soldiers while watching a military parade. Vice President Hosni Mubarak takes over as President.

■ Poland's Solidarity movement, led by Lech Walesa, holds its first national conference in Gdansk.

■ Walter Polovchak, a twelve-year-old who remained in the U.S. after his parents returned to the U.S.S.R., is granted political asylum against his parents' wishes.

News and Lifestyle

■ John Hinckley shoots President Ronald Reagan, Press Secretary Jim Brady, and two others outside a Washington, D.C. hotel.

■ The TGV, the world's fastest passenger train, begins service in France between Paris and Lyons.

■ Prince Charles and Lady Diana Spencer announce their engagement, and are married in St. Paul's Cathedral on July 29.

■ America's largest naturalization ceremony is held at Memorial Stadium in Los Angeles, with 9,700 becoming citizens.

■ Roughly 12,000 air traffic controllers go on strike in the U.S., and are dismissed from their jobs.

Sports and Games

■ The twenty-second Olympic Games begin in Moscow.

- The New York Islanders win hockey's Stanley Cup for the second consecutive year.
- Muhammad Ali retires from boxing with a career record of 56 wins and five defeats.
- Major league baseball players in the U.S. go on strike from June 12 to August 9.

Arts and the Media

- Walter Cronkite retires from regular television broadcasting.
- Soviet conductor Maxim Shostakovich and his son defect to the West.
- "Double Fantasy" by John Lennon and Yoko Ono wins the Grammy Award for best album.
- Washington, D.C.'s National Gallery conducts the largest exhibition ever of sculpture by Rodin.
- Australian Rupert Murdoch buys the Times Newspapers, Ltd. of London.

Deaths

- Jamaican reggae musician Bob Marley, born in 1945, dies.
- Five-star General Omar Bradley dies at the age of 88.
- Joe Louis, world heavyweight boxing champion from 1937 to 1949, dies.
- American poet Isabella Gardner, born in 1915, dies at the age of 66.
- U.S. novelist William Saroyan dies at the age of 73.

25th Anniversary ... 1976

Science and Technology

- IBM introduces the ink-jet printer.
- Steve Jobs and Stephen Wozniak establish Apple Computer, Inc. in California.

- The National Academy of Science reports that gases from spray cans can damage the earth's ozone layer.

Government, Politics, and History

- The first debate between candidates for the vice presidency is held October 15, with Democrat Walter Mondale facing off against Republican Robert Dole.
- North and South Vietnam are reunited as one country after 22 years of separation. The country is named the Socialist Republic of Vietnam and its capital is Hanoi.
- The U.S.S.R. and the U.S. sign a treaty limiting the size of underground nuclear explosions for peaceful purposes. It is the first treaty to include provisions for on-site inspections.

News and Lifestyle

- U.S. military academies begin admitting female students for the first time.
- Barbara Walters becomes the first woman to anchor a network news program, appearing on April 22 on ABC News.
- Supersonic passenger service begins between Europe and the U.S., with two Concorde flights—one from Paris and one from London—landing in the U.S.
- Fourteen people are killed as Idaho's Teton River Dam collapses.
- The U.S. celebrates its Bicentennial with events in Philadelphia, Washington, D.C., and other cities nationwide.

Sports and Games

- At college football's first Independence Bowl, held in Shreveport, La., McNeese State beats Tulsa, 20–16.
- The Twelfth Winter Olympics are held at Innsbruck, Austria, with the

IDEAS

team from the U.S.S.R. taking home 13 gold medals.

■ Four American Basketball Association teams merge with the National Basketball Association as the ABA disbands.

The Arts and the Media

■ *One Flew Over the Cuckoo's Nest* sweeps all five major Academy Awards, including honors for best picture, best actor (Jack Nicholson), best actress (Louise Fletcher), best director and best screenplay. It is the first film to accomplish such a sweep since 1934.

■ Saul Bellow wins the Pulitzer Prize for fiction for *Humboldt's Gift*. Michael Bennett's *A Chorus Line* wins for drama, and also wins a Tony award.

■ Books issued this year include Alex Haley's *Roots*, *The Final Days* by Robert Woodward and Carl Bernstein, and Leon Uris's novel, *Trinity*.

40th Anniversary ... 1961

Science and Technology

■ Soviet astronaut Yuri Gagarin, piloting a six-ton satellite, becomes the first man to orbit the Earth.

■ Alan Shepard, Jr. makes the first manned U.S. space flight, aboard Freedom 7.

■ U.S. researchers Robert Hofstadter and Rudolf Mössbauer receive the Nobel Prize for Physics for their research into nucleons and gamma rays.

■ The Tanganyika Conference moves to protect wildlife in Africa.

■ The Atlas computer is installed at Harwell.

Government, Politics, and History

■ John F. Kennedy is inaugurated as the thirty-fifth, and youngest, president.

■ Kennedy meets with Soviet Premier Nikita Khrushchev to discuss disarmament.

■ The Berlin Wall is constructed. Vice President Lyndon Johnson tours Berlin.

■ Exiled Cuban rebels—trained and supplied by the U.S.—unsuccessfully attempt to invade Cuba at the Bay of Pigs. President Kennedy acknowledges full responsibility for the failed invasion. (Earlier in the year, the U.S. severed diplomatic relations with Cuba.)

■ All synagogues in Moscow are closed.

News and Lifestyle

■ Dag Hammarskjöld, winner of the 1961 Nobel Peace Prize, is killed in an airplane crash.

■ The Orient Express takes its last trip between Paris and Bucharest.

■ Freedom Riders, a group of white and black liberals organized to test and force integration in the South, are attacked and beaten by white citizens in Anniston and Birmingham, Ala.

■ Farthings are no longer accepted as legal tender in Great Britain.

Sports and Games

■ Bobby Fischer defeats Hungarian Grand Master Paul Benko to win the U.S. chess championship for the fourth time.

■ The New York Yankees beat the Cincinnati Reds four games to one to win the World Series.

■ Jack Nicklaus wins the U.S. Golf Association Amateur Tournament, and Gene Littler wins the U.S. Open.

■ Floyd Patterson retains the world heavyweight boxing crown by knocking out Ingemar Johansson.

Arts and the Media

■ Soviet dancer Rudolph Nureyev leaves the Kirov Opera ballet group and asks for political asylum in France.

■ Goya's portrait of the Duke of Wellington is stolen from the National Gallery in London.

■ The Museum of the Chinese Revolution is opened in Peking.

■ Henry Miller's *Tropic of Cancer* is published legally for the first time in the U.S. Also released are Steinbeck's *The Winter of Our Discontent*, Irving Stone's *The Agony and the Ecstasy*, and Joseph Heller's *Catch-22*.

Deaths

■ Baseball great Ty Cobb dies at the age of 75.

■ Painter Anna Mary Moses, better known as Grandma Moses, dies at 101.

■ Sam Rayburn, elected Speaker of the House for ten terms, dies at the age of 72 and is succeeded by John McCormack.

50th Anniversary ... 1951

Science and Technology

■ Chinese immigrant An Wang founds Wang Laboratories with $600.

■ Nuclear fission is used to generate electricity at an experimental atomic power plant in Idaho.

■ The first computers—called UNIVACs for the Universal Automatic Computer—are now commercially available.

■ Alcoholics are treated with antabuse, a compound that causes a painful reaction if alcohol is consumed.

Government, Politics, and History

■ The Twenty-Second Amendment to the Constitution is enacted, limiting Presidential terms to two.

■ Juan Perón is re-elected as President of Argentina.

■ King Abdullah of Jordan is assassinated in Jerusalem.

News and Lifestyle

■ The first simultaneous transmission of a television program occurs. The broadcast, covering President Truman's remarks at a conference in San Francisco for the signing of a Japanese peace treaty, is carried by 94 television stations.

■ Julius and Ethel Rosenberg are sentenced to death for espionage against the U.S.

■ CBS broadcasts the first commercial television program in color, a one-hour show featuring Arthur Godfrey and Ed Sullivan.

Arts and the Media

■ Books released this year include *The Catcher in the Rye*, J.D. Salinger; *The Caine Mutiny*, Herman Wouk; and *Lie Down in Darkness*, William Styron.

■ Abstract expressionism first garners public attention in the U.S. at a major exhibit at the Museum of Modern Art in New York, N.Y.

■ Frank Lloyd Wright designs Friedman House in Pleasantville, N.Y.

■ *The King and I*, a musical by Rodgers and Hammerstein, premiers in New York.

Sports and Games

■ The first Pan-American Games are held in Buenos Aires, Argentina, and

IDEAS

feature victories by the Cuban baseball team, the U.S. basketball team, and the Argentinian soccer and boxing teams.

■ "Jersey" Joe Walcott knocks out former champion Ezzard Charles in the seventh round to win the world heavyweight boxing title.

■ Michigan beats California by a score of 14 to 6 to win college football's Rose Bowl trophy.

75th Anniversary ... 1926

Science and Technology

■ The first wireless voice transmission across the Atlantic is broadcast on March 7.

■ American scientist Robert Goddard launches the world's first liquid-fueled rocket, which flies to a height of 184 feet.

■ Lt. Cmdr. Richard Byrd makes the first flight over the North Pole, a round trip flight that originated from Kings Bay, Spitzbergen, and lasted 15 hours and 51 minutes.

■ Kodak produces the first 16 mm movie film.

■ American biologist Herman Muller discovers that x-rays produce genetic mutations.

Government, Politics, and History

■ Congress establishes the U.S. Army Air Corps.

■ Hirohito succeeds his father, Yoshihito, as Emperor of Japan.

■ A slate of reforms passed in Turkey includes the abolition of polygamy, modernization of female attire, the prohibition of the fez, and (two years later) the adoption of the Latin alphabet.

■ Fascist youth organizations "Balilla"

and "Hitlerjugend" are founded in Italy and Germany, respectively.

News and Lifestyle

■ The first regular airplane service is established with a mail flight from Los Angeles to Salt Lake City, Utah, operated by Western Airlines. Passenger service is added by putting folding chairs next to the mail sacks.

■ Q-tips are first developed, and pop-up toasters are first marketed.

■ Book clubs are first introduced in the U.S., with one group—The Book of the Month Club—gaining 40,000 subscribers in its first year.

■ Delta Airlines, United Airlines, Deutsche Lufthansa, and Northwest Airlines are established.

Arts and the Media

■ Chicago opens its museum of Science and Industry, and the Rodin Museum is opened in Philadelphia.

■ Ernest Hemingway's *The Sun Also Rises* is published, as are Eugene O'Neill's *Desire Under the Elms*, A.A. Milne's *Winnie the Pooh*, and T.E. Lawrence's *The Seven Pillars of Wisdom*.

■ William Randolph Hearst creates the *National Enquirer* as a Sunday afternoon tabloid.

■ Sinclair Lewis turns down the $1,000 Pulitzer Prize for his novel, *Arrowsmith*.

Sports and Games

■ New York's Gertrude Ederle swims the English Channel in 14 hours and 34 minutes, becoming the first woman to do so, and beating by two hours the record time set by a man.

■ The cushioned, cork-center baseball is introduced.

- Golf's Bobby Jones, defeated by George Von Elm in the U.S. Golf Association Amateur Championship, goes on to win the U.S. Open.
- St. Louis (NL) beats New York (AL), four games to three, to win baseball's World Series.

Deaths

- Magician Harry Houdini dies from peritonitis caused by a blow to the stomach. The anniversary of his death is celebrated as National Magic Day.
- American newspaper man Edward Scripps, born in 1854, dies.
- Actor Rudolph Valentino dies after finishing the film *The Son of the Shiek.*

100th Anniversary ... 1901

Science and Technology

- Italian electrical engineer Marchese Gugliemo Marconi makes the first long-distance broadcast of a radio signal. Signals broadcast from the southeastern coast of England are received in Newfoundland, roughly 2,000 miles away.
- A U.S. medical commission concludes that Yellow Fever is transmitted by mosquitoes, confirming a discovery made one year earlier by Walter Reed.
- Daimler Technical Director Wilhelm Maybach builds the first Mercedes car.
- The first British submarine launches.
- The hormone adrenaline is first isolated by researchers.

Government, Politics, and History

- President William McKinley dies eight days after being shot by an assassin while attending the Pan-American Exposition in Buffalo, N.Y. Vice President Teddy Roosevelt succeeds him as president.
- W.H. Taft becomes Governor-General of the Philippines.
- The Hay Paunceforte Treaty is signed, allowing the U.S. to build the Panama Canal.
- Queen Victoria II dies and is succeeded to the throne by Edward VII, her son.
- The Social Revolutionary Party is founded in Russia.

News and Lifestyle

- More than 900 students at 67 test centers nationwide take the first college entrance examinations, which include questions in English, language, mathematics, history, chemistry, and physics.
- Africa's Mombasa-Lake Victoria Railway is completed.
- J.P. Morgan organizes U.S. Steel Corp.
- The Trans-Siberian Railroad reaches Port Arthur.
- Switzerland's Henri Dunant and France's Frédéric Passy are awarded the Nobel Peace Prize.

Arts and the Media

- Dvoràk's opera, *Rusalka,* premieres in Prague. Rachmaninoff's Piano Concerto No. 2 is also released this year.
- Walt Disney is born on December 5 in Chicago, Illinois.
- Ragtime jazz develops in the U.S.
- Picasso's Blue Period begins (and will end in 1905).

Sports and Games

- Professional baseball teams from eight cities (Baltimore, Boston, Chicago, Cleveland, Detroit, Milwau-

IDEAS

kee, Philadelphia, and Washington, D.C.) form the American League of the Professional Baseball Association.

■ England recognizes boxing as a legal sport.

■ The first American Bowling Club tournament is held in Chicago.

Deaths

■ French painter Henri Toulouse-Lautrec dies at age 37.

■ Composer Guiseppi Verdi, born in 1813, dies.

200th Anniversary ... 1801

Science and Technology

■ Italian astronomer Giuseppe Piazzi discovers the first asteroid, which he names Ceres.

■ Johann Ritter, a German physicist, discovers ultraviolet radiation.

■ The first submarine capable of diving, resurfacing, and running while submerged is invented by American Robert Fulton.

■ The first system to identify and organize animals without backbones is created by Jean-Baptiste de Lamarck, a French naturalist who also created the science of invertebrate zoology and coined the terms "invertebrate" and "vertebrate."

■ The first suspension bridge in the U.S. is constructed by James Finney and spans Mahantango Creek in Uniontown, Pa. The longest suspension bridge of all time, 244 feet, also opens over the Merrimac River in Newburyport, Mass.

Government, Politics, and History

■ Thomas Jefferson is inaugurated as the third president of the U.S. and the first inaugurated in Washington, D.C.

■ Tripoli declares war on the U.S., marking the first assignment for the U.S. Marine Corps.

■ The Union Jack becomes the official flag of Great Britain and Ireland.

■ The Peace of Lunéville, between Austria and France, marks the actual end of the Holy Roman Empire.

■ Lord Nelson destroys the Danish fleet off Copenhagen.

■ The U.S. Congress assumes jurisdiction over the District of Columbia.

News and Lifestyle

■ Josiah Bent opens a bakery in Milton, Mass. that makes biscuits so crisp that they're renamed "crackers" for the sound made when they're chewed.

■ E.I. du Pont de Nemours and Co. is founded by Pierre du Pont and his son in Wilmington, Delaware, to manufacture gunpowder.

■ The first iron trolley tracks are built in Croydon-Wandsworth, England.

■ Population totals in Europe: Italy, 17.2 million; Spain, 10.5 million; Britain, 10.4 million.

■ The University of South Carolina is established in Columbia.

Arts and the Media

■ Alexander Hamilton creates the *New York Evening Post*.

■ Ludwig von Beethoven composes the Sonata in C Sharp Minor ("The Moonlight Sonata").

■ *The Maid of Orleans* is published by Friedrich von Schiller.

■ William Dunlap's play, *Abellino, the Great Bandit*, opens on February 11, beginning a 25-year run.

300th Anniversary ... 1701

Science and Technology

■ Children in Constantinople are the first vaccinated against smallpox.

Government, Politics, and History

■ Fort Pontchartrain, later renamed Detroit, is settled in the territory of Michigan by Antoine de la Mothe Cadillac.
■ Elector Frederick III of Brandenburg crowns himself King Frederick I of Prussia.
■ James II of England dies, and the French king, Louis XIV, recognizes the Old Pretender, James Edward, son of James II, as King James III.
■ A town meeting in Boston, Mass. authorizes street naming, making it the third city (along with Newport, R.I. and Philadelphia) to have named streets.
■ The War of Spanish Succession, or Queen Anne's War, begins, marking Louis XIV's last attempt to extend his rule in Europe.
■ London's Board of Trade proposes placing all colonies under jurisdiction of the Crown.

News and Lifestyle

■ Yale College is founded in Killingworth, Conn., as the Collegiate School. It is relocated to New Haven and renamed Yale in 1745.
■ "Captain" William Kidd is hanged for piracy. He was commissioned by royal order in 1695 to attack pirates preying on English ships, but turned to piracy when his mission was unsuccessful.

Arts and the Media

■ The first artistic engravings in the U.S., completed by Thomas Emmes, are published in Boston.
■ Music publisher Henry Playford establishes a series of weekly concerts at Oxford.
■ Jeremy Collier publishes *The Great Historical, Geographical, Genealogical, and Political Dictionary*, a two-volume work.

400th Anniversary ... 1601

Science and Technology

■ Johann Keppler is appointed astronomer and astrologer to Emperor Rudolf II.
■ East India Company's James Lancaster gives his crew lemon juice at the Cape of Good Hope, before traveling to Madagascar to take on more citrus fruit. His crew of 200 is the only crew not decimated by scurvy.

Government, Politics, and History

■ The English Parliament establishes the first official public welfare legislation, which includes provisions for creating jobs and apprenticeships and for aiding those unable to work.
■ The Earl of Essex leads a revolt against Elizabeth I, is tried for treason, and executed.
■ The Hungarians assassinate Michael, the prince of Moldavia.
■ Claiming to be a son of Czar Ivan IV, the "False Dimitri" appears in Poland and wins support for an invasion of Russia.
■ Mexican Gov. Juan de Onate returns to the colony of San Gabriel, Mexico, from a six-month search for Quiviria to find the colony deserted.
■ Dutch navigator Olivier Van Noort returns from circumnavigating the

IDEAS

world, a trip begun in 1598 and the fourth since Magellan's journey.

News and Lifestyle

■ Coffee brought from Turkey by explorer Anthony Sherley is introduced in London, selling for £5 an ounce.
■ France and Germany finalize a postal agreement.
■ John Lancaster leads the first East India Company voyage, from Torbay to Sumatra.
■ Monopolies are abolished in England.

Arts and the Media

■ Shakespeare finishes *Troilus and Cressida*.
■ Caravaggio completes "The Conversion of St. Paul."

500th Anniversary ... 1501

Government, Politics, and History

■ A papal bull orders the burning of books that are contrary to the authority of the Church.
■ Pedro Cabral completes a voyage that establishes Portuguese trade with the East Indies.
■ England's Henry VII declines the Pope's request to lead a crusade against the Turks.
■ Ivan III invades Lithuania.
■ The Anglo-Portuguese Syndicate makes its first voyage to North America.
■ Spain's King Ferdinand issues directives to Colonial Governor Nicolas de Ovando, setting up a system of tribute and labor for natives in the colonies.

News and Lifestyle

■ The first black slaves are introduced in Santo Domingo by Spanish colonists, marking the first arrival of blacks in the New World.
■ In Lisbon, fifty natives sent by explorer Gaspar Corte-Real from south of Cape Breton arrive to be sold into slavery.
■ Rodrigo de Bastides explores the coast of Panama.
■ Card games, first introduced one hundred years earlier, gain great popularity throughout Europe.
■ Book printing and typography develop swiftly, with some 1,000 printing offices producing 35,000 books and 10 million copies.

Arts and the Media

■ Michelangelo completes the Pietà, commissioned by the abbot of St. Denis, and begins work on the statue of David.
■ *The Palice of Honour*, a dream allegory by Scottish poet and bishop Gawin Douglas, is published.
■ In Nuremberg, playwright Conradus Celtis discovers manuscripts of plays written by a nun, Hroswitha of Gandersheim, who lived circa 1000.

INDEX

A

ABC-Clio, 180, 181
Abigail Adams, Witness to a Revolution, 229
Abrahamson, David, 92
Abramowitz, Joan, 52, 54, 58
Achauer, Hilary, 172, 174
Addison Wesley Longman, 3
   (See also Scott Foresman-Addison Wesley.)
Advances *(See Payment.)*
Adventures with Nicholas, 9, 48
Advertising, 65, 90
African-American Heritage and Achievement,
   18, 67, 70
   (See also Cobblestone Publishing.)
African-American, writing and publishing,
   18, 27, 88, 193
Agenda, 11
Agents, 106, 107, 108, 109, 137, 138, 140,
   155-168
Agincourt Press, 95
Ake and His World, 266
Aladdin Books, 3, 9, 51 *(See also Simon &*
   Schuster.)
Allen, John D., 218, 221, 223, 225, 226
All the Lights in the Night, 282
Allure, 44
Amelia Bedelia, 15
America the Beautiful, 307
American Adventure series, 181
American Association of Publishers, 47
American Book Producers Association, (ABPA),
   81, 95
   directory, 100
American Bookseller, 28
American Booksellers Association, 15, 120
   Pick of the Lists, 32
American Booksellers Book of the Year, 11
American Cheerleader, 37
American Girl, 70
   books, 16
   magazine, 14, 73
American Historical Publications, 64
American Library Association (ALA), 3, 12,
   29, 37, 69, 120, 132
   Best Book, 301
   (See also Caldecott, Newbery, Scott O'Dell
   Award)
American Society of Journalists and Authors
   (ASJA), 116
American Society of Picture Professionals, 209
Among the Orangutans, 125
Amsco School Publications, 84
Anastasia Krupnik books, 285, 286
Anderson, Laurie, 32, 34
Angelou, Maya, 193
Animal Monsters: The Truth About Scary
   Animals, 205

Animorphs, 10, 14
AppleSeeds, 18, 67, 70
Archer, Peter, 7
Archives, 230-231
   appointments, 231
   archivist interview, 231
   fees, 231
   model letter, 232
Archway Paperbacks, 6, 55
Aristotle, 173
Armstrong, Jennifer, 96, 100
Art in America, 209
Arthur, 54
ArtNews, 209
ASCAP, 116
Asher, Sandy, 138, 139, 140, 142, 143
Assignments, articles, 223
Association of Booksellers for Children (ABC),
   120
Atheneum Books, 8, 18, 28, 30, 51, 275, 314
   (See also Simon & Schuster.)
At-Home Mothering, 7, 67
Atkins, Laura, 23, 24
Atlanta Parent, 87, 91
Author associations *(See Writers' organizations.)*
Author copies *(See Contracts.)*
An Author's Guide to Children's Book
   Promotion, 122
Authors' Guild, 13, 107, 116, 118
Authors' Registry, 116, 118
Avisson Press, 9
Avon Books, 4, 9
   Avon Hardcover, 9, 48

B

Babcock, Denise, 70, 71
Babybug, 69, 72, 172
   (See also Cricket Magazine Group.)
The Baby-Sitters Club, 287
Backlists, 54, 57, 131
Badger's Bad Mood, 282
Bagenal, Elinor, 4
Balan, Bruce, 125, 126, 127, 128, 134
Balgassi, Haemi, 30, 32
Balzer, Alessandra, 9
Bank Street College Children's Book Award, 11
Bantam Doubleday Dell, 6, 9, 13, 21, 52, 55,
   57, 100, 119, 122, 124, 139
Barbour & Company, 181
Barnes and Noble, 54, 294
Barrett, Tracy, 228, 229230
Barron's Educational Series, 82
Basket Moon, 266, 267
Batson, Coy, 120, 121, 125,
Bauer Publishing, 14, 43, 65
Bayard Presse Canada, 14, 64
Bay Area Parent, 88, 91

Beaufort Books, 138
Beautiful Warrior: The Legend of the Nun's Kung Fu, 281
Beauty and fashion, 66
Belle Prater's Boy, 8
Bennett, William, 16
The Berenstain BearScouts, 6
Berg, Susie, 14
Bergen, Lara, 6, 10
Berger, Lori, 14, 38, 39, 66
Berlitz Kids, 9, 48
Bertelsmann, 13 *(See also Bantam Doubleday Dell)*
Better Homes and Gardens, 92
Bibliography, 180
Bicknell, Elizabeth, 4
"Big Fat Fibs and Little White Lies," 187
Biographies, 227, 229
    picture book, 28
    young adult, 182
Blackbirch Press,
    blackbirch picturebooks, 16
    packager, 98, 100, 101
Black Child, 88
Bloor, Ed, 76, 80
Blue Jean, 69
Board books, 54
Bober, Natalie, 227, 229, 230
Bokram, Karen, 185, 187
Bologna Book Fair, Children's Book Award, 11
Bone Chillers, 98
Book clubs, 54, 109
Book Industry Study Group, 47
Book publishers,
    educational or textbook, 70, 75-84, 106, 110
    mass-market, 106
    packagers, 95-102, 106
    religious, 106, 110
    small presses, 106
    trade, 106
    (See also Contracts; Payment; Promotion.)
The Book of Virtues, 16
Books of Wonder, 9, 48
Books plus, 54, 143
Bookstores, 29, 54, 106, 120, 124, 125, 128, 143
BookWire, 4
Bortz, Fred, 218, 220, 221, 222, 224, 225
Boston Globe, 209
Boston Globe-Horn Book Award, 265, 289
Bourland, Annette, 25
Boyds Mills Press, 23
Boyles, Andy, 217, 219, 221, 222, 223, 224, 225
Boys' Life, 7, 73, 174, 175, 297-300
Boys' Quest, 73 *(See also Hopscotch.)*

The Boy Scout Handbook, 298
Bradbury Press, 314
Brand,
    identity, 53, 54
    loyalty, 69
    (See also Licensing and tie-ins.)
Brian, Sarah Jane, 14
Bridge to Terabithia, 301
Bridgewater Books, 76
Briley, Dorothy, 32
Broadwater, Robert, 53
Brooks, Donna, 17
Brosnan-Workman, Rosemary, 16, 21, 23
Brown Bear, Brown Bear, What Do You See?, 54
Brown, Marc, 54
Brown, Margaret Wise, 8, 57
Brown Publishing Network, 80
Buchholz, Rachel, 186
Buckley, Virginia, 17, 302
Budka, Shaun, 93
Bunting, Eve, 227, 228
Burke, Judy, 25
Burnett, Frances Hodgson, 174
Byline, 179, 180

C

Cahners Publishing, 4
Caldecott Medal, 8, 29, 132, 265, 266, 281
California Cobblestone, 18, 67, 70
    (See also Cobblestone Publishing.)
The Call of the Wild, 136
Calliope, 73, 207 *(See also Cobblestone Publishing.)*
Calmenson, Stephanie, 262, 263
Candlewick Press, 4, 11, 51
Carapetyan, Francelle, 204, 205, 207, 209
Carney, Mary Lou, 24, 25, 43, 175, 176, 177, 185, 187
Carson-Dellosa, 12
Cartwheel Books, 6
Carus, Marianne, 64, 69
Carus Publishing *(See Cricket Magazine Group.)*
Cary, Elizabeth, 182
Casanova, Mary, 121, 122, 124, 128, 129, 130, 133, 134
Cascardi, Andrea, 49, 51, 52
Catalogues, book publishers, 120, 228
The Cat in the Hat, 3
Catwings, 278
CD-ROMS, 116, 118, 210
Celebrities, 66
Chan, Janet, 7, 85, 91
Characters,
    description, 191
    development, 57
    and plot, 172-174, 176
Charlesbridge Publishing, 4, 12, 47, 49, 53

educational publishing, 82
Charlotte's Web, 273
Charts and Graphs,
   advances, religious publishers, 140
   advances, trade publishers, 136-137
   book manuscript purchases, 59
   book publisher list sizes, 60
   circulations over one million, 63
   educational publishers, 79
   family and parenting magazines, 86
   launches, 67
   magazine circulations, 62
   magazine market overview, 72-73
   magazine submissions and purchases, 68
   mass-market publishers, 55
   multicultural book publishers, 31
   multicultural magazine markets, 33
   new imprints, lines, series, 48-49
   projected juvenile book units, 50
   religious teen magazines, 42
   royalties, religious publishers, 141
   royalties, trade publishers, 138-139
   teen magazines, 40-41
Chelsea House, 96
Chickadee, 14, 64, 72
   (See also Owl Communications.)
The Children's Audiobook of Virtues, 16
Children's Better Health Institute, 145, 152
   Children's Digest, 73
   Children's Playmate, 72
   Humpty Dumpty, 72
   Jack And Jill, 73, 115, 171, 186
   Turtle, 72, 149
Children's Book Council, 12
Children's Book of the Month Club, 54
Children's Book Press, 23, 24
The Children's Book of Virtues, 16
Children's Books and Their Creators, 311
Children's Digest, 73
   (See also Children's Better Health Institute.)
Children's Literature Web Guide, 127, 128
Children's Playmate, 72
   (See also Children's Better Health Institute.)
Children's Press, 4, 305, 307, 308
   (See also Grolier.)
Chirp, 10, 61, 64, 67, 72
   (See also Owl Communications.)
Christensen, Deborah, 93
Christian Service Brigade, 93
Christian Science Monitor, 209
Christopher, Matt 18, 53
Chronicle Books, 172, 175
Churchman, Deborah, 174, 175
Cicada, 37
CINAR Films, 12
Circulation, 62, 63, 65, 116
Cirone, Michael, 3

Civilization, 209
Clarion Books, 27, 29, 32
Classic Frights, 9, 48
Click, 10, 61, 64, 67, 72
Clifford, Gale, 80, 81, 84
Clips *(See Credits.)*
Cloverdale Press, 96
Clubhouse, 10
Cobblehill Books, 17, 50
   (See also Penguin Putnam)
Cobblestone Publishing, 18, 61, 70, 71
   Calliope, 73, 207
   Cobblestone, 73, 207
   Faces, 73, 207, 208
   Odyssey, 73, 204, 206, 207, 209
   (See also Simon & Schuster.)
Cohl, Claudia, 14
Cole, Brock, 18
Cole, Joanna, 261-264
Coles, Katherine, 198
Colette, 199
Collins, Richard, 12
Coman, Carolyn, 177
Conferences and conventions,
   reading and library, 120, 131, 132
   writers', 371-395
Conflict, 172, 176, 181
Connections, 7, 67
Contests and awards, 319 -370
Contracts, 105-118
   books,
      advances, 111-112
      agents, 106, 107, 108
      audio, 109
      author copies, 107, 114
      book club sales, 109
      books, 105, 107, 109-114
      British publication, 109
      clauses, 109
      commercial rights, 109, 110
      copyright, 109
      dangerous-instruction, 113
      deadlines, 110
      discounts, 111, 114
      delivery, 110
      design and production, 108
      editing and form, 113
      educational publishing, 106, 112
      escalation clause, 111
      electronic rights, 109, 110
      financial report, 111
      first book, 110
      first-, second-line publishers, 108
      flat fees, 109, 111, 112
      grant of rights, 109
      indebtedness, 114
      joint accounting, 114

INDEX

lawyers, 107, 108
mass-market, 106, 110, 112
merchandising, 109
miscellaneous clauses, 114
negotiations, 107, 108, 109, 111
option clause, 113
oral contracts, 114
out-of-print, 113
packagers, 106, 112
paperbacks, 109, 110
payment,109, 110-112
photographs, 205
picture books, 110
promise to publish, 110
religious books, 106, 112
remainders, 114
return of rights, 113
royalties, 110-111
serialization, 109
small presses, 106, 112
split, 109
subsidiary rights, 109
termination clause, 112
terms, 107
television and drama, 109
trade books, 105, 106, 110, 111
translations, 109
warranties and indemnities, 112
work-for-hire, 109
magazines, 105, 115-118
acceptance letter, 115
all rights, 116, 117
author card, 115
Authors' Guild, 116
Authors' Registry, 116
designation of rights, 115
electronic rights, 116, 118
first North American serial rights, 117
first rights, 115, 117
first serial rights, 115, 117
holding system, 115
lawyers, 117
licensed material, 116
National Writers' Union, 116
newspaper rights, 116
notification letter, 115
one-time rights, 117
payment, 115, 116
periodical rights, 116
publication date, 115, 116
Publications Rights Clearinghouse, 116
purchase process, 115
reprint rights, 117
reproduction rights, 118
second rights, 115, 117
second serial rights, 117
simultaneous rights, 117

software rights, 116
syndication rights, 117
title, 116
transfer, 115
resources, 118
David C. Cook Publishing, 4
Cooney, Barbara, 265-268
Copyright *(See Contracts; Rights.)*
Cosby, Bill, 6, 10
Coscient Group, 14, 64
Joanna Cotler Books, 11
Courses, writing, 22
Cover letter, 81
Covey, Stephen, 9, 56
"Creative Playtime," 187
Creative Teaching Press, 83
Credits, publishing, 22, 23, 81, 179, 180, 234
Cricket Magazine Group, 10, 37, 61,
    64, 65, 69, 70, 145, 172, 175
    Babybug, 69, 72, 172
    Cicada, 37
    Click, 10, 61, 64, 67, 72
    Cricket, 69, 73, 209, 218, 223, 234
    Ladybug, 69, 72, 172
    Muse, 64, 73, 223, 234
    Spider, 69, 72, 153, 172
Crown Books, 49 *(See also Random House.)*
Crystal Ball, 7, 37, 67
The Cuckoo's Child, 5, 11, 174
Cunningham, Barry, 4
Curious George, 8, 54
The Cut-ups, 15
Cuyler, Margery, 5, 9, 16, 56
Cyber.kdz, 125, 128, 134

D

Daly, Joe Ann, 17
Dance Spirit, 18, 37, 67
Dancing on the Edge, 18, 228
Danny and the Dinosaur, 15
Databases, 116, 118
Daughters of the Law, 138
Davy, Diane, 64
Deadlines, 110
de Angeli, Marguerite, contest, 57
Dear America, 10
Degen, Bruce, 261, 262
de Jenkins, Lyll Becerra, 11
Delacorte Press, 138, 139
    contest, 57
Dell *(See Bantam Doubleday Dell.)*
Delta Education, 7
Demographics, and magazines, 85, 90, 93
Description, 189-194
    action verbs, 189, 191
    analogy, 189
    character, 191

exercises, 190, 192
experience, 193
imagery, 193
metaphor, 189, 191, 193
plot, 191
poetry, 193
senses, 191
simile, 189
Design and production, books, 95, 96, 97, 108
Development companies, 75, 80, 81
   (See also Educational publishing; Packagers.)
Dial Books, 8, 50, 282
Dial an Expert, The National Directory of
   Quotable Experts, 221
Dialogue, 229
Didax Educational Resources, 82
Dinosaurus, 14, 67, 71, 72
Disney,
   Disney Press, 9, 13, 15, 57
   Walt Disney Corporation, 16
   magazines, 65
   (See also Hyperion Books.)
Disney Adventures, 299
Disney's Hercules: Zero to Hero, 12
Doherty, Sally, 15
Dolphin Log, 73
Dorling Kindersley, (DK Publishing), 4, 5, 9,
   12, 17, 30, 313
   DK Ink, 4, 29, 48
Doubleday Books, 3
The Double Diamond Triangle, 7
Doubletake, 209
Dove Entertainment, 12, 16
Dutton Books, 8, 17 *(See also Penguin Putnam)*

E

The Ear, the Eye, and the Arm, 35
The Earthsea Quartet, 277, 278, 279
Eaton, Deb, 77
Edcon Publishing Group, 83
Editorial Directions, 16, 305
Educational Press of America (EdPress), 63,
   65 , 209
   awards, 18
Educational publishing, 70, 75-84, 106
   big books, 76
   chart, number of books, 79
   classroom texts, 75, 76, 77, 84, 106
   community standards, 77
   contracts, 106
   deadlines, 78
   development companies, 75, 80, 81
   early childhood education, 84
   emergent readers, 76, 78, 83
   foreign language, 84
   high school, 84, 180
   language arts, 75

little books, 76, 77
math manipulatives, 82
middle school, 84
music education, 84
parent involvement, 83
packagers, 80
payment, 110, 112, 140
phonics, 77, 80, 82
reading levels, 77, 78, 84
supplementary materials, 76
teachers' guides, 76
whole-language, 75, 76, 77
Educational Development Corp., 4, 5
Edwards, Marilyn, 172, 175, 176
Edwards, Virginia, 115
Ehrlich, Amy, 4
Element Books, 4
Elizabeth Cary: Writer of Conscience, 182
Ellis Island series, 294
Elsevier/Nelson, 138 *(See also Dutton Books.)*
E-mail, 127
Emergent readers, 76, 78, 83
Emery, Dr. Francenia L., 35
Enchantment of the World, 307
Etherington, Vanessa, 71
Evan-Moor Educational Publications, 83
Evans, Marilyn, 83
Every Writer's Guide to Copyright &
   Publishing Law, 118
Expert sources, 217-226
   connecting with, 223-224
   contacting, 222-223
   Dial an Expert, The National Directory
      of Quotable Experts, 221
   finding, 220-221
   interview preparation, 222-223
   online, 218-219, 242
   (See also Market research, magazines;
   Photographs, research; References,
   writers'.)
Exploring, 297

F

Faces, 73, 207, 208
   (See also Cobblestone Publishing.)
The Facts Speak for Themselves, 18
Fairchild Publications, 65
Falling Up, 11
Family *(See Parenting.)*
FamilyFun, 89, 90
Family Life, 89, 90, 92
Fantasy *(See Science fiction.)*
Farmer, Nancy, 8, 29, 35
Farrar, Straus & Giroux, 11, 143
   Frances Foster Books, 8, 11
Fear Street, 56
Fear Street Sagas, 56

Feiwel, Jean, 10, 49, 50, 53, 58
Feldman, Thea, 4
J G Ferguson, 306, 307
Ferrari, Christina, 7, 38, 39, 44, 66, 269-272
Fiction,
    historical, 180, 181, 229, 230
    queries, 21-25
    series, 282, 283
    research, 227, 229, 230, 231, 233
The Fiddler of the Northern Lights, 8
The Field Book, 298
Finestone, Jeanne, 52
First for Women, 14
First-Time Dad, 93
Fish, Becky Durost, 181
Fisher, Peter, 4
Fisher Price, 6
Fitness and health, 66
Fit Pregnancy, 65
Flat fee *(See Contracts; Payment; Work-for-hire.)*
Flower, Mary, 107, 108, 109, 110, 111, 139,
    140, 141, 142
Focus on the Family, 89
Focus on the Family Clubhouse, 25
Fogelman, Sheldon, 106, 107, 108, 109, 110,
    111, 112, 113, 114
Folktales, 28, 30, 77
Forgotten Realm, 7, 48
Forster, E.M., 173
For Whom the Bell Tolls, 179
Frances Foster Books, 8, 11
    (See also Farrar, Straus & Giroux.)
Foundation for Concepts in Education, 17
Four Winds, 314
Fox easy readers, 15
Franklin Watts, 4, 305, 307, 308
    (See also Grolier.)
Freedson, Grace, 82
Freeman, Suzanne, 5, 11, 174
Freeze, 18, 37, 61, 65, 67
Frith, Margaret, 282
Frog and Toad, 15
*From the Mixed-up Files of Mrs. Basil E.
    Frankweiler*, 273, 274, 275
From Sea to Shining Sea, 308
Front Street Books, 18, 119, 124, 130, 1423
171
Frost, Robert, 228
Full-Time Dads, 92

G

Gallardo, Evelyn, 122, 125, 128, 129, 130,
    131, 134
Gareth Stevens, 5
The Gator Girls, 262, 263
Gauch, Patricia, 173, 176, 177
Gave, Marc, 5

Gaynor, Charlene, 63, 65
Geck, Steve, 54, 58
Geist, Ken, 13, 57
George and Martha, 15
Get Ready, Get Set, Read!, 82
*Getting to Yes: Negotiating Agreement
    Without Giving In*, 118
Ghosts of Fear Street, 56
Giblin, James Cross, 27, 137, 140, 141, 142
A Girl Named Disaster, 8, 29
Girls' Life, 73, 185
The Giver, 177
Glassman, Bruce, 98, 100, 101
Glassman, Peter, 9
Globe Fearon, 7
Glossy, 10, 37, 43, 44, 67
Goddy, David, 61, 65, 70
Godwin, Laura, 5
The Golden Compass, 11, 282
Golden Family Entertainment, 4, 9, 10, 12,
    16, 49, 55, 56
    Smart Pages, 12, 49
The Golden Goblet, 291
Golden Kite, 229 *(See also Society of Children's
    Book Writers & Illustrators.)*
Goldsmith, Sarah, 44
Golem, 8, 29
Goosebumps, 10, 14, 53, 282, 287
Gore, Ariel, 89
Grammar, 195, 197, 199
Grann, Phyllis, 6
The Graphic Alphabet, 8
The Great Gilly Hopkins, 302
Great Snakes, 76
Green, David, 10
Greenwillow Books, 5, 8, 11, 23, 174
    (See also William Morrow.)
Griffen, Regina, 24
Griffin, Adele, 18
Grolier, Inc., 4, 5, 9, 12, 219, 307, 313, 315
    Children's Press, 4, 305, 307, 308
    Franklin Watts, 4, 305, 307, 308
    Orchard Books, 4, 5, 8, 9, 29, 313, 315, 316
Grosset & Dunlap, 6, 50, 55
    (See also Penguin Putnam.)
Grosz, Gabe, 88
Grove, Karen, 227, 229
Growing Tree, 16
Grune, George, 17
GT Publishing, 13, 48
Guess How Much I Love You, 54
Guidelines, 150, 151, 152, 180, 183
Guideposts for Kids, 24, 43, 175, 176, 185, 187
Guideposts for Teens, 37, 43

H

Hallock, Ann, 89

Hall, Donald, 266
Harcourt Brace, 4, 5, 18, 139, 172, 175, 227, 229
   educational publishing, 76, 80
   promotion, 120, 125
HarperCollins, 5, 9, 11, 13, 15, 16, 18, 47, 54, 55
   Joanna Cotler Books, 11
   Growing Tree, 16
   HarperActive, 5, 48, 54, 55
   HarperFestival, 5, 9
   Harper & Row, 137
   HarperTrophy, 5, 9
   I Can Read Books, 15
Harper's Bazaar, 44
Hatch, Tom, 97, 98, 99
Hattie and the Wild Waves, 267
Hayashida, Ralph, 84
Hayes, Clair III, 84
Hayes, Donna, 7
Hayes School Publishing, 84
Heins, Ethel L., 11
Help Wanted: Short Stories About Young People Working, 311
Henkes, Kevin, 11, 17
Henry, Marguerite, 3, 8
Herbst, Peter, 90, 92
Hercules: The Heart of a Hero, 12
Highlights for Children, 11, 25, 65, 72, 115, 171, 217, 223, 234
HIP, 130
Hip Mama, 89
Hirschman, Susan, 174
History,
   fiction, 180, 181, 230, 291
   history-mystery, 294
   photographs, 205, 207, 208
   research, 228
   young adult, 182
The Hobbit, 279
Hoffmann, Nina, 13
Holiday House, 24
Henry Holt Books, 5, 16, 32, 174, 175
   educational publishing, 80
Ho, Minfong, 8, 29
Honey Hill Publishing, 94
The Honorable Prison, 11
Hopscotch, 73, 115, 172, 175
   (See also Boys' Quest.)
Horn Book, 11, 119, 309, 310
Houghton Mifflin, 15, 24, 47, 54, 309, 310
   educational publishing, 80
Howard, Elise, 4
How to Promote Your Children's Book: A Survival Guide, 125
How to Write and Sell Children's Picture Books, 275

Hudson, Cheryl, Katura, and Wade, 27
Hugo Award, 277
Humpty Dumpty, 72
   (See also Children's Better Health Institute.)
Humpty Dumpty Award, 17
Hunter, Lynda, 89
Hunt, Laura, 97
Hurd, Clement, 8
Hurd, Edith, 8
Hush! A Thai Lullaby, 8, 29, 30
Hyperion Books, 5, 9, 13, 18, 53, 57
   (See also Disney Press.)

I

I Am Regina, 173
I Can Read Books, 15
Idea generation, 399-406, 407-456
   book catalogues, 228
   fiction idea, form, 146
   nonfiction idea, form, 147
   research process, 227
Illustration, 110, 113, 205, 265-268
Imprints, 48-49, 50
Inchworm Press, 13, 48
In His Steps, or What Would Jesus Do?, 136
InKNOWvations, 4
Innelli, Hope, 5
Institutional markets, 28, 50, 119
   (See also Libraries; Schools.)
International Reading Association (IRA), 120, 132
Internet, 106, 118, 308
   book promotion, 126-127
   bulletin boards, 221
   expert sources online, 218-219, 221, 242
   global Internet searches, 237
   mailing lists and newsgroups, 127, 218-219, 220
   news sources, 240-241
   online databases, 241-242
   pay database services, 238
   search engines, 127, 219, 236, 237, 238, 239, 240, 241
   websites, 238
   writers and writing, 242-243
   (See also World Wide Web.)
Interrace, 88
Interviews, 217-226, 231-232
   accuracy, 225-226
   archivists, 231
   connecting with subject, 222-223
   contacting, 222-223
   fact-checking, 225
   follow-up, 225-226
   notes or recording, 224
   preparation, 222-223
   protocol, 224

quotes, checking, 225
(See also Expert sources; Market research, magazines; Photographs, research; References, writers'.)
InTime, 11, 67
Island Boy, 267
I Spy Challenger, 10

J

Jack And Jill, 73, 115, 171, 186
(See also Children's Better Health Institute.)
Jackson, Richard, 29, 313, 315
Jacob Have I Loved, 301
Jacobs, Erica, 172, 175
Jacobs, Michael, 17
Jaguar, 123
James, Sister Kathryn, 7
Jane, 14, 65, 67
Jane on Her Own, 278
Jennifer, Hecate, Macbeth, William McKinley, and Me, Elizabeth, 273
Jensen, Patty, 10
Jip, His Story, 11, 301, 303
Jonah, the Whale, 281
Jordan, Denise, 153
Jump, 14, 37, 38, 39, 61, 65, 66, 67
Junior Scholastic, 15, 70 *(See also Scholastic.)*
Just like Jenny, 139
Just Us Books, 27

K

Kaplan, Simone, 16
Karl, Jean, 8, 29, 275
Katcher, Ruth, 9
Katz, Susan, 57
Keehn, Sally M., 173
Keeper of the Light, 78
Kehret, Peg, 17
Keiner, Jo, 13
Keller, John, 47, 53, 54
Kelly, Joe, 66, 69
Kennedy, Martin, 82
Kent Publishing, 97, 98
Kessenich, Diane, 17
The Kidnapping of Christina Lattimore, 293, 294
Kids Can Press, 9
Kids Discover, 73, 209
KidStyle, 14, 67
Coretta Scott King Award, 8
King of Wreck Island, 266
Kinsey-Warnock, Natalie, 8
Kirchoff/Wohlberg, 80, 81
Kirkus Reviews, 119
Kittinger, Jo, 229, 230
Klutz Press, 13
Alfred A. Knopf Books, 9, 11, 35, 49, 52, 53, 96, 282

Knopf Paperbacks, 6, 48
(See also Random House.)
Knowlton, Laurie, 99, 100, 101
Konigsburg, E.L., 8, 29, 273-275
Koeppel, Ruth, 6
Koop, C. Everett, 6
Korman, Judy, 10
Kriney, Marilyn, 13
Kroons, Linda, 13
Kroupa, Melanie, 29, 30, 35, 313
K-III Holdings, 5
Kurtz, Jane, 28, 34, 35, 119, 121, 124, 127, 132, 133, 134

L

Lacrosse, 18
Ladybug, 69, 72, 172
(See also Cricket Magazine Group.)
Lamb Chop, 56
Lassie, 56
Launches, 67
Leadership, 93
Leahey, Joe, 61, 64
The Learning Journal, 4
Lee & Low Books, 24, 27, 28, 30
Lee, Daniel, 115, 171, 172, 186, 187
Lee, Philip, 28, 30
Le Guin, Ursula K., 277-280
L'Engle, Madeleine, 131
Length, word, 22, 23, 25, 149, 150
Lenz, Tom, 82
Lerner Publications, 315
Levine, Abby, 24
Levine, Arthur, 281-284
Lewis, Shari, 56
Libraries,
 author visits, 131
 librarians, research, 230
 market, 53, 106, 119
 multicultural books, 28
 (See also Institutional markets.)
Licensing and tie-ins, 48, 51, 54, 56, 57
 (See also Brand identity; Rights.)
Lightstone, Rod, 12
Lilly's Purple Plastic Purse, 11, 17
Lindstrom, Elizabeth, 204, 205, 206, 208, 210
Listservs and newsgroups, 127, 218-219, 220
 (See also Internet; World Wide Web.)
List sizes, 50
Literacy campaigns, 15
Literary Market Place, 81, 100
 award, 11
Literature,
 across the curriculum, 82
 in magazines, 69
 literary books, 106

plot, 177
Little Bear, 15
Little, Brown and Company, 47, 53, 54, 266, 309
Little People Playbooks, 6
Little Simon, 55, 97 *(See also Simon & Schuster.)*
Living Books, 6
Living Fit, 14, 65
Living with Teenagers, 90
Lodestar Books, 11, 16, 17, 21, 50
   (See also Penguin Putnam.)
Lombardi, Lisa, 15, 43
London, Jack, 136
Lothrop, Lee & Shepard, 137
Love Stories, 98
Love You Forever, 6
Lowry, Lois, 285-288
Lowry, Shannon, 174, 175
Lucent Books, 233
Lupine Award, 265
Lurie, Stephanie Owens, 10, 23, 27, 28, 29, 30, 119, 120, 121, 124
Lynton, Michael, 6

M

Macmillan, 314, 315
   McGraw Hill, 80
   (See also Simon & Schuster.)
Madame Bovary, 199
Magazine Publishers of America, 63
Magic Attic Club, 78
Mahoning Valley Grandparent, 94
Mahoning Valley Parent, 94
Maisy's House, 11
Magazines,
   market research, 145-153
   parenting, 7, 85-94
   teens, 37-44, 65, 66, 69
The Magic School Bus, 261, 262, 263
The Magic School Bus and the Electric Field Trip, 262
"Make Mine Meat," 187
Mander, Lelia, 81
Manuscripts, unsolicited, 21-25
Marcus, Barbara, 17
Marketing, 122
Market research, magazines,
   contributor copies, 152
   credits, clips, tear sheets, 151
   editor needs, 148
   fiction idea, form, 146
   guidelines, 150, 151, 152
   mastheads, analysis, 150, 152
   nonfiction idea, form, 147
   payment, 151
   résumé, 151
   rights, 151

sample copies, 149, 152
submission format, 150
targets, 145
themes, 152
word count, 149, 150
Markets,
   chain stores, 52
   institutional, 50
   library, 53, 106
   mass-markets, 54, 55, 56, 106
   new sales outlets, 48
   nontraditional, 52, 53
   religious, 106
   schools, 28, 106
   retail, 53
Markle, Sandra, 228, 230, 233
Marshall Cavendish, 5, 47, 49
Marshall, James, 15
Mary Poppins, 287
Mass-market, 54, 55, 106, 110, 112
Master Cornhill, 291
The Master Puppeteer, 301
Math Power, 10
Maugham, Somerset, 199
Mayer, Margery, 13
Mayes, Walter, 119, 122, 123, 124, 125
Mazer, Norma Fox, 281
McCall's, 270
McClanahan and Company, 5, 52, 55, 82
   (See also Scott Foresman-Addison Wesley.)
McCully, Emily Arnold, 282
McCutcheon, Marc, 221
Margaret K. McElderry Books, 3, 8, 51, 314, 315 *(See also Simon & Schuster.)*
McGraw, Eloise Jarvis, 8, 289-292
McGraw, William Corbin, 290
McGuigan, Mary Ann, 18
McIntyre, Patty, 116
McLaughlin, James, 92, 93
Meade, Holly, 8, 29, 30
Mean Margaret, 18
Media Equities International, 12
Media Projects, 81
Medill School of Journalism, 87, 92
Merchandising, 109, 143
   (See also Books plus; Specialty books.)
Meredith Corporation, 87, 92, 93
Metaphor *(See Description.)*
Meyers, Walter Dean, 8
Midlist writers, books, 50, 143
Mid-South Independent Booksellers for Children Association, 17
The Midwife's Apprentice, 177
Mighty Spiders, 76
The Millbrook Press, 5, 10, 16, 47, 81
Minarik, Else Holmelund, 15
Minstrel Books, 6, 55

Mirette on the High Wire, 282
The Missing Cat, 9
Miss Rumphius, 267
Miss Spider's New Car, 10
Misty of Chincoteague, 3, 8
Mittler, Kathy, 91, 94
Moby Dick, 78
Mochizuki, Ken, 28
Modern Curriculum Press, 99
Modern Dad, 93
Modern Publishing, 55
Moeckel, Sandy, 88, 91, 94
Monfried, Lucia, 17
Montgomery, Gwen, 9
Monty: A Story of Young Harriet Tubman, 8
The Moorchild, 8, 289
Moore, Mary Alice, 9
Moore, Pat, 75, 81
Moose Tracks, 122, 129, 130, 134
Morgan Reynolds Press, 182
Morgenstein, Les, 98, 99, 101
Morrison, Toni, 282
Morrow, Paula, 172, 175, 176
William Morrow, 5
    Greenwillow Books, 5, 8, 11, 23, 174
    Morrow Junior Books, 16, 21, 53
Morton, Colin, 199
Muchnik, Irving, 116
Multicultural publishing, 27-35
Multicultural Resource Center, 35
Munsch, Robert, 6
Muse, 64, 73, 223, 234
    (See also Cricket Magazine Group.)
My Friend, 7
My Many Colored Days, 11
My Very First Mother Goose, 11
Mysteries, 230, 293, 294, 295

N

Nam, Victoria, 69
Nancy Drew books, 174
National Book Award, 18, 228, 277, 301
National Children's Book and Literacy
    Alliance, 15
National Council of Social Studies, 84
National Council of Teachers of English, 120
National Geographic Books, 13
National Geographic World, 73, 299
National Museum of American History, 64
National Writers' Union, 107, 116, 118
Natural History, 209
Ndito Runs, 32
Nebula Award, 277
Negotiating a Book Contract, 118
Nelson, David, 5
Nenneker, Kathy, 65, 66

Newbery Medal and Honor books, 8, 12, 29, 35,
    132, 273, 274, 277, 285, 286, 289, 291, 301
New England Book Award, 8
New Moon, 66, 69
New York Times Company, lawsuit, 118
Nicholson, George, 138
Nickelodeon, 14, 17, 307-308
Nickelodeon, 299
Nixon, Joan Lowery, 293-296
Nobisso, Josephine, 17
Nolan, Han, 18, 228, 230
Nonfiction,
    books, photos, 205
    expert sources, 217-226
    invented dialogue, 229
    magazines, 64, 70
    multicultural, 28
    research, 217-226
    payment, 112
    queries, 21
Nordstrum, Ursula, 15
Northland Publishing, 6, 47, 49
Not Just for Children Anymore, 12
Novelty books, 51
NTC Publishing, 294
Number the Stars, 285

O

O'Brien, Anne Sibley, 78
Oceans Apart, 199
Scott O'Dell Award, 11, 301
Odyssey, 73, 204, 206, 207, 209
    (See also Cobblestone Publishing.)
Odyssey of the Mind, 71
Officer Buckle and Gloria, 282
Oldacre, Ellen, 90, 94
O'Neil, Alexis, 203, 204, 206, 207, 210
On the Father Front, 93
Only a Pigeon, 35, 119
Openings, 171-172, 198
Opie, Iona, 10-11
Oram, Hiawyn, 282
Orchard Books, 4, 5, 8, 9, 29, 313, 315, 316
    (See also Grolier.)
Orphan Train, 294
The Other Side of Dark, 294
Ottaviano, Christie, 174
Ottenheimer Publishers, 101
Oughton, Jon, 197
Our Little Friend, 72
Owen, J.D., 297-300
Richard C. Owen Publishers, 10, 49
Owl Communications, 14, 64, 73
    Chickadee, 14, 64, 72
    Chirp, 10, 61, 64, 67, 72
    Owl, 64, 73

P

Packagers, 95-102
  advantages, 96
  assignments, 97
  contracts, 106, 112
  cost-effectiveness, 97
  educational, 80, 81, 97, 98
  idea development, 97, 98
  tasks, 96
  work-for-hire, 101
Pages Inc., 13
Paper Bag Princess, 6
Paperbacks, 53
  promotion, 120
  rights, 109
The Paperboy, 8
PaperStar, 50 *(See also Penguin Putnam.)*
Parenting, 7, 85, 91, 269
Parenting publications, 7, 85-94
  chart, 86
  niches, 88, 89, 92
  regionals, 88, 91
  sidebars, 187
Parenting Publications of America, 91, 94
Parents, 87
Parent's Choice Silver Honor, 289
Passage to Freedom: The Sugihara Story, 28
Pat the Bunny, 56
Paterson, Katherine, 11, 301-303
Payment,
  books, 109, 110-112, 135-143
    advances, 107, 111-112, 136, 137,
      138, 139, 140, 141, 207
    calculation, 111
    deep discount sales, 111
    earnings, 135
    educational, text, 110, 140
    escalation clause, 111, 142
    first novel or nonfiction, 141, 142
    flat-fee, 109, 112, 135, 136
    mass-market, 110, 111
    nonfiction, 112
    novels, 112
    paperbacks, 110, 140, 142
    picture books, 110, 112, 140, 141
    printruns, 111
    profit sharing, 135, 136
    religious, 110, 140, 142
    rights, 109
    royalties, 107, 110-111, 136, 137, 138,
      142
    small presses, 110
    specialty, 111
    trade, hardcover, 110, 140
    work-for-hire, 109, 112
  magazines, 115-116
    all rights, 116
    process, 115-116

    scale, 116
    schedule, 115
    photographs, 207
    (See also Contracts.)
Peacebound Trains, 32
Pearl Moscowitz's Last Stand, 282
Pearson, *(See Penguin Putnam.)*
Pelletier, David, 8
PEN Center, 17
  USA West Award, 17
Penguin Putnam, 6, 10, 17, 21, 50, 51, 54,
  55, 56, 57
  Cobblehill Books, 17, 50
  Dial Books, 8, 50, 282
  Dutton Books, 8, 17
  Grosset & Dunlap, 6, 50, 55
  Lodestar Books, 11, 1617, 21, 50
  PaperStar, 50
  Playskool Books, 17
  Price Stern Sloan, 10, 50, 55
  Putnam and Grosset Group, 50, 282
  Viking Books, 50
People, 7, 269, 270, 271
Pernick, Nancy, 80, 81
Petersen Publishing, 8, 15
  'Teen, 8, 11, 15
Peterson, Kristina, 17
Pfitsch, Patricia Curtis, 78
Photographs, research, 203-216
  advances, 207
  age-appropriateness, 205
  author role, 206, 208
  book sources, 211
  collections, 206, 209, 210, 214-216
  copyright, 206
  costs, 205, 207, 209
  credits, 203, 206
  design, 204, 206
  directories, 211-214
  electronic media, 205
  history, 205, 207, 209
  illustration, 205
  image identification, 203
  good photos, determining, 204, 208
  magazines and pamphlets, sources,
    211-214
  nonfiction books, 205, 207
  organizations, 211
  paperwork, 204
  permission, 203
  photocopies, 203
  picture agencies, 203, 208, 214-216
  picture puzzles, 204
  prints, 205
  queries, 204
  record-keeping, 209
  resolution, 210

INDEX

rights, 206, 209
science 205
sources, 203, 206, 207, 209, 210, 211-216
technology, 209, 210
Picture books,
  biographies, 28
  contracts, 110
  manuscripts, 24
  multicultural, 28
  payment, 112
Pilkey, Dav, 8
Pines, Nancy, 6
Pinkney, Jerry, 8
Pittsburgh's Child, 94
Planet Dexter, 3
Playskool Books, 17 *(See also Penguin Putnam.)*
Pleasant Company, 16 *(See also American Girl.)*
Plot, 171-177
  action-driven, 174, 176
  adults, 176
  beginning, 171-172
  character-driven, 172-174, 176
  coming-of-age novel, 174
  complexity, 176
  conflict, 172, 176, 181
  descriptive language, 191
  ending, 172
  focus, 172
  historical fiction, 181
  improving, 175
  language, 177
  middle, 172
  originality, 177
  problem, 176
  situation, 173
  slice-of-life, 172
  story, 173
  target age, 176
  tone, 177
  vehicle, or object, 176
The Poky Little Puppy, 56
Pocket Books, 6
Pockets, 116
Edgar Allan Poe Award, 293
Poploff, Michelle, 52, 57
Porter, Neal, 313, 315
Posey, Kirby G., 135
Postage, 23, 145
Potter, Beatrix, 278
Powers, Joan, 17
Pratt, Jane, 14
Prentice Hall, 7
Preston, Marcia, 179, 180
Price Stern Sloan, 10, 50, 55
  (See also Penguin Putnam.)
Primm, E. Russell III, 305-308
Pringle, Lawrence, 204, 205, 206, 207

Printruns, 57, 111, 142
Promotion, authors and books, 119-134
  author promotion coordinators, 131
  author responsibility, 121, 124
  author tours, 120, 132
  biography, 129
  bookstores, 120, 128, 131
  brochures and flyers, 121, 124, 125, 131
  catalogues, 120
  conferences, 120, 131, 132
  conventions, 120
  Internet, 126-127
  library visits, 131
  media attention, 128, 129
  media campaigns, 132
  niche markets, 130
  nonprofit organizations, 130
  postcards, 120, 121
  posters, 121
  press release, 129
  promotional packet, 129
  radio and television, 129, 130
  reviews, 119, 120, 123
  school visits, 122, 131
  signings, 128, 131
Proposals, nonfiction, 179-183
  book proposal package, 181
  credits, clips, 179, 180
  guidelines, 180
  historical fiction, 180, 181
  magazine proposal package, 180
  need, 182
  originality, 182
  query, 179, 180
  résumé, 179, 180
  sources, 179, 180
  (See also Queries.)
Publications Rights Clearinghouse, 116, 118
Publicists, 122-123, 129, 130, 131, 133, 134
  (See also Promotion.)
Publicom, 75
Publishers Weekly, 54, 119, 285, 313
Pulling the Lion's Tale, 28, 34
Pullman, Philip, 11, 282
Punctuation, 195, 199
Pushcart Prize, 277
Putnam and Grosset Group, 50, 282
  (See also Penguin Putnam.)
Putnam Berkely, *(See Penguin Putnam.)*

Q

Queries,
  fiction, 21-25
  nonfiction, 21, 182
  picture research, 203
  (See also Proposals.)

R

Raab, Susan, 122, 123, 128, 134
Raab Associates, 122, 128
Radio AHHS, 129
Raising Teens, 87, 92
Random House, 3, 6, 15, 17, 48, 52
    Crown Books, 49
    Alfred A. Knopf Books, 9, 11, 35, 49, 52,
       53, 96
    Knopf Paperbacks, 6, 48
Ranger Rick, 73, 174, 175
Rathmann, Peggy, 282
Ray, Mary Lyn, 266
Raymo, Margaret, 47
Reader's Digest, 6, 17
Reading level, 77, 78, 84, 149
Read to Your Bunny, 15
Real Kids, 61, 64
Real Monsters, 17
Redbook, 270
Red Wagon, 4
References,
    books, 180, 228
    electronic, 235-236
    writers', 245-258
Reginald, Steve, 96
Religious publishing,
    contracts, 110, 112
    magazines, 149
    magazines, chart, 48
    payment, books, 110, 140, 141
Research,
    accuracy, 225-226, 234
    archives, 230-233
    expert sources, 217-226
    fact-checking, 225, 234
    fiction, 227, 229, 230, 233-234
    idea generation, 227
    information-building, 230
    interplay with writing, 233
    interviews, 217-226
    museums, clubs, historical places, 228,
       230, 233
    newspapers, 229
    model letter, archivist, 232
    nonfiction, 228
    online, 218-219
    organization, 228, 230
    process, 227-234
    subject identification, 227
    (See also Market research, magazines;
    Photographs, research; References,
    writers'; Research, electronic.)
Research, electronic, 235-243
    CD-ROMs, 235
    encyclopedias, 236
    expert sources, 218-219, 242

    global Internet searches, 237
    news sources, 240-241
    online databases, 241-242
    pay database services, 238
    references, 235-236
    search engines, 219, 236, 237, 238, 239,
       240
    websites, 238
    writers and writing, 242-243
    (See also Expert sources; Internet; Market
    research, magazines; World Wide Web.)
Résumé, 81, 129, 179
Returns, 53
Revision, self-editing and, 195-199
    asides and digressions, 199
    characters, 197
    checklist, 196
    dialect, 198
    dialogue, 197
    fragments and run-ons, 198-199
    grammar, 195, 197
    imagery, 197
    opening, 198
    punctuation, 195, 197, 200
    quotes, 197
    spelling, 195, 198
    theme, 198
    typos, 198
    word choice, 199
Reuther, David, 53
Rey, H.A., 8
Rey, Margaret, 8, 54
Richter, Rick, 51, 52, 57
Rights,
    books,
       audio, 109
       British, 109
       commercial, 110
       electronic, 109, 110
       grant of rights, 109
       merchandising, 109
       paperback, 110
       payment, 110
       return of rights, 113
       serialization, 109
       split, 109
       subsidiary rights, 109
       television and drama, 109
       translations, 109
    magazines,
       all rights, 116, 117
       author card, 115
       Authors' Guild, 116
       Authors' Registry, 116
       designation of rights, 115
       electronic rights, 116, 118
       first North American serial rights, 117

first rights, 115, 117
first serial rights, 115, 117
holding system, 115
lawyers, 117
licensed, 116
market research, 151
newspaper rights, 116
New York Times Company, lawsuit, 118
notification letter, 115
payment, 115, 116, 151
periodical rights, 116
Publications Rights Clearinghouse, 116
purchase process, 115
reprint rights, 117
reproduction rights, 118
second rights, 115, 117
second serial rights, 117
simultaneous rights, 117
software rights, 116
syndication rights, 117
transfer of rights, 115
photographs, 205
(See also Contracts; Payment.)
Riley, John, 182
Rising Moon, 6, 49
Robb, Don, 82
Robinson, Fay, 76, 77
Robinson, Marileta, 171, 172, 176
Robinson, Richard, 14
"Rocks in My Head," 176
Rocky and His Friends, 17
Roome, Hugh, 14
The Rosen Publishing Group, 233
Rowland, Pleasant, 70
Roxburgh, Stephen, 119, 120, 121, 124, 130, 131, 133, 171, 172, 173, 174, 177
Royalties *(See Payment.)*
Roy, Robin, 23, 24
Rubel, David, 95, 96, 97, 101
Rugrats, 17

S

Sage, Juniper, 8
Saint Mary's Press, 6, 49
The Sandman's Eyes, 138
Sassy, 8, 11
Sawdust in His Shoes, 290
Sawicki, Norma Jean, 315
Frank Schaffer Publications, 99
Scholastic, 14, 15
    books, 6, 8, 10, 11, 17, 49, 53, 58, 76, 100, 282, 315
    magazines, 11, 13, 18, 61, 65, 70
    school/educational, 13, 18, 80
Scholastic Literary Cavalcade, 18
Scholastic News, 70

School book fairs, 13
School Library Journal, 119
Schools,
    author visits, 122, 131
    markets, 28, 119
    (See also Educational publishing; Institutional markets.)
Anne Schwartz Books, 7
Science fiction, 277, 278, 279, 280
Science, and technology, 64, 70, 71, 262-263
    expert sources, 217, 218, 221
    photographs, 205
    research, 228, 229
Scott Foresman-Addison Wesley, 76, 78, 82
Scouting, 38, 297
Scoutmaster Handbook, 298
Scribner, 314
The Sea King's Daughter: A Russian Legend, 28
The Seance, 294
Search engines, 127, 219, 236, 237, 238, 239, 240
The Secret Garden, 174
Seidler, Tor, 18
Self, 270
Sendak, Maurice, 15, 57
Send Me Down a Miracle, 228
Series fiction, 282, 283
Dr. Seuss, 3, 11
Sevastiades, Patra, 233
The Seven Habits of Highly Effective Families, 9, 56
Seventeen, 38, 66
Seymour, Lesley, 11
Shabanu: Daughter of the Wind, 35
Shape, 14, 39, 65
Sheldon, Rev. Charles Monroe, 136
Shepard, Aaron, 28, 30
Shoofly, 72
Short Circuit, 294
Short stories, 24
Sidebars, 185-188
    format, 187
    planning, 186
    transitions, 186
    varieties, 186-187
    word count, 187
Sierra Club Books, 14
Silver Burdett Ginn, 7
Silverstein, Shel, 11, 57
Silver Whistle Books, 5
Silvey, Anita, 309-311
SingleLife, 187
Single-Parent Family, 89
The Sinister Smoke Ring, 6
Sinykin, Sheri Cooper, 78
Simon & Schuster, 3, 7, 10, 16, 17, 18, 23, 27, 28, 30, 34, 35, 51, 54, 55, 57, 78, 315

Aladdin Books, 3, 9, 51
Atheneum Books, 8, 18, 28, 30, 51, 275, 314
Cobblestone Publishing, 18, 61, 70, 71
Little Simon, 55, 97
Margaret K. McElderry Books, 3, 8, 51, 315
promotion, 119
Simon Spotlight, 10, 17, 49, 51, 54, 55, 97
Sis, Peter, 8
Skiing, 65
Slam!, 8
Slattery, Joan, 6
Smalley, Richard, 221
Small, Jonathan, 15
Small presses, 106, 110, 112
Small Steps: The Year I Got Polio, 17
Smart Pages, 12, 49
(*See also Golden Family Entertainment.*)
Smith, Roland, 122, 123, 128,
Smithsonian, 65, 209, 234
Smithsonian Institution, 64
SNAP!, 14, 63 (*See also Twist.*)
Snyder, Richard, 4, 56
Soap Opera Digest, 15
Soccer JR., 73
Society of Children's Book Writers and Illustrators (SCBWI), 81, 106, 118, 126
Golden Kite, 229, 289
Solimene, Philip, 83
Something's Waiting for You, Baker, D., 137
"Song for the Old Ones," 193
Sons of Liberty, 18
"Sophie and the Christmas Crib," 176
Sources, 179, 182
Specialty books, 111
(*See also Books plus; Merchandising.*)
Spelling, 195, 198
Spider, 69, 72, 153, 172
(*See also Cricket Magazine Group.*)
Spinner, Stephanie, 9
Split, rights, 109 (*See also Contracts; Rights.*)
Sports, 39, 65
Sports Illustrated, 93
Sports Illustrated For Kids, 8, 73, 299
Staples, Suzanne Fisher, 35
Starry Messenger, 8
Stein, Ellen, 16
Stephens, Sarah Hines, 24
Stepping Stones, 6
Stevenson, Robert Louis, 173
Steward, Melissa, 219, 220, 225
Stine, R.L., 56
Stock picture agencies (*See Photo research.*)
Stoll, Don, 65, 70, 71
Storyworks, 73
The Stupids, 15
Submissions, 63, 68, 150

(*See also Queries; Proposals.*)
Submit-it.com, 127
Sullivan, Patty, 4
A Summer Before, 137
Summer Begins, 138
Summer Smith Begins, 138
SuperScience Red, 10
Sweetland, Helen, 14
Sweet Valley High, 98, 99, 101
Synopsis, 22, 23
Szabla, Liz, 24
Szumski, Bonnie, 233

T

Tae's Sonata, 32
Tales from Earthsea, 278
Talewinds, 49
Technology (*See Science and technology.*)
'Teen, 8, 11, 15, 38
Teen People, 7, 37, 38, 61, 66, 67, 269, 270, 271, 272
Teens, 37-44, 65, 66, 69, 269, 270, 271, 272
magazines, chart, 40-41
parenting, 87, 90, 91, 92
Tehanu, 278, 279, 280
Texas Press Association, 298
Theme, 23, 24
"There's a Tomb Waiting for You," 294
The Thief, 8
3-2-1 Contact, 73
Thunder Cave, 123
Time For Kids, 11, 61, 63, 67, 69, 70
Time Machine, 15, 64
Times Mirror Magazines, 18
Together Time, 72
To Kill a Mockingbird, 179
Tolkien, J.R.R., 279
The Tombs of Atuan, 277
Topspin, 15, 37, 61, 65, 67
Torstar Corporation, 7, 14
Totally Fox Kids, 73
To the Young..., 220
To the Young Scientist, 221
Troll Books, 10, 14
Troop, Beth, 23
TSR Books, 7, 14, 48
Turner, Megan Whelan, 8
Turtle, 72, 149
(*See also Children's Better Health Institute.*)
Twenty-First Century Books, 16
Twist, 15, 37, 43, 61, 63, 65, 67
Tyler, Anne, 282

U

UCLA Extension Writers' Program, 203
UnCover, 116
Underdown, Harold, 12, 53, 58

U*S*Kids, 72
U.S. Census Bureau, 37, 93, 135, 270
U.S. Tennis Association, 15, 37, 65

V

Valdata, Pat, 198
Van Metre, Susan, 17
Veronis, Suhler & Associates, 53
    Industry Forecast, 47
Viacom, 10
Victor Books, 4
Vogel, Valerie, 204, 205, 207, 208, 209, 210
The View from Saturday, 8, 29, 273, 274, 275
Viking Books, 50 *(See also Penguin Putnam)*
Viner, Michael and Deborah Raffin, 12
Virden, Craig, 9
Vogue, 44
Volunteer Lawyers for the Arts, 118

W

W, 44
Walker Books, 139
Wallace, Rich, 115
Wallis, Claudia, 69
Walske, Christine, 145, 153
Wan, David, 7
The Watsons Go to Birmingham—1963, 281
Weather Channel books, 17
Weider Publications, 14, 39, 65, 66
Weismann, Daniel, 10
Daniel Weiss Associates, 96, 98, 101
Wells, Rosemary, 15
Whalen, William, 9
Whaley, James, 9
What Jamie Saw, 177
When She Was Good, 281
Where Did All the Dragons Go?, 76
Where You Belong, 18
White, E.B., 273
White, Liz, 87, 88, 91
White, Ruth, 8
Whiteman, Douglas, 10, 50, 51, 54, 56, 57, 58
Albert Whitman and Company, 24
Why Our Schools Are Failing and What We
    Can Learn from Japanese and Chinese
    Education, 7
Who's Who, 221
Wilburn, Deborah, 87
John Wiley & Sons, 314
Williams, Carolea, 83
Willis Stein & Partners, 8
Wilson, Judy, 5, 313-316
Windsor, Pat, 137, 140, 143
Winslow Press, 17, 49
Wirkner, Linda, 78
Wiseman, Paula, 5
Wisniewski, David, 8, 29

Wizards of the Coast, 14
A Wizard of Earthsea, 278
Wojtyla, Karen, 21, 23
Wolaner, Robin, 269
Wolf Shadows, 121
Wood, Dan, 101
Work-for-hire, 101, 109
    (See also Contracts; Payment.)
Working Mother, 87
World Book, 4
World Wide Web, 118, 126-127, 210
    mailing lists, newsgroups, 218-219, 220
    expert sources, 218-219, 221
    search engines, 127, 219
    (See also Internet; Research, electronic.)
Writers,
    educational, 76, 77, 78, 80, 81, 82, 83
    midlist, 50
    new authors, 57, 101, 107, 112, 115, 123,
        138, 145, 223
    published, contracts, 107, 111, 142
A Writer's Guide to a Children's Book Contract,
    107, 118, 139
The Writer's Law Primer, 118
Writers' organizations, 106, 116

Y

YM, 7, 11, 38, 66
Yoder, Carolyn, 11, 234
Yoo, Mary, 7
Young adults,
    fiction, 289, 291
    history, 182
    mystery, 295
    novels, 120, 138
    science fiction, 277, 278, 279
    (See also Teens.)
Young Musicians, 149
Your Big Backyard, 8, 64, 72

Z

Zach, Cheryl, 229, 230
Ziccardi Publishing Group, 17
Zillions, 73
ZooBooks, 209
Zrike, Stephen, 4